Running Across America

50 States of Leadership

#92

Jeffrey M. Fazio, M.Ed.

Ruth,
You have been such a
wonderful part of my ITHOC
experience. I'm so glad we
are friends. I hope you enjoy the
book and find it inspirational.
Thank you for
being you,

4/3/15

JFazio
BOOKS

Jeff Fazio Books

Dedicated to Dee Gerber for hitting 'Send'

and

Ardell Simon, my incredible mother,
for inspiring all that is good in me.

"The person who says it cannot be done,
should not interrupt the person doing it."

—Chinese Proverb

CONTENTS

Chapter 1

Write, Delete, Write, Send
Harrisburg, Pennsylvania
June 20, 2013

On June 20, 2013, my life changed. That day I received an Email from a colleague, Deanne "Dee" Gerber, with the simple subject line "non-work." That Email changed my life. It changed Dee's life. It changed hundreds of lives and we hope that it will someday affect thousands.

But I'm getting ahead of myself. Before I can talk about life-changing Emails, it's prudent to put that Email into context. After all, things happen the way they happen. Let's rewind 5 months.

***

On a very cold morning in February of 2013, exactly 138 days before receiving that life-changing Email, I stepped out of my home to run a mile. I had something to prove—that I could actually run one mile. How hard could that be?

At 39 years of age, I considered myself physically fit. I regularly biked, hiked, and kayaked. Free weights and I were friends; we had consistent dates two or three times per week. Surely I was capable of running a mile.

I wasn't.

Having "accurately" measured a mile on Google maps using landmarks along the recreational path that runs alongside the Susquehanna River in Harrisburg, PA, I stepped out of my home wearing ugly sweats and a very old pair of generic sneakers. Several blocks passed under foot as I walked to the designated starting point.

Time was ready to be measured on my cell phone's stopwatch feature. A few deep breaths and I was off. I was running. Fast. I maintained a solid 6-minute-per-mile pace for an impressive 200 feet. The pace slowed abruptly to 7-minute/mile and then just as abruptly slowed again to slower than 8-minute miles. Why couldn't I breathe? What was going on with my chest?

I was done. I could not go any farther. As I took notice of my stopping point, I realized I couldn't see the finish landmark. How could this be?

I turned and started what felt like an incredibly long walk home. I was dejected. I was humbled. This was much harder than I thought it would be. After walking several blocks, I thought I would give running another shot. But my heart and lungs seemed more intent on laughing at me than assisting in propelling me forward, so I quickly dropped back to walking pace.

At home, I calculated the distance where I ran out of steam. I had barely traversed half a mile. It was done in 4 minutes, so I was averaging an 8-minute pace, which would be pretty impressive having not run in over 20 years, if I had *actually been able to run a complete mile.*

This was not acceptable.

A week later I went out for another run—with a different attitude. This time, I was going for a healthy jog. There was no need to finish fast. The need was just to finish.

For the second attempt, I stayed closer, running around the lake directly across the street from my place. Using Google Maps again and confirming with my car's odometer, I measured a mile around the lake.

I managed to get around the lake in less than 10 minutes, precisely the time I ran 24 years earlier in the 10th grade Presidential Physical Fitness experience. I had my 1-mile pace, and this was enough to propel my obsessive personality into beating that time.

A few times a week, I ran my mile around the lake, getting quicker and quicker. By the end of March, I was getting around the lake in an impressive 7:30. I even had a couple of 2-lap runs; once I did 3 laps in just under 30 minutes.

Things were getting serious. It was time to buy my first pair of real running sneakers—a pair of Nike 5.0s. I ordered the Nike+ runner's watch by TOMTOM. This watch was going to be my key to accurate timing and measurement.

It's hard to explain the feeling I had the first time I went out with my new sneakers and watch, running around the lake at an impressive pace. The elation of that run quickly evaporated like my post-run deep breaths when I realized that I had gone only 9/10ths of a mile. Surely this was a joke. All those days running around the lake, had to be miles—right? How could I be 520 feet short?

After several days with the GPS watch monitoring me like an NSA staffer, it became clear that I was not running as far as I had thought. A mile, after all, is mile.

I am highly competitive and my favorite challenger has always been myself. By mid-April I was fixated on improving my times. A friend told me about a 5K race taking place in a few days a few miles from my home. What's a 5K? I asked. It's a running race that traverses 3.1 miles.

So, I entered my first 5K race. On April 13, 2013, I showed up and registered for the "Jersey Mike 5K" on beautiful City Island in Harrisburg, PA.

*"**Jersey Mike 5K:** This 5-kilometer (3.1 mile) race was developed by the K+L Guardian foundation, which was formed to benefit concert promoter "Jersey" Mike Van Jura's children after he died suddenly from a heart attack in 2012 at only age 36." ***

*Race descriptions are quoted from each event's websites.

It was 70 days since my 1-mile failure and 68 days before my life was changed by a simple Email. My goal was to finish the 5K in under 30 minutes. I got talking to a fellow racer who had been running only 2 years, and he indicated that he typically runs a 5K around 26 minutes. That number startled me. How could a guy my age run that fast? It seemed an impossible time. I was so naïve. Little did I realize the fast guys my age were running 5K in under 17 minutes!

I decided to do my best to keep this guy in my sights. When the gun sounded, I realized two things about my 5K style: I like to be out front with the faster runners—and I don't have what it takes to be out front with the faster runners.

The Jersey Mike 5K was a scenic run along the banks of the Susquehanna River, and although I took off at great pace, well ahead of the guy I had talked to pre-race, it didn't take him long to pass me. I corrected my thinking and paced more reasonably. I managed to keep him in my sights. By that I mean I could see the color of his shirt when he finished as I was contemplating how far away the finish line felt. Regardless, I was ecstatic at my first 5K time of 28:29.

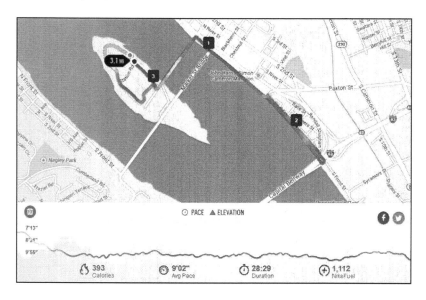

Until this first 5K, I had run alone. I was surprised by how different it felt to run with hundreds of other people. The other runners push you along at a faster pace than you would normally keep on your own. Running with others also feeds more visual data for the brain to work with than running solo. Running with others simultaneously distracts you from the effort of and also keeps you focused on the act of running.

This new experience was invigorating. Over the next 2 weeks, I was frenzied to improve. The 26s that gentleman spoke of no longer seemed unreachable. My training consisted of 1-mile sprints and 5K distance on the street. About this time, a friend, Adrienne Thoman, invited me to join her running group. Adrienne and her friend Mandie Levan ran with 3 to 5 runners on Tuesday nights. Their runs were much longer than I had been doing. They typically run between 5 and 7 miles at conversational pace. This was new to me, and it changed the way my body responded to running.

I spent much of my life using weights and bicycles to train my muscles. I trained my brain through books and schools. It never occurred to me how beneficial improving my lungs and heart could be. Running has enhanced my perspective on being healthy.

Two weeks after experiencing my first 5K, I found myself back at City Island, signing registration forms and waivers to enter the "Race Against Racism" 5K. How much had I improved in the span of 2 weeks? Would it be much different? Had the training paid off?

> *"**Race Against Racism 5K:** The ninth annual Race Against Racism will take place on City Island on Saturday, April 27th. The Race not only raises significant funds to support the YWCA of Greater Harrisburg's racial justice programs, but also promotes awareness of the issues that surround racial injustice in our community."*

It had been nearly 3 months since my dismal failure at running a mile and here I was, running my second 5K. When the start gun went off, there were 2 things I did not know: First, in 1,581 seconds I would demonstrate an improvement of over 2 minutes in my official 5K race time; and, second, in 54 days, Dee Gerber would change my life.

When I crossed the finish line, I was shocked by my time of 26:21. At the start of any new endeavor, it is always encouraging to see the quick improvements one can make as the mind and body acclimate. Two minutes fell from my race time faster than I could have imagined.

The next 2-minute reduction would take nearly 4 months—4 months of training and 9 more 5K races in 8 States. Of course, by then, my life had already been changed by Dee's Email. I wasn't sure when (or whether) another 2 minutes would fall, but I was committed to trying.

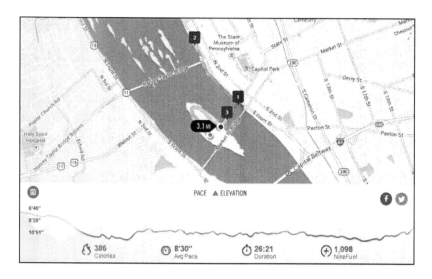

PACE ▲ ELEVATION

| 386 Calories | 8'30" Avg Pace | 26:21 Duration | 1,098 NikeFuel |

***

In May of 2013, I had a 2-week vacation planned to visit my girlfriend in Kingston, Jamaica. She was also a runner, and I was excited that she included a 5K in our itinerary. In Kingston, I ran every few days to keep up with training. The first weekend, I entered a Hash run. Regardless of Jamaica's reputation for being open minded about the highs of leafy weeds, a Hash run has nothing to do with marijuana. Hashes take place all over the world and are hosted by hundreds of Hash groups. In Jamaica, I ran with the Hash House Harriers. Like most Hash organizations, they describe themselves as a "drinking group with a running problem."

A Hash run is like a "choose your own adventure" book with only one ending. One member of the group acts as the hare (rabbit) who marks a course for others (the hounds) to run. Along the way, the Hare occasionally puts down a directional symbol that indicates that runners have a choice of directions. Only after running a decent distance do you reach either affirmation that you chose the correct path or a demarcation that clearly indicates you chose the wrong path (think the Dark Side in *Star Wars*). If you unfortunately chose the wrong direction, you must return to the decision point and pick another, hopefully correct, direction to run.

Hashes take place on all sorts of terrain and at distances of 2 to 5 miles. The one I ran was short at just over 2 miles, and I was grateful, as I baked in the Jamaican sun and humidity. The possibility of the hare throwing you off course adds a sense of excitement (and frustration) to the experience. Although it induces a healthy shot of adrenaline when you realized you made an error, the frustration far outweighed the benefits for me. I was grateful for the experience, but I will most likely not run another Hash.

A week later, my girlfriend registered us for the PUMA/Fortis 5K in Kingston. We had decided to run together, at her pace. This offered me an opportunity to enjoy the run without having to worry about my competitive nemesis—myself.

> *"**PUMA/Fortis 5K:** The inaugural PUMA/Fortis 5K slated for Sunday, May 26, seeks to raise funds for the Alpha Boys Home and the students of Kingston College."*

As we lined up for the race, a significant cultural difference between the U.S. and Jamaican events was apparent. Many of the Jamaicans were dressed in full cross-country racing uniforms as teams. At the time, I had run only 2 events in the U.S. and didn't realize how unique it was to see teams of runners compete in an open 5K. Don't misunderstand me; most of the Jamaican runners were not there as part of teams, but it was clear that most of the top runners were there with teammates. It was refreshing to see the support they offered each other and to hear the competitive banter between teams. Having now run a 5K in all 50 states, I can attest that this is a cultural difference. In America, running is a solo sport on this level.

The Jamaican 5K was a beautiful, although very hot, run through the capital city of Kingston. Although I ran at my girlfriend's pace, resulting in my slowest 5K to date, I was still very pleased that we came in under the 30-minunte mark at 29:37.

I had completed my third 5K in another country. I found an added sense of excitement from being a foreigner in a new land. Little did I know that feeling was a seed that would be nurtured by an important message that would arrive in my in-box 26 days later.

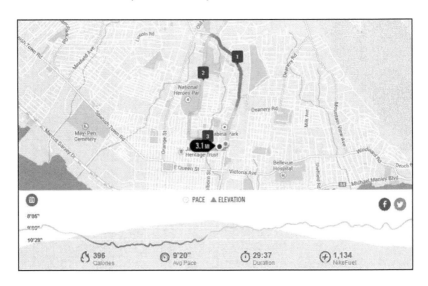

It would be easy to assume that such a significant Email between colleagues must have occurred between two people who work closely and have built a bond beyond their jobs. That couldn't have been farther from the truth. At the time "The Email" arrived, Dee and I were just getting to know each other. I was finishing my second year of employment at the college where we work.

Our college, HACC, Central Pennsylvania's Community College, has 5 campuses and serves over 20,000 students. My role is Director of Student Life, Multicultural Programs and Judicial Affairs at the largest campus, in Harrisburg. I work with student clubs & organizations, campus events and activities, student leadership development, and student conduct.

Dee works in the college's Accounts Payable office, which, at the time, was located in a central office building that was exactly 3.1 miles—a 5K— away from my office. That said, Dee and I rarely saw each other, though we communicated each week on payments for student organizations.

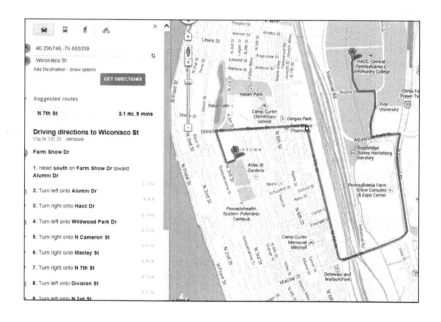

In my first 2 years at the college, I recall being in Dee's physical presence only twice, both to pick up checks we couldn't wait to receive through inter-office mail. The first time I met Dee, she was in a scooter, and the second time she was getting around her office with some sort of leg brace. Clearly, she had ambulatory challenges, but those were never discussed.

Around the time I was learning that I couldn't actually run a mile, I was also being inundated with challenging payment requests from my student groups. These challenges led to me to talk to Dee more often, as she is a wizard at working through the college's labyrinth of payment protocols.

This increased communication led to a Facebook friend request. Since this Facebook friendship coincided with the start of my running endeavors, Dee was privy to all my updates on adventures in running. (In fact, the Nike+ watch has an option to update Facebook on your runs, showing a route map, distance, and elapsed time.) Dee frequently "liked" these updates. Considering how little we knew about each other, it was awkward for me to receive "likes" to my running activity from someone who evidently had challenges walking.

That was all about to change, as were my life and hers.

My date with that life-changing Email was fast approaching, and on Thursday, June 20, 2013 at 1:07 p.m. it arrived:

— — — — — — — — — — — — — — — — — —
Subject: non-work
From: Gerber, Deanne   **To:** Fazio, Jeff
HAPPY (HACC version) Friday!
Are you running this weekend??
— — — — — — — — — — — — — — — — — —

She is saying Happy Friday on Thursday because HACC is closed on Fridays during the summer. Staff work longer hours Monday through Thursday, so Thursday *feels* like our Friday. My reply:

— — — — — — — — — — — — — — — — — —
Subject: non-work
From: Fazio, Jeff   **To:** Gerber, Deanne
Hey Dee,
I am hoping to do a 5K Saturday morning … we shall see. I haven't run/exercised all week. I was taking a self-imposed sabbatical. I am planning on doing something tonight. We shall see.
— — — — — — — — — — — — — — — — — —

I took a break from running because my knee was bothering me (runners frequently have problems with their knees). I had jumped into the sport so fast and hard it was not surprising to have body parts screaming.

Her reply changed everything—everything:

Subject: non-work
From: Gerber, Deanne   **To:** Fazio, Jeff

Anyway ... Silly little favor ... If you do run this weekend... when you get to mile 1—just think of those who can't... I won't bore you with the details, but been having a lot of issues with the MD—I have to go for more tests next month UGH—the THRILLS of it all.

My response:

Subject: non-work
From: Fazio, Jeff   **To:** Gerber, Deanne
Hey Dee,
I assure you that I think of those less able often, but I will make a point of it every time I run a mile. I don't think I shared with you that when I was in college I dated a girl who was the only ... only ... female in her entire family (extended included) that did not have MS. In her house she had 2 sisters, her mom and an aunt. There were all sorts of ambulatory issues to overcome and I know she had a lot of guilt for being the only able-bodied female in the house.
{{ hugs }}

This was such a simple Email exchange, but the evolution of the dialogue would ultimately have year-long implications that would provide a lifetime of memories, lessons and friendships—enough to fill a book.

Dee told me that she wrote the "little favor" Email, deleted it, wrote it, deleted it, and wrote it again. *He's going to think I am nuts. SEND!*

Sometimes the send button sends an Email. Sometimes it sends a snowball down a hill with such momentum that no one can predict how far it will grow or how big it will become.

Friday afternoon I was feeling pretty great and decided to ride my bicycle to pre-registration for Saturday's event. If my knee felt good after pedaling the 10 miles there, it should be good enough to run the next morning in the Hoot-N-Howl 5K.

Muscular Dystrophy Facts *from the Centers for Disease Control and Prevention*

"Muscular dystrophies are a group of diseases caused by defects in a person's genes. Over time, this muscle weakness decreases mobility and makes the tasks of daily living difficult."

Source: www.cdc.gov/ncbddd/musculardystrophy/facts.html

"**Hoot-n-Howl 5K:** The proceeds from this event benefit the Central Pennsylvania Animal Alliance (CPAA). The Central Pennsylvania Animal Alliance is an all-volunteer, non-profit alliance of local animal rescues working together to save dogs/cats through spay/neuter programs, adoptions, fostering, public outreach and education. CPAA believes that through working together and networking in our community, we can create a better community for both people and animals."

All seemed well, so I registered. That 20-mile bike ride provided ample thinking time. I thought about Dee and the previous day's Email correspondence. I thought about the fact that I would run a 5K the next day, and that running a race was not something Dee could ever do.

That evening, on my home computer I printed a 2" square of paper with two bold-faced, san serif characters: **4D**

I intended to pin this to my tank top much like runners pin race bibs to their shirts. Knowing Dee is an avid Facebook user, I'd tag Dee in the photos from the event.

When I arrived at the race, I got into what was becoming my pre-race ritual of eating a banana, drinking some water, and squeezing a tasty, 1-ounce GU Energy Gel into my mouth. Other runners were talking about the big hill on the course. Hill? What hill? Running is a flat sport—isn't it? Who would put a hill, a significant hill, in the route of a 5K? I was so naïve.

As I started contemplating the idea of running up a rather large hill, the second bomb hit—it's a 2-lap course! Surely they must be joking. Who would run up a big hill twice? But I am always open to trying new experiences, so I would suck it up and give this running up hills thing a shot.

I was not prepared for this. I had not trained for this. I didn't even realize this was a possibility.

When the race started, I was toward the front, as I like to be, for the first quarter mile or so. That was when the hill began. It was impressive and rising fast. My breath became heavier, my legs began to complain, and that is when I questioned the logic of riding my bicycle 20 miles the previous day. As we approached what appeared to be the top of the hill, the road turned—and the hill kept rising.

As I started the second leg of this never-ending hill, a beautiful young lady pranced by. As she passed, I was able to read the back of her custom-made jersey. It read, "Some girls chase boys, I pass them." That was a rather deflating message to read as I was trying to recall how to simultaneously breathe and make my legs work.

The top of the second rise was really just the beginning of the third. I was seriously dismayed and concerned about being able to complete a second lap. Flashbacks came of the horrible feelings I had 140 days earlier when I walked home crushed from failing to run a mile.

Other, crazy, runners were passing me at an impressive rate. Why would anyone have a hill in a 5K? Did I have second lap in me? Why put myself through this misery? I could just stop.

I could just run back down the hill and finish the first lap, jump in my car and leave.

The top of the hill was the 1-mile mark. In my mild relief at ending the climb, I remembered the 4D pinned on my shirt. I thought about Dee and others who can't run.

Who was I to question a second lap when so many don't have the option of attempting a first? How selfish was it for me to stop running because it was tough? I wasn't running just for myself. Today, I was also running for Dee. I pressed on, over the crest, thankful for the aid of gravity as I ran.

I would have quit that race if it weren't for Dee Gerber. That was the first of many hills Dee would push me up. Dee has pushed me through running ill, and she has pushed me through running cold, tired and exhausted.

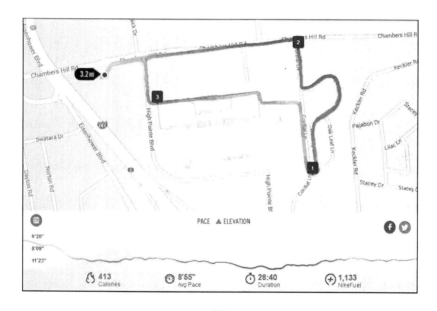

***

Facebook has power.

When I got home, I posted photos from the event on Facebook, along with my race results. I had actually completed that challenging, hill-laden course in 28 minutes and 16 seconds. I was very pleased that it wasn't my slowest attempt. Clearly, I was getting stronger and faster.

Dee was excited about the 4D on my shirt, and with her permission I tagged her as that little piece of pinned printer paper on my jersey. The power of Facebook took over from there, with *her* friends taking notice of my running efforts and asking questions. In an instant, a simple agreement between colleagues became something others would witness and applaud.

The metaphoric 4D snowball had been pushed down a hill and momentum was building. Little did Dee and I know that the hill this snowball was descending was infinitely taller and steeper than the hill that almost broke my will. Dee and I talked about how the D in 4D was intended for her, but could have wider implications by also representing *dystrophy*. The 4D experience had begun and we didn't even know it.

Muscular Dystrophy Facts *from the Centers for Disease Control and Prevention*

"Different types of muscular dystrophy affect specific groups of muscles, have a specific age when signs and symptoms are first seen, vary in how severe they can be, and are caused by imperfections in different genes. Muscular dystrophy can run in the family, or a person might be the first one in their family to have the condition."

Source: www.cdc.gov/ncbddd/musculardystrophy/facts.html

Chapter 2

Van Cortlandt Track Club 5k Cancer Challenge
Bronx, New York City, New York
June 30, 2013

The following weekend I ran my first 5K in a state other than my home state of Pennsylvania. My favorite aspect of living in central Pennsylvania is our proximity to so many amazing places. Our area is ripe with incredible day trips. Beyond all of the wonderful things to see and do in my home state, I am within 3 hours of New York City, Atlantic City, Baltimore, Washington, D.C., and the shores of New Jersey, Delaware, and Maryland. My weekends are often filled with one- or two-day trips.

The last weekend of June, 2013, I had planned a camping trip to the beach at Gateway National Park in New Jersey. Having used the website www.runningintheusa.com to find local races, I explored the site's ability to locate races in other areas. I found a 5K race in the Bronx, New York City, in Van Cortlandt Park and decided I would give it a shot.

At Van Cortlandt Park I was struck by how different the place was from my home 200 miles away in Pennsylvania. I was still in the U.S., still in the Mid-Atlantic, but the environment was completely different. I, once again, had that stranger-in-a-strange land feeling that I had when I'd run in Jamaica. When you travel outside of familiar areas, everything seems new. You notice small things again, like signs, trees, stores and restaurants. Familiarity allows us to take our environment for granted. Being somewhere new makes you feel alive. It crossed my mind that I enjoyed that feeling of being a newcomer and that running was a great way to socialize and meet the locals.

Before the race, I realized I'd forgotten my paper 4D, so I scrambled—or rather scribbled—4D onto a fast-food napkin and pinned it on my jersey. With such a great response to the first 4D race, I couldn't run without it!

When I approached the registration table, another runner pointed to my scribbled, 2-character napkin-badge and asked if that was what the race bibs looked like. That joke allowed me to talk to her for a moment about what it meant. That opportunity was my first 4D "elevator speech" as I completed registration for the Van Cortlandt Track Club's 3rd Annual VCTC 5k Run Cancer Challenge.

*"**VCTC 5k Run Cancer Challenge:** A fast, Personal Record-setting course. Consists of 3 laps on the track then a loop of the Van*

Cortlandt Parade Grounds (the Flats) with an exciting detour up the cow path coming back to the Flats at the north end for the run in, some asphalt but mainly the new cinder track, then re-enter the stadium for an athletic finish. All proceeds go to the American Cancer Society - Bronx Region."

The woman at the VCTC registration table looked at my form and noted Harrisburg, PA, as my city of residence. She asked me why I was running an event in New York since I live over 3 hours away. On a little high from having just talked about the 4D experience, I had one of those moments where the mouth says something that the brain has not fully checked out. Impulsively, I blurted out that I was running a 5K in all 50 states in honor of a colleague with Muscular Dystrophy.

She thought that was terrific and quickly shared with two older gentlemen who were standing nearby. I was thinking "What have I just said? What did I just do?" Suddenly, there was some chatter among the people around me and one of the guys said that it was a really cool goal. He asked how many states I had completed.

Rather embarrassed and pretty shyly, I admitted that this was going to be my first out-of-state run.

I received a gentle, knowing smile from those two men and they politely wished me well. I suspect they had more insight, than I did, into how intense the journey of running all 50 states was going be. It was an interesting moment. This was only my second event running with the 4D badge on my shirt and somehow I'd managed to proclaim that I am going to run a 5K in all 50 states.

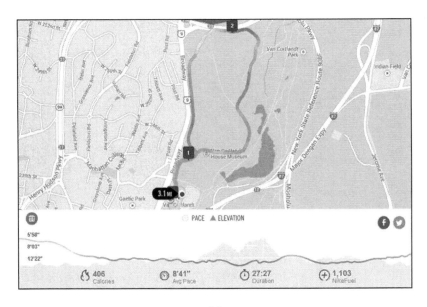

Whenever someone first shares their vision, it is always interesting to see how the outside world responds. All too frequently this type of declaration is met with discouragement or, at best, the polite good-luck-with-that smile I received.

I had a lot to think about during my 27-minute run through Van Cortlandt Park.

The run was an appropriate place to clarify my vision for what I wanted to do. I decided that I was committed to running a 5K in all 50 states and that I wanted to do this in honor of "Dee and others who can't run." It was also going to be important to share information about Muscular Dystrophy along the way. 4D was going to become a nationwide experience.

***

After declaring my commitment, it was clear that this effort was going to be bigger than printer paper and napkins. That said, I created a logo for 4D with the word "dystrophy" inside the letter D and added a slogan. Then I uploaded it to www.cafepress.com so I could order real pins to wear when running. When you upload a logo to Cafe Press, the site automatically populates a store for you filled with dozens of products. The 4D Cafe Press site is located at www.cafepress.com/4d4d.

Within a day of sharing the link to the store on Facebook, I got questions from bikers, hikers and swimmers about their willingness to support. So the next day I opened www.cafepress.com/4d4dswim, www.cafepress.com/4d4dhike, and www.cafepress.com/4d4dbike. The initial profits from the stores were used to purchase pins to hand out to runners. As the stores become more profitable, the intent is to donate to the Muscular Dystrophy Association (MDA).

On July 11, my first batch of 4D pins arrived and I was shocked 6 days later when Brad Bansner, someone I did not know, shared a photo on Facebook of himself running wearing a 4D pin! It had begun so fast. In such a short amount of time, there were other runners seeing the value in running for those who can't. I started the 4D Facebook page at www.facebook.com/Run4D.

***

Life offers us endless opportunities to reflect and learn. Through each state (and, consequently, chapter), I'll reflect on aspects of leadership that were learned through the various experiences.

Declaring a goal of running a 5K in all 50 States while standing in the middle of a park in the Bronx registering for the first out-of-state race might seem, depending on your perspective, foolish or inspirational. It might even seem ill-informed, improbable or naïve. The beauty of hindsight is that it allows us to evaluate the motivation, passion, and, ultimately, the commitment of those who announce lofty aspirations.

Leaders need the ability to set clear goals based on a solid, but evolving vision. Furthermore, they need the ability to communicate this vision to others and inspire them to follow. After all, without others following, there is no leadership. Special attention should be given to vision that is supportive of others. Humans are social creatures, and a good leader makes sure other people's needs are met too.

Part of sharing vision is the ability to handle naysayers and critics. No matter how great our ideas, not everyone will see it that way. Leaders need the ability to keep focus and dedication to a goal when faced with those who do not deem what we are attempting is possible or worthwhile. Leaders need the ability to persist.

***

I learned a few other important lessons that day running in Van Cortlandt Park. When I started running 5Ks, I never dreamt of actually winning anything and I surely didn't win anything that day, but I could have. That realization was incredibly eye-opening.

Typically 5Ks award top 3 male and female runners overall. They also usually award top 3 men and women in age groups. Some events do age groups by decades and some do them in 5-year increments.

From the start, I have always thought that finishing was winning, and I still feel that way. My biggest competitor in all aspects of life has always been myself. When I run, I am trying to beat me—trying to set a new personal record (PR).

That 5K in the Bronx was a wakeup call to my potential and the need to start paying attention to other runners more closely. Why? I finished 4th in my age group (Males, 30-39). I finished 13 seconds behind the gentleman who earned 3rd place and there were no runners between us.

I was very aware of his passing me in the last tenth of a mile, but I was not aware that he was in my age group. If I had been, would I have found a little more inside myself to compete? Could I have pushed harder for a little longer? I don't know, but I do know that I may have missed out on earning my first medal that day.

When I crossed the finish line, I did have a medal put around my neck. This medal wasn't for placing, but for finishing. Many running events offer finishers' medals as a sign of accomplishment for completing the entire run. This was my first finishers' medal and it did exactly what it should do: It made me feel proud and as if I had accomplished something. It was recognition of my efforts. It showed that all my training and hard work had value and was appreciated.

**

New York Leadership Lesson:
Know the Competition, Reward People

_____

As leaders it is important to know the competition and to be aware when they are starting to pass us by; otherwise, opportunities will be missed. It is always important to know the rules and who you are up against. You never know when a competitor will push you to a new level of achievement.

Receiving a finisher's medal at a race is a reaffirmation that you accomplished something. Your time and effort had value. It's a sign of appreciation and recognition. As a leader, make sure you are taking time to acknowledge team members and give rewards as appropriate. It is very inspiring for those who follow your lead. If it is not fiscally possible to offer rewards, then show gratitude through words. Saying "Thank You" for a job well done has no cost, but incredibly high value.

Muscular Dystrophy Facts *from the Centers for Disease Control and Prevention*

"Muscular dystrophy is rare, and there is not a lot of data on how many people are affected by the condition. Much of the information comes from outside the United States. CDC scientists are working to estimate the number of people with each type of muscular dystrophy in the United States."

Source: www.cdc.gov/ncbddd/musculardystrophy/facts.html

Chapter 3

Jersey Shore Undy 5000 5K
Long Branch, New Jersey
July 20, 2013

As mentioned previously, I tend to take a lot of day trips on weekends, and 4 weeks after the Bronx run, I found myself headed back to Gateway National Park in Sandy hook, New Jersey. Gateway National Park is a beautiful place to relax on the beach and is close to New York City and other attractions, so I end up there frequently over the summer.

Fortunately there was a 5K scheduled 30 minutes away in Long Branch, New Jersey, on July 20. This was to be my second state in as many months. It was also to be my second themed run.

***

Previously, my Tuesday night running group convinced me to join its team, Rockin' Rosado, for a huge theme race in Philadelphia. So I joined Adrienne Thoman, Mandie Levan, Jodi Stuber, Shawna Strine and five of their other friends for my first themed run on July 13. Our team had entered into The Color Run—Philadelphia.

> **"The Color Run:** The Color Run was founded in January of 2012 as an event to promote healthiness and happiness by bringing the community together to participate in the "Happiest 5k on the Planet". We are the original paint race and have created a completely new genre of running events that continues to grow exponentially. Now the single largest event series in the United States, The Color Run has exploded since our debut event. We have more than tripled our growth, hosting more than 170 events in 30+ countries in 2013."

The Color Run is an exciting event where volunteers throw huge plumes of colored powder at the runners at various locations throughout the course. By the end of the event, runners are covered in bright colors from the powder. It was a wonderful event to run with a group of friends.

Although this run was incredibly fun and encouraged me to look at themed runs, it is not included in this book as its own chapter, since it was not scheduled as part the 4D 50-State 5K experience, the impossibility of "running" the event, and because the race fell drastically short of a 5K. My Nike+ watch barely reached 3 miles at the finish and that was including a lot of extra running. At one point, Jodi, Adrienne, and I turned around and ran the wrong direction to find some missing teammates. That distance we ran back had to be redone to get to the finish line, so we traversed a significant portion of the course 3 times!

Regardless of the event's shortcomings (literally), it was a remarkable experience to run with 26,000 other runners. The energy that such a large group brings is impressive. Unfortunately, a group that large combined with all of the crazy and colorful distractions encourage a lot of non-running behaviors. There is a lot of people traffic on course from participants that are not running. The Color Run is a blast, but is not a 5K race.

***

So, the New Jersey event was to be my first themed run of the 50-state experience. This 5K was in support of colon cancer services. I suppose when you work with a tooshie, I mean touchy, subject like colon cancer you must have a sense of humor. The event I entered was the Undy 5000.

> **"Undy 5000:** The Undy 5000 is one of the Colon Cancer Alliance's signature fundraising events and is an important revenue source for furthering its mission of knocking colon cancer out of the top three cancer killers. Money raised through the Undy 5000 supports both local and national colon cancer services."

The name is a play on words that references one of the most famous automobile races in the world, the Indy 500. The automobile race has its name because it takes place in Indianapolis, IN, and traverses 500 miles. The running race is called Undy because runners race in underwear to bring awareness to colon cancer concerns, and 5000 because there is that many meters in a 5K.

The race took place on the boardwalk in Long Branch, NJ. As one might imagine, it is an interesting experience to have over 350 runners in their underwear heading down the boardwalk. The reality is a bit tamer than the imagination might provide. Most of the runners wore the skin-tight, spandex infused running shorts with their underwear layered on top.

I anticipated the possibility of setting a new personal record at this event, as it was a very flat course and basically at sea level. Sadly, I did not get much sleep the night before. I was camping at Sandy Hook that night and the tent experience was less than ideal as people in the other tents nearby enjoyed their Saturday evening into the wee hours, not an environment conducive to getting rest. Regardless, I put in a solid effort and missed a PR by 14 seconds with a time of 26:34.

Although my primary goal for this event was to set a new PR, I also had to wrestle with the secondary experience—running in just a pair of boxer shorts. Our cultural upbringing has strange effects on how we think we *should* behave. For a guy to go shirtless with a pair of shorts or a bathing suit in public is no big deal. Put that same guy in a pair of underwear and have him walk around bare-chested, suddenly we have an issue. Psychologically, it was bizarre running down a New Jersey boardwalk in just a pair of boxers and running sneakers.

It's even worse for ladies. Walk the board walk in a bikini? No problem. Walk the boardwalk in a bra and panties? Someone's calling the police. Our sense of modesty is really displayed through a unique prism of ambiguity.

In an odd, counter-intuitive display, most runners wore the tight, black running shorts *beneath* their undergarments—myself included. In a bizarre role reversal, our outerwear became underwear and vice versa.

As a man, running in boxers really didn't challenge my modesty any more than regular shorts. I wore the skin-tight running shorts under the boxers for added support. It would be another 17 states before I learned that men don't really need *that kind of support* while running.

Beyond having us run in our undies, the race organizers added another unique and amusing feature to the course. About 200 yards from the start/finish line they had a fire truck parked to shoot a huge arc of cold water across the boardwalk for the participants to run under.

When we first started running, you could see the large arc of water spewing from the truck and you just knew that we were going to be running under it. My knee-jerk reaction was that it was a wasted novelty at the beginning of the race when we were not sweating. After I ran through the blast and felt the cool water, the light switch went off, and I realized we would be running back this way when we finished. Suddenly, it was something to look forward to.

The Undy 5000 was a very well organized and enjoyable event. I would run in my undies again to support the Colon Cancer Alliance.

***

New Jersey Leadership Lesson:
Get Outside Your Comfort Zone

Leadership sometimes puts us in positions that make us uncomfortable. Leaders need to get used to that feeling and still maintain focus. For most people, running down a boardwalk in underwear with hundreds of strangers, also in their underwear, is not a way to find comfort. Regardless, 359 people found the courage that day to participate and support a great cause. Often, in Intro to Speech courses, nervous students are told to imagine the audience sitting in their underwear to help take the edge off of public speaking. In a leadership role, you can step that game up by imagining yourself speaking about your vision in your underwear. Are you willing to bare yourself to inspire others to follow your vision?

Muscular Dystrophy Facts from the Centers for Disease Control and Prevention

There are eight major types of muscular dystrophy:

Duchenne/Becker (DMD/BMD)

Myotonic (MMD)

Limb-Girdle (LGMD)

Facioscapulohumeral (FSH)

Congenital (CMD) and myopathies

Distal (DD)

Oculopharyngeal (OPMD)

Emery-Dreifuss (EDMD)

Source: www.cdc.gov/ncbddd/musculardystrophy/facts.html

Chapter 4

Run to Read Races 5K
Fairmont, West Virginia,
July 26, 2013

With 2 states down, it was apparent that I needed to look at more efficient ways of completing states or this project might take years to complete. Anyone who knows me knows that when I set sight on a goal, I put 110% into it. I have also earned a reputation for achieving goals quickly. The word "idle" is not often used in my lexicon.

Besides the efficiency of time, I also realized that travel costs could get exponentially expensive as I got farther from Pennsylvania. If I was going to make my goal happen in reasonable time (whatever that is) and within a reasonable budget (whatever that is), I was going to have to make my plan significantly more efficient.

My first step in logistical efficiency was attempting to complete more than one state per weekend. I am fortunate that my job becomes a 4-day work week from the middle of May to the middle of August. That extra day was going to come in handy as a travel day for weekend running.

The Friday after I bared my chest and heinie-in-boxers along the beach in New Jersey, I set out in the opposite direction—west—to run West Virginia and Ohio. Faced with driving 673 miles over 2 days, I decided it was prudent to start planning some sight-seeing along the way. As they say, "all work and no play make Johnny a dull boy." If you are going to attack a massive goal, you might was well enjoy the trip. Before I left, I logged onto www.roadsideamerica.com to plan stops along the way.

The Roadside America motto is "Find Attractions and Oddities." The site lists thousands of interesting things to see and do while you are traveling within the United States. This was the first, crucial piece in planning some interesting stops. Roadside America served me well on this journey and it was a great starting point. Sixty-one days after I set out for West Virginia, I would get a simple, two-word Email from *another colleague* that would drastically alter my perspective on how I was planning to do all 50 states, but that is a story for another chapter.

From here on out, I will include a section titled "Sights along the Way" that will give a list of the things I stopped to investigate in my travels. Since tourist attractions are not the primary focus of the book, I will let readers decide whether the list of sights is worth their time for further exploration.

***

I woke up early on a Friday morning for a road trip to Fairmont, WV, for an evening run. To get to Fairmont, I immediately exited Pennsylvania to the south and crossed Maryland. This day, like many in my future, would consist of traveling on interstate highways with planned exits for sight-seeing. Considering how many other states are physically closer to my home, it was peculiar to think that West Virginia would be state #3 and I was excited to be running in Ohio the next morning.

WEST VIRGINIA
Sights Along the Way

Cooper's Rock State Forest: Cooper's Rock and Rock City

Don Knott's Hollywood Star in Morgantown

Skyrock at Dorsey's Knob

As I drove, I contemplated the 5K I would run that evening. With a starting time of 6:30 p.m., this would be my first evening race. It was in West Virginia, so I anticipated there might be some hills. At the time, I didn't know enough to be aware of the difference in elevation, but the run took place at just under 1000' so the difference in oxygen content in the atmosphere was not significantly different from what I was used to in Pennsylvania.

Years ago, I used to race cars, and like all types of racing, my life was dominated by times. Time in the racing world is a measure of performance. It's a measure of improvement. Dedication to improving times is an addiction, and it feeds progress. I was addicted once again and eager to see improvement in my 5K time. Having completed two 5Ks in the 26s, I was hungry for a 25-anything run.

I arrived early to the East-West Stadium in Fairmont, WV, and volunteered with the set-up crew to carry bottled water and Gatorades to the finish line. This was going to be a neat finish as we were completing the race on an actual track-n-field running track. The run in the Bronx also finished (and started) on a running track, which adds a special feel to a 5K.

There was still plenty of time before the crew would be ready for registration, so I decided to drive the course. It seemed to be a pretty clear loop through the town of Fairmont. The route featured 6 to 7 rolling hills; they seemed steep, but short. As quickly as we would run up one, we could catch our breath and run down the other side. I thought this might be helpful in trying to break the 26-minute barrier. I was ready to run.

I enjoyed the rest of the drive as I ate my banana and drank my vitamin water. I would wait until 15 minutes before the start to consume the Energy Gel. My pre-race ritual was becoming a ritual.

Once everything was prepared, the registration lines opened, and I stepped up with my registration fees. Once again, the registration worker commented on my 4D pin, and I was able to share the 4D story with her. I completed my registration for the 15th Annual Run to Read Races 5K

"Run to Read Races 10K/5K: *Event benefits Literacy Volunteers of Marion County, a United Way agency & a 501©(3) entity."*

This event featured another first for me. The event kicked off with a 10K. Although I had run over 6.2 miles (10K) on the street for training purposes, I hadn't actually attended a 10K event. The 10Kers were going to run the 5K course twice and about 30 minutes later the 5K race would begin.

Watching the 10K race was very motivating. The winner came in at 34 minutes and 12 seconds running 5.30-minute miles! His 10K time beat the race times of the last 10 runners in the 5K! He also passed the police car that was leading the race, twice!

When it was our time to run, we lined up on Virginia Avenue. The gun fired and we were off. The rolling hills that I had driven were fast approaching, but the runners out front were turning. I was confused, where were we going? This wasn't the direction I had driven. As I turned with the lead runners, they turned again onto a road parallel to the one with the rolling hills.

This road didn't have the hills. It was just a steady decline. This was fabulous news, I could keep increasing my speed and have a shot at a record-setting 25-anything run! As the road continued onward and downward at seemingly increasing steepness, my brain started doing the math on the harsh reality that somewhere, somehow, I would have to run back up this elevation. As much as this concerned me, it motivated me to go downhill even faster because I knew I was going to lose a lot of time on the way back up.

When we reached the bottom of the hill, we made a left and continued on relatively flat terrain for about half of a mile. Then we made another left turn to go up THE hill. This hill was almost a mile long, which meant there was no hope of seeing its peak soon. But I had mentally prepared myself for the long haul and was committed to just plowing along at a significantly slower pace.

I started to ascend the hill and a woman about my age flew passed me at an incredible pace. As I began to contemplate how she could be running so fast and how long she could possibly keep up that pace, she abruptly stopped running and started walking. That cleared up that mystery as soon as it began.

I plugged along at my steady pace and eventually passed her. A few moments later, she went zooming passed me again at a fast pace and, once more, abruptly stopped running and started walking. As we both attacked the hill with very different strategies, she passed me and went back to walking 7 or 8 times. It was incredibly distracting. The hill was wearing me down physically and I was becoming very realistic that running a new PR, much less a 25.XX, was not likely.

She raced passed me one last time right as we approached the peak of the hill and she was gone. By the time I got to the top, she was barely visible as the road wound on a slight downhill. I am 6' and my long legs do me well when running downhill. I started picking up speed and distance in long strides.

By the time the course flattened out, the run-and-stop woman was back within a visible distance and the gap was closing quickly. We were also fast approaching the running track that was home to the finish line. Could I catch her? It was doubtful with the amount of distance left, but the possibility motivated me to push harder.

We entered the track at the top of the oval and had to run 3/4 of the track to reach the finish line. My flying-by-the-seat-of-my-pants plan was to close the gap as much as possible and then sprint hard as we rounded the top of the oval at the end of the track.

This worked miraculously, except I underestimated how long the top of the oval was. I was closing in on her fast but running out of steam even faster. I backed off a bit and paced her until the oval straightened and I could see the finish line.

I mounted one last charge and was in full-out sprint. As she heard my increased pace she stepped up into a sprint. We were racing side-by-side in a blindingly fast sprint as the finish line approached. The finish line, for whatever reason, was not actually on the track, but about 15 feet off the track in the infield.

In the craziness of our sprint, we misjudged our lines into this last curve and she crashed into me, pushing me over the line in front of her. We managed to stay upright, but we were a momentary tangle of arms and elbows. What an incredible finish, regardless of the actual elapsed time.

When I looked at the race results, I spotted her time first. She scored a 26:00.8! How incredible, that means I had to have managed to set a new PR in the 25s. My final result was a 25:58.8, a new personal record.

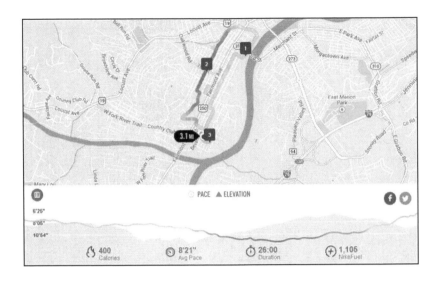

PACE ▲ ELEVATION

6'25"

8'05"

10'54"

| 400 Calories | 8'21" Avg Pace | 26:00 Duration | 1,105 NikeFuel |

***

Keep Steady, Let Others Push You

There are two important lessons from this race. One is the age-old question of the race between the tortoise and the hare. Clearly, I was the tortoise in this race. What I experienced was that although the hare I was racing got within closing distance of the finish line well ahead of me, I had a lot more "fuel in the tank" left to sprint at the end. I needed to make up the distance I was down and have enough left to sprint passed her.

The second lesson is that sometimes it is good to use other people's momentum to push you farther than you would otherwise go on your own. I suspect that without her pushing into me, I would have claimed the 26:00, which would have been frustrating even though it would have been a new best. Sometimes a split second makes a very big difference.

Muscular Dystrophy Facts from the Centers for Disease Control and Prevention

Duchenne/Becker (DMD/BMD) more commonly affects men. "In 2007, 349 out of 2.37 million males aged 5-24 years were reported to have DMD or BMD in the United States. This means that about 15 out of every 100,000 males ages 5-24 years were affected that year.

In 2009, 233 out of 1.49 million males were reported to have DMD or BMD in Northern England. That is, about 16 out of every 100,000 males were affected that year."

Source: www.cdc.gov/ncbddd/musculardystrophy/facts.html

Chapter 5

Scrappers 5K
Niles, Ohio
July 27, 2013

With West Virginia checked off, I headed north to the Ohio 5K, taking place 12 hours after I completed the WV run. Inside those 12 hours, I needed to complete a 2.5 hour drive, find food, and a safe place to sleep, and actually get some rest.

As it was still summer and warm, I considered saving money by camping in my car overnight, but by the time I arrived in Niles, OH, I was dying for the comfort of a bed—any bed. I pulled into the first dive-looking motel I could find and hoped it would be $40 (or less) for the night.

I entered the lobby, a dirty little space scratched up—from what, I have no idea. Next to the glass window with the opening to talk through was a buzzer to notify staff you were in need of service. As I waited for a response, I read the "No Hand Guns Allowed On Premise" sign. It was very reassuring and I felt much safer.

The place cost exactly $40 for a night's stay, which was probably $20 too much, but in my current state well worth it. After all of that driving and running, I was asleep in seconds. Thankfully, the stay was uneventful. I was able to shower and get to the morning's race with no issue.

The Ohio contest was taking place at Eastwood Field, the home of the Mahoning Valley Scrappers' minor league baseball team. It was to be my first of two 5Ks at minor league fields. On the morning of July 27, I entered the Scrappers 5K in Niles, OH.

> **"Scrappers 5K:** This event donates $3 from each entry to the Akron Children's Hospital Mahoning Valley."

The course started, and finished, on the training track around the baseball field. Although the course began in the stadium, it quickly left and looped through their parking lot then continued with a giant loop around a shopping mall. The race was much earlier than mall hours so traffic was not an issue. For all intents and purposes, this course was completely flat.

If I had just touched a 25-minute run last night, imagine what I could do on a flat course in the morning, when I am typically faster.

By this time, my training included 1-mile sprints, 5Ks on the street, longer runs with my Tuesday-night running group, weight training, and a lot of cycling. I was feeling pretty fit and healthy. Ever since my first race, I tried to talk to other runners to get a sense of their times so I could see if there was someone to pace or keep an eye on.

As I walked around pre-race, a gentleman just a few years older than I struck up a conversation. I asked him what kind of times he was running. He said, rather modestly, that he was a medium-fast runner. I asked what that means. He said he typically only runs 19- to 21-minute 5Ks. That is a time I could only dream of. In this particular race he ultimately ended up taking 3rd

OHIO
Sights Along the Way

Eastwood Field

*Niles Iron and Metal Co.
Iron Man Sculpture*

David Grohl Alley

*Sight of Neil Armstrongs's
First Flight*

A Christmas Story House

overall in the men's open with a PR of 18:44—absolutely amazing.

I laughed and said that was incredible. I said I was just hoping to get solidly into the 25s. He looked surprised and told me that he came over to see what I was about because he thought I would be competition, as he hadn't seen me around before. He thought I would be much faster by the way I looked. I told him that I had only been running for a few months and he assured me that I was going to be significantly faster next year.

In running races there are elapsed time and gun time. Elapsed time is the actual time it takes a runner to go from the start line to the finish line. The gun time is the time it takes the runner to finish from the moment that the gun went off. If a runner starts toward the back of the pack, it could take several seconds, sometimes even more than a minute, to cross the *starting* line.

I tend to be one of the first people to move up to the front of the line before the race starts. I like to be able to click on my Nike watch just as the race timer starts. If all goes well, my Nike+ watch time, elapsed time, and gun time are very close.

As we lined up for the race, I went toward the front. No matter what state I run in, people just don't like to go up front. Even the fast runners don't seem as if they are eager to walk up to the actual starting line. Frequently, I am standing there by myself until people begin filling in. The second person to the line was a woman much older than I, but clearly in very good shape.

She appeared to be in her late 50s or early 60s. A few family members there showed her support and took photos. It was evident that she had been a runner a long time, clearly experienced. As I was 10-to-20 years her junior, I thought she might be an ideal candidate for me to pace.

When the race started, I was behind her, matching her speed easily. The first part of the course circled the training track that surrounded the baseball field. It was exciting to run inside a stadium, and I started looking at all the spectators, appreciating the view that minor leaguers get to enjoy.

As we completed the lap inside the stadium, I refocused on running and navigating the exit into the parking lot. That is when I realized the woman I was pacing was no longer in front of me. I hadn't even realized I passed her so quickly. As I exited the stadium, I glanced back to see how much distance I had put between us, but I did not see her.

Running into the parking lot to start our trek around the outside of the stadium, I saw her again, well ahead of me and turning the first corner. It was a very humbling moment, but I was confident I could catch her. I stepped up my pace, and as I turned the corner she had just tackled, I looked ahead and barely saw a glimpse of her as she made the next turn!

I never saw her again. I would have sworn that she completely vanished if I hadn't seen her after I finished the race. She had been done for some time and was enjoying a post-race water and banana. As the old adage goes, don't judge a book by its cover.

Regardless of my time and haven taken a pounding from this older woman, I was ecstatic to see that I clocked a 25:13. I managed to shave another 45 seconds off the previous evening's PR! Not only did I prove that I could tackle two 5Ks in fewer than 24 hours, but I could do it while performing at peak performance. The fruits of my training were ripening.

***

Never underestimate the competition, and don't judge people based on age, sex or appearance. It is all too easy to see someone's age and make assumptions about their abilities. Leaders should look for a variety of strengths from everyone on their team, without making assumptions about their abilities based on appearance. Unless you take the time to learn, you may never know what level of talent, training or expertise someone possesses. My expectations of the older woman's ability were exactly as erroneous as the assumptions of my running ability made by the gentleman I spoke to pre-race. We tend to jump to conclusions when sizing up the competition. Be wary of letting these thoughts alter your decisions, as you may miss important opportunities.

Muscular Dystrophy Facts from the Centers for Disease Control and Prevention

Myotonic (MMD) affects men and women equally. "In 2009, 316 out of 2.99 million individuals of all ages were reported to have MMD in Northern England. This means that about 11 out of every 100,000 people were affected that year."

Source: www.cdc.gov/ncbddd/musculardystrophy/facts.html

Chapter 6

Spartyka Fallen Heroes 5K
Virginia Beach, Virginia
August 4, 2013

Three states had been raced during July, taking the total to 4. Having finished my first full month of attempting 5Ks in other states, it seemed that accomplishing 3 races per month was very reasonable. Fortunately for my goals, I can be very unreasonable. In the near future, my dedication and obsessiveness would show that accomplishing *significantly more* than 3 states per month is not only possible, but absolutely probable in my world.

When attempting a 50-state challenge of any sort, it is smart to go through your list of friends and family (and their friends and family) to see if there is any chance of getting assistance along the way. My list of family members is rather short, but I am fortunate that some of them live out of state.

Although we both grew up in Pennsylvania, my brother John has been living in Virginia for nearly 20 years. He did a 4-year stint in the Navy in the early '90s and was stationed in Norfolk. He never left and Virginia has been his home ever since.

Toward the end of July my brother announced that he was moving from Suffolk, VA, back to Virginia Beach. He put the call out for movers and I immediately started looking at maps and race schedules. My brother's move was going to happen on Saturday, August 4, and there was a really interesting 5K taking place on Sunday in Virginia Beach. This would work out well.

After a 7-hour drive, I arrived at my brother's place Friday night, and he had, thankfully, already had a majority of his home packed into the moving truck and ready to roll. My parents were already there, so we were all set for the big move the next morning. Saturday was an early wakeup call and we all got to work right away. The move went very smoothly and we finished in plenty of time to relax and share a family meal. I was going to be able to race the next day and was thrilled that my family was going to watch.

***

The next morning I headed to the Virginia Beach Sportsplex to register for the event. The stadium at the Sportplex was decorated with giant banners that read "Wounded Warrior," "Spartyka," "We Support Our

Troops" and "Fallen Heroes 5K." Most 5Ks support one cause or another and it is impossible to rate one as more important than another.

The reality is that some causes just touch individuals more than others. I am fortunate that I do not have family or friends who have been wounded or killed in combat, but I read a lot of news. The death, misery and human destruction of war just always feels so useless and unnecessary. Humans cause themselves so much pain over confrontations. This event was going to pull some heartstrings, and I am grateful that I had the opportunity to run in the Spartyka Fallen Heroes 5K.

> "*Spartyka Fallen Heroes 5K:* In honor of the daily sacrifices made by the brave men and women in all branches of the United States Military, Spartyka Nation is proud to host the Spartyka Wounded Warrior 5K to benefit the Wounded Warrior Project, a national organization supporting wounded veterans."

My girlfriend was visiting from Jamaica and also registered to run. Having registered, we took some time to walk around and look through the Wounded Warrior and Spartyka merchandise. I was eagerly waiting for my parents to show up. There was something novel about being 39 years old and excited that my parents were coming to watch me run. I guess that is not something you ever lose—look Mom! Are you proud of what I am doing?

A call for the runners to come to the field was announced. This event, like a few of the others, started on an actual running track. Unlike any of the other races, this was a cross-country course, which meant we were going to leave the track and run through woods and fields. The running terrain was grass (and some mud), much different than the hard asphalt I had been running and training on.

The event had a very formal pre-race presentation, honoring a family who had lost their son in the war. The family was recognized and given a folded US flag. Other notable mentions were made in support of the day and our troops. There was an ROTC honor guard also on the field. The National Anthem was sung. Whenever I hear the National Anthem, I get choked up. So many thoughts go through my head when I hear that song and this day was particularly moving.

I was thinking about the freedoms and prosperity we enjoy in this country and what the cost of that freedom is. Time was spent thinking about all who served and are serving. There I was, enjoying the opportunity to travel to other states on a whim to race 5Ks while other Americans were in combat losing limbs and lives.

The fact that I was a White American standing there holding hands with my girlfriend who was a Black Jamaican emphasized how wonderful this country is. The diversity of the U.S. is truly amazing. It was important that we could be there, together, and for the most part be accepted. It is lawful for mixed couples to be together. In so many places this is still extremely taboo, illegal, punishable.

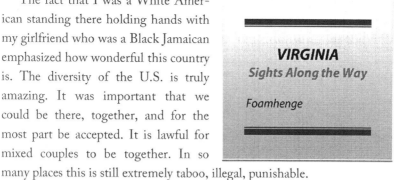

VIRGINIA
Sights Along the Way

Foamhenge

My thoughts also went to the efforts that my girlfriend was going through to gain legal entry to the United States in hopes of a better life. I spent time with her in Jamaica and she has a pretty decent way of life. She is doing better than many Jamaicans, but you get the sense that could change quickly. The United States really is home to opportunity, if you know where to look and how to invest in yourself.

My attention turned toward the stands. I was wondering how the pre-race show was affecting my brother. He is a veteran and although he hadn't seen combat, I know he still has very real connection to our troops.

As I looked up to the stands at my brother, mother and stepfather, I was struck by another thought. Life sure does change over time. Twenty years earlier, I would have been in the stands watching my brother play high school football. In school, he was always the athlete. I was the lanky 6'-tall, 130 lb. president of the chess club. For me, playing the part of athlete does not come naturally. It will probably always feel weird when someone uses the word "athletic" in the same sentence as my name.

It was time to line up and I was curious how a run through the woods on soft ground was going to work. I hadn't run a trail race before and I was grateful that I was going to run at my girlfriend's pace so I could pay attention to the experience. If you are a runner, and haven't ventured off the pavement, you really need to give it a shot. Generally speaking it is so much nicer on your joints, especially the knees.

We were off to a good start and she was keeping a much quicker pace than she had 3 months earlier in Jamaica. This was going to be a pretty decent run. We started to emerge from the woods and could hear the music at the finish line. There was a lengthy clearing in front of us with no runners in sight, and as we got a couple of hundred feet into this space I looked back to see if there were runners behind us.

She asked if there was anyone back there and I said no. This would be a nice finish, with just the two of us and my parents watching, but then I heard a noise. I looked back and a guy about my age was pounding the ground with each step while pushing one of those running strollers—one for two children! Please tell me this was not happening. I know we were not running at my full potential, but we were still running pretty quickly.

It happened. That guy passed us like we were walking, and just as quickly he was out of sight. His calves were the size of my thighs.

I was monitoring the race on the Nike+ and realized the finish line was coming up much more quickly than the 3.1-mile reading so I told her that I was going to overrun the finish line. I tend to get pretty frustrated when courses are not a full 3.1 miles. She and I sprinted to the finish. As we crossed the finish line, a volunteer handed us our medals and I kept going around the track. It took nearly 3/4s of the running track to complete a full 5K with a time of 27:31.

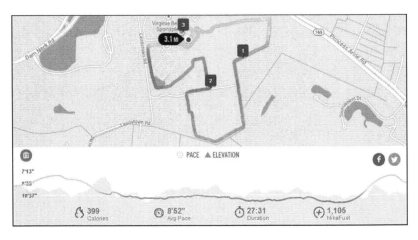

***

Virginia Leadership Lesson:
Honoring the Fallen, Respecting Diversity

As we lead, many people will follow and some will stay to the end and others you will lose along the way—hopefully none to death. No matter how you lose team members, remember to honor those who contributed to your vision, even when they are not there to hear the accolades. It is the right thing to do and sends the message to your current team that you will value their contributions even if they ultimately depart.

The second lesson I took from Virginia is the need for a commitment to diversity. Although this has long been engrained into my thinking, sometimes a reminder surfaces with such distinction it causes me to stop and consciously think about its importance. I'm not suggesting that leaders need to date interracially, but I do believe that leaders need to be open to, and even seek out, all people regardless of race, age, sex, national origin, sexual orientation, gender identity, or physical ability to be part of the team.

Chapter 7

Krumpe's Donut Alley Rally
Hagerstown, Maryland
August 9, 2013

Bobby Hall is a student. He's a student of life. He is one of those true life-long learners. I met him when he enrolled at the college that I work for.

Part of my professional responsibilities includes oversight of student clubs and organizations. I am also the advisor the Student Government Association (SGA). Bobby first came around when he tried to jump-start the campus Business Club which had been defunct for years. His efforts led to his seeking guidance and assistance from the SGA.

As SGA's will do, they noted his talents and saw that he could be an asset to their organization. In fairly quick order he was appointed a Senator within SGA. A few days after his appointment, he walked into my office and asked if I had a minute. I said that I did, and he immediately said, "Good. Someday you are going to be a reference for me and I want to get to know you."

He said this because he saw that two of the three degrees hanging on my office wall are from Kutztown University and he had intentions of attending there. I was impressed with his forthrightness and the clear vision he had for his future. Over time, I learned that whenever Bobby came into my office, he had something worthwhile to share or ask.

Toward the end of the summer, Bobby came into my office and declared that he wanted to run a 5K with me. I had been posting a lot on Facebook about my travels and sharing the 50-state 4D experience, and it was clear that he knew what I was doing. He also confessed that he had never run a 5K, but was getting in shape to join the service to help pay for his studies. He wanted to know what my running schedule looked like.

Throughout this experience, I have had a number of friends, students and colleagues share with me that they were starting to run or, at the very least, considering it. This was very rewarding for me, as I was also brought into the world of running by friends and colleagues who were posting about their running experiences. The running bug is contagious and I hope it continues to spread.

After going over my proposed race schedule, Bobby decided he wanted to join me for my run in Maryland. It was one of the closest runs, just over an hour away, and it was on a Friday night, which was schedule-friendly.

On August 9, we headed to Hagerstown, Maryland for Bobby's first 5K and my 11th. On the way, I fielded all the first-timer questions and let him know what to expect. We arrived to a light rain and found our way to the registration table. We plopped down our $30 and entered the 2013 Krumpe's Donut Alley Rally.

> **"Krumpe's Donut Alley Rally 5K:** *The 5K Run/walk will be an evening event benefiting the Wounded Warrior Project. 100% of net proceeds (i.e. gross receipts minus event expenses) will be paid to Wounded Warrior Project within 30 days of event."*

We decided to go for a walk to check out the course. The route took us through a neighborhood in Hagerstown and then turned into Rose Hill Cemetery for a rather intricate loop. Ultimately, we would come back onto city streets to make our way back to Krumpe's Donut Shop.

There were 561 participants in this event, which is a lot of people to line up on a side street. Race etiquette dictates that the fastest runners and those going for Personal Records (PRs) line up toward the front, while the slowest runners and walkers line up toward the rear. This keeps the speedy runners from stampeding those who are slower off the line.

I am almost always going for time, so I usually line up toward the front. Bobby decided to move farther back in the group, as he wasn't sure what kind of time he could run.

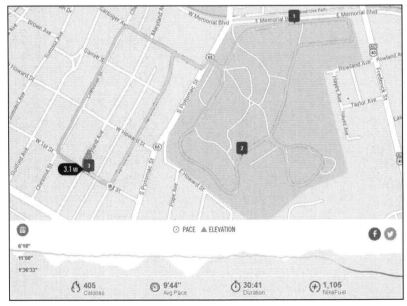

My finishing time was 25:26, which placed me 117th overall. Bobby came in at 33:11 running under 11-minute miles! His first outing was very successful. My favorite part of this event was watching Bobby finish. The last 1/10 of a mile was downhill, and he came barreling to the finish at an incredible pace. The finish line of a running race has a gravitational force that compels runners to give up what they have left, when there isn't anything left to give. The sprint to the finish is always exhilarating.

It was very moving watching Bobby experience the finish-line rush and the complete exhaustion that comes from giving something your all. Afterward, we grabbed a bite to eat before getting on the road for home. We asked a couple local old timers for a recommendation and were directed to a neighborhood deli.

As we dined, we shared our war stories from the race. It is amazing how much can happen and be told about running 3.1 miles with several hundred strangers. There is so much drama stuffed into that time. I witnessed Bobby's excitement and could see the satisfaction he'd earned. I too was extremely pleased, not so much for the time that I ran, but that I was fortunate enough to have been able to share the experience with someone else.

***

Maryland Leadership Lesson:
Inspiring Others

Leadership is not just about having vision and setting clear goals. It is about inspiring other people to follow your lead so they can find their success and/or add to yours (or your organization's). I know that I made a difference in Bobby's life. I hope he realizes someday how much he did for me.

People who follow remind those who lead that they are not completely crazy or foolish, that their message is not only understood, but appreciated and capable of moving others to act.

Sometimes your best is not measured in the race time you post, but rather in the race time you inspire someone else to post.

***

Summer was coming to a close and the school year would be back in full swing in a couple of weeks. This meant that my traveling was going to be inhibited, and it would eventually start to get too cold to run. I mean, it does get too cold to run—right?

Looking ahead to Labor Day weekend, I was able to easily plan three states in three days over the holiday. One of the benefits of starting a project like this in Pennsylvania is that we are close to large groups of other states (i.e. New England, Mid-Atlantic and the Appalachian Highlands), which can make it easy to complete multiple states in a single weekend.

My Labor Day weekend was going to include Rhode Island, Massachusetts, and New Hampshire. All three races were within a 2-hour drive of each other. I also added to my schedule runs in Connecticut and Vermont later in September. That would complete 5 of the 6 New England States. All that would remain is Maine. Maine—all the way up there, Maine.

The thought of running Maine after September was not appealing. The risk of snow and the plummeting temperatures in a few weeks would make Maine an undesirable place. However, the thought of knocking out all of New England before breaking for the winter sounded like a good goal.

With a few weekends left in August, it was time to see how I could make Maine happen.

Muscular Dystrophy Facts from the *Centers for Disease Control and Prevention*

Limb-Girdle (LGMD) affects men and women equally. "In 2009, 68 out of 2.99 million individuals of all ages were reported to have LGMD in Northern England. This means that about 2 out of every 100,000 people were affected that year."

Source: www.cdc.gov/ncbddd/musculardystrophy/facts.html

Chapter 8

MS Harborfest Shoreside 5K
Portland, Maine
August 18, 2013

The challenge for me to run Maine in a single weekend is that just getting to Portland, ME, is an 8-hour drive from Harrisburg, PA, and Portland is less than an hour inside of the New Hampshire/Maine border. 16 hours of driving over two days does not leave much time for anything else.

I located a 5K on Sunday, August 18 in Portland down at the harbor. That gave me all day Saturday to drive, but I would have to get back on the road right after the race to arrive home at a reasonable time. This was doable. A friend, David Mena, lived in Portland for a few years, and it would be nice to revisit the area. David is one of two friends responsible for getting me into running.

As I planned the trip, I went to the trusty Roadside America website to find interesting sights along the way. I wasn't planning to make any stops until I got to Maine, as I knew I would be visiting the pass-through states in a few weeks and could check them out then.

Another aspect of all of this traveling struck me—the solitude. Although I have always been comfortable with my-self and alone time, I am also a very social creature and enjoying meeting new people. From time to time, I have dated online, as I feel it is a great way to meet people. The creative side of me wondered whether I could use online dating sites just to meet up with locals to share meals and learn about their areas.

I had a few weeks before the Maine run so I started reaching out to women on one of the dating sites to see whether anyone was interested in

MAINE
Sights Along the Way

York Harbor, Beach

Sumner Winebaum's "Pleasure Ground" sculpture of miniature sunbathers, York Harbor

Fort Allen Park, Portland, ME

Mast of U.S.S. Portland, which accepted the Japanese WWII surrender

Portland Harbor front and downtown shopping

Fences of Love at Portland Harbor

meeting for dinner in Portland. As luck would have it, I was able to connect with someone inclined to meet for dinner knowing that there were no romantic expectations, as I was traveling from pretty far away.

She was from Burundi, Africa, and had been living in the U.S. a number of years. Wonderful company, she suggested a terrific restaurant, the Sebago Brewing Company. We enjoyed a nice dinner, and she offered to help me find a cheap hotel for the night.

It did not take us long to realize that there were no cheap hotels in Maine that time of year. August is their main tourist month. Even the dive motels were close to $200 a night. As I contemplated the just-in-case tent and sleeping bag in my trunk, she offered to make a call for me.

She said that normally she would offer me her couch but her brother was staying with her. He would find it culturally offensive for an unmarried man to stay the night in the home of his unmarried sister, and she did not want to offend him, which I completely respect.

I was delighted that she was able to secure me a couch with friends. These two ladies recently moved to the U.S. from Africa. One was home when we arrived and she did not speak English. It was an interesting night of miscommunication, but I was able to sleep the night and shower in the morning.

***

After an early rise, I stopped at a convenience store for a banana and vitamin water to supplement my pre-race GU Energy Gel. Aren't we all creatures of habit? This is what I was eating before every race, and it seemed to be working—so why change?

I arrived at the top of the hill that overlooks Portland Harbor, home to the beautiful Fort Allen Park, where the race started and finished. I registered for the MS Harborfest Shoreside 5K.

> *"**MS Harborfest Shoreside 5K:** Your participation in the MS Harborfest Shoreside 5K Run provides help for today and hope for tomorrow through education, support, advocacy, and research funded by the National Multiple Sclerosis Society, Greater New England Chapter. And that makes a huge difference to the 3,000 people and their families in Maine (and 400,000 nationwide) who must live with MS every day of their lives."*

The race route started on Eastern Promenade in front of the park and after two blocks made a right into the park and down the steep hill to the Harbor front. How steep was the hill? The elevation dropped over 140' in the first half mile of the race. This was perfect for running my PR in the 1 mile, but it had ominous overtones as the finish line was back up there—where we started. That meant, sometime in the near future, the gravitational pull that accelerated towards the harbor was going to act like a reverse-bungee and try to pull us down that hill when we needed to run back up.

This time, I was well aware I was required to run up the equivalent of a 14-story building. Knowing how poorly I'd done on my first real hilly course, reading about this 140' incline had me concerned before I ever left home. My mind wandered back to this worry several times in the weeks leading up to this event.

As I mentioned at the beginning of the book, I used to race cars. I raced in hill climbs, drag races, autocrosses, and road courses. One of the things I learned when hill climb racing was the power of visualizations. When athletes use visualization, they are thoughtfully imagining themselves doing the physical act before they actually perform it. It's practicing in your mind. When I raced cars, this allowed me to imagine where I could go faster, giving more gas or where I might take a turn at a slightly different radius to keep speed up.

Knowing that I feared my performance on this hill, I used visualization on and off throughout my 8-hour drive to the event. I kept envisioning myself running and the ground rising in front of me. I concentrated on keeping my pace and breathing easily as I imagined this, and I forced myself to think about finding extra energy reserves when the hill approached.

It was race day and no longer time to visualize. It was time to realize.

The gun fired and we were off. I always start off fast and my pace declines as a race goes on. This is how I prefer to run. I have tried starting at a consistent pace or even slowly, and I still end up losing a similar amount of momentum, so it makes sense for me to start off quick.

This race was no different. I left the starting line very fast, and in a couple of hundred feet we were descending at an incredible rate. At 6' tall, I have pretty long legs and I don't typically feel they are very advantageous when I run. This day was different. I was able to take long strides and keep my feet under my body weight. The momentum built like a turbocharger and my pace was increasing at an amazing rate, without any apparent deficit to my respiratory and cardiovascular needs. I was flying!

Intuitively I knew this was the fastest mile I had ever run—and it was at 6:56. It was amazing to complete a mile in less than 7 minutes. It would be the first, but not the last, time I would eclipse the 7:00 minute barrier in the first mile of a 5K.

From that point, we were cruising along the harbor. The view of the harbor filled with sailing ships in the early morning light was beautiful. The

Portland Harbor is filled with ships moored in place out in the open water, not at docks. It gives the impression of more boating activity than is actually going on, which adds to the picturesque view. It was a perfect day for a run.

As we rounded the end of the peninsula, it was time to start our climb back to the top. The climb took place on a surface street that wound back on itself like a snake slithering up a mountain. With each turn, our view was more hill. It felt endless. As I approached another turn, a police officer there monitored vehicle traffic to keep runners safe. I called out to ask if this was the last turn.

I felt myself winning against the rise of the hill, but the mind starts over-thinking experience. You are simultaneously concentrating on breathing and stride while fending off thoughts of doubt, concern, and fatigue. Thankfully, I had spent so much time visualizing that I had prepared myself for this mental chess game.

I had looked at a course map before we started, but I lost track of how many turns we had completed. The officer shrugged and said he didn't know. I decided to treat that turn like it was the last one and dug deep inside to find energy to race up the last of the hill. Thankfully that was the last turn and we had a lot of straight hill left to traverse. After that, the course leveled out and we had to run a few blocks back toward the park.

As we turned the corner toward the finish line, I could see the timing lights scrolling into the 23s and this energized me. I couldn't believe I was seeing a number that low. It was an incredible run and it felt like I did really well. I ended running PRs in the 1K, 1-mile and the 5K at this event! My finishing time was 24:29 on the Nike watch, a full 45 seconds faster than my previous best in Ohio.

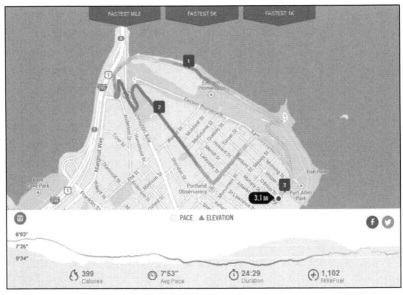

Facing Fears, Visualizing, and Cultural Competence

We all have fears. The difference between those with leadership skills and the rest is the ability to cognitively evaluate those fears and prepare to meet fears head on. I could have easily avoided races with hills. I could have simply accepted that I would always have poor race times when I run an event with a significant hill, or I could plan and prepare for hills. I now include hill running as part of my regular training, as do most serious runners.

A second lesson to take away from Maine is the power of visualizations. People perform better when they are familiar with an experience. In times when you can't practice something before you perform, try visualization. You will be amazed at how easy it is to have that "I've done this before" feeling, even though the experience might be a completely new.

Lastly, know the importance of multiculturalism. It would have been easy and more comfortable to avoid spending the night in the home of foreigners who do not look like me or share my language and culture, but that would not have provided any growth. When we allow ourselves to enter uncomfortable situations, we give ourselves the gift of growth. Are you willing to grow?

***

When I returned from Maine, I posted the photos I took to my Facebook page. My friend Jessica Harper posted this comment on my album: "Way to pursue your goals!" I appreciated her sentiment, but also smiled knowingly when I read it. If she thought driving 8 hours to Maine and back in a weekend was evidence of my commitment to this goal, she (and a lot of others) had some surprises coming.

Muscular Dystrophy Facts *from the Centers for Disease Control and Prevention*

Facioscapulohumeral (FSH) affects men and women equally. "In 2009, 118 out of 2.99 million individuals of all ages were reported to have FSH in Northern England. This means that about 4 out of every 100,000 people were affected that year."

Source: www.cdc.gov/ncbddd/musculardystrophy/facts.html

Chapter 9

Warrior Dash
Long Pond, Pennsylvania
August 24, 2013

Long before I started this journey of running a 5K in all 50 states in honor of my friend and colleague, Dee Gerber, while raising awareness of Muscular Dystrophy, I had paid my registration for a 5K event with military-style obstacles. These types of events, of various distances, have become incredibly popular over the last few years and are quite expensive to enter. Typically, entrance fees are discounted the farther in advance you register.

These events get thousands of runners and can sell out, so advanced registration is a must. I had pre-paid to race in a Warrior Dash, a series of races that take place all over the country. I had paid to enter their event in Long Pond, Pennsylvania.

> *"**Warrior Dash:** Seeing a distinct need for a fun, challenging way to stay healthy and get fit, Red Frog Events (an event company based in Chicago, IL) unleashed Warrior Dash in 2009 and has been a forerunner of the event production industry ever since. The first Warrior Dash was held in Joliet, IL and we've come a long way in the past four years! Over a million Warriors have stormed The Battleground and raised $7.5 million and counting for St. Jude Children's Hospital. More than 150 Warrior Dashes have taken place on the most rugged terrain across six countries and four continents. We're no scientists, but that's a ton of mud, sweat and beer."*

What exactly is a Warrior Dash? This is the description on their website: "Warrior Dash is the world's largest obstacle race series, held on the most rugged terrain in more than 50 locations across the globe. Participants earn their Warrior helmet by tackling a fierce 3-4 mile course and 12 extreme obstacles."

The obstacles include running through fire, crawling (as fast as possible) under barbed wire, running through muddy trenches, crawling through mud under more barbed wire, climbing rope walls, crawling through rope tunnels, scaling plywood walls—all while intermittently being bombarded by large amounts of water. Obviously, this sounds like something worth getting involved in.

The Pennsylvania event was taking place on the grounds of Pocono International Raceway. This is a fairly remote area of PA, and I recalled that a former student of mine, Patrine Lewis, lived in that part of the state, graduated and was working in her first professional position. One of the benefits of working in higher education is the opportunity to reconnect with former students years later.

The Poconos are about an hour and a half from my home, so this was a short ride compared to other states. Since Warrior Dashes attract thousands of runners, runners are corralled into waves that take off every 15 minutes for most of the day. Since my run group wasn't scheduled until after noon, I met Patrine for breakfast.

Prior to meeting Patrine, I stopped by the event to pick up my race materials. I also had time to watch the first wave of runners finish. Two teenage boys were the first to be seen approaching the final 4 obstacles. The boy who was leading after the first obstacle we could see was not the boy who was leading after the second obstacle. They switched positions, passing each other from obstacle to obstacle.

One boy was clearly in the lead as he rounded the last corner, a 180-degree hairpin. As soon as he made the turn, he stopped and waited. What a strange thing to do in the middle of a "race"! Was he toying with his competitor? Was he teasing him before taking off to the finish?

No.

He stuck his hand out and the other boy grabbed it. They ran together, holding hands, through the two rows of fire (the second to last obstacle) and then they dove together into the mud-under-barbed-wire to get to a photo finish. 7,116 other runners followed them through the mud over the next several hours. None of them beat the elapsed time of these two friends.

My innate character is competitive—at times to a fault. Those two teenagers taught me something. Watching them finish together was more enlightening and motivating than if I had witnessed a finish-line victory. They redefined "photo finish."

***

I had a few hours until my turn through the fire and mud, time to catch up with Patrine. I hadn't seen her in nearly 4 years. Patrine had earned her bachelor's degree and was working in a lab.

Patrine didn't have to work until later in the afternoon, so I convinced her to tag along to the event. I was glad when she accepted, as I knew it would be fun to introduce her to such an unusual activity and, rather selfishly, I was going to appreciate having someone take a few photos for me. This is the type of event that you want to remember.

At the racetrack, I took Patrine around the grounds to show her where we would be running and the best vantage points to take some photos. Near the finish line is always good for photos of people running through fire or diving into mud. Immediately after the finish line are make-shift showers for everyone to clean off the layers and layers of mud.

***

I entered the corrals. When it was our turn, many of us took off running, but more people took their time. They were not racing, just managing their way through the course. Waves of runners were released every 15 minutes so those of us running quickly caught up to walkers from the previous corral, which made for some serious congestion.

As I approached the various obstacles, there were sometimes lines of competitors watching others attempt the obstacle crossing. They were wasting valuable time trying to decipher the best course of action. I ran by these groups of talkers and attacked each obstacle. Although I hadn't specifically trained for any one obstacle, I was grateful for the many outings I have had at high ropes courses and zip-lining. Each obstacle's solution seemed intuitive, and something I could just jump into. In fact, I was able to get by every obstacle on the initial try.

When you are going for time in this type of event, body stress compounds. Running a 5K is enough to get your heart racing and your lungs pumping like a steam engine, but the stakes are raised when every 1/8 of a mile you need to duck, dive, climb, leap or otherwise meet a new physical challenge. Adrenaline rushes through your system, and with competitors all around, you have the sense of being in a combat zone trying to escape as fast as possible.

The ninth obstacle was a 12' rope-net wall to be scaled from muddy ground. When I got there, 70 competitors must have been standing watching others attempt the ropes. I ran up, knew there was no time to watch, so I ran past the lookers and jumped up the wall as high as I could grab the ropes. I made quick work of scaling to the top.

As I got to the top and stood, an overwhelming amount of information drowned my thoughts: The surface I was standing on was only a foot wide and a dizzying 12' high and I was not alone. A dozen other people were also perching precariously on top of this wall. I knew from watching this obstacle before my run that the other side of the wall was a reverse rock climb: we had to scale the wall down to the ground while being hosed by high-powered water. From the top of the wall, the water's intensity was painfully apparent.

All of this struck me at once, in the same moment my brain was struggling to remember to breathe while instructing my heart to keep pumping. It was an awful moment and I felt lightheaded and as if my heart were going to jump out of chest. The top of a narrow wall seemed a poor location for cardiac arrest, so I forced myself to pause a moment in the middle of the chaos.

After a few deep breaths to calm down, I started my descent. The climb wasn't bad, but it was very challenging to see the climbing holds with water being sprayed at us. As soon as I felt comfortably close to the ground, I let go and leaped. Unfortunately the ground wasn't the solid experience I was anticipating. It was over a foot of very wet mud, so I landed farther down than I was expecting and got a rather huge splash of mud all over me.

Jeff Fazio, muddy and tired, completed the 2013 Warrior Dash in Long Pond, PA.

Out of that mud pit and into the last leg of the run brought me to the dual rows of fire. If a blind person ran through these rows, they might not be aware of the fire. The obstacle goes by so quickly that you do not feel the warmth with your already elevated body temperature. The fire obstacle is purely for visual excitement and I suppose could be a mental challenge for some. For me, it was just the cool photo op that everyone uses it for. It is the image that makes you look like a "warrior."

The last mud pit with its ceiling of barbed wire is the organizer's last attempt to force you to get muddier than you would like, and it works. I doubt that anyone chooses the barbs over the mud, so everyone ends up coated with mud.

I was ecstatic when I saw the final results. I had finished 202 out of 7,118 entrants. That had me finishing well in the top 3%. Not bad for a guy who 6 months earlier couldn't run a mile!

After the finish, it was my turn for the showers. Patrine declined my proposed mud-filled hug. Apparently she wanted to stay clean and neat for work. I walked her back to her car and headed out to my mother's for dinner. When I arrived, she asked to see my finisher's medal. That is the moment I realized that I was never given one.

***

It is always an awful moment when you realize you forgot or did not receive something you paid for and earned. Mistakes happen. With 7000+ runners, it is probable that the volunteers would miss giving a medal to a runner or two coming across the finish line.

I figured this would not be a big deal; I would contact them and get my medal. Sadly, life is sometimes not as easy as it seems. I sent an Email to the organizer, Red Frog Events, and posted on their Facebook page. I noted that at least one other runner also posted on Facebook. I even provided a photo of me with the other finishers, all clearly wearing their medals and me without one.

By Monday I hadn't heard anything so I called the company. The woman who answered apologized and said it was company policy to never mail medals. I said I would pay for the shipping and she said she couldn't. It was simply against policy to mail medals and ended the call.

This weighed on me all day. It wasn't right. I had earned my medal; it wasn't my fault that it was not given to me, and I really didn't appreciate being pushed aside on the phone the way that woman had. I made a second call to Red Frog Events and spoke with a gentleman there. I explained what had occurred and that I was dissatisfied with my previous phone call.

He apologized again and said that he wanted to make things right. He reiterated that it was company policy to never ship medals. He said it would be okay though. He said that if I was willing to register for next year's event, he would make sure that I received two medals next year. Seriously!?

I pointed out that this was ridiculous. Not only should I not have to wait a year for my medal, it wouldn't even make sense, as the medals have the year of completion listed on them. I also shouldn't have to make a second purchase to receive items that I paid for the first time around. Again, that call was ended.

This bothered me all day. The next day I checked the details of the "purchase" of registering for a Warrior Dash. I called back on Tuesday and spoke to a third employee. I explained everything that had occurred up to this point. I explained that I was a customer who made a purchase and did not receive my products. I had paid online via my credit card and if I was not supplied with all items I paid for, I would be challenging the charge.

Their response, "No problem Mr. Fazio, this happens all the time. We have a list right here by the phone of people that didn't receive medals and need them shipped. Let me get your information."

Wow. Why did that take three phone calls? I received my medal about 10 days later through the mail. So much for company policy. So much for my positive feelings about an otherwise great event.

***

Pennsylvania Leadership Lesson:
Competition, Keeping in Touch, Preparedness, Taking Breaks, and Customer Service

This event was ripe with leadership lessons. It was a beautiful moment to watch those two teenagers finish 1st and 2nd—together. It was incredibly mature of them. Most people, in their position, would have sprinted to the finish to see who was best. Clearly, being together was more important than proving who was best. These two friends must be incredibly content with each other and comfortable with themselves to feel no need to prove anything. When we lead, we do not always have to finish first.

Reconnecting with Patrine enabled me to keep in touch with the past. In our fast-moving world, it is easy to lose sight of those we have come in contact with. Thankfully, social media makes this easier, but only if we choose to use it. I could keep in contact with Patrine for the rest of my life through Facebook, but an occasional face-to-face experience enhances any relationship. My fear is that the internet is diluting the population's ability to interact in real time, in shared space. As a leader, make a conscious effort to stay in touch with those you have met along the way.

I would be remiss to write a chapter on an obstacle-laden 5K and not address the importance of being prepared for challenges that come your way. It is important for leaders to know, understand and even expect serious challenges. I was confident going into the Warrior Dash that I could handle most of what they were going to throw at us. For those who are not as sure, their Red Frog Events website has videos of the obstacles and suggestions for training. YouTube is loaded with videos that racers have shot of the various obstacles. Although we will not always know what is coming our way, that doesn't preclude us from being prepared. Do your research.

We also have to know when to take breaks. This can be hard, as those with a natural tendency to lead often do not have a natural tendency to slow down. It is imperative that we look for times to get needed rest. I have no idea what would have happened if I had pushed myself when I reached the top of the rope wall, but whatever it was, it would not have been good. My body wanted to shut down and I am grateful that my brain allowed me to take a moment for everything to synch. When proceeding was safe, it was clear.

Lastly, I want to say a word about customer service. There is a great business leadership book "Give 'Em the Pickle" by Bob Farrell that explains customer service beautifully. Red Frog would have left a lasting, positive impression, if my third phone call was the first. I would have shared my overwhelmingly positive experience with the Warrior Dash with everyone and had a good feeling about the organization. Unfortunately, two phone calls happened first and they left more of an impact on my feelings about the Warrior Dash and Red Frog than the ultimate, satisfactory resolution to my concern.

When I was a child, my mother worked for a restaurant that intentionally overbooked reservations on Mother's Day knowing that customers would be forced to wait as all other restaurants were packed as well. When my mother pointed out that this decision was not customer friendly, she was told that the county was big enough that the restaurant could "afford to piss off everyone at least once." The restaurant, as you might imagine, has been out of business for decades now. As a leader, do not take customer service for granted.

Great customer service makes an event great. It's a way of thinking—not an add-on.

***

When I first started talking about running a 5K in all 50 States I had no sense of timeline. It was just something I was going to accomplish … eventually. When? I had no idea.

Originally, the goal was to be a weekend warrior and hit states as the race schedules made it convenient to do so. I figured I would finish the project when I finished. Those who are closest to me know that when I am passionate and dedicated about something, I become borderline obsessive. Okay, who I am kidding? It just becomes a flat-out obsession.

As I looked at the calendar and saw Labor Day weekend was up next, it dawned on me that I would be running 3 states in 3 days. That would take the number of completed states to 11. That means I would have run 22% of the country in the first 10 weeks. Ten weeks is 19% of the year. The percentage of States completed was happening slightly faster than the pace of passing weeks.

In the early evening of Tuesday, August 27, 2013 I sent this message to Dee on Facebook:

"Pretty sure I just figured out how to complete 25 states and DC by January 1st!!!! That is 1/2 the country in the 6 months since my first out-of-state race on June 30."

With the popularity of 5K racing, I realized that it might actually be easy to keep stringing together a few states each weekend. This would be cost effective, as I could travel once and complete 2 or 3 states. This inspired me and enhanced the challenge to see whether I could run all of the states in a relatively short time frame.

If I could run half of the States in half of a year, then what would stop me from completing the second half of the country in another 6 months? The new goal was set: run a 5K in all 50 states … *in 1 year.*

The reality was that I did not actually complete 25 States in the first 6 months—I completed 39.

Oh, and Washington D.C. too.

Muscular Dystrophy Facts from the Centers for Disease Control and Prevention

Congenital (CMD) and myopathies affects men and women equally. "In 2009, 68 out of 2.99 million individuals of all ages were reported to have CMD in Northern England. This means that about 2 out of every 100,000 people were affected that year."

Source: www.cdc.gov/ncbddd/musculardystrophy/facts.html

Chapter 10

PAWSOX 5K
Pawtucket, Rhode Island
August 31, 2013

I don't get sick. In fact, it's been a choice not to get sick. I am really terrible at being sick, so about 10 years ago I decided to just not be sick any more. It's worked for me. Other than the two times I consumed foods that I shouldn't have, being sick has not been part of my experience in over a decade. The last week of August 2013 was going to end that streak in a horrible way.

The college I work for has a huge welcome back event for students every fall called "Fall Free 4 All" on the second Wednesday of the semester. Most offices on campuses come outside to staff information tables under 4 huge tents in the quad. They are joined by the student clubs and organizations.

The big tents are surrounded by DJ music and a long line of students and staff waiting by grills for free hotdogs, chips, cookies and drink. There are games, activities, scavenger hunts and prizes galore. Welcome back to campus everyone!

Ultimately, the responsibility of this day falls on me, or rather a strong committee of staff and students that I chair. We have a strong team that pulls off this big event every year. The event formally kicks off at 10:00 a.m., but I was there by 7:00 a.m. to set up.

By 10:30 a.m. I was not feeling well. A crippling exhaustion came over me. Lifting another case of soda onto the cart destined for the food lines seemed as likely to me as lifting a bus. This came on quickly and I immediately lost all appetite. From what I was told, I looked awful. I could read the concern in my colleagues' faces as they approached me over the next hour. By noon, my Dean sent me home.

I went home and rested and felt incredibly worse by Thursday. I called off work.

Friday came and I still felt awful, but I am not one to miss work. I peeled myself out of bed, took a shower, and threw on something resembling work clothes. By 11:00 a.m. my boss had sent me home—again.

Regardless of my inability to function at work, I had a second dilemma: This was Labor Day weekend and I was planning to run 5Ks in 3 states in 3 days in New England. I had just declared my intent to run all 50 States in one year. How could I miss an opportunity to knock out 3 in a single weekend? I couldn't.

The registration for the race the next morning in Rhode Island opened at 8:30 a.m. There were 6 hours of driving between that race and me, not counting stops for food, gas, and bathrooms. When I got home from work, I put a little food in my stomach and went to bed.

When the local radio station blasted from my alarm clock at 1:00 a.m., I wasn't feeling much better. Regardless, I found my way to an upright position, located that bathroom and the shower faucet. The steaming shower fell over me while I pondered the insanity of driving nearly 1,000 miles over the next 3 days while running a 5K every 24 hours.

I had at least made arrangements with my stepfather's sister and husband to stay at their home in Foxborough, MA, on Saturday night, but I didn't have a solid plan on where I was going to stay Sunday. I had a tentative reservation at a hostel outside of Boston, but I had serious doubts, as I had never hosteled before.

The nearly 7-hour drive was uneventful and I made it in plenty of time to the race start at McCoy Stadium, a Minor League Baseball venue. This was my second visit to a Minor League stadium in the first 9 states. Was there some connection to baseball and running that I was unaware of? Either way, I paid my fees to run in the PAWSOX 5K.

"PAWSOX 5K: *To Benefit the Pawtucket Red Sox Charitable Foundation and the Rhode Island Veterans Home."*

After registering, I went for a walk to check out the race route. On my way around the blocks surrounding the stadium, I stopped into a corner market to pick up a banana and vitamin water. I was exhausted from the drive and being ill, hoping my pre-race fix would give me enough energy to make it through the event. As I was checking the assortment of bananas, I heard the old man behind the counter talking to another old fellow who was obviously a local, regular.

At first I thought they were messing with me because it sounded like they were making odd sounds rather than words. My brain was not processing these foreign-sounding noises that clearly weren't foreign words. Somewhere under the thick shellac of accent I heard something resembling English.

It just wasn't hitting me that I was in New England. It just wasn't hitting me that their accents could really be that thick. I had been to New England many times and I have heard the New England accent before, but this was so extreme it felt like an over-done caricature of a New England accent. Apparently, I had stumbled into a local market with some deep roots.

I headed back to my car to enjoy my breakfast and drop off the bag of swag that was given to me at registration. As I was leaning against my car, I noticed another runner, a few cars away, trying to take a selfie with the stadium in the background. I wandered over to offer my assistance with the camera.

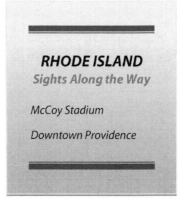

RHODE ISLAND
Sights Along the Way

McCoy Stadium

Downtown Providence

She seemed surprised to see me and declined the offer. After introductions, I explained who I was and why I was in Rhode Island to run. She told me her story. Her name is Kristy Higham and she was entering this 5K as part of her training for an upcoming half marathon.

We walked over to the event together and continued our conversation. I offered her a 4D pin and she graciously accepted and affixed it to her tank top.

The course was relatively flat and on the paved streets surrounding the baseball stadium. Considering the condition I was in, I was grateful for level terrain. I always take off fast in a 5K and spend the race fighting the body's tendency to slow down and ultimately tire out. When the finish line is within sight, I burst into a full sprint, digging deep for whatever reserves I might have left.

Other runners have suggested maintaining a steady pace or even starting out slow and building up speed over the 3 miles, but that doesn't work for me. I have found, no matter where I start, I end up tiring into 8-minute miles by the end. It just makes sense for my body and mind to start off fast.

The race started and I took off as much as I could after driving all night. Running exhausted and sick is not pleasant. My mind was swimming with thoughts of how challenging this is, but knowing that it was nowhere near the daily challenges Dee faces living with Muscular Dystrophy. Who was I to complain? I ran on.

Since I start off fast and slow down, other runners will eventually start passing me. As that happens, I try to resist the pass and even 'hold onto" them when they go by. Each faster runner is a little burst of inspiration to push a little more. About a mile into the race, Kristy passed by me swiftly. I tried to hold on for a few blocks but couldn't. Her steady pace was just too strong, and although inspired, I didn't have it in me to hold on. She eventually went out of sight.

The finish line in Rhode Island, like the one at the Scrapper's baseball stadium in Ohio, was on the training track inside the stadium. There is something exciting about entering a "real' athletic field to end a race. The stadium, the professionally manicured field and the overall sense of a competitive environment exudes from professional sports facilities. This was the second time that I got to run (around) the bases of a minor league field, and I was so grateful to see the finish line.

Although it was far off of my new best, I was not displeased with posting a time of 26:43. Kristy did very well with a time of 26:00. In fact, she placed 3rd in Females 20–29 years old. It was her first medal and she was the first person to medal wearing a 4D pin!

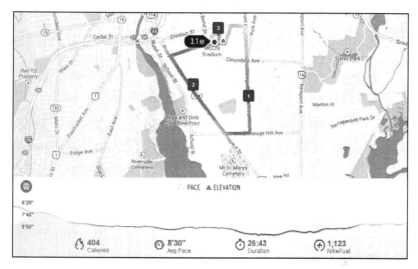

This had the making of a great story and a wonderful friendship. We ended up having lunch and she was gracious enough to show me around downtown Providence, RI. We also became Facebook friends. I was really excited to see her post a few weeks later that she completed the half marathon she was training for. I was even more excited to see she did it wearing her 4D pin!

We live in a world where many people would graciously accept a small gift like a 4D pin, maybe wear

Kristy Higham and Jeff Fazio pose at the 2013 PAXSOX 5K in Pawtucket, RI.

it once and then forget about it. It says a lot about Kristy's character that not only did she keep the pin, but she made it important enough in her life to remember to wear it. It's no surprise that Kristy was destined to be the first 4D-pin bearer to cross the finish line of a marathon, but that chapter comes later.

***

Rhode Island Leadership Lesson:
Making Connections

When you are in a leadership position, it is important to always look for connections. You never know who you will meet and how they will help you. It is even possible they will also pick up your cause and champion it. Be intentional about connecting with new people and sharing your vision. You never know who will be key in taking you and your vision to the next level.

When I arrived in Rhode Island, I had just finished driving 6 hours and I was sick. Not saying hello to Kristy would have been the easiest thing in the world (okay, the easiest thing in the world would have actually been staying in bed, but I digress). We walk past strangers all the time without knowing the potential they have for our lives and what potential we have in their lives.

I'm not sure what value you would put on the life of another, but I am guessing it would be far greater than twenty dollars. We wouldn't walk by $20 lying on the ground without picking it up, yet we walk past strangers every day without determining their value.

Yes, I was sick and I was about to run over 3 miles. Kristy was a healthy distraction to that. Why sit and stew over the poor hand I was dealt that weekend, when I could talk to the dealer and trade in a card?

The connection to Kristy kept my mind off not being 100% and gave me something interesting to focus on.

And what was the return on that minimal investment? I have a friend for life and 4D has a runner for life. I couldn't begin to guess how many 4D pins I have handed out all over the country. There are many runners who wear them, but I am sure there are more who have received the pin and do not wear it. It takes a special person to maintain that connection after the race where the pin was given.

For those of us who proudly run with the 4D pin, it feels weird getting ready for an event without the pin. In fact, if I raced without the pin on, I would feel more naked than when I ran the 5K in Texas.

Ok, not that naked. When you get to the Chapter on Texas, you will understand.

To this day, Kristy runs wearing her 4D pin. Some people will surprise you. That is why you should say hello. How many surprises have you walked past this week? Month? Year?

Chapter 11

Labor Day 5K for MS
Raynham, Massachusetts
September 1, 2013

After leaving Kristy, I headed to my stepfather's sister home in Foxborough, MA. I mentioned earlier that when you are attempting to accomplish any goal in all 50 states, it makes sense to look up friends and family. I was fortunate that my step-aunt Mary and her husband Mike were going to provide a wonderful, warm place to sleep for the evening. Thankfully, their home was not far from the Rhode Island event and was even closer to the Massachusetts run the next morning.

While I was catching Mike and Mary up on the tales of my travels, I started to lose my voice—completely lose it. It was really awful, and I still wasn't feeling great. Mike took me out for a quick run to a drug store to get some throat lozenges.

They had plans to go out that evening for their anniversary. I had plans to meet up with Victoria Nayiga, a woman from one of the dating sites. We were meeting for dinner and I had texted to let her know I had lost my voice. She was kind and still willing to meet for dinner. She is from Uganda and had been working professionally in the U.S. for over 7 years. Dinner was splendid and we made sport of writing notes back on forth on a tablet in lieu of being able to actually speak. It was a unique first meeting, but it was not destined to be our last.

***

I was up early on Sunday and headed out to the town of Raynham for my Massachusetts run. It was an overcast, dreary morning. There was moisture falling from the sky, but it was so slight that it almost felt as if it was hanging in the air. The droplets gave my skin the sensation of perpetually walking through spider webs—it just touched skin everywhere and nowhere all at once.

My motivation was as drained as my voice, but I was intent on completing this 5K even if it took all day. There was too much invested to risk losing a single state on this trip, so, as my friend David would say, "It must be done!" I dragged myself to the registration table and signed up for the Labor Day 5K for MS.

*"**Labor Day 5K:** Your participation in the Labor Day 5K for MS Run provides help for today and hope for tomorrow through education, support, advocacy, and research funded by the National Multiple Sclerosis Society, Greater New England Chapter. And that makes a huge difference to the 3,000 people and their families in Maine who must live with MS every day of their lives."*

This event was organized by the same group from MS that hosted the event in Portland, ME two weeks earlier. It was nice that the race director recognized me from the earlier run. It was really unique for me to be out of state and recognize someone I met on another out-of-state run.

The event was relatively small with 81 runners, but it was not surprising considering how unpleasant the morning's weather was. We were in a fairly remote area and would be running along the shoulders of various roads. We were warned that there was a pretty good hill, not too steep but very long.

That unfortunately turned out to be accurate. Imagine running in a cold morning drizzle while sick and having no voice. Then imagine a hill in front that is a steady increasing slope with no apparent end. Running up that hill that morning was like bad sex. It wasn't any good and it seemed to last forever.

As I was dying on the hill, my thoughts went to Dee and that first 5K I ran with 4D pinned to my tank top. If it weren't for the 4D on my chest, I would have given up on that hill at that first event. I wasn't about to give up this time, even though it crippled my lungs and my legs had no enthusiasm for forward motion. A quick check on the Nike+ watch confirmed, via global-positioning data, that I was losing pace—fast.

***

The Monday before I left on this 3-races-in-3-states-in-3-days trip over Labor Day weekend, Dee took me to a regional Muscular Dystrophy Association dinner. After the formal part of the dinner was over, we were all joking around and having a good time. As we were goofing around, I teased Dee about giving me a ride on her scooter. Little did I know she was willing to oblige! I stood on the back of the scooter and she gave me a short trip around the banquet room.

Dee "4D" Gerber gives Jeff Fazio a ride on her scooter at an MDA dinner.

It was fun and is a great memory. The second time I rode on the back of Dee's scooter was for the CBS news cameras, but I am getting way ahead of the story. Let's get back to Massachusetts.

***

So there I was, facing an unrelenting hill straining the life out of me. As I was acknowledging pain, my mind wandered to earlier that week, when Dee gave me the ride on the scooter. Imagining her zipping around the hotel with me hanging on the back started to bring a smile to my mind (not enough energy to actually bring it to my face). It was a pleasant memory.

I started thinking how nice it would if Dee showed up and gave me a ride up this hill. Then I thought that would not be fair, as my feet wouldn't be on the ground. I compromised: Dee could use the scooter to push me. That didn't feel as much like cheating. Yeah, that would work. Where is Dee? Why isn't she pushing me up this god-forsaken hill?

As these stream-of-conscious scooter-pushing images popped into my head, I started to notice something else. Was the misty rain coming down faster? No, it wasn't, but it was hitting my face and arms faster. What was going on? I looked down again at the Nike+ and, sure enough, my pace was picking up. How incredible is that? As I was picturing Dee pushing me up the hill, my pace actually increased almost a full minute-per-mile. It's really interesting and it is documented on the run record with Nike.

Somehow I managed to turn a 26:32 in the 3.1 miles that I timed. That was 11 seconds faster than the day before, though I felt much worse and there was that hill. I stopped the Nike+ when I got to3.1, but we still had a pretty good amount of course left. I think we ran an extra quarter mile or so.

I was beat. I was tired. Massachusetts was done and so was I—at least for the day.

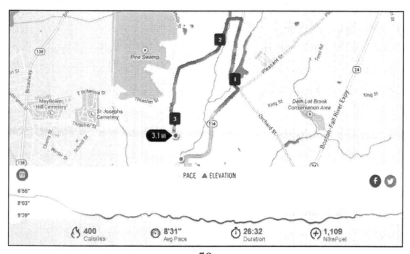

We choose our goals and frame our vision, but we can't always control outside factors that will try to sidetrack us from meeting those goals. Sickness is one of those factors. I'm not suggesting that leaders must work when ill, but I think the possibility always merits consideration.

It would not have been the end of the world if I canceled the 3-race weekend. It wouldn't even drastically affect any outcome in life if it took me longer than a calendar year to run all 50 states because I got ill before one particular trip. Who wouldn't understand that? It would still be a great feat to run all 50 even if it took more than a year to do.

So why travel and run when sick? Simply because I knew I could still do it. Somewhere inside, I knew it wasn't so bad that I couldn't overcome and press on. It was just hard. We can't fear the difficult.

A second lesson from this run is the power of positive thinking. In this instance, I am not referring to the type of positive thinking that the little train expressed with "I think I can, I think can." That was direct positive thinking about accomplishing the task at hand. What I am referring to, is actually having positive thoughts. When I started thinking about Dee giving me a ride on her scooter, it lifted my spirit. That positive affect on my psyche is what started to propel my running forward at a faster pace.

MASSACHUSETTS
Sights Along the Way

Cape Cod

Dr. Seuss National
Memorial Sculpture
Garden

Keep your mind full of positivity. Life is too short to dwell in the negative.

Muscular Dystrophy Facts *from the Centers for Disease Control and Prevention*

Distal (DD) affects men and women equally. "In 2009, 10 out of 2.99 million individuals of all ages were reported to have DD in Northern England. This means less than 1 out of every 100,000 people were affected that year."

Source: www.cdc.gov/ncbddd/musculardystrophy/facts.html

Chapter 12

St. Charles Children's Home 5K
Portsmouth, New Hampshire
September 2, 2013

One of the things that made running the 3 states over Labor Day weekend a little more palatable was the fact that all of the races were within 2 hours of each other, so the drives were not too bad. My run the next morning was in Portsmouth, NH, which was not far beyond the Massachusetts-New Hampshire border.

I technically still had a reservation for Sunday night at the hostel, but I preferred the idea of staying in place more comfortable. I sent a text to Victoria, the woman I met the night before. As we exchanged messages throughout the morning, we decided to meet again for dinner. I was extremely grateful when she offered me her place to stay. She was terrific company and I really wasn't sure about my feelings on a hostel—especially when not feeling 100%.

We had a great time our second night and I started to get my voice back a little so communication was a bit easier. I stayed as quiet as possible and enjoyed hearing her Ugandan accent. She asked about joining me in the morning for the New Hampshire 5K, which I thought was a terrific idea.

She considered entering the event, but when we woke, it was raining. The forecast for New Hampshire was worse. I definitely understood that she didn't want to run.

When we got to the event, it was pouring. Fortunately, the race organizers had ordered a huge tent, so registration and the morning snack items were covered. Unfortunately, the rain was coming down so hard there was a "river" several inches deep through the middle of the tent. This had the making of a very unpleasant morning.

Victoria stayed in the car while I slalomed over-sized puddles to get to registration for the St. Charles Children's Home 5K. The turnout was amazing, with nearly 1,000 runners. It was inspiring to see so many people willing to brave the rain to run.

"St. Charles Children's Home 5K: The race has a flat, fast course and cash awards for fast runners. At the same time it welcomes children, beginners and walkers. Don't miss this encouraging

I was grateful that the event was taking place, rain or shine, as I had traveled so far and really wanted to complete these closely connected states. As race time approached, the rain went from torrential to a steady rain. Somehow that seemed like a big improvement.

Runners were called to the line and an army of nearly one thousand organized behind the designated spot. The official gave us instructions, "The Star Spangled Banner" was sung, and then a priest led the group in a prayer. This is to be expected when you are running in a "nun run."

As the priest offered his prayer, he included a request for the rain to stop for the event. The rain stopped. The sky became a little bit brighter.

This was a unique experience. Runners looked around at each other. Spectators looked at the sky. The rain was mostly gone. Large puddles still dotted the course, but we were apparently not going to have to be soaked as we ran.

The course was relatively flat and uninteresting, perfect for my current level of engagement. Sometimes you just need to get a task completed, and this was going to be one of those states. After 2 days of racing, traveling and illness, an easy course was welcome. My race time was 26:50.

My weekend triple resulted in times of 26:34, 26:32 and 26:50. Although these times were well over 2 minutes slower than my best, I was very pleased at the consistency. Not bad for a weekend of unhealthy running.

***

Interestingly, this race was won by Ethiopian Demesse Tefera from New York with a time of 15:31. The winner of the women's race was Hirut Beyene posting a 16:50 run. To put that in perspective, they completed the entire 3.1 miles of the course while I was finishing mile 2. This is not so interesting in and of itself. What was really noteworthy about this accomplishment is the fact that I recognized these two.

This pair of accomplished runners had also won the PAXSOX 5K in Rhode Island two days earlier. It made me wonder if they were *winning* a 5K in all 50 States. If so, were they doing it in a year?

***

What stops the rain when you need it? Is it your faith? Is it luck? Is serendipity influencing your course? When I arrived in Portsmouth, NH, I knew to expect rain—lots of rain. I was mentally prepared to run through gobs and gobs of H2O falling from the sky.

Although it was miraculous to hear a man of the cloth pray for the rain to stop and witness it actually occur, as a leader, I wouldn't put a lot of faith in that as part of my plans to achieving a goal. We are best served dealing with the reality we are facing and negotiating through as best we can. If another influence (be it luck, faith or serendipity) happens to open up the sky of opportunity, by all means, let's enjoy the good fortune. I just don't think it is advisable to plan for it.

A second take-away from the New Hampshire experience is the amazing feats by the Ethiopian runners. They are accomplishing some amazing running results. Whatever their personal goals are, they are not competitors of mine. They are apparently playing a similar game in a similar field, but we are on very different levels. I have all the admiration in the world for their abilities, but my focus remains on my goal and my vision. I am running in honor of Dee, 4D. The running of the 50 states was done for Dee and the others who can't run. Nothing changes that. Best wishes to Demesse and Hirut.

Muscular Dystrophy Facts from the Centers for Disease Control and Prevention

Oculopharyngeal (OPMD) affects men and women equally. "In 2009, 4 out of 2.99 million individuals of all ages were reported to have OPMD in Northern England. This means that less than 1 out of every 100,000 people were affected that year."

Source: www.cdc.gov/ncbddd/musculardystrophy/facts.html

Chapter 13

National Press Club 5K: Beat the Deadline
Washington, D.C.
September 7, 2013

The United States is made up of 50 States and a variety of other geo-political constructs. Within the purview of the U.S. government, there are commonwealths (*that aren't states*), territories, protectorates, reservations, and one federal district, Washington D.C.

The intent of the 4D 50-State 5K mission was primarily the running of the actual states; however, as Washington, D.C. holds a special place in America's heart, it seemed appropriate to include it in when "Running Across America." Besides, it's only a two-drive, so why not?

As it turned out, I was the only thing that moved fast in D.C. in 2013.

***

Going to Washington afforded me the opportunity to connect with Erik Hein, a great friend I had not seen in way too long. Erik and his partner, Matthew Rogers, live in a fabulous home in the heart of D.C. I arrived at their home on Friday, September 6. We went to a terrific restaurant for dinner and caught up on all of life's happenings.

I needed to be in bed relatively early as the next morning's run had a 7:30 a.m. start. Matthew was kind enough to drop me off at the event so I could leave my car at their place and not deal with D.C. parking. There I was, in the Capital of the nation, at 6:30 a.m. holding a bottle of Vitamin water, a banana and a GU Gel pack.

My illness from the previous week got its butt kicked from some healthy antibiotics and I was feeling much better. In fact, I wasn't aware of just how much better I was, but I was about to find out. I just knew I was ready to run. I entered the Beat the Deadline 5K hosted by the National Press Club (NPC).

> *"**Beat the Deadline 5K:** Benefits the ongoing work of the National Press Club Journalism Institute. The Institute is committed to helping working journalists improve their skills through ongoing training and programming of future journalists through scholarships that promote diversity within our profession."*

This event drew in over 400 runners. The course was relatively flat. We were starting fairly close to the White House and were going to run near the Capitol and back. The starting line was on F Street and at the end of the block turned onto 13th Street, which provided a steep, short decent to Pennsylvania Avenue, which leads to the Capitol.

Knowing this was the route, I had decided to run with my point-n-shoot camera. I was hoping to get some good shots of the runners heading toward the Capitol and maybe a decent selfie with the Capitol behind me on the return trip.

The pre-race festivities included a warm-up directed by Tony Horton, creator of the P90X extreme fitness program. I wasn't aware of who he was, but I had heard of the P90X workout. I chose not to participate in the pre-race workout. For better or worse, I do nothing physical before a run—not even stretching. I prefer to hold onto whatever fuel I have and use it only on the event. I happily watched everyone else do the warm up. Tony was a true professional up there, inspiring and motivating everyone into all sorts of exercises and positions. He was clearly in fantastic shape.

***

The race began and, as always, I started as close as possible to the actual start line. We were off and I ran fast off the starting line. The turn down 13th Street came quickly and my pace increased fast running downhill. As we turned onto Pennsylvania Avenue, I saw the Capitol in the distance.

D.C. is a competitive town, so I was not surprised at the caliber of runners involved in this race. I was doing my best to keep pace; a seemingly endless crowd of runners was passing me. As we got closer to the Capitol, I started taking photos while I ran. Frankly, I got distracted from running, as I was more engaged with the "how do you take good photos while running fast problem." Having taught and worked in the photography industry for several years, this was a new and exciting challenge for me to wrestle.

Jeff Fazio takes a 'selfie' while running passed the U.S. Capitol.

We hit the turn-around, and it was time to try to get my selfie with the Capitol in the background. Sadly, the lighting was working against me and I wasn't in a position of authority to move the sun, so I did what I could. Overall, I am happy with the shots I got. The memories are there.

That drop down from F Street to Pennsylvania was something we were going to have to attack in reverse on the way back. Although it is only a block and a half, it rises quickly. I dug in and brought what I could. I managed to slightly *increase* my pace going up the hill and as I turned the corner on F Street, I could see finish line and the timer. It was ticking through the 23s and I was racing down the street toward it.

I couldn't believe that I had run so fast when I had paid so little attention to my running on this course. I blew through the finish line and the clock said 24:07, so did the Nike watch. That is when the Nike watch lit up with the light display of digital fireworks that shows you set a new personal record.

I had clocked 24:06 in Maine, so I was curious to see what the watch was fussing about. The watch said I had a new fastest 1K at 3:53. That is great, but who talks about 1K? It then went onto another screen indicating that I had also completed my fastest mile at 6:35! That was truly incredible, as I had only run under 7 minutes for a mile once, and that was in Portland, ME, when we ran downhill for almost the entire first mile. Even that mile was 15 seconds slower than this one.

The competitive D.C. crowd must have really pushed my body's limits to go fast, but the big surprise was the new fastest 5K at 23:34. It turns out that the course was just a little bit longer than 5K and the GPS'ed Nike+ indicated that at the actual 5K mark, I broke the 24-minute barrier.

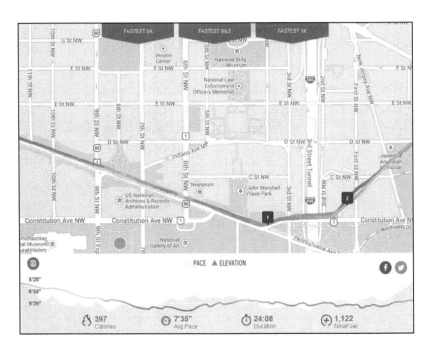

***

I have been living over 20 years without cable TV so I occasionally miss out on some pop-culture. That said, when I got to the race and people were talking about Tony Horton doing the pre-race warm up, I didn't know who he was or that he was a big deal in the fitness community. I had, however, heard of the P90X workout products and I knew they were a big deal.

As someone with only cursory knowledge of the P90X world, it was mildly intriguing that the "P90X guy" was at the event and doing the warm up. What ended up being very interesting to me was when I got home, read a few articles about the event and realized that Tony Horton had also run in the race!

I just had to know. How did I stack up against this fitness guru? Right then, I went online to see exactly how far behind this great trainer I finished. The difference in our times was 1 minute and 38 seconds. That is how long he finished *after me*.

***

Washington D.C. Leadership Lesson:
Pushing Yourself Without Pushing, Be Leery of Heroes

I would have bet anything that my absolute best (PR) run would come from 100% focus and commitment to the act of running. It would be derived from pure concentration on breathing, emphasis on perfect form, devotion to a fast pace and above all, 100% effort in moving those arms and legs as fast as possible.

The reality is that my Personal Record 5K and 1 mile still remain in Washington, D.C. I have gone out on the street with the intent to run a single mile as fast as I possibly can and my best has been 6:52.

Think about that. I rarely break the 7-minute mark when I am trying to run a single mile, but I have done it twice within a race setting. Other runners, other competitors, push us toward our goals.

What does it say that my fastest time came while not focusing on total performance? I think that day preparation met opportunity (that is how some people define luck). I was done being sick, I had trained for months, it was a great course on a good day at a reasonable elevation. There was also a solid group of faster runners showing me the way. Be cautious of putting too much effort into a single performance. Instead, put all that effort into the training and practice so when the right moment comes, you are prepared to excel naturally.

This is why we say professional athletes "make it look easy." They can do this because they spend hours upon hours in the gym making it incredibly hard on themselves. When it comes down to game time, they can enjoy the moment. The big event becomes play, fun. It is the party after the hard work.

Lastly, a word about Tony Horton. He seems to be a great guy and clearly knows something about physical fitness. He is in amazing shape for his age. Actually, he is in amazing shape for someone half his age. However, that does not make him an all-round athletic deity. He excels in areas and does not in others, as we all do. Be leery of expecting too much from heroes; they are human too.

To his credit, Tony increased his race time by 2 minutes and 30 seconds from the previous year. That is quite an accomplishment! And even as a fitness celebrity, he is not afraid to not be the best at everything athletic.

Muscular Dystrophy Facts *from the Centers for Disease Control and Prevention*

Emery-Dreifuss (EDMD) affects men and women equally. "In 2009, 4 out of 2.99 million individuals of all ages were reported to have EDMD in Northern England. This means that less than 1 out of every 100,000 people were affected that year."

Source: www.cdc.gov/ncbddd/musculardystrophy/facts.html

Chapter 14

Nun Run 5K
Newark, Delaware
September 14, 2013

The following weekend I was scheduled to run in Delaware. I've always said the thing I love about living in Central Pennsylvania is our proximity to so many other places. Newark, DE, is under two hours away, so it was an easy down-and-back day-trip.

Eventually I would run out of states convenient to drive to. Until then, I was going to check off, as quickly as possible, all states I could get to in a weekend. In less than a month, I was going to learn that almost all states can be done in a weekend—even multiple states, even when flying. When you put your heart and mind into it, a lot can be accomplished in 48 hours.

The Delaware race started at 9:00 a.m., and I like to be there about an hour before race time. To make that happen, I was up by 5:00 a.m. and on the road by 6:00. That put me at the registration table for the Nun Run 5K with plenty of time to spare.

*"**Nun Run 5K:** Raises funds for the Sisters to care for the needy aged in the Delmarva area, in the Jeanne Jugan Residence. For over 100 years they have offered quality care in a loving home atmosphere to thousands of elderly persons of low income."*

The 5K brought in nearly 500 runners, a good crowd. The course was a relatively flat "out and back," that means we run away from the starting point 1.55 miles, hit a turnaround, and head back to the start, which now becomes the finish line.

Typically, the turnaround is just one or more orange cones with volunteers to guide runners back around. On the way back, runners have to watch for on-coming runners, which can be motivating for both sides.

Before I make it to the turnaround, I look at the runners coming at me and admire how fast they are. It also gives me a chance to figure out how well (or poorly) I am doing in the field. After the turnaround, when I see everyone who is behind me, I jokingly make myself feel good by saying things in my head like, "Yep, I am faster than him. Yeah, I am faster than her. Look at that, I am ahead of him."

No matter which side of the turnaround I am on, I find a reason to spin the positive on my position. It's one of the great things about running. How often can you get 500 people together and get them to be unanimous about where they are going, how there are going to get there, and agree to keep moving?

The sheer number of nuns who ran and walked in the event was impressive. I suppose they embrace their slogan which reads "Nun Run, Make It A Habit."

After the race, there was a variety of photo opportunities. The nuns were, of course, available for photos. There was a giant Snoopy mascot from Met Life. Miss New Castle County (Delaware), Stephanie Bailey, was on hand for photos. She also sang the National Anthem before the race.

Sister Elise, Jeff Fazio, and Sister Emmanuel completed the 2013 Nun Run.

It was a decent event for me. It wasn't my strongest showing, as I posted 24:39, but I am at a point where 24-anything is satisfying. I didn't dawdle in Delaware after the race. I just jumped in the car and headed home.

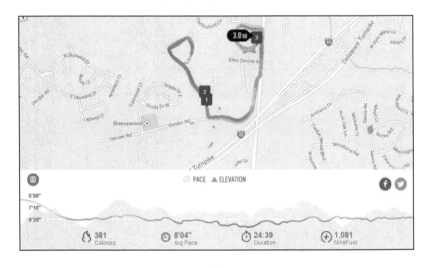

***

Throughout this whole experience, I was intentional about considering the leadership principles I was learning and observing traveling around the country. On the way home, I started thinking about what I learned in Delaware. What stood out? What was meaningful?

Frankly, nothing struck me. I went over every detail and thought about every angle. There was seemingly no profound moment or message from this event. How was I going to be able to write about "50 States of Leadership" if there wasn't an important message from one of the states?

After many weeks of contemplating the Delaware run, it hit me. Delaware was to be the 'Seinfeld' of this experience. 'Seinfeld' was the television show about nothing, but it was still incredibly important. It was part of the bigger picture of the entertainment world and that show amused us for years and still does on reruns.

Delaware is the 2nd smallest state in the Union. It is one of five states in the Mid-Atlantic Region of the United States. The U.S. is divided into 10 geographic regions: New England, Mid-Atlantic, Appalachian Highlands, Southeast, Midwest, Heartland, Southwest, Mountain, Pacific Coast, and the two Noncontiguous States.

I had already run Pennsylvania, New Jersey, New York, Maryland, and even Washington D.C. The only remaining State in the Mid-Atlantic to run was Delaware, and therein lies the lesson from Delaware.

***

Delaware Leadership Lesson:
Size Doesn't Matter

Delaware was an inconsequential event. Nothing amazing or fantastic happened there. Regardless, it was key to completing the first section of the United States, and it was, ultimately, necessary to run Delaware in order to meet the entire goal. Don't underestimate the importance of the small pieces of your plan. Everything plays a role in bringing a vision to fruition.

It would not have been incredible to say, "I ran 49 States. I just missed Delaware." This book would inherently be lacking if it was titled "Running Across America: 49 States of Leadership."

Value everything that contributes to your goals.

Muscular Dystrophy Facts *from the Centers for Disease Control and Prevention*

"The change in the gene that causes Duchenne/Becker muscular dystrophy (DBMD) happens on the X chromosome. A boy gets an X chromosome from his mother and a Y chromosome from his father. Only the X chromosome can have the changed gene that causes DBMD. Females almost never have DBMD because they have two X chromosomes. Even if a female has one X chromosome with the DBMD gene, her second X chromosome usually will make enough dystrophin to keep her muscles strong."

Source: www.cdc.gov/ncbddd/musculardystrophy/facts.html

Chapter 15

5K FOR ONLY YOU
Fairfield, Connecticut
September 21, 2013

Having already demonstrated my ability to go to sleep right after work on a Friday, wake up before the drunks think about leaving the bar, drive 6+ hours to register and race in 5K while sick; I was confident that I could handle a similar feat while feeling terrific. The go-to-sleep-after-work Friday plan was going to be used twice more in September to check off 5 more states. Up next were Connecticut and Vermont.

I made sure I was amply tired so that I could fall asleep by 6:00 p.m. on Friday, September 20, 2013. This middle-of-the-night adventure would take me to Fairfield, CT. Thankfully, it was a much shorter drive than the last one to Rhode Island.

I made it to Fairfield before the event registration crew arrived. I also beat the morning sun. The run was going to start at the end of a parking lot along the beach front. My early arrival allowed me the opportunity to take a walk on Jennings Beach and enjoy the sunrise. It was going to be a beautiful day, I just didn't know how beautiful.

***

Along this journey, I have been asked many times how I chose which 5Ks to run. That is not a simple question, as many factors went into deciding. Frankly, the most important deciding factor was logistics. When I figured out which weekends I could get away to run, I started scouring RunningInTheUSA.com to see what my options were. As I went along, I started visually connecting which states could be conveniently done in the same weekend. From there, it was a matter of seeing which pair, or sometimes trio, of states could be mapped out.

The second factor that went into deciding was looking at the cause. Most 5Ks support something, and it was often compelling to see which charity I would be supporting. Next, I would look at the costs of the event and what kind of swag came with registration.

Most events give runners an event t-shirt, but I have also received pajamas, socks, head bands, hoodies, and even a pair of boxers. Although it is common for marathons and half marathons to give a finisher's medal, that is not the norm with 5Ks. I have to admit that knowing I would receive a medal at the end was often a worthwhile incentive to enter a particular race. Besides getting the medal, my experience has been that the events that provide finishers' medals tend to be some of the best organized events.

All of these factors brought me to Connecticut for the inaugural running of the 5K For Only You.

> **"5K For Only You:** Only You is a non-profit organization started by Mike and Kelly Fedak to honor the memory of their son Mikey. Mikey had special needs and passed away unexpectedly in April 2013 at the age of 10. He was a truly special child, who in his brief time here, worked very hard to overcome his many challenges, but also really enjoyed life. He was always very happy and had a positive effect on everyone he met."

There is a huge difference between reading a story online and meeting the people involved. I am sure that is true of books too. I suspect meeting Dee and me in person would be a very different experience than reading my words written here. This was amply true of Mike and Kelly Fedak.

Prior to the race, I happened to be talking to a volunteer who is a family friend of the Fedaks. She asked me who I was and why I was running. I told her the 4D 50-state story. She asked me if I knew what today's event was about. I showed her the flyer given at registration and told her I had read that. She gave me more insight into the situation.

Mike is a Wall Street guy and the Fedaks are doing well. Their son Mikey was a special needs child, and they were fortunate to be able to afford the extras that come along with caring for a child in his situation.

Sadly, Mikey unexpectedly died in April of 2013. In response to his passing, the Fedaks wanted to share Mikey's positive impact with others. They realized that not everyone is in a position to afford the expenses of caring for a special needs child, so they founded Only You, a 501(c)(3) to assist these families.

With the start of this new initiative, they boldly laid out plans to a host a 5K in September to raise funds for Only You and to spread awareness. In addition to the 5K, they were organizing a kids' 1-mile race. They were hoping, and optimistic, that they could achieve their goal of 100 runners and walkers for this first event. When the day was done, they surpassed that conservative expectation with 430 participants—a very great turnout.

***

The course was flat and fast. Being close to the beach, we were not running much above sea level, so our lungs would not be taxed. It was early enough in the morning that temperatures were not too hot. This all added up to one of my fastest runs with a time of 24:11 minutes. As I continued through the states, it became apparent that a solid performance for me was in the 24:05–24:15 range, an average of 7:45-minute miles.

While I was catching my breath after the finish, I saw Mike Fedak coming in for his finish. I took the opportunity to introduce myself, offer condolences and thank him for such an amazing event. The event was a resounding success.

I was walking around with my camera taking photos of the awards table when Kelly crossed the finish line. It was a magnificent moment to see her reaction to finishing the run and making eye contact with Mike. They ran into each other's arms, hugging and crying.

The exhaustion from the run, from organizing the event, founding Only You and, of course, mourning their son was apparent in their embrace. It was an amazing culmination of human emotion. It was beautiful to witness and I was grateful that I had my camera and was able to take some photos from a respectful distance. It was an incredibly moving moment.

Kelly and Mike Fedak embrace after completing the inaugural For Only You 5K they held in remembrance of their son.

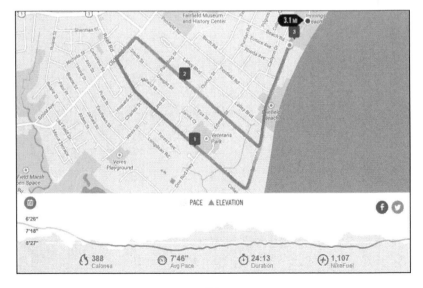

Connecticut Leadership Lesson:
Being Prepared to Shatter Goals, Allowing Emotions

The Fedaks had very realistic goals for their first 5K—100 runners. As the registration came rolling in, they saw the magnitude of what was coming and prepared. This event had beautiful, custom-made finishers' medals and t-shirts. Their initial plans for 100 items was going to have to change along with everything else associated with properly running a 5K (bananas, water, etc.). The 5K for Only You was one of the best organized events I attended nationwide. Clearly, they knew something about organization and leadership.

It's one thing to be prepared for success, but it is another to be prepared to smash your goals.

Another point worth mentioning is the openness with which the Fedaks shared their emotions. This event was clearly a result of their passion and their commitment. There was no need for them to hide the emotional import of their achievement. Too many leaders feel compelled to hide their emotions in order to show a "strong presence." I would argue that is far stronger to allow others to see your emotions and share the importance of events. So much of human communication happens through non-verbal communication. Why would we want to inhibit that for appearance sake?

CONNECTICUT
Sights Along the Way

P.T. Barnum Statue

PEZ Factory Visitors Center and Store

Muscular Dystrophy Facts *from the Centers for Disease Control and Prevention*

"Because a female can carry (or have) one Duchenne/Becker muscular dystrophy (DBMD) mutation and not be affected, she is referred to as a carrier. As a carrier, a female does have a risk of passing the same mutation on to her children. Each son born to a carrier female has a 50% chance of inheriting the DBMD mutation and having MD. Each daughter born to a carrier female instead has a 50% chance of inheriting the DBMD mutation and becoming a carrier like her mother."

Source: www.cdc.gov/ncbddd/musculardystrophy/facts.html

Chapter 16

Trapp Cabin 5
Stowe, Vermont
September 22, 2013

Speaking of being prepared, I was completely unprepared for Vermont. Unfortunately, I would be there in a few hours.

I tend to be optimistic—at times, overly. This is what allows me to get into my car, drive several hours, and not really be concerned about finding a place to stay. There are affordable motels and hotels everywhere, right? Sure, I had a close call in Maine, but I managed to spend the night on the couch of some friendly foreigners. See, it always works out. What could possibly go wrong?

In preparation for my trip to Vermont, I literally prepared nothing. I hadn't located a motel, nor had I made a connection through online dating for someone to join me for dinner. In short, I had zero solid plans in Vermont other than the chosen 5K.

Knowing that everything would always be okay, I meandered my way from Connecticut to Vermont. I took my time at the PEZ Visitors Center in Connecticut and the Dr. Seuss National Memorial Sculpture Garden in Massachusetts. When I got relatively close to my destination in northern Vermont, I started looking for motels. They were scarce, but every now and then I could find one. I wasn't worried.

So I traveled on to see other sites before I lost daylight. I took notice of the shockingly large number of old hot rods, custom cars and street rods that were seemingly everywhere. The juxtaposition of the cars against the fantastic mountain and forest landscapes was not lost on me.

VERMONT
Sights Along the Way

Sea Serpent, Brattleboro

The Round Church

Flying Monkeys in downtown Burlington

I continued on with a stop to see The Round Church and spent time in downtown Burlington. It was starting to get late and dark, time to find a place to stay for the night. Burlington is a large college town, and there are many motels, both nice and divey. Each lot I entered, I negotiated my car around the fancy collectible cars occupying every spot. Every place I stopped either had no vacancies or the rooms were over $200! Apparently, one of the country's largest car shows was taking place that weekend in the greater Burlington area, motels were full even at skyrocket rates.

There was no way I was spending two Benjamins on a room that I wouldn't use to avoid the police, so I left Burlington and headed east toward Stowe, VT, where the race was in the morning. When the sun goes down in northern Vermont, it gets dark—very, very dark. If it were not for the headlights of traffic, the interstate would be pitched black.

As I drove along I-89, it started to drizzle. I ventured on, waiting to see one of those big blue interstate signs acknowledging the presence of lodging at the next exit. They came rarely and when they did, I could either not locate the place referenced or it was grossly overpriced. The outlook on finding a warm bed and hot shower was gloomy.

I made it all the back to the area of Stowe and started heading off the interstate toward the Trapp Family Lodge, where the event would be the next day. I didn't know much about the facility but it sounded like a nice place where I could possibly grab a cheap room.

A few minutes after leaving the interstate, I entered pure darkness. Occasionally, my headlights would illuminate a Moose Crossing or Speed Limit sign. Near the middle of Stowe were few inns and motels. Even this far out, the endless hot rods made parking lots and room rates overflow. This could not be happening.

I eventually made it up the mountain to Trapp Family Lodge and was shocked by what I saw. I suppose my family was not affluent enough to have heard of this place, but it was clear that people with dough knew of its existence. The place was incredibly busy, incredibly fancy, and outrageously beautiful. Up to that moment, I was thinking "cabin" when I heard "lodge," when I should have been thinking Kellerman's from *Dirty Dancing*. There was no way this place would be in the budget.

This can't be happening. I'm in the middle of nowhere in northern Vermont, a light rain surrounded by pitched darkness. Right about then, I was expecting to hear scary music, with slowly increasing volume as a hand-carved, wooden sign that read "Camp Crystal Lake" appeared in sight through the falling rain. Of course, that didn't happen, but it might as well have. I was stuck.

I drove off the mountain and down to I-89, and headed back toward Burlington. What was I going to do? My back-up plan had always been my tent and sleeping bag in the trunk, but the idea of pitching a tent in the rain was not appealing. Besides, where would I pitch it? I couldn't see anything.

As I did a second lap on I-89, the glow of the distant highway rest area shone ominously. After two more laps on I-89, I accepted fate and pulled into the rest area and visitor center. I was able to use the bathroom before it was locked for the night. I parked my car next to a small outbuilding that offered shade from the intense parking lot lights. My sleeping bag made its way into the back seat of my car, and I built the best cocoon I could.

This was going to be a long, cold night, but at least there would be running water in the morning. I locked the doors and tried hard to fall asleep with the sound of rain pelting the roof. A few hours later, I was awakened by a very bright light in my eyes. As I put my glasses on and looked up, I realized another car had parked facing me. After quite a long while, it was clear they had no intention of shutting those headlights off.

I scrambled back to the front seat and went for a drive up the highway, turned around and stopped back at the other rest area—the one facing Stowe. I climbed into my cocoon and revisited thoughts of sleeping. Needless to say, this was not the best night of sleep I have ever had, but was worth saving $200.

***

In the morning, I unkinked myself from the evening's contortions and made my way to the restroom to make myself resemble a human being again. A quick sink wash-up and I was on the road back to the Trapp Family Lodge for the Trapp Cabin 5K.

> **"Trapp Cabin 5K:** *Beginning and ending in the Trapp Family Lodge Meadow, the races wind through 800 vertical feet [342 feet for the 5K] of idyllic forest, bubbling streams, and wild flowers. The race follows a dirt road briefly before merging with double track cross country trails. The 5K diverts at Old County Road and follows Russel Knoll Trail back to the finish. The 10K continues on to the cabin. These beautiful trails are not accessible to the general public so this is a special opportunity to run in a unique location.*
>
> *The races benefit Friends of Stowe Adaptive Sports is a Vermont-based non-profit founded in 2010 on the belief that access to sports and recreational programs are a powerful means for people with disabilities to develop independence as well as physical and mental well-being."*

It seemed like a nice connection to go from supporting Only You in Connecticut, which supports families with special needs children, to Stowe, VT, to support adaptive recreational equipment for those with disabilities.

***

Apparently not having a place to sleep for the night wasn't the only thing I had not properly prepared for in order to complete Vermont. Although I had been running hills during my practice runs and I had confidently attacked the 140' incline in Portland, ME, the hill on this course was to prove very different.

This was a trail run, so no smooth paved roads. I would have to negotiate a wild terrain of roots, rocks, edges, trees, and brush—all while ascending over 340'. This race's elevation gain was over two hundred feet higher than that of the Maine run. With rain the night before, the ground was sure to be slippery. We were also running at an elevation of nearly 1,600', one of the highest elevations I had run so far.

The factors were not adding together for a positive equation for the day.

The beginning of the race was confusing for me as there was a 10K sharing the start with the 5K. We raced across a marked path, in an open meadow to the edge of the woods and took off upwards. When I got to the split where the two races diverged, almost everyone went toward the 10K. One woman directly ahead of me turned toward the 5K. She was the only one I could see going that direction.

This made me enthusiastic; maybe I was doing well in the 5K field. I yelled to a course worker and asked if any other runners had gone this way—pointing toward the 5K route. She yelled back, "Plenty!" So much for that optimism. I raced onward.

The 5K route took us more directly up the hill along an old gravel road. It was steep, which at least meant we wouldn't be traveling on the road long, but it was extremely tough. When I hit a hill, my pace crashes like an airplane with a stalled engine.

Three women passed me on the way up. One ran briefly with me and we talked about how grueling this was, and then she was off. Somewhere close to the top, I called out to her, as she had missed the turn which led down into the woods. I was able to beat her to that turn, and I was not expecting what I saw.

The course entered a marked mountain bike path for our descent. The path was barely 18 inches wide. We were no longer on solid ground. The footing was mostly large stones, smaller rocks, boulders, downed trees, roots, and any other natural debris with no flat land. This descent was also happening incredibly fast. My feet barely made contact with one obstacle as my mind strategized the next. At times, my brain went from seeing a tree root to seeing one of my arms broken. This thought was quickly replaced with the next rock or tree limb.

Gravity pulled me forward at an ever-increasing pace and my long legs chewed up distance faster than I could adequately comprehend. My rate of acceleration was increasing. It was a borderline controlled fall. The surroundings were a complete blur. In the world of *Star Wars*, I had just entered warp speed.

The distance between me and the next runner was decreasing rapidly. I could tell she was taking a much safer approach to this downhill, and she stepped aside as I came clambering past her. The course had dozens and dozens of tight switchbacks that added to the sensory overload.

Just as I passed her, I entered a fast switchback that was sort of flat and definitely muddy. The transition from rocks to mud in my sneakers-designed-for-the-street was about to become comical as my feet went out from under me ala Scooby Doo. I managed a few, rapid woop, woops with my feet to locate something resembling traction, and I was off on my way. Luckily, I did not fall and introduce myself to the local shrubbery and rocks.

After a few more slippery turns, I was headed back to somewhat level ground and a clearer path. Back on a wide gravel road, I was happy to leave the claustrophobia of the bike path. Soon after, the woman I had passed on the downhill passed me a second time, and it was obvious I would not be seeing her until after the finish. She had lot more left in her tank than I had in mine.

As the road came to an end, my Nike watch was clicking off 3.1 miles and I stopped its recording, as that was officially 5K distance for me. The finish line was nowhere in sight and I thought about stopping. I had completed the 5K distance and I was exhausted. But I could see the meadow where we started, and if I kept running I would get back quicker than if I walked, so I kept at it.

The woman who had missed the turn off for the downhill cruised by me and asked if the course was long. I told her we had passed 5K a while back and she said she thought so. My goal was now to keep her in sight and try to run it off for the finish. As we got about half-way through the meadow, the path became obvious and I found that extra energy that always seems to be available for a maniacal sprint to the finish. She geared up as well, but I had the jump on her and took off. It was a good race, considering how tough the course was. The extra half mile that course contained was, however, unnecessary roughness.

It was very humbling to see some of the 10K racers finish just a few minutes after we did. I couldn't help thinking they had run more than twice the distance and climbed over twice as high. There are some truly amazing, unknown athletes hidden in the world of running.

There were not a large number of entrants and the field was split between the 5K and the 10K. I decided to hang around and see if there was a chance that something might have gone my way. As it turns out, today was to be my day. I managed to claim 1st place in my age group.

This was my first, but not my last, time visiting the podium on my 50-state mission. If only there was actually a podium.

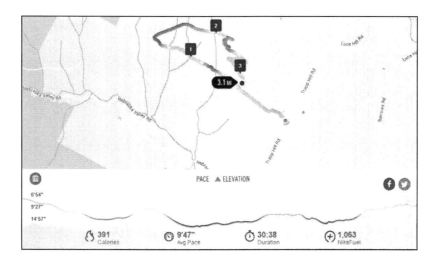

***

Being Prepared When You Are Unprepared

What do leaders do when they are unprepared? Part of leadership is never being completely unprepared. At the very least, we need to be incredibly adaptable. Although my lack of preparation left me with less than ideal options for spending the night, I still managed to get through the evening safely. If push came to shove, I had the resources to spend $200 for a nasty motel room, but I was able to weigh the value of that room.

As for the treacherous run, it was tough. In fact, one of the race sponsors was a company called "Darn Tough Vermont." It was more than I had trained for, but I had trained. I wasn't completely lacking in ability when I entered the event. It was just beyond my preparation level. I accepted the spots that were going to be challenging and slowed down so I could keep going. I also took calculated risks in the places I could gain back lost time.

Being unprepared is devastating only if "unprepared" is the way you see yourself. I prefer to see times of less-than-perfect preparation as an opportunity to use creativity to engineer solutions on the fly. These contrasting perspectives are sometimes the difference between surviving and perishing.

Chapter 17

Latonia 5K
Covington, Kentucky
September 28, 2013

It's interesting how two words can completely change your perspective on a project. I had posted a status on Facebook asking if friends wanted to join me on some of my crazy weekend trips. A few people sent messages in regards to possibly joining me to some of the more obvious, more popular states, like Hawaii, Alaska, California, etc. One particular response stuck out.

Sheila Ciotti, an associate dean at the college I work for, sent me an Email indicating that she might be interested in joining me for South Dakota. South Dakota?

I couldn't for the life of me imagine why anyone would choose South Dakota. Honestly, my knowledge of the U.S. Heartland was limited to images of endlessly flat fields with perfectly squared off roads. Why would anyone want to see that?

I sent her message looking for clarification:

Subject: South Dakota
From: Fazio, Jeff   **To:** Ciotti, Sheila
Is there a particular part of SD you want to see?

My ignorance of United States geography hadn't prepared me for her simple, two-word reply:

Subject: South Dakota
From: Ciotti, Sheila   **To:** Fazio, Jeff
Mount Rushmore

Mount Rushmore? Mount Rushmore! I stared blankly at my computer screen, letting "Mount Rushmore" sink in and all those words implied.

As ridiculous as this might sound, that was the first moment that it hit me that I was actually traveling throughout the *entire United States of America.* What was I thinking? What wasn't I thinking!? It never occurred to me that I would ever see Mount Rushmore in my life, much less on one of these trips. Why hadn't that occurred to me? Why didn't I know that Mount Rushmore was in South Dakota? What else didn't I know? What else might I see?

This innocuous exchange made an immediate and permanent change in how I would view traveling throughout this 50-state 4D challenge.

***

Completing Vermont and Connecticut finished off the New England states. It was the second section of the country to be completed, and it was time to turn my attention, literally, in another direction. Fall officially arrived during the Connecticut/Vermont weekend and the clock was quickly ticking away the number of weeks left for reasonable running weather. I would come to learn that "reasonable" can be very negotiable when I am on a mission.

Leaving Vermont, I had completed 6 States in September, the largest one-month total thus far. There was still one weekend left in the month, plenty of time to complete more states.

About this time, I started thinking about the benefits of running at other hours of the day. After all, not all 5Ks were morning events. In fact, there are a whole lot of novelty-themed runs that happen in the evening. There are neon runs, flashlight runs, glow runs, and more. This opened up the possibility of doing more than one run in a day, assuming I could figure out the travel logistics.

This inspired an internet search for late-night runs. Success came quickly with a "Glow Trot" 5K in Tennessee on Saturday, September 28. I logged back onto RunningInTheUSA to see what I could piece together with this run. It turned out there was an early morning run in Kentucky the same day and an early evening run the following day in North Carolina.

This was possible. By possible, I mean it was within the realm of being able to accomplish if I could figure out how to drive 1500 miles (about 24 hours of driving), run three 5Ks, and have time for meals and sleep within 48-hours. Clearly, this would be a great time to share the 4D experience, and driving.

My friend, Angela Gorman agreed to take on the adventure. This was going to be an awesome road trip with a good friend. Sharing driving would be a massive help and we could each sleep while the other drove. To sweeten the deal, we used Angela's car, which was significantly better on fuel than mine.

Angela was the perfect companion for this trip, as she also committed to running all three events. She is an accomplished Spartan; the Spartan events are typically 13.1-mile (1/2-marathon length) trail runs loaded with military-inspired obstacles. These events are not for the weak of heart or body. In fact, Angela was running the Spartan in Vermont the previous weekend when I was running at Trappe Lodge. She also sports a 4D pin. Tearing up three 5Ks inside of 32 hours was not going to tax her abilities.

**

At 1:00 a.m. on Saturday, September 28, 2013, we loaded our bags into Angela's car and we were off for a 6+ hour drive to Covington, KY. The wee hours of the morning are the only time interstates are truly magnificent and work as efficiently as they are designed to. The rest of the day, they are clogged arteries filled with the cholesterol of left-lane drivers who do not pass and 18-wheelers that try to pass but can't get out of their own way. It's at these incredibly late hours (or incredibly early hours, depending on your perspective) that the estimated times of arrival on a GPS are accurate.

KENTUCKY
Sights Along the Way

Notre Dame Cathedral Replica, Covington, KY

Covington, KY, sits across the Ohio River from Cincinnati, OH, so our early-morning route took us clear across Pennsylvania and Ohio. We arrived very early for the event, so we had time to check out one of the main sights in town, the Notre Dame Cathedral Replica. Our final destination in Covington was in the neighborhood of Latonia, where we registered for the Latonia 5K.

> *"**Latonia** 5K: We are Latonia residents and business owners working for Latonia's bright future! The 5K course showcases Latonia's gorgeous Craftsman, Victorian, Queen Anne, and Bungalow homes while celebrating the incredible history of the Latonia Race Track, around which many of the neighborhood's homes were built. All funds raised from the event will go towards the new Latonia Cardinal's Community Park at Latonia Elementary School."*

As we watched other people show up to register, I began taking notice of the folks attending. This was a small community event and it appeared as if the locals were coming out to support the race. The turnout was great for a community event, but not big from what I have seen at most 5Ks. As with any competition, odds of winning an award go up when there are fewer challengers.

There is a certain air given off by really fast runners. Even if you do not know a lot about running, you still can probably point to the people most likely to place near the top. A certain level of fitness is evident in their physiques, a certain flavor to how they hold themselves and the not-to-be-mistaken, dead give-away of knowing how to stretch before they race. I still don't stretch prior to running. Maybe someday I will be good enough to justify stretching.

Anyway, I wasn't seeing any of "these" people walking around. Everyone I saw, were mere mortals. They looked like a wonderful group of real human beings. I had been running faster and faster and who knows, maybe I had a chance to place well in this small-town event. I made a comment to Angela about this and she agreed.

I went to the registration table to look at the course map while I consumed my morning gel pack, Vitamin water and banana. In the unlikely scenario that I was anywhere close to the front, I wanted to have an idea of where I was going. The course was clearly designed to show off the neighborhood with as many as 28 turns! That is roughly 9 turns per mile. The map looked like connect-the-dots that ultimately would create an abstract design.

This was going to be an interesting experience.

We lined up in front of the Latonia Elementary School for the start of the race. The gun went off and the first three turns took us around the outside of the school yard. By the second turn, I was in the lead. Since I generally take off fast at the sound of the gun, it is not unusual for me to be out front for the first couple of hundred feet, but this already felt very different.

As I ran, the distance between me and the pack grew. This was crazy. Was I really leading a 5K? This was pretty exciting. I wondered if I could hold onto the lead for the entire first half mile.

Most 5Ks have some sort of directional, fixed signage or arrows painted on the ground to direct the runners. Some 5Ks even have a lead vehicle to guide the front runners. I have seen this done by bicycle, 4-wheeler and even police cars.

Since we were making so many turns and running around blocks, we repeated intersections. In an effort, I can only imagine, to be efficient, this race had volunteers holding signs with arrows so they could move and change the direction of the arrow depending on which direction a runner was approaching from. This proved to be a terrible idea when runners started coming from two directions—inevitable as the race field spread out.

As the race leader, I yelled to volunteers to get their attention when we came through intersections the second time. They were so focused on the long train of runners coming through for the first pass that they were surprised by the lead runners returning from a different direction. This caused a lot of confusion as volunteers had to quickly think which way to point the arrow when I called to them. It would have been comical if it were not so stressful.

Yelling to course workers also robbed valuable energy and concentration. During the times I did not have to get their attention, I was struck by how incredibly lonely it is being out front. It was an odd feeling to run by myself, even knowing dozens of people were chasing me.

Jeff Fazio leads the 2013 Latonia 5K with Kevin Hester closing in fast.

A quick glance at the Nike confirmed that I was fast approaching the first mile and I was still in the lead, although I could hear at least one pair of sneakers not far behind me. I wondered how long I could hold off this mystery runner.

As we completed 1.55 miles, exactly half of the course, he passed me, a young guy, about 18 years old, running a strong pace, but not completely leaving me in his dust. A quick glance over my shoulder confirmed that no one else was close to us. This race was on.

The former chess player inside me strategized keeping pace with him at a distance of 50–100 feet. I hoped I had enough in reserves to sprint at the end. I focused on his shoulders and tried to match his stride.

As we approached another section of corner workers, I noted that he did not call out to them. I was hoping he knew where he was going. The course workers jumped up, startled that we were fast approaching, and they fumbled with the arrow sign. After flip flopping it a few times, they finally chose a direction to point us. I had no confidence that was the right way, but what choice did I have?

We kept running, getting closer and closer to the edge of town, until it was absolutely clear we would be leaving town, not just the neighborhood. He stopped in frustration and yelled—I think we were sent the wrong way. I said I was certain of it.

Frustrated and out of breath, we stood there together trying to decide what to do. Soon, three other runners joined us—two men and a woman. They all started talking about what to do and I decided to run back. The clock was still ticking after all and I wanted to see what I could salvage. Later we learned that course workers not only had us in the wrong direction, but they were actually standing at the wrong intersection, so there was never a chance they could have directed us correctly.

This was heartbreaking, as I could never imagine a scenario where I might have a chance at actually wining a 5K. As I ran back, sorting through my disappointment, I heard a car zoom down the street, beeping its horn. It was the race director. Her window was down and she was yelling for me to get in.

As I got into her vehicle, the other runners caught us. The female runner joined me in the car; the two older guys pretty much said the heck with this and started to run back to the course. The young kid who was leading at the time of the "course malfunction" seemed aggravated and started walking back.

The race director was on her phone letting people know that she found us and that she would be bringing us back. She apologized to us numerous times. I made the comment that this was so unfortunate because that kid probably would have won. She asked which kid and I indicated the boy who was leading the race when we were sent off course.

The whole time she was on the phone, her car was just sitting there, idling in the middle of the street. I couldn't believe we were just sitting still! The race was still on. A clock was ticking off our time! I regretted getting in the car. She eventually pulled off the street and found a place to turn around.

She got us back to the intersection where we had been misled, and I could see the other two guys running down the street. I am pretty sure I was out of her car before it came to a complete stop. I was running down the street, reeling those two guys in as quickly as I could. I eventually caught them and as I passed them, one of them yelled to me that I was missing yet another turn on the course.

I double-backed and could see the playground where we'd started. I wondered how far back in the pack we had dropped. In my mind, I wanted to at least race these guys to the finish. As I rounded the last corner, I looked across the school yard and there was a strange absence of runners. I could see the finish line and I bolted full steam ahead, putting distance between myself and those two other guys.

As I came through the finish line, there was a volunteer handing out finishing cards. I had never seen this before or since. I grabbed my card and slowed to walking pace. As I caught my breath, I looked down at the card and saw a laminated square with one digit on it: 1.

Could this be? After that fiasco, had I managed to come in first? — overall?

Through all of the confusion and course chaos, I had, in fact, crossed the line first. But it didn't feel good. It would have been nicer to race that young guy for all the glory to a second place finish that was not disputable.

From what I understood from Angela, on another section of the course, some mid-pack runners also got sent the wrong direction. It was an ambitious goal to create a course that showed off so much of the neighborhood, but there were simply too many turns, not enough volunteers, and a complete lack of fixed, directional signage to accurately keep runners on course.

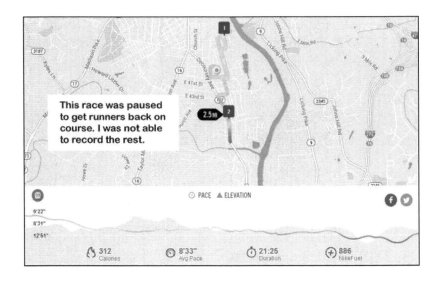

This race was paused to get runners back on course. I was not able to record the rest.

***

As we waited around for the awards ceremony to being, the race director approached me. She apologized again for the course errors. She also asked for a favor. She indicated that the 1st place prizes were an oil painting of a local horse racing track and a 1-year membership to a local gym. She wanted to know if I valued either of these prizes and I said that I did not. She asked if it would be okay to award them to the younger guy and I said absolutely.

When it came time for awards, they listed him as first in men's and myself as the fastest, overall runner. He got the prizes and I got the microphone. The race director had asked if I would say a few words about why I was there and the 4D experience. That was the first, but not the last, time I found myself in the front of a group, talking through a microphone explaining about me, Dee, 4D, and this crazy goal of running a 5K in all 50 states in one year.

It felt terrific to share the message—even better than collecting the "1" finishing tag.

***

Losing Your Way and Winning, What to Do When Things go Wrong

Sometimes we need to get lost to find our way. When we are leading and we lose our way, it just might be an opportunity to take a moment to pause, look around and reassess where we are. Going off course every once in a while can build character, patience and perspective. What we do when we lose our way says much more about our character than the fact that we lost our way in the first place.

We tend to focus on our experience. When the other runners and I realized we were off course, it was something we perceived that happened to us, just us. We were aware of the race clock ticking and that we were losing time. The reality was that the disorganization affected many runners, not only our isolated group. Once we gathered ourselves, refocused, we each still had an opportunity to win. All was not lost in getting lost.

Another important leadership perspective from this race was how the race director handled the chaos. I think she handled everything as well as possible given the circumstances. After things go afoul, it is hard to make the situation right. Her choice to acknowledge me as the first runner across, but still show "1st place" to the other runner was a good compromise.

The persons who may have been the most negatively affected were the two older guys who placed 2nd and 3rd as they had committed themselves to running the rest of the race. The young man who was given 1st place chose to jog back and apparently "gave up" on the run. I never had a chance to talk to those two guys to get their feelings.

Either way, the race director was in an uncomfortable position, as the chaos compromised everyone's times and distances. I was left with a positive feeling about how she resolved everything as fairly as possible.

Taking advantage of an opportunity to speak is always important. A mentor of mine once counseled me that "If you can speak in a situation, you can affect the situation." When I was given the opportunity to address everyone at this event about the 4D mission, I jumped at the chance. It is important to get the message out about what you are doing and what you hope to achieve. If you find yourself in a position to promote your vision, take it!

Chapter 18

The Glow Trot 5k
Maryville, Tennessee
September 28, 2013

Angela and I didn't dawdle in Kentucky. We had another 5K to run in 9 hours and we had a 4-hour drive ahead. Assuming reasonable stops for food, gas and sightseeing, it was going to be a packed day of traveling.

We stopped to see a few random attractions along the way, but spent most of our sightseeing in Knoxville, TN. Among the interesting sights, we stopped at the World's Largest Rubik's Cube (you have to love Roadside America), which sits in the lobby of a hotel in downtown Knoxville. When you zigzag the entire United States you are bound to cross your own path from time to time. Let's just say this wasn't going to be the last time I would see this Rubik's Cube on my journey. The second time would be under very different circumstances and with a really unique individual. As you might guess, that is a story for a later chapter.

||*

We settled into our hotel and made our way to Maryville, TN, for our 8:00 p.m. event—The Glow Trot 5k.

> **"The Glow Trot 5k:** *The Glow Trot is a locally run 5K to help support ReachHaiti Ministries. Overcome your fears and love others by supporting this event. Come join us to light up the darkness with a night of glow swag, black lights and music, while helping support ReachHaiti Ministries."*

This was another novelty event. The run was at night, in the dark. As part of the registration swag, all runners were given neon glow bracelets and a glow necklace. Runners did not just stop there—many brought lots of extra glow items and used their creativity to fabricate all sorts of self-illuminating items for the run. It was pretty wild seeing the fun that people had embracing the neon glow concept of the race.

There were, of course, those diehard runners who showed up only because someone had taken the time to measure 5 kilometers and stick a timer at each end. They were there to race—novelty be damned. The darkness did not concern them. The circus of illumination around them offered no distraction. In a Vin Diesel-inspired way, these runners were there because they live their lives 3.1 miles at a time.

I'm always looking around for someone I think I might be able to pace. It can be motivating to have a target to measure yourself against when you are out on course. If I were a better judge of age, I would also eye up my age-group competition. This rarely works out for me, as I have trouble discerning the ages of other men. However, this time would be different.

As I looked through the growing mass of runners, one guy clearly stood out. He was wearing only a pair of black, light-weight running shorts and his sneakers. His shirtless body was exposed and his dedication to the gym was clearly evident. This man was built. He was a tank.

There are those guys who live in the gym and appear to feast on pallets of eggs while gargling with steroids. Their muscles expanding outward like bread rising in an oven until their necks disappeared. That was not this guy.

This guy was the poster boy for the word "ripped." His photo might appear near the definition of "shredded." He was lean, cut and apparently found the secret to dissolving body fat. The man was a chiseled rock—the epitome of physical fitness. He was also clearly in my age group.

I pointed him out to Angela and said, "There's the guy that is going to win my age group." Oh, how prophetic. I've noticed that runners who show up shirtless, typically are very fast. Their motivation for lacking upper-body garments is not to show off their body, but rather to remove any sense of restriction and weight that might get in the way of the few seconds of a new PR. In fact, these guys—and I say guys,

TENNESSEE
Sights Along the Way

Giant Christian I-75 Cross

Big Dragon Statue

The Sunsphere

World's Largest Rubik's Cube

Woman's Basketball Hall of Fame

Gatlinburg, TN

Smokey Mountains

Clingmans Dome

Spaceship House

Martin Luther King Jr. Assassination Location

Graceland

because I've only seen women run shirtless at one event, a week later in Texas. The Texas 5K was to be a very different type of novelty run, held in a very *natural setting*.

This guy's name was Jay Reggio. Maryville is his hometown. He runs triathlons and a variety of other events. He is built for competition. When I asked about how fast he typically runs a 5K, he indicated that he is usually in the 18-19 minute range. He also said there was no way he would be that fast this evening though, as he wasn't supposed to be running yet as per doctor's orders. You see, he was still in the early stages of recovery from spine surgery—SPINE surgery.

Are you kidding me? If my spine was ever the main course of a surgery, I am not sure how long it would take me to exert myself in a physical competition. I imagine it would be years, surely not weeks before recovery was declared by the doctors. This guy was intense.

It looked like I had my goal for this particular event: try to keep Jay within visible range. As the race started, I positioned myself about 4 feet directly behind and decided to just concentrate on watching his shoulders. I wanted to keep the distance between me and his shoulders consistent. I thought if I could concentrate on such a specific goal, I might not think about the impending strain on my muscles, lungs and heart.

This race had a very unique layout. Most 5Ks are either out-and-back or a loop. Some races have a smaller loop that runners take two laps around. This race combined elements. There was a 2-lap loop, but in the middle of the second lap, the course turned down a small road through a cemetery, and that small portion was out-n-back.

The race started in a parking lot, made a right onto a main road that had a slight, gradual incline. About a quarter mile into the race, I was concerned with how much this incline was going to affect me, as I lose an awful lot of time on hills, even small ones. At the risk of fatigue, I pushed hard early to keep Jay in my sights.

When we turned off the main road, we enjoyed the benefits of going uphill as we were rewarded with a descent. I made up some ground that I'd lost. Regardless, I was using a lot more energy than I am used to, and I had just run the Kentucky 5K hours earlier. I was feeling it.

The end of the first mile had us cutting across another parking lot to head back toward the starting line to complete our first lap. That is when Jay really started putting some distance between us, and I knew he would be gone soon as we had a second round of that incline.

By the time I reached the top of the incline and made the turn for the descent, he was no longer in sight. Well, he may have been, but we were running in complete darkness and it is really hard to distinguish runners, even when one of them is not wearing a shirt. I figured I would be able to get an idea of how far ahead he was when we hit the out-and-back portion along the cemetery. However, I had not counted on how incredibly dark and impossible it would be to see when we entered the cemetery.

As we made the turn into the cemetery, I immediately worried about my feet. It was a very narrow lane we were on and the edge of the asphalt provided ample opportunities to twist an ankle or lose footing. This was enough of a distraction that I never saw Jay come back at me after he made the turn-around.

I had lost my target before completing mile 2. The last mile of the race my eyes were playing tricks on me thinking I was catching a glimpse of him. When I made it to the finish, he was there drinking a glass of water. We congratulated each other on a good race. I knew I did well, and having him there pushed me harder. I managed a 24:22 which is a solid run for me, especially after having raced in the morning and driven many hours between. I was happy to claim 2nd in my age group and 13th overall out of 156 runners. Jay ran 23:37, winning our age group and placing 9th overall.

Angela's goal for the weekend was to run a 30-minute or better 5K to get her new PR. The run in the dark worked for her, as she came in 5th in her age group with a time of 30:06. It was a good night for running. Two races in one day were done, but we were still hundreds of miles and one more 5K away from home.

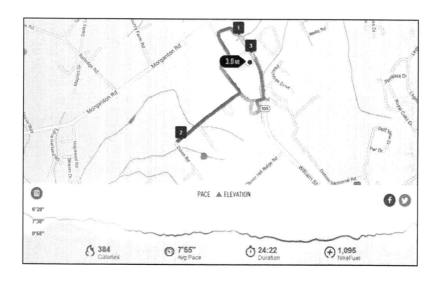

***

Tennessee Leadership Lesson:
Finding Your Inspiration, Finding Your Way in the Dark

If we look, we will find inspiration all around us. Solid leadership includes being able to identify those with superiors skills, talent and/or knowledge. True leaders are inspired by, not intimidated by, seeing excellence in others.

When I saw Jay Reggio, I immediately realized he was in my age group, and after speaking to him it was clear that he was in a very different league.

After realizing how strong a runner he is, I was motived—not to beat him, but merely to be able to keep him within sight. If not for the darkness, I may have achieved that goal as I finished only 45 seconds behind him. When confronted with someone of greater ability, leaders do not discount them, disregard them, or in any way treat them with negativity. Those are all signs of a weak ego. In fact, I encourage leaders to seek out those who have achieved more, so that they can see what is possible and learn from others.

I played tournament chess in high school. My skill at chess improved tenfold when I was willing to play stronger players and take a beating. When I played them, I didn't just sit and get whooped. I sat and studied. It was class time for me and my focus was on playing as well I could while learning from the better player.

Another point worth making about the Tennessee run is the moment that we left the main course and ran the tangent out and back through the cemetery. It was pure darkness. The illumination from our glow sticks and necklaces did very little to combat the overwhelming pitch darkness of night. It would have been easy to lose my way or misstep. Darkness can be intimidating and disorienting.

Many people talk about negotiating the dark times by looking for the light. We have heard that cliché ad nauseam. My undergraduate degree is in fine art photography, so it might be that I spent a lot of time in darkrooms, but my feeling on darkness is very different. I do not have a need to "strive toward the light," but rather to find my way through the darkness. You just might find that navigating the darkness is not too difficult if you simply stop looking for the light and concentrate on finding your way. The lightness will just eventually come as assuredly as the morning sun.

Chapter 19

Rotary District 7710 Global Run 4 Water
Cary, North Carolina
September 29, 2013

Need a cure for insomnia? Run a 5K. Drive several hours to another State. Run another 5K.

Angela and I were drained and promptly crashed when we got back to the hotel room. It was an exhausting day, but we had the hardest run of the weekend ahead of us—we just didn't know it.

Part of traveling is debating the wake-up time to hit the road. The run the following day was late in the afternoon so we had plenty of time to get there. We could sleep in the next morning or we could get up to see more sights along the way. Angela was on board with an early departure, which was a terrific choice for sightseeing, but not so great for race preparation.

Our drive took us from Knoxville, TN, to Cary, NC. Leaving early allowed us to take an indirect route through the Great Smoky Mountains. That was a beautiful choice.

Prior to this trip, I had never heard of Gatlinburg, TN. I didn't even realize there was going to be something significant on our route toward the Great Smoky Mountains. When you are driving in the pre-dawn hours on roads you are not familiar with, the last thing you expect to drive upon is Time Square or the Vegas Strip. These just aren't places you accidently drive into.

Gatlinburg, TN, was that type of experience. We were driving along in near darkness and then suddenly, right in front of our eyes, the world was lit up as if it were daytime. The bright lights for shows, clubs, and restaurants were everywhere crowding each other like spectators at the Super Bowl. Layers upon layers of illumination overwhelmed our senses. There were advertisements for amusement parks, go-karts, and comedy shows.

The time of day made it an unusual experience. The effect was almost eerie, as we were there so early there were no other people out and about and very few cars. It gave the impression of being in a post-apocalyptic entertainment world that was 100% entertainment but zero audience. Neither of us would have been shocked to see zombies walking down the on-coming lane.

As we were just passing through and nothing was *really* open, we just drove through light after light of this visual stimulation. The only thing more sudden than the arrival of all these lights was how immediately they all disappeared. When you hit the edge of Gatlinburg and enter the Great Smoky Mountains, everything is immediately and completely shut off.

It was like walking through an overly bright room when the lights unexpectedly go out, except that we were traveling at 50 mph. The time for your eyes to adjust became rather important, but I managed to keep on driving, and we had the opportunity to explore the beautiful American wilderness for at least a few hours.

***

We made it to Cary in plenty of time to compete in the Rotary District 7710 Global Run 4 Water 5K.

> *"**Global Run 4 Water 5K:** Our mission is to help needy people in the world have clean drinking water, because safe water helps to liberate people so they can live healthier, fuller, and more productive lives. At the same time we are going to raise awareness among Rotarians of the worldwide water crisis, and improve Rotary's public image as a major player in the water and sanitation cause."*

This was one of those events that just happened to fit into the schedule. It was conveniently located and the timing was right for my travels. I can't really say that I had any perspective on what we were running for; I just needed to check North Carolina off the list.

Once I arrived, the impact of what we were doing was much more meaningful. The run was hosted by a local Rotary Club and was a fundraiser for their Global Water Initiatives. In addition to the run, they had other activities set up to draw attention to concerns about clean and healthy drinking water. One of the activities involved teams of people carrying long pieces of bamboo with water jugs hanging off them.

Most 5Ks are held as fundraisers and, like most fundraisers, they benefit a local organization, charity, or person. This event was unique in that it was helping raise funds for an issue outside of the U.S. While running 5Ks all over the country, I was used to supporting causes that I might have been familiar with, but accepted that my money was going to help the locales where I was competing. This was the first time that I entered an event that supported people elsewhere.

This allowed me to reflect beyond the local activities and think about our impact on a much larger scale. It was satisfying to think that participating in a healthy activity, like running here in the United States, could impact unhealthy living conditions elsewhere in the world.

***

As for the actual run, the course featured two laps that were not exactly identical, but both included an awful hill. I look forward to a day that hills stop cramping my style. Until then, I accept that when I see a serious gain in elevation on course, it is going to have proportional gain in my race time.

Considering the early morning drive, running two events the day before, and the healthy hill on course, I was not entirely displeased with placing 18th and completing the course in slightly over 27 minutes. Angela was also more than 3 minutes off her best run, but we both made it. We both completed three 5Ks in fewer than 32 hours in three different states.

Completing North Carolina also meant that I finished my third section of the country, the Appalachian Highlands (VA, WV, KY, TN and NC). North Carolina was also my 9th state in September. I ran as many states in September as I did in June, July, and August combined. My pace of completing States just skyrocketed. I was on a roll. It started to become clear that completing the entire U.S. in one year was very possible, if not entirely probable.

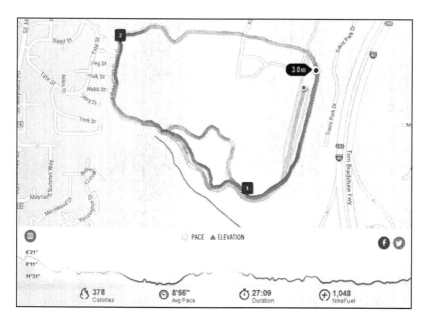

***

Leaders should always keep an eye on the big picture. The big picture will not only include your group's primary goal, but also the effect that reaching that goal will have on the macro environment. Depending on your initiative, that may be looking at the effects you will have on the county, state, country, or world-wide level. Always keep any eye out for opportunities to maximize your impact.

Taking on three states in one weekend was ambitious. It would have been naïve to think that all three races would be accomplished at top performance. Leaders have to make decisions sometimes between quantity and quality. For this weekend, it was more important to finish more states and make progress toward the 50-state goal than it was to post a new best time. Although setting PRs is wonderful, it is not the primary objective and leaders need to always be vigilant about the primary goal.

Muscular Dystrophy Facts *from the Centers for Disease Control and Prevention*

"Pediatricians need to regularly screen, identify and evaluate babies and young children for delays in motor development, according to recommendations in a new clinical report funded by the Centers for Disease Control and Prevention (CDC). Motor development is how a child's brain and muscles become able to move parts of the body like arms, fingers, legs, and head, and to work together so the child can get around (such as in walking, running, and climbing)."

Source: www.cdc.gov/ncbddd/musculardystrophy/facts.html

Chapter 20

Bare As You Dare 5K
Alvord, Texas
October 5, 2013

There are all sorts of 5Ks that take place all over the world. There seem to be endless themes for runs and novel ways to twist the typical 3.1-mile run. To keep this project fresh and engaging, I made a point all along to look for interesting runs (i.e. the Undy 5000 and the Glow Trot). Later chapters will cover some really clever ideas for races, but this chapter might take the cake as the most titillating event of them all.

One evening I was scouring the Internet for races that took place at odd times of day, like the Glow Trot. Finding these races made it easier to slip an extra state or two into a weekend, so it was important to find them and see what was available in the area.

My search landed me on a website for an interesting run in Florida. The race date had already passed so it was not an option for this project, but the idea of the race caused me pause. This particular 5K was done in the nude.

Nude?

Do people really run races naked? As naked as a deer sprinting through the woods? Could this be? Really?

I shot a message to my friend David and asked him if he realized that there was nude run in Florida. He replied back quickly and said that he wasn't aware of that one, but he was aware of a nude run in Oregon. People run naked on both coasts? This was becoming more interesting. I was intrigued.

I asked him to send information on the Oregon run, but he could not find it. A quick Internet search revealed that Google really does know everything. If one was willing to peek under the covers, one just might find nude runs happening all over the country. In fact, there is a nude running series, with points! And awards!

Was this something to include in this project? Could I really bare it all and run a 5K? In Chapter 3, I wrote about leaders being willing to bare themselves to gain attention to their cause, but that was in reference to running in your underwear. But nude?

Why not?

One of my favorite phrases is, "I rather live life saying 'Oh, well!' than saying 'What if?'" I dove into the race listings to see if there were events that made sense with my travel options. October was around the corner and it was starting to get colder outside. States that made sense to run in the nude were running in short supply for this time of the year, but I managed to locate one in Texas—the Bare As You Dare 5K at the Blue Bonnet Nudist Park. The acronym for the race is, of course, *BAYD*.

> **"Bare As You Dare 5K:** The 5K race course is definitely cross-country. It is a fun and challenging course laid out on gravel roads and trails that are enclosed entirely within the resort. For safety reasons, no pets, bicycles, strollers, baby joggers, or in-line skates will be permitted on the course. The race will be electronic chip timed.
>
> Bluebonnet, a naturist park, rests on 66.5 acres adjacent to Caddo and LBJ National Grasslands. Guests are able to relax and find refuge from the pressures of urban life. Our resort adds a new dimension to the clothing optional experience by offering a secure and serene environment. We welcome the experienced and the uninitiated nudist to enjoy our hospitality."

I was going to Texas.

***

The Blue Bonnet Nudist Park is a 21-hour drive from home. It was time to park the car and hitch a ride on something faster. Texas was going to be the first state I flew into as part of this project. Adding the costs of airfare was going to put pressure on the budget. It was also going to become imperative to do more than one state in a weekend whenever possible.

Flying to an event added emphasis to my concern about events potentially being canceled. Airline tickets are cheapest 35-45 days before you need them, but that is too far out to predict weather. How awful would it be to buy a ticket and have an event canceled? *(Truly terrible!)* How much more money would it be to keep buying the ticket insurance? *(Hundreds of dollars more)* How many flights would I need to complete this project? *(15!)*

The Blue Bonnet is located in Alvord, TX, about an hour from the Dallas/Fort Worth International Airport. It also happens to be about an hour from the Oklahoma border. In looking at Google maps and the Running In The USA website, I was able to find a run in Lawton, OK, the same weekend as the nude run in Texas.

Finding a flight to get me in and out of Dallas was not a problem. The plan was set: I would be gone 52 hours, flying from Harrisburg to Dallas, renting a car and completing 5Ks in two states, and making it back to

Dallas for my flight home, all in time to be ready for work on Monday morning.

This was going to be interesting.

My next challenge was going to be sorting out where I would stay. I was coming into Dallas just before midnight on Friday. Ideally I would have a place to stay Friday night and Saturday night, but with a project as expensive as traveling throughout the entire U.S., I needed to watch every expense.

In talking with Dee about this, I had shared that I was planning on just "spending the night" in the airport. Not only would this save a night of hotels, it would also save many hours of car rental. Dee had a better thought. She has an aunt and uncle who live 10 minutes from the DFW Airport. I was so thankful that they agreed to pick me up, let me use their spare bedroom, and take me back to the airport in the morning for my rental car. This was perfect.

That still left Saturday night. I am a very low-needs traveler. I am quite happy with something to sleep on and a place to shower in the morning. That said, I was on a hunt for the lowest-of-the-low dollar motels. I have learned that if you look at Google maps, and zoom into the map between major cities and type in the word "motel," it will highlight the little mom-n-pop motels. This scavenger hunt led me to the Ranch House Motel in Burkburnett, TX, for $40 for one night's stay.

With the flight booked and the room and rental car reserved, all that was left was paying my race registrations. I took care of that online as well. Texas and Oklahoma would be the first races of October, on the 5th and 6th of the month.

***

A few days before the race, the forecasters were calling for a pretty solid chance of light rain in Alvord. I sent a message to the Facebook page for the race to confirm that the run was rain or shine. I explained that I was coming from PA and wanted to be sure that I would be able to race. I got a message back from the Resort's owner, Lourdes Brioso Moss Keep. She confirmed that the event was on regardless of the weather. She also asked why I was coming in from Pennsylvania for the run.

I explained the 4D experience to her and what it all meant. She shared details about a different medical issue that a very close loved one had to deal with and how that impacted her. It was nice to build this bond with her as it gave me comfort "knowing" someone where I would be racing. I hadn't realized how impactful our bond was until I arrived at the resort. Lourdes had some surprises up her sleeve.

A few days later I boarded a plane in Harrisburg and started my journey to Texas. Dee's Aunt Pam and Uncle Scott met me at the airport and were incredibly gracious hosts. Not only did they supply a place to stay and the ride back-and-forth to the airport, they also took me out for a nice Texas breakfast. Their hospitality was far beyond what I could have expected and light-years beyond what I would have supplied for myself. Their contribution to this project was greatly appreciated.

***

After breakfast, I grabbed my rental car and checked out some sights in Dallas before heading to the Blue Bonnet. This was my first time entering a nudist resort, although I had previously been to a nude beach a few times. The experiences were very different.

For some reason it feels more natural to me to be around nude people at a beach where everyone is laying out and getting tan. Beaches, by their nature, entice people to wear very little clothing, so losing the inconsequential garments people have on at the beach doesn't seem like a very big deal. The resort was very different.

People were camping in various ways and the main building had space for cooking and hosting large groups. It was a very chilly day so people were in various stages of undress, but most had on some amount of clothing. I guess what was really different for me was being inside with so many naked people.

I located the registration table and as I was standing in line I started chuckling to myself over the irony of receiving race t-shirt for a nude run. Just then, the woman next to me asked, "Hey, isn't that you?" as she pointed to an A-frame easel. My brain was thinking "She got the wrong guy. I've only been in Texas a few hours ... but ... wait ... huh? ... that is me?!"

I was shocked to see a framed poster on the A-frame that detailed

Jeff Fazio and Lourdes Brioso Moss Keep pose with the 4D Mission donation station at the Bluebonnet Nudist Park.

the 4D project, had photos of me, Dee, and the map of the U.S. I was creating out of my race bibs. Below the posting was a hanging bag with a sign that simply read "voluntary donations." There are no words to explain how that moment felt. To see another person, unsolicited, make something to help the 4D cause was beyond touching. I was incredibly moved. I sought out Lourdes immediately.

Lourdes is an incredible person. Her heart is huge. As they say, everything is big in Texas. She has been such a support to the 4D experience and continues to stay in contact with both Dee and me. Her donations to the cause offered much needed help as the expenses were growing quickly.

Next, I was curious how they were handling race numbers for a nude run. It became clear when I saw a woman with a sharpie writing a race number across another woman's chest. It was my turn and the black sharpie drew a large "69" on my left pectoral muscle. This was fodder for all sorts of questions and comments. I'm not sure how that ended up being my race number for a nude run—just lucky I guess.

I made my way back to my rental car to strip off the rest of my clothes. I also had to resolve the 4D pin and where on Earth would I put the key to the rental car. I didn't want to hold it when I was running. The answer to both questions ended up being my sneakers. The pin went through the laces and the key was tucked between the side of my foot and the sneaker.

TEXAS
Sights Along the Way

30' tall eyeball in downtown Dallas.

Giant Chrome abstract people sculptures, downtown Dallas

JFK Memorial

"The" Grassy Knoll

Glenn Goode's Big People, Gainesville, TX

Lady Bug VWs

Things I don't do every day: get out of my car in a parking lot wearing nothing but sneakers and contact lenses. This was really putting myself out there for a cause. My mind wandered to thoughts of the nude women who protest for People for the Ethical Treatment of Animals (PETA) all over the world. Animals should really feel loved.

This was the 23rd year for the Bare As You Dare 5K. It has become tradition for all runners to pose for one large, nude group photo prior to the race and a second photo wearing just the race shirts. Beyond the novelty of taking a naked group photo, it also provided the only visual memory of the event, as it is nudist etiquette to not take photos.

Prior to heading to Texas, I had several people ask me if I was concerned about running with a "lack of support" or if I was concerned that certain body parts might get squished in the process of running. From what I can tell, our bodies are designed to run and we are born naked. It felt like a very natural thing to do and "everything" seemed to stay in front of the legs just fine.

Now, I must say that part of the experience was lacking as it was chilly—just barely 50° outside—and there was a light drizzle. My mind raced with flashbacks from Seinfeld with George Costanza screaming "There was shrinkage!" Let's just say running naked posed no problems.

It was good run and a fun course. It was mostly a trail run, but there were some parts on gravel roads that lace through the resort. Considering the random terrain, I was very pleased with a 24:28 time, good enough to take 1st place in my age division. I was the fastest naked guy in his late 30s there. This as the only event I have entered for which adding a medal to my outfit significantly increased the coverage of my body.

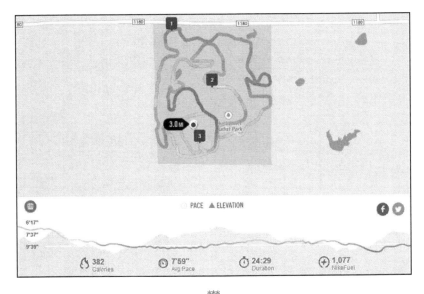

***

Texas Leadership Lesson:
Leaving Yourself Exposed, Accepting a Helping Hand

Earlier, I referenced the naked protesters from PETA. Why do they do what they do? The slogan they often use is "I rather go naked than wear fur." There is a logical connection between their statement and posing nude. It even conjures images of the human form as animal, but is that why they do it? It is probably safe to say that they do it because it increases their press coverage.

What are you willing to do to advance your cause and meet your goals? Getting naked isn't the answer to every problem, but are you willing to find the right answers, no matter how uncomfortable they might be to follow through on?

It would be fair to say that I did not need to do a nude run to complete the 4D 50-State 5K mission. I also didn't need to do a neon glow run, a Color Run or Warrior Dash. Each of those events added to the overall story. What is important for me isn't so much that I completed a nude 5K, but that I didn't avoid doing a nude 5K. I didn't let that be a barrier or an obstacle.

The second big lesson from Texas was accepting help from a stranger. Granted, Lourdes is no longer a stranger, but she was when she took the initiative to set up donations for 4D at her event. I still can't wrap my brain around someone so willing to help a stranger with his cause. It is all very touching. Part of leadership is accepting help like this. When someone makes a sincere donation to your cause, make sure to accept it graciously. There is nothing wrong with accepting help. In fact, it feels pretty great—for both parties.

Muscular Dystrophy Facts from the Centers for Disease Control and Prevention

"No two people with Duchenne or Becker muscular dystrophy (DBMD) are exactly alike. Therefore, the health issues will be different for each individual. Living a full life with DBMD may involve health care providers who know about different parts of the body all working together to address the needs of each individual. Most people who have Becker muscular dystrophy (BMD) receive treatments similar to those people who have Duchenne muscular dystrophy (DMD)."

Source: www.cdc.gov/ncbddd/musculardystrophy/facts.html

Chapter 21

Spirit of Survival: Superhero 5K

Lawton, Oklahoma
October 6, 2013

The Ranch House Motel might very well be one of the best bargains in cheap travel. At least this was before I found a little gem in South Dakota on my way to the 5K in Minnesota, but that is four states from now. Let's stay on track with the trip to Oklahoma.

When I originally called the Ranch House to make my reservation, the guy just said to call this same number when I arrived and he would bring a key to me. That seemed odd, but then he explained that they owned another motel a few miles away and operated only one front desk. Fair enough.

So I left the Blue Bonnet and traveled to Burkburnett, TX, to get my room for the night. The motel was extremely close to the Oklahoma border, so I did not have a long drive in the morning to get to the OK 5K (Yes, that was fun to type OK 5K), about 40 minutes away, 30 minutes closer than I ended up driving for dinner or, more accurately, a burger.

For my $40, I got an entire motel to myself for the night. There was not another soul, not even an employee. It was clean enough and it was quiet. Thankfully, all the lights in the parking lot worked without flickering; otherwise, I would have been up all night watching for Norman Bates and his mother.

The room was small, but included a complete kitchen. Again, it is hard to find a deal like that for $40. It provided a satisfactory place to lie down for the night and rest up for the morning's race.

***

Even before I purchased my airline ticket, I knew the event in Lawton, Oklahoma was going to be huge—HUGE. The quality of their website and the sheer quantity of events they had planned were very impressive. In addition to a 5K, they were hosting a half marathon, quarter marathon, kids marathon, and a spirit walk.

So I was prepared for big, just not THIS big. When I pulled into the parking lot of the registration location, I pulled in between two tour buses loaded with participants and the lot was full. I saw a sea of people, dozens of port-o-potties, and some really large tents. I made my way amongst thousands of people to get my registration packet for the Spirit of Survival: Superhero 5K.

> **"Spirit of Survival: Superhero 5K:** *This event is a 3.1 mile USATF Certified and ChampionChip timed race. The 5K Superhero Race will have placer's medals for the top three finishers in each age division & category and will provide trophies for the top three overall male and female winners.*
>
> *For people with a cancer diagnosis, this spirit of survival, combined with the strength and support of a community of family and friends, is critical. And above all, patients need ready access to the advanced medical treatments that give them the best opportunity to win the fight."*

It was an unusually cold morning. It was a windy morning. Neither made my tank top and running shorts a good idea. Other runners had on long pants and long-sleeve shirts. I was seriously underdressed and shivering beyond control. When people gave me strange looks, I awkwardly said, "From Pennsylvania" in teeth-chatter English as if that was all that was necessary to explain my lack of weather preparedness. Most just smiled and said, "Welcome to Oklahoma" in the tone of *this is how it is here.*

Regardless of the weather, the event was extraordinary. The banners, lights, start/finish arches, timing equipment, tents, booths, and the layout of the courses were second to none. This was one of the largest races that I had attended. It was clear that the entire town was behind this event.

Between the 3 adult races, there were over 1,600 runners. I can only imagine how many more people participated in the walk and the kids' marathon. There were just lots and lots of people with race bibs on everywhere you looked. It was going to be one of those days were you get lost in the crowd and just run as best you can. Between the cold, traveling and large crowds, my mind wasn't entertaining thoughts of winning a medal on this day.

The energy of a really large event is something that surges through each person. You feel part of something big. It feels like you are about to accomplish something important. You are a cog in a very essential wheel.

The half- and quarter-marathons left the starting line 10 minutes before the rest of us. Having previously enjoyed my pre-race banana and Vitamin Water, I sucked down the gel pack and got myself ready by shaking out the last of the shivers. When it was our time to go, I made sure I was close to the front of the group, as I always like to take off quick from the start.

The starting line was inside Elmer Thomas Park, but we quickly left the park for our first mile out and back into Lawton. When we came back to the park, we turned and went about a 1/3 of a mile along the outside and then darted right into the park for the rest of the course.

Crossing the finish line felt amazing. There was such a large crowd cheering us on, the announcer calling out information on the finishers and cameras. Volunteers were placing finisher's medals around our neck. This piece of memorabilia seemed to be heavier than all of my other medals combined. It was huge, multi-colored, and really beautiful. The weight around my neck was a consistent reminder of my accomplishment. It was a rock-star-finish and amazing race.

Fairly close to the finish line was a large, flat-screen TV updating results. My Nike+ was indicating a 24:20 run, which was one of my quickest, averaging 7:41 minute miles. It took a while for the age group results to start scrolling, and, even then, the lists were long since there were so many competitors. Runners were still finishing so the numbers kept updating in real time. Everyone doesn't necessarily start precisely at the same time, because people farther back in the pack take longer to get to the starting line. That is why I always try to be close to the line. Anyway, as you watch the results come in, it is possible for someone to beat you, even if you got to the finish line first.

This was a very important point for me as I watched the screen because I was listed as 1st in my age group. There didn't seem to be any way that was possible, as I was pretty sure that half of Oklahoma passed me on the course. I suppose it was possible they weren't in my age group or were in one of the other races. It was really disorienting with several different races running through the same city.

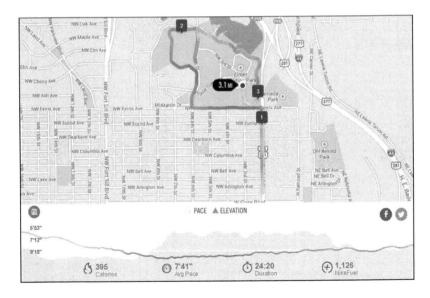

I had a date with a plane 2 hours and another State away, so I couldn't wait for the award's ceremony. I tracked down the race director. I told her I thought there was a chance that I won my age group, but couldn't stay for the awards. She said no worries; the medals for the top placers hadn't come in on time for the event so they had to be mailed regardless. I thanked her and took off for my car.

OKLAHOMA
Sights Along the Way

Meersburgers

I was heading back to the airport with two 1st places in two days in two states. It was a terrific weekend and I was inspired anew.

Although I have appreciated every single event on this journey, there are only a handful of events that I would consider traveling back for. The Spirit of Survival is on the top of that list. It was an impressive event, great people and truly high-caliber experience.

***

Oklahoma Leadership Lesson:
Small Fish, Big Pond; Quality

At the start of the Oklahoma race, I wouldn't have dreamt of medaling. I was just happy to be part of something so big and beautiful. I felt like a small, but significant fish in a very large pond. I was there to do my best and to race my fiercest competitor, myself. Sometimes when we focus on ourselves and our goals, even when surrounded by something massive and magnificent, we can accomplish great things. We shouldn't shy away from the "big show," because we don't think we are fit to compete. As long as you always try your hardest accomplishments will keep rolling in.

It is worth commenting again on how impressive this event was. As leaders, when we put something together, whether it is a business plan or a 5K, we should do our best to make it top-notch. Anyone can accomplish the mundane. It takes a dedicated leader with clear vision to make something truly marvelous. Seek out those who make amazing things happen and learn from them.

Chapter 22

Zombie Chase 5K
Pittsburg, Kansas
October 18, 2013

Months in advance I had scheduled 12 days off work in October to go to Jamaica to visit my girlfriend. We broke up in September and I started thinking about how I could use that time off to maximize completing states. How many states could realistically be done in 12 days?

Most 5Ks are scheduled on Saturdays and Sundays. Occasionally, there might be one on a Friday night. If I was lucky, I might find another evening Saturday run to get three states in a single weekend. A massive investigation began into logistics and race schedules.

If I was going to invest the time and money into this 12-day "vacation," I needed to shoot for the maximum number of states—I figured 6 States in 12 days. Having completed 40% of the country in the first 100 days, I had 30 states left to choose from.

I began my research with nailing down every Friday night run I could find. That list was pretty short as the weather, in mid-October starts getting colder and darkness comes earlier. On the positive side, Halloween inspires some themed 5Ks that would potentially work for me.

I found about a half dozen states with Friday night 5Ks on either weekend that I needed. The two most promising were Kansas and Minnesota. Thankfully, those states are really close. Right? If you look at a typical map, they are only 2 inches away. How far could that be?

The foundation was laid with those 2 states bookending the Friday nights. Now it was time to fill up those Saturdays and Sundays. By the time all this homework was done, I had drawn up a tentative itinerary of running Kansas the first Friday, Nebraska the next morning and Wyoming on Sunday. That meant I had to cross the entire state of Nebraska on Saturday.

That would leave me with 4 days to get from Wyoming to Minnesota to race the following Friday night, which would include a drive across the entire state of South Dakota. There was a run in North Dakota on Saturday morning so there would be late-night driving after the run Friday night. If I spent all of Saturday crossing the entire state of North Dakota I could get to a run in South Dakota on Sunday morning.

One of the things I have learned with all of this traveling is that it is incredibly expensive to return a rental car to a different airport than the one where you picked it up from. Sometimes it is close to an extra $100 per day! For a trip this long, it was going to be imperative to fly in and out of the same airport. The best option for airfare ended up being Omaha, NE.

Flying in and out of Omaha, meant after the Sunday run in South Dakota I would have to drive, for a second time in a week, across the entire State of South Dakota. For the reader adept at counting while reading, that is a total of four "*entires*" in 12 days of travel. I was going to need a rental car with unlimited miles.

***

This trip was going to take me through South Dakota several times. That was the state that my colleague, Sheila Ciotti, wanted the opportunity to consider joining me for, as she wanted to see Mt. Rushmore. It would have been ideal as the 5K in SD was really close this national monument, but this trip was not going to work out for her. We both work in higher education and taking off in October is rare. Secondly, my driving plan was taking me all over the place, so for her even to consider finding flights in and out of a state where I was when she might travel would have been a logistical nightmare. Sadly she wasn't going to make it, but I will always credit her with inspiring how wonderfully this trip ended up.

Cleary, I was going to make a point to see Mt. Rushmore on this journey, but what else could I see? After all, I would have 4–5 days of travel and sightseeing between races. When I started looking at maps, I became incredibly enthused. With "slight' detours, some of the most amazing features of the United States would be on my route: Split Rock, the Grand Tetons, Yellowstone, Old Faithful, Deadwood, Mt. Rushmore, Crazy Horse, the Badlands, and Devils Tower.

These are all parts of the United States that I have heard of, but I never imagined in my life that I would invest the time or money to see. In the words of my students, this trip was going to be "epic."

This was a dream I hadn't had come true.

***

Now that I was clearly at the point of flying into states and renting cars, it was going to be imperative for me to be smarter about making sure I had safe places to spend the night. It was time to say goodbye to relying on luck, cheap local motels, and leads from people I met on dating sites. I needed to find accommodations that were not going to inflate an already ballooning budget, but were reliable.

~ 111 ~

I wish I could recall who gave me the best travel tip I ever received, but my memory has failed me. I do not recall who directed me to www.CouchSurfing.org. This website has changed my life—forever. If I had unlimited piles of cash, I would still use this site to travel. It adds a layer of interest to traveling that you cannot find elsewhere.

The website connects travelers (Couch Surfers) with hosts who can offer a free couch. Free. What in this world is free anymore? That is exactly the point of the site! Travelers help each other and you can avoid paying high fees for hotel rooms. Some folks are only hosts and some are only travelers, but many do both.

KANSAS
Sights Along the Way

Roland Sherman Carvings

Fritz's Railroad Restaurant

Like most websites for social interaction, it takes a while to build your reputation and get to be known. I was fortunate that my local CBS affiliate did a feature on Dee, me and the 4D experience. I was able to share that video, the Google map I created of my runs and my online professional portfolio to let potential hosts know who I was.

My first "accept" on the site came from Jayne Mosley in Mobile, AL. I was going to be staying with her in a few weeks when I ran Louisiana and Alabama. For the present trip, I lucked out with finding 7 potential Couch Surfing hosts for my 12-day, 11-night trip. That left me with four nights in motels. For those nights, I found the cheapie little motels I use when I am traveling light.

So, this 6-state journey started with my landing in Omaha, NE on Thursday, October 17, 2013. When I picked up my rental car, I verified that it was truly "unlimited miles." I told the woman at the rental desk, "That's good. This car will need an oil change when I bring it back." She laughed and said, "Yeah, sure it will." In 12 days I would have the last laugh.

My first stop after getting the rental car was going to the grocery store to load the car with 12-days' worth of supplies. In addition to food and snacks for the long drives, I wanted to make sure I had some emergency food in the event of, well, an emergency. Two weeks prior to my arrival, the Heartland had been hit by a freak snow storm that devastated farms and killed thousands of cattle. The forecast was good for my trip, but I wanted to be prepared. This stop was also imperative as I needed to stock up on Vitamin water and bananas for my pre-race rituals. I had packed enough GU Energy Gels for all of the races, so no need to grab more.

I was fortunate to find a Couch Surfing host for both Thursday and Friday nights. Kenny Ludacka was a perfect host, and I am glad he took my Couch Surfing virginity. He and his dog Buddy share a beautiful apartment overlooking Old Market in downtown, Omaha, NE.

He gave me a tour of Omaha both by car and by foot. Later that evening we went out for sushi with a good friend of his. Buying my hosts sushi has become a tradition for me. There seems to be a nice connection between people who are willing to host travelers and also willing to eat sushi. I will let the sociologists investigate that correlation. For me, they both just mean the person is awesome.

I left Kenny's in the morning for my first 5+ hour drive of this multi-state adventure. I was heading to Pittsburg, KS, for a Friday evening race. I had a date with Zombies.

***

In hindsight, it is almost comical how little I learned about the actual 5Ks I was traveling thousands of miles to run. I put a lot of faith in other people and I took some risks based on what I read online. I am forever the optimist. Things always have a way of working out. Right? It's only 3.1 miles, so how bad can things be?

The forecast for Pittsburg was bleak. It looked like it was going to be a cold evening with a solid chance of rain. I sent out a message to the race director via Facebook. I wanted assurance that the race was going to happen regardless of weather. I explained that I had flown many hours from PA into NE and would be driving many more hours to KS. The race director, Carol Meza, assured me that this race was going to happen. No matter what, the Zombie Chase 5K was transpiring.

*"**Zombie Chase 5K:** Dress your best for this event. Dress as your favorite character or whatever you want to be. We want to have as many participants as we can. We will also have a best dressed contest and the winner will receive a prize :) $15 for Non-students, $10 per student and $5 for children 12 and under. Registration starts at 6:30pm and event starts at 7:30pm."*

Based on her confidence that this event was definitely on, I started my long drive of sightseeing on my way to the race. As I drove into Pittsburg, rain and night followed right behind, holding hands like a conspiring couple. Sadly, this couple had a very cold heart and the temperature started to drop. This was setting the stage for an awful night to run.

Pittsburg, KS, is a typical college town. By typical, I mean it is clear that the town often gets drunk on beer and school pride. Gorillas, the school mascot, leered at me from every corner of town. At times, this added to the ominous atmosphere.

After driving around town, I made my way to Pittsburg State University, the site of the 5K. After getting help at the college welcome desk, I was able to locate the football field. Race registration was taking place behind the stadium. As I entered the rain-coated parking lot behind the stadium, I saw nothing–nothing.

There was no registration table or tent. There were no people. There were no signs. There was just a poorly lit, empty parking lot. This was a bad sign. I couldn't believe I had driven this far and there was apparently no race. I did what every good son does in a situation like this. I called my mommy.

Even at 39 years of age, it's amazing how comforting your mother's voice can be. I didn't feel like driving back and I wanted to stick it out in case "something" happened, so I sat in the parking lot, talking to my mom while listening to the rain pitter-pattering on the roof of my rental.

After a few minutes, a couple of cars rolled into the lot. They all parked next to each other and were trading glances between the rain drops, as no one apparently wanted to get out in the downpour. Eventually, people made their way to a pavilion that offered some protection.

That is where I met Carol. She had the registration materials and said the event was still on. I learned that she was senior majoring in sociology and this 5K was her senior project, so it *had* to go on. There were only a few of us there to run. A cold, dark, and rainy Friday night on a college campus doesn't make for a popular 5K. She was visibly disappointed with the turnout and the weather. I am sure when she was planning this event, she was optimistic about hosting a "cool" college-party-Zombie-themed, Halloween 5K that would be the stage for incredible memories.

Jeff Fazio, with two Zombies and race director, Carol Meza (far right) pose before the Zombie 5K.

The cold was a gigantic exclamation point on the moment. Having worked many years in student activities, I have seen my fair share of well-planned events fall flat because turnout was dismal. It is always a tough call to fold up shop or hold onto the old adage, The Show Must Go On!

Carol was amazing. Although it was clear she was unhappy, her fortitude and dedication to her mission were just as clear. This all made perfect sense weeks later when I learned that she is a soldier.

In all, I think we had about 13 runners and 5 zombies. You know what else we had? An awesome time.

It was a really fun event. The course was laid out well and was easy to follow. It was mostly flat, which allowed for quick times. The rain had lightened up for the run, so we just dealt with a wet, misty cold atmosphere, which added to the zombie effect.

Pre-race, I was talking to a college couple who was running. He indicated that he typically runs a 23-minute 5K and she said she was typically around 25. I ran a 24-flat on this course, which was enough to claim 2nd place overall, right between these two.

Regardless of the low turnout, I was extremely happy to place 2nd considering I was the oldest person there running among traditional college-aged students. I was even more pleased that Carol had finisher's medals for us. That was a nice surprise!

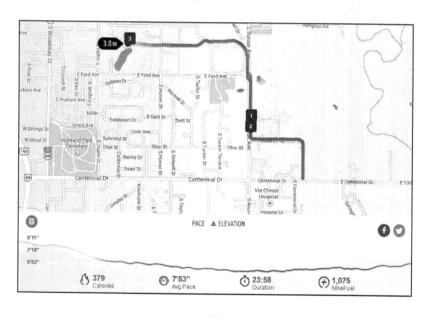

***

Kansas was the first of the Heartland states to feel the oscillating pressure of my running sneakers upon its ground. Four more states in the Heartland would be checked off in the next 11 days. For now, it was time to get back into the car for the 5-hour drive back to Omaha. I was hoping to be back to Kenny's and asleep by 1:00 a.m., as I had to be up by 7:00 a.m. for the next run.

Sometimes we feel that things need to be grandiose in order to be successful, and that is simply not true. Months earlier, when Carol first planted the seeds of her 5K, I have no doubt she imagined hundreds of costumed runners being chased by dozens of zombies enjoying a radical Halloween inspired 5K while potentially fundraising thousands of dollars. For her sake, I hope she hasn't measured the success or failure of the event based on that measuring stick. Having traveled thousands of miles to be there, I felt the event was a complete success, and I left with the feeling that Carol is an extraordinary woman.

Regardless of our hopes, dreams and visions, it is possible to find success somewhere close without achieving every single objective we set out for. One of my favorite quotes "Shoot for the moon. Even if you miss, you'll land among the stars." Carol is definitely amongst the stars.

***

By this time, I was being intentional about writing leadership notes from each state. It offered me a chance for much needed introspection. This journey was starting to develop many interesting layers.

The primary layer was, of course, honoring Dee and others with Muscular Dystrophy by spreading awareness with each step. Secondarily, there was the actual running from the stand point of health and fitness. As race times improved, the running also became competitive.

This 50-state journey also included sightseeing of national monuments, historic sites, significant geological features, important locations, a variety of national and state parks along with the wide array of novelty locations. When I was back in Omaha, I photographed a rather beautiful memorial to the victims of the September 11, 2001 terrorist attacks. That was a seed planted, and I started documenting 9/11 memorials around the country as part of my travels.

There was an underlying theme of people being met and connections being made. There were the fellow racers, race organizers, and spectators. There were news people, people I connected with through the dating sites, and, now, the Couch Surfing hosts and hostesses.

Chapter 23

Free to Breathe Omaha Lung Cancer 5K
Omaha, Nebraska
October 19, 2013

Leaving Kansas, I made the 4+ hour drive back to Omaha and Kenny's place to crash for the night. It was a long, exhausting day and I was grateful for the warm, safe couch and Buddy snuggling with me. Kenny's dog is truly a sweetheart, and this is coming from someone who is not a dog lover.

Unfortunately, Saturday was one of those mornings when you wake up feeling like you had just gone to sleep; that groggy feeling that leaves you wondering if a night time phantom stole the hours you were hoping to rest. Nevertheless, I was up and in the shower being careful to not wake Kenny. I got my running gear on and quietly let myself out.

Thankfully, Kenny's place was just a few minutes from the *race location*. Race location? Well, that is where I thought I was going. I was about to get a lesson in reading fine print.

I made my way to Miller's Landing along the Missouri River

Jeff Fazio stands on the Nebraska/Iowa with Kenny Ludacka, his first Couch Surfing host.

where the event was set up. There was much fanfare with balloons, welcome signs, and music. After parking, I made my way to the registration table and signed up for the 4th Annual Free to Breathe Omaha Lung Cancer 5K

> ***"Free to Breathe Omaha Lung Cancer 5K:*** *The 4th Annual Free to Breathe Omaha Lung Cancer 5K Run/Walk is a non-competitive event that provides an opportunity for lung cancer advocates, survivors and the community to come together to raise awareness and support in the movement to defeat lung cancer. All proceeds will benefit the National Lung Cancer Partnership's research, education and awareness programs."*

Registration seemed pretty typical. We received our race bib, commemorative t-shirt, and some swag. More often than not, the timing chips for recording race elapsed times are embedded in the race bibs. Sometimes the chip timing is done with a chip that is anchored through the laces in a sneaker. In the worst case scenario (or what I thought was worst case scenario up to this point), timing was done by pulling off a tab on your race bib when you cross the finish line and hand it off to a person recording the times. As you can imagine, this can be inaccurate for timing, but pretty accurate for finish order.

NEBRASKA
Sights Along the Way

Malcolm X Birth Site

On The Wings of Angels 9/11 Memorial

Joslyn Castle

Old Market, Downtown Omaha

Missouri River

Bob Kerrey Pedestrian Bridge

Gerald Ford Birth Site

Warren Buffet's home

Scout's Rest: Buffalo Bill's home

I noticed that the race bibs were not chipped and there was no easily seen place to pick up a timing chip for my shoe. I went back to the registration table and asked where the chips were. I was greeted with a confused look. Realizing that she thought I meant a snack food, I clarified that I meant a timing chip. She got my meaning and told me that the race wasn't timed. Wasn't timed?

She said it was a non-competitive fun run and that there was no official times given. I asked, "If times are not recorded, why do we have race bibs?" She just shrugged and said they were fun to have and that I didn't need to wear it.

An untimed run—this was a shock, but not a huge blow as I always have my Nike+ to record my times. Needless to say, I was confused when I saw the trophy table for the top finishers. So it was a non-competitive run with trophies for the overall winners. Ok, I got it now.

The run started on a road that led through the parking lot of Miller's Landing and then made some unique turns, and eventually we were on a running/biking path that meanders along the Missouri River. There was supposed to be a golf cart to lead the front runners through the course, but the race started without it, as it was still being used to guide the 1-mile walkers who hadn't returned yet.

So the race begins, I bolt out front and somehow find myself leading another 5K. In rather short order, I was putting distance between myself and the 100+ other runners. There were a handful of people staying relatively close, but we were spreading out fast. The course was not clearly marked and I was having flashbacks of the Kentucky fiasco, and I surely didn't want to be responsible for taking the entire event off course. I did my best to follow the little pink arrows directing us.

After about a half mile, a rather fit guy in his 20s started pacing with me and asked where we were going. I did my best to point out the little pink arrows that I was following. We ran together for quite a while, but I could feel fatigue setting in. No matter how slow or fast I start out, the same level of fatigue hits me about the same time, and my pace dwindles. He seemed to be running strong.

As we approached the first mile, the golf cart finally caught up to us and zoomed past. With the confidence of having a clearer path to follow, this guy took off pacing the golf cart, and I wished him well. There was no way I had the steam that he had. I did my best to keep him and the golf cart in sight which I was able to do until we got back to the parking lot where we would eventually finish.

When I entered the parking lot, I could just barely seem him and the golf cart make the turn toward the finish line. I wasn't that far back, but I was very confused, as the Nike+ was only registering 2.5 miles. How could the finish line possibly be in sight at this point?

Regardless of the race seeming short, I was grateful to see the finish line, as I was quickly running out of steam. I was also becoming aware of other runners who were very far back not being so far back. I made my way through the parking lot and ran through the finish line, clicking off the Nike+. The watch flashed its end-of-run "CONGRATULATIONS!" and then the stats screen popped up indicating that I ran 22:08. I was shocked by that inconceivably fast time until I noticed that it also said that I only ran 2.8 miles. The course was nearly a 1/3 of a mile short.

I suppose it was a fun, non-competitive run. The guy who passed me deservedly won his trophy for winning the non-race. Meanwhile, I was pleased to have claimed 2nd place for the second time in 2 days.

***

Nebraska Leadership Lesson:
Non-Competition Competition, Measuring Up, Trusting Strangers

———————

Humans are competitive by nature. If we can measure it, we want to improve it. That is why we keep building taller buildings, shortening travel times, increasing Gross National Product (GNP). We fall over ourselves watching the latest contest, whether it is the NFL, Jeopardy, or UFC. It is not realistic to gather over a hundred people together, put them on a closed course with a start line and a finish line, and expect it to be non-competitive experience. It only takes two to make it a race and a race it was. The organizers of the Omaha run intuitively knew this; otherwise, there wouldn't have been trophies for 1st place. So why not have timing? My best guess, from my years of racing cars, is that it may have made a difference in their insurance rates. Then again, maybe it was just cost savings.

As leaders, we need to be aware of the competitive environments we enter, regardless whether or not they are billed that way. It is important that we are always "on our game" and ready to be challenged. We can't be "asleep at the wheel" when "opportunity knocks." You get the point.

Additionally, we need to be able to measure or at least make sure someone on our team can measure. It is pretty bad to advertise something as 3.1 miles when it is actually 2.8 miles. That is a 10% margin of error! When we offer data points, they should be accurate. Granted, with something like a running race, individuals will take slightly different steps to get from point to point, so distance will not always be 100% precise, but it would fall within .05–.15 of a mile. When you are in a leadership role, others count on the information you supply—make sure it is accurate.

Although I Couch Surfed the night before the Kansas run, I am including it in this chapter because my host was located in Omaha and that is where the surfing officially began. Sometimes when we are trying to achieve a goal, we need to trust strangers. If you read the news, it feels like the world is filled with evil and there are truly horrible people out there. That type of news that grabs headlines.

The news fails to report the infinite number of kind gestures we do for each other every day. People are mostly good and it is those good people who make something like CouchSurfing.org work to the benefit of all. Couch Surfing has changed the way I travel and the way I view people. If I had unlimited funds, I would still use the site to find places to stay. The people who you can meet and the friendships that can be made are astounding. Couch Surfing instills a lot of faith in humanity. Amazingly, two of my hosts on this trip were not even home when I stayed. One left a spare key for me, and one simply left the house unlocked. If staying with complete strangers seems odd to you, I can only tell you that letting yourself into their home, when they are not home, is truly bizarre—and beautiful.

As William Butler Yeats said, "There are no strangers here; only friends you haven't yet met."

Chapter 24

Laramie Blizzard Blast
Laramie, Wyoming
October 20, 2013

In life, sometimes you have experiences you never want to have again. Driving straight across the State of Nebraska is one of those experiences. It is truly dreadful when the display on your GPS indicates 243 miles until your next exit.

I was leaving Omaha on my all-day journey to Laramie, Wyoming, for a 5K the next day. The week before I got on the plane that deposited me into the Heartland of the United States, I read an article on altitude sickness, specifically about how high altitudes affect runners. I actually looked for an article on this, as I knew I would eventually be running in Colorado and there was a good chance that it would be in Denver, the Mile High City.

As I read about all of the awful things that can happen to you at high altitudes and low levels of oxygen, one sentence jumped out at me. It read, "One of the worst places to run in the country, is Laramie, Wyoming." I immediately recognized the name of that infamous city and realized that I was scheduled to run there the following Sunday. I wasn't mentally prepared for dealing with elevation. What would this mean? How hard would it be?

I had reservations about running Denver at an elevation of one mile, 5,280'. Laramie is nearly 35% higher at roughly 7,200'. How was I supposed to prepare to run Laramie in less than a week?

The article indicated that one of the best things you could do was be at the high elevation at least 1 day in advance and sleep in that environment.

WYOMING
Sights Along the Way

Split Rock

Matthew Shepard Memorial

Matthew Shepard Murder Location

Wyoming Territorial Penitentiary

Dinosaur Fossil Cabin

Virginian Hotel, Medicine Bow, WY

Grand Tetons

Yellowstone

Old Faithful

Buffalo Bill's Irma Hotel

Devils Tower

Apparently, the body does magical things while you sleep to adjust to the lack of oxygen. Drinking lots of water is also highly recommended.

I was pleased that I had managed to find a couch in Laramie for the night before. Fay Bisbee was my hostess for the evening, and she was able to provide a bedroom instead of a couch. I was going to be living it up in Laramie. Making a connection with Fay was wonderful. As we shared basic information about ourselves, we realized that we had exactly the same birthday—exactly—same day *and year*. I was born a few hours before her. She took this as an opportunity to point out that she was younger and I pointed out that I was more mature. It was the beginning of a new friendship.

***

The following morning, October 20, I rose extra early, as I wanted to see two sights, the Matthew Shepard Memorial and his murder location. It was 15 years and eight days since Matthew had been murdered in Laramie for being homosexual. His death sparked the national movement "A Day of Silence," something I work with students on each year.

I first stopped by the University of Wyoming to see the Matthew Shepard Memorial. It might be more accurate to stay that I stopped by to see a bench with a 3" x 10" placard honoring Matthew and wishing peace to those who sit on the bench. That is what they call a memorial—the bench. I personally found it to be a dishonor to his memory.

Laramie wants to forget. They so much want to forget, that they have changed the names of the roads where his body was found. Homeowners have installed signs labeling public roads as "private" and warning of trespass.

They don't want visitors. I visited.

It was cold and desolate, hard to imagine a young man tied to a fence, bleeding to death in a cold October. What kinds of monsters leave someone in that condition to die? The morning was eerily quiet. I got the sense I was being watched, and when I turned around, across the way, in someone's yard were 6 or 7 deer eating. It felt as though they were secret security and the act of eating was a cover to justify their presence, in this space, watching over Matthew's memory. Their presence was comforting.

***

After a somber morning, I found my way to the race. Registration was located inside The Pitch, Laramie Blizzard's indoor soccer facility. I went in and registered for the Laramie Blizzard Blast.

"Laramie Blizzard Blast: *The Second Annual Laramie Blizzard Blast Costume Run is a fun running and walking event organized by the Laramie Blizzard Soccer Association to support youth soccer in the Laramie Area. The events will include a 5K run (3.1 miles), a 5K walk and a 10K run (6.2 miles). Costumes are strongly encouraged."*

It was 33 degrees with light flurries. Immediately prior to the start of the race, those flurries changed into full-blown snow coming down hard and sideways due to wind. If you are going to run at extremely high elevation, it makes sense to pick a day that is slightly above freezing, snowing and windy. At least it was warm enough that the snow was not accumulating. Regardless, this was going to be an interesting event.

Surprisingly, I felt great. I kept thinking about my breathing and heart rate. Everything seemed normal. It didn't *feel* like I was at high elevation, but what did high elevation feel like anyway? I was 15 minutes away from that answer.

We lined up for the race and I decided I was just going to go for it. If it was bad (how bad could it be?), I could always slow down—right?

The race started and I was off. I shot to the front and held that lead for at least 50 feet, but by 1/10th of a mile I was having problems. All at once, it felt as if I were running up a steep hill while trying to breathe through a cocktail straw. It was an overwhelming, horrible feeling. I might as well have been drowning, as I was lacking oxygen.

Slowing was not only an option: it was a requirement. My pace plummeted and the masses of runners who did not know the benefits of oxygen flew past me. How did these people get used to lacking something as critical to life as oxygen? How is it that I suddenly felt like a lifetime chain smoker competing against well-trained athletes?

Not being able to run fast also meant that I was going to experience more of the cold and for a significantly longer time. This run was going to be long and terrible. With wind and snow in my face, I wanted to quit.

Although it was awful, at least continuing to run was an option for me. Who was I to complain when people with Muscular Dystrophy, people like Dee, don't even have the option to enter this event? It was bad, but it was survivable.

As I approached the end of mile 2, a strange sensation started from my arm pits to my fingers. At least I think it went to my fingers. I couldn't feel them any longer, even with two layers of gloves. It was a weird vibrating tingle. It didn't feel good and it seemed to be increasing intensity as I ran, but what to do about it? I was nowhere near assistance and it was incredibly cold. I just kept running and tried to shake my arms out a bit. I didn't have much farther to go to get back to the finish line. Somehow I managed to keep my time under 28 minutes.

This run really felt like I was going through Hell. In hindsight, it would actually be another 40 days until I would be in Hell, but I did end up there, *for real.*

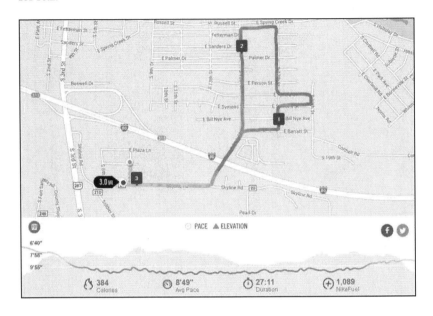

***

Wyoming Leadership Lesson:
Risk of Elevated Success, Weathering the Storm

When you are achieving success, be cautious if that success quickly escalates. As we approach higher altitudes, the game changes and success on a lower level does not guarantee success at a higher one. As with any change, we need to be cognizant of how the change affects our methodologies. We may need to adapt or train in a different way to achieve success at this new level.

Even when things are going well, we may have to weather a storm from time to time. Unfortunately, the snow storm that hit the runners in Laramie was more stress added to the high elevation and cold temperatures. The storms you may have to weather in pursuit of your goals might be literal storms, but they also might just be dark, cloudy times that attempt to distract you from the good work you are doing. As with all storms, seek shelter, be cautious and patient while you navigate a challenging time. As the old saying goes, "This too shall pass."

Chapter 25

Scare in White Bear 5K
White Bear Lake, Minnesota
October 25, 2013

With completion of the Wyoming 5K, I had 4 days until my next race in this trip, hundreds of miles away in the Twin Cities of Minnesota. Considering my current location in the United States, I took advantage of those days and my unlimited rental car miles and ventured forth to see some of the most amazing parts of this country: Grand Tetons National Park, Yellowstone National Park, Old Faithful, Devils Tower, Mt. Rushmore, and the Badlands.

There was much more, but those are some of the highlights. Over the course of those days, I spent two nights in cheapie motels and two nights Couch Surfing. The first night of Couch Surfing was with a couple who lived a few miles from the entrance of Grant Tetons National Park. He is a hunter and recently brought home an antelope which she made into a lovely dinner.

The second night of Surfing was spent in Cody, WY, just outside Yellowstone. My hostess was a landscaper for a ranch, and her employment includes a beautiful little cabin at the base of the Rockies. I awoke to the sunrise illuminating the Rockies and about a dozen deer roaming her yard. You just can't get hotel rooms like that.

It was an amazing 4 days filled with beauty and reflection. It was impactful enough that I almost didn't mind the 6-hour drive crossing South Dakota on my way to Minneapolis. Somewhere during that monotonous drive, Dee texted and asked what my favorite part of the trip was thus far. I told her it was texting her and sending her photos.

MINNESOTA
Sights Along the Way

Sod House on the Prairie

Charles Shultz's Peanuts Statues in the Twin Cities

Minneapolis Sculpture Garden

The Mall of America

This journey wasn't just about running for Dee and others. I was her legs on and off the 5K course. My opportunity to go out and see the country was also Dee's opportunity to follow along in a virtual seat, getting first-hand updates and photos. Sharing with Dee made the trip not so lonely. She was always right there, sort of in the passenger seat, following along at home on Google maps.

***

The run in Minnesota was in the town of White Bear Lake, just northeast of the Twin Cities, Minneapolis and St. Paul. It was an evening event on the Friday preceding Halloween, themed for the holiday. It was the Scare in White Bear 5K.

> **"Scare in White Bear 5K:** *Famously referenced by Mark Twain in, "Life on the Mississippi," White Bear Lake is named after its largest lake. Once proclaimed, "One of the most popular resorts in the magic northlands," White Bear Lake has retained its small-town charm and is located on the north-eastern edge of the Twin Cities metropolitan area. Distinct for its small town character, the beautiful downtown area of White Bear Lake hosts many events showcasing some of the greatest things about this lakeside community. The "Scare in White Bear 5k" begins at West Park, closest to the downtown area and along scenic Lake Ave. Be sure to join the post-race reception for performance and costume awards ceremonies which will take place at the park."*

Prior to heading out for this trip, I knew that several of the races had a Halloween theme and encouraged runners to wear costumes to embrace the holiday spirit (or *spirits*—boo!). I am pretty strict about traveling with only carry-on bags so space is at a premium in my luggage. Costumes were not happening for me.

It seemed like most people entering this event were embracing the theme. There were all sorts of costumes. Photos were taken everywhere and people were enjoying observing each other. By now, I was used to showing up alone and meeting other runners, but this environment was not conducive to that. Themed races tend to bring our people in groups, and people in groups tend to stay together. Layers of costumes make it even harder to break the ice with strangers. Nighttime had crept in, eliminating any hopes of making new bonds.

In the back of my mind, I also was thinking about my schedule for the next 14 hours. This race wasn't starting at 7:00 p.m. and, if I was lucky, I might be on the road by 8:00–8:30 p.m. I had a motel reserved for the night about 2 hours away, traffic permitting. The race the following morning started at 8:00 a.m. and I wanted to be there by 7:00 a.m., though it was just over 2 hours from my motel.

That schedule had me getting up at just after 4:00 a.m. to shower, breakfast and drive 2+ hours for the next event. I was scheduled for a late check-in after 10:00 p.m. I wasn't getting much sleep and was lacking a good plan for food beyond the stash in my car. All that said, my focus was not 100% on where I was and what I was about to do. Sometimes "next" takes our brain well beyond "now."

The merriment surrounding me was interrupted by the race director calling everyone together for pre-race information. As he explained the details of the run, I was caught by surprise when he said, "And, is Jeff Fazio from Pennsylvania here?" I was standing close by and raised my hand. He made a quick announcement about my 50-state mission and running for those who can't. The round of applause was greatly appreciated and brought me back into the moment.

The course was an out-and-back along a section of road that circumvents White Bear Lake. It was pitch black by now, so the visual effect of running near water was lost, but the cool air from the lake was omnipresent. As we lined up along the starting point, I looked at the road ahead. About a hundred feet from us was a lone street light that illuminated that path we would be running on. From there, it seemed like an incredibly long distance to the next light, with a span of pure darkness between.

It was an eerie scene. The atmosphere filled with costumes added to the surreal feeling. As always, I was lined up close to the front. My thoughts centered on the task of running into the darkness and not knowing where we were going. Would the turnaround point be obvious?

About this time, a woman made her way next to me, and she was pushing a man who was nestled into some sort of a cart. There was lots of conversation going on around them, all kidding about his getting a new personal best this evening in the 5K. I recalled thinking he must be a seasoned runner and they are teasing him about getting a new best because she was pushing him.

I didn't really focus on them, and in the darkness I wasn't really sure what they were up to. I recall having the impression that they must have made up some sort of costume that involved her pushing him in the run. Maybe they were a couple and it was a challenge for her to push him? Maybe he thought she couldn't do it? They were most likely goofing around for the holiday. Surely they weren't serious runners, here to race.

My brain was back on task. This was a flat course at an elevation closer to what I was used to running. This might be a chance for me to lock in a fast run—and here she was moving in front of me. Was I really going to have to deal with this over-sized two-person costume in my way at the beginning of a race? Apparently so.

The race actually started off a little differently than I expected. Instead of running straight out the road in front of us, we first made a lap around the park where registration was located. By the time we got to the end of the block, I had easily passed the woman-pushing-the-man-in-cart experience and I was off. I felt great and was running solid.

We spread out as we ran along the lake we could not see. As always happens for me, the runners who carry a stronger pace started passing me. I try to hold onto them as long as I can, but they eventually steam away from me. It was strange, but seemed to make sense to be passed by Superman and the occasional monster.

As we approached the turnaround point, I sensed another runner catching to make a pass. As I maintained my line so they could get clear, I became aware of the wheel. The wheel rolled into my peripheral vision. It was that guy being pushed by his girlfriend! She was really running, her breathing was intense and she was focused. Could she really be this serious about running with her guy? *Like this?*

I could see the turnaround point fast approaching and I let them by, as I knew I would quickly overtake them again. From my days of racing cars, I learned a thing or two about passing in turns. This was all made easier by the fact that their setup wasn't the easiest thing to get around the turnaround cone.

I passed them as they got hung up turning, and passing inspired me to run faster. There was simply no way I was going to be beaten by someone pushing someone else in a cart. I hadn't been running a year yet, but surely my training had me at a point of being able to beat two adults running as one. Sure, I had been passed by Herculean men pushing babies in those made-for-running strollers, but they had clearly trained that way. They were not having some pre-Halloween fun.

My satisfaction grew as I sensed that I was putting real distance between me and them—again. That distance, apparently, was only good for keeping them at bay for another half mile. Although I was doing fairly decently with maintaining my pace, she had something inside of her that I could not fathom. She eventually passed me with ease, and it was clear I was not going to finish in front of them.

As often happens when we do not take the time to look at details, I made some assumptions about what was going on. This wasn't two people having fun, although it was, but not how I thought. The woman was Elizabeth Jensen, avid runner. The man in the chair was Mike Ewaldt, half of Team Heart.

At 18 months old, Mike was diagnosed with encephalitis and has been in a wheelchair since. Mike's older sister, Niki Ronnan, staring running three years prior to Beth and Mike lining up against me in White Bear. Niki has taken to running with Mike. Together they make up Team Heart and run all sorts of races.

The Sunday before the White Bear 5K, while I was internally whining about running 3.1 miles in an elevated snow storm in Laramie, WY, Niki was running 26.2 miles with Mike in the Mankato marathon. Two weeks earlier, when I was running through Lawton, OK, she and Mike were starting the Twin Cities Marathon. By the time White Bear came around, she was in need of a rest, so Beth offered to run with Mike.

In our race, Mike came in 11th overall with a time of 23:49 and Elizabeth running-as-Niki came in 12th one second later. I ended 15th overall with a time of 24:10. It was one of my better runs and I couldn't have lost to a better team.

I'm grateful that I remain undefeated against Niki (okay, we never raced each other, but still) and that she and her brother are such an inspiration. She is living the 4D slogan, "I Run For Those That Can't," in ways that I can't comprehend.

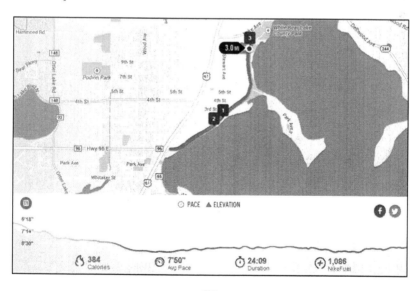

***

Minnesota Leadership Lesson:
Carrying Extra Weight

How much can you carry? What weight are you willing to put on your shoulders or push in front of you? Sometimes leaders, by their very nature, need to take on something extra. When it's your time, will you be ready? Capable? Sometimes it is simply not good enough to do your thing and do it well. Sometimes you need to bring someone along with you.

Just because someone does not have the same abilities that we have does not mean they are not entitled to enjoy similar experiences. How many of us take walking, much less running, for granted? How many people out there can only dream of running? Dancing? Climbing?

When someone with a specific ability takes the time to assist and share with someone without that ability, we all benefit. The world becomes a richer place for us all. Instead of always looking to see where you can climb next, take a moment to see who you can help pull up to where you are already.

Muscular Dystrophy Facts *from the Centers for Disease Control and Prevention*

"*Care for DMD includes monitoring muscle health. Muscle weakness happens in BMD as well, but usually at a slower rate. People who have DMD experience progressive muscle weakness because they do not have enough dystrophin (a protein) to help keep the muscles strong and healthy. Although every person is different, the muscle weakness in DMD often follows a certain path. The problems caused by muscle weakness can include difficulty learning to crawl and walk, trouble getting up off the floor, trouble climbing stairs, difficulty falling more often than other children, and difficulty with joints locking in one position.*

Regular medical check-ups are important to measure how well the muscles are working, and find out if treatments are needed. Treatments can include steroid medications to maintain muscle strength as long as possible; stretching and other exercises specifically designed for people with muscular dystrophy; braces and splints; assistive devices such as wheelchairs, computer technology, and lifting devices to help people with DBMD continue their daily activities; and surgery to prolong walking.)"

Source: www.cdc.gov/ncbddd/musculardystrophy/facts.html

Chapter 26

Sheyenne Valley Shuffle
Valley City, North Dakota
October 26, 2013

When you wake up at 4:00 a.m. in a cheap motel to shower, put on running clothes and drive over 2 hours to run 3 miles with 50 strangers in the bitter cold, you have to pause for moment and ask yourself, "What am I doing?" Thankfully, I had a good answer for that. I was doing the 4D 50-State 5K mission, and I was doing in honor of Dee and others that can't run.

Was this an ideal morning for me? Not at all.

Was this how I would normally invest a "vacation day?" Not at all.

Was it worthwhile? Absolutely.

Runners everywhere frequently get up at odd hours and drive long distances to support various causes and their own health. The few uncomfortable mornings I have had on this adventure pale in comparison to the discomfort I know Dee faces daily. Who am I to complain? Who am I not to run?

Although Dee can't run, she can get up early and stay up late. I know. I've gotten her texts at all hours. She wears her 4D pin and supports from a distance and participates in the trips via real-time updates. One time she was even up before me and sent me a "wakeup" text that wasn't meant to be a wakeup call. It happens when people are in different time zones. Her heart is always in the right place, and I've appreciated her support through this crazy adventure. She started it and she has kept it going.

***

Just before 5:00 a.m. I was on the road leaving Minnesota on my way to Valley City, ND. When I started planning trips around the country, it seemed like North and South Dakota would be the biggest challenges as it didn't seem they hosted many races and rarely on the same weekend. Until I decided to do this 6-state trip, my best bet was a weekend in February with back-to-back races in the Dakotas.

The Dakotas in February? I don't think so.

This October trip worked out perfectly, and I was grateful to get these two states checked off the list. Registration for this event was at Shelly Ellig Field at Lokken Stadium of Valley City State University. I arrived early and picked up my materials for the Sheyenne Valley Shuffle.

It was a very cold morning. Everyone was visibly shivering. Although registration was inside the stadium, the indoor space was not heated and did not offer much protection from the Artic temperatures. As I am always a planner, I had packed plenty of cold weather running clothes.

I was wearing doubled-up running socks, spandex running underwear and a pair of long spandex underwear. Over those, I wore a pair of Nike running pants. Up top I had on a spandex t-shirt that was covered with a thick, insulated running mock-turtleneck. A third layer consisted of a zippered long-sleeved V-neck running shirt punctuated with a 4D pin.

Additionally, I had on two layers of gloves, the Nike+ watch and a pair of wristbands. I always wear wristbands when I am running. When it is hot, I use them to wipe sweat from my forehead. When it is cold, they help keep my wrists warm as they swing through the cold air.

From years of racing cars, I had learned the importance of proper equipment. It makes life easier and allows you to be more comfortable.

As I was standing around trying to keep myself warm, I noticed a young boy awkwardly staring at me. Sometimes, it is cute when kids are so obvious about staring. Other times, like this time, it is just uncomfortable. There wasn't really any place for me to go to escape his gaze, and I had no clue why he kept looking my way.

There were not many people at the event so there wasn't much opportunity to get engaged in conversation. It seemed like a small town event and everyone knew everyone. No one knew me. Maybe that is why this kid was staring at me? It was probably obvious that I wasn't "from around here."

There were about 50 runners total and I was grateful for the start of the run. Getting the event underway was a good way to get the heart rate up to warm the body and to get away from the can't-stop-looking-at-you boy. We lined up, the gun went bang, and we were off. The course took us through the town of Valley City. At that hour, the only traffic was a pair of police vehicles that would direct cars away from us, if there were cars. There weren't.

We ran down the center of the street and as seems to be my luck in small towns, I was leading the race. I didn't keep the lead very long, as stare-boy came running up next to me and matched pace for a while.

Eventually, he started to pull away at a pretty good speed, and I wondered if he was going to tire by going too fast, too soon. A few other runners passed.

The run the night before, travel and lack of quality sleep really took their toll on me, and I just did not have reserve energy, even with sucking down my pre-race GU Energy Gel. When I crossed the finish line, the Nike+ indicated a 26:02—nearly 2 minutes off my normal time. That was still good enough for 3rd in my age group and 8th overall. I was grateful this run was done.

It turned out that the winner of the race was that 11-year-old with the eye fixation. He came over after we received our medals and he said, "You know. I was worried you were going to beat me today. I figured you were going to be my competition."

I thanked him for the compliment and told him that I had only been running since February, which really surprised him. I encouraged him to stick with it and I asked him why he thought I was going to be his challenge for the day.

He simply replied, "You were the only one wearing the right running gear."

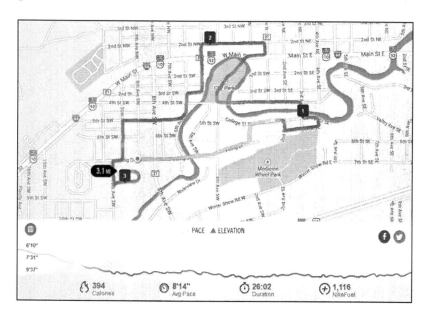

***

North Dakota Leadership Lesson:
Dressing the Part: Proper Gear

Life is not a dress rehearsal. Every day we are front-and-center on the stage of our world and our life. Wearing the proper clothes and having the right gear for whatever endeavor you are involved in is not a matter of being a fashionista. It is a matter of making sure you are ready to perform your best.

Ballerinas do not wear clogs. Olympic swimmers do not race in trench coats. We don't show up to professional job interviews in shorts and we certainly don't wear a clown suit on a first date. What we wear assists us in performing better. That is why they tell you to still wear a suit for a phone interview even though the other party can't see you. It puts you in interview mode. It keeps you from being too casual.

Having the right gear makes things easier. When we are striving for our goals, it is imperative to grab any edge we can to ensure success. Never underestimate the benefits of proper attire and gear.

***

My next run, and the last one for this trip, was at 1:00 p.m. the next day in Rapid City, SD. I was heading back to the Mt. Rushmore area, which meant a drive across the entire state of North Dakota. By the end of the day, I learned there is only one thing worse than driving across Nebraska: driving across North Dakota.

NORTH DAKOTA
Sights Along the Way

World's Largest Buffalo

Space Aliens Grill & Bar

Enchanted Highway

Muscular Dystrophy Facts from the Centers for Disease Control and Prevention

"Doctors can use different types of steroid medications to help maintain muscle strength as long as possible. These medications are the only ones currently available that can help slow the muscle damage caused by DBMD. A doctor might prescribe steroids when a person with DBMD is still active, or when he becomes less active. Steroids can have serious side effects. It is important that people with DBMD tell all of their health care providers that they are taking steroids. This is especially important when people who have DBMD are having surgery, have an infection, or are injured."

Source: www.cdc.gov/ncbddd/musculardystrophy/facts.html

Chapter 27

Halloween Sock Hop
Rapid City, South Dakota
October 27, 2013

Running in Rapid City, SD on my last day of this trip meant that I would need to cross South Dakota *a second time in a week* to return to Omaha, NE, for my flight home. All this driving was well worth it. This was an exciting, sight-filled 12 days, but I was ready to go home.

***

I was also enthusiastic about the run being at 1:00 p.m. It was predicted to be a clear, sunny day which meant this would be the only race of the trip that I could be in shorts and a t-shirt. When I arrived at the race, my excitement increased when I realized that the course was mostly flat.

With the level of confidence that comes from being well-rested, I started thinking about the possibility of setting a personal record. This was my 25th state in just 4 months, and it was 13 races since I PR'ed in Washington, D.C. I was sure today would be the day that I'd break 24:00 again and, hopefully, even lower for a PR.

Registration for the Halloween Sock Hop was at Canyon Lake Park. It was a beautiful place and they had a decent turnout for the 5K and the kids' costumed 1-mile run.

> **"Halloween Sock Hop:** Come in costume or run with friends as a centipede. Fun for all ages. Prizes for costumes. We are helping the KOTA Care & Share Food Drive - bring a non-perishable food item if you'd like to join in!"

Before the race, I got into several conversations about the 50-state 4D experience. I met a runner who was 62 and had run all 50 states, at various lengths between 5K and marathon. He was impressed that I was trying to do all 50 in year, as it had taken him 29 years to complete his journey. It was inspiring to meet another 50-stater.

The conversation turned to how many states I had accomplished, and we realized that this race in South Dakota was #25. That made SD the half-way point! It was the "turn around state." From this point forward, each state would bring me one step beyond halfway. Appropriately enough, the day's race was an out-and-back course with a turnaround point.

The course meandered through the picturesque park. I started feeling very solid, but I just couldn't seem to catch my breath. I was getting winded faster than I was used to. The Nike+ confirmed that I was struggling to maintain what is for me a fast pace. It just seemed like I was slightly off, even though I was physically and mentally prepared for this race. I couldn't tell what was going on, but started to resign myself to the fact that my pace would not pick up no matter how much I was instructing my legs to move and my lungs to breathe.

When I completed the race I was disappointed to see my time of 25:05. I was off by a full minute. What was going on here? I talked to one of the faster runners. Although the course seemed relatively flat, it was actually on a steady grade. This should not have affected my time though, because it was an out-and-back course, so any negative impact on my time from the uphill would have been outweighed by the speed on the downhill.

After talking with some other people, I finally realized what I had been missing all along. We were running at over 3,200' of elevation. This was the second highest run I had done and was more than 3 times the elevation of my typical run. No wonder I couldn't catch my breath. There was significantly less oxygen available than I am used to. Things are not always as they seem.

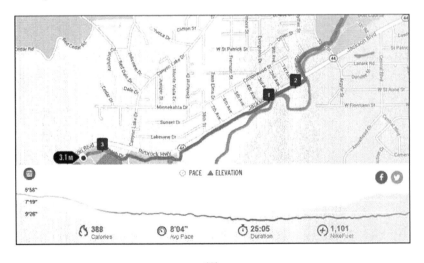

***

South Dakota was the 8th state run in October, bringing the total to 25. 50% of the country was done in the first 30% of the year. I was elated and glad to be heading back to the airport. True to my word, the rental car's "oil change" light came on during my trip back to Omaha. The car was returned, 12 days after I rented it, with 4,560 miles added to its odometer.

***

South Dakota Leadership Lesson:
Things Are Not Always As They Appear

Things are not always as they appear, and we need to be prepared for performance that might not meet expectations when we are missing an important factor. Everything for this run seemed to indicate my potential to do extremely well, but my time came up short. I was missing one very key piece of information—the elevation. It only takes one factor to throw off calculation.

Make sure you do your research—all of it. Calculate the potential outcomes, and, in the end, if you missed something you just might come up short on your expectations. It will be up to you to decide how much that might affect your goals.

SOUTH DAKOTA
Sights Along the Way

Belle Fourche, Geographic Center of the United States

Rapid City Presidents of the United States on Street Corners

Deadwood

Mt. Moriah Cemetery, Burial Place of Wild Bill Hickok and Calamity Jane

Mt. Rushmore

Crazy Horse

Wall Drug Store

The Badlands

Muscular Dystrophy Facts from the Centers for Disease Control and Prevention

"Muscle weakness, lack of movement, and taking steroid medicines to help maintain muscle strength can cause bones to be weaker among people who have DBMD. Bone problems can include the spine curving to one or both sides, which might cause breathing difficulties; bones becoming weaker and thinner, which increases the chances of a fracture (breaking a bone); and fractures in the legs and spine. Doctors can test for bone strength and spine health, and can prescribe medications and vitamins."

Source: www.cdc.gov/ncbddd/musculardystrophy/facts.html

Chapter 28

Mock the Clock
Seattle, Washington
November 3, 2013

After driving over 4,500 miles and running 5Ks across 6 states, most people would probably take a weekend off. I'm not most people, and I was cognizant of the approaching winter months. If I was going to complete the entire U.S. in one year, letting up was not an option.

If I knew I was going to go this far with this project, I would have attacked more states in July and August. At this point, there would be no rest for the weary. I was back to work for the week, and by Saturday morning I was on another plane.

More than any other weekend, this one was going to be about *time*. I flew out of the Philadelphia airport at 5:50 a.m. on Saturday, November 2, and returned at 11:55 p.m. on Sunday. I was gone for 30 hours and 5 minutes and managed to explore two states, albeit in not much detail, and run two 5Ks. One of the 5Ks was the strangest event: I finished the race 35 minutes before I started it!

***

My plane landed in Portland, OR, at 10:30 a.m., crossing three time zones en route. I grabbed my rental and headed north into the state of Washington. My destination was Seattle, my race was 15 hours away, and I was 100% certain I was going to run a new fastest time. In a matter of hours, I was going to set a new personal record in the 5K with a time that will probably never be broken. It practically defies logic and was, more or less, guaranteed.

Portland, OR, to Seattle, WA, is a

WASHINGTON
Sights Along the Way

Tacoma Museum of Glass

Space Needle

Chihuly Garden and Glass

Snoqualmie Falls Park

3-hour drive, a bit longer with sightseeing stops. I crammed as much in as I could in the few hours I was there. By 9:30 p.m. I needed to check into a motel and get some sleep. I didn't bother Couch Surfing on this trip as I only needed a place to sleep one night, and I was going to be keeping a rather bizarre sleep schedule and did not want to be a rude guest.

I was asleep by 10:00 p.m. for only a few hours of Zzz's as I was up just after midnight to get ready for my run. Yes, this 5K was happening in the wee hours of the morning. Generally speaking, I run my best just after waking up, but that is usually after a full night's sleep. On just over 2 hours, I wasn't sure how things would work out. I just knew it would be my best run to date.

Most 5Ks give registrants a commemorative T-shirt, but since we were running after 1:00 a.m., they gave us PJs: it was a nice touch. The run took place on the campus of the University of Washington. Running through a college campus at 2:00 a.m. with 300+ other people really gave the feeling that I was back in college and misbehaving.

It was a very good time, but my random sleep schedule did not have a positive impact on my running. I was well off pace and the course was frustratingly short at 2.8 miles. I will never understand how course designers can be a ¼-mile off an accurate distance.

On a good run, my pace is around 7:40 minutes per mile. On this run, I was well off that pace as I averaged 8:30. Yet, in complete disobedience to the natural order of time, I ran a new personal best.

You read that correctly. I ran 40-seconds per mile slower than I normally run, but I posted my quickest time ever in a 5K!

My recorded time was -35:36 minutes. That is not a typo. That is a negative number. *I finished the run 35 minutes and 36 seconds before I started the run.*

How can this be? It's simple really. I mocked the clock.

"Mock the Clock 5K: *Defy time - finish before you start! The Mock the Clock 5K Run/Walks (formerly known as Anything is Possible 5Ks) will be held in cities across the U.S., all starting at 1:50 AM on the night that Daylight Savings Time ends and clocks get turned back."*

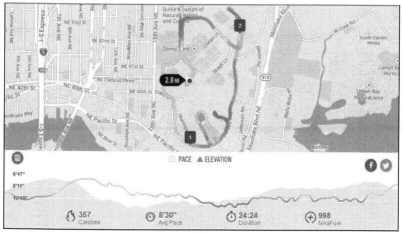

Whenever we are leading, we can be inundated with data. All sorts of information is available to evaluate our performance, monitor our progress in meeting goals, and compare us to our competitors. Data can be confusing, and it has been said that statistics can always be manipulated to tell the story you want to tell.

For example, during the Cold War, there was an International race and a Russian newspaper listed the results. They said that Russia came in second place and that the United States came in second-to-last place. This was true and accurate data; however, they failed to mention that they were the only two countries competing!

Make sure you question data, especially if something seems awry (like a negative 5K time!).

Keep in mind that anyone who shares data with you has an agenda for sharing it. Always ask yourself why is this person sharing this data? What is their goal? What does it mean to me? Does it appear accurate? Does this warrant further investigation?

Muscular Dystrophy Facts *from the Centers for Disease Control and Prevention*

"DBMD affects muscles in the heart. As people with the condition grow older, their heart muscles get weaker. The heart muscle becomes weak and might not pump blood into the body properly. The heart also might beat either too fast or too slow. People with DBMD should have their heart checked regularly. Cardiologists—doctors who specialize in caring for the heart—can perform tests to monitor heart health. Medications can be prescribed to prevent or treat heart problems."

Source: www.cdc.gov/ncbddd/musculardystrophy/facts.html

Chapter 29

Run for the Hole
Portland, Oregon
November 3, 2013

Following the Mock the Clock, I found my way back to my motel and collapsed on the bed by 2:30 a.m. I had to be up by 5:30 a.m. to get back to Portland, OR, for another race. Yes, I was running two 5KS in two states within 7 hours of each other.

After this morning's 5K, I was going to have to get back to the airport, return the rental car, and fly home in time for bed so I could get up for work on Monday morning. Visiting two states in less than 48 hours does not leave a lot of time to dawdle. My scheduling was really getting interesting, but I was checking off states at an amazing rate.

***

The Portland, OR, run was in downtown along the Willamette River. Registration was a block away from Waterfront Park in an open-air plaza of a business building. The start/finish line was also there, which was unusual as the only way out of the plaza has 4 stairs. Apparently we were going to run across the starting line and up 4 individual steps. If only I knew that this was an awful case of foreshadowing.

I made my way over and signed in for the Run for the Hole 5K while finishing my banana and GU Energy Gel, not realizing it would be the last time I consumed one of those gels before a race.

> *"**Run for the Hole:** A family-friendly fun-filled 5K run in downtown Portland. You'll burn enough calories to enjoy the sweet treat at the finish line all while getting the satisfaction of also participating in an event that helps those battling cancer. Run for the Hole ... for a whole lot of reasons!"*

Disregarding my state of general exhaustion, I had it in my mind that I might be able to PR in this event. The run was at 50' above sea level, so elevation wasn't a factor. It was chilly, but after the crazy trip through the middle of the U.S., cold running was no longer an issue.

The course went down along Waterfront Park, along the river, crossed a bridge, and continued up the other side of the river before taking us back over another bridge. After crossing that bridge was another leg through Waterfront Park before crossing the street to the finish line in the plaza. The layout of the course is what made me think I had PR-potential that morning. Running up and down both sides a river meant the course was going to be, more or less, flat.

So I thought.

At the beginning of the race, part of the announcements addressed the 4 stairs staring directly at us in front of the start line. We were told that when the *race* starts, we were supposed to walk up the stairs quickly, not run, for everyone's safety. At the time, I thought it odd to tell runners not to run. In hindsight, requesting we not run up four stairs was even stranger, considering an obstacle waiting for us about a quarter mile into the course.

The race started, we quickly made our way up the 4 stairs, took a hard left to run down the block to a police officer waiting with stopped traffic. We crossed the street and ran into the park to make a right along the waterfront. I was feeling good, dreaming of a new PR, and then I saw the strangest thing. The runners ahead were going underneath a bridge, making an immediate right and disappearing.

I was completely confused as to where they went. As I approached the bridge, I happened to look up and saw competitors, race bibs flapping, running across the bridge. Are you kidding me? How did they get all the way up there?

As I ran under the bridge, I saw an awkwardly steep, two-story stairwell. By awkward I mean something you would never, ever choose to run up. I have no way of knowing what your running experience is or how you train, but throwing stairs into a race, especially at the beginning, is just cruel.

When I was battling with my fears of running up hills, I started training on stairs. It is a great leg workout. It is not something I include *in the middle* of a run. Who does this?

With only moments to decide how to attack this obstacle, I decided to charge and get it over with as fast as I could. On the positive side, I made it up those stairs quickly, but I was not going to be leaving them behind. The damage to my legs and my lungs was lasting. Whatever momentum I had prior to those stairs gave on the spot and jumped over the bridge. My pace slowed as I watched my momentum splash in the river below, and a steady stream of runners started passing me.

My focus was shot, but I was still intent on doing well. I found something else inside and pushed on as hard as I could. I was still doing reasonably well and my breathing was starting to recover. Was a PR still possible?

As we approached the second bridge, I was elated to see that it was on river level, so no more stairs to run up (or down). Since we came back down to river level, which means the slight elevation decline was working in my favor, maybe I could start making up lost time. I started running faster.

Ahead, I saw runners darting through the park toward the street, crossing where the policeman had traffic stopped. I did a quick glance at the Nike+ to check pace and realized that I still had a long distance to go. I was nowhere near 3.1 miles.

For the second time in 7 hours I crossed the finish line of a 5K while logging only 2.8 miles instead of the correct 3.1. How could Seattle and Portland both come up so short? And by the exact same amount? Regardless, my 7:58 minutes-per-mile pace wouldn't have been enough for the ever-elusive PR.

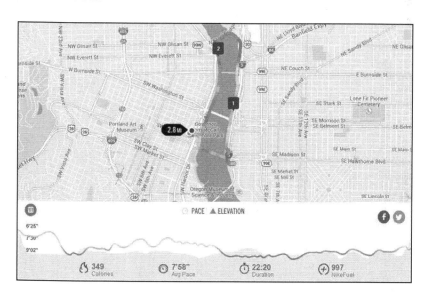

***

Sitting on the plane, it occurred to me that I had now run Portland, Maine, and Portland, Oregon, coast-to-coast. What an experience this whole endeavor has been! Twenty-seven states were completed and Washington and Oregon were just the beginning of November. By the end of the month, 7 more states would fall.

Life throws us all curveballs. You are running on an even-keel course and suddenly there are two flights of stairs in front of you. You will need to decide your course of action. Maybe running full blast up the stairs was not my best option, but I made it to the top and continued on. Maybe I would have been better with a quick jog up, keeping some reserve energy. The only wrong answer would have been not to attempt the stairs at all. What will you do when large, imposing obstacles come between you and your goals? Will they defeat you or inspire you?

We can't really prepare for surprises, otherwise they wouldn't be surprises. What we need to do is prepare as best we can for the goals ahead and to accept that unplanned experiences will invade our space and try to divert us from reaching our goals. Make sure you're ready, mentally and emotionally, for the unexpected.

Muscular Dystrophy Facts from the Centers for Disease Control and Prevention

"As people with DBMD grow older, the muscles that support breathing get weaker. Signs of trouble with breathing can include shortness of breath, fatigue (that is, being very tired all the time), headaches, and trouble sleeping. People with DBMD might have trouble breathing at night and might need to use a machine to help take a deep breath. Over time, they might find it difficult to breathe during the day, and might need a machine to help them both day and night.

As the condition progresses, the lungs become weaker. Preventing lung infections, such as pneumonia, is important for healthy breathing. It is important that people who have DBMD get vaccinations to prevent pneumonia. They also might need manual and mechanically assisted support to stimulate coughing when they have a cold or infection."

Source: www.cdc.gov/ncbddd/musculardystrophy/facts.html

Chapter 30

Crescent City Fall Classic
New Orleans, Louisiana
November 9, 2013

The second weekend of November was going to provide two more states to the growing lists of territories conquered. This time I was heading south to the land of Mardi Gras.

The night before the flight I realized that I was out of GU Energy Gels. There was no way to get to a sporting goods store prior to my departure. I was flying into Mobile, AL, at night for an extremely late check-in at a Motel 6. I had only enough time to get to the motel, sleep, and get up for the early morning drive to New Orleans. Stopping for a GU Energy Gel was not an option.

Thoughts of the Energy Gels were in my mind throughout the flight. I questioned how much a difference they really made. I had never run an event without them. What was the worst that could happen? I train on the street without them and my times never seemed drastically different. But I have never run 10K training runs without that extra boost of energy.

I decided to run New Orleans without consuming the gel—not as if I had much choice. The banana and Vitamin Water would stay as part of my pre-race ritual, but if I was going into the land of voodoo, I should take a look at my own superstitions. If my 5K time was drastically affected by not ingesting an energy gel, I could always repent and go back to my full ritual in time for the next day's event in Alabama.

LOUISIANA
Sights Along the Way

Voodoo Museum

French Quarter and Bourbon Street

French Market

St. Louis Cathedral

Louis Armstrong Park

New Orleans Museum of Art Sculpture Garden

***

The Color Run in Philadelphia, PA, and the Warrior Dash in Long Pond, PA, were the two largest races I entered with 26,000+ runners and

7,000+ runners, respectively. They were both all-day affairs with runners taking off in waves of several hundred at a time. They both had a massive party atmosphere. When you parked your car, you could hear the music, see hundreds of people walking toward the same general location, and feel the energy. They weren't just a 5K, they were a happening.

This run would have as similar feel. The event was held inside of New Orleans's City Park. I managed to find parking a few blocks away and the energy was immediately evident. There were droves of people, clad in running attire, converging on the park. It didn't take long to get close enough to hear the music. This was going to be big.

In fact, the Crescent City Fall Classic 5K was the largest 5K race I had entered in which all runners started together. This was huge and it was a race—none of this silly runners leaving in waves business. All 2,495 of us got the signal *to take off together.*

> *"**Crescent City Fall Classic 5K:** Held the second Saturday in November, this race has multiple audiences. Serious runners can use this event as a qualifier to earn a prime starting position in the Allstate Sugar Bowl Crescent City Classic 10k. This is the ONLY opportunity to run a qualifying time at the 5k distance!"*

Large running experiences are one of the few times that you can get several thousand people to do the same thing, in the same place, at the same time, and actually be quiet. At one point we turned onto City Park Avenue, a significant roadway. The road was blocked to traffic for the event.

With over 2,000 runners, you are constantly passing, being passed and pacing several others. I ran down City Park Avenue with several hundred runners, the only sound the soft beating of thousands of sneakers against asphalt keeping time with a harmony of intense breathing. It felt I was part of a living river. Nay, we were blood cells rushing through the heart of the city. It was incredible, fascinating.

We eventually left the main street and turned back into the park. A very fit woman cruised past me at a good clip as we approached two 90-degree left turns. As I saw her complete the first turn, my eye caught another woman ahead lose her footing in the second turn. She went crashing down, not too hard, but I am sure it was hard enough. The woman who had passed me ran right to the fallen female and offered assistance.

I caught up and passed them as I heard some sincere words of encouragement from fit-lady to fallen-lady. I could tell they were back on their feet and running again. Sometime, not too far into the future, fit-lady buzzed by me for the second time.

This event could be used as a qualifier for a much bigger event that was very hard to get into. It struck me that it was probable that fit-lady was trying to qualify for the other race. Yet she stopped and offered assistance.

As for me, I was feeling solid with my run, and I kept on pushing myself. When the finish line was in sight, I found that extra little bit and sprinted to the end. I turned in one of my best times at 24:07 on a perfectly measured course. That averaged out to 7:37 minute miles.

With a field that large and that competitive, my time was only good enough for 38th in my age group. Regardless, I felt like a winner and realized I could give up my voodoo. I was going to be saving money—no more GU Energy Gels.

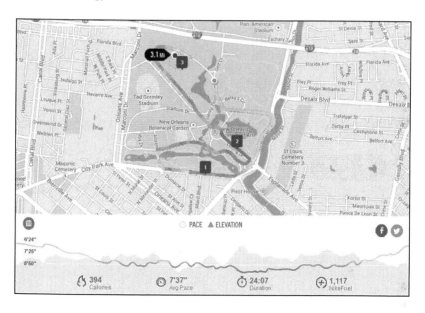

***

Louisiana Leadership Lesson:
Giving Up Superstitions, Helping Those Who Stumble

I ran over 30 events before I questioned the merits of the GU Energy Gel and then, only because I didn't have an option. How did I manage to convince myself that I needed that little pack of energy in order to run? It didn't even make logical sense, as I never used the supplement when I was training.

We need to be cautious of our rituals. Are our decisions logical? Rational? Are we doing something merely because it was advised? Maybe we read something that made it sound like a good idea. Yes, we should be open to trying new things and hearing other people's advice, but we ultimately have to analyze whether what we are doing really makes sense.

The reality is that I was probably getting something from that little pack of gel, but I am doubtful it was significant. I suspect that it was probably more the calming affect that ritualistic behavior gives us. It provides a sense of normalcy to states of confusion, or in my case, confusing states.

And, what about that other runner, the fit lady, who stopped her effort to help someone else? What does her action say about leadership? Is she a poor leader for losing sight of her goals or is she a strong leader for stopping to assist someone else? That might be a personal judgment, but it may also be that we do not have enough information to decide.

Having been there and witnessed her actions, it appeared to me that she was "doing the right thing," and that, I feel, is one of the first requirements of being a leader. If I would have been the next runner to get to the fallen runner, I would have stopped to assist. These are decisions we have to make all the time. Do we go ahead alone or help someone win their fight too? It's a question of values, not just goals.

Muscular Dystrophy Facts from the Centers for Disease Control and Prevention

"People with DBMD can have diet, nutrition, and digestion issues. These problems can change over time and include being underweight or overweight, and having swallowing problems, heartburn, and constipation (bowel movements which are infrequent, difficult, or both). Maintaining a well-balanced diet and healthy weight is important. As they get older, people with DBMD can develop swallowing problems that can cause weight loss and unhealthy eating. A doctor might recommend using a feeding tube to assist with proper nutrition."

Source: www.cdc.gov/ncbddd/musculardystrophy/facts.html

Chapter 31

Stamp Out Muscular Dystrophy 5K
Mobile, Alabama
November 10, 2013

It might seem strange, but as soon as I was done with the 5K in New Orleans, I jumped in the rental and left town. I did not spend time looking at a single sight in New Orleans (there are sights listed on the things I saw, because I spent time in the city 2 months later when I ran Mississippi—long story for another chapter). That may seem odd, as it is such a cool city, but I had been there before and I had a cool experience waiting for me back in Alabama—my Couch Surfing hostess!

Although the big 12-day trip through the center of the country was the first time I Couch Surfed, it actually wasn't my first "accept" on the Couch Surfing website. The first "accept" came from a wonderful woman named Jayne Mosley. Jayne lives outside the Mobile, AL, area and agreed to host me for the Louisiana/Alabama weekend. I was also Jayne's first "accept," so it was going to be a new experience for both of us.

It was evident that Jayne was excited about being a hostess, as she was making really great suggestions on things we could do while I was in Alabama. Her enthusiasm was contagious and inspiring, and that is why I left New Orleans right after the run. I was excited to explore Alabama with a seasoned tour guide.

Jayne is the embodiment of Southern hospitality. She was both gracious and generous with her time, sharing local events with me. She took me to an Oyster Festival and, later in the day,

---

ALABAMA
Sights Along the Way

USS Alabama Battleship Memorial Park

Gulf Shores

Mobile Museum of Art

Bragg Mitchell Mansion

Little River Canyon National Preserve

Noccalula Falls Park

Birmingham, AL – Civil Rights locations

Birmingham 9/11 Memorial

Vulcan Park

Montgomery, AL – Civil Rights locations

Bamahenge

Dinosaur Sculptures

an Italian Foods Festival. These were not activities I would have ever found traveling on my own.

Couch Surfing has really changed the way I view travel and people. It has been a reaffirming experience. It restores faith in people's ability to be kind to a stranger and to offer assistance. If I had a million dollars in the bank, I would still Couch Surf.

Jayne Mosley and Jeff Fazio hang out at "The Hangout" in Gulf Shores, AL.

***

Meanwhile, back in Pennsylvania, Dee was busy reaching out to race organizers, letting them know that I was coming. She is a great PR-person and was taking advantage of my travel to help spread the word about Muscular Dystrophy and the 4D 50-State 5K experience.

For both Dee and me, the run in Mobile was going to hold a special place in this journey. After running 29 races all over the country supporting all sorts of other causes, it was time to run a 5K raising funds and awareness about Muscular Dystrophy. It was time to run the Stamp Out Muscular Dystrophy 5K.

> **"Stamp Out Muscular Dystrophy 5K:** Benefits: Muscular Dystrophy Association. Organized by the National Association of Letter Carriers, Branch 469."

Dee was in contact with Kiesha Cordier, race director and letter carrier. The group was excited that the 4D mission was coming to their event. When you are running for a cause and you show up to an event supporting that cause, it is like finding family you didn't know you had. There is an immediate connection and understanding of what you are doing and why.

The race was taking place in Langan Park in Mobile, Alabama, home to the Mobile Museum of Art. The run the previous day in New Orleans was through a park that was also home to a museum, the New Orleans Museum of Art.

The park, museum, and race in New Orleans were significantly larger than Mobile, but that did not overshadow the importance of running for Muscular Dystrophy. I was very grateful for the opportunity to run in this event. The letter carriers were an amazing group of caring people who devoted a lot of time and energy to their event.

It was a beautiful course through the park and was accurately measured. It is unfortunate that I am at a point where I feel like celebrating when a course actually comes out to 3.1 miles on the Nike+. The juxtaposition of running with 32 other runners a day after running with 2,494 other runners was not lost on me. In fact, I was thankful for that opportunity too. I can't imagine doing *anything* in all 50 States without an appreciation for variety.

Kiesha Cordier and Jeff Fazio met prior to the beginning of the Alabama 5K.

I posted a decent time of 24:17, only 10 seconds slower than the previous day. The time was good enough to earn second place in my age group.

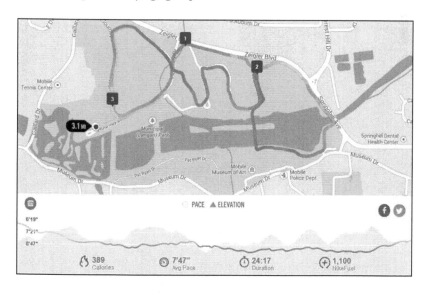

***

Alabama Leadership Lesson:
Keeping Focus on Real Goals

We started the 4D 50-State 5K experience to spread the word about Muscular Dystrophy and raise awareness. That has always been the primary goal. As leaders, it is all too easy to get wrapped up in secondary goals like running and visiting 50 states. Running in Mobile at an event supporting MD was a grounding reminder of why we were doing what we were doing. As leaders, we need to keep our focus on the primary goal. Everything else is, after all, secondary.

Muscular Dystrophy Facts *from the Centers for Disease Control and Prevention*

"People with DBMD might have issues that affect how they interact with others. These issues might be caused by the condition, they might be side effects of using medications to treat health issues, or they might be a result of the emotional and mental health challenges that accompany living with muscular dystrophy. Mental and emotional issues should be addressed by a health care professional who is an expert in these conditions, such as a psychologist, psychiatrist, or social worker.

Treatment of emotional and mental health might include encouraging independence and involvement in decision making; receiving help in developing social and learning skills; receiving psychotherapy, such as individual or family therapy; or using medications for treatments. There are organizations that provide support for people and families affected by DBMD. Some offer programs such as sports teams and summer camps for people with special needs. People who have DBMD also might enjoy engaging in equine and water therapy, participating in art activities, and communicating with others on the Internet."

Source: www.cdc.gov/ncbddd/musculardystrophy/facts.html

Chapter 32

Philadelphia GORE-TEX® Marathon
Philadelphia, Pennsylvania
November 17, 2013

Back in Chapter 10, in the first weekend of September, I introduced Kristy Higham. She is the runner I met in Rhode Island on Labor Day weekend who ran with a 4D pin and, a few weeks later, ran a half marathon sporting the 4D pin. The 4D-"I Run For Those That Can't" pin is now a permanent part of Kristy's race gear.

While I was running around the Dakotas (literally), I received a message from Kristy on Facebook letting me know that she was running the Philadelphia Marathon on November 17. She wanted to know if I could make it there to support her. It looked like she was going to be the first person to run a marathon with a 4D pin: Yes, I was going to do my best to make it there.

Some folks have questioned my mental health since I took on running 3.1 miles of each state in the Union. I wonder about the sanity of people who run a marathon—26.2 miles at *one time*.

I digress. Anyway, I enthusiastically agreed to meet Kristy and her family in Philadelphia to support her in this endeavor. This would be the first, but certainly not the last, time that I would get to re-connect with a "stranger" whom I met on my around-the-country travels. Kristy is terrific and I was enjoying our growing running-addiction friendship through Facebook, so I was excited to be able to hang out with her again.

As this would also be the first time someone was running a marathon sporting a 4D pin, it was important for me to be there. For Dee, for this cause, for me, this was an incredibly big deal, and I was excited that Kristy was championing the 4D story in such an amazing way. The plan was set. The only weekend in November that I was not running in a race of my own in some distant state, I would be headed to Philadelphia to support a fellow runner in *her goal.*

***

I met up with Kristy, her mother and father at the hotel in Philly. We went out for a nice pre-race dinner with her aunt and uncle. Afterward, the four of us piled into the hotel room and tried to grab some sleep. The next morning was going to come very fast. I'm not sure how Kristy was able to sleep at all.

29,394 runners.

That is how many people completed the 2013 Philadelphia GORE-TEX® Marathon & Half Marathon. The breakdown of participation was 14,163 entries in the marathon and 15,231 entries in the half.

> *"Philadelphia GORE-TEX® Marathon: In Philadelphia, we redefine the experience of what a marathon should be. A beautiful course, an engaging atmosphere—it's no wonder we're consistently listed among the top ten courses in the country, recognized for our flat terrain, mellow weather and spirited fans."*

It is impossible to describe what nearly 30,000 people running down a main street in Philadelphia looks like. What it feels like. What it sounds like.

It is also really hard to describe what running 26.2 miles *at one time* is like. Of course, it might be easier to describe if I ever done it. I haven't and I will not.

Kristy did it. Kristy is amazing. She is a pillar of dedication and commitment. She is also a killer athlete.

***

I was Kristy's personal photographer for the day. For the first location, I stationed myself at mile 1 atop a concrete entrance to a parking garage. It gave me a good 10' of height over the runners. Thankfully, I had found a way to get myself higher. With the number of people who came running at me, it would have almost been impossible to see Kristy.

Mile 1 is precisely at the point where runners leave Ben Franklin Parkway and turn onto Arch Street in downtown Philadelphia. My parking garage spot was on the outside of the turn and I could just barely see down the Parkway. The first participants to complete the first mile were the wheelchairs and handcycles. The crowd roared for these athletes as they powered past.

A few moments later, the on-foot leaders came around the bend. It was a group of about 30 runners who were just charging along. The crowd burst into cheers for them as well. We were all eagerly awaiting the masses.

Here they came; a few hundred runners came around the turn. I had memorized Kristy's outfit. She was wearing very distinct and unique colors. Unfortunately, there were about 75 other women with that particular combination. I suppose with 15,000 runners you are bound to find some who picked the same colors. I went to work. I snapped dozens and dozens of photos of women who *looked like* Kristy.

The interesting thing about a few hundred runners coming around a turn toward you is that it is only impressive until several thousand come after them in never-ending waves. All at once there were thousands of runners rushing towards us like water coming from a broken damn. They were flowing into the path of least resistance, which was the space between the crowds on both sides.

Things were being thrown at me. En mass, runners began shedding clothes. It was a cold morning, but as any runner can tell you, it is only cold outside until you start running. Once the heart starts pumping blood around your system, you warm up quick. In Philadelphia, that day, that happened around mile 1.

I was thankful that the first item "littered' was a pair of black, soft cloth gloves. I jumped down and grabbed them, as my hands were freezing. From what I understand, Philadelphia sends trucks after the runners picking up these "donated" clothes and takes them to the homeless.

Kristy came by and I was so grateful to be able to get shots of her. Because where I stood above the crowd, she easily spotted me and was able to "smile for the camera." My biggest fear was that I would not get any photos of her. With several good shots committed to pixels, I could relax and not worry the rest of the day.

After she passed, I jumped down and walked three blocks to Chestnut St. It would take her another 5 miles and not quite an hour to get there. At the intersection of 17th and Chestnut, I found a trashcan I could climb on top of. The street was lined with a mob of cheering people. This street was much narrower than the previous, so everyone was squished tight.

As I waited at mile 6 for her I thought about the fact that my "long training runs" were 10K or 6.2 miles. When Kristy passed us, she would have to repeat that distance over 3 more times! By mile 6 my legs are killing me and I am dying of boredom.

Kristy's parents were at the starting line, a good distance away, but there was enough time for her parents to catch up with me at the Chestnut Street location. I am glad they were there, because I would have missed Kristy otherwise. It was very chaotic, but I was able to snap a few more photos of her from that location.

After she passed, Kristy's parents and I walked back toward the starting line area. Just north of that location was the 13.1 mile-mark—the half-way point of the race. It was a good 20-minute walk for us, but over an hour (and another 7 miles) for Kristy to get to that point.

Once we took photos of Kristy passing at the half, she would be gone until the finish. The second half of the course leads runners along Kelly Drive and the Schuylkill River until they reach the turnaround point.

We took the opportunity to seek out breakfast. We walked around Philly for a bit and got recommendations for places to eat. We went into a nice little corner place and sat at the counter. We got our food and relaxed over conversation and food. The whole time, I kept thinking about Kristy.

She was pounding out miles at quicker than a 10-minute-per-mile pace. If she kept that pace, she would not be done for another 2 hours. She had already been out there over 2 hours. It was unfathomable to me that she was doing 10-minute miles for 4 hours. What an incredible feat! Or should I say *incredible feet?*

After our breakfast, we meandered back to the finish line and waited for Kristy. She was right on schedule. In fact, she was a tad early. She had actually picked up her pace slightly in the second half of the race.

Her mom started screaming to her and Kristy spotted us through the endless crowd of cheerer-oners. When Kristy saw us, she smiled and smiled big. If her smile was any bigger she would have knocked over a few other runners. And then her hands came up, along with her thumbs. She was finishing like a champ.

Kristy Higham finished her first, but not her last, marathon sporting the 4D pin.

Kristy Higham, from East Greenwich, RI, wearing Bib #13872 finished the 2013 Philadelphia GORE-TEX® Marathon in 4 hours, 13 minutes and 6 seconds. Her average pace was 9:39/mile. November 17, 2013, was her day. She was a rock star. I was proud to be a groupie.

***

Philadelphia Leadership Lesson:
Knowing Your Limits

Leaders need to know their limits. I said that while Kristy was running the second half of the marathon I was enjoying breakfast with her family and thinking about her out there running. That is true. It is also true that it gave me a lot of time to reflect on me and what I was capable of. Having been an avid runner for 8 months, I knew enough to put into perspective what it meant to run under a 10-minute mile and I could imagine what it would be like to attempt to do that for over 4 hours.

When I run long (for me) distances, somewhere between 5 and 6 miles, I start feeling it in my knees— and it feels bad. I also have a short attention span, so even when running at a conversational pace with a group of 5 or 6 other runners, by 7 miles I am simply bored. I am tired. Not physically tired, but mentally just done—checked out.

I know my limitations and you should know yours. I am up for most challenges, but I am also smart enough to know the things I am not built for. Marathons are not in my future. I am okay with that.

Do you know your limitations? Are you comfortable with them?

Lastly, don't confuse your limitations with things you are afraid to do or are lacking confidence in. They are not the same thing. Never let your mind limit what you're able to achieve.

Muscular Dystrophy Facts from the Centers for Disease Control and Prevention

"It is not known exactly how many people of all ages in the United States have DBMD. An estimated 1 of every 5,600 to 7,700 males 5 through 24 years of age had DBMD. That is approximately equal to a prevalence of 1.3 to 1.8 per 10,000 males 5 through 24 years of age in the four states."

Source: www.cdc.gov/ncbddd/musculardystrophy/facts.html

Chapter 33

'STACHE DASH 5K
Wauwatosa, Wisconsin
November 23, 2013

There are certain races I specifically sought out. During the month of November, or as some call it, Movember, men are asked to let their facial hair run wild. Let it grow and be free. Why?

> *"**No-Shave November:** The goal of No-Shave November is to grow awareness by embracing our hair, which many cancer patients lose, and letting it grow wild and free. Donate the money you usually spend on shaving and grooming for a month to educate about cancer prevention, save lives, and aid those fighting the battle."*

All around the country, there are 5Ks inspired by this shave-less month. These races are fondly referred to as mustache dashes (or some variation thereof). I scoured the Internet trying to find a mustache-themed run in a state I had not already completed or scheduled. This was beginning to get tricky, but I managed to find an event in Milwaukee, WI, on November 23. I was able to identify another 5K the next day in Iowa. Perfect. I scheduled my flight and started scouting out couches to surf.

***

Travel can be funny. Sometimes it can be significantly more affordable to fly into one state even though your target is another. For this trip, I flew into Chicago, rented a car, and drove to Milwaukee. Since Chicago is a major hub for airlines, it was a lot cheaper to fly there, and I could fly direct.

I landed in Chicago Friday evening, grabbed the rental, and headed out to meet my Couch Surfing hostess for the evening. My hostess, Brandy Koch, is an architect and I stayed in her beautiful brownstone in Chicago. After a great night of conversation and sushi, I got up very early for the 1.5-hour drive to Milwaukee and, of course, some sightseeing.

The race was actually in Wauwatosa, close to Milwaukee. Wisconsin was experiencing an extra cold blast of air for the time of the year, so race registration for the event was moved inside. Everyone met at Leff's Lucky Town, a local Sports Bar & Grill. The run was not scheduled to start until noon, but the late start did very little to ward off the 32-degree weather. It was cold, literally freezing cold. Regardless, I plopped down my money to enter the HOG's 'Stache Dash.

> **"The HOG's 'Stache Dash:** Join 102.9 The Hog, Leff's Lucky Town & Silver Circle Sports Events for the Hog's 'Stache Dash in support of Movember. Movember is an international movement to raise awareness for prostate cancer and other men's issues. As part of The Hog's 'Stache Dash, we will make a Movember contribution."

While hanging out at Leff's waiting for the wall clock to tick away enough minutes to start the ticking of the race clock, I met a really interesting couple, Kate and Reto Gugerli. People are fascinating and traveling the country meeting them has been an added bonus to this 50-State experience. Reto is Swiss and they met in Switzerland when Kate was visiting her aunt (who also married a Swiss man). They typically run together once per week and they ran a half marathon in Switzerland. This was to be Reto's first 5K in the U.S. Why this event? He had been working on his handlebar mustache for Movember and thought it was a good time and place to spotlight it.

***

Running in 32-degrees can always be worse—just add wind. That is precisely what Wisconsin did. The wind chill brought the effective temperature down to 9 degrees. How do you dress to run in temperatures this cold?

I was wearing running underwear, running long-underwear, running pants and a pair of running shorts. I doubled-up my socks and was wearing two, long-sleeved running shirts. I also had on a running jacket, two pairs of gloves and wrist bands. I was grateful that the swag bag for the race included a head band. I wrapped it around my ears. I had brought ear muffs, but they broke when I tried to put them on.

WISCONSIN
Sights Along the Way

Easter Island Head

The Bronze Fonz

Lady Bug Building

Harley Davidson Museum

Frank Lloyd Wright designed home

Lake Michigan

Lincoln Statue at Lake

Mitchell Park Conservatory

Old North Point Water Tower

Pickup Truck in Tree

Even with all of that clothing on, I was frozen. At least I was until we started to run, then the body temperature came up, and I was actually okay except for my nose. I was very grateful that for the previous 6 weeks I had grown a full beard and mustache.

Not everyone layered up for this event. 47-year-old Robert Zimmerman had a very different take on how to dress. Robert showed up wearing only an old-school wrestling singlet, knee-high socks, sunglasses, and the swag-bag headband. I doubt his handle bar mustache offered much cold-weather protection.

When I say "old school" wrestling singlet, I mean the type that only has the very thin straps that cover the nipples or, as in Robert's case, didn't really cover them at all. He looked more like he was wearing skin-tight shorts with suspenders. Frankly, he looked ridiculous, and I am sure he knew it.

His "outfit" garnered a lot of attention, quite a few laughs, and many pointing fingers. He was quite the spectacle and took center stage when he could. When we lined up to race, we stood front-and-center. I couldn't believe he was not suffering from the cold, much less that he was actually going to run dressed like that.

A funny thing happened when the gun went off for the race. Robert took off. He ran. He was gone. I don't think anyone was laughing anymore. He put himself out there in such a fun and silly way, but he had what it takes to back it up. The man can run and run he did!

There were 283 participants in the HOG's 'Stache Dash and Robert came in 11th with an incredibly fast time of 22:35. I was pleased with my official race time of 23:50, but the Nike+ indicated 23:58. It was also a 1/10 of a mile off so the actual 5K time for me would have been an incredibly low 24. It was one of my best runs.

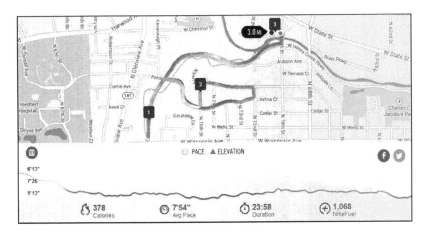

After the Stache' Dash, I went out for a wonderful brunch with Reto and Kate. We suffered through a long walk in the cold to a terrific restaurant and traded travel stories. Like many of the wonderful people I have met along the way, they have become really good "Facebook friends." It's fantastic that so many people have maintained the connection after our serendipitous introductions.

Kate and Reto Gugerli relax post-race with Jeff Fazio.

Brunch was followed by exploring Milwaukee on my own. I was spending the night in the city on some strangers' couch. Apparently, I wasn't the only one with that idea as my Couch Surfing hosts had a full house, or rather, a full living room. The couple I was staying with pretty much accept any Surfers they can physically accommodate.

On their living room wall hang two gigantic maps—one of the U.S. and one of the world. They have their Surfers use a black Sharpie to sign their names over their home cities. These maps are covered—literally, cities all over the world. It was impressive.

The array of people staying with them that night was equally impressive and just as worldly. I was on the couch. Next to me, on the floor in a sleeping bag was a gentleman from Ecuador. At the other end of the room was a row of sleeping bags that kept three female travelers warm. They were from Japan, South Korea, and Brazil. Three continents and five countries were represented by the handful of people staying over that night—only in the world of Couch Surfing!

***

Wisconsin Leadership Lesson:
Risking Ridicule

In Chapter 3 (Undy 500) and Chapter 20 (Bare As You Dare 5K) we talked about the benefits of leaders getting outside of their comfort zones to meet their goals. What about risking ridicule? If you knew you had the perform-ance to back up a ridiculous display and it would benefit your long-term goals, would you do it?

I don't know what Robert Zimmerman's agenda was. Maybe he is just the stereotypical class clown. Maybe he lost a bet. Maybe he misread the weather forecast.

Or maybe, he was embracing his own mission and found a way to meet his goals through a unique public display. Who knows? He might own a wrestling singlet manufacturing company and wanted to demonstrate how they hold up under extreme duress.

Most likely I will never know, but what I do know is that he had the performance to back up his display. He drew everyone's attention and ran with it (literally). He also made everyone smile.

Muscular Dystrophy Facts from the Centers for Disease Control and Prevention

"Economic costs pertaining specifically to DBMD have not been reported. The MarketScan Commercial Claims and Encounters Database for the period 2001-2004, which includes paid medical and prescription drug claims of people covered by employer-sponsored health insurance, was used to calculate money spent on care for all types of MD.

The yearly average cost in 2004 for medical care for privately insured individuals with any type of muscular dystrophy was $18,930, ranging from $13,464 at 5 through 9 years of age to $32,541 at 15 through 19 years of age."

Source: www.cdc.gov/ncbddd/musculardystrophy/facts.html

Chapter 34

Run for the Red
DeWitt, Iowa
November 24, 2013

With a 1-year goal in place, some states were simply not going to receive a lot of exploration time—Iowa was one of them. To get to the Iowa event, I entered the state by barely 20 miles from the east and the sum total of my Iowa experience was confined to less than 4 hours. Although not much, that proved to be more than enough time to meet some fantastic people, have a great 5K run, and have a few minutes left for a TV news interview.

So my Iowan readers do not feel completely slighted, I did spend some time exploring the western side of the State when I was in Omaha, NE. Honestly, that wasn't much time either. Sorry, Iowa, I didn't get to see much of you.

What I did see, was DeWitt, IA, on a Sunday: small town America, angled downtown parking, churchgoing traffic, and the one police officer who pulled out to follow the out-of-state rental car I was driving clear across town (all 12 blocks) to make sure I wasn't up to no good. DeWitt is quaint.

The run was taking place on the Paul Skeffington Memorial Trail in Westbrook Park, and with registration at the Lions Shelter—which is exactly where I went to sign up for the Run for the Red 5K.

*"**Run for the Red:** Take this opportunity to help us show the community and your employees, members, students how much fun wellness can be – all the while supporting the work of YOUR American Red Cross. Help us exceed our past event participation record of 175 runners/walkers."*

In what was going to become a theme for the next 4 months, the day was cold. I even planned "warm" states over the winter and each had a cold front come in (literally) the night before I arrived. Iowa was no different. With such chilly weather, everyone huddled around the heaters in the pavilion at registration.

At one point I ducked out to use one of the luxurious bathrooms that decorate 5K venues across the nation—the portable toilet. I always enter one of these plastic hovels to take care of a pre-race sprinkle. Although having to pee can sometimes provide a faster race time, it also makes for a very uncomfortable 5K. Have no fear, I did not find a leadership lessons to share from inside this vestibule of human waste. I mention this experience only because of what took place as soon as I exited.

As I looked around, I noticed a nice-looking, young gentleman with camera and a large lens pointed directly at me. Having participated in all sorts of events in my life, I have gotten used to cameras being pointed at me *during the activity*—not when leaving a portable restroom.

I always try to find out who a photographer is shooting for so I can find the images later online, I walked his way. When I got to him, he was engaged in a phone call so I waited. That is when I noticed three other people standing near him also carrying impressive camera equipment. I said hello and asked them what they were shooting. They said hello and shot each other concerned looks. It seemed they didn't want to answer my question.

About that time, the first guy ended his phone call and said hello. I asked him what his group was shooting and he gave his friends a quick look. He looked back at me oddly and said, "You."

I said, "Excuse me, I don't understand."

He replied, "We are here to shoot you. Your name is Jeff—right? You're running all 50 states?"

I was blown away. He said he had seen my picture online and the 4D pin on my shirt confirmed my identity. Who was he shooting for? I had to know. He explained that he and his friends are part of the Ashford State University Photography Club. He said the race director contacted them about covering the event and asked them to make sure they got photos of the guy running a 5K in all 50 states.

Jeff Fazio poses with the paparazzi from Ashford University, from left, Adam Cauley, Christie Dillie, Alexander Richie, and Melody Williams.

How cool was that? It was a very small taste of celebrity, and it surely gave a boost to my ego. It was a really great feeling and a pleasure to meet Alexander Richie and his fellow club members, Christie Dillie, Melody Williams, and Adam Cauley. We chatted for a while, and I thanked them for coming out, especially on such a cold day.

While we were talking, I noticed the local news, WHBF-TV CBS Channel 4, setting up equipment. I made my way over and landed a 60-second spot talking about the 4D campaign. It was a great opportunity to share the story, and I was grateful for the newscaster taking the time to hear Dee's and my story.

When the race started, I was keenly aware of the ASU students' cameras all along course. It was a surreal feeling running knowing that there was a talented group of strangers around the course taking your photo. Having just photographed Kristy's Philly Marathon the previous weekend, I could relate to what these students were doing—running from one location to another trying to get as many photos as possible while the "target" keeps moving. I kept seeing Alexander's red jacket. At times, I could hear the rapid clicking of their shutters.

The course was relatively flat with some undulations, and I was pleased turning in a 23:51 for the 3-mile course. The course, by my Nike+, was .1 short, which would have pushed me well into the 24s, so the Washington, D.C., record was still firm.

Iowa was done. That was 31 states and D.C. in the bag: 60% of the country was completed in the first 5 months, and I still had another weekend left in the month. Surely I could squeeze 3 or 4 more states in before the end of November.

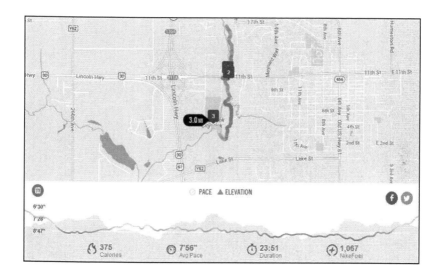

***

Iowa Leadership Lesson:
Be Prepared for Paparazzi

When you take on a goal worthy of attention, you just might receive it. It had been nearly 5 months since the guys at the Van Cortlandt Track Club in New York City gave me the "yeah, right" look about running a 5K in all 50 states. At the rate I was pounding states into the log books, there were few doubters left. This goal was being accomplished and people were starting to talk about it.

Once you achieve and advance in a leadership experience, you have to anticipate the news and the paparazzi. It is worthwhile to engage those interested in covering your story. It helps spread the word on your mission, externally substantiates your achievements, and opens doors to critique and observations those close to you might miss. And let's be honest, talking to the news is kind of cool.

Depending on your particular leadership position, talking to the press may be a downright necessity. If you are confident in your goal and secure in your position, talking to journalists should come easily and be an opportunity you seek.

The news is always looking for the news. Make it easy for them to find.

Muscular Dystrophy Facts from the Centers for Disease Control and Prevention

"The Centers for Disease Control and Prevention (CDC) funds the Muscular Dystrophy Surveillance Tracking and Research Network, known as MD STARnet. MD STARnet is collecting critical information about muscular dystrophy that will improve care for those living with the disease."

Source: www.cdc.gov/ncbddd/musculardystrophy/facts.html

Chapter 35

Howell Fantasy 5K
Howell, Michigan
November 29, 2013

Like millions of Americans, I got up extremely early on Black Friday. Unlike millions of Americans, I got up extremely early to drive over 8 hours to an evening 5K several states away.

In fact, I might be the only American who did that. Even if I am not, I am positive I am the only one who did so after running a 5K the day before and 2 on the day after. What can I say? Goals do not achieve themselves.

If you are ever concerned about the outrageously high calories you consume on Thanksgiving, I assure you running four 5Ks in four states in 3 days is a proactive way to combat bulge. I am certain I lost weight over Thanksgiving weekend 2013.

On November 29, 2013, Black Friday, I was on the road by 6:00 a.m. to drive from Harrisburg, PA, to Howell, MI, for a 6:00 p.m. 5K. The previous day, Thanksgiving, I joined the ladies from the Tuesday night running group for a Turkey Trot 5K at home.

My 3-day plan was to reunite with friends for the run in Pennsylvania and then leave early Friday for Michigan. From there, I would drive a few hours overnight toward Chicago, where I would run a 5K in Grant Park at 9:00 a.m. on Saturday to complete Illinois. If I left Chicago immediately after the run, I would have precisely enough time to make a 3:00 p.m. run in Indianapolis, IN.

My goal was to be on the road after the Chicago race by 10:00 a.m. to make the 3-hour drive to Indianapolis. Since that journey crosses the boundary of the Central and Eastern Time zones, I would lose an hour, making it effectively a 4-hour trip. That places me in Indianapolis at 2:00 p.m.—one hour before race time. My desire is always to be at an event roughly an hour prior to the start so I can check-in, gather my materials, and get ready to run.

This plan was contingent on nothing going wrong. My itinerary for this trip was so tight that I did not have time on Saturday for lunch, traffic, getting lost, or cracking the radiator in my car. I had packed plenty of snacks to ward off lunch, I travel with two GPSs so no worries on getting lost, and my driving abilities tend to get me through even the worst traffic.

The only thing I wasn't prepared for was the car's coolant system failing on one of the first truly cold weekends of the year.

***

I went through Hell to get to Howell, MI.

It wasn't exactly on my way, but I made it a point to stop. Most people wouldn't go out of their way to get to Hell, but I did. Hell is about 3 miles southwest of Pinckney, MI. The unofficial census says that population of Hell is 266. If that number is close to being accurate, then many religions have it wrong as to how many people actually end up in Hell.

Hell was not as I have been told my whole life it would be. None of my friends were there. I was allowed to leave. Truth be told, it wasn't even hot in Hell. In fact, it was pretty darn cold. They even sell T-shirts indicating that Hell has frozen over

Welcome to Hell.

and, being in Michigan, there is no doubting the truth of that statement.

Hell was what I expected it to be—a tiny tourist trap. It was worth the stop. The town is very small. It would be easy to drive right through it and not know it except for the two tacky tourist shops screaming all sorts of HELL messages announcing your arrival. As you can imagine, the two shops have a lot of fun at the expense of the town's name.

Beyond those two stores, there isn't much else noteworthy. There is a church. Yes, you read that right. There is a church in Hell. One of the novelty store proprietors said the church does host weddings. In his words, "A marriage that starts in Hell can only go up."

Once per year, the town hosts a late-night, naked 5K. Crazy. Who would run a 5k naked?

***

Somewhere between Hell and Howell, the temperature gauge in my car started to rise. Not enough to cause concern, but enough to catch my eye. I kept driving and I made my way into Howell, MI, and located the church where the race registration was located. I was blown away when I saw the main street of Howell. It was lined on both sides, in both directions, with hundreds of folding chairs. The police were starting to block off streets.

I couldn't believe that this many spectators would come out to a 5K. This town must really be supportive of racing, I thought. After walking around and talking to the locals, I realized that our 5K was 6:00 p.m. and the Parade of Lights was at 7:00 p.m. How brilliant! Having the 5K an hour before a huge holiday parade was a great way to bring out spectators to encourage the runners.

Another key feature of this event was the layout of the route. We started on a side street next to the church and immediately made a right onto the main street, running for a half mile in front of hundreds of spectators, music, and announcers, until we turned around and ran back. After running three quarters of a mile in that direction, we turned around again and ran a full mile back down the same street, in front of the same spectators. At the end of that mile, we turned around one more time, and ran passed everyone for a fourth time on our way to the finish. It was sort of like a human version of the carnival game Duck Shoot.

The overall effect was a magnified sense of runners and spectators. They really got the most mileage out of the event. I have never seen a course designed where any spectator could see so much of a race without moving position.

The town was lit up—literally—for this event. The feeling of the holiday season was everywhere. I was glad I was able to compete in the Howell Fantasy 5K.

> **"Howell Fantasy 5K:** *Light up the night in the Fantasy 5K Run, a nighttime run down Grand River in downtown Howell. As part of the Fantasy of Lights Parade festivities, the run starts at 6 p.m. at the First Presbyterian Church."*

Even after driving 8 hours and exploring all day, I posted a decent time (for me) of 24:19. That was good for only 8th in my age group

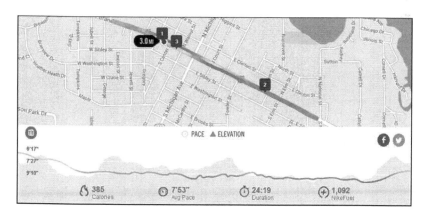

***

Hanging out in Howell for the after-race parade was not an option. I had a couple hours of driving to do to get to my motel in Indiana, and I needed a really good night of rest as I was running two 5Ks the next day. There was also the concern of getting my car out of its on-street parking spot and away from of the vicinity before the parade started. Having closed roads trap me was a serious concern. I fired up the car and GPS and headed out of town.

Once onto the highway, the coolant temperature in my car escalated at an alarming rate. There was also a need for refueling, so I made a stop for gas and to see what was going on with my radiator. My coolant was low. I surmised that since I had been using more water than coolant over the last year or so, I may have lost a lot over time to evaporation. I hadn't checked it in forever. I added some coolant and was on my way.

The temperature held rock-steady for nearly an hour before the engine overheated again. By the time I got to the next exit, the car was full-blown smoking, and spewing my recently purchased coolant everywhere. Strangely, I lost the heat inside the car, which is a bit of an automotive oxymoron— overheating engine and no cabin heat.

Anyway, I added more coolant and got back onto the highway. I had two more states, two more 5Ks, and over 1,000 miles of driving to go. Although it was freezing inside my car, this trip was really beginning to feel like Hell.

> **MICHIGAN**
> *Sights Along the Way*
>
> *Pete's Garage Restaurant*
>
> *Wm C. Sterling State Park*
>
> *Lake Erie*
>
> *Sculpture of Jesus sitting at a Table with 12 empty seats*
>
> *Hell*

***

Michigan Leadership Lesson:
Going Through Hell to Meet Goals

When you take on a serious goal, all sorts of obstacles will come your way. At times, it will seem like you are going through Hell to achieve your goals. If you set a high enough goal for yourself, it will be challenging to achieve; otherwise, everyone else would have done it. Those challenges are when your resolve will be tested. There will be tough times, but therein lies the heroic stories for future telling.

Ironically, when I was in Hell, MI, I thought that I might eventually write a chapter on going through Hell to meet your goals. I thought this chapter would be a bit tongue-in-cheek, since I literally drove through Hell (the town) to get to the 5K. Little did I know that I would actually drive through Hell (over a 1,000 miles of driving on a cracked radiator) in order to get home.

I went through 5 bottles of coolant and numerous unplanned stops, but I did it. I made it through Hell and lived to tell. So can you.

Chapter 36

Grant Park Turkey Trot 5K
Chicago, Illinois
November 30, 2013

If you are going to run three 5Ks inside 21 hours in three different states and do all of the driving that this task requires, you had better have a plan. My strategy for this weekend was pretty straightforward. I was going to run my ass off in Michigan and go for my best possible time. The early-morning Chicago run was going to be a time to take it easy, since I would need to run again in a few hours. The afternoon 5K in Indianapolis was a trail run, which tends to be on softer ground, easier on the legs. I figured that would be a good thing as I anticipated my legs getting tired from the first two races and sitting stagnant in a car for hours between.

The Chicago run was downtown in Grant Park and was aptly named the Grant Park Turkey Trot 5K.

> *"**Grant Park Turkey Trot 5K:** Come run or walk a 5k the Saturday just after Thanksgiving at Chicago's famous Grant Park. Work off your thanksgiving feast with family and friends and don't forget to bring the little ones for the Free Kid's Dash. All 5k participants receive a long sleeve souvenir shirt. The run benefits Playworks. Playworks is reducing bullying, making kids feel safer, returning classroom time back to teachers for instruction, all while getting students more physically active."*

Chicago is a big city. Grant Park is a big park. Upon entering the park, it was not clear where registration was and a runner had just slowed for a break near me. I asked her where the registration was for the 5K. She sarcastically laughed and asked, "Which one?" I said, "The one here, in Grant Park." She replied, "Yeah well, there are like three of them today. Good luck" and ran off while putting her ear buds back in.

Now I was really confused. Not because I couldn't find the event, but because I suddenly felt like I was back East in New York or something. Thanks for the attitude, fellow runner.

Wandering through the park, it was clear there were multiple events going on. There was much activity and different race bibs. It almost felt like a running festival (*if there are such things*).

This event was put together very well. Not only were runners getting a beautiful finisher's medal, but the race swag included a hoodie. When most

5Ks are handing out t-shirts, getting a quality hoodie was a pleasant surprise.

I felt good and I was ready to run. Grant Park sits right between downtown Chicago and Lake Michigan. It is beautifully trapped between skyscrapers and the Great Lake. I can only imagine how amazing this park must look in all its glory during springtime. Since my plan was to take this run easy, it was the perfect time to run with the camera, like I did in D.C.

ILLINOIS
Sights Along the Way

Gold Pyramid House

Ferris Bueller's Day Off Garage Scene Location

Grant Park

Lake Michigan

Downtown Chicago

Unlike other runs, I did not push my way toward the front of the pack at the starting line. This was my time to cruise and not stress about race time. I was going to simply enjoy a run through the park.

When the race started, I was enjoying myself, taking photos of the tall buildings and shooting some hard-to-time selfies along the Lake. It was a fairly relaxing run—that is, as relaxed as you can get while running with hundreds of strangers in a metropolitan city.

Coming across the finish line, I was surprised to see my finishing time starting with a 25. After many runs ending in the low 24s, I figured running at a casual pace would have put me well into the 27s or 28s. The course was perfectly mapped out at 3.1 miles and my Nike+ time was 25:40. I wasn't sure if I should be happy that I ran so well taking it easy or if I should be bothered that I burned up more energy than I was planning on before my afternoon run.

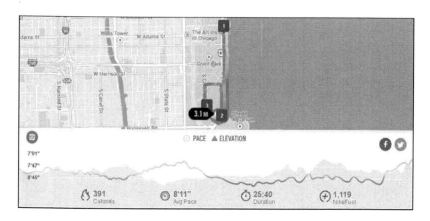

Speaking of that run, I needed to get going. I had just enough time to get from Chicago to Indianapolis and my car was still bleeding coolant. This 3-hour drive was going to be an adventure for sure.

At least the Indy run was a trail run and the soft ground would be easy on my legs and knees—right?

**

Illinois Leadership Lesson:
Permission to Take It Easy

Leaders wouldn't be in their roles if they didn't get things done. The motivation that moves leaders to achievement at times also pushes them to exhaustion. When you are leading, especially on a huge project, it is easy to burn yourself out. Look for times to take it easy, and give yourself permission to do so. These times of rest can be crucial for allowing you to energize and reinvigorate. Sometimes slowing down allows you to go faster; ask any race car driver.

Another key point of slowing down is that it is not stopping. There is still forward movement. There is still progress toward the goal. Well-timed relaxation periods may provide the opportunity to be better prepared what is coming next. That is why race car drivers sometimes slowdown in order to go faster. It sounds like an oxymoron, but it is isn't.

Imagine a race car going as fast as possible down a short straightaway. That car is going to need to brake heavily to slow down for the next turn. Braking hard kills momentum, and that momentum needs to be built back up after exiting the corner. If the corner is followed by a really long straight section, then that lost momentum will negatively affect the elapsed time.

It may be smarter to not go as fast on the short straight so you can carry more momentum through the turn and exit at a higher speed. That small advantage will be magnified on that long straight. Make sure you take it slow before your long straights, and you, too, will reap the benefits.

Muscular Dystrophy Facts from the Centers for Disease Control and Prevention

"In late 2014, CDC awarded grants for the next phase of MD STARnet research. These organizations and the states or regions where they will collect data are:

University of Iowa, Colorado Department of Health and Environment, New York State Department of Health, Research Triangle Institute, South Carolina Department of Public Health & Environmental Control, University of Utah."

Source: www.cdc.gov/ncbddd/musculardystrophy/facts.html

Chapter 37

Leftover Turkey Trail Run
Indianapolis, Indiana
November 30, 2013

As I crossed the finish line at the Chicago event, I slowed to a walk, grabbed my medal, grabbed a handful of the finishers' snacks (granola bars and bananas) and kept going. I had no time to waste. A quick stop at the portable restroom was followed by a short jog back to the car a few blocks away. Those snacks were "lunch," and I really needed my car to behave for a few hours to get to Indianapolis.

Having completed so many states, I was used to running and jumping in a car for a long drive; however, my legs hated it. They get stiff and sore. At times, they don't even want to move when I try to get out of the car, much less support my body weight. I tried to do miniature leg lifts and calf flexes while I drove.

My car mostly behaved on the ride. I needed only one stop to add coolant. Traffic mostly behaved too. I made it on time to the Leftover Turkey Trail Run just outside of Indianapolis, IN.

> *"**Leftover Turkey Trail Run:** For most of us, the weekend after Thanksgiving is synonymous with one thing: leftover turkey. But now you have something else to look forward to: Upland's Leftover Turkey Trail Run and Novemberfest! Join us for a chip-timed run through Eagle Creek Park followed by a party featuring an open beer bar, food, and live music."*

My sore legs were grateful to see the field that spread out in front of the registration tables. The ground looked and felt soft. This was going to be a swift run through fields and woods while not taxing my knees too much. After running two events on hard asphalt, the actual Earth was going to be joyously forgiving to my bouncing feet.

This event featured a 10K in addition to the 5K. The longer-distance runners headed out 15 minutes before us and took a different path. I was anticipating having a fast run and getting started on my 8+ hour drive home (car issues ultimately made it closer to 9.5 hours).

The 5K'ers got their start and I was out front where I like to be at the beginning of a race. Strange thing, the ground felt significantly softer when running than when I was walking across it. It had rained the night before, so the turf was saturated. No worries, the water just made the surface even softer on the ole legs.

I lost steam just beyond the first quarter mile and my pace slowed more than normal. We also left the field and entered woods, where things started to get a tad trickier—narrower and more tree roots.

About three quarters of a mile into the run, we started to descend. I picked up some of the speed I had lost, but something else was changing drastically—the quality of the ground. We dropped about 80' in elevation in a short time. All the water that had made the ground above soft had found its way down to this lower elevation and terrain changed abruptly to mud.

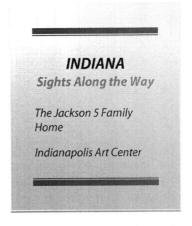

INDIANA
Sights Along the Way

The Jackson 5 Family Home

Indianapolis Art Center

Running through woods, avoiding tree roots and rocks while nearly leaping on what you are hoping is dry ground between all of the clearly muddy spots is incredibly stressful. The course was also getting significantly narrower as it was the width of only one-and-a-half bodies.

I misjudged what looked like a piece of solid ground and my foot slid away from me, twisting my knee and summarily notifying me of its extreme displeasure. There were two immediate consequences to this—pain and a lack of trust in my footing.

My heart rate and breathing accelerated their already intense pace. This was turning out awful. I slowed. I had to. Even with this adjusted pace, I managed to step more than a handful of times in places I shouldn't have, twisting the other knee or an ankle. So much for a trail run being easier on my legs. So much for thinking I had escaped Hell.

Regardless of the situation, there were two things that compelled me to keep running. The first is the thing that always keeps me moving when a run is horrible or painful or grossly hilly—Dee. She can't do this, so I need to. Secondly, I was in the middle of the woods and I needed to get out in order to see my car again. I pressed on.

As I was questioning my sanity for continuing at anything resembling a running pace, I saw runners coming at me. How could this be? This path wasn't wide enough for two runners. Were these the 10K runners using our path in the opposite direction? No, I recognized these guys. They had passed me at the start of the 5K.

This had all sorts of horrible implications. I would have to run back up the muddy drop that I came down. The bulk of the race field was behind me, which meant that I would have to negotiate running past them on this limited footpath on my way back. It also signified that I hadn't even made it to the halfway point. I wanted my mommy.

As the front runners came at me, we instinctively made side steps to share the path and avoid each other. On a few occasions there was just enough room for us to pass without much concern, but it was incredible having someone pass you so close by, at speed, while you are avoiding rocks, roots, mud, and whatever else was out there. There was no thinking, just reacting—fast-paced reacting.

My pace had dropped to nearly 12-minute miles, but I was still moving forward. When I reached the turnaround point, I found some motivation and picked up my pace. I wanted this experience to end. I wanted to see that finish line. I was now the salmon and the stream was the bulk of slower runners coming at me.

I ran up a rise in front and as I crested the hill I noticed, too late, two women running toward me, together. For some reason, they thought it would be fine to run next to each other (as much as you could) and talk. This course was not conducive to running with a friend like that. My brain had only enough time to read this situation as I shouldered the woman closest to me and nearly sent her sailing backward. It was a solid hit and how neither of us fell over is beyond me. My legs kept moving, without stumbling, and I was vaguely aware that she was continuing on. This was getting worse and I wasn't even back to the incline.

My pace flagged between 10 and 12 minute miles. When I hit the ascent, pace plummeted to the bottom of that range and my feet fought to find a way up without sliding. It might be worth mentioning that *trail runners* have trail running shoes. Since I run everything, I just have standard running shoes, which are not designed for this abuse. My knees reminded me of this frequently. I needed to be done with this one.

Elation set in when I made my way back onto the field. The claustrophobia of the woods was behind me and my pace picked up, but not much even though I found that "little extra" as my body screamed to see the finish.

So many people passed me on that open field that any chance I had of placing reasonably well was shot. I wasn't sure how many people passed me on the course. The more I thought about it, the more I couldn't recall many people passing me, as the trail was so narrow.

My time was horrible at 28:56. That was 16 seconds slower than the first race I entered with the 4D on my chest and suffered up that terrible hill—twice. 28:56 was also 27 seconds slower than my first ever 5K back in

April before I started to train specifically for 5Ks. This run would not hold great memories for me, but it was done.

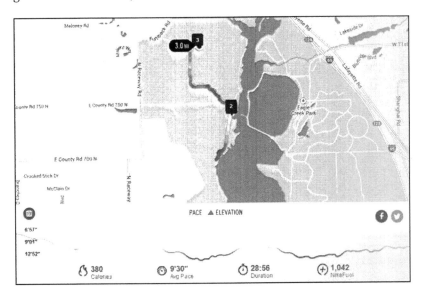

PACE ▲ ELEVATION

6'57"
9'01"
12'52"

380 Calories   9'30" Avg Pace   28:56 Duration   1,042 NikeFuel

***

Life sometimes plays tricks on us. It turned out that most of the runners who passed me in the field were 10K runners. It was also true that not many people passed me out on that treacherous course. My "horrible" time was good enough to place me 9th overall out of 159 competitors.

***

I would not stop to see the sights in Indiana that I had planned to. My car was broken. My body was battered. My brain was exhausted, but I'd done it, I'd run three 5Ks in three states in under 24 hours. The ride home was long and filled with many stops to let the car cool down and refill coolant. It was one of the worst drives of my life, but I still had an overall sense of immense satisfaction.

Back on August 27 I had sent that e-mail to Dee indicating I might be able to accomplish 25 states by January 1. Rounding up these states finished off 26 in just three months (Sept.–Nov.). Indiana was the 34th State completed, and it happened exactly 5 months from the start of this project in New York. Knocking these three states out also checked off another section of the United States: the Midwest was now complete.

Before I left on this trip, I had said that this would be the worst of it. It was. I survived. I was still running for those who can't.

Indiana Leadership Lesson:
Slippery Slopes

_____

Leaders plan out solid paths forward. No matter how much planning is done, no matter how solid the path forward appears, there will be spots with slippery slopes. The drops will set you back and twist your path. They might even leave you hurt, but they do not have to beat you. Like any obstacle, the slippery slopes are navigable. They may require slowing down, being more cautious. In the end, you will still be moving forward. You will still be making progress.

Be aware of slippery slopes, but do not fear them.

***

After this trip I enjoyed dinner with a good friend and colleague, Rose Miller. She had made a comment that what I was doing was terrific, but she wished I was seeing more of each state—spending more time exploring. I said, "Really?" and asked, "Have you looked at my Facebook photo albums?"

She replied, "No, every time you post photos there is 200-300 images. I am just not going to go through all of that!"

"And you wish I was seeing more? How many more photos would be in my albums?" I asked. She laughed at that point. In another 4 months, I would punctuate that last laugh when Rose joined me on one of my trips. She got to see firsthand just how much of each state I was able to see in a short visit.

Muscular Dystrophy Facts *from the Centers for Disease Control and Prevention*

"Soon after birth, all babies born in the United States are checked for certain medical conditions. This is called newborn screening. Finding these conditions soon after birth can help prevent some serious problems, such as brain damage, organ damage, and even death. Each state decides which conditions are tested among newborns.

It is possible to test for DMD at birth, but currently it is not part of newborn screening for a number of reasons, most notably the lack of a proven intervention that must be administered very early in life to prevent death and disability."

Source: www.cdc.gov/ncbddd/musculardystrophy/facts.html

Chapter 38

Come Run with Santa 5K
Las Vegas, Nevada
December 21, 2013

A side benefit of this mission was reconnecting with long-lost friends. A couple of hundred years ago (actually 8 years) my friend Ron Paukovits and his wonderful wife, Nanette, moved from Pennsylvania to Phoenix, AZ. Ron would probably switch the order of that and tell you that Nanette moved to Phoenix and brought Ron (and his toys) along with her. The truth is, they moved together to start a new life in a place devoid of snow shovels.

NEVADA
Sights Along the Way

Las Vegas Strip

Valley of Fire

Hoover Dam

Ron is an old racing buddy—cars, not running. We keep up with each other on Facebook, but haven't had a chance to really connect in years. Sometime, before I started Couch Surfing, I asked on Facebook whether anyone had friends I might be able to stay with in other states. Ron was the first to respond, and said he would gladly host me in Arizona. This was no surprise as Ron has always been the guy to offer help—even to strangers.

After his offer came through, I scoured race listings to see what state could be connected with Phoenix, AZ, and, preferably, over the colder Pennsylvania winter months. I found a pair of races in the same weekend in Las Vegas, NV, and Phoenix, AZ. The cities are about 5 hours apart, which was as good as I could hope for.

Plans were made. Flights were booked. I was going to see Ron and Nanette the weekend before Christmas.

***

I can be a foolish romantic. Throughout these months of running, I had it in mind that I could run all 50 states on the same pair of shoes. I fantasized about building some sort of showcase for that pair of shoes. I dreamt of going back in time and buying a red-white-and-blue pair specifically for this mission. I wanted to point at a *single pair* of shoes and say those are *the ones*.

This would have been a reality if I hadn't been racing on the same shoes that I was using for training and other events. At nearly 300 miles on the odometer, my shoes were toast. The pain in my knees after my Black Friday triple-race weekend confirmed that they were no longer giving needed support. It was time to let them go.

Although, I bought a new pair of shoes, when I flew into Las Vegas, I carried those old ones with me. I just couldn't let them go.

***

Working in higher education has great time-off benefits. Luckily, my college was closed for over a week during the holidays. This allowed me to slate 6 races between December 21 and January 1 in what were, presumably, warmer states. I even had time to stop at home for Christmas.

This leg of the 4D 50-State 5K mission began when I took off for Las Vegas on December 20. Ron picked me up at the Vegas airport at 11:30 p.m. My race was scheduled for 7:00 the next morning. The good thing about 7:00 a.m. races is that you have the entire day after to do whatever you want. The bad thing about 7:00 a.m. races is that they are at 7:00 a.m.

With such an early start, my reunion with Ron on Friday night was short lived, or rather postponed, until after the race. I needed to grab what sleep I could before the run. As I fell asleep it occurred to me that I hadn't needed a rental car or hotel reservations. Ron had taken care of everything.

I didn't know where the race was in relation to the hotel. The pair of GPS units that I typically travel with were safe at home in my car. My on-time arrival for this event was 100% in Ron's capable hands. As someone who is Type A, or rather Type **A**, I found it hard to give up so much of my planning. I was on a trip without an itinerary. My fate was not under my control.

Yet, I knew everything was going to be alright. Ron had this.

***

Ron had me up early and on time for the Come Run with Santa 5K.

"Come Run with Santa 5K: 15th Annual Come Run with Santa 5K & 1 Mile Walk."

When I imagined running a 5K in Las Vegas, I saw glitz, lights, show girls, and random men dressed as Elvis. I anticipated a circus of humans. Running a race in Vegas just sounds like a spectacular thing to do.

The reality of this event is that it was hosted at a Chevrolet dealership just off an Interstate exit. The course took us around the block that surrounds the dealership twice and then down the service road that runs parallel to I-215. There was a turnaround point and we headed back for another trip around the block to the finish line.

The dealership and highway were a scene right out of "Geography of Nowhere." The only saving grace was the backdrop of desert which was barely noticeable beyond the mundane foreground. There was not much to see or do between the start and the finish line 3.1 miles away. The multiple laps around the same block gave the vague impression of being inside a human hamster wheel. We kept going around and were still seemingly in the same spot.

I had a decent run at 25:17. Taking into account the long flight, the lack of sleep, the new shoes and the somewhat high elevation (over 2000'), I was pleased with my result. It wasn't earning any medals, but it was still a decent time.

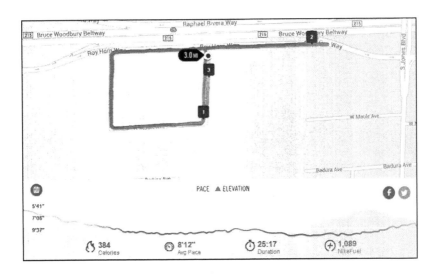

***

Nevada Leadership Lesson:
Knowing When to Give Up

Part of being a good leader is knowing when to give something up. Sometimes you must give up control. Other times you might have to part with an item that outlived its usefulness. It can be hard to part with articles that seem integral to your goals. Realizing that something incredibly useful one day now lacks functional value today can be taxing.

Could I have run all 50 States on the same pair of shoes? Yes, of course. I would have needed to plan it better. Although I could have physically run the last 16 states on those original sneakers, what would have been the cost to my legs? To my knees? To my back? It was time to give them up, and I had to admit it and accept it.

Another, larger element that I gave up on this trip was control. Here I was, in the middle of one of the biggest endeavors of my life, and I gave up complete control of getting myself to and from events. My success in these two states rested completely in trusting that Ron would get me to both events on time.

The new running shoes did what they were designed to do. Ron did what I trusted him to do. Giving things up isn't always bad. It was nice to enjoy a trip without having to worry about details or deal with driving. I suspect that Ron might not realize how big his gift to me was or how much I appreciated it.

Muscular Dystrophy Facts from the Centers for Disease Control and Prevention

"Facioscapulohumeral muscular dystrophy is named for the areas in the body that are affected most often: muscles in the face (facio-), around the shoulder blades (scapula-) and in the upper arms (humeral). Weakness in the facial muscles can make it difficult to turn up the corners of the mouth when smiling, drink from a straw, or whistle. Weak shoulder muscles tend to make the shoulder blades "stick out" from the back, and weakness in the shoulders and upper arms can make it difficult to raise the arms overhead. FSHD worsens slowly over decades and can lead to a condition called foot drop which affects walking and increases the risk of falls. Muscle weakness in the hips and pelvis can make it difficult to climb stairs or walk long distances."

Source: www.cdc.gov/ncbddd/musculardystrophy/facts.html

Chapter 39

5K Jingle Run
Phoenix, Arizona
December 22, 2013

Planning to run events in the "warm states" over the winter was the logical thing to do. However, Mother Nature cannot be outwitted. The schedule held 9 races from December through March. Every one of those states had a cold front come in the night I arrived. No matter where I traveled, no matter how far south or west, I was running in 30-degrees.

Arizona was no different. At least it was sunny.

Ron was amazing throughout this whole weekend. He took care of all of the driving and navigation. He and Nanette were splendid hosts. Ron's on-time-delivery service had me to the 5K Jingle Run with plenty of time to spare.

> *"5K Jingle Run: Join us on December 22nd 2013 at Bullard Wash for this wonderful event. With holiday spirits in the air, Race Timers will be hosting the 5K Jingle Run & 1 Mile Bell Run: Blanket & Toy Drive which will consist of a 5k Run/Walk and a 1 Mile Fun/Run/Walk. Both events will be chip timed by Race Timers using a disposable chip system. Blankets and toys will be donated to local charities in the Phoenix Metropolitan Area."*

I was excited for this run. The race was 1000' feet lower than Vegas, so there was a bounty of oxygen available. The course was flat. I felt strong in spite of the cold weather. This would be a good day.

There was not a huge turnout for this event—only 72 runners and 8 walkers. I had learned many states before that big numbers are not needed to have a terrific event. I made my way to the start line and Ron fired up the digital camera.

The course was fast and I ran strong. I chose not to watch my Nike+ throughout this event. My concentration was on running fast, not on monitoring my digitally-recorded pace. Intuitively, I knew I was doing well.

The miles flew by and I could see the blow-up arc of the finish line across the park. We had one last loop to complete and then it was slight downhill to the finish—always a great way to end a race strong.

I was elated when I crossed the finish line and finally looked at the Nike+. The little screen was flashing "Way To Go" and read 24:04. It was one of my quickest runs.

I made my way over to Ron. He showed me the photos he had taken of me, from crossing the start line through crossing the finish line. We walked back over toward timing as they had a flat screen with times and finishing places. When my age group popped up I was listed as 4th with a time in the 26s. The 26s? How could it be that far off? My Nike+ is typically within 1 or 2 seconds of official race time, not off by well over 2 minutes.

Ron suggested looking at the time stamp on the digital photos. The starting line photo was taken precisely 24:04 minutes before the finish line photo. With my watch and camera as evidence, I walked to the timing table.

ARIZONA
Sights Along the Way

Hoover Dam

Grand Canyon National Park

Monolith Garden Trail

Sedona

Wild Side Restaurant

Tempe, AZ, Waterfront

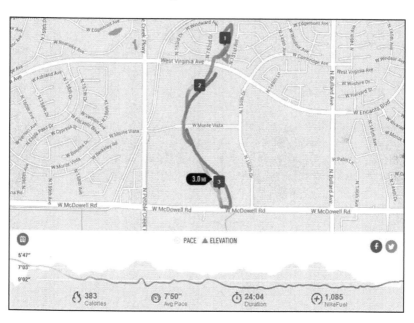

I explained to the lady at the table my concerns and asked if something was up with the times. She said she thinks everyone's times might be off by 2 minutes. She was looking through her materials and another runner came over to double check her time. She thought her listed time was too fast. She said it would be a huge PR for her. That being said, the 2 minutes would have drastically improved her time which didn't seem possible (to her).

The lady kept saying she thought something was wrong with everyone's time. In that case, it would not affect my finishing within group. As we were talking, the guy who was working the equipment at the finish line walked over and asked what was going on. We explained.

He said, "Yeah, I remember you finishing. For some reason it didn't beep and I was looking into it. I just ended up clicking you as done." I showed him the watch and camera and he adjusted my official race time to match my data. I went from finishing 4th in my class to finishing first.

I am so glad I took the time to ask and share the evidence that I had. It was the difference between leaving with a medal and leaving without one.

***

Arizona Leadership Lesson:
Challenge Appropriately

There are times in life when things simply do not add up. That should be a flag to ask questions. Results, data, information all matter. When something appears awry, gather your evidence and question the source appropriately.

What does appropriately mean? It means do not attack, but be inquisitive without passing judgment. If two people have sources of information that should match and do not, then one is clearly incorrect. Keep in mind it might be your mistake. If it is your mistake, how would you want the other person to approach you and point out the error? That is what challenging appropriately means.

Leaders need to be assertive, not aggressive. Without asserting yourself, it is easy to get walked over or miss opportunities. In my mind, I went back and forth on challenging the race results. I could have just left. It would have been easy enough and Ron wouldn't have been kept waiting. My life wouldn't have changed much by not receiving another medal. But in my heart, I felt something wasn't right, and that would have bothered me for a very long time. It was better to ask and to know.

***

I am convinced that accomplishing any goal that requires travel to all 50 states, especially in 1 year, requires either a tall pile of cash or a wide array of friends, family and the occasional stranger. I accept that I do not have tall piles of cash, so I am eternally grateful for being able to enjoy the latter. The 4D 50-State 5K Mission simply would not have been possible without the help of some truly great people. Ron and Nanette Paukovits are truly great people, and I am fortunate to call them friends.

An old African proverb says: "If you want to go fast, go alone. If you want to go far, go together." This adage was in my mind often throughout this experience. I find that both phrases applied to me at different times. Maybe the secret to getting through life is finding a balance between traveling alone and traveling with others.

Muscular Dystrophy Facts *from the Centers for Disease Control and Prevention*

"There is no specific treatment to prevent or stop muscular dystrophy. Physical and occupational therapy, respiratory therapy, speech therapy, orthopedic appliances, and assistive technology may improve quality of life. Medications can help maintain muscle strength."

Source: www.cdc.gov/ncbddd/musculardystrophy/facts.html

Chapter 40

Biggest Loser Run
Panama City Beach, Florida
December 29, 2013

Christmas Eve morning I returned home from the Las Vegas–Phoenix trip. I enjoyed a quiet holiday with my family and spent Christmas night packing for a 7-day road trip which would allow me to finish the remaining four states east of the Mississippi River: Mississippi, Florida, Georgia, and South Carolina. I had 6 couches set up for my travel and was grateful to save the expense of motels.

My car is getting older and memories of the 12-hour, stop-and-fill-the-coolant trip across the Midwest were still fresh in my mind. I rented a car for this 2,400-mile trip. Actually, a relative of Dee's paid for the rental car. Throughout this experience, all sorts of people stepped up and offered assistance.

On December 26, Pennsylvania sent me off on this trip with a 2-hour delay due to snow. Thankfully, it did not take long to escape the weather and make my way south to warmer, but not warm, weather. I spent two days driving from Harrisburg, PA, to Mobile, AL. My midway stopping point was Knoxville, TN.

This was my second time in Knoxville and the realization that I would be in Mobile for the second time the next day struck me. I was crisscrossing the nation enough now that I was starting to cross my own, previous paths.

My night in Knoxville was spent on the couch of a Trinidadian doctoral student studying in the U.S. a number of years and had a great appreciation for Couch Surfing. I awoke that morning to a distinct reminder that I was getting older. It was December 27. It was my birthday—a milestone. I turned 40 or rather, in the spirit of my mission, maybe it is more accurate to say I turned *4D*.

***

My birthday was spent exploring the state of Alabama. Although I had already checked this off my list, I didn't get to explore the state much on my first go around. Traveling through the state from the north would offer the opportunity to see many noteworthy sites.

During my trip through Alabama, I visited a national park and a local park that both included beautiful waterfalls: Little River Canyon National Preserve and Noccalula Falls Park.

The rest of the day I spent exploring the significant Civil Rights locations and memorials in Birmingham and Montgomery, AL, places where truly awful things happened to people because of the color of their skin. Too much of American History is ugly.

When I completed the drive for the day, I thought of the waterfalls and how they erode and cleanse the history of the environment while making it beautiful. I wish parts of Birmingham and Montgomery would turn into waterfalls

***

Couch Surfing hosts and those who surf are only strangers when they first meet. My experience has been that you typically leave with a new friend. And like most friends, it is great to keep in touch and see each other again.

If I was headed to Mobile, I was certainly going to visit Jayne Mosley again. It was such a pleasure meeting her the first time and her Southern hospitality is greatly appreciated. Jayne was the second person I met in my travels across the country who I was able to revisit.

The careful reader may have caught that the first state I was to run on this particular adventure was Mississippi, but this chapter is ultimately about the run in Florida. Jayne intended to ride along with me to the Mississippi run even though it meant a very early rise. We were both up and ready to go on time, but the forecast was less than friendly. It was already raining in Mobile and the wet weather was to arrive in Mississippi as well.

I had sent text messages to the two individuals listed as race directors to confirm the race was happening rain or shine. We loaded the car, and headed out hoping for the best. We stopped a few miles from Jayne's to get gas and a breakfast snack. That was (thankfully) enough time for one of the race directors to call and let me know the race was postponed until the next day. Unfortunately, that would not work for me as I was racing then in Florida.

Two days of travel to get to Mississippi and the race was canceled. Life happens. Weather happens. On the bright side, 36 states were completed before I encountered a cancelation or postponement, although it would not to be the last. In other positive news, I was still scheduled to check off three more states on my way home over the next 4 days.

Jayne and I used the free morning to explore sights around southern Alabama, and then I hit the road to Florida.

There was not much on the itinerary to see in Florida, as I had been to the state several times before. This was my first time on the panhandle though. My destination was Panama City Beach, FL, allegedly an awesome spring break location. I say allegedly only because I was there on December 29 and it was far from beach weather—unless you enjoy cold, windy beaches.

It is always strange to be in a beach town during the off season. It's like sitting in an empty theater. You are left wondering what happened to the show and where all of the people went. It just doesn't seem like you should be there either. But I was there and I wasn't alone.

There were 479 other 5K runners, joined by 397 half marathoners and 333 walkers. Over 1200 people came to participate in (and who knows how many more came out to support) the Biggest Loser RunWalk Panama City Beach 2013.

FLORIDA
Sights Along the Way

Spaceship House

Panama City Beach

*"**Biggest Loser 5K:** Start your own success story this New Year at the Biggest Loser RunWalk in Panama City Beach. Run, walk and be inspired as thousands embark on a 3.1-mile journey along the white sand beaches of Panama City Beach, Florida. The Biggest Loser RunWalk offers a non-intimidating environment to allow you the freedom to achieve your goal, whether it's setting a new personal record or making it to the finish line!"*

Apparently this Biggest Loser business is, well, big business. There was a huge crowd. I'm a little clueless on all things TV, but I knew enough to gather this event was sponsored by a TV program centered on weight loss. There were lots of positive weight loss messages and all sorts of encouragement for healthier bodies.

People were pointing at the TV personalities on stage making announcements and getting the energy flowing. It was an exciting event and the energy was phenomenal. I was feeling good and I was ready to run.

The course was flat and fast. It looped back on itself twice and had a short leg that ran to a turnaround. There was plenty of space to adjust the length of the leg with the turnaround point, so I was really troubled that the event came in at 2.9 miles by my GPS. It would have been easy enough to move the turnaround a 1/10 of a mile for an accurate course.

Although 2/10 of a mile might not sound like much, if you are running an 8-minute mile pace, that shaves off over 1.5 minutes —a huge amount.

My watch and the race time matched at 23:32. Add in the missing 2/10 and I was looking at a 25-flat actual 5K time. It was a decent run, but not good enough to earn a medal—in my new, older age bracket.

Age is a funny thing in racing. Beyond the 20-somethings, age brackets get more competitive for several decades so I was not pleased about my new age group. My 23:32 earned me 4th spot in the 40-44 age group. If this event happened 3 days earlier, I would have placed 1st in the 35-39 age group. What a difference a day (or a few days) makes.

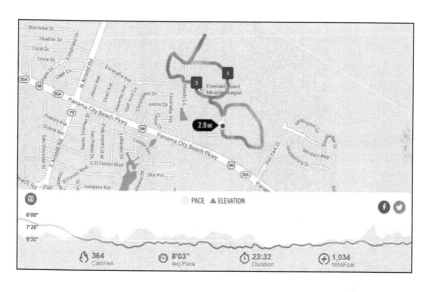

***

Florida Leadership Lesson:
Canceled Events, Physical Fitness and Changing Class

There is so much beyond our control. As leaders, we just need to accept that. We need to work within the realm of what we can control. Was it frustrating to drive two days to Mississippi and have the event rained out? Absolutely. Could anything be done about it? Not at all. It just happens.

The key is to not let frustration affect resolve. Setbacks are a chance to reevaluate and find a new path forward. I will never know what experiences I missed because that Mississippi run was canceled. What I do know is the value of the experiences I had, not going to that event, but from attending a different run in that state. Accept that life will supply obstacles, and look for positive ways to move forward.

Do you need to be physically fit and in great shape to be a strong leader? No. Does it help? Yes.

This was another concept I thought about in Florida. A focus on health and nutrition makes us feel better, stronger, and more confident. When we are in our best physical shape, our minds and emotions also benefit. The Biggest Loser RunWalk, not surprisingly, had more an emphasis on the health and fitness aspect of running than most running events. Their concentration is on weight loss, and running is a great way to work toward that goal.

It was wonderful observing individuals within the Biggest Loser community demonstrate leadership. It was evident not just in the words of the talking heads on the stage, but also in the actions and words of participants who shared stories and celebrated successes.

Another facet of leadership worthy of discussion here is the impact of changing the realm within which you compete. In this case, the calendar flipped a page, which impacted which age group I was competing in. The 40+ age group is typically faster than the 30+ age group. My birthday ushered me into a more competitive field. In running, birth dates directly impact what the competitions looks like.

There are other factors, beyond age, that may affect who your competition is. It might be volume of sales. It might be a change in geography or size of the region. Maybe your group has competed within your home country and competing internationally changes your game. The number of participants might change the dynamic of your experience. Many other factors could change the competitiveness of your group. Be mindful of significant changes within you or your group that may affect your goals.

Muscular Dystrophy Association (MDA)

"The Muscular Dystrophy Association is the world's leading nonprofit health agency dedicated to finding treatments and cures for muscular dystrophy, amyotrophic lateral sclerosis (ALS) and other neuromuscular diseases. We do so by funding worldwide research; by providing comprehensive health care services and support to MDA families nationwide; and by rallying communities to fight back through advocacy, fundraising and local engagement. It's special work powered by special people who give generously."

Source: mda.org/about

Chapter 41

Flashlight 5K
Lawrenceville, Georgia
December 31, 2013

New Year's Eve 2014 was spent driving to Lawrenceville, GA, for a 6:00 p.m. 5K race. At that time of year, it is dark outside at 6:00. To battle the darkness, organizers came up with a novel approach: numerous volunteers spread throughout the course with flashlights. Runners would follow a path of lights through the neighborhood.

Runners were encouraged to bring small flashlights and other illuminating accessories. Fittingly, the event was called the Flashlight 5K.

> **"Flashlight 5K:** *The Flashlight 5k is entering its ninth year. For nearly a decade, the race has served as a fundraiser for a variety of charities serving the poor and vulnerable in our community. Over the past three years, the race has raised more than $30,000, with all the proceeds benefiting the Lawrenceville Cooperative Ministry Food Bank. Click here to learn more about the Lawrenceville Co-Op or to make a donation."*

I had a decent run considering I am not my best in the evening. The early morning is when I seem to run my fastest times. For this run I managed a 25:22. That was not enough to get me anywhere close to placing, leaving me 9th in my new age group.

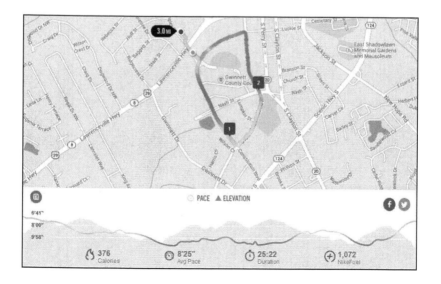

After the race I hung around talking to other runners and race organizers. I share the 4D message whenever I can. It was a genuine gift to meet so many amazing people on these trips. At this event, I met a woman in her 60s and, here, on the last day of the year, she had completed her 101st race of the year! The year! I couldn't believe it. I would have bet that had to be close to some record somewhere until her friend, a gentleman her age, pointed out that this was his 198th of the year. How is that even possible? This was truly remarkable and inspiring.

I also got talking to a woman who was part of the organization team. She found the 4D 50-state story interesting and asked if I would be willing to tell my story during the awards. Since I always take advantage of opportunities to share the 4D message, I told her that would be great.

When I agreed to speak at the awards ceremony, I didn't realize it was taking place in the main worship space of a church and I would be speaking from the pulpit on a microphone. This was going to be a new experience. Working

GEORGIA
Sights Along the Way

Shri Swaminarayan
Mandir, Hindu Temple

9/11 Memorial –
Suwanee, GA

9/11 Memorial –
Tucker, GA

in higher education, I am comfortable talking to large crowds and using a microphone. I am not, however, used to hearing myself over the mic in a church.

I tend to just roll with whatever happens so I ran with this. Although it was not the most comfortable situation, I did my best. After all, this wasn't about me: this about the 4D mission and sharing the message about running for those who can't while raising awareness about Muscular Dystrophy.

After leaving the awards presentation, I had to get on the road. My holiday season of 5Ks was not finished. I had a run the next morning in South Carolina and I had some miles to put on the car in order to get there.

I had couches lined up for this entire trip, but my host for this evening canceled last minute because several family members had gotten very sick. As inconvenient as it was to find another place to stay, I was grateful for not spending the night in a home filled with illness.

My backup plan is always one of the lower-priced chain motels, and I was able to reserve a room at a Motel 6 on the route to my next race. I spent my NYE driving from Lawrenceville, GA, toward South Carolina and sleeping at Motel 6 surrounded by rooms filled with people celebrating the holiday in their own, mostly noisy, way. It was not destined to be a night of good sleep. It is safe to assume that I will not have another New Year's Eve quite like that one.

***

Georgia Leadership Lesson:
Public Speaking

The average American fears public speaking more than death. It always amazes me when I hear this statistic, but facts are facts. Years ago I would have described myself as dreading public speaking. The change happened for me when I got into higher education and realized I would be speaking often in my new career.

To deal with this, I accepted every opportunity I could to speak. I hated it. I wasn't comfortable, but I knew that experience is the key to slaying fears. Over time, I have gotten used to public speaking, but every now and then I will get thrown a curve (i.e. speaking in front of high-level people, speaking from the pulpit at a church, etc.)

If you are going to be a leader, you are going to need to be able to speak in front of groups. Even if you can make it through your goals without addressing a large public audience, you will, from time to time, have to address your followers. Being able to speak in front of a room is a skill. Since it is as skill, it can be learned and refined. Don't fear it. Just do it.

Muscular Dystrophy Association (MDA)

MDA "Assists Families with Life-Changing Support:

MDA clinics 200 locations, including at many of America's top hospitals, meet challenging health care needs of families through expert, team-based care.

Summer camps enable thousands of children with muscle disease to enjoy a week of barrier-free fun as they build confidence and independence.

Durable medical equipment assistance provides powerful, practical support for daily living from the loan of a shower chair to the repair of a power wheelchair.

Support groups and educational resources give families real-world tools for managing complicated diseases."

Source: assets.mda.org/your-contributions-at-work

Chapter 42

Rock Hill Striders Ring in 2014 5K Trail Race
Fort Mill, South Carolina
January 1, 2014

The first day of 2014 was going to be spent following through on a resolution I'd made on June 30, 2013: to run a 5K in all 50 states. I never understood why we need one day each year to declare new goals for ourselves. An argument could be made that it makes sense to declare these commitments to ourselves on any other day of the year, as it seems New Year's resolutions have a reputation for not being completed. It almost seems as if declaring a resolution on the first of the year has a built-in excuse not to follow through.

January 1, 2014 was exactly 6 months from the beginning of this campaign, and South Carolina was going to be the 39th state completed. Although there would not be many races in January and February, the remaining 11 states would not have insurmountable challenges in planning and running.

The 4D 50-State 5K mission was going to be completed. The commitment was made not just to me, but to Dee, everyone else who can't walk, and anyone who has been inspired by the story. Some commitments just have to be finished—no excuses.

***

The South Carolina event was another trail run. After the slippery slopes of the Indiana trail run, I now approached trails with a level of respect and slight distrust. No longer did I see a trail run as an opportunity to take it easy on my legs. I was prepared for anything—or so I thought.

It was a cold day. This would be my 11th consecutive race in cold-weather running clothes. This was getting old, but I had four more cold runs to go, even though I was heading to warmer climates.

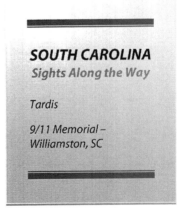

SOUTH CAROLINA
Sights Along the Way

Tardis

*9/11 Memorial –
Williamston, SC*

The Ring In New Year's Trail Race was scheduled for 10:00 a.m. at the Anne Springs Close Greenway in Fort Mill, SC (about 20 minutes from Charlotte). The ASC Greenway is a nature preserve.

*"**Ring In New Year's Trail Race:** The Ring In trail races are held annually on January 1 at the ASC Greenway. The length, and price, of the race depends on the date. The 2014 race will be a 14K and cost $14, for example. There is also a 5K option and a 1.2 mile fun run."*

The 5K had 46 registrants and the 14K had 63. This event was hosted by a group of runners called the Rock Hill Sliders. This is a tight running group, and it seemed everyone literally knew everyone. They were very welcoming to an out-of-state visitor, and I was happy to join some of them near the fireplace in the pavilion while we waited for race time.

Instinctively, I had brought the pair of running sneakers that I started the 50-State project with. I had assumed that with a trail run there would be risk of getting my running shoes mucked up. Ultimately, that was a brilliant choice, as my feet ended up stepping in places that I had not expected.

The difference in elevation from the highest point to the lowest point of this race was only 67', but we went up and down significant slopes more than 10 times. It is very hard on the legs and knees to transition like that especially over varying terrain.

There is another element that makes trail running unique to me—panic.

It might just be me, but running through the woods with people behind gives the impression of a chase, not a race. Maybe my mother shared too many horror films with me as a child, but if I am in the woods running and someone is chasing me, I have no intention of slowing down. Add to that a complex matrix of branches, roots, mud, rocks, and whatever else is out there and you have an intensified feeling of being hunted—hence, the panic. The undulations of the topography amplified this feeling.

This particular course had a distinctive feature. The path crossed seven creeks—only three bridges. The first bridge didn't count. It was a rope bridge and we were told that if we chose to go over the bridge instead of the through the water, we would have to walk as the bridge could not withstand running.

Photo by Don Rice

Sometimes you have to just step in it to reach your goals.

I was being chased. I chose the water. When the temperature is 32 degrees and you run through a creek that has recently seen even colder temperatures, your body has a nearly immediate reaction, it is not pleasant. The sensation of cold is magnified. My legs wanted to cramp, but there wasn't time. As soon as I was in the water, I was out again and needed to keep running—I was being chased.

Running in the cold can be uncomfortable. Running in the cold with wet legs can be painful. As the race continued, it seemed my legs dried off some. About the time I got comfortable with my situation, we would hit another creek, sometimes with a bridge and sometimes not. In all, I went through 5 creeks and was feeling pretty miserable about it. On the positive side, I was very proud of myself for attacking each waterway.

Between the wet legs and the up-and-down of the path, I was becoming exhausted. My brain focused on two things: moving forward and the fact that I am doing this because Dee can't. I would get through this.

As if I needed any more punishment, the Nike+ clicked the 5K mark and the finish line was nowhere in sight. I couldn't see the end of this race because it was a 1/4 of a mile away up 50' hill. My time came in at 31:35. This was my only event that I had an official time over 30 minutes. If we stopped at the 3.1 mile mark, I would have been well under 30-minutes, but the race goes until the end.

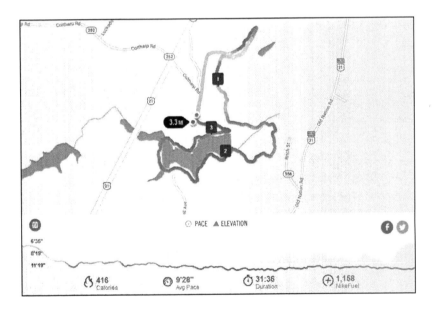

I was surprised that I finished 10th overall. My time was enough for 4th in my age group. If it wasn't for that pesky birthday, I would have been 3rd in my division.

It was time to start the 8-hour drive home. So much was accomplished in the first 6 months. I spent my New Year's Day 2014 feeling beat up and exhausted. It is also true that I spent it feeling encouraged and proud.

***

South Carolina Leadership Lesson:
Resolutions, Sometimes You Just Have to Step In It

_____

Leaders do not wait until January 1 to make a resolution. They make them when the time is right and it is imperative to set goals and a plan to achieve them. If you wait until the first of the year to make such declarations, ask yourself if you are waiting for that day for the built-in excuse to fail.

An integral part of leadership is having vision. An important part of having vision is goal setting and building a plan to achieve those goals. When those pieces are in place, you have an opportunity to prove your resolve, regardless of the calendar.

We have all heard the clichés of the "road less traveled" and the risks of taking the "easy path." Well, they wouldn't be clichés if there wasn't an ounce of truth in them. Regardless, sometimes you do not have a choice and have to take a more challenging path.

At times in this race, I could have picked an easy path over a bridge, but I would have lost momentum and time. In other instances, I had no choice. I had to run into the creek. Either way, I had to step in it and keep moving. As leaders, sometimes we need to get our feet wet (literally) and keep pushing on. Sometimes it is enough to make that first, unwanted step to get through an obstacle we would rather avoid. Even if that step is as bad as we feared, at least it is over quickly and we can keep moving forward. When you face fear, make contact with it, you often learn that it is not as bad as you had imagined.

Muscular Dystrophy Association (MDA)

MDA "Rallies Communities To Fight Back

Advocacy amplifies the voices of people with neuromuscular disease, ensuring that legislators and policymakers are aware of issues of importance to our community.

Community events create greater awareness of muscle disease, and provide local families and volunteers with an effective way to fight back against muscle disease."

Source: assets.mda.org/your-contributions-at-work

Chapter 43

Long Beach Carnival Classic 5K
Long Beach, MS
January 25, 2014

The original plan was to rest from running and traveling during January and February with the exception of January 1st. Besides not having many good, viable options for those months, I wanted to give my body and bank account a break.

When you are working on a mission this large, plans are always fluid—always. The canceled Mississippi run needed to be made up and it would have been taxing to add it into the schedule between March and the June finale. I was going to have to head back to the Gulf Coast sooner than I expected.

The task of scouring websites for races and flights began immediately upon returning to Pennsylvania. I had a sense of pressure to schedule this makeup run sooner than later to retain flexibility should something sidetrack this state again. With only one cancellation in 40 races, I was on edge that another could happen. As the months were checked off the calendar, there was less and less time to negotiate cancellations. I was heading back to Mississippi in 23 days.

MISSISSIPPI
Sights Along the Way

*9/11 Memorial –
Hattiesburg, Mississippi*

Red Bluff

*Chua Van Duc Buddhist
Temple*

***

With such a relatively short time to plan a trip, I was concerned about finding a Couch Surfing host for the two nights I would be in the state. When I registered for the event, I reached out to the race director with my concerns and one of the members of her committee offered to put me up on Friday night before the race. This was terrific news, as I was adding on the huge expense of another flight and rental car. Fortunately, I was able to also score a couch for Saturday evening.

Everything was set for this trip except weather. When my plane landed in Biloxi, the car rental agent warned me about icing on the roads. I couldn't believe I was on the Gulf of Mexico and had to worry about ice!

Apparently Mississippi was hit with an unusually cold blast of winter the day I arrived. Mother Nature was intent on having me run in the cold yet again.

I made my way to the Friday night race registration and packet pick-up at church that sits right on U.S. 90. This highway wraps the edge of the Gulf through Mississippi. As I got close to the beach, the icing changed to a light drizzle. The people at registration were optimistic the run in the morning would be dry, but cold. No matter what, the Long Beach Carnival Classic Half Marathon and 5K were happening, rain or shine—no cancellation here.

> **"Long Beach Carnival Classic Half Marathon and 5K:** *This event is a primary fundraiser for the Carnival Association of Long Beach, Inc., which provides cash grants for local non-profits in the Mississippi Gulf Coast Community. This event fosters healthy living, a family atmosphere, and supports Mississippi pride."*

It was one of those mornings I just hid in my rental car. It was cold and, being right on the Gulf, a breeze chilled to the core. It was damp and ugly. I had no desire to be outside longer than I needed to be.

The course was a beautiful route along the coast right on U.S. 90. The lanes closest to the Gulf were closed for the event, the other lanes were split to allow two-way traffic. It was an out-and-back run, so 5K runners raced out 1.55 miles to a turnaround while half marathoners would not turn back until the 6.55 mile mark.

This would have been an amazing event in nicer weather. It is a shame that the cold put such a damper on an otherwise wonderful location.

There would 128 people running in the half marathon and another 64 in the 5K. All 192 of us started the race together. A third of the group would simply be heading back much sooner than the rest. We were told that the turnaround for the 5K was *clearly marked* and that a volunteer *was there*.

The race started out normally enough, and I had a strong pace. I was feeling great about my chances of a fast run. For the first part of the race, I was out with the front runners, which I didn't feel was unusual, as the half-marathoners were probably starting out with a more conservative pace and there were not that many 5K participants.

I was eagerly anticipating the turnaround to see just how many of the people in front of me were in my race. As my Nike+ indicated the 1.35 mile mark, a handful of people were running back toward me and I was excited that there weren't many of them. I was doing great and might place well.

Around the 1.4 mile mark I passed a woman sitting in a lawn chair next to the course. It was too soon to be the turnaround so I smiled and kept running. Right after passing her, I passed a parked police car with an officer standing nearby. Clearly he wasn't the volunteer telling me it was time to head back, so I forged onward.

The Nike+ clicked over 1.55 miles—the half-way point of a 5K—and there was no sign or volunteer, so I kept running. I noticed there were no on-coming runners and I'd started to fear that I missed the turnaround point. Just then, a few other runners near me started expressing concern that we missed our mark and my Nike was zooming passed 1.75 miles—clearly too far.

I turned around, frustrated and annoyed, and started to run back. On the way, I saw someone righting the 5K turnaround sign that had blown over. Seriously? It was also clear that other runners saw the mark and were turning back. The handful of us who ran too far ultimately ran an extra ½ mile. Besides the sign being knocked over, the volunteer was also at a location a good distance from that sign.

Realizing that you have run too far is a surefire way to suck the wind out of your sails. I tried to transform my irritation into positive, kinetic energy to keep me moving. Who knew how many finishing places I (and the other runners) lost because the sign was down and the volunteer incorrectly situated?

As we crossed the finish line, several of us voiced our displeasure in an exhausted chorus. The race director immediately responded to the concerns and learned what had occurred. There wasn't anything that could be done at that point as it would be impossible to know: Who had turned around at the correct spot? How far did the other runners go and at what pace? In short, accurate results blew away with the fallen sign.

A few of us were chatting with the race director and another runner came up to talk to her. He indicated that he was confident he took 3rd place overall, but he couldn't wait for the award ceremony as he had plane to catch. He wanted to confirm that they would mail his medal to him. The race director affirmed that they would mail it if he was not present.

I did not recognize this man, but I certainly recognized the feeling of thinking you placed, wanting your medal and having to catch a plane. I knew that scenario all too well. After the director left, I asked the man, "Are you running a 5K in all 50 states?"

He smiled and said, "Yes." I just met my doppelganger. He wanted to know how I knew and I explained what I was doing. His name is Matthew Warren and his work takes him to various States. He tries to get in an event whenever he can and is not on any set deadline to finish the states. He couldn't believe I was doing it in a year—of course, neither could I.

When the awards ceremony began, I was pleased to hear that Matthew did claim 3rd place overall. As it turned out, I was 10th overall and took 1st place in my age group. Ironically, at this event my recent birthday worked for me. If I would have stayed under 40, running against Matthew, I would have been 4th. As it turned out, that extra few days on the calendar bought me a 1st place medal.

I couldn't believe it. How could I run an extra half mile and still win? When the full results were posted, I noticed that I was the *only person* in my age group. 1st is still 1st.

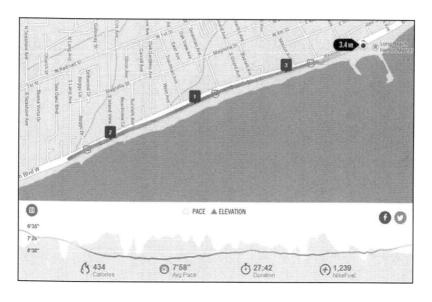

***

Mississippi Leadership Lesson:
Meeting Your Double, 1st is 1st

Matthew Warren is less than a year younger than I am. He runs at a far superior pace. I am running the states at a far quicker rate. We are similar and different. As leaders move about and pay attention, they are bound to find other, motivated people tackling similar goals. This is a wonderful opportunity to expand our learning and share what we have learned along the way. I did not see Matthew as competition, but rather a kindred spirit. There is plenty of success out there for all of us.

Some have criticized this 1st place win as not really being a win, as there were no other men in my age group. That is certainly their right to feel this way, but I beg to differ. The original race I scheduled in Mississippi was postponed to a date I could not run. I made all sorts of commitments, in both time and money, to get back to this state to run this event. It was an early morning and very cold and damp. If I was a local, I may have shut off the alarm clock and said forget about this. I didn't do that.

I traveled and woke up early. I put my game face on and I did my very best. I earned that medal, regardless of who did (or did not) finish after me. I beat the millions of 40-year old men who could have run this race but did not. Our successes are not defined by who we beat but rather how much we achieve.

If you need a loser to call yourself a winner, you will never be the latter.

Muscular Dystrophy Association (MDA)

MDA "Funds Research To Find Treatments and Cures

Basic research grants lead to the discovery of new treatments and potential cures.

Grants for clinical trials and translational research move promising discoveries along the drug development pipeline toward becoming approved therapies.

Clinical research networks and disease registries advance the understanding of muscle disease and lead to improved health outcomes.

Conferences and symposia catalyze research progress by bringing together top scientific minds to collaborate and share insights.

Source: assets.mda.org/your-contributions-at-work

Chapter 44

Leprechaun Lane 5K
Kansas City, MO
March 8, 2014

History has a way of repeating, as they say. On March 7, I found myself flying into Kansas City, MO. This was the second time a 4D 5K trip took me through this city, but that is not the interesting part of my history repeating itself. The noteworthy recurrence would happen the following morning when I arrived at the 5K, but we will get to that in due time.

This was the Friday of my college's spring break, and I had planned on running 4 states over the course of the week. Three of the four races were themed for Saint Patrick's Day. The first week, I would accomplish my goals in Missouri and Arkansas, followed by a Tuesday flight to New Mexico. From there, I would run Colorado on Saturday, New Mexico on Sunday, and grab a flight back to Pennsylvania in time for work Monday.

We have to play the cards we are dealt, and I was dealt a canceled 5K in Arkansas. Sadly, the race was cancelled after I booked flights and rental cars, so I was still making the trip and would knock out Missouri at least. I would have to come up with a Plan B for Arkansas.

If I had my druthers, I would have planned to run a 5K in St. Louis, MO, but the routing was easier to connect the Kansas City run to an Arkansas run.

MISSOURI
Sights Along the Way

National World War I Museum

City Block of Library Books

Stonehenge

Branson, MO

Wild Bill's Shootout Location – First Shootout in U.S. History

9/11 Memorials
– Fenton, MO
– Hannibal, MO at Lover's Leap
– Hannibal, MO at 911 Call Center
– St. Charles, MO
– O'Fallon, MO
– Walnut Shade, MO
– Springfield, MO

Hannibal, MO

Lover's Leap

Citygarden Sculpture Park

The Gateway Arch

Buried Giant

World's Largest Chess Piece

World Chess Hall of Fame

Cathedral Basilica, St. Louis

Laumeier Sculpture Park

St Louis Walk of Fame

With that cancelation, I didn't have as much need to run Kansas City, except for the fact that I was landing there the night before, and I had a date to repeat history in the a.m. My Missouri run was going to be where it was originally planned.

Serendipity has a way of serving up opportunity. If I would have gone with the original plan, I would not have had enough time to check out St. Louis and the infamous Gateway Arch. The cancellation freed up part of my weekend, so I was able to add several interesting Missouri cities, St. Louis, Branson, and Springfield, to my itinerary.

Prior to this trip, I thought of the Gateway Arch as just another must-see-when-you-are-there. Really, it was so much more. I was not prepared for the awesomeness of this creation. It is one of those human achievements that must be experienced in person to comprehend the full effect, and when you are there, it is almost incomprehensible.

Of course, the trip around Missouri visiting the Arch and those cities came after the 5K. In typical 4D 5K fashion, a cold front rolled into Missouri with my plane, which secured another race in the cold. At least I would not be running alone for this event.

***

As the states rushed by, my Facebook friends list was growing. I posted frequently on Facebook about my plans for making upcoming races. Carol Meza, the race director from the 5K in Pittsburgh, KS, noticed that I was coming back to Kansas City to race on the Missouri side of the city. She and I have been Facebook friends ever since I outran her zombies in October. She saw this run coming up, and we discussed meeting to run this 5K together.

The event wasn't far from her home, and we agreed to meet there. Carol would be the third person I met on a 4D 5K trip who I was able to revisit on a second trip. It is one thing to travel the entire country and meet people. It is something extra special to be able *run* into them again. This was another layer added to this experience, and I was really excited that Carol made the hour-plus drive to Lee's Summit, MO, for the Leprechaun Lane 5K.

> **"Leprechaun Lane 5K:** See if you can find the pot of gold in this year's Leprechaun Lane 5K or 10K. The race benefits the Uplift Organization. Uplift is a completely volunteer-run homeless outreach program in Kansas City, MO, that relies completely on donations and personal commitments to feed and clothe the area's homeless."

Whenever two people are running a race together, you have to decide if you are both going for your best race or if you are going to run side-by-side. When we first made plans to meet at the race, I think we were both assuming we would run our own races.

Plans have a way of changing. I hadn't run a race in six weeks and Carol was recovering from a knee injury. As we caught up and discussed the day's race, we decided to run together. It was a great decision for both of us. We didn't exactly take it easy, but we didn't push hard either.

Running with someone in a race is a unique dynamic. When I run with others while training, it is usually at a pace at which we can talk and run comfortably. The race dynamic changes that. The sense of urgency that comes from all the other runners pushes you faster than conversational pace. There is also the unspoken battle of each runner not wanting to be the slow one and, simultaneously, not being the one pushing too hard.

Jeff Fazio and Carol Meza display their finishers' medals after the Leprechaun Lane 5K.

You can actually see this phenomenon in the Nike+ watches tracking of the run. The software shows your course mapped in colors relative pace. Green is fast. Red is slow. Orange and yellow are mixed paces in the middle. The map from this run shows our pace starting really fast and then pulsating between red and yellow. That is when we took turns pushing and slowing each other down. When the finish line is in sight, the line starts getting much greener.

The course was relatively flat and we maintained 8:45–9:45-minute miles. Amazingly, we finished with exactly the same time, down to the second at 26:38. For my age group, that wasn't worth much. For Carol it worked out terrifically. She placed 2nd in her group!

Yes, she was wearing a 4D pin. There seems to be something with people wearing a 4D pin and placing in their age groups. Kristy did it in her first run wearing 4D in Rhode Island, and now Carol did it in Missouri.

Maybe when we run for those who can't, we perform better. Or, maybe Dee and the others who can't run are silently pushing us farther, faster, and harder.

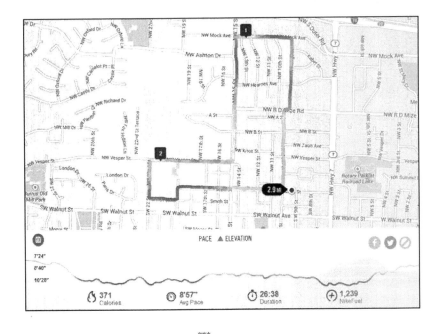

7'24"

8'40"

10'28"

🔥 **371** Calories

⏱ **8'57"** Avg Pace

⏰ **26:38** Duration

⊕ **1,239** NikeFuel

***

Completing Missouri finished off the U.S. Heartland. That was the 5th section of the country fulfilled. The first state that I ran in the Heartland was Kansas, Carol's event. The last Heartland race, Missouri, I ran with Carol. Somehow that seems like a nice pair of Heartland bookends.

***

Missouri Leadership Lesson:
Non-Compete Clause

If you create good rhythm on your team, you can move the group forward without in-group competition. Having team members push each other and, also, slow each other down can have many positive effects. You got solid forward movement on your project without burnout. Everyone knows how they are affecting the group and they can see the results of their input. The success is shared without the sense of one person's doing more than any other.

Carol and I had a great run. Either of us probably could have run faster alone, but we performed better together. We were not overly exhausted when we finished. It just felt a like an incredibly satisfying workout with some solid returns.

Chapter 45

Lucky Laces 5K
Denver, CO
March 15, 2014

After completing Missouri on Saturday, I enjoyed 3 days exploring Missouri before my flight left Tuesday for New Mexico. I landed in Albuquerque, NM, at 7:15 p.m.—10 minutes before my friend Rose Miller's plane landed next to mine. Rose is the good friend and colleague who made the comment wishing I would see "more of each state."

Rose accepted my offer to join me on a trip. She flew out for Colorado and New Mexico. Rose was in for an experience. She was going to see just how much adventure can be crammed into a few short days.

She was great sport and embraced the adventure. We slept little and drove lots. Interesting sights streamed past us over 4 days of exploring these two magnificent states. Even with swift travel, we did not manage to see everything on our wish list, but I am sure we saw more than most would in such a short time.

COLORADO
Sights Along the Way

9/11 Memorial – Ft. Carson, Colorado

9/11 Memorial – Broomfield, CO

Garden of the Gods

Balanced Rock

Manitou Cliff Dwellings

The Airplane Restaurant

Cathedral Basilica

Bishop's Castle

Great Sand Dunes National Park

***

For this trip I had pre-registered for all of the events, so we just needed to pick up my race packet for the Denver race the day before the event. The packet pick up was at a Sports Authority location. For whatever reason, they used a different store location on each of the two days prior to the race. I mistakenly went to the first store listed, the wrong store for that day. Apparently, Sports Authority is not in short supply in Denver, they seemed to be everywhere.

After wrestling with big-city traffic, we found the correct location. I grabbed my packet and we were off. For this race, my bib number was 4222. At first I thought they really had a huge turnout, but they most likely are working their way through a huge packet of numbers over several races.

So, Colorado would be the 42nd State completed. The race was in City Park in Denver. The event drew a healthy crowd—over 900 runners for the 5K and over 340 for the 10K. The park was full of activity. All sorts of St. Patrick's-themed fun happened everywhere we looked.

Being in the infamous mile-high city, I was concerned about another high elevation run. This time, I would just take it easy and pace myself. I had my sights on finishing, not on a new personal best. There isn't enough luck in the world for me to PR at high elevation, so the luck would have to be used on someone else running in the Lucky Laces 5K.

> **"Lucky Laces 5K:** If ya' wait a wee moment, you'll find that the awards for the 3rd Annual Lucky Laces include a wine & dine, a spit & shine, room for two & a bit o' brew! This is just a clue, but stay tuned and all the details will be revealed! The race benefits Denver Urban Ministries."

The race took us through the park, between Duck Lake and Ferril Lake, with the last mile bringing us all the way around Ferril. The lowest point was 5,260' of elevation, just below a mile. Twice during the race we hit a maximum elevation just over 5,300'.

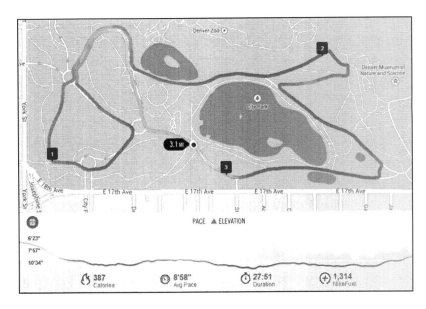

I was able to maintain a pace about a 1 minute slower per mile than my really good runs. Considering the lack of oxygen at those elevations, I was pleased to record a 27:51 minute 5K. It wasn't good enough to place among a field of experienced high-elevation runners, but it was respectable for me. I ended up 17th in my age group and 172nd overall.

***

Colorado Leadership Lesson:
Reading is Knowledge

___

The name "Lucky Laces 5K/10K and Little Leprechaun Kids Run" has 42 characters.

With the completion of Colorado, the number of States that I ran 5Ks in numbered 42.

I finished 172 out 911 runners and the 344 who ran the 10K, ran farther than I. Those numbers combined have me performing in the top 42%.

My race bib was 4222.

The difference in elevation from the highest to the lowest point of the race was 42'.

Every time I noticed another 42, I smiled knowingly. I knew it was the answer to the Colorado leadership question. It is, after all, the answer to everything.

What is all of this business about "42?" 42 is the answer to the "great Question of Life, the Universe and Everything" as per Douglas Adams' in his book The Hitchhiker's Guide to the Galaxy. This novel is famously the first of five books in the trilogy by the same name. Yes, I did say trilogy and referenced 5 books. If this seems odd to you, you must not have read the books!

These books are classic (ok, maybe cult classics). The references to the answer to everything being 42 are all over, an "in joke" between millions of people. Life is filled with these types of references and the people who get them are well read.

Part of leadership is having knowledge and understanding the world around you. In order to do that, leaders must be well read. No one has ever wasted time reading.

Muscular Dystrophy Association (MDA)

MDA will "assist 100,000 people this year with individualized care and support, one person at a time and fund 250 different research projects totaling $33 million with the hope of someday saving lives."

Source: assets.mda.org/your-contributions-at-work

Chapter 46

Shamrock Shuffle 5K
Albuquerque, NM
March 16, 2014

When Rose and I left Colorado to head back to New Mexico, our schedule moved quickly. After a short stop for some wonderful Thai food in Santa Fe, we arrived back in Albuquerque late Saturday night. The 5K was early Sunday and we would need to jet right afterward to make our plane home. There was not much time for exploring New Mexico so I am grateful that we had spent a few days exploring the state before heading up to Colorado. It was time well spent, especially since we were not going to have a spare moment on our second time through.

The New Mexico event included four different races: 10-Mile, 10K, 5K and Kids 1K fun run. The three adult races brought out 500 runners. All the races shared the same finish line, but had different start locations. Registration was in the same building for everyone, so there was a lot of shuffling as we picked up packets for the Shamrock Shuffle.

NEW MEXICO
Sights Along the Way

Valley of Fires

Three Rivers Petroglyphs

World's Largest Pistachio

White Sands National Monument

Very Large Array

Bandelier National Monument – Cliff Dwellings

Pecos National Historic Park

Oldest House in the U.S.

9/11 Memorial – Rio Rancho

"Shamrock Shuffle 5K: Join RunFit for the 11th Annual NM Shamrock Shuffle -- a must for one and all. All events (10-Miler, 10K, 5K and Kids K) start and finish at the Rio Rancho Aquatic Center. RunFit launched the spring of 2006 as a bold initiative aimed at curbing the growing epidemic of childhood obesity by creating a running and/or walking program for children at after-school (or before school) programs across the district."

There ended up being 145 runners in the 10-Miler, 141 in the 10K and 211 of us in the 5K. I didn't see any documentation on how many kids participated in the Kids 1K fun run. A lot of people were wandering around preparing for races.

Before heading to Colorado, Rose Miller and Jeff Fazio explore Bandelier National Monument

As Rose and I walked around, I contemplated leadership lessons. This was one of those events where I specifically looked for something to learn. My attention was waiting to be grabbed.

Yes, this was another run that started at a mile-plus in elevation, but I had done a few like this, though—not exactly unique. The weather was sunny, but cold. After running so many cold races, that was hardly exceptional. Rose and I walked down the hill from the finish line toward the start line about 1/3 of a mile away.

Part way down the hill, we saw him.

He was nearly 9' tall, wide and green. He claimed to be fast and seemingly unbeatable. No, it was not the Incredible Hulk. It was a guy in a giant green bean outfit.

He claimed to run the 5K in the 20–21 minute range. That is quite a bit faster than I run, so I began to prepare myself for the possibility that

The race was set in New Mexico, Jeff Fazio versus a giant green bean.

a giant green bean might beat me in a foot race. My mind started sorting what hidden lesson could be learned by being trounced by a 2-legged vegetable.

Ultimately, that was not time well spent, for several reasons. For one, I never figured out the lesson there, although I still feel there might be one. Two, it was a moot point, as the green bean finished over 6 minutes after me, with 75 other runners between us.

This was not destined to be a fast run for me, but at least I was faster than a speeding green bean.

The course was a giant right triangle with a curved hypotenuse. The starting line was about a 1/3 of the overall length of the hypotenuse from the first turn, while the finish line was a 1/3 of the length of the hypotenuse from the last turn. The other 1/3 was the space between that Rose and I were walking when we met the green bean.

The race started relatively flat and then climbed. We made the first hard right and the road rose rapidly. My mind kicked and told me I could get up this hill. The pinnacle was clearly in sight and I had this. After some hard running uphill in thin, high-altitude air, I could see myself cresting the top.

Sadly, that wasn't the top of the hill. The road kept rising all the way to the next intersection, where the 90-degree turn was for our second change of direction. When I made it there, I was exhausted and saw that the road continued to rise, albeit at a lesser grade for the foreseeable future.

All in all, this course had us running uphill for the first 2 miles of 3.1-mile race. The Nike+ statistics show the increase in elevation at 208': I ran up a 20-story building with no oxygen. The only thing keeping me moving was the thought that whatever goes up, must come down.

As I caught my breath and took longer strides downhill, it occurred to me that we were well past the halfway point, which meant we would not get as much downhill distance as we had uphill. In fact, we were given back only about half of the elevation gain before we started back uphill!

Between hard exhales, I realized the implications of having the start and finish line so far apart on a hill. I am really not a fan of big hills on 5K courses, but you get what they give you. Hills are bad enough, but when the race starts farther downhill than it finishes, there is very little reprieve for the weary.

My finish time showed this. It was one of my slowest runs at 29:13. Somehow, that was good enough for 4th in my age group and 58th overall (211 runners in the 5K).

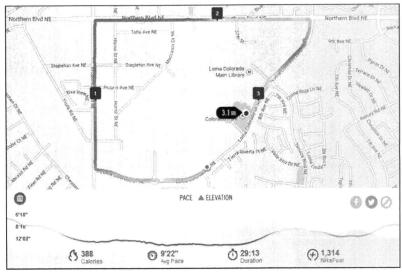

The states were flying by now, and the end was starting to come in sight. Seven states were left. Completing New Mexico finished the last of the Southwest states, the 6th area of the country finished.

It would be six weeks until my next run, and it was safe to assume that it would be cold.

New Mexico Leadership Lesson:
Life Isn't Fair

_____

We all know that life isn't fair, but this lesson still stuns us from time to time, so it is worth mentioning. There is an inherent assumption with most 5Ks that you will end up where you started.

This hides another, unstated assumption—that the rise and fall of the terrain will be equal. It will be fair. As a runner, you can normally bank on having just as much free energy running downhill as you exerted going uphill. After all, that is fair.

The reality is things will not always be this way. It is possible that you will end up at a higher elevation than you started, running an energy deficit. If I would have invested more time analyzing the course and comprehending that we walked downhill so far to get to the start, I may have adjusted my initial running pace to better serve my pace and sanity.

Leaders need to be aware of times when they are literally and figuratively fighting uphill battles. Pay attention to the landscape, as the terrain might not match your assumptions.

Muscular Dystrophy Association (MDA)

"Since MDA was founded more than 50 years ago, advocacy always has been the undercurrent of our programs and services. In September 2007, MDA launched a formal National Advocacy office to effectively project the voice of our MDA community, and protect the interests of the individuals and families we serve.

Source: mda.org/advocacy

Chapter 47

Montana Made Run
Missoula, MT
April 26, 2014

During my January through February break, I put a lot of effort into plotting the last 7 states so that I would have a clear plan to finishing this journey by June 30. Part of my planning included contacting potential Couch Surfing hosts. Since I was contacting these people months in advance, most of them offered "maybes," with an understanding that we would confirm details closer to the travel date.

The schedule for Montana had me landing in Missoula on Thursday, April 24, and leaving on Sunday the 27th. Securing a Couch for Friday and Saturday night came quickly with a 29-year-old guy I will call Mark. Mark said it was no problem to stay and that we could finalize plans later. Thursday night was a bit more challenging, as my plane would land late and I am uncomfortable asking a stranger to put me up a night when I know I am arriving late and leaving early. It just seems a lot to ask.

I assumed I would just find a cheap motel for the night. As luck would have it, a Couch Surfing hostess, Heather Morris, responded positively to my request for Friday and Saturday night. I told her that I had a place lined up, but could really use something for Thursday night. She was incredibly gracious about accommodating me Thursday evening, and she lives just minutes from the airport. All was seemingly set.

Mark and I had friended each other on Facebook and communicated plans there for touching base. The week before my trip to Montana, I sent him a message on Facebook requesting his phone number and address. The messaging software on the site allows you to see when someone reads your message; Mark had and I was surprised that several days passed without a response.

Saturday night before my trip, I was concerned that I still had not heard from Mark. I was flying in 5 days. I sent another request for information on meeting, including another request for his phone number and address. Again, the message was read, but he did not respond.

I sent him one last message indicating that I'd had only positive experiences on Couch Surfing and was starting to fear I would be left without arrangements for this trip. I also sent a message to Heather asking about staying multiple nights at her place. Heather got back to me right away. Staying with her all three nights was not a problem.

A few hours later, Mark sent a message apologizing and requesting my phone number. My number was already listed in our message exchange, but I sent it again. He called later on Tuesday afternoon and told me all was set. He apologized for the lack of communication and said he was really busy with work. He also indicated that he doesn't own a cell phone and only has a house phone.

He gave me his address and a lot of detail on how to find his home. That seemed a little odd, as it was a simple city address. It seemed as if he was being overly cautious about directions.

I let Heather know that Mark had contacted me and that I was going to give his place a shot, since he was the first to accept my request. She understood and told me to let her know if anything changed.

***

The flight to Missoula was uneventful. Finding Heather's place was simple and I was able to fall asleep quickly. She and I had a great conversation in the morning over tea, and I told her that I still had some reservations about staying at Mark's. If it ended up being awkward could I come back to her home on Saturday? She said that would be fine.

It was Friday morning and she was off to work while I was off to explore Montana. My day was going to be filled with sightseeing and meeting up with Mark for dinner at 6:00 p.m.

Mark lives in downtown Missoula and his street was easily found, but when I first drove passed his place, I completely missed it. The number before his was a rundown second-hand shop and the number after his was boarded up—neither instilled confidence. What confidence I had left was eliminated by not seeing his house number on any of the buildings. I was in city traffic and had to keep moving.

I wasn't due to meet him for a few more hours, so I continued to explore Missoula. Specifically, I went to find the location for the race the next morning, at McCormick Park. I relaxed by the park and worked on my computer. Around 5:40 I gave Mark a call and the number just rang and rang. I knew that he was working and assumed that he just might not be home yet.

A few minutes later I drove over to his end of town, now bustling with rush-hour traffic and people filling bars and restaurants around his place. Parking was a nightmare. Circling his block a few times, I finally saw that there was, in fact, a door between the other two addresses. It was easily missed, as it was faded and the house number was all but invisible from years of wear. The door was simple glass with a ragged drapery.

I wasn't sure what to do about parking, and it was getting close to 6:00 so I called Mark again, and there was still no answer. The house phone kept ringing. Eventually, I found street parking about two blocks away and found myself at his door. There was no doorbell or knocker and it seemed that beyond the curtain was a vestibule. I gently tugged the door, which opened into a very small foyer. An old glass door inside was secured with a push-button lock system that appeared to be from the early '80s. There was still no doorbell, so I called Mark again and let it ring and ring and ring. The call was never answered, not even by voicemail.

Having nothing to lose, I tugged at this second door and, to my surprise, it opened to a steep staircase, covered with an old rug. The walls were lined with interesting art work that included mannequin parts and dim lights. I called out, "Hello?"

A sultry woman's voice responded back, "Helllooooooo." But I did not see where the voice was coming from. Tentatively, I threw out another hello. This time she said hello again as she came to the top of the stairs. She was an attractive 20-something wearing a strappy-top, exposing a variety of tattoos on her arms and chest. A black dog joined her.

I said I was looking for Mark. She offered an evil laugh, waved her arms, and said, "He is here somewhere, go find him," and promptly vanished.

I wasn't sure whether I should proceed up the stairs or leave. This was the oddest entrance I have ever made into someone's home. Going against my better judgment, I ascended. When I reached the landing, I saw a hallway that turned back and ran the length of the stairwell to another set of stairs leading to a third floor. The second floor had many rooms, most with the doors open, and I could hear people inside talking or watching TV. The hall was covered with more unusual artwork and mannequin parts. I anticipated the stench of marijuana, but it did not appear.

It didn't feel like a space I should be in. I risked a third "hello."

MONTANA
Sights Along the Way

Garden of One Thousand Buddhas

Flathead Lake

Glacier National Park

Miracle of America Museum

National Bison Range

The Lady of the Rockies

Cathedral of St. Helena

Liberty Bell (copy)

Berkeley Pit

Evel Knievel's Grave

Garnet, MT Ghost Mining Town

The Missoula "M"

The mysterious woman appeared again and said hello as if it was the first time we had met. I introduced myself. She said her name was Crystal (*I wondered if her last name was Meth*). Again, I explained I was here to see Mark and that I was supposed to be staying there overnight. She looked momentarily confused, and then pointed to a white board with a notation: "Mark has a Couch Surfer in the yoga room tonight." She smiled and said, "You must be the Couch."

I confirmed and she said Mark was around. She urged me to walk around and call out his name. She vanished again. With all of these people, how could no one hear the house phone I was calling?

Anyway, I walked on wondering what I had gotten myself into. As I reached the end of the hall, my phone rang with an unknown number. I answered and heard Mark say hello, both over the phone and in-person: he was calling me from the top of the 3rd floor stairs.

When I reached the 3rd floor I found another level filled with more rooms and more people. Mark offered a friendly hello and walked me to the end of the hall. The last room had a glass door, offering no privacy from the rest of the residents. The only furniture was a couch and a TV. An older man sat on the couch staring at the television. He didn't acknowledge that we had walked into the room. It appeared that he was in the state immediately preceding catatonic. I anticipated the sight of his drool, but it did not appear.

Mark pointed out the couch as a sleeping option and then point upward to a set of stairs that came out of a ceiling loft. He informed me that there was an actual bed up there if I was willing to climb the rather rough looking set of stairs.

Looking around the room, thinking about the many people living in the place and realizing there were all sorts of nightlife going on outside, there was no way I could sleep comfortably there. I needed to be prepared for my race in morning and this place was telling me many things, but rest was not among them.

I declined Mark's offer of a place to stay as respectfully as I could and left quickly. Thankfully, Heather understood, and I enjoyed the rest of my weekend at her quiet, comfortable home. I took her and her boyfriend to dinner Saturday night and he explained that the building Mark lives in was an old hotel converted to an artist colony. That explained the many open rooms and the unique artwork. He also said he could understand why I wouldn't have been comfortable there.

***

In the week leading to the 5K in Montana, the weather was consistently predicted to be cold and rainy, just what I needed for another high-elevation run. I learned in my time in Montana that if you do not like the weather in April, wait 30 minutes and it will change. This was true for the precipitation, but not the cold. It stayed pretty cool throughout my 3 days there, but we experienced everything from sunshine to rain and snow.

On my way to the 5K, I was grateful that it appeared that we would run without precipitation. I made my way to McCormick Park and picked up my race packet for the Montana Made Run.

"**Montana Made Run:** *Participate in the 6th annual Montana Made Run on Saturday, April 26, 2014 in Missoula, MT. This race supports and features Montana Made Business and Products, with all proceeds going to the International Association of Firefighters Burn Foundation.*"

This event featured a 10K, 5K and a 5K Donut Challenge. Those racing in the donut challenge had to stop at each mile and eat a corresponding number of donuts: 1st mile one donut, 2nd mile two donuts, and three donuts at the 3rd mile. Human beings find bizarre ways to challenge themselves.

It was chilly, so I waited in my car for the start of the race. When I pulled my Nike watch out of my bag, it was blank. The battery had died. This was unusual, as I had unplugged it only 36 hours earlier from a full charge that typically lasts a few days. I plugged it into the car hoping that it would receive enough of a charge for the race, but I wasn't confident, as race time was less than 30 minutes away.

As I left my rental car, I noted that the battery life on the Nike was well beyond half-way, so I felt assured it would last to the end of the race. We lined up for the beginning of the race and I started the Nike watch. It flashed "low battery" and showed the last bar. Seriously? Now it didn't seem it would make it until the end.

I felt strong for this event and was ready to attack the course. The near-death Nike watch was going to increase the level of immediacy to the run. Would I make it to the finish before the watch made it to its?

The run started strong enough. I felt great, considering the cold and the elevation. After I completed the first half mile, I settled into my normal race stride. As faster runners came up to pass me, I would surge as much as I could to hold them off. As they eventually passed me, I would repeat this for the next faster runner. This is one of the benefits from racing. When I run on the street, I do not get a push from other runners.

The farther into the race I got, the more concerned I became about the watch. It, too, was urging me to move faster and faster. At any moment, it could go totally blank and I was powerless to do anything about it. This gave me the sense of being in an action movie and racing against time to save the hostage. I just had to get their before the timer went off!

In all of my runs, I am racing against the clock, but this was the first time I was running to beat the clock's death. The proverbially water broke and I needed to get to the emergency room as soon as possible. Look out! Coming through!

In the midst of this added stress, I was keenly aware that the woman leading the female donut challenge had passed me three times. I was thankful that she would need to stop a tenth of a mile before the finish to eat three more donuts. That was clearly the only way I was going to finish before her.

I kept moving, trying to eat up ground as fast as I could. My breaths and heart beats were like accentuated ticks coming from the dying clock.

Okay, okay, that is being melodramatic. The watch, after all, is digital and doesn't actually tick, but work with me here. I am trying to convey the sense of urgency I felt to get to this particular finish.

When the finish line finally arrived, or rather when I finally arrived at it, the watch was still counting seconds and parts of miles. I made it. Frustratingly, the watch recorded the run at 2.8 miles—over a quarter mile short. A woman who finished right behind me had a watch from another manufacturer and hers read precisely 3.1 miles. This race course is a known route used before, so it has a solid history of being the correct distance.

My Nike and the race time were accurate to the second. It is almost always within 1-2 seconds off posted race time. I am just very skeptical of its accuracy in regards to distance. Before I left on this trip, I went out for a training run with a colleague who also has a Nike watch. Our times were nearly identical, but my watch showed me running significantly less distance than hers.

Regardless, this was my fastest high-elevation run at 24:44, quick enough to win my age group. I was very pleased, as the last thing I expected was to place in any of the Mountain states.

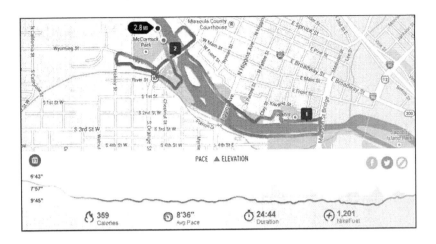

***

After the run, I explored Montana. My plan was to head east to see the capital, Helena, and then travel south to the city of Butte. From there, I would complete the triangle and return to Missoula to have dinner with Heather and her boyfriend.

When I travel, I plan my itineraries in advance, but I will occasionally pick up travel books at welcome centers. I was having some frustration exploring Montana as it was April and spring there doesn't arrive until June, so many sightseeing opportunities were closed or limited by closed roads. Having the travel books came in handy to check other sights I had not planned on.

As I was traveling east on Interstate 90, I checked some of the state travel books. There were many references to historic gold mining towns hundreds of years old and kept in original condition. These abandoned towns were rumored to have ghosts and are apparently very cool places to visit. The brochures listed several of these locations but only one on my route—the tiny little town of Garnet, MT. It sounded fabulous and right off I-90 somewhere. By somewhere, I mean that the brochure did not list any directions or routes through the town. The supplied map merely had a dot noting the town's existence in the middle of an otherwise empty area.

No worries. I always travel with two GPS units. I plugged Garnet, MT, into one and then the other. Neither found Garnet. How can several brochures indicate this as a cool place to see, without a way to get there? I had no way to find it.

Several minutes later, I dug out an old-school Atlas I carry with me just for times like this. In the general area of the brochure-indicated dot, there was, sure enough, a red dot—"Garner Ghost Town."

Garner? How could the brochures have the town name wrong! It was Garner, not Garnet. I quickly plugged Garner into my twin GPSs—my second strike. By now, I was traveling so fast at highway speeds I was far beyond where this town could possibly be—so strike three, I am out. I was not going to get to see Garnet or Garner or ghosts. I went onward to Helena and Butte for my regularly scheduled program.

On my way back to Missoula, I touched based with Heather and she indicated that she and her boyfriend would be ready for dinner much later than my estimated return time. I suddenly had an extra 2 hours to kill. My mind wandered to Garnet. I was going to find it!

From my seat-of-the-pants research, I ascertained that Garnet existed somewhere between Drummond and Clinton. Zooming in really close on my GPS map, I could see tiny lines that sort of looked like they might be roads. One of them had to be the way to Garnet. I took the exit for Drummond and stopped at a gas station.

I asked the woman behind the counter, "Do you know where Garnet is?"

She stared at me blankly and said, "Yup."

I asked, "How do I get there?" to which she replied, "You can't."

She went on to explain that the road to Garnet was closed until at least June. It would be covered with very deep snow and even if the snow had melted, the road would be impassably thick mud. She did say that I might be able to get there if I went around to the other entrance from the Highway 200 side of the mountain, 45 miles out of my way. I did not have time for that.

Garnet, apparently, was going to be another site I could not see on an April Montana trip. I decided to take the back roads out of Drummond, since I was not in a rush to get back to Missoula. As I left town, there was a simple green sign that mockingly read "Garnet" with an arrow pointing straight ahead.

I continued on my way. A few miles down the road, I came to another green sign for Garnet with an arrow pointing to the right, down a dirt road. It indicated that Garnet was a mere 10 miles away. I made the right turn.

After I drove the dirt road for some time, I came to a sign indicating the roadway had two-way traffic. That seemed comical, considering how narrow it was. The next sign indicated the road was closed 6 miles ahead. Doing quick math, 10 minus 6 was 4, and I had already driven some distance. That said, if I drove to the where the road was closed, I would have roughly a 5K to hike to Garnet.

I had time. I was motivated and up for a challenge. I could do this. I kept driving.

My eyes were locked on both the rocky-dirt road and the odometer. I really wanted to have an accurate idea how far I might have to walk, run, or hike to get to Garnet when I finally made it to the closed portion of roadway. Well beyond the 6-mile mark, I came to a clearing, a parking area of some sort, though it was just a dirt lot.

At the end of the dirt lot, was a sign, about a foot tall and at least 6 feet to the side of the roadway that said "Road Closed." Funny thing was, the road didn't appear to be closed. Nothing was *physically* stopping me from making one of the dumbest decisions of my life.

I rationalized that I would drive back as far as I felt safe and when the road conditions seemed to worsen, I would park and decide about hiking the rest of the way. At this point, every tenth of a mile I could drive would save a lot of time hiking.

After 2 miles of driving, the road suddenly got steeper and muddier. It wasn't alarming, but I was aware that it was getting a worse. I came upon a 180-degree turn with three really old buildings—clearly not Garnet, but quite interesting nonetheless. There was no place to park, but I stopped and took some photos from the car.

When I started to drive forward all sorts of horrible things happened at once. The road became steeper, narrower, and muddier. The mud was thick and there was no guard rail. The passenger side of the road also now had no shoulder. It fell off into oblivion—steep oblivion.

It was impossible to turn around. It was impossible to attempt to drive backward down this mess and it was frightening to go forward. The road started to turn around another, even steeper 180-degree turn. The mud was really thick and I could feel the tires sliding. If the car slid backward on this turn, there was no guard rail or trees to stop me from slipping over the cliff. This was terrible. No one even knew I was back there. It's amazing how fast life can change. One minute you are fine and the next it is perilous. My only choice was to keep moving forward, slowly and carefully.

I am writing this chapter, so, clearly, I survived or was at least found alive. In the end, I did make it to Garnet. It was buried in 3'-5' of snow which made it lonelier, quieter and creepier. I was also still dealing with scary-drive aftermath.

My plan for escape was to leave out of the back of the town and head toward Highway 200, as that was only 3 miles, but that plan was thwarted: A gate at the end of town *actually* closed the road. After all of that treacherous driving, and here is where they put a gate? My only option was to return on the muddy-slope I had risked driving up to get there.

A lesson was learned. That will be the last time I drive passed a Road Closed sign.

Some people work well under pressure. Some do not. Which are you? When the clock is ticking, do you find your zone and become super focused? No matter what field we are in and no matter what goal we pursue, there will be situations where we find ourselves in time pressure, and we need to be able to handle that.

Planning helps avoid time crunches. Working on large projects in smaller pieces will also help ward off the looming tick, tick. Many strategies can help us avoid positions where time is of the essence, but inevitably we will occasionally find ourselves there. Leadership is accepting this, finding focus and being able to move forward. Stress and worry never add time to the clock.

The dying battery in my Nike watch inspired me to run faster. When the clock is ticking down on your goal, what will you be inspired to do?

Another aspect of leadership that offered itself while I traveled Montana was risk management.

Leaders must constantly weigh the benefits versus the risks of each situation. Is a free night stay worth being uncomfortable the night before an important experience? Is the sight you are going to see worth the risk of driving beyond the "Road Closed" sign?

I am pretty sure that Mark and his artist colony would have been a safe place to sleep. I'm not entirely sure it would have been as quiet as I would have liked, but I am confident that nothing horrible would have happened to me if I had stayed. Regardless, I was more comfortable leaving and going to a known, quiet place to rest for the evening.

Although I survived the trek back to the town of Garnet, I never actually got to explore it as I would have liked. Besides being covered in deep snow, I was such a mess from the ride that I didn't enjoy the experience. Chances are I will never get back to that area of Montana, so was it worth it? That's hard to say. If I knew then what I know now, I wouldn't have driven passed the sign.

Risk assessment is an ongoing process. At least until the moment we fail to safely assess the risk.

When in doubt, err on the side of caution. You will most likely sleep sounder.

Chapter 48

Law Day 5K
Jonesboro, AR
May 3, 2014

Fun Run 5K
Marion, AR
May 3, 2014

When I flew out in March to run Missouri and Arkansas, the latter event was cancelled. I would have to return to run Arkansas and because I didn't have a desire to explore that state, I wanted to be certain that I could check this state off on my next trip. That said, I booked my flight for a weekend with listings for two 5Ks, over an hour away from each other. In the event that one event was cancelled, I could, hopefully, still make the second. I had a "Plan B."

One of my best friends, David Mena, was planning on flying out and meeting me for this weekend. It was so apropos that David was joining me for this race. First, he is one of the primary people responsible for getting me into running. Second, we were flying in and out of Memphis, TN, where he had lived for a few years. As life had it, the years he lived in Memphis I was not in a position to visit him there. We were now going to get to spend some time together in Memphis, and, for the first time, race together. The races in Arkansas were just across the border, so we used Memphis as our home base for the weekend.

The weather forecast for the races was fabulous, so I decided that I would race in both. Why not? Arkansas canceled on me on my first trip, so I would make up for that by running the state twice—in the same day.

Although David is an accomplished marathon runner and could easily knock out two 5Ks in a single day, he had no desire to run any distance on a really hot, sunny day. After many months running dozens of states in bitter cold, I was more than eager to throw on shorts and tank top. I had never looked forward to sweating so much.

As I traveled the U.S. running 5Ks, David is the person who I most wanted to run with. He has inspired and challenged me in more ways than he will ever know, and I credit him with my running.

Now that the weekend was finally here, I had concerns about our running together. David and I are both extremely competitive. In fact, if there was a competition to spell "competition," we would surely compete. We would probably debate for weeks before on the best strategy, who had the better chance, and what the odds were of the other one pulling out a win anyway. Afterward, we would dissect what actually occurred and how it could have been different.

It's not that we are *really* competitive. We are just both used to winning and rather like that feeling. We do what we can to ensure that wins happen over and over. Sometimes we get in each other's way with that goal. After all, only one of us can win.

That said, I had some reservations on how this "race" would affect our friendship. That's not fair. Our friendship is solid. It would be more accurate to say that I was concerned how the race would affect the quality of our weekend together.

David is a seasoned runner. I thought he should trounce me. In his eyes, I had been running and training consistently for months, specifically for 5Ks, and he hadn't been running as much.

The difference in our racing styles would also make this an unusual encounter. I take off when a race starts and accept that my pace will fall off over the course of the race. David runs at a pretty steady pace. The tortoise meets the hare. I was keenly aware that I would be taking off and that David would be hunting me down—in no time. Win, lose or draw, I only wanted to share a good race with us both giving our best.

***

On May 3, we awoke in our hotel room in Memphis, TN, and traveled across the Mississippi River via the Memphis-Arkansas Memorial Bridge. Our journey took us just over an hour into Arkansas to Jonesboro. We picked up our packets for the Law Day 5K.

> **"Law Day 5K:** The 2nd Annual Law Day Running Festival will feature both a 10K and a 5K. Runners and walkers will be treated to flat and fast courses designed to showcase the historic and cultural center of Northeast Arkansas. This year's race will be held on May 3rd, 2014. Legal Aid of Arkansas is proud to host the Law Day Running Festival in honor of the American Bar Association initiative, Law Day 2014."

The Law Day Running Festival will help benefit the work that Legal Aid of Arkansas does every year for thousands of low-income Arkansans. All money raised in connection with the Law Day Running Festival will go directly to Legal Aid of Arkansas to help it better serve those in need.

The course was relatively flat and traversed secondary roads through the town of Jonesboro. As predicted, I took off with front runners and held onto them as long as I could. It does not take me long to start backing off, as the leaders are able to maintain a tremendous pace and I do have some sense of self-preservation. In this particular race, I tried harder to stay in longer knowing that David was behind me.

This was the first race when I genuinely felt chased. It was an eerie feeling knowing that he could, more than likely, see me—his target. From my perspective, I had no idea whether he was 5 feet behind me or 50 yards. I just knew he was there. I could sense that he was back there somewhere.

I'm not sure how far into the race it was that he passed me. My hunch is that it was before the first mile, but after the first half mile. Holding him off even that long was a small, but valued, victory.

He passed by with some words of encouragement and started adding distance between us. I was grateful that the distance, although increasing steadily, wasn't increasing rapidly. My adjusted goal was to be in a position that I could see him finish, which was accomplished, although not easily.

David won our age group with a 24:21-minute run to my third place effort at 25:08. A local runner finished just ahead of me at 25:03. I generally have a great ability to sprint at the finish; however, on this particular course, I was robbed a bit because what appeared to be the finish line was not.

As I hit the timing maps, I clicked off my watch and slowed down, but everyone started screaming at me to keep running. That cost me precious time, cost me a 24.XX run and it very well may have cost me 2nd place. It is

David Mena won 1ˢᵗ place and Jeff Fazio took 3ʳᵈ place in their age division in the Law Day 5K in Jonesboro, AR.

unfortunate, but things like this happen. It wasn't the Olympics. It was a local run supporting a local charity, so mistakes are bound to happen.

I got to run with David. We both walked away with medals (okay, this time it was actually coffee mugs). Running in a 5K with David added an immeasurable value to the Arkansas trip.

After the race, David and I headed back into Tennessee to clean up and go on with the rest of our day. His day included lunch with a friend from when he lived in Memphis. My day was going to include a little exploration of Memphis before crossing the Mississippi again, for my second Arkansas 5K.

When I arrived in Marion, AR, for the 4:00 p.m. run, the skies were clear and sunny. The course had almost no shade. It was hot. I could hear David's voice saying how much he disliked running on sunny, hot days. After many months of running in cold weather, I was prepared to make the best of the heat. At least that is what I was telling myself.

Regardless, I had paid and was registered for the Marion Chamber of Commerce Fun Run 5K, and there was no turning back. Although I had run multiple races in the same day twice before, this was my first time running two in the same state in one day. Interestingly, there was another runner at this event who had also run the morning race.

> **"Fun Run 5K:** The seventh annual Marion Chamber of Commerce 10K/5K, benefitting St. Jude Research Hospital, is a community, county and Mid-South event whose goal is to promote the City of Marion and its Chamber of Commerce. Funds raised will be used to promote new business opportunities for our growing city, and a portion of the proceeds will go to St. Jude. Click here to visit St. Jude's website and contribute to the St. Jude family."

When they made the pre-race announcements, they described the arrows we would follow along the course—signs and markings on the ground. It seemed straightforward enough. The route took us around a park and through a neighborhood. It eventually came back into the park. The course did not have any extreme elevation changes and would have been an ideal course to go for a quick time, if it weren't for the blaring sun and the fact that I had already pushed my body once that day.

As a race progresses, the field spreads out. The very fast runners get by me and I hold on as long as I can, though I typically finish trailing the runners turning quick times. I am used to a healthy gap behind me and the next batch of runners.

That is how this race was going until just beyond the 2-mile mark. Heat and exhaustion were wearing on me and my pace was plummeting. The next batch of runners was catching up, but I was still maintaining a reasonable lead. I started focusing on not letting anyone else pass me. I sensed the park was getting close, and I wanted only to hold my position.

When the park finally appeared, just before the entrance were bright orange arrows spray-painted on the asphalt indicating we should turn right which lead perpendicularly away from the park entrance. According to my Nike watch, we didn't have enough distance left to run much farther without entering the park. As doubt set in, I saw the next arrow point straight ahead, offering reassurance I was going the correct way.

Other runners called out to me to question whether I was on the correct route, and I yelled back confirming there were arrows. The road I was on approached a busy street, and it didn't seem logical we would be running that far, and the next turn would take us even farther from the finish. Doubt set in deeper, and that is when I saw the big orange arrows painted on the ground indicating a turnaround point. Usually turnaround points have an orange cone marking where runners should pass to make the turn, but I simply accepted what was given to me by the arrows.

As I ran back this leg of the course, I had runners in the on-coming lane. We exchanged confused looks as to why we were running blocks off course to turn and run back. I was happy to be entering the park and was ecstatic to see the finish line. The dream of running across the finish line faded fast when I realized no one was there. There was no timing equipment. There was no one with water. There was just the giant inflatable start/finish line, which turned out to be the start line only—a giant tease. I had to keep running.

By this point, I was well beyond 3.1 miles and feeling beat. I could at least hear the music, which implied that the finish line festivities actually existed. I needed to find my way there. It turned out that I was not supposed to run down that short leg prior to entering the park. That extra run added nearly a quarter mile to my overall distance and to all the runners who followed me. The prevailing theory was that some local jokesters may have painted the additional orange arrows the night before.

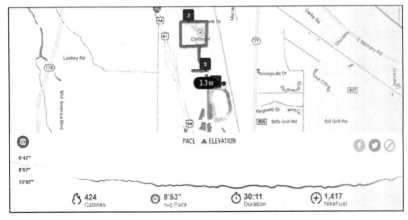

Somehow, my effort, even with all of the extra running, was enough to earn 1st place in my age division. It was one of the slowest times I have recorded at an event, but it still felt good to claim the division.

**

Leaving Arkansas closed the books on the Southeast United States. Another section of the country was added to the completed pile along with the Mid-Atlantic, New England, Appalachian Highlands, Midwest, Heartland and Southwest states. With 7 down, only 3 sections were left to complete. The Mountain and Pacific Coast states would be done by the end of May. That left the two non-contiguous states, Alaska and Hawaii, for June.

Aloha was fast approaching.

**

Arkansas Leadership Lesson:
Friendly Competition, Importance of "Plan B" & Doing Twice as Much

Competing with friends can be a wonderful experience. Friends can help inspire us to do more and we can return the favor. There is a difference between competing with friends and being competitive with friends. Be cautious that the latter does not burden the former. If you are a truly competitive spirit, this can be really tough task, but remember that friendship runs deeper than bragging rights. If you are truly good friends, just as much joy can be found in sharing another's victory as you would find in your own. Remember those two teenagers from the Warrior Dash?

Smart leaders always have a "Plan B." Why? Because they know that the unexpected can happen. For most of these trips, I had planned multiple states to ensure that I was as efficient with my time and money as I could be. It was taxing to go back to Arkansas, but knowing that I had a second option for an event in case one got canceled bought me security in the investment. If I had only one option, a cancelation could have cost me the goal of accomplishing all 50 states in 1 year as time was running out.

Don't get caught by surprise, especially when you are nearing the finish of a goal. You are not across the finish line until it passes under you, so don't let up or take for granted that you will make it just because you can see it.

Once you have become proficient at a skill or task, challenge yourself to double output. You might amaze yourself at what you can accomplish. Arkansas would have been a spectacular weekend if I had simply left after the first event with my 3rd place finish while watching my friend nab 1st. However, I had challenged myself to do a second race that day. I pushed myself to accomplish twice as much and was rewarded for my effort. I was able to leave with my own 1st place prize. What can you achieve if you go for twice as much? What if you challenged your team to double their efforts? Even if the increase is only 50%, that is significantly more than you may have achieved if you hadn't challenged yourself (or your team) to go for more.

When looking at doubling efforts, make sure that the goal remains reasonable and possible; otherwise, you risk demotivating yourself or the group with an overwhelming expectation. Make sure your group knows they are supported, and make the challenge a point of inspiration. Let them know that getting anywhere close to achieving this increased goal would be a success worth celebrating.

Chapter 49

Famous Idaho Potato 5K
Boise, ID
May 17, 2014

In my first 39 years of life, it never occurred to me that I might visit Idaho. It never even crossed my mind as something I might want to do. About a decade ago, my mother visited Boise, ID, for work, and I did not listen attentively to the details of her trip because I didn't see why anyone would spend time or money to go to Idaho. I was Idaho ignorant.

My Idaho ignorance ended when I started researching "things to see in Idaho" while planning the last states. Originally, I thought I'd do Idaho and Montana the same weekend, but two things became apparent. One, they are both very large and distances between the major cities where 5Ks are more likely to happen are far too great to cover by car in a single weekend. Second, I realized, there are many wonderful sights worth seeing in both states, and I did not want to rush those experiences. Montana and Idaho were scheduled for their own weekends.

Any remaining traces of my Idaho ignorance were eliminated when I landed in Boise on May 16. The United States is really an awesome—*awe-inspiring*—country. The differences between the areas of the country are astounding, beautiful, and wonderfully surprising.

***

By this time I was accruing travel rewards, points, and frequent flier miles, and it was time to cash in. I traded in enough points to stay the first night at the Super 8 in Boise for under $2. The next two nights would be spent Couch Surfing in Twin Falls and then back in Boise.

My flight landed early enough on Friday that I had ample time to go exploring and grab my race packet for the Famous Idaho Potato 5K (part of the Famous Idaho Potato Marathon festivities) before having to turn in for the night.

*"**Famous Idaho Potato 5K:** The YMCA Famous Idaho Potato Marathon, presented by the Idaho Potato Commission, is a fun full marathon, half marathon, 10K or 5K course along the Boise, Idaho greenbelt. All courses are flat and fast! This marathon can be used to qualify for the 2015 Boston Marathon. Bring the entire family out for this event! We have a distance that will work for everyone."*

This race was going to be very different than all the others. The start line and finish line were not in the same place. Although that was true for the New Mexico run, those were at least close enough to share a parking area with a short walk between.

For the Idaho run, start and finish were nearly 3 miles apart. The race provided a free shuttle, but I can be leery of relying on someone else for transportation to the start of a race. If something goes wrong on their end or I can't find the correct pick-up location, I am stuck.

I perused the maps and discovered three viable options. Get up extra early, park at the finish line, and walk nearly 3 miles to the start. Park at the start line and walk back to my car after the race. Or, park in the middle and split the distance. All of these options were unattractive for various reasons, so I decided to bite the bullet and rely on the provided shuttle. This proved to be incredibly easy and convenient, as it was only minutes from my hotel. I got to the starting area with plenty of time to relax pre-race.

Hundreds and hundreds of people were there. A DJ was playing music and a race official was making announcements about the race and people attending. I approached him and introduced myself. He liked my story and made a point of announcing it. There was a pleasant round of applause and the people in my general vicinity gave me some congratulations. I wandered off through the crowd.

I found my way to the top of a little hill so I could get a photo of everyone

IDAHO
Sights Along the Way

Ahavath Beth Israel Synagogue

Temple of the Church of Jesus Christ of Latter-Day Saints

Abe Lincoln Statue

Boise Capitol Building

Liberty Bell (copy)

Human-sized Chess Board

Marvin the Martian ACME Rocket

Bogus Basin

Boise Depot

Mountain Home Idaho Penny Relief Mural

Balanced Rock

Minidoka National Historic Site

Snake River

Shoshone Falls

Perrine Memorial Bridge

Evil Knievel Jump Site

Twin Falls Park

Hagerman Fossil Beds National Monument

Bruneau Dunes State Park

Bruneau Overlook

Zoo Boise

milling about. After the photo, I made my way back in the crowd and was shocked when a woman stopped me and said, "Hey, you are that 4D guy." I figured she'd heard the announcement, and I confirmed that it was me. It turns out she actually recognized me from my posts on Facebook about running the 50 states and my intention to be at this particular run in Idaho. It was extremely flattering that she had followed the story.

He name is Janine Johnson and she was running the race with her father, Rick. It was a pleasure meeting them both. I loved that they were running together. Meeting someone who knew about the 4D story before I told them about it was a feel-good moment. Word was getting out.

***

In the weeks prior to the Idaho run, I had finally pestered my brother Johnny enough to get him out and running. The last few years have been trying for him. It seemed life kept throwing obstacles his way. I kept trying to instill in him that running makes you feel awesome, allows you to sleep better, and boosts confidence. I am also convinced that it is a fountain of youth.

My brother got outside and started to run. He started putting in his first few miles and was feeling energized. That meant so much to me. He was getting excited and sharing updates. I was eager to see him get hooked, to catch the running bug. Throughout the course of the 50-state 4D Mission, it has been motivating to see how many people have picked up running after following the story or, at the very least, started talking about trying.

I sent my brother a text from Boise that morning telling him that I was dedicating the Idaho run to him. Hey Bro, this one was for you.

***

The course was fairly flat and pretty fast. Considering I was back to running at high elevation, I was grateful for a run without significant hills. We ran westward along the Boise River through a couple of parks.

My performance was unremarkable. There weren't any interesting mid-race challenges. It was just a solid, quick run. I was pleased to clock a 24:40, especially at elevation. When the full results came in, my time was enough to earn me 3rd in my age group.

With my 5th Mountain state out of the way, I had only one more high elevation run, and that would happen in one more week under a veil of utter darkness.

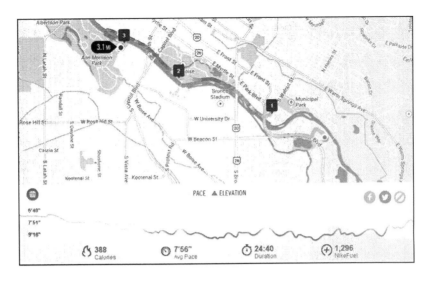

***

Idaho Leadership Lesson:
Help Getting Started, Motivating Others

Leaders tend to be incredibly self-reliant people, sometimes to a fault. This is particularly true when they are getting started. Often, we do not think of the assistance we could use just to get moving. The Idaho run provided a terrific shuttle service to get runners to the faraway starting line. I wasted too much time and energy trying to engineer a way to not use this service. Why? Because sometimes it's hard to rely on someone else. It gets even harder when we do not know the person or area—and that is precisely when we might need to trust them more.

The year spent running the 50 states was punctuated by friends, family, colleagues, and students talking to me about getting into running. It was extraordinarily moving to watch people start running or even consider it. But, none impacted me as much as my brother. I cried when I received the first text that he went outside and ran. When leadership is done right, it motivates others, sometimes very significant others.

Chapter 50

Midnight 5K
St. George, UT
May 23, 2014

As I worked through the country, it was important to me to find a trip I could share with my mother. As I considered the options, I kept coming back to my mother's bucket list where one item was to see the Grand Canyon. Although she traversed the country twice, and drove to the canyon, she had actually never seen it.

On her first trip, fog was so thick she couldn't see anything. On the second trip, an unpredicted snow fall came down so hard she was denied her view once again. The Grand Canyon cuts through Arizona, but I had already run that state, so it was time to get creative.

***

Utah and California were the last two contiguous states left for me to run. Having previously run Arizona and Nevada meant the last two states were not sharing a border. Since they are on the opposite side of the country from me, it was imperative to get them both in on the same plane ticket. A quick look at the map showed the easiest place to fly into between Utah and California was Las Vegas.

California and Utah are separated by the pointy southern tip of Nevada, home to Vegas. Directly east of that point is the Grand Canyon. It seemed as if life was pointing me and my mother to Las Vegas for an epic trip.

This escapade was to happen over Memorial Day weekend. We would fly into Vegas on Thursday night and spend Friday exploring the Grand Canyon. Late Friday night, I would run a Midnight 5K in St. George, Utah, and Saturday we would explore the national parks in Utah. All day Sunday would be a massive drive from the far side of Utah to the opposite side of California. Our destination was a Memorial Day race in Los Angeles. There would be enough time after the race to make it back to Las Vegas for our return flight.

The plan was set: 4 states in 4 days

***

Friday morning my mother and I got up extremely early for the nearly 5-hour drive to the Grand Canyon. We debated as to which location of the

Canyon to visit. The South Rim is most popular, but had the worst forecast. The other options, the North Rim and the western Indian Reservation, are both appealing as well, but the South Rim was the real draw for my mother, and I wanted this experience to be for her. I just wanted to ensure she would finally see the Grand Canyon.

As the sun came up, it revealed a beautiful day. We were in luck. As we drove, we enjoyed glorious sunshine and clear skies. Sure, there some really dark and stormy clouds in the distance, but they had to be hundreds of miles away. In fact, they were.

Of course, our destination was also hundreds of miles away.

As we drove, the clouds were getting closer but seemed to be keeping a

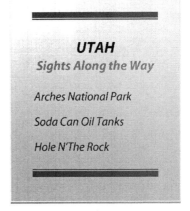

UTAH
Sights Along the Way

Arches National Park

Soda Can Oil Tanks

Hole N'The Rock

respectful distance. I felt we were going to be okay. Besides, you need clouds for good photographs, as they add atmosphere and diffuse light.

Within a mile of the entrance to Grand Canyon National Park is a collection of roadside stands selling all sorts of items to lure tourists. My mother has a supernatural attraction to cash registers. If you ever accidentally bury a cash register and forget the location, she can find it for you. Needless to say, after such a long drive, we were both ready to get out of the car to stretch our legs and wallets. My mother was perusing the local wares and I was keeping an eye on those clouds which, for some reason, did not seem to be quite as far away as they had been a few hours earlier. We needed to get going.

We entered the park, and the clouds got closer. We made our way through the parking lot maze hoping to find an open space. The place was packed. The only spot we found was at the end of the second lot, practically off asphalt into landscaping. It was one of those days where everyone was getting creative with making parking spaces.

Tiny sprinkles of rain poked at us as we got out of the car. Mom shot me a knowing, concerned looked. I assured her everything would be okay. As we walked across the lot, the rain picked up, but it was still a light, manageable drizzle. Once we got onto the sidewalks that lead through the visitor center, benches, and park maps, the rain picked up. Although we were getting wet, we were determined to reach the end of the main lookout to see the Grand Canyon. My mother was going to see this canyon and no amount rain was going to stop us.

My mother stepped foot onto the main concrete pad of the primary viewing area and it happened. It happened all at once. The temperature seemed to plummet 20 degrees, the rain gained speed and volume, but it was no longer rain—it was a snowy, hail. Mom was dressed in all black. Maybe she was prepared to mourn her chances of seeing the canyon. Regardless, her black outfit was quickly changing to white. I was trying to snap photos, but my bare arm was getting coated with frozen water and starting to feel numb. It was too much, we had to retreat. I thought she was going to cry.

We huddled with a handful of strangers under one of the park's roofed information displays. I assured her that everything would be okay. We stood shivering and trading travel stories with the other people as we waited out this mini storm. Within half an hour the weather decided to go annoy other people elsewhere and the skies opened back up. We had a beautiful day exploring the Grand Canyon's various lookout points. My mother finally saw her canyon.

***

The late-night Friday run was in St. George, Utah, at 11:00 p.m., though it was called the Midnight 5K.

> **"Midnight 5K:** A spectacular course at the former municipal airport. Participants will get to race down the airport runway with fantastic views of the entire town. This event is a can't-miss race with lots of rocking tunes, amazing glowing giveaways, and glow awards!"

The race organizers heard I was coming and offered me a complimentary race. Having spent thousands of dollars on this 50-state project, every bit helped, and I graciously accepted their offer for a free ride (or free run in this case).

Having a midnight run pretty much guarantees it is going to be dark, unless it happens to be in Alaska. I wouldn't experience the 24-hours of daylight up north for another 3 weeks, so I was prepared for the dark—so I thought.

The race was themed as a glow run. This was not new to me, as I had run a few states in the dark (Tennessee, Minnesota, Kansas, Michigan, Washington, and Georgia) and at least one was a dedicated glow run. But this Utah race was on an unused runway. Planes, not fashion.

The challenge with a runway is you can't put real effort into lighting it up, as you wouldn't want red-eye flights catching a glimpse and thinking it might be a fun place to stop. This run was going to be dark, real dark. Sure, we were all decorated with glow bracelets and necklaces, but there was little to no ambient light out on the course.

They told us the course was flat and well paved. We couldn't see it to confirm. We had to trust that we were not running into anything danger-ous: potholes to twist ankles, curbs to stub toes or random drop offs into vegetation. What we did have, unless you were the fastest runner, was the person in front of you. If they were not stumbling into a pile of surprised chaos, then it was probably a safe you could run where they just were.

After I got about 20 states into this 50-state mission, I became hyper vigilant about avoiding activities that could injure my legs. I stopped riding my bike and didn't even look at my roller blades. Walking on winter ice took on a whole new meaning. I worried that a leg injury would impact my ability to complete this goal within one year, so running through a seem-ingly infinite, black space was not in my current comfort zone.

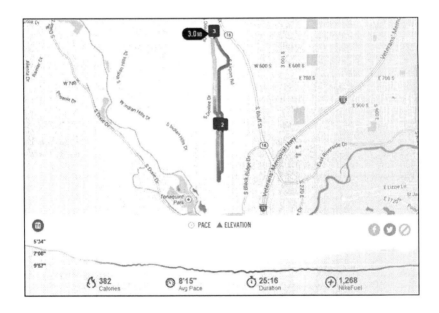

Yes, we were all adorned with glowing paraphernalia, but the illumina-tion from those items is not much when you are in vast, complete darkness. Even the items on your own body do not light up much of the world around you when you are running through empty space—there's nothing for the light to illuminate.

A large portion of this event required blind trust.

Thankfully, the course was an easy route as we ran out the runway and turned around with minimal twists and turns. The race organizers did a ter-rific job keeping us safe and away from hard objects and holes. For my part,

I did not let my fears hold me back. I just kept running even when no other runner was directly in front of me. I survived and managed to clock a decent low 25-minute run. It was not enough to place within my age group: I just missed the podium with a 4th place effort.

It was nearly midnight and Utah was completed. The Mountain states were completed. I was more than ready to dissolve into my bed at the hotel.

***

Utah Leadership Lesson:
Determination and Blind Trust

When you set out on achieving your goals, you need to be determined. Leaders can't falter over every setback. Taking on the entire country in a project like running a 5K in all 50 states in a year required a certain level of resolve. My mother's determination to see the Grand Canyon led her to some of the most amazing views she had ever seen, but it took her three attempts, all at great expense. We had our goals and we had a plan in place and we stuck with it. When obstacles arose, we regrouped and headed back out. Life doesn't happen smoothly. Use determination to get through the rough spots and find a way to achieve your goals.

At times, leaders will be challenged by not seeing a clear path forward. You might literally find yourself in the dark. When preparation and knowledge come together, you can confidently move forward even without the benefit of sight. Sometimes, it is safe to run in the dark, fly in the clouds, or dive into deep, dark water. Blind trust is not to be feared, but is to be prepared for and expected.

Chapter 51

Walk For Warriors Memorial Day 5K
Los Angeles, CA
May 26, 2014

When trying to see the entire country in one year, while still working full-time, managing a social life, and writing a book, it is not unusual for the GPS in your rental car to display the estimated time to your destination as 11 hours. That was the estimated time of travel from Moab, UT, to Los Angeles, CA. That Sunday, Mom and I were setting out on a seriously long road trip. We had a full day to accomplish it, and we plotted some sights along the way, namely Valley of Fire in Nevada.

That drive, and the rest of that long weekend, was terrific mother-and-son time. I have always appreciated time away with my mother. This drive was also laced with anticipation of California. I had been to Los Angeles twice before, so the excitement was not about the California sights, but rather the prospect of completing the 48 adjoining states. In my mind, this was a major accomplishment and signified that coming up fast was the finale: a 12-day trip to tackle Alaska and Hawaii.

CALIFORNIA
Sights Along the Way

Hollywood

Beverly Hills

Santa Monica

Mark Twain Statue

***

The morning of Memorial Day Monday was spent running a 5K in honor of our veterans. Running for those that have risked their lives so I can run is the least I can do.

California would be the seventh and last state in which I had a friend run with me. A few times earlier in this book, I mentioned one of my best friends David, who got me into running. David's fiancée, Taleen Maranian, lives in the greater Los Angeles area and decided to run the Memorial Day event with me. After a couple of rounds of phone tag, we found each other in the registration area for the Walk for Warriors Memorial Day 5K.

*"**Walk For Warriors Memorial Day 5K:** Walk for Warriors will take place this Memorial Day, Monday, May 26th on the Veterans Affairs Campus in West Los Angeles. Walk for Warriors is a wonderful opportunity to bring together all members of the Los Angeles community for one common cause—to support New Directions' programs for struggling veterans and their families."*

The course took us through the campus of Veteran Affairs in West Los Angeles. After a quick, flat start, we hooked left up a decent hill into a long loop we would ultimately do twice. It was a nice course, filled with equal up and downhill portions. I liked that we looped through the registration area twice, as it allowed spectators, my mom included, to cheer us on several times.

I was really grateful that Taleen showed up to run. It is always great to have a friendly face find you when you are 3,000 miles from home. The presence of another known human makes the whole experience a little more meaningful and adds to the memories. It is also nice to know that

Taleen Maranian participated in the Walk for Warriors Memorial Day 5K in Los Angeles, CA, with Jeff Fazio.

friends and family have been supportive of the 4D 50-state 5K goal.

***

This California run was happening 1 year and 2 weeks from my very first race, the Jersey Mike 5K. The Wounded Warrior 5K was my 57th 5K in that timeframe and would complete the Pacific Coast states.

A year earlier, when I ran the Jersey Mike 5K, was the first time I ran with other people. For 2 months prior to that race, I trained by myself. I hadn't run with friends or anyone until the day I showed up at City Island in Harrisburg, PA, for that race. In Chapter 1, I wrote about the difference I felt running with a large group of people. I also wrote about the guy I met pre-race and how I used him to gauge my pace and as motivation to push harder.

When I wrote about that first race, I left out another motivating factor I recognized that day. Honestly, I left this motivating factor out of several other chapters between then and now, too. I guess I thought we needed time to get better acquainted with each other before I shared this detail and, well, since we are nearing the end, it is time to come clean and tell you about "The Butt."

During that first race, I ran as fast as I could while keeping an eye on the pre-race guy. As my pace steadied, the legitimately faster runners started passing me. About a half-mile into the race she passed me. I don't know who she was, but she was clearly an avid runner. You could tell by her stride, by her confidence, her physique and, well, her butt.

Her butt was amazing. It was mesmerizing and, more importantly, it was motivating.

I was motivated to try my best to keep up, but the reality is that the work she put into sculpting her backside was more work than I could ever imagine putting into running and the distance between me and the pleasant sight of her running tights was getting bigger and bigger. Eventually, it was gone from view.

This exact scenario unfolded many times throughout 5Ks all over the country. Each provides a burst of inspiration for me to keep a faster pace than I am prepared for while enjoying a distraction from my breathing. And each time "The Butt" powered away, never to be seen again.

Back to the California 5K, shortly after the start, we headed up a gradual, but significant, hill. Since it was at the start and I tend to take off, I was doing pretty well on the hill, keeping a quick pace. In the back of my mind, I was telling myself that we had to do two laps and I would need to retrace each of these steps. It was not pleasant foreshadowing.

About halfway up the hill, she passed me and there it was: "The Butt." Considering how much a hill can kill my momentum, "The Butt" was both a healthy distraction and inspiration. Regardless, I was losing ground quickly as she powered on.

Running up hills tends to cost me several positions in a race, but I can often make some of them back up on the way down. As we crested the hill and started to turn back down, I could still see "The Butt" a couple of hundred feet ahead.

When I start going downhill, I am very comfortable extending my stride and letting gravity pull me. Many runners I have spoken to hold back their pace downhill, as it sometimes has an out-of-control feel or because they worry about their knees. Apparently, running downhill can be painful for some people at that joint. However, I feel free and can relax my breathing while dramatically improving my pace. Maybe it is from years of racing cars, but I am quite comfortable with out-of-control speed.

We started down that hill and my legs started stretching out and the ground under me started flying by. I was catching "The Butt" at a considerable speed, but the course started leveling and took my pace with it.

I was still approaching her, and closing the gap, and it seemed as if I would be able to pass her. I was actually going to pass "The Butt" for the first time ever in a race!

It was a glorious victory, but I knew it would be short-lived. When the uphill came back into view, I knew it was only a matter of time until she retook her spot ahead of me. I ran as fast as I could, but the hill loomed before me as we passed the half-way point of the race. My pace would start to plummet, both because of the hill and time into the course.

I fought as hard as I could and kept an eye on those passing me. The wait for "The Butt" to pass me seemed forever. It made the hill seem longer. "The Butt" transformed from a motivating factor for running quicker into something emphasizing the length of the hill. I wished she would pass me and get it over with so I could go back to being motivated to keep her pace.

She never passed me. I do not know how close she got to a second pass, but I never saw her again. Once I was over the crest for the second time, I knew she wouldn't pass me again. The legs came alive, the breathing was back under control, and I was gliding downhill toward the finish. It was the first time I ever beat "The Butt."

When Taleen and I met after the race, I told her about "The Butt." She gave me the "you're a typical guy" look until a few minutes later when I spied "The Butt" walking around the post-race crowd. I pointed her out to Taleen and I believe she understood. "The Butt" was clearly a sign of hard work and dedication to sculpting and I have always appreciated art.

Considering I ran up two hills, I was very pleased with a 24:22. In many 5Ks that time would have had a good chance of placing in my age group; however, this was beautiful, socially competitive Los Angeles, and it was barely good enough for 10th. It didn't matter though. I beat "The Butt" and felt incredibly victorious.

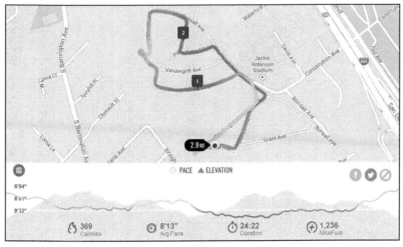

California Leadership Lesson:
How To Beat Your Nemesis

All too often leaders get caught up in beating their nemesis when their fiercest competitor ought to be themselves. If you really want to defeat your nemesis, then figure out how to beat yourself. You are the one standing in the way of conquering all of your rivals. I have been racing 5Ks, and I previously raced cars, and in both experiences I concentrated on improving myself and my times. At some point, the scale tipped, and I started besting my competitors too. Use those challengers as inspiration to push yourself farther to increase your own standard performance. The other victories will come in time, and they will be more solid because you concentrated on beating yourself and not the other person.

Chapter 52

Redemption Run 5K
Ottawa, Canada
June 7, 2014

Sometime after I ran the 25th state, South Dakota, people really started paying attention, recognizing that I was serious about making this goal happen inside a year. At various times, the same question kept being proposed to me: "So, what's next?"

What's next? Really?

I am running a 5K in all 50 states in 1 year and people want to know, "What's next?" My standard reply has been, "Does there really need to be more?" and people responded, "Yes."

There will be a next. However, the "next" will not have a deadline as this amazing "year" had. A time deadline adds an enormous amount of pressure and it eliminates a lot of wonderful options in exchange for expediency.

So, what is next?

A month before starting the 50-State 4D 5K Mission, I ran that 5K in Kingston, capital of Jamaica. During the 50-State 5K Mission, I also ran that 5K in Washington, D.C., the U.S. capital. Those two capital cities held the seeds of the next idea—run a 5K in the capital cities of the world.

There is no rule that states you have to finish one goal before you start the next. On June 7, 2014, I scheduled myself to run a 5K in Ottawa, capital of Canada. I also registered and booked the flights to run 5Ks in George Town, Grand Cayman Island on July 5and San Juan, Puerto Rico, on October 5.

As time, finances and opportunity allow, I will make 4D a capital experience around the world. There is no deadline. There is just a mission. I will continue to run for those that can't, wherever I can. As long as Muscular Dystrophy robs people of the ability to run, those of us who can run need to run for those who can't. This story will continue.

***

The Pacific Coast states moved onto the completed list which finished the 48 contiguous states and I had a free weekend before heading to Alaska and Hawaii. Ottawa, Canada, is only a 7-hour drive from my home—easily a 3-day weekend trip after what I had already accomplished. The plan was set and the alarm went off very early on June 6. I was on the road, driving to another country to run another 5K for those who can't.

On Saturday morning, I arose and got myself to the registration table for the Redemption Run 5K.

> **"Redemption Run 5K:** Each participant will receive a t-shirt and unique wooden medal. The race will be timed and each participant will pick up a chip on race day. There is a pancake breakfast for all participants after the race. Proceeds from this race will benefit Harvest House Ministries."

Like many events, this race offered runners multiple distances. They were hosting a 5K, of course, but also an 11K and a 21K. These distances for a race seemed unique to me. The 21K comes out to a half marathon. The 11K is not quite 7 miles.

Several options for distance at one event often increase my chances of placing within my age group, as it spreads runners out. Often, faster runners prefer longer distances. I'm impressed with those who have the fortitude to run long distances. For me, anything beyond a 5K seems like something to survive, not race. I've done 10Ks during training often and I can't imagine trying to go for time in those races.

The course was a simple out-and-back on a country road outside of Ottawa, so there was no worry of getting lost in Canada. As always, I took off at a quick pace and did my best to hold onto it. The faster runners caught me and started to pass.

About a half mile into the run, another runner caught me and started to pass. He was much younger than I and had a very steady stride. As soon as he started to pass, I could tell that his pace dropped slightly. He was slowing. I began closing the very small gap he created.

As I approached him, he picked up slightly and I may have slowed slightly. We settled into our pace and ran, shoulder-to-shoulder, out Ramsayville Road in search of a turnaround point.

His breathing was intense and his steps powerful. His breath reminded me to concentrate on mine. The louder he got, the more I tried to keep my breathing controlled and steady while maintaining his pace. Or was he matching my pace? We were running together like friends, although we had never met. The silence between us was broken only by the pounding of our shoes and air escaping our lungs.

The longer we ran, the more our pace matched. We were having an unspoken negotiation in pace as we wordlessly agreed to run together. As we ran, in subtle moments we seemed to push one another to increase the pace gently, and occasionally we gave each other permission to slow. We took turns playing each other's shadow.

I rarely take water from the midway-point station in a 5K. If anything, I yell to the volunteers to just throw it on me if I am really hot. My new partner dashed over to the station to grab a cup of water, a move that always costs time. I didn't have to take that turn as wide or slow down to grab the water, so I was able to put some distance between us.

It didn't take my shadow long to catch up and we returned to jockeying for position. We both knew that if we put serious effort into pulling away from the other, the energy expended would cost long-term and likely push us backward. The short-term gain was not worth the long-term risk.

We were on our way back and, magically, the course seemed uphill in both directions. We had now been running "together" for well over 15 minutes without any verbal communication. Our conversation was maintained in breath and stride.

The harder his breathing, the more I concentrated on controlling my own. Since I started running 5Ks, I have noticed that no matter how exhausted I am, I can find an enormous pocket of energy to blast to the finish line in a crazed sprint. When I cross the finish, my chest is ready to explode, with my heart racing out of control, my lungs sucking up atmosphere, and my pores releasing buckets of sweat.

About a quarter mile from the finish line, the road rose in front of us again. It was not a significant incline, but it was

CANADA

Sights Along the Way

Parliament of Canada

Supreme Court of Canada

Notre-Dame Cathedral Basilica

Giant Spider at the National Gallery of Canada

Major Hill's Park and the Rideau Canal

Steel Atlas Rocket

Armenian Embassy

Little Italy

enough to be enough already. Our breathing strained more and our pace slackened. I managed to blurt, "Another hill." He managed a quick reply, "Yeah, really." That was enough for both of us. We couldn't utter more than two words each without overdrawing the account.

The more he pushed and increased his breathing, the more I told myself I have reserves. I can generally sprint the last tenth of a mile, but that can be tricky, as not all courses are measured accurately. I now start my sprint based more on perceived distance to finish.

As the finish line came into view, we each picked up pace. We were taking turns pushing ever so slightly quicker and quicker. Then it happened. My blast.

I'm not sure how I do it, but I absolutely love the feeling of releasing 100% of whatever is left inside of me. It's my body's equivalent of going completely insane.

He ran too. He ran hard, but I had reserves. I had him by 4.9 seconds. What a rush.

I placed 16th overall and took 3rd in my age group (40-49) with a 26:30.7 run to his 17th place overall and 4th in his age group (19 and under) with his time of 26:35.6.

Once I caught my breath and dumped water over my head, I looked for him to congratulate him on an awesome run. From what the race volunteers told me, his parents were waiting for him, and they left together right after he finished. I really wish I could have shaken his hand. He was a serious motivator for me that day.

***

Canada Leadership Lesson:
Conspiring with the Enemy

Sometimes it pays to conspire with the enemy. Of course, sometimes it just pays to stop thinking of others as enemies. Either way, those who appear to be adversaries can often benefit us, and we can do the same for them. Everyone who runs does so for some reason. They have their own, individual stories and motivations.

I don't know the story of the guy who ran with me in Canada because he escaped before I learned it. Maybe that was the best 5K of his life and our fast-paced dance got him to a new level of performance. Maybe it was his first event and he found inspiration running with someone else. Maybe, just maybe, he dedicated his run to someone who can't. I will never know.

What I do know is what I got out of the run and how much his run pushed mine. He got me closer to my goal and added a new experience to the 5K for me. Be careful of who you consider an enemy as they may be an ally in disguise.

Chapter 53

22nd Annual Mosquito Meander 5K
Fairbanks, AK
June 14, 2014

If I was asked a year ago to make a list of ten things I would probably never do in the United States, visiting Alaska and Hawaii very well may have been on that list. Of course, many of the 50 states would have been on that list, but especially *those two*.

They are really far away from Pennsylvania, which makes visiting there a big investment in time and money. I enjoy traveling, but spending an entire day to get somewhere, especially by plane, is not enjoyable. But it had to be done.

On June 12, with 17 days left on the 1-year clock, I left home for a 12-day trip to complete Alaska and Hawaii. It was going to take me two cars, two trains and two planes to get to Alaska. At least that was the plan. Plans change.

The first two car rides were no issue and I made both trains without a hitch. That got me as far as the Philadelphia airport. US Airways flight 483 was scheduled to depart Philadelphia at 3:54 p.m. for Seattle, where I would have a 2-hour-and-7-minute layover until my flight to Anchorage, Alaska.

While I was sitting at the boarding gate, they announced a mechanical issue with the plane. Boarding would be delayed at least 45 minutes. It ended up an hour. After the extra wait, we finally boarded and the plane pulled away from the gate. We rolled onto the tarmac to get in line for the runway and the plane stopped. We sat there for about 10 minutes before the pilot announced that there was a mechanical issue with the plane and we had to go back to the gate.

We sat for another hour inside the plane while they tended to the issue. Since we could be pulling out at any moment, we were not allowed to leave our seats. We couldn't use the restroom and we were not offered any beverages. We just sat.

My layover in Seattle had been whittled to 7 minutes, and it was highly unlikely, even if I gave my best finish-line-is-coming-sprint, that I would make it to my Alaska Airlines plane to get to Anchorage.

We pulled away from the gate and got into line for the runway. The pilot announced we were safe to fly, but that we were now 27th in line for the runway, so it would be at least another 45 minutes until we actually took off. There went any chance of making Alaska that day.

I have spent too many hours of my life in traffic jams in Philadelphia, PA, but this was a first—traffic jam on airport tarmac. There were two long lines of planes waiting for their turns. It was just like being on I-76 in Philadelphia most days.

When I finally made it to Seattle, US Airways was not accommodating stranded passengers with rooms. They said everything in Seattle was booked and that it was up to us to find our own hotel rooms and contact their customer service department for reimbursement. The closest room I could find was in Tacoma, WA—a $90-taxi ride away.

US Airways was also not able to get me onto another plane to Anchorage early enough to have time to drive to Fairbanks for my run Saturday morning. Alaska Airlines came to the rescue as they were able to move me to a flight right into Fairbanks. That was the only solution for me to get to my race on time, but it meant that I would have to pay, out-of-pocket, for another flight from Fairbanks to Anchorage in two days to make my flight for Hawaii.

In all, I was out nearly $500 because US Airways ran late. The customer service department at US Airways eventually responded to my complaint. They offered $100 off my next flight—if I booked it directly through their agents, not online. Feel free to revisit Chapter 9 and my comments on customer service.

ALASKA
Sights Along the Way

North Pole (the town)

Santa Claus House

Alaska Pipeline Visitor Center

Alaska Zoo

Chugach State Park

Kenai Peninsula

Exit Glacier

Kenai Fjords National Park

Portage Valley

Byron Glacier

Eisenhower Alaska Statehood Monument

Anchorage Light Speed Planet Walk

Captain James Cook Statue

MLK Memorial

Mirror Lake Park

Thunderbird Falls

Eklutna Historical Park

Although I never had an intrinsic desire to see Alaska, Dee did. It was a bucket list item for her. She has family in Alaska whom she had never visited and she has always wanted to see the state.

By the time I got on the flight to Alaska, I had run 58 5Ks—55 of them "For Dee." Seven of them were at home in Pennsylvania; yet, Dee had never actually seen me run. Watching me race for her was also on her to-do list. Somehow it had just never happened.

As the excitement was building over the foreseeable completion of the 4D 50-State 5K Mission, Dee's family rallied and purchased tickets for her and her mother to fly to Fairbanks, AK, so she could finally see Alaska. So she could finally see me run.

Even with my US Airways runaround, I was able to get to Fairbanks a few hours ahead of Dee. I was delighted to meet a woman at the airport who was a volunteer with the Muscular Dystrophy Association in Alaska. She was there with a scooter for Dee to use while she visited the state. Through the MDA network, Dee was able to let them know she was coming and to see what sort of assistance they could offer. A scooter was the perfect accommodation. Dee was able to rent an appropriately-sized SUV for hauling the scooter, so she was set.

This type of service is why it is so important to donate to MDA. The opportunities and support MDA offices are able to provide those living with Muscular Dystrophy are truly life-changing. Back home, Dee has her own SUV that she purchased and MDA was able to provide her scooter and the modifications to her SUV to

Dee "4D" Gerber finally made it to Alaska with the assistance of family and the Muscular Dystrophy Association (MDA). Her mother, Pat Arms, joined her on the trip and Jeff Fazio met them at the airport in Fairbanks, AK.

accommodate the scooter. That included a mini-crane mounted in the back which picks up the scooter and places it down for her.

***

Dee and her mom had reserved a hotel room. I was, of course, Couch Surfing. I stayed with a group of people sharing the rental of a home just outside Fairbanks. My main hostess was Naomi O'Neal from Illinois. She does research for the University of Alaska and spends a lot of time exploring the Alaskan wilderness. Naomi is also a runner.

She agreed to run the Mosquito Meander 5K with me.

"22nd Annual Mosquito Meander 5K: *This is a flat looped course. The race benefits Fairbanks Counseling and Adoption".*

This was going to be the only time a Couch Surfing host ran one of the 5Ks with me, and that added a little something to the connection. Throughout this whole experience, I intentionally looked for things that made each event unique, and Naomi's running in the event was a nice addition. Some of the locals she typically runs with were also present at the event and I was able to meet a few of them.

As we talked about running and the race the night before, Naomi left out the part about her being a pretty fast runner. Although I took off fast from the start, it did not take her long to sail passed me. She is a strong, confident runner, and it was clear I would not be seeing her again until the finish line.

In many of my runs, there have been times I thought of Dee. Usually this happens when the run is particularly hard or a hill is feeling insurmountable. Dee has gotten me through the toughest parts of my races when I most felt like giving up or at least stopping to walk. At those times, the same thought kept running through my mind over and over as a motivating mantra: "You have to keep going, because she can't. It's hard for you, but impossible for her. At least you can do this; so do it."

Alaska was different. It was not a challenging run. It was a flat, fast course. The weather was perfect, slightly leaning to hot. With 649 runners, there was plenty of traffic to play in. It was a great day for a run, but I managed to think about Dee throughout most of the course. I knew she would be at the finish line, camera in hand, and I did not want to make her wait.

She had followed the year's events closely, so I knew she had an idea of when I would be coming if I had a good run—somewhere just after 24 minutes. I also knew that every minute after 24 would be a minute she'd wonder whether the run was okay and how I was doing. Really, I just wanted a solid run to make her happy. I wanted her to see one of the "good ones," especially because she sometimes tells me about the really "bad ones."

Of course, her "bad ones" are not days spent running, but rather days that muscular dystrophy seems to be winning the fight over her body's control. I can't imagine the struggle—the frustration that must accompany your muscles' not following direct orders. Those are her bad days.

I was grateful for the easy course and the opportunity to do well for her. I posted a solid 24:30-minute time, which placed me 36th overall out of

649. The time was not good enough for the top 3 in my age group, but I was a solid 4th.

Meanwhile, Naomi really kicked butt with a 22:23-minute run, which earned her 2nd place in 20-something women and 7th overall for the women. She was the latest runner to medal wearing a 4D pin.

Alaska was posted into my record books. Alaska was checked off Dee's bucket list.

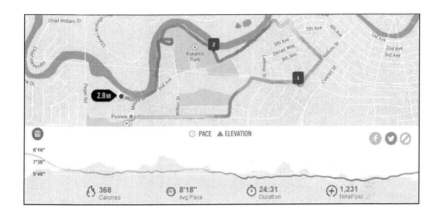

***

Alaska Leadership Lesson:
Embracing the Bucket List

Far too many people think of their bucket list as something for retirement or to do later in life. It gets put off from tomorrow to another day and then to another. It gets added to the "eventually" or "someday" pile. Leaders do not put things off. They plan and prioritize their "to do" lists.

It was a gift seeing how much joy Dee experienced being in Alaska. It is something she always wanted to do, and I suspect it may have happened regardless of the 4D campaign; however, I am certain it happened sooner because we were sharing the 4D 50-State 5K challenge. It is wonderful to think my insane mission inspired her to check something off of her bucket list.

I'm not sure that I really have a true bucket list, but if I did there would have been many things checked off that list as I traveled the country. Leaders should look for ways to accentuate their goals by accommodating other goals (like bucket lists) along the way. It adds to the experience and is efficient use of time. Leaders should also keep an eye on the "to do" lists of those around them and see if they can inspire others to check items off their lists while supporting their own causes. It creates a win-win for everyone and makes for lasting bonds and tremendous memories. Keep an eye on your bucket list, as you just never know when opportunity will knock.

Chapter 54

Kona 5K
Kailua-Kona, HI
June 22, 2014

One of the most emotional moments of my life was when Alaska Airlines 870 landed in Honolulu, HI. It meant that I had actually, physically made it to all 50 states in one year. It meant that I was going to make the Hawaii run in six days. This amazing journey would be successful. The mission would be completed.

I was in Hawaii, about as far from a continent as anyone could be on Earth and stand on dry land. I was in Hawaii. Growing up, we never had much money. I know that sounds like such a cliché coming from an author (does anyone who grows up *with money* write?), but it is true. Our vacations mostly centered on stealing a few days, maybe a week, at the Jersey shore. The idea of vacationing somewhere with blue water wasn't even a dream: it seemed impossible. Never had I entered one of the states with such an overwhelming sense of being there—*there*.

In a way, landing in Hawaii was more emotional than crossing the finish line of the Kona 5K a few days later. I knew that finish line was coming, but sometimes approaching the end is more impactful than the end itself. Months of buildup and anticipation were coming to an end. The naysayers had long been silenced. The supporters were poised for celebration.

Thankfully there were six quiet days between landing of the plane and running of the race. It was time to reflect. My eyes welled up often that week. This whole experience was so much bigger than me or Dee. Like many of my friends, family, and the people I met along the way, I often felt like a spectator to this achievement. I have done a lot of interesting things, but never have I been so aware of achieving while it was happening. This amazing journey was on the last chapter—well, almost the last chapter.

There was one more race that needed to happen to truly complete the 4D 50-State 5K mission, but let's finish Hawaii first.

***

Of all the states, I made sure to give myself the most time in Hawaii—a full week. This decision wasn't made because I was enthralled with traveling to Hawaii, but the exact opposite. I wasn't looking forward to getting to Hawaii. It is too expensive in both time and money. For that reason, I don't anticipate ever going back and I wanted to make sure I had enough time there, this time, to satisfy any curiosity I might have about the place.

Although I landed in Honolulu, I spent no time there. Our plane was a bit late, and we were literally rushed from one plane to the next to get to the Big Island. My entire experience in Hawaii would be on the Big Island. I would not visit the name-droppers of Honolulu, Waikiki, Maui, or Pearl Harbor.

That was fine by me. I had six days to explore the Big Island before my race Sunday. So explore I did, Couch Surfing the whole way. I met some great people and stayed in some wonderful homes. The Big Island has much to offer, and I was thankful I was able to set up hosts around the entire island, so that each day I could explore another aspect of the place.

***

A few months earlier, when I was planning the last few states, I had reached out to the race directors to let them know I was coming. The director of the Kona Marathon, Sharron Faff, responded and offered to get me a complimentary room at the Sheraton Kona Resort & Spa in Kona the night before the race if I was willing to give a talk

HAWAII
Sights Along the Way

Pu'uhonua O Hōnaunau National Historic Park

Whittington Beach Park

Punalu'u Black Sand Beach

Hawaii Volcanoes National Park

Wailuku River Rainbow Falls Section

Wailuku River Boiling Pots Section

Kamehameha The Great Statue

Lili'uokalani Gardens

Hilo Bay

Coconut Island

Onekahakaha Beach Park

Lava Tree State Park

Kapoho Point

'Akaka Falls State Park

Laupahoehoe Point

Waipio Valley Lookout

about my experience running the 50 states. I gladly accepted this offer. After a week of Couch Surfing, spending a night in the Sheraton sounded wonderful.

I arrived back in Kona on Saturday, June 21st to pick up my race packet and deliver my talk. It was a fitting end to this experience. It was a pleasure to have the opportunity to talk about my experience and the nice room was greatly appreciated.

The rest of Saturday was spent relaxing in the water around the hotel. I even made a few attempts at snorkeling. I was eager for Sunday. I knew I would have a lot to think about during that final run. Hawaii was the last state added to the union, and it would be the last state run in my 50-state challenge. I was ready for the Kona 5K.

> **"Kona 5K:** The 5K start is at the Keauhou Shopping Center on Ali'i Drive just south of Kailua-Kona, Hawaii. The course begins heading north on Ali'i Drive then doubles back for the remaining miles to the finish at the Sheraton Kona Resort and Spa at Keauhou Bay."

The Kona 5K started at a shopping center a few miles from the Sheraton and ended at the hotel. A shuttle from the hotel to the start line was provided to runners. I took the opportunity to get chatty with other runners on the bus. I spoke mostly with a woman from California, Anna-Maria Orlando.

The Kona Marathon had several races of various distances as part of a full day of racing. Anna-Maria was running the 10K. She listened intently to my story of 4D and how I was finishing the saga that day. She then opened her heart and told me her story. She had started running with her teenage son, Robert Orlando, a few years earlier. She enjoyed her time running with him, but he was senselessly killed at 17 years-old as a passenger in a car few months earlier. She hadn't run a race since.

Friends and family encouraged her to get back out there and run, run for her son. Run with her son. She wore his image on a necklace and took him with her that day. She was running for someone who couldn't in an entirely different way—a way I could not have imagined when we crafted the slogan for 4D.

My race went well. It was hillier than I expected for a coastal run on an island, but I barely noticed. Every step of that race my mind was filled with thoughts of Dee and of 50 states filled with unimaginable travel, unbelievable sights, incredible memories, amazing people, and many, many 5K races. My heart was full, my mind overrun, and my lungs were recycling air as fast as they could in pace with my feet chasing each other along Ali'i Drive.

The finish line was fast approaching. This goal was going to be achieved 51 weeks after it was started. All 50 states and Washington D.C. were run with a week to spare, and there was one more, very important race planned for that last week.

The finish line in Kona was reached in 25 minutes and 54 seconds. It wasn't my fastest run. It wasn't my best effort. But it was the last state and it was memorable.

My time earned me 2nd place in my age group and 35th overall out of 471 runners. It was a great way to complete the states.

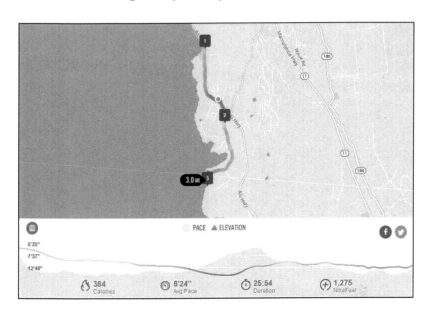

***

While I was wandering around post-race, catching my breath, guzzling water, and peaking at my 2nd place award, I saw Anna-Maria coming into finish her 10K effort. I ran to the finish line and cheered her in, giving her a high five.

A few days later I received the most touching message from Anna-Maria on the 4D Facebook page. She told me how much it meant to her that I was at the finish line, as she did not know a single person at the race. She appreciated that I took the time to hear her and her son's story. It meant so much to her. I had no idea. I was just doing what I do—which just goes to show how much of an impact we can have on one another.

Anna-Maria and I have since connected on Facebook, and I enjoy her posts about her running. She is still running with her son on her necklace, and with a 4D pin on her shirt. She will be one of those who will always run for those who can't.

***

Hawaii Leadership Lesson:
Achieving Your Goals

A crucial aspect of leadership is following through—completely—on what you started. The pyramids were not half built. The constitution was not partially written. Broadway shows do not end at intermission. Leaders need to find the path that leads to achieving their goals. There are many distractions that try to take us away from fully investing ourselves in our primary goals. We need to keep our focus and stay driven. Only with passion, dedication, and determination will goals, very large goals, be realized. If your ambitions are worthy of your time and attention to start, then they are worth the effort required to complete them.

Chapter 55

4D 5K
Lebanon, PA
June 29, 2014

Back in October of 2013, when I was approaching only the half-way mark of this adventure, on the 12-day journey across Wyoming and 5 of the Heartland states, Dee and I texted a lot. I understand the dangers of texting and driving; however, I think the cautions on texting while driving in some states may need to be reconsidered, namely North and South Dakota.

There is so much in both of these states to *not see* while driving that texting is almost a necessity. The views are largely bland, expansive and seemingly never-ending. North Dakota is the only place in the 48-contigious states where I was able to get myself 100 miles from the closest McDonald's. These states are, for the most part, remarkably unremarkable.

When you are on a 12-day drive that covers 4,500 miles while crossing the Dakotas three times, I highly encourage you to text while driving. In fact, not only do I encourage you to text while driving, but also suggest making coffee (fresh, grind the beans while driving), do crossword puzzles, analyze Einstein's theory of relativity, and try to count to a million using only prime numbers. Do what you need to do to stay awake and alive on those long, straight, boring interstates. Texting while driving kept me alive in the Dakotas and it felt significantly safer than the woman I passed reading the hard-backed book resting on her steering wheel.

During one of our texting sprees, I mentioned to Dee that it would be awesome to end this journey back in Pennsylvania with our very own 4D 5K. I immediately acknowledged that it probably wouldn't be possible, but was a fun idea. As a second thought, I suggested seeing how many runners with 4D pins we could get to show up to the same event. 4D runners could just crash someone else's party and support their cause while spreading the word about ours.

Dee's response sent me for another loop. She said that her local fire department used to host a 5K to raise money for the Muscular Dystrophy Association, but hadn't done so in a number of years. She said she would reach out to them and see if they would bring the race back.

After I returned from that trip, Dee caught me up-to-speed with her conversation with the firefighters. They said they would gladly support the

5K and would offer volunteer help, but they were not able to organize and plan the event.

We decided to bring together a group of talented individuals who might have an interest in serving on the inaugural 4D 5K race committee. Could we pull this off? We had about 6 months to get everything set up and ready to go—actually less, as we needed to be ready well in advance so runners could sign up.

Our team included Dave Berger, Blair Ciccocioppo, Chase Dubendorf, Dawn Losiewicz, Jess Matarazzi , Rose and Myles Miller, Adrienne Thoman, Bob Tier, and Audrie Yetter. We set our race date as June 29, 2014— exactly one year, to the day, of the first out-of-state 4D run that took place on June 30, 2013 in New York City.

We had a lot of work to do. We needed to secure site permits and race insurance, gather volunteers, solicit donations, advertise the event, make signs, hire a timing company, and determine where we were getting bananas and water, and much, much more. It was a task—a task worth undertaking. We were going to have our event, and the proceeds would go the local Muscular Dystrophy Association.

***

Hosting large events open to the public can be unnerving, as you never know whether you are going to get 30 people or 3,000 to show up. We hoped for 300.

Our race registration opened February 24, and 15 people signed up the first week. They were all people who knew someone on the race committee. It was a start and we had 4 months to go. Each week, a few more registrations came in, but not in huge numbers.

People who I had met along the way started signing up, which was an incredible surprise. The Tuesday night running group that ran the Philly Color Run together came out to support the race: Mandie Levan, Shawna Strine, Jodi Stuber, and Adrienne Thoman.

My good friend David Mena, who got me into running and joined me for one of the Arkansas runs, drove from New York for the 4D 5K.

Brad Bansner, the first person who I did not already know who posted a photo online running with a 4D pin, attended the race. It was an honor to meet Brad, as he competes in a variety of races and is an incredibly strong runner.

Kristy Higham, the first person to complete a marathon sporting the 4D pin, committed to coming to our event all the way from Rhode Island. She took the train to Philadelphia to pick up her marathoning friend, Laura McCarthy. They drove together to the 4D 5K.

Lourdes Moss-Keep, the owner of the Blue Bonnet Resort in Texas, flew out with a friend to participate. This was truly magnificent. I had traveled the country meeting extraordinary people, and they were returning the favor.

Not everyone could travel, but they supported the event by entering "virtually" in the 4D 5K. Our virtual runners included a few people I met while traveling the 50 states. Carol Meza, the race director of the Kansas run, who ran with me in Missouri, supported us from afar.

When I ran the 'Stache Dash in Wisconsin, I met Kate Gugerli, and her husband, Reto. Kate also participated virtually.

When I ran in South Dakota, Erika Winchester, working the race registration enjoyed hearing about the 4D 50-State 5K Mission, and she also supported our event from the comfort of her home state.

It was truly touching to Dee and me that so many people supported this event in so many ways

***

On June 29, 2014, a year to the day of the start of the 4D 50-State 5K Mission, I put on a race bib for one more 5K—our 5K—the 4D 5K. It was a beautiful morning and between runners and walkers we had just over 200 people line up at the starting line. That wasn't a bad turnout for our first time hosting an event like this. I was ready to race the 4D 5K.

> **4D 5K:** Not all of us can run. Do you ever think of those that can't run? We too often take our ability to run for granted. The 4D 5K is a fundraising event for the Muscular Dystrophy Association (MDA) and is held in honor of those who can't run. 4D: Run For Those Who Can't.

It was a great run; the course was a bit long, which I would prefer over short. We had some issues with course design that will be easily rectified for 2015. Turnout was great. The weather was a bit hot, but manageable.

Based on this experience, I don't recommend that race directors run in their own events. There is so much going on the night before and the morning of, that you will most likely not be in good condition to run. I was definitely not feeling 100%, but I ran happy, watching people enjoy our event.

My marathon-running friend David sailed passed me early on. Later in the course, he waited for me to catch up. He is such a good guy. I huffed out, "I'm not feeling it today."

He replied, "It doesn't matter. You don't have to feel this one. You have already proved what you can do. This is just a victory lap. Enjoy it."

I just about lost it—many emotions overcame me at that moment. I was so exhausted—too exhausted to cry, but I wanted to. What an incredible year. What an amazing journey. What awesome people. What a great friend.

I gathered what energy I could for one more blast to the finish, and David graciously made way, allowing me by to claim 3rd place in our age group. It was the best gift, from one of my best friends.

When the final numbers came in, I posted a 27:17-minute run to David's 27:18 (my time on the graphic is slight quicker than race time because I did not start the Nike+ watch until we were a bit into the race). He really didn't need to do that, but that is why he is a terrific person.

Dee Gerber and Jeff Fazio celebrate the end of an amazing 365-day journey.

The 4D 5K was a perfect last chapter, for this adventure and for this book. The year-long buildup was coming to an end and the whole host of characters who were introduced throughout the story came together for the crescendo. There was laughter. There were tears. There was a well-deserved celebration.

And one last leadership lesson: When people come together, amazing things are possible.

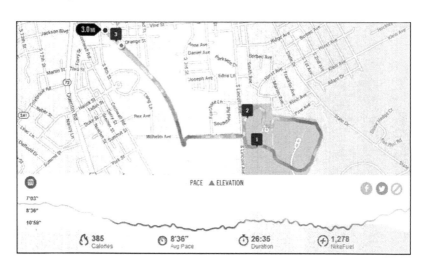

AFTERWORD

The 4D 50-State 5K experience remains the most complex task I have ever taken on. It has changed much about my life. I am fairly certain it changed Dee's life. By the feedback we have received, it is also apparent that it has made a difference in the lives of many others.

So many people have been motivated to run, to learn about Muscular Dystrophy, or to donate their time or money. This whole experience has been incredibly humbling. It has been, and will continue to be, an honor to "Run For Those Who Can't."

June 30, 2013 through June 29, 2014 was an unbelievable year. It far exceeded any expectations I could have mustered at that start, if it would have ever occurred to me to have any. It is hard to describe all the places I have seen, the races I ran, the lessons I learned, the people that I met and the life-long connections I made. It is my hope that this book was able to capture some of the magic that took place during those 365 days.

It's amazing what can be accomplished in the time it takes the Earth to take one lap around the Sun. It would be wonderful if this book inspired you—*yes, you*—to do something on your next trip around our star that is amazing and impactful. *You can do it*, and you can do it in honor of someone who can't.

As for me, in reflection on the last year, I leave you with these words:

I've run in Portland, Maine, and Portland, Oregon.

I've run in Fairmont, West Virginia; Fairmont Park in Philadelphia; Fairfield, Connecticut; and Fairbanks, Alaska.

I've run in Long Branch, New Jersey; Long Pond, Pennsylvania; and Long Beach, Mississippi.

I've run in heavy snow, light rain, direct sunlight, and complete darkness.

I've run at 2' and at 7,100' elevation.

I've run to celebrate Labor Day, Halloween, Thanksgiving, Christmas, New Years and St. Patrick's Day.

I've run in tank tops, cold-weather running pants, boxer shorts, and the nude.

I've run 51 different 5Ks and collected 45 race shirts, a hoodie, a head band, a pair of boxers, pajamas and socks.

I've run on main streets of cities, side roads in rural towns, boardwalks on the beach, paths through parks and cemeteries, up forested mountains, through cold creeks and down a steep, curvy road to a harbor.

I've run for Muscular Dystrophy, but I have also run for the American Cancer Society, Colon Cancer Alliance, Prostate Cancer, National Lung Cancer Partnership, Providence Cancer Center, Red Cross, National MS Society, Wounded Warrior Project, St. Jude Children's Hospital, Akron Children's Hospital, Literacy Volunteers, Pawtucket Red Sox Charitable Foundation, St. Charles Children's Home, National Press Club Journalism Institute, Little Sisters of the Poor, Only You Foundation, Stowe Adaptive Sports, REACH Haiti Ministries, Global Water, Cancer Centers of Southwest Oklahoma, Jason's Friends, Team Red White and Blue, Playworks Chicago, Lawrenceville Cooperative Ministry Food Bank, Carnival Association of Long Beach, Uplift Organization, Denver Urban Ministries, International Association of Firefighters Burn Foundation, Legal Aid of Arkansas, St. Jude Research Hospital, YMCA, Fairbanks Counseling & Adoption Center, New Directions, and Harvest House Ministries.

I am lucky, not because I was able to travel to all 50 states to run, but because I am able to walk. Not all of us can, please think of those who can't.

4D—Run For Those That Can't

SPECIAL THANKS

I can never express enough gratitude to the plethora of people who made the 4D 50-State 5K Mission a reality. At the very least, I would like to recognize many of them here:

THANK YOU to the runners that inspired me to put on my sneakers and go outside: David Mena, Matthew R. Shupp, and David Satterlee.

THANK YOU to the runners and friends who motivated me, ran with me or helped me: Adrienne Thoman, Mandie Levan, Jodi Stuber, Melissa Mahoney, Shawna Strine, Rose Miller, Angela Gorman, Lola Fabros, Patrine Lewis, Robert Hall, Ron Paukovits, Natalie Rose, Jeffrey Herstine, Sarah Cazella Solomon, Carol Meza, Sherry Christian, David Mena, Taleen Maranian, and Bim Angst.

THANK YOU to the people who have made donations to this cause and helped make this experience possible: Lourdes Brioso Moss Keep, Peter Doane, Ardell Simon, Robert Simon, Kyron Banks, Vee Insixiengmay, Rose Miller, Myles Miller, Yolanda Perez, Amy Withrow, Dee Gerber, Chris Coia, David Mena, Kate Chescattie, Karen Rollins, Thad Sampson, Debbie Bucks, Tammy & Amos Gebhard, Victoria (on the plane to Omaha), Reto Gugerli, Kim Kelsey, Tim Banks, Dwayne Hunt, Michael Sandy, Emily Jayne Wagner, Ron Paukovits, Gail Chatfield, Kristy Higham, David Surratt, Julie from SC, Sheila Ciotti, Ruth Purgason, and Bim Angst.

THANK YOU to my Couch Surfing Hosts: Mary and Mike Lane, Victoria Nayiga, Erik Hein, Matthew Rogers, Dee's Aunt Pam & Uncle Scott, Kenny Ludacka, Fay Bisbee, Christina Gonzalez, Danielle Rodier, Arik from S.D., Stephanie Strand, Jayne Mosley, Brandy Koch, Melissa Green, Paulson Skerrit, Susan and JP, Aysun Ulusan, Brian Dear, Devin Dillon, Basia Muż, Heather Morris, Jim Musser, Erik Jonsson, Kelly Redmond, Joe Krueger, Susan and John Hendricks, Wes Owens, Claire Lettow, Jeffrey Werle, and Naomi O'Neal.

THANK YOU to the runners and supporters I met along the way: Kristy Higham, Sherry Christian, Sarah Solomon, Carol Meza, Gail Chatfield, Laura McCarthy, Julie Addis, Kiesha Cordier, Kate and Reto Gugerli, Ashley Foley, Melody Williams, Christie Dillie, Alexander Richie, Lauren Mulac, Julie Faust, Niki Ronnan, Mike Ewaldt, Lisa Holbrooks, Debbie Milligan, Julie Nickelson, Daniela Petkova, Francesca Fontana, Melissa Tabor, Nancy Winmill, Janine Johnson, Kiley Macdonald, Anna-Maria Barrett Orlando, Adeline Besse, and Liane Völker.

THANK YOU to the friends I have made through the Muscular Dystrophy Association: Dave Berger, Karen Lindeman Corp, Anastasia Corp, Audrie Yetter, Deanna Stuart, Karen Rollins, and Heather Boydston.

... and a **HUGE** THANK YOU to the inaugural 4D 5K Race Committee: Dee Gerber, Rose and Myles Miller, Adrienne Thoman, Blair Ciccocioppo, Audrie Yetter, Jess Matarazzi, Dawn Losiewicz, and Bob Tier.

... and, a special thank you to Bim Angst for, well, being Bim Angst.

50-STATE STATISTICS

Mileage:
>78,066 – Total miles traveled on the 50-State 4D 5K Mission
>50,319 – Miles on planes.
>19,749 – Miles in Rental Cars.
>7,660 – Miles on my car.
>176.7 – Miles ran in 5Ks from 6/30/13–6/29/14.
>161.2 – Miles ran in 5Ks ran as part of the 50-state challenge.

Costs:
>$20,289.99 – Total expense of this mission.
>$5,928.04 – Price of all flights.
>$4,682.68 – Cost of all food on the trips.
>$3,859.06 – Cost of fuel for my car and rentals cars.
>$2,935.48 – Fees for rentals cars.
>$1,532.90 – Registration fees for the 5K races.
>$790.74 – Parking, Tolls and Trains.
>$561.13 – Cost for Motels (Thank you Couch Surfing!).
>$397.84 – Average cost per state.

Medals/Placing:
>1 – 1st place overall
>2 – 2nd places overall
>9 – 1st places age group
>3 – 2nd places age group
>5 – 3rd places age group

Other interesting numbers:
>52 – The number of 5Ks officially part of the 50-state experience.
>57 – The number of 5Ks actually ran from 6/30/13–6/29/14.
>36 – The number of motel nights saved by Couch Surfing.
>27 – Number of trips taken to complete the 50 states + D.C.
>15 – Number of flights taken to accomplish this goal.

RESOURCES

Website for the Muscular Dystrophy Association (MDA)
        mda.org

Website for the Center for Disease Control and Prevention MD facts
        www.cdc.gov/ncbddd/musculardystrophy/facts.html

Website for this book and more information on the 50-State 4D Mission
        www.running-across-america.com

Website for the 4D 5K
        www.4D5K.org

Facebook pages for 4D:
        www.facebook.com/Run4D

Website for ordering 4D products for
        Runners: www.cafepress.com/4d4d
        Cyclists: www.cafepress.com/4d4dbike
        Hikers: www.cafepress.com/4d4dhike
        Swimmers: www.cafepress.com/4d4dswim
        Triathletes: www.cafepress.com/4d4dswimrunbike

Websites for finding 5Ks around the United States:
        www.runningintheusa.com
        www.race360.com
        www.roadracerunner.com

Website for finding some of the best people in the world
(and free places to stay while traveling):
        www.couchsurfing.com

Website for finding unique roadside attractions around the United States
        www.roadsideamerica.com

Website for those that have visited all 50 U.S. states
        www.allfiftyclub.com/

REFERENCES

Race links are listed in the order they were accomplished.

PA: Jersey Mike 5K: jerseymikerun.com/#cause

PA: Race Against Racism 5K: www.ywcahbg.org/events/race-against-racism-2013

JAMAICA: PUMA/Fortis 5K: www.runningeventsja.com/events/fortis-2013.html

PA: Hoot-n-Howl 5K: www.turnerkia.com/hootnhowl5k.htm

NY: VCTC 5k Cancer Challenge: www.vctc.org/page/5k2m-cancer-challenge

NJ: Undy 5000:
support.ccalliance.org/site/PageServer?pagename=undy_about_landing

WV: Run to Read Races 5K: www.runningintheusa.com/run2read/

OH: Scrappers 5K: gopherarun.com/races/2013-mahoning-valley-scrappers-5k.html

VA: Spartyka Wounded Warrior 5K: www.spartyka.com/sww5k/

MD: Krumpe's Donut Alley Rally:
krumpesdonuts.com/event/krumpes-donut-alley-rally-2013

ME: MS Harborfest Shoreside 5K:
eventmam.nationalmssociety.org/site/TR?fr_id=21396

PA: Warrior Dash: www.warriordash.com

RI: PAWSOX 5K:
www.milb.com/content/page.jsp?sid=t533&ymd=20120613&content_id=33238228

MA: Labor Day 5K for MS:
eventmam.nationalmssociety.org/site/TR?fr_id=22287&pg=entry

NH: St. Charles Children's Home 5K: runningnuns.com/labor-day-race/race-details/

DC: NPC's Beat the Deadline 5K: press.org/5k

DE: Nun Run 5K: www.nunrun5k.org/race.php

CT: 5K For Only You: www.onlyyoufoundation.org/1st-annual-5k.html

VT: Trapp Cabin 5K: stoweadaptive.org/Trapp%20Cabin.htm

KY: Latonia 5K: latonia5k.wordpress.com

TN: The Glow Trot 5k: lovegreater.org/glowtrot5k/

NC: Global Run 4 Water: www.rotarydistrict7710rotaryglobalrun4water.com

TX: The Bare As You Dare 5K: www.bluebonnetnudistpark.com/bayd

OK: Spirit of Survival: Superhero 5K: www.spiritofsurvival.com

KS: Zombie Chase 5K: www.facebook.com/events/376875795759282/

NE: Free to Breathe Omaha Lung Cancer 5K: omaharun.org/events/

WY: Laramie Blizzard Blast: blizzardblast.org/blast/blast.html

MN: Scare in White Bear 5K:
trifitnesswbl.com/as_scare-in-white-bear-overview#schedule

ND: Sheyenne Valley Shuffle: runningintheusa.com/Race/View.aspx?RaceID=60127

SD: Halloween Sock Hop: www.blackhillsrunnersclub.com/halloween-run

WA: Mock the Clock 5K: www.mocktheclock5k.com/locations/2013/seattle.php

OR: Run for the Hole: runforthehole.com

LA: Crescent City Fall Classic 5K: www.ccc10k.com/crescent-city-fall-classic

AL: Stamp Out MD5K: productionsbylittleredhen.com/raceinfo_s.asp?raceid=SOMD13

PA: Philadelphia Marathon: philadelphiamarathon.com

WI: The HOG's 'Stache Dash: www.silvercirclesportsevents.com/hogs-stache-dash

IA: Run for the Red: www.redcross.org/news/event/ia/clinton/Run-for-the-Red

MI: Howell Fantasy 5K: howellfantasy5k.com/signup.php

IL: Grant Park Turkey Trot 5K: www.allcommunityevents.com

IN: Leftover Turkey Trail Run: uplandbeeradventures.com/event/leftover-turkey-trail-run

NV: Come Run with Santa 5K: www.lasvegasrunningteam.com/events.htm

AZ: 5K Jingle Run: racetimers.com

FL: Biggest Loser 5K: www.biggestloserrunwalk.com

GA: Flashlight 5K: flashlight5k.org/

SC: Ring In New Year's Trail Race: rockhillstriders.org/ring-in-new-years-day-trail-races.html

MS: Long Beach Carnival Classic 5K: www.facebook.com/lbcarnivalclassic

MO: Leprechaun Lane 5K: www.bodiespersonaltraining.com/leprechaun-lane-5k-10k-race.html

CO: Lucky Laces 5K: www.runningguru.com/EventInformation.asp?eID=9929

NM: Shamrock Shuffle 5K: www.irunfit.org/sports/icalrepeat.detail/2014/03/16/86/-/nm-shamrock-shuffle-2014

MT: Montana Made Run: www.montanamaderun.org

AR: Law Day 5K: www.jonesboro10k.com

AR: Fun Run 5K: www.marionchamberrun.com

ID: Famous Idaho Potato 5K: www.ymcatvidaho.org/fip

UT: Midnight 5K: www.sgcity.org/running/midnight.php

CA: Walk For Warriors Memorial Day 5K: walkforwarriors.org/faf/home/default.asp?ievent=1093361

CANADA: Redemption Run 5K: www.harvesthouse.org/fund/redemption_run.html

AK: 22nd Annual Mosquito Meander: www.fcaalaska.org/race_information.html

HI: Kona 5K: www.konamarathon.com

PA: 4D 5K: 4D5K.org

Made in the USA
Middletown, DE
20 February 2015

THE SEX OF ARCHITECTURE

Editors

Diana Agrest

Patricia Conway *managing editor*

Leslie Kanes Weisman

DIANA AGREST

DIANA BALMORI

ANN BERGREN

JENNIFER BLOOMER

M. CHRISTINE BOYER

LYNNE BRESLIN

ZEYNEP ÇELIK

BEATRIZ COLOMINA

MARGARET CRAWFORD

ESTHER DA COSTA MEYER

DIANE FAVRO

ALICE T. FRIEDMAN

GHISLAINE HERMANUZ

CATHERINE INGRAHAM

SYLVIA LAVIN

DIANE LEWIS

MARY MCLEOD

JOAN OCKMAN

DENISE SCOTT BROWN

SHARON E. SUTTON

SUSANA TORRE

LAURETTA VINCIARELLI

LESLIE KANES WEISMAN

MARION WEISS

Harry N. Abrams, Inc.,
Publishers

EDITOR: Diana Murphy
DESIGNER: Judith Hudson

LIBRARY OF CONGRESS CATALOGING-IN-
PUBLICATION DATA

The sex of architecture / editors,
Diana Agrest, Patricia Conway, Leslie
Kanes Weisman.
p.   cm.
Includes index.
ISBN 0-8109-2683-0 (pbk.)
1. Architecture and women. 1. Agrest,
Diana. 11. Conway, Patricia. 111. Weisman,
Leslie.
NA2543.W65S48 1996
720' .82—dc20   96-5552

Printed and bound in Japan

The quotation in M. Christine Boyer's
caption to fig. 3 is taken from Malvin
Wald and Albert Maltz, "*The Naked City*":
A Screenplay (Carbondale and Edwards-
ville: Southern Illinois University Press,
1948), 3.

Front cover: Erwin Blumenfeld. Lisa
Fonssagrives on the Eiffel Tower, Paris.
1938. Collection Kathleen Blumenfeld;
courtesy French *Vogue;* © 1996 Artist
Rights Society (ARS) New York/ADAGP,
Paris

CONTENTS

Acknowledgments

The essays in this book have been developed from selected papers delivered at a conference entitled "Inherited Ideologies: A Re-Examination," held at the University of Pennsylvania on March 31 and April 1, 1995, and attended by more than four hundred people from all over the East Coast and as far away as California, Canada, and Australia. The spirit of that conference was a conversational one: a dialogue among women theorists, historians, educators, and practitioners concerned with critical issues in architecture and the related fields of urban design and landscape architecture. While not a feminist conference *per se*, many of the papers presented there were informed by a gendered perspective – a perspective that eventually determined the contents of this book.

So far as we know, "Inherited Ideologies" was the first all-women academic assembly on architecture in the United States, and credit for bringing together its remarkably diverse participants is due to the program organizers – Diana Agrest, Diana Balmori, Jennifer Bloomer, Lynne Breslin, Zeynep Çelik, Patricia Conway (conference chair), Mildred Friedman, Susana Torre, and Leslie Kanes Weisman – who had been meeting regularly in New York City since 1992 as part of a larger group of professional women. When Penn's newly formed Annenberg Public Policy Center announced a year-long series of university-wide conferences on "Women in the Public Sphere" (1994–95), Conway, then dean of Penn's Graduate School of Fine Arts, conjoined the planning for her school's conference with the emerging interests of the women with whom she had been meeting in New York. Out of this collaboration, the program organizers enlisted the participation of women colleagues around the country who were doing work that, broadly construed, related to the themes of public place and private space around which the Graduate School of Fine Arts "Inherited Ideologies" conference was being developed.

All of the foregoing is by way of saying that to properly acknowledge the efforts that have gone into the making of this book, we must first thank the Hon. Walter H. Annenberg, a part of whose extraordinary gift to the University of Pennsylvania helped to fund the "Inherited Ideologies" conference; and Kathleen Hall Jamieson, dean of Penn's Annenberg School for Communication and director of the Annenberg Public Policy Center, whose leadership mobilized an entire university around an issue, "Women in the Public Sphere," that, heretofore, had received insufficient attention. In addition, we are grateful to those women who, while choosing to remain anonymous, have made important contributions to the success of these endeavors. For their unflagging energies in compiling and processing the contents of this book, Joshua Gesell, Eva Gibson, and Margaret Braver deserve special mention. We are also indebted to Diana Murphy, Senior Editor at Harry N. Abrams, Inc., who guided the progress from wide-ranging conference proceedings to a more topical collection of essays. Finally, our deepest appreciation goes to the authors, whose provocative essays collectively express the power and diversity of women's views on architecture today.

Diana Agrest
Patricia Conway
Leslie Kanes Weisman

Foreword

Today women are playing more important roles in the production of architecture
than at any time in this country's history. A growing number are succeeding in
smaller, critical practices that tend to lead the larger, more commercial firms
toward the cutting edge of design; they are entering – and winning – their fair
share of public-sector competitions, traditionally the first step toward a distinguished career in architectural design.

At the same time, women continue to encounter obstacles created by
gender prejudice at defining moments in their careers. For the last two decades,
they have constituted nearly half the enrollment in this country's most prestigious
architecture programs – programs from which they are consistently graduated
at the tops of their classes. Yet in 1995, only 8.9 percent of registered architects
and 8.7 percent of tenured architecture faculty in the United States were women.

Almost no women are recognized as name partners in large commercial
firms, nor has any woman in this country ever been commissioned to design a
nationally significant building on the scale of, say, Ada Karmi-Melamede's
Supreme Court in Jerusalem or Gae Aulenti's Musée d'Orsay in Paris. Moreover,
the number of women holding top administrative positions and named chairs
in American university architecture programs remains shockingly low; and since
the retirement of Ada Louise Huxtable from the *New York Times*, no woman
has had a commanding voice as architecture critic for a major city newspaper or
weekly newsmagazine. It comes as no surprise, then, that although at least
two women have received the RIBA Gold Medal in Great Britain, no woman
has been awarded either of this country's highest architectural honors: the AIA
Gold Medal or the Pritzker Prize.

Nevertheless, it is critical practice and competition entries that exert the
most powerful pull on the discourse of architecture, and in this discourse women
have a remarkably strong presence. Writing as theorists, critics, historians,
educators, and practitioners, women are at the forefront of the debate in architecture today – a debate that is reshaping the way we think about our built
environment at the millennium. Inevitably one of the most controversial issues
to surface in this debate is gender: a seemingly circular discourse that begs, yet
refuses, closure.

P.C.

Introduction

Sex. The word is layered with meaning and provocation. Embedded within it are the corporeal and the carnal, sensuality and desire, male and female, human reproduction. The inscription of the sexualized body is a central and recurrent theme in Western architecture, but that body is neither innocent nor androgynous. It is a reification of the male longing to appropriate an exclusively female privilege: maternity. Thus the insistence, in ancient and contemporary discourse, that male architects "give birth" to their buildings. Implicated in man's inevitable state of childlessness, which gives rise to an obsession with "reproducing himself," is the systematic erasure of woman and her contributions.

If sex condenses the notions of body and power that have permeated architectural criticism since the Renaissance revival of Classicism, an analysis of gender in modern architectural criticism reveals a social system that has historically functioned to contain, control, or exclude women. It is from these perspectives that the twenty-four authors in this book, all of whom are women, more closely reexamine some long-suspect "truths": that man builds and woman inhabits; that man is outside and woman is inside; that man is public and woman is private; that nature, in both its kindest and its cruelest aspects, is female and culture, the ultimate triumph over nature, is male. These and other gender-based assumptions – in particular those associating men with economic production, wage earning, and the city, and women with consumption, non-wage earning domestic labor, and the home – are the subjects of many of the essays in this volume.

Perhaps a reexamination of such "truths" might begin with the concept of "otherness" originated by Simone de Beauvoir more than fifty years ago and here explored philosophically by Mary McLeod in her critique of Foucault. Esther da Costa Meyer considers the same concept, but from a psychoanalytic point of view, in her investigation of agoraphobia, that puzzling disorder afflicting primarily women, to which Lauretta Vinciarelli responds with some sociological observations. Indeed, almost all of the essays in this book identify, explicitly or implicitly, the female as "other," and it is from this marginalized position that women writing on architecture today are exploring history, the uses of public space, consumerism, and the role of domesticity in search of "ways into" architecture, often through alternative forms of practice and education. We are now in an era where discourse is as important as design, often more important, and a number of authors address their subjects from this perspective. Catherine Ingraham, for example, confronts the prevailing and clearly gendered bias in favor of images over words, a view with which Diane Lewis emphatically disagrees; and Jennifer Bloomer writes with nostalgic longing about domestic space in order to examine important architectural questions of matter, materiality, and gravity in the age of non-physical, electronic communication.

Throughout many of these essays there runs a current of struggle: the struggle for active participation in the modern project. Nowhere is that struggle made more vivid than in those essays dealing with the city. M. Christine Boyer's proposition of the *femme fatale* as urban allegory in film noir is particularly intriguing in this regard, as is Margaret Crawford's extension of the argument to include the genre of the hard-boiled detective novel. It is through the Greek play that Ann Bergren takes us back to an ancient text, Aristophanes' *Ecclesiazusae*, wherein women rebel against the Classical architecture of the house and the city. Looking at a more recent past, Diana Agrest critically reexamines modernist urbanism and scientific discourse to explain the absence of nature from urban discourse over the last fifty years. Still on the subject of nature, Diana Balmori gives us a narrative that reveals another missing character, Culture.

War, occupation, and violence, including the violence of poverty and the breakdown of traditional cultural values – which afflicts millions of women no longer protected by traditional social structures – are also recurring themes. Just as Zeynep Çelik's essay on colonial Algiers traces the subversion of male/public versus female/private spaces in a war for independence, so Susana Torre chronicles the transformation of the main square in Buenos Aires by mothers in their struggle to account for thousands of people who "disappeared" during Argentina's repressive military dictatorship. Beatriz Colomina documents the invasion of Eileen Gray's private space, the home she designed for herself at Roquebrune-Cap Martin, by Le Corbusier's essentially public act of painting murals on her walls – an act because of which many historians later credited Le Corbusier with the design of Gray's house. Sylvia Lavin replies to Colomina's thesis by analyzing Gray's house and the *cabanon* Le Corbusier built to overlook it in terms of primitive hut-making and the desire for escape.

The concept of "home" is explored in a very different way by Joan Ockman, to whose critique of the redomestication of American women following World War II Denise Scott Brown replies with a discussion of the architectural strategies that accompanied women's newly defined roles of consumption. Alice T. Friedman analyzes the formative role of women as clients for certain "signature" houses designed by "star" (male) architects, while

Ghislaine Hermanuz focuses on women as shapers of the domestic program within the political framework of race and class.

Other authors discuss the uses of architecture and discourse to confront bigotry and prejudice, marginality and powerlessness. Lynne Breslin, for example, analyzes exhibitions on anti-Semitism and racism to illustrate how the museum can be designed to serve as an instrument of public education and personal transformation, while Diane Favro summarizes the history of American women as chroniclers of the profession from which they were largely excluded. Marion Weiss documents a project – the Women's Memorial and Education Center at Arlington National Cemetery – that is both about the recognition of women's achievements and symptomatic of it. Leslie Kanes Weisman describes a feminist vision of architectural education and practice dedicated to fostering human equity and environmental wholeness, and Sharon E. Sutton replies to Weisman by counting the personal and professional costs of teaching and practice in service of social justice.

A word about the structure of this book. The pairing of certain essays with responses not only echoes the dialogue format of the "Inherited Ideologies" conference but also helps to illuminate common themes running through a remarkably diverse body of work. Yet it is also possible to make these connections in different ways. For example, Bergren's essay can as usefully be read with Ockman and Friedman on domesticity as with Boyer, Crawford, and Çelik on the city, or with Ingraham and McLeod on discourse; Agrest also can be read with Ingraham and McLeod as well as with Balmori on nature, or with other essays on the city; and so on. For this reason, no attempt has been made to group texts in rigid categories. Rather, readers are encouraged to construct their own sequences, to explore the multiple ways of reading this book that will continually shift its meanings.

D.A., P.C., L.K.W.

"Other" Spaces and "Others"

MARY McLEOD

One of the primary preoccupations of contemporary architectural theory is the concept of "other" or "otherness." Members of the so-called neo-avant garde – architects and critics frequently affiliated with publications such as *ANY* and *Assemblage* and with architecture schools such as Princeton, Columbia, Sci Arc, and the Architectural Association – advocate the creation of a *new* architecture that is somehow totally "other." While these individuals repeatedly decry utopianism and the morality of form, they promote novelty and marginality as instruments of political subversion and cultural transgression. The spoken and unspoken assumption is that "different" is good, that "otherness" is automatically an improvement over the status quo.

This tendency is most clearly evident among so-called deconstructivist architects and critics, who advocate strategies such as disruption, violation, and break as a means of dismantling architectural forms and creating a new architecture that is somehow "other." Previously, I have raised questions about the limits of linguistic analogies inherent in deconstructivist theory and its equation of formal change with political change.[1] In this paper I would like to turn instead to another strain in contemporary architectural theory that also emphasizes, indeed validates, "otherness." This alternative view is articulated by a diverse group of architects and theorists, such as Anthony Vidler, Aaron Betsky, Catherine Ingraham, and Stanley Allen, who have been influenced by Michel Foucault's notion of "heterotopia."[2] They also often endorse deconstructivist architecture (and what might be considered historical precedents, such as Piranesi's Carceri or Campo Marzio), but they embrace its colliding, fragmented forms as embodiments of Foucault's more politicized concept of heterotopia, or "other" spaces.[3] Here the notion of "other" refers to that which is both formally and socially "other." Difference is a function of different locations and distributions of power, as well as of formal or textual inversion. "Other" therefore encompasses physical and social arenas outside of or marginal to our daily life.

Foucault gives his most complete discussion of heterotopia in his essay "Des Espaces autres," a lecture he delivered at a French architectural research institute in 1967 and which was not published in English until 1985.[4] Since it was written as a lecture, it lacks Foucault's usual rigor; his argument seems loose, almost conflicted at times, as if he were groping for examples. But it is also his most comprehensive discussion of physical space,[5] and its very looseness may be one of the reasons for its influence in recent architectural discourse.

In this essay Foucault distinguishes heterotopias from imaginary spaces – utopias – and from everyday landscapes. He proposes that certain unusual, or out-of-the-ordinary, places – the museum, the prison, the hospital, the cemetery, the theater, the church, the carnival, the vacation village, the barracks, the brothel, the place of sexual initiation, the colony – provide our most acute perceptions of the social order (figs. 1–6). These perceptions might derive either from a quality of disorder and multiplicity, as in the brothel, or from a kind of compensation, a laboratory-like perfection, as in the colony, which exposes the messy, ill-constructed nature of everyday reality. Many of the spaces cited, such as the prison or asylum, are exactly the arenas that Foucault condemns in his institutional studies for their insidious control and policing of the body. In this essay, however, his tone is neutral or even laudatory of those "other" spaces. Foucault suggests that these heterotopic environments, by breaking with the banality of everyday existence and by granting us insight into our condition, are both privileged and politically charged. He asserts that they "suspend, neutralize, or invert the set of relationships" that they designate.[6]

What are explicitly omitted from his list of "other" spaces, however, are the residence, the workplace, the street, the shopping center, and the more mundane areas of everyday leisure, such as playgrounds, parks,

FIG. 1

Thomas Wright. Kirkdale House
of Correction, near Liverpool.
1821–22

FIG. 2

Libéral Bruand. Hôtel des
Invalides (a hostel for wounded
soldiers), Paris. 1670–77

FIG. 3

Charles Garnier. Opéra, Paris.
1861–75

FIG. 4

E. Angelou. Prostitute in a French brothel during the Belle Epoque. Stereoscopic photograph, ca. 1900

FIG. 5

John James Burnett (for Imperial War Graves Commission). British Military Cemetery, Jerusalem. 1919–27

FIG. 6

Albert Laprade. Central axis of Parc Lyautey (now Parc de la Ligue Arabe), Casablanca. 1915. Foucault writes of heterotopias: "On the one hand they perform the task of creating a space of illusion that reveals how all of real space is more illusory, all the locations within which life is fragmented. On the other, they have the function of forming another place, as perfect, meticu-lous, and well-arranged as ours is disordered, ill-conceived, and in a sketchy state. . . . Brothels and colonies, here are two extreme types of heterotopia"

FIG. 7

Mom's house, Wheaton, Maryland.
1951. For Foucault, the house is
an "arrangement of rest" and thus
not a heterotopia

sporting fields, restaurants, and so on (fig. 7). (Cinemas, paradoxically, are both excluded and included as heterotopias.) Indeed, in his emphasis on isolated institutions – monuments, asylums, or pleasure houses – he forsakes all the messy, in-between urban spaces that might be considered literally heterotopic. For most American architecture critics, the political ambiguity and two-sided nature of Foucault's notion of heterotopia (its diversity or its extreme control) has been ignored. Following Foucault's brief commentary in *The Order of Things*, they interpret the concept simply as incongruous juxtaposition – exemplified by Borges's Chinese encyclopedia or Lautréamont's pairing of the umbrella and the operating table [7] – all too frequently equating Foucault's notion of "otherness" with Derrida's concept of *différance*. With a kind of postmodern ease, critics have often created, themselves, a heterotopic tableau of theories seeking to undermine order. [8]

Foucault's conception of "other" stands apart from Lacanian and Derridean models in that it suggests actual places, in actual moments in time. It acknowledges that power is not simply an issue of language. And this insistence on seeing institutions and practices in political and social terms has been welcomed by many feminist theorists. Yet one of the most striking aspects of Foucault's notion of heterotopia is how the idea of "other," in its emphasis on rupture, seems to exclude the traditional arenas of women and children – two of the groups that most rightly deserve (if by now one can abide the term's universalizing effect) the label "other." Women are admitted in his discussion primarily as sex objects – in the brothel, in the motel rented by the hour. (And what might be even harder for most working mothers to accept with a straight face is his exclusion of the house as a heterotopia on the grounds that it is a "place of rest.") Foucault seems to have an unconscious disdain for sites of everyday life such as the home, the public park, and the department store that have been provinces where women have found not only oppression but also some degree of comfort, security, autonomy, and even freedom. In fact, Foucault and some of his architecture-critic followers (most notably, Mike Davis) display an almost callous disregard for the needs of the less powerful – older people, the handicapped, the sick – who are more likely to seek security, comfort, and the pleasures of everyday life than to pursue the thrills of transgression and break. In applauding the rest home, for instance, as a microcosm of insight, Foucault never considers it from the eyes of the resident. Knowledge *is* the privilege of the powerful.

Another major, and all too obvious, problem is the exclusion of minorities, the third world, and, indeed, most non-Western culture from Foucault's discussions of "other" and, by extension, from criticism written by his architect-followers. One of the most paradoxical aspects of Foucault's notion of heterotopia is his example of the colony. Although since World War II the concept of "other" has had a powerful influence on third-world political and cultural theorists (from Frantz Fanon to Edward Said[9]), Foucault himself never attempts to see the colony through the eyes of the colonized, just as in his earlier institutional studies he avoids the prisoner's viewpoint in his rejection of a certain experiential analysis. In poststructuralist philosophy and literary criticism, a major claim for political validity is the notion of dismantling European logocentricism. Yet despite this embrace of the "other" in some of its theoretical sources, contemporary theory in architecture, echoing the unconscious biases of Foucault, appears to posit a notion of the "other" that is solely a question of Western dismantling of Western conventions for a Western audience. In other words, "others" are "the other" of a white Western male cultural elite. Instead of asking what is the avant-garde's desire for "other," architects and theorists might better ask what are the desires of those multiple "others" – actual, flesh-and-blood "others"? Difference is experienced differently, at different times, in different cultures, by different people. The point is not just to recognize difference, but all kinds of difference.

Thus far, this argument about the exclusion of "others" in the concept of the "other" has been limited to theoretical propositions that have at best – perhaps fortunately – only marginal relation to the architecture admired by advocates of heterotopia (above all, the designs of Frank Gehry, Bernard Tschumi, Peter Eisenman, and Daniel Libeskind[10]). And by no means is the negative tone of these remarks meant to disparage the incredible aesthetic energy and invention of many of these designs. What is disturbing is the link between theory and the architectural culture surrounding this theory. In the United States the focus on transgression in contemporary architecture circles seems to have contributed to a whole atmosphere of machismo and exclusion. One is reminded how often avant-gardism is a more polite label for the concerns of angry young men, sometimes graying young men. All too frequently lecture series and symposia have at best a token representation of women – and

no African-American or non-Western architects except perhaps from Japan. One of the most telling examples was the first Anyone conference, staged at the Getty Center at immense expense. A conference supposedly about the multiplicity, diversity, and fluidity of identity had, in a list of some twenty-five speakers, only two women; the rest were American (white), European (white), and Japanese men.[11] In fairness, it should be noted that this exclusionary attitude is not the sole province of the deconstructivist architects or poststructuralist theorists. American and European postmodernists and proponents of regionalism are equally blind to the issues of the non-Western world. Most recently, the same charge might be brought against the "Deleuzean de-form" nexus, despite its rhetoric of continuity and inclusion.[12]

These blatant social exclusions, under the mantle of a discourse that celebrates the "other" and "difference," raise the issue of whether contemporary theorists and deconstructivist architects have focused too exclusively on formal subversion and negation as a mode of practice. Undoubtedly, the difficult political climate of the past fifteen years and the economic recession of the late 1980s and early 1990s have contributed to the profession's hermeticism (namely, its rejection of constructive political strategies and institutional engagement), but the consequences of this retreat are now all too clear. Are there other formal and social options – options beyond transgression and nostalgia, deconstructivism and historicist postmodernism – that might embrace the desires and needs of those outside the avant-garde?

The seduction and power of the work of Foucault and Derrida, and their very dominance in American academic intellectual life, may have encouraged architects and theorists to leave unexplored another position linking space and power: the notion of "everyday life" developed by

Henri Lefebvre from the 1930s through the 1970s (a peculiar synthesis of Surrealist and Marxist ideas), and which Michel de Certeau gave a somewhat more particularist, and less Marxist, cast shortly thereafter.[13] Both theorists not only analyze the tyranny and controls that have imposed themselves on "everyday" life; they also explore the freedoms, joys, and diversity – what de Certeau describes as "the network of antidiscipline" – within everyday life. In other words, their concern is not simply to depict the power of disciplinary technology, but also to reveal how society resists being reduced to it – not just in the unusual or removed places but in the most ordinary as well. And here they place an emphasis on consumption, without seeing it as solely a negative force, as some leftists have, but also as an arena of freedom, choice, creativity, and invention.

De Certeau, who dedicated his seminal work *The Practice of Everyday Life* to the "ordinary man," is strangely silent on the issue of women (except for one female *flâneur* in his chapter "Walking the City"). Lefebvre, however, despite moments of infuriating sexism and disturbingly essentialist rhetoric, seems to have an acute understanding of the role of the everyday in woman's experience and how consumption has been both her demon and liberator, offering her an arena of action that grants her entry into and power in the public sphere. This argument has been further developed by a number of contemporary feminist theorists, including Janet Wolff, Elizabeth Wilson, Anne Friedberg, and Kristen Ross.[14] What these critics share, despite their many differences, is an emphasis on pleasure, the intensification of sensory impressions, and the positive excesses of consumption as experiences that counter the webs of control and monotony in daily life. Here "other" refers not only to what is outside everyday life – the events characterized by rupture, schism, difference – but also to what is contained, and *potentially* contained, within it. In short, their emphasis is populist, not avant-garde. They articulate a desire to bring experience and enrichment to many, not simply to jolt those few who have the textual or architectural sophistication to comprehend that a new formal break has been initiated. Certainly, these two goals need not be mutually exclusive.

1. Mary McLeod, "Architecture and Politics in the Reagan Era: From Post-modernism to Deconstructivism," *Assemblage* 8 (February 1989), 23–55.

2. See Anthony Vidler, *The Architectural Uncanny: Essays in the Modern Unhomely* (Cambridge, Mass.: MIT Press, 1992); Aaron Betsky, *Violated Perfection: Architecture and the Fragmentation of the Modern* (New York: Rizzoli, 1990); Catherine Ingraham, "Utopia/Heterotopia," course description of class given at Columbia University in 1989, and "Deconstruction III," in Andreas Papadakis, ed., *Architectural Design* (London: Academy Editions, 1994); and Stanley Allen, "Piranesi's Campo Marzio: An Experimental Design," *Assemblage* 10 (December 1989), 71–109. Other individuals who have been influenced by Foucault's notion of heterotopia include architects Diana Agrest and Demetri Porphyrios, and geographer Edward Soja. See Diana Agrest, "The City as the Place of Representation," *Design Quarterly* 113–14 (1980), reprinted in *Architecture from Without* (Cambridge, Mass.: MIT Press, 1991), 109–27; Demetri Porphyrios, *Sources of Modern Eclecticism: Studies of Alvar Aalto* (London: Academy Editions, 1982); and Edward Soja, *Postmodern Geographies: The Reassertion of Space in Critical Social Theory* (London: Verso, 1989). Although Vidler does not specifically mention the notion of heterotopia in his book *The Architectural Uncanny*, he cites Foucault on numerous occasions and adopts David Carroll's notion of "paraesthetics," which is indebted to Foucault. See David Carroll, *Paraesthetics: Foucault, Lyotard, Derrida* (New York: Methuen, 1987). In several publications, Manfredo Tafuri also alludes sympathetically to Foucault's notion of heterotopia, and Tafuri's interpretation of Piranesi's work as encapsulating the crisis of capitalism reveals certain parallels with Foucault's claims for heterotopic environments. See especially Manfredo Tafuri, "'The Wicked Architect': G. B. Piranesi, Heterotopia, and the Voyage," in *The Sphere and the Labyrinth: Avant-Gardes and Architecture from Piranesi to the 1970s*, trans. Pellegrino d'Acierno and Robert Connolly (Cambridge, Mass.: MIT Press, 1987). The complexity of Tafuri's project of ideological demystification and its multiplicity of intellectual sources, however, separate Tafuri's interest in Foucault from the instrumental applications of many architecture critics.

3. For most architecture critics who are adherents of Foucault's heterotopia, this does not preclude an endorsement of Derridean precepts. The Italian philosopher Gianni Vattimo also uses the notion of heterotopia, though in a different manner from Foucault. For Vattimo heterotopia alludes to the plurality of

norms that distinguishes late-modern art (since the 1960s) from modern art. See Gianni Vattimo, "From Utopia to Heterotopia," in *Transparent Society*, trans. David Webb (Baltimore: Johns Hopkins University Press, 1992), 62–75. The writings of Vattimo have been influential in European architectural debate, but they have had little impact on American architectural theory.

4. Michel Foucault, "Of Other Spaces: Utopias and Heterotopias," in Joan Ockman, ed., *Architecture Culture 1943–1968: A Documentary Anthology* (New York: Rizzoli, 1993), 420–26. The paper was first delivered at the Centre d'études architecturales, Paris, in March 1967. A brief account of its publishing history is given in Ockman, 419.

5. Despite Foucault's interest in institutions and his insistent use of spatial metaphors, discussions of physical urban space such as cities, streets, and parks are rare in his work. The philosopher Henri Lefebvre charged, probably legitimately, that Foucault was more concerned with a metaphorical notion of space – "mental space" – than with lived space, "the space of people who deal with material things." See Henri Lefebvre, *The Production of Space*, trans. Donald Nicholson-Smith (Oxford and Cambridge, Mass.: Blackwell, 1991; original French ed., 1974), 3–4. Besides his paper "Des Espaces autres," Foucault's most concrete discussions of physical space can be found in interviews, which occurred in the last decade of his life. See, for instance, "Questions on Geography" (1976) and "The Eye of Power" (1977), in Colin Gordon, ed., *Power/Knowledge: Selected Interviews and Other Writings, 1972–77* (New York: Pantheon Books, 1980); "Space, Knowledge, and Power" (1982), in Paul Rabinow, ed., *Foucault Reader* (New York: Pantheon Books, 1984); and, especially, "An Ethics of Pleasure," in Sylvere Lotringer, ed., *Foucault Live (Interviews, 1966–84)* (New York: Semiotext[e], 1989), 257–77. In the last interview, Foucault distinguishes architects from doctors, priests, psychiatrists, and prison wardens, claiming that the architect does not exercise (or serve as a vehicle of) as much power as the other professionals. Again Foucault's own class status and power emerge when he states, "After all, the architect has no power over me. If I want to tear down or change a house he built for me, put up new partitions, add a chimney, the architect has no control" (267). Surely, few occupants of public housing projects or nursing homes could or would make the same statement.

6. Foucault, "Of Other Spaces," 421–22.

7. Michel Foucault, *The Order of Things: An Archeology of Human Sciences* (New

York: Vintage Books, 1970), xv–xx. Foucault does not cite the poet le Comte de Lautréamont (pseud. of Isidore Ducasse) by name but rather alludes to the novelist Raymond Roussel, a favorite of the Surrealists. For examples of architects' use of Foucault's Preface to *The Order of Things,* see Porphyrios, 1–4; Allen, 77; and Georges Teyssot, "Heterotopias and the History of Spaces," *A+U* (October 1980), 80–100.

8. This is especially notable in Ingraham's and Allen's work. My objective, however, is not to expound on the distinctions between Foucault's and Derrida's versions of poststructuralism in terms of architecture. Nor is this the opportunity to expand on the philosophical differences raised by the meanings of the word *other,* namely the differences between Sartre's reworking of a Hegelian other in existentialism and Lacan's notions of split subjectivity and linguistic drift. Though certainly significant in philosophical and literary discourse, these distinctions, for better or worse, are typically blurred in architectural theory. For a concise historical account of "the problem of other," see Vincent Descombes, *Modern French Philosophy,* trans. L. Scott-Fox and J. M. Harding (Cambridge: Cambridge University Press, 1980), and Elizabeth Grosz, *Sexual Subversions: Three French Feminists* (Sydney: Allen and Unwin, 1989), 1–38. For a discussion of the notion of the "other" and its relation to gender and colonial/postcolonial theory in the context of architecture, see Zeynep Çelik and Leila Kinney, "Ethnography and Exhibitionism at the Expositions Universelles," *Assemblage* 13 (December 1990), esp. 54–56.

9. Recently, postcolonial critics such as Homi K. Bhabha and Gayatri Spivak have challenged the manichaeism or binary logic implicit in Fanon's and Said's understanding of colonial identity. See especially Homi K. Bhabha's essay "The Other Question: Stereotype, Discrimination and the Discourse of Colonialism," in Homi K. Bhabha, ed., *The Location of Culture* (London and New York: Routledge, 1994) for a critique of phenomenology's opposition between subject and object – and its extension into the discourse of colonialism as a rigid division between colonizer and colonized.

10. Certainly, La Villette and the Wexner Center, the two iconic built projects most cited by poststructuralist architectural theorists, are enjoyed by women and children as much as men, with the possible exception of the predominantly female staff at the Wexner, who are squeezed into extremely tight quarters.

11. One of the women, Maria Nordman, limited her remarks to a request that the

windows be opened to let in light and that the method of seating be decentralized. She chose to sit in the audience during her presentation. See the conference publication, *Anyone* (New York: Rizzoli, 1991), 198–99. A third woman, Cynthia Davidson, the editor of *Anyone,* might arguably be included, although this publication does not include a short biographical statement for her, as it does for the speakers. Subsequent *ANY* events have included more women, perhaps in response to public outrage, although minority architects have yet to be involved. Perhaps even more scandalous is the track record of the evening lecture series at Columbia University's Graduate School of Architecture, Planning, and Preservation, an institution that prides itself on being avant-garde. Not once in the past six years has the semester series included more than two women speakers (most have featured only one), and there have been no African-American speakers.

12. It can be argued that decidedly masculine assumptions underlie this new current in architectural theory, which seems to have its greatest energy in New York and almost exclusively among men. While Deleuze and Guattari reject the bipolarity latent in much Derridean thought, their "becoming – animal, becoming – women" suggests their (*male*) desire. As in Foucault's work, what is neglected in their exhilarating vision of fluidity and flow (for instance, domesticity, children, the elderly) is telling, and strikingly reminiscent of the machismo of some of the male leaders of the New Left in the 1960s.

13. The notion of "everyday life" can be frustratingly amorphous, and Lefebvre's intensely dialectical approach, combined with his rejection of traditional philosophical rationalism ("truth without reality"), makes the concept all the more difficult to decipher. Lefebvre's description of "everyday life" might best be understood as embracing a series of paradoxes. While the "object of philosophy," it is inherently non-philosophical; while conveying an image of stability and immutability, it is transitory and uncertain; while unbearable in its monotony and routine, it is festival and play. In brief, everyday life is "real life," the "here and now," not abstract truth. Lefebvre's description of everyday life as "sustenance, clothing, furniture, homes, neighborhoods, environment" – "material life" but with a "dramatic attitude" and "lyrical tone" – contrasts sharply with Foucault's concept of heterotopias as isolated and removed spaces. See Henri Lefebvre, *Everyday Life in the Modern World* (New Brunswick, N.J., and London: Transaction Publishers, 1984); Henri Lefebvre, *The Production of Space,*

trans. Donald Nicholson-Smith (Oxford and Cambridge, Mass.: Blackwell, 1991); Michel de Certeau, *The Practice of Everyday Life,* trans. Steven Rendall (Berkeley: University of California Press, 1984); and Michel de Certeau, *Heterologies: Discourse on the Other,* trans. Brian Massumi (Minneapolis: University of Minnesota Press, 1986).

14. See Janet Wolff, *Feminine Sentences: Essays on Women and Culture* (Berkeley: University of California Press, 1990), esp. 34–50; Elizabeth Wilson, *The Sphinx in the City: Urban Life, the Control of Disorder, and Women* (Berkeley: University of California Press, 1991); Anne Friedberg, *Window Shopping: Cinema and the Postmodern* (Berkeley: University of California, 1993); Kristen Ross, Introduction, *The Ladies' Paradise* (Berkeley: University of California Press, 1992), and *Fast Cars, Clean Bodies: Decolonization and the Reordering of French Culture* (Cambridge, Mass.: MIT Press, 1995). Of the critics cited here, Ross is the most indebted to Lefebvre, and, like Lefebvre, she stresses consumption's double-sided nature. For an insightful discussion of consumption and women's role with regard to architecture, see Leila Whittemore, "Women and the Architecture of Fashion in 19th-Century Paris," *a/r/c,* "Public Space" 5 (1994–95), 14–25.

Missing Objects

CATHERINE INGRAHAM

Recently[1] I was trying to untangle the famous aphorism "A picture is
worth a thousand words." The more I tried to penetrate this equation,
the more peculiar it became. We know, generally, the circumstances
under which this phrase is uttered, circumstances where a certain crisis
has arisen between two values, the value of the word and the value of
the picture (to which I want to append everything grasped visually,
although this poses problems). Although the import of the aphorism is
that it takes many, many words to achieve what a picture can achieve
all by itself, and all at once, the number 1000 is low when it comes to
words. One thousand words represents about three pages of written text,
about six minutes of continuously spoken language, about ten minutes
of conversation. One thousand pictures = a million words, or one one-
thousandth of a picture = one word, would be a more accurate way of
stating the force of this aphorism. The issue of value and worth, so
slyly persuasive in this equation, is related, then, not to some carefully
weighed economy of words and images but to a tacit politics of expen-
diture that counts words as cheap and insubstantial and, therefore,
proliferative, and images as substantial and dear and, therefore, unique.

I am belaboring this aphorism because I am interested in the
equation between words and images, words and things, words and
objects (fig. 1). At the same time, I recognize the ugliness and difficulty
of words compared to things – how small and petty words are, how
promiscuous and entangling. This ugliness is part of what aesthetically
magnetizes me about words – that is, I am attracted by the possibility
of writing them grossly at the scale of buildings much as, say, Barbara
Kruger or Robert Venturi have done, taking them at face value, so to

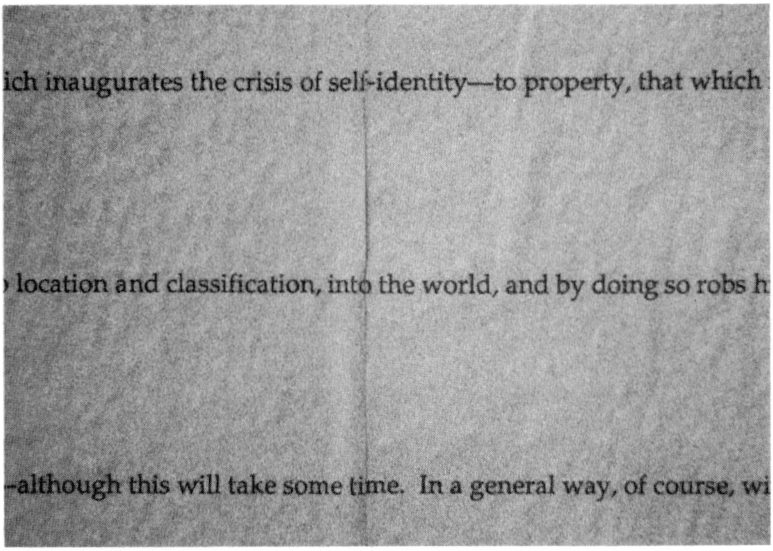

ich inaugurates the crisis of self-identity—to property, that which

location and classification, into the world, and by doing so robs h

—although this will take some time. In a general way, of course, wi

FIG. 1

One Text = One Wall, installation in *Architexturally Speaking*, Gallery 400, Chicago, 1992. The project was, in theory, very simple: to cover one wall (8 ft. 3 in. high x 15 ft. 5 in. long) with one (10-point) text that could be read from left to right as if the wall had become the book. It turned out to be extraordinarily difficult to mount one 15-foot line of 10-point text on a wall, much less cover the entire wall. Ordinary photographic and computer graphic technologies had not envisioned, for obvious reasons, this precise task. In the end, I used a tiling program that took three days of continuous day and night operation to produce three hundred pages of text because each time one page was produced the computer had to reread the entire book. The text was an early version of my book manuscript, "Architecture and the Burdens of Linearity," which is, in part, about the issues of line and surface raised by the project

speak; and yet, simultaneously, I am struck by their formal irrelevance to the world of built objects. The smallness of words – their relative cheapness, proliferative character, and lack of materiality – is their point, almost.

Taking this aphorism, "A picture is worth a thousand words," at face value is an oblique way of looking at a far more difficult set of problems having to do not only with the particular kind of architectural practice that might lead us to question the economy between words and things, but also with a strange, ongoing lament in architecture about words and objects, and, lastly, with the realm of invention. Invention was a key word in the proposal Francesca Hughes recently made to those writers invited to contribute to a book she was editing on women in architectural practice.[2] The proposal was that women had more cause to *invent* an architectural practice because they hold an ambiguous position with respect to architecture; they are both outside and inside architecture. Hughes suggested that this "architecture" be rendered "Architecture" with a capital *A* to indicate the entire culture of architecture – the profession, the discipline, the building. She wanted to underscore the idea that "invention" was not utopic in the sense that it pointed to some more idealized state of female practice with respect to architecture. I agree with her, but I have an aversion to a capitalized architecture since it is lower case architecture that signifies for me the massive plurality of architectural meaning. And "a" is a letter that cannot be capitalized with impunity; we have been warned, persuasively I think, against the "kingdom of the a, the silent tomb, the pyramid."[3]

But let me return for a moment to the aphorism "A picture is worth a thousand words." The spirit of the aphorism recognizes the mediating function of words and the apparently unmediated meaning of the image. The attempt of words to represent pictures or images or objects, according to this aphorism, not only happens outside the image or object (as a kind of excess of clothing around the image or object) but also results in a proliferation of multiplicities (1000) that is offensive to the apparent singularity of meaning that is the image or object. The themes that we might locate here – the mediation of meaning, competition between outside and inside, the ever-present problem of representation, systems of value, the frame and its economy, multiplicity and singularity, the politics of meaning – are some of the themes of my architectural practice, and I think they belong to everyone practicing a critical architecture today. The material implications of these themes, that is, what can be built from them, are not as elusive as both theorists and practitioners make them out to be. Materiality is relatively easy; it lays in wait for metaphysics and philosophy at every turn.

Taking an aphorism at face value is tactically adiaphoristic; it breaks into the formal closure of the aphorism. But taking something at face value is also a material moment, in the sense that it deals with the formal and material propositions of something – the dimensions, quantities, literalness of that thing (in this case, language). The sense in which language is revealed to have a surface meaning that casts doubt on its deeper purposes is peculiar since language is nothing but surface to begin with, although we know from Jacques Lacan that the "nothing" in the "nothing but surface" must also be taken into account. The formulation "nothing but surface" refers, as Jean-Luc Nancy and Philippe Lacoue-Labarthe have written, to Lacan's "rejection of any mythical notion of the unconscious as the seat of instincts, a rejection of any sort of depth psychology. The subject – that is, the subject revealed by psychoanalysis – is to be understood simply as an effect of the signifier, a subject of the letter."[4] The reason why the "nothing" must be taken into account is that it is, of course, too glib to say everything is nothing but surface since the very enunciation of this principle is, itself, calling on a forgotten substance or a forgotten depth, a refused depth.

The matter of depth and surface invariably leads to an irritating but instructive contortionism in our thinking. For one thing, once things are recognized as surfaces, things surface and we get a look at what lies deeply within. Certainly a great deal of contemporary architectural theory has been interested in the relation and identity between two surface practices, language and architecture, but the comparison between the surface of writing and architecture can only be held together for a split second.

Let me quickly review the grammatology of this situation – quickly not because it is irrelevant but because Jacques Derrida's work is by now known to most people. But there is one small, prior remark I want to make. The fact that one thing leads to another in philosophy or any kind of work, such that everything is formed on already existing forms (either as the sort of extensive cross-referencing – the hypertext – of philosophy, or the use of precedent in architecture), is a fact that architecture finds both appealing and appalling throughout its own history. Whenever I return to Derrida in the middle of a discussion about architecture, I am reminded of how completely thought and action must already be structured in order to operate. Derrida's insights on the matter of structuring and structurality speak precisely to this point, and architectural theory was right, I think, to have found a (troubled and temporary) home inside poststructural philosophy.

On our way back to the aphorism, then, through Derrida. It is not enough to say that words are the "other" of the image, or vice versa. One must further divide words into the spoken and the written. Written language is the "image" of speech:

"Has it ever been doubted that writing is the clothing of speech? . . . One already suspects that if writing is 'image' and exterior 'figuration,' this representation is not innocent. The outside bears with the inside a relationship that is, as usual, anything but simple exteriority. The meaning of the outside was always present within the inside, imprisoned outside the outside, and vice versa. Thus a science of language must recover the *natural* – that is, the simple and original – relationships between speech and writing, that is, between an inside and an outside."[5]

The clothing of speech by writing, the clothing that makes a word an image, produces a perplexing shift between what we have always held to be exteriority (images, objects, writing) and what we have always held to be interiority (speech). To extract one more turn from this most salient of passages on writing: Derrida speaks of our attempt to recover the "natural" relationship between inside and outside, a "natural" relationship that would have been "inverted by the original sin of writing." The mythology of an "original speech" that was later sullied by writing, by civilization, by genealogical anxiety, is the mythology and theology of the Garden of Eden itself, which was, above all, a place where inside and outside were fixed. Derrida goes on to say:

"Malebranche explained original sin as inattention, the temptation of ease and idleness, by that *nothing* that was Adam's distraction, alone culpable before the innocence of the divine word: the latter exerted no force, no efficacy, since *nothing* had taken place. Here too, one gave in to ease, which is curiously, but as usual, on the side of technical artifice and not within the bent of the natural movement thus thwarted or deviated."[6]

Adam's distraction, then, creates a slippery surface upon which the imperatives of the divine (of origin, of the clarity of boundary that is the garden, of original speech) cannot get a grip. And this distraction is a kind of technique for evading the theology and authority of the "natural." The surface, where nothing happens, becomes a place where traditional deep oppositions such as inside/outside, original/copy, object/word, are in a kind of suspension.

There is another piece to this, mainly the presence of Eve. What is Eve doing? Eve is either complicitous in the politics of distraction or not. Perhaps she has easily given up on the natural and is busy conspiring with the serpent to take advantage of Adam's distraction – to get a ticket out of the garden, so to speak, on the back of Adam's nothingness. Or perhaps she already inhabits the "nothing but surface" condition of the cosmos and makes use of specific surfaces, like the red of the apple, to ease out from under divine scrutiny. The problem of Eve is, in a sense, the problem of how to account for the persistence of an opposition (between writing and architecture) in the face of multiple and clever arguments to the contrary. Why is it so difficult for us to hold to the surface and see the alliance between surfaces? Eve, or rather Eve's gender, puts some kind of wedge into the equation.

The spirit of Hughes's use of the word "invention" is that women invent a way into architecture by inventing different kinds of practice: small practices, hybrid practices, practices in theory. The one architectural practice that resists, or proves difficult for, this type of invention is building buildings. Either invented practices are too small, too hybrid, too theoretical to attract major building commissions, or the very form of a (so-called) invented practice has a puzzling and problematic relationship to buildings. While it would be a kind of theoretical folly to pursue the history of the architectural object, the building, with respect to some generalized gender condition called "woman," there are a number of mythologies, theories, and histories that situate women with respect to objects. Generally these mythologies provide conflicting accounts of women and objects. Some suggest that women are acquisitive of objects, and themselves objects to be acquired; others that women are expert purveyors of words, but have an imperfect or weak relationship to objects. Words are cheap, objects are dear, except where the woman herself is an object, in which case objects are cheap, too. Women acquire objects but they produce words. One thinks, as always, of Penelope (the shroud and the suitors), Helen and Paris ("the face . . ."), Scheherazade and her endless tale, certain African societies that equate women with semi-precious objects, the relation of women to jewelry and money, property ownership histories, domestic engineering and Taylorism, Melanie Klein and other object theorists, Lacanian psychoanalytic theory, and contemporary feminist theories of female identity; one thinks also of the adjectives that have traditionally described women's speech/objects/properties such as babble/bauble and chatter/chattel. As we might discover in different ways from the preceding list, and as we already know from the spin of the aphorism "A picture is worth a thousand words," the opposition between words and things, or words and objects, is difficult to uphold and, more specifically, difficult to genderize.

But it is possible to say that whenever we find a surfeit of stereotypes and exclusions, in this case women from the practice of building, we might suspect that there is some kind of identification crisis under way. How does the (other) saying go? "Necessity is the mother of invention." Invention is mothered forth in response to a lack – the same lack as always – the lack of an object. Architecture is not, contrary to its reputation, an object profession, but it fetishizes the object with impunity; very few architects actually build, in a physical way, the buildings they design (fig. 2). It is a profession of object thinkers who grapple with the living condition of the object as a condition that is other to itself (one of the conditions for fetishization). The carpenter or electrician, the trade person who actually carries out the instructions specified by the architect, is a different order of being from the architect and this is testified to by the massive legal, cultural, and material conflict between these two worlds. What the architect has, among other things, is a knowledge of materials, and this knowledge is in perpetual negotiation with the actual material practices that the architect must marshall to his/her cause. Without exploring all the multiple dimensions of how architects identify with the construction of the buildings to which they never, literally, put a hand, one can say that the sense of object-loss or object-lament is a very long and deep strand in architectural history. I want only to touch on this history obliquely by means of another history, the mythical history of the American West.

Jane Tompkins writes of how, in the film genre of the western, a certain concept of the masculine is aligned with the need to become as total, as dense, as present as an object. She quotes Peter Schewenger: "To become a man . . . must be finally to attain the solidity and self-containment of an object."[7] And she quotes Octavio Paz, whose definition of "macho" is a "hermetic being, closed up in himself." "The interdiction masculinity places on speech," Tompkins says, "arises from the desire for complete objectivization. And this means being conscious of nothing, not knowing that one has a self . . . nature is what [the hero] aspires to emulate: perfect being-in-itself."[8]

The western is, of course, a parable of American identity that bears specifically on the settling of the West and the relationship of men and women to that settlement. In this parable, women are the protectors of proper speech, which is the speech of the schoolteacher and the society woman imported from the East. The identification of women with proper speech is synonymous with the proprietorial role women played in the West as those who "settled" a mobile population into proper houses, schools, towns with libraries, and so forth.[9]

But the house itself, the building and ownership of the house, belongs to the other side of the parable, the man's side. Owning property, which was, of course, part of what the settlement of the West involved, was related in some intimate way to the male identification with land as object. Turning the West into real estate, and subsequently towns and cities, required both the "silent" identity with objects (the image) and the "talkative" identity of social propriety (the word).

FIG. 2

Robert Longo. *Pressure.* 1982–83.
Two parts: painted wood with lac-
quer finish, and charcoal, graphite,
and ink on paper, overall 8 ft. 6
3/8 in. x 7 ft. 6 in. x 36 1/2 in. The
Museum of Modern Art, New
York. Gift of the Louis and Bessie
Adler Foundation, Inc., Seymour
M. Klein, President

FIG. 3

Mies van der Rohe + object

Architecture's identification crisis, at least in part, also belongs to a version of this parable. The sense in which the discipline of architecture stands back from the object, and simultaneously desires the object (fig. 3), guarantees the anxiety associated with the admission of women into its ranks. For mastery over the object, becoming one with the object, is not possible in architecture (in fact, it is possible nowhere), and women, in spite of their conflicting history, have traditionally almost always stood for the failure of that mastery. To invite women in is simultaneously to invite in the idea that the route, however mistaken, to (masculine) identity through architecture and the object will be foreclosed; the *owning* of identity through the *owning* of objects is also foreclosed. The architecture of the American West – which is the scene of Tompkins's observations – is a landscape of solid monumental forms (buttes, mesas) seen against a horizon. In his search for perfect objecthood and the hermeticism of *machismo*, and ultimately property, the western hero tries to assimilate himself to this landscape totally. But this architecture – and now we see it is a mistake to call it architecture – is *nothing like* the architecture of the architect. The architecture of architects is hollow inside, not dense, not solid. So if this parable of American (and to some extent, European) masculinity, the western hero, falls short of becoming one with the densely formed landscape, how much more will a voided architecture fail to deliver its object-promises?

It seems, then, that, women are on the surface of things; certainly they are nothing to the discipline of architecture. But it also seems as if women invert something by being nothing, not because of some hidden or gender-specific power, but because of this strange condition of architecture as also being on the surface. There is an isomorphism between the surface and face practices of women (their words and appearances) and the practice of architecture.

But it is, of course, foolish to isolate some generalized (object) position for women or men. I have entertained this opposition only for its suggestive power. How else can we explain the strangeness of historical relations between men and women and architecture? Jacqueline Rose, in the introduction to Lacan's book *Feminine Sexuality*, reminds us of how generalizing the categories of "male" and "female" is fatal to the project of understanding the difficulty of sexuality:

"Sexuality belongs in this area of instability [the arbitrary nature of lan-guage] played out in the register of demand and desire, each sex coming to stand, mythically and exclusively, for that which could satisfy and complete the other. It is when the categories 'male' and 'female' are seen to represent an absolute and complementary division that they fall prey to a mystification in which the difficulty of sexuality instantly disappears. . . . Lacan therefore argued that psychoanalysis should not try to produce 'male' and 'female' as complementary entities, sure of each other and of their own identity, but should expose the fantasy on which this notion rests."[10]

Instead of speaking of "women" we should speak of the unstable and shifting equations produced by the conjunction of architecture + female + male + architecture, or architecture + word + object + architecture; and we would have to specify which part of architecture we meant, and so on. This would be the project that would discover what the ambiguity of outside/inside and invention might mean for women in architecture.

1. "Recently" now refers to two years ago, when I was writing an article on John Hejduk for a Canadian Centre for Architecture symposium in Montreal. This (pres-ent) essay has been difficult to put to rest because many of the issues I am writing about here intersect with larger unresolved problems. Also, uncharacteristically for me, this essay will be appearing in three different forms in three different places. All of these versions start with the same "Recently . . ." sentence, but then subtly begin to diverge from each other as I keep trying to straighten things out. For the other versions, see Francesca Hughes, ed., *Reconstructing Her Practice* (Cambridge, Mass.: MIT Press, 1996), and my book manuscript, "Architecture and the Burdens of Linearity," currently under review by Yale University Press.

2. Private correspondence with Hughes.

3. I am thinking of that amazing passage in "Différance," where Derrida speaks of the complication of the "a" insinuated into the word "différence." See Jacques Derrida, *Margins of Philosophy*, trans. Alan Bass (Chicago: University of Chicago Press, 1982).

4. Jean-Luc Nancy and Philippe Lacoue-Labarthe, *The Title of the Letter: A Reading of Lacan*, trans. François Raffoul and David Pettigrew (Albany: State University

of New York Press, 1992), x.

5. Jacques Derrida, *Of Grammatology,* trans. Gayatri Chakravorty Spivak (Baltimore: Johns Hopkins University Press, 1974), 35 (his emphasis).

6. Ibid. (his emphasis).

7. Jane Tompkins, *West of Everything: The Inner Life of Westerns* (New York: Oxford University Press, 1992), 56.

8. Ibid.

9. The prostitute, who preceded the "proper woman," is not usually depicted as antithetical to the female project of settlement. Her house is lavishly and permanently furnished, and she "entertains." Men have to get clean of the land before they go to this house, and their manners matter. But, strictly speaking, the prostitute is a woman who wanders and, in this, she resembles the man who wanders.

10. Jacqueline Rose, introduction to Jacques Lacan, *Feminine Sexuality* (New York: W. W. Norton, 1982), 33.

Present Tense: Reply to Catherine Ingraham

DIANE LEWIS

For the furies, muses, and goddesses who came to speak in Lou Kahn's city

ANTIGONE, THE FIRST FEMALE HERO,
ENTRAPPED IN A LEGALISTIC AND LITERAL ERA, ASKS:
"OH, GOD, WHO WILL BE MY ALLY
WHEN PIETY IS MY CRIME?"[1]
THE PIETY I CHOOSE TO REPRESENT HERE
IS THE PIETY OF ARCHITECURE AS A DISCIPLINE.

Writing as practice is neither literature nor discipline. It is not the same as the language of architecture, an abstract language of dots and lines and voids into which is imbedded desire, structure, concept, and imagination of the universe, *if* it is studied carefully enough to carry such meaning. Contrary to Jennifer Bloomer's contention that the wall could never carry desire (see her essay in this volume, p. 161), I posit that any and every condition with which the imagination can confront the wall can be imbedded into the notation and the construction of the wall *if* the language of architecture is read, drawn, and understood as a poetic discipline.

THE RELATION OF ARCHITECTURE TO LITERATURE
THE LITERATURE OF ARCHITECTURE
ARCHITECTURE AS THE LITERATURE OF CIVILIZATION
ARCHITECTURAL LANGUAGE AS A LITERATURE OF ITS OWN
THE DISCIPLINE OF THE PLAN AND THE SECTION

This highly structural, historic and poetic set of relations is the antithesis of the postmodern position posited in Catherine Ingraham's essay, which analyzes the implications of what she calls an aphorism, "A picture is worth a thousand words."

"A picture is worth a thousand words" is a quotation, printed on March 10, 1927, by Fred Barnard, the famous New York critic and poet, in his magazine, *The Printers Ink,* where he goes on to say that he was inspired by the original and very ancient Chinese proverb, "One *look* is worth a thousand words" (my emphasis). So we see that "A picture is worth a thousand words" is not an aphorism but a quote – a quote with a particular history and a specific source. A typical malaise of postmodernism and deconstructivism is the erasure of the source, the erasure of attribution, in order to construct a history of anonymous collective acts, as opposed to a history of ideas attributed to their makers. Ingraham implies that the "aphorism" carries a value commonly acknowledged by a collective, anonymous objectivity: the value of images over ideas, built works over written concepts, male acts over female processes. The value implied by the "aphorism" is then analyzed for a polemical purpose, while the meaning or root of the "aphorism" (quote) is ignored.

I prefer an existential and literary approach learned from Sartre who, on the subject of history, explained that the interest is not to know its objective, but to give it one. Quite the contrary from Ingraham, I relish the exclusivity of experience within the domain of language; the invisible boundaries between the expression that different languages provide; the erotic sense of the untranslatable states of the exquisite difference between disciplines. Such is the "rub" to which Hamlet refers, a boundary between sleeping and waking, dreams and existence, the physical and the imaginary. The conscious discomfort and knowledge of this is the threshold of the modern. The "rub" of Hamlet became the *frottage* of Surrealism. I am interested in upholding and exploring the boundaries. The presence of the mind is confirmed in the ability to suspend or sustain the knowledge of the existence of contradictory realms, exclusive but simultaneous. Such a faculty is necessary to be an architect, and to make architecture.

My interest in the quote lies in the fact that it deals with the limits of language and must be studied in those terms. "A picture is worth a thousand words" even questions the difference between the nature of the history of images and the history of words. Challenging the limits of these families of histories, I will employ it to address the diverse disciplines and the conditions that confront the boundary between word and image in philosophy, architecture, art, propaganda, and my own history.

Philosophy

"A picture is worth a thousand words" is the quotidian way of expressing a great philosophic recognition best stated in this century by Ludwig Wittgenstein in his discussions of the limits of language. When he says, "What can be shown cannot be said. What we cannot speak about we must pass over in silence,"[2] it is clear that he means that the language of the image, the seen, imparts and contains different knowledge than the written or spoken word.

Architecture

The silent language of architecture speaks about the structure of civilization and the forces of gravity; its letter and words are best described in the seminal tract that Frank Lloyd Wright acknowledged to be his inspiration:

" Architecture began like any other form of writing. It was first of all an alphabet. A stone was set upright and it was a letter, and each letter was a hieroglyph, and on each hieroglyph a group of ideas rested like the capital on a column. . . . later on they formed words. . . . the Celtic dolmen and cromlech, the Etruscan tumulus, the Hebrew glagal are words. . . . Finally they wrote books. . . . architecture evolved along with the human mind; while Daedalus who is force, measured, and Orpheus who is intelligence, sang, the pillar which is a letter, the arcade which is a syllable, the pyramid which is a word, simultaneously set in motion both by a law of geometry and a law of poetry, formed groups, they combined and amalgamated, they rose and fell, they were juxtaposed on the ground and superimposed on the sky, until at the dictate of the general idea of an epoch, they had written those marvelous books which are also marvelous buildings: the Pagoda of Eklinga, the Ramesseum of

Egypt, the Temple of Solomon. . . . the Temple of Solomon was not merely the binding of the sacred book, but the sacred book itself."

– Victor Hugo, "Ceci Tuera Cela"
(This Will Kill That)[3]

When Hugo wrote these words, he desired that the name of the great cathedral become a title binding a book to demonstrate his point. He mourns the change in the position of architecture in history as a result of the invention of the printing press. Architecture – the literature of civilization, a physically inscribed tectonic manifestation of oral tradition – was usurped by the imaginary space of the book. Hugo proposed that the next great architecture would arise from a new literary spatiality.

When Wright was asked about the crisis of the machine age and the subject of "modern" architecture, he argued that the book had replaced the cathedral, that the threat of the machine age had been the printing press, and he quoted Hugo's words, "this will kill that." Because the obvious root of Wright's spatially explosive free plan was the continuation of bare structural and mythic elements of classical thought, it innately held a concern for the historical memory of the power and purpose of architectural structure and space, for democratic ideals of freedom in the classical tradition, and for the survival of the individual and the imagination. *Plan libre* was the name the Europeans gave to Wright's structural concept, which was his spatial manifestation of an American ethical ideal, born constitutional, a set of principles.

In French, *histoire* means both "history" and "story," and the English dictionary reveals a shift between these two meanings, from an account of events both real and imaginary (first definition) to, later, an account of only those events deemed real. It is with the shift of boundaries between real and imaginary that the nature of history is redefined, and with it the limits of the concrete manifestation of its individual and collective acts: architecture.

Each city is a volume of civilization, a physical record of the decisions of individuals, imbedments of their thoughts and acts over centuries. The historic transition of an architectural work from collective attribution to individual authorship is a critical issue to *any* position on urbanism from the nineteenth century through the present. In a postmonarchial civilization new programs for architecture had to be derived: the church, the piazza, and the palace were no longer the only work for the architect. New institutions, organs of a new civic corporeality and evolved social contract, had become necessary. Thus the pursuit of this century was not utopian design formalism, attributed to the modern movement by Philip Johnson and his followers to deride that movement as a failure, but the new potentials for a fusion of structure and program implicit in the democratic spatiality of the free plan.

ARTICULATION OF STRUCTURAL FROM NON-STRUCTURAL
ARTICULATION OF EARTH AS OPPOSED TO GROUND ZERO
ORDER OF GRID AS DISTINCT FROM THE RANDOM
SPATIAL THEORY
ICONOGRAPHY OF AUTONOMOUS PROGRAMMATIC ELEMENTS
EXPRESSION OF GRAVITY EQUIVALENCE IN PLAN AND SECTION

. . . are some of the objective breakthroughs in twentieth-century architectural language which have borne the subjective nuance of the individual imagination. The discipline of architecture is within this language, a text of space and structure expressed in the binary opposition of architectural notation, articulate of the most subtle qualities and dimensionalities.

In a time when science is equated with objectivity, the nuance of the literary is devalued; technocratic language is employed to represent anonymous collective objectivity. There is a confusion about the value of subjectivity and the responsibility of authorship to the discipline and the poetics of architecture.

The "modern" space, in the strict meaning of the word as "definitive of its time," is and was always literary in the richness of the imagination of its inhabitation at every scale and in every state of its existence. One draws a plan as one writes a story: each detail is remarked, each event is set in a time passage, a spatial frame. The *plan libre* and the *nouveau roman* were the foundation for a new vision of locations and relationships for facts and circumstances to become ideal. Thus Hugo's prophecy has been realized in the innovations in literary and architectural language of the twentieth century.

Art

"My dear friend,
The real danger you point out to me, one cannot take for a condition of the mind. Whenever we meddle with the differences between words and things, between the mind and our body and our ideas, the differences become even greater. But in order to see them we have got to be there. . . . To deny them would be to deny the mind."

– René Magritte[4]

Propaganda
Again, Magritte: *"Ceci n'est pas une pipe"* (This is not a pipe; fig. 1).

THE POSTMODERN MOTIVE

SEPARATES LANGUAGE AND IMAGE

SEPARATES MIND AND BODY

DE-CORPORALIZES ARCHITECTURE

THE SINGLE LINE

ELIMINATION OF THICKNESS

UNINHABITED TERRAIN

HISTORIC VS. MODERN

HITCHCOCK AND JOHNSON'S *INTERNATIONAL STYLE* CREDO

SETS UP A FALSE OPPOSITION WITHIN WHICH

AMERICAN ARCHITECTURAL CRITIQUE IS STILL IMPRISONED

ASSUMING A DISCONTINUITY OF TIME

A EUPHEMISM MASKING AS OPPOSITION OF

COLLECTIVE VS. INDIVIDUAL

IN GUISES OF

VERNACULAR VS. AUTHORED

AN AMERICAN VERSION OF *DER VOLK*

COMMERCIAL BECOMES EQUIVALENT TO PUBLIC

PUBLIC BECOMES POPULAR

LEWIS

Ceci n'est pas une pipe.

FIG. I

René Magritte. *The Treachery of Images.* 1929. Oil on canvas, 23 5/8 x 31 7/8 in. Los Angeles County Museum of Art, purchased with funds provided by the Mr. and Mrs. William Preston Harrison Collection

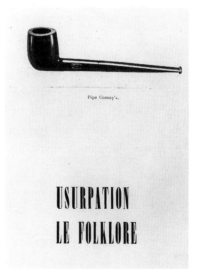

Pipe Comoy's.

FIG. 2

Le Corbusier. From *L'Art décoratif d'aujourd'hui,* 1925

USURPATION
LE FOLKLORE

USURPATION OF THE CIVIC

DECONSTRUCTIVISM IS THE DESTRUCTION

OF THE MEMORY OF

IMBEDMENT OF CONTENT IN ARCHITECTURAL NOTATION

THE ERASURE OF THE VALUATION OF INDIVIDUAL SPIRIT

IN COLLECTIVE LANGUAGE

THE SUPPRESSION OF EROS IN THE ART OF ARCHITECTURE

NOT A FEMINIST ISSUE ONLY

LEWIS   AN EROTICIST ISSUE

THE STRUGGLE FOR THE POSITION OF THE INDIVIDUAL

ARTIST IN HISTORY

RIMBAUD AGAINST *LEARNING FROM LAS VEGAS*

My History

In 1976 my aunt and guardian, Ann Heller, cousin of Joseph, graduate
of Barnard in the 1920s, dedicated to women's education, spent her final
days in a series of very directed conversations with me. She prefaced
the last with a discussion of "A picture is worth a thousand words." She
informed me that the pictorial days of *Life* and *Look* were past, and that
she recognized the creeping presence of the kind of separation of fact
from image that she had witnessed during the Nazi era. Debilitation of
language was the purpose: both the language of words and the poetry of
images; and in such erosion was a great threat to freedom. For, ultimately,
your freedom is in the quality of your language.

1. Sophocles, *Antigone*, trans. Kenneth McLeish (New York: Cambridge University
   Press, 1979).

2. Ludwig Wittgenstein, *Tractatus Logico-Philosophicus*, trans. D. F. Pears and B. F.
   McGuinness (London: Routledge and Kegan Paul, 1961).

3. Victor Hugo, *Notre Dame of Paris*, trans. John Sturrock (London: Penguin Books,
   1978), 189.

4. René Magritte, letter to Camille Goemans, September 27, 1928, in *Magritte/
   Torczyner: Letters Between Friends*, trans. Richard Miller (New York: Harry N.
   Abrams, 1994).

The Return of the Repressed: Nature

DIANA AGREST

"As nature came to seem more like a machine, did not the machine come
to seem more natural?"

– Sandra Harding[1]

This essay originated with the China Basin project, a theoretical urban
proposal for San Francisco developed with my office for the exhibition
Visionary San Francisco, held at the San Francisco Museum of Modern
Art in 1990. We were given a text from which to work, a detective story
à la Hammett, in which the China Basin area in San Francisco was the
cause for intrigue and murder. This area became the site for the project.
While the project was an instinctive response to the question of the
American city and urbanism today, its retrospective reading led me to
focus on the question of nature. Although the project preceded the text,
I have reversed the order of their presentation here, thus providing a
framework for the understanding of the project rather than presenting
the project as an application of it.

For more than fifty years the question of nature has been conspicuously absent from urbanistic discourse. This symptomatic absence has
generated the critical examination of ideology that this text represents.
This work explores the conditions that articulate and structure the notions
of nature, architecture, and gender in the ideology of modernist urbanism.

The American city, a city that regulates (suppresses or generates)
enjoyment through the presence of object buildings, plays a key role in
the unraveling of this complex articulation, indicating the repetition of a
symptom that goes back to the original (American) urban scene/sin: the

violation of nature by the machine; a confrontation where, in the struggle between the machine and the forces of nature, woman is suppressed.

Nature has been a referent for Western architectural discourse from Vitruvius through the Renaissance, when beauty, the most important property of buildings, was supposed to result from the re-presentation of nature. Only in the nineteenth century, with Durand's critique of architecture as representation, was there a break with this tradition.[2] It is in the twentieth century, in Le Corbusier's *Ville Contemporaine*,[3] *Plan Voisin,* and *Ville Radieuse,*[4] that nature reappears in the urban discourse, not as part of an architectural metaphoric operation but as an element in an urbanistic metonymic construct. It is not only in the European urbanistic discourse that we find clues to the absence of nature, but also in the American ideological construction of the relationship between nature and city and its articulation with the process of urbanization. The current absence of nature from urban discourse is related precisely to the suppressed relationship between European urbanistic discourse and the American city. The American city – that place where urban development directly coincides with the westward displacement of the frontier, where a rational order was applied to virgin land – presents the most pertinent example of the relationship between nature and the city in twentieth-century urbanism as ideology and its articulation with the real.[5]

The development of the American city can be explained through the opposition between nature and culture, between wilderness and the city. In this equation city, considered as evil, as the place of sin, was assigned a negative "sign" or value, while nature was equated with God and embodied everything that was positive. "By the time Emerson wrote *Nature* in 1836, the terms God and Nature could be used interchangeably." Ideas of God's nature and God in nature became hopelessly entangled.[6] The moral and aesthetic qualities with which nature was imbued were considered far superior to economic and urban forces and the potential for development those forces represented. The pastoral ideal was a distinctly American theory of society and an all-embracing ideology; America was seen by Europeans as a place that, as virgin land, offered the possibility of a new beginning for already developed Europe.[7] However, when the frontier began to be pushed westward and wilderness was to be conquered, the city, by necessity, was assigned a positive value since towns were necessary in order to facilitate the development of the land; nature, which came to represent the danger of the unknown, became the negative "sign."[8] This conflict between city and country is already present in Jefferson's *Notes on Virginia,* in which he recognizes both the great political and economic potential of the machine and the fact that it will alter rural life.[9]

The machine, a product of and vehicle for the scientific revolution, made industrialization possible in a manner apparently consistent with the democratic project; at the same time, it both became and symbolized a threat to the pastoral ideal. The greatest manifestation of this conflict appears in the form of the locomotive, the machine that disturbs the peaceful rural idyll, as Hawthorne so vividly describes in *Sleepy Hollow,* his reaction to the process of urbanization.[10] The locomotive that slashes and scars the virgin land is the machine that makes possible the westward conquest of the wilderness, paradoxically destroying what it wants to discover (fig. 1). The more nature was conquered and exploited, the more a growing consciousness of its value as wilderness developed in anticipation of its ultimate destruction. Suddenly Americans came to the realization that as opposed to Europeans' historical past, their true past was nature itself. Extraordinary views of nature afforded by the new accessibility to the wilderness became equated with the beautiful and the sublime as defined by European Romantics;[11] and in the arts, it was in painting that the sublime in nature was most powerfully manifested. Nature was equated with God, and painters who could portray nature as God's work were close to being emissaries of God on earth. But paradoxically, "the new significance of nature and the development of landscape painting coincided with the relentless destruction of the wilderness into the early 19th century."[12] Thomas Cole represented this paradox in his series of paintings *The Course of Empire – Savage State, Pastoral State, Consummation, Destruction,* and *Desolation* (fig. 2).[13] However, the locomotive crossing the virgin land "was like nothing seen before," and in order to reconcile the power of the machine with the

FIG. 1

Frederic Edwin Church. *Twilight in the Wilderness*. 1860. Oil on canvas, 40 x 64 in. The Cleveland Museum of Art. Mr. and Mrs. William H. Marlatt Fund, 65.233

FIG. 2

Thomas Cole. *The Course of Empire – Pastoral State*. 1836. Oil on canvas, 39 1/4 x 63 1/4 in. The New York Historical Society

beauty and peacefulness of the rural countryside, a discourse in which the power of the machine could be praised – a technological sublime – had to be developed.[14]

The mid-nineteenth century ideology of science, in which the entire universe was seen as a mechanism and the machine was viewed as part of this natural universe, provided the mediation that made the machine acceptable. However, this philosophy, while neutralizing the contradiction of accepting the machine as a positive force, facilitated the destruction of the very landscape that represented the ideal of pastoralism.[15]

The ideological displacements that make possible the notion of the machine as mediator in the opposition between nature and city cannot be properly understood without introducing the problematic question of nature and science, in particular as it relates to scientific discourse, considered by philosophers as the "mirror" of nature. But for the ideology of that discourse to be understood in its many implications, another term needs to be added: that of gender, as it relates to both nature and to science.

In exploring the relationship between nature and science it is important to recognize the equivalence between nature and woman that, historically, scientific discourse has developed. Nature, gendered female, has been seen in philosophy and throughout the history of science as either an organism or a mechanism.[16] According to the first view, nature was feminine and passive while husbandry, the active exploitation of nature, was masculine. Thus, the male was made essential to the cultivation of nature's latent fertility, just as in procreation, where the egg was seen as passive and the sperm as active, making the male "essential" to the process.[17] This equivalence between nature and female is key to understanding the struggle for power and the engendering of the parties in that struggle, where power is gendered male, making possible the displacement of the double image of woman/nature. Nature is seen as a virgin nymph or fertile and nurturing mother "in loving service of mankind," or as "a wild willful creature generating chaotic states that needs to be controlled," and, even worse, the bearer of "plagues, famines, and tempests."[18] Nature, identified with the female sex, was to be enslaved, inquisitioned, dissected, and exploited – an identification that

53

FIG. 3

Hans Baldung Grien. *The Witches.*
1510. Woodcut. Bildarchiv
Preussischer Kulturbesitz, Berlin

justifies the search for power over nature and over woman. Woman was seen as a virgin if subjected to male desires, as a witch if rebellious; adored as a virgin, burned as a witch (fig. 3). (Witches, symbolizing the violence of nature, were believed to control natural forces like storms, illness, and death. In addition, the fact that "women also seemed closer to nature than men and imbued with a far greater sexual passion" became one of the major arguments in the witch trials of the sixteenth century.[19])

After the scientific revolution of the sixteenth century, the mechanistic view of the universe secured domination over the female attributes of nature. The virgin earth was subdued by the machine for the exploitation of the goods of the earth in a race where industrialization and technological progress, backed by an ever-more rationalized view of the world, made the development of capitalism possible.[20] The process that privileged the mechanistic over the organic was also needed to control, dominate, and violate nature as female while excluding woman from socially and economically dominant ideology and practices. This approach to nature was based on a double system: one factual as it related to scientific laws; and one symbolic as machines transcended their own specific primary functions to give rise to a world of metaphoric and analogical relationships, ranging from the body to the entire universe.[21]

From a general opposition of nature/culture, other dichotomies more specific to architecture develop: nature/city and nature/architecture. Nature/city was already present – through the oppositional relationship between nature and machine – at the conquest of the American wilderness and concomitant development of the agrarian countryside. Throughout this process the mechanistic view of nature prevailed in consonance with the scientific revolution, and it continued to prevail on both sides of the Atlantic, certainly until Le Corbusier's *Ville Contemporaine* of 1922.

The locomotive, the machine that traversed the yet undeveloped land, generated another phenomenon: the appropriation and subdivision of land for towns and cities (figs. 4–6). The formal instrument that shaped this appropriation is Jefferson's one-mile grid, which also became an urban footprint regardless of topographical conditions, transcending the

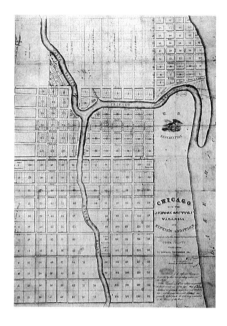

FIG. 4

Plan of Chicago, Illinois. 1834

FIG. 5

View of Oklahoma City, Indian
Territory. 1890

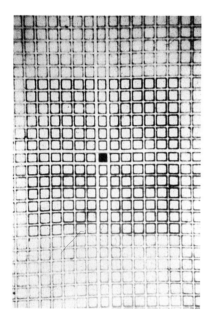 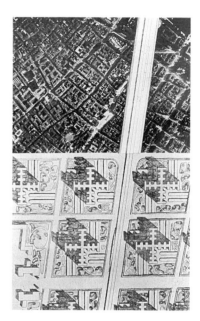

FIG. 6

Plan of the Far West, Missouri.
ca. 1836

FIG. 7

Le Corbusier. The historical city
and the modern city. From *The
City of Tomorrow*, 1929

opposition between country and city. Grids were drawn over the natural terrain as if on a blank piece of paper: cities without history. The grid as a spatially open-ended, nonhierarchical system of circulation networks anticipated what communications would produce later in a non-physical, spatial way. The gridding of America should be seen as the creation of the real modern city – an abstract Cartesian grid with no past traced on virgin land, a condition claimed by Le Corbusier in his *Plan Voisin* of 1922, specifically, and in early modernist urban design in general (fig. 7).

While modern cities were being built in America, modern examples of urban theory such as Le Corbusier's *Ville Contemporaine, Plan Voisin,* and *Ville Radieuse* were being developed in Europe.[22] It is in these early twentieth-century projects that nature appears as a major element in urban discourse. *Ville Radieuse* offers an excellent compendium of urbanistic ideology: "I go where order is coming out of endless dialogue between man and nature, out of the struggle for life, out of the enjoyment of leisure under the open sky, in the passing of the seasons, the song of the sea. . . . The idea of the Radiant City was born over a period of years from observation of the laws of nature."[23]

It is worth looking into the apparent paradox in Le Corbusier's urbanism, where nature has an essential role in his critique of the conditions of the historical city and in his development of an urbanism and an architecture whose avowed referent is the machine. To better understand this we must examine not only his writings but also his projects. Le Corbusier's critique of the historical city is based on establishing the opposition between historic city/nature, which could be translated formally into fabric/nature as stated in his critique of "the corridor street" in *Précisions.*[24] The green plane, as a metonymic presentation of nature, provides the formal background for the modernist notion of the city of object buildings as an alternative to the historical city of fabric. In the *Ville Contemporaine,* a paradigmatic example of modern urbanism, the American city's "gridded nature" is metaphorically (and unconsciously) transformed into an abstract gridded green plane dedicated to the movement of cars, while buildings (on pilotis) and pedestrians are lifted from the ground.[25] Nature becomes an element in the machinery of circulation, or part of the modernist *visual field*. This field is not an organic entity but an artificial construct formally organized as an abstract horizontal plane where geometry imposes order and formal control. "In order to save himself from . . . chaos . . . man has projected the laws of nature into a system that is a manifestation of the human spirit itself: geometry."[26] While the incorporation of nature as an element of the modernist city was essential in generating the opposition between fabric and object, in its application this opposition becomes autonomous of nature, which, as if by legerdemain, disappears. Nature is first suppressed, via a metaphorical manoeuvre representing it as a "green plane," as part of the urban machine; it is then relegated to a background, finally to be expelled by the economic-political forces of capitalism in a globalized market economy based on the exploitation and destruction of nature.

In modernist urbanism, where the city becomes the subject of architecture as a reaction to the historical city, the general opposition between nature and culture is transformed into the more specific opposition between nature and architecture. This new opposition is further articulated in the form of fabric/object, entering the architectural urban discourse as the historical city-of-fabric versus the modern city-of-objects on a green plane, thus generating a new morphology. In its subsequent application, however, what remains of this morphology is just the object, while the green plane – nature, which was the essential condition for the emergence of this opposition and morphology – curiously disappears. Nature then reappears in the discourse of modernist architecture and urbanism in a manner consistent with the mechanicism of the scientific ideology that is at its base, represented in the imaginary of modernist urbanism as an artificial construct or as mechanized nature: in the *Ville Radieuse* sun, air, and light, absent from the historical city, reappear managed and controlled by the machine (that is, "exact air" and "artificial building site"). "To build houses you must have sites. Are they natural sites? Not at all: they are immediately *artificialized*. This means that the natural ground is limited to but one function: withstand the strains, the weight of the structure (law of gravity). Once this is done we say 'goodbye' to the natural site, for it is the *enemy of man*. A home on the ground (beaten earth) is frightfully unhealthful; you no longer find it anywhere but in artificial sites."[27] The countryside is now "gay, clean, and alive," always placed in the context of the machine age. It is the artificial architectural order of modernism that regulates the relations between nature, city, and technology. The ideology of modernist architecture and urbanism is still based on the mechanistic scientific ideology, taking the form of *machinism,* an ideology that implicitly sanctions the repression/suppression of woman. Le Corbusier writes, once more in *Radiant City,* this time on "Laws":

" The laws of nature and the laws of men.
We live in the presence of three spheres:
Our dictator, the sun
The globe on which we live out our destinies: the earth
And a companion forever whirling around us: the moon
. . . .
Woman, that power in conjunction with which we work,
is ruled by this lunar month.
We the men are ruled by the solar year."[28]

The urban realm thus discloses the historical role of the alignment of nature and gender, an identification that is once again key to the struggle for power and the engendering of power. The conception of the world as a machine in a fetishistic architecture that is the result of the application of the principles of modernist urbanism allows the double domination (or negation) of nature and woman.

INSCRIPTION OF NATURE: THE CHINA BASIN PROJECT

The city as object of desire is transformed into the city as the place where the forces of desire are set free. The China Basin project, much like Donna Haraway's cyborg, is "about transgressed boundaries, potent fusions and dangerous possibilities."[29] This project is a provocation. It is, to paraphrase Haraway, a fiction mapping our urban, social, and ideological reality, resolutely committed to partiality, irony, and perversity. It is antagonistic, utopian, and completely without innocence.[30] The project serves as a unique opportunity to examine some of the pressing questions concerning the place, role, and form of urban development and questions about nature in urbanistic discourse at this moment in time (figs. 8–13).

The China Basin is a 300-acre site sloping down from the Embarcadero Freeway toward San Francisco Bay. The scheme assumes the creation of a new natural urban datum plane related to that of the existing freeway, which in turn is rendered obsolete and transformed into a residential structure. The freeway both defines one edge of the site and indicates the highest point above sea level. The China Basin Canal bounds the northwestern edge of the site, and San Francisco Bay lies to the east. An undulating blanket of nature covers the site and is punctuated by curvilinear public spaces varying in function and depth.

In the China Basin project, the smooth surface of nature replaces the striated fabric of the city in the form of various street grids; the fabric in turn is buried under the site: a seamless continuity of activity flows under the smooth surface of nature, a continuous flux without delimitation. This project addresses and encourages active production rather than the passive consumption that characterizes most urban developments, a condition manifested in the proposed program.

Zones of programmatic superimposition and interrelation radiating out of each "courtyard" are created, thus defining a *public place*. The boundaries determining various programs are left in suspense, undetermined, creating areas of programmatic instability, dissolving the barriers of institutionalized practice and reflecting the chance process of urban change over time. Intermediate levels provide most of the routes of movement. An intricate machine comprised of rotating, interlocking reels and platforms allows pedestrians to travel from one place to another in horizontal, vertical, and diagonal movement. At other levels, more traditional communication routes are present as well. This project proposes to explore the possibilities of using other geometries than Euclidean, which is at the core of the Cartesian grids of both the American city and early twentieth-century urbanism.

FIG. 8

View of San Francisco showing the China Basin area and the Mission District grid, ca. 1860

FIG. 9

Mapping San Francisco: reading the city through a mystery (story), a different city is revealed

FIG. 10

China Basin, site plan

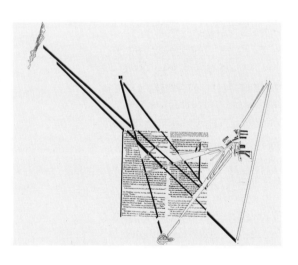

Programs

1. AMPHITHEATER 2. GENETIC RESEARCH CENTER Here, a place for the Genome
Projects: the body as machine is scrutinized on the most scientific and analytic
levels. 3. MUSEUM OF THE TWENTIETH CENTURY 4. OLYMPIC TRAINING CENTER
The Olympic Training Center is organized in linear fashion for swimming, running,
jumping, skating, and so on. The machines for exercising the body further elaborate the relationship between body and machine. 5. RADIO TOWER 6. WORKSHOP
The workshop is a center for production. Space is available for individual or group
work in disciplines ranging from the fine arts and literature to cooking and computer animation. Spaces are oriented radially, with the most concrete of physical
activities – those requiring the most space – occurring closest to the center. Moving
outward, the space becomes more limited and the activities more abstract and conceptual. Sectionally, each discipline occupies an L-shaped space. The individual
spaces are stacked vertically while the horizontal space is maintained as a communal area for the exchange of ideas within a discipline. Acting as a two-way panoptic
device, the workshops accommodate visual interaction between different disciplines. 7. SEAT-IN SCREENING The screening studio is a dual "seat-in" open-air film
theater with screens oriented back to back. The occupants are protected from the
elements and audio linkup is provided at each seat. The studio is intended to present sporting events and those films not shown in the popular commercial cinema,
including experimental films, documentaries, foreign films, and low-budget films.
8. MARKETPLACE The marketplace is a mega-automat, where a structure rotates
within a series of walkways. The structure itself is composed of four levels where
the exchange of merchandise may occur. The consumer travels exclusively along the
peripheral walkways, while the central structure rotates around its own axis, thereby
making products accessible to the public. Adjacent to the marketplace are agricultural fields and workshops, where items are collected and produced for sale. Only
those items produced on the China Basin site would be sold at the marketplace.
9. AQUARIUM AND OCEANOGRAPHIC RESEARCH CENTER A semi-circular wall with
a diameter of 500 feet defines the entire site of the aquarium and oceanographic
research center, which is composed of three major elements: a primary research
tank connected to the China Basin Canal, an elevated aquarium tank, and, adjacent
to the primary tank, a three-dimensional grid of pathways giving access to research
floor space. 10. BATHS The notion of *dépense* underlies the program, and the plea-

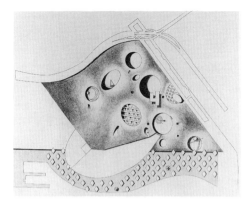

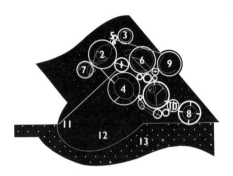

FIG. 11

China Basin, plans at highest level and circulation level showing the public places and the blanket of green

FIG. 12

China Basin, section showing circulation level and open public spaces

FIG. 13

China Basin, view of model

sure of free bodies can express itself. The baths symbolize the intentions of the project as a whole. In this natural forum for the discourse on the body, the public is encouraged to develop a new vision for the twenty-first century. 11. BASEBALL FIELD 12. FIELDS Here, activities of agricultural experimentation take place, generating products that may be obtained at the market. 13. FIELD OF SOLAR COLLECTORS

THE FORCES OF INSCRIPTION

The city as object of desire is transformed into the city as the place where the forces of desire are set free (fig. 14).

AGREST

Nature and machine join in the creation of collective territories. Residues of the forces that traverse the subject – the memories, the emotions, the rationalizations, the history, the stories, the assumed knowledge – are fixed by lines, by marks that project the forces of desire: "the survival of an experience."

In a movement that flows through earth and body, reaching through the gaze and into the depth of the universe, in the framing of infinitude, in the folding, collapsing of the sky onto the earth, through edges, borders, the borders of the body. Orifices and borders that are the makings of a body.

Border, edge, frame; the capturing and losing focus in an oscillating movement between the recognizable and the unknown.

Window, border, frame protecting the interiority of the subject from the collective outside while allowing the eye as shifter to bridge both worlds, as the mirror reflects the gaze back (to us).

A seamless continuity of activity (of program) flows under the smooth surface of nature. A continuous flux without delimitation.

The natural machine, the point where nature, body, and the machine intersect, placing the subject and object on the same plane.

FIG. 14

Diana Agrest. *The Forces of Inscription.* 1992. Photomontage

The traces of a body of woman which embodies desire, which is itself and the other.

Woman as gender constructing a new nature. It displaces the city to another place, which does not depend on the fetishistic object-building to achieve an "urban pleasure."

1. Sandra Harding, *The Science Question in Feminism* (Ithaca and London: Cornell University Press, 1990), 116.

2. Jean Nicholas Louis Durand, *Précis des lessons d'architecture* (Paris, 1817).

3. Le Corbusier, *Urbanisme* (Paris: Editions Vincent, Fréal & Cie., 1966).

4. Le Corbusier, *Radiant City* (New York: The Orion Press, 1964).

5. John W. Reps, *The Making of Urban America* (Princeton, N.J.: Princeton University Press, 1965).

6. Barbara Novak, *Nature and Culture, American Landscape and Painting 1825–1875* (New York and Toronto: Oxford University Press, 1980), 3.

7. Leo Marx, *The Machine in the Garden* (London, Oxford, and New York: Oxford University Press, 1964), 4, 99.

8. Reps.

9. Marx, 88.

10. Ibid., 15.

11. Ibid., 96; Novak, 5.

12. Novak, 4.

13. Ibid., 10.

14. Marx, 195, 206.

15. Ibid., 162, 165; Carolyn Merchant, *The Death of Nature* (San Francisco: Harper and Row, 1989), 194, 227–29.

16. Merchant, 2–5, 20, 99, 214.

17. Ibid., 149–163.

18. Ibid., 2, 20, 127.

19. Ibid., 130–32.

20. Ibid., 2, 192.

21. Ibid., 192, 227.

22. Le Corbusier, *Radiant City* and *Urbanisme*.

23. Le Corbusier, *Radiant City*, 85.

24. Le Corbusier, *Précisions* (Paris: Editions Vincent, Fréal & Cie., 1964).

25. Ibid.

26. Le Corbusier, *Radiant City*, 83.

27. Ibid., 55 (my emphasis).

28. Ibid., 76.

29. Donna J. Haraway, *Simians, Cyborgs, and Women* (New York: Routledge, 1991), 154.

30. Ibid., 151.

The Case of the Death of Nature: A Mystery

DIANA BALMORI

Nature is dead. Murdered, in fact. Or so I was told. I was assigned to the case — it'll be a year this August — much to my chagrin. I didn't have a choice about it either. If I wanted to go on working I had to tackle it. All I was told was that Nature was killed or that she disappeared somewhere around July 1989. Causes unknown; attackers (if any) also unknown.

It was a very hot July when I started, hardly a propitious time to begin an investigation. I escaped the office — the air conditioning was on the fritz — and brought a few books to the house that could tell me something about Nature's life as a way of getting started. I got a cool breeze going by opening the door to the porch and the window to the garden and immersed myself in Raymond Williams's *Keywords* and C. S. Lewis's *Studies in Words,* both of which devoted great attention to our subject. These biographies gave me a sense of the complicated life Nature had led and of her many career changes over time.

The bios and some conversations I had soon after with some of her friends did seem to point to a particularly close tie between Nature and women. This picture was reinforced by many rumors about her troubled relationship with Culture, her male companion and lover, shortly before her demise. They were often seen arguing in public.

Her special relationship with women was based, I suppose, on the fact that she, herself, was female. But others speculated that it had to do with the group she was a part of, a women's group that met informally to discuss diverse topics. I spent some time investigating one particular session to get the flavor of these gatherings and of the participants. This session discussed the Roman physician Celsus: he had stated that woman's nature was based on the good functioning of her reproductive organs and that a woman at the peak of her powers is equivalent to a male child, an old man, or a "castrato," a eunuch.[1] They discussed the fact that Celsus had saved all his praise of women's physiology for the womb – using the epithet *mirabilis* for it (*"ante omnia natura mirabilis"*) and had adjudicated the womb to Nature. They noted, too, Nature's name shared a common root with *natus* (birth).

The group also discussed how the Greeks and Romans had called female genitalia "natural parts" but had not applied that term to male genitalia.[2] Then they also brought out other words that the Greeks and Romans had used as euphemisms for female genitalia, words such as garden, meadow, field, farm, furrow,[3] which, as Nature herself pointed out at that meeting, were her bailiwick.

A look at the list of women who had been present at the meeting told me immediately that she was running around with a rather wild pack; these women were not the kind that appear on newspaper society pages. Many of them had been in skirmishes with the law, others had been ostracized for crossing moral lines (codes of morality for women always being much stricter than those for men, as several pointed out to me in the interviews). Of course, once Nature was identified with this group, it affected her reputation and she kept being portrayed as a weak victim, always in some rural setting, and often with these female acolytes. Meanwhile, Culture, her companion, got good press: he was always seen in the company of captains of industry, usually against the background of gleaming machines and cities. I heard it often, this bit about Nature's special relationship to women and Culture's to those who made things happen in the world, so often that it seemed more and more like a stereotype. Maybe it had sprung up in Nature's early days and nobody had bothered to adjust the picture. Of course, early days can mark out a course in a person's life or in a person's makeup. Maybe the way she started out branded her so that she fell into marginalized groups for company from then on.

But a lot of this stuff about her just didn't ring true. I'm reading through my old notes now and I see a major gathering of artists with her – this was years earlier – where she was honored by both male and female artists from all over the world. They had declared her to be the model they sought to imitate – in fact *had to* imitate, if they were to amount to anything as artists. But that had been many years ago and now, in talking to contemporary artists about her in private, they told me that they were through with her, that she certainly was not their model any more. Some artists said outright that it was all Culture now and that in fact he may well have had a hand in her disappearance.

I looked for witnesses to the alleged murder, someone who actually knew or had some confirmation of her death. I found two: Carolyn Merchant in *The Death of Nature* and Bill McKibben in *The End of Nature* were both emphatic about her death, though neither had actually witnessed it. They both presented convincing evidence of plans to harm Nature. But it was clear, too, that each one had known only one aspect of her – her life's geography in one case, her relation to gender issues in the other – and couldn't tell me much about other parts of her complex life. They had known her while she was mucking around in ecology and trying to sell something called ecosystems to municipalities, without much success. At town meetings, people kept telling her to stick to trees, rocks, and rivers: that was her stuff. At any rate, my notes say that she managed to get a resolution passed in some municipalities, putting towns under her jurisdiction, though not without some strong holdouts everywhere she went, the opposition coming from those who said towns were Culture's domain.

"Talk to Culture," my notebook says in early September. I tried several times but could never get beyond one of his agents. He was much too busy, I guess, with his various multinational ventures to give an unknown gumshoe like me the time of day. Notes from these interviews say Culture had been setting up some joint ventures with Nature just before she disappeared. When I asked what kind of joint ventures, and how come Nature had not been given credit for any that I knew of, the agent excused himself to take an international call.

Note from February 6th: "Culture, when did this liaison with Nature start?" From that date on, this became a central question in the investigation. Clearly I had to look at it more closely. Some people who knew her – I couldn't tell how well – said it was a late affair and that Nature

had been at her best before he showed up; that she had been a creature
of spontaneous unmediated responses, a pure-hearted, innocent, playful,
and delightful creature; that even of late, when she left for her ranch in
the Sierras, a rather primitive outpost she was very fond of, she reverted
to her old self and was in peak form. When I tried to get a fix on when
he'd made his appearance, a most surprising piece of information came
to light: I got different time periods from each of the respondents. When
I double-checked their answers, it became clear that Nature and Culture
must have known each other since childhood and must have actually
grown up together (if, that is, we can trust my respondents' accounts: I
still can't quite make heads or tails of the many different dates given to
me). At some time in adulthood they had become lovers and they had
also spent long periods as enemies. They had been everything to each
other, it was clear, at one time or another. They had been less than everything to each other, too; there were many tales out of school about each
one's dalliances. At any rate, Nature and he had had a big row at a public restaurant. Nature stomped out, and this had been the last Culture
had seen of her. Poof – disappeared without a trace July 26, 1989 – that's
what Culture's agent told me. If nobody had gone out to look for her
sooner, it was because she had complained of wanting to be left alone.
Culture maintained he hadn't seen her since that night.

   Ah, yes. In my notes for October – I'm backtracking here – there
were some jottings about her being seen in Indonesia as part of a rice
symposium, an unlikely venture it seemed at first, but as I was reviewing
my notes – cryptic as they were – something caught my eye. Through
the centuries rice diseases were regularly overcome by crossings with
the many wild varieties of rice. Nature's outfit in Southeast Asia was
demonstrating the value of biodiversity, at least within one species, and
this had become a new trump card. While there, she visited rice planta-
tions (she was with Culture on that trip) and spoke out publicly in favor
of terracing the rice paddies on the sides of hills, saying that terraces
did what was needed to slow the flow of water while handling a lot of
water without problems of erosion. She praised the Southeast Asians'
use of the terrace on convex slopes and said they had understood what

she had done in the landscape of New England with hammocks (low mounds) and hollows – free form terraces – where the eroded soil went to fill hollows. They had understood, too, how she controlled erosion in streams by the sequence of pool (an area of deep still water which slows water flow), riffle (an area of fast running shallow broken water), pool.

More facts. But where did they fit? After spending three days alternately walking around my desk and tidying it up, I decided I needed help to see if I could make sense of all this (it always helps to have a friend look at the same thing you're looking at). So I went to see my friend H. B. After he'd heard me out, he said, "The trick in these things is to find the relevant piece to analyze. Where can you track her behavior? Is there any way you can get an overall sense of what she was doing in a discrete chunk of time?"

It seemed worth a try, so I started to organize the data on the basis of those activities of Nature that had come to light rather recently and seemed to be outside the activities she had been usually associated with. Like the Indonesian rice fields, this strategy brought up some unexpected places and topics, which, if anything, made things more confusing and difficult rather than simpler or clearer.

Going back to some August notes (I'm skipping again) I found "mosaic": take a landscape with patches of different elements – rocks, woods, roads, ponds, houses; Nature was reported to have said something about finding the system's boundary and measuring the input and output flow across that boundary and then, by altering the input into any one piece of the mosaic, affecting the whole of it. The mosaic could have many and varied pieces: some natural, some cultural; the mix was possible.[4] Bingo! That was the track I'd been looking for.

It's April and I'm stuck again. No progress. I know where to go, but not how. Late call to a Seattle friend, C. S. She suggested putting down the data I now thought relevant and moving each piece around to see if it clicked with any other. It did.

Moving into late May. Morning fog, and the sun hitting hard in the afternoon. No obvious progress, but it feels closer. Then anxiety sets in; I have a clear sense now of how serious the plot against Nature had been and, if it has not already succeeded, how serious it continues to be. It was early June when, through tips, questioning, and some lucky guesses, I traced her disappearance to an underground group who admitted kidnapping her for a few months and barricading themselves with her in some rugged hills in northern California. They had notified police as to how they would keep Nature there, intact: a royal prison with electrified barbed wire where not a blade of grass, rock, or tree would be interfered with. With this admission, I knew that I had enough to charge them with intent to kill. They were – the whole group of them – however, hardly the answer to the question, since in fact she had escaped; nobody knew how or where to. Her jailers had been the first to be surprised. After long interrogation, it became quite clear that they had no idea where she was; and that they had little, if any, understanding of her. They had, as most others, fallen for the cliché: romanticized her, and tried to make her fit their expectations.

Weekend of July Fourth: everybody out of town. On the phone with D. P., who's working on a grant proposal this weekend. I told him I was writing about the investigation, putting what I knew down on paper as a way of clarifying it for myself, and that just as I thought I had arrived at a solution and found the culprits, I discovered they were guilty only of intent and that Nature was, in fact, still alive. My so-called solution had vanished.

I decided to catch Culture off guard and appeared at his place unannounced. I saw the car in the garage when I pulled up. Somebody was home. I rang the doorbell. Silence. The door was slightly ajar. I pushed it open and called out, "Hello. Anybody home?" More silence. I could hear birds singing in the background, that's how silent it was. I looked out toward the yard and saw on the veranda a table with a large dish of fresh oysters on ice, still unopened. I smelled the smoke of a charcoal grill somewhere. There was a strong scent of eucalyptus out there, too, and of dry heat. Then a splash. I followed the sound and saw a long lap pool running into the dry landscape and a figure swimming away. It was not quite visible. I stood at the end of the pool to make myself seen and called out again. It was dusk, and some dark clouds swallowed up the oranges and reds of the sunset. It was strange, this place so full of the marks of habitation and still so empty. I sat on the edge of the deck and waited.

Perhaps it was the lack of light, or my own letting go in the peacefulness of the place – sunset has always been my favorite hour – but I did not see the figure till it was by me. It was Nature's face, I thought, but dressed as a man. Or was it Culture with the mien and hands of Nature? I said nothing, just looked.

The charade was over. My companion knew it and didn't even attempt an explanation. The gendering, the interplay of conqueror and victim, had all been real – yet they were never separate, just contained in the same being. Virginia Woolf had caught a whiff of it when inventing Orlando, male in one era, female in another, a succession of roles and a multitude of careers.[5] It had been useful to one group or another to depict the separateness, to present it as if they were apart from the rest of us. But they were not.

We sat in silence for a while and later, when invited, I shared the meal. Oysters, grilled tuna, corn, fresh fruit. The image of the mosaic floated through from the corn, grilled fish, oysters, and fruit to rocks, woods, paved roads, a lake, and houses. As I sat there, I had the clear sensation of being by myself. My companion was silent and absorbed in the food. Had I not been so aware of the changing features of everything on the table and of the face, gestures, eyes of my companion, I would have said I was alone contemplating my own nature.

I turned in my report on July 15, 1995. In my notebook, I wrote: Nature found. With Culture. Nature was Culture's idea. Culture, when it wants to convince anybody that it is really right, just says that it's Nature.

1. Heinrich von Staden, "Apud nos foediora verba: Celsus' Reluctant Construction of the Female Body," in Guy Sabbah, ed., *Le Latin medical: La Constitution d'une language scientifique* (Sainte-Etienne: Publications de l'Université de Sainte-Etienne, 1991), 271–96.

2. C. S. Lewis, *Studies in Words* (Cambridge, Mass.: Cambridge University Press, 1960, reprinted 1990).

3. Von Staden.

4. F. H. Borman and G. E. Likens, "Catastrophic Disturbance and the Steady State in the Northern Hardwood Forest," *American Scientist* 67 (1979), 660–69, and *Pattern and Process in a Forested Ecosystem* (New York: Springer-Verlag, 1981).

5. Virginia Woolf, *Orlando, a Biography* (New York: Harcourt Brace Jovanovich, 1992).

BALMORI

Female Fetish Urban Form

ANN BERGREN

Female, fetish, and urban form are mutually fashioned in a fifth-century Greek comedy by Aristophanes called the *Ecclesiazusae*, which means "the women who take over the *ecclesia*," the male-only legislative assembly of Athens. The play shows a group of women successfully mounting a rebellion against the Classical architecture of the house and the city. Through their revolution, the play addresses questions left unspoken in canonical architectural history and theory: What will a woman build, if left to her own devices? In the construction of Western culture, why must we restrict her so severely? In her urban form, answers the play, the female will build the "death of the fetish."

The play opens in the predawn darkness as the leader of the plot, Praxagora, invokes a ceramic lamp, explaining why it is the right sign by which to signal the other women to assemble (fig. 1).

"O shining eye of the wheel-driven lamp,
among clever men a discovery most noble and fair –
we shall disclose both your birth and your honors:
driven by the wheel and born from the potter's thrust
you hold in your nostrils the shining honors of the sun –
rouse up the agreed-upon signs of light.
For by you alone do we fittingly reveal our signs, since
indeed in our bedrooms as we make our heroic trial
of the tropes of Aphrodite you stand near beside and
no one bars from the house your eye as superintendent
of our bodies curved with heads thrown back.

FIG. 1

Attic ceramic lamp with burning
flame, from the time of Socrates,
425–400 B.C.

Alone into the unspeakable recesses of our thighs
you shine as you singe off the flowering hair.
And with us as we furtively open the full storehouses
of grain and flowing wine you stand beside.
And although you do these things with us, you don't babble to those
who are near.
Because of all these things, you will be a witness of our present plans as
well,
as many as were ratified by my woman friends at the ritual of the Skira."[1]

This lamp is crucial to understanding the architectural meaning of the
play, for it will illuminate the ideal, institutionalized relation in Greek
thought between architecture and the female body. In being a molded
clay vessel and an instrument of depilation, the lamp will show, indeed,
why and how architecture in its Classical foundation is precisely a matter,
both for men and for women, of forming the female body. As a work
of the potter's wheel, the lamp evokes the fundamental analogy, figured
in the myth of Pandora, between the female body, the ceramic jar, and
the *oikos* or "household." This analogy is an ideological construction,
designed to mold women who will mold themselves according to the
architecture of father-rule.[2] A salient instance of this self-formation is
the Greek woman's depilation of her pubic hair. As tool of such auto-
architecture, the lamp displays women who have graduated with honors,
so to speak, from male-designed architectural school: women who act
as properly male-formed architects by using their architectural power
first and foremost to fashion themselves, so that the man will least fear
and take most pleasure in the female *sexe*. By giving us this glimpse of
how the architecture of the *oikos* normally regulates the female, Praxagora's apostrophe of the lamp also predicts, in effect, how the women
will rebel against it. Indeed, this is perhaps the most ironically valuable
and disturbing implication of the play's architectural meaning: that the
women's strategies for resisting male constructions are themselves built
into the original structure of household and city alike. With this prefab-
rication in mind, let us examine more closely the function of the lamp
as ceramic jar and instrument of depilation.

Female Body as *Ceramic Jar* as Oikos *Form: "My Mother, the House"*[3]

Tracing the implications of the lamp as "driven by the wheel and born
from the potter's thrust" takes us outside the play to two other texts:
first, the myth of Pandora, which establishes the analogy between the
female body, the ceramic jar, and the form of the *oikos*; and second,
the *Oeconomicus* by Xenophon, which details the ways in which the
household works as the woman's architectural school. Pandora, the first
female and founding model of all the rest, is molded by Hephaestus,
male god of craft, out of earth and water. Although a jar, she is also a
building, with lips as door. In the words of the myth, "there in the
unbreakable halls hope alone was remaining inside under the lips of the
jar, and it did not fly out from the door."[4] So Pandora as ceramic container is thus a body and (as) a house. This identification of body and
house is embedded in the Greek language itself, in which the word for
"own" (*oikeios*) is an adjectival form of the word for "house" (*oikos).* Your
"own" thing is the thing of your house and your house is your "ownership" – your "ownness" itself – an identification that will be crucial to
Praxagora's urban form, when her operation upon the *oikos* demolishes
the distinction between own and other's.

The analogy posed by the myth of Pandora is not a simple assimi-
lation of separate and equal male-molded containers. Within their
relation of mutual likeness is the hierarchy of original over copy and
container over contained with the jar as mediator. The female is modeled
upon the jar, being herself ceramic and male-molded only in metaphor,
and she is subordinated to the house that encloses her, molding her as
an image of itself, a domestic container like the jar.[5] What the woman
(as contained by the house) is supposed to contain is the female's architectural power, that capacity the Greeks call *mêtis.*[6] This tricky power of
reversal and transformation is cast as originally female in the myth of
the goddess Metis, whom Zeus marries and swallows, when she becomes
pregnant. Zeus himself then gives birth through his head to their child,
the goddess Athena, who teaches women to weave, weaving, along
with such transformations as making bread from grain and children from
seed, being a signal manifestation of the female's *mêtis.* If the architec-

ture of the *oikos* works, the female will imitate it. She will confine her shape-shifting to the edification of her husband, limiting her plastic production to the weaving of his walls and her sexual reproduction to the bearing of his legitimate children. Such is the lesson we learn from Xenophon's *Oeconomicus*, a text in which a husband tells Socrates how he taught his bride, who comes to him knowing nothing except how to weave, everything else she needs to know.

His first lesson is the coincident aetiology of marriage and architecture itself.[7] Not simply to produce children or to care for the aged, the *zeugos* or "joining" that is marriage derives from what makes humans different from animals: the need for shelter instead of living in the open air. Humans need the joint that divides – or the division that joins – inside and outside, and with it, the divisive joint of female and male. But in order to have something to bring inside the shelter, so the husband reasons, the man must go out to work in the open air, while the woman remains inside, devoting her *mêtis* to transforming what he brings in – sperm into children, grain into bread, and wool into woven cloth – acting, in this role, like a "general bee" (*hêgemôn melissa*, compare "hegemony") who "weaves the cells" of her domestic hive. All the physical and psychological differences between male and female were created by "the god himself," master architect of this marital "joint," to fit the sexes for this basic spatial division.

The sexual spaces of marriage, however, are far from "separate, but equal." For it is the male outside who functions as architect, teacher, and model of the female and the *oikos* inside. And, paradoxically, the male's design to maintain the female's architectural difference – indeed, to maintain female as architectural difference – does not make her different.[8] Rather, in anticipation of the function of the psychoanalytic fetish, the male design of female difference makes her a parodic imitation of himself.

Female as *Parodic Male*

The husband constructs the woman's realm – from the innermost recesses of her mind and body to the organization of the *oikos* itself – as a microcosm of the roles, institutions, and ideals of the exterior, male world. Like the job of architects working in the office of a star, it is the wife's duty to devote her architectural talent to realizing her husband's design.

The consummate architectural virtue that the wife must emulate in the *oikos*, in her body, and in her deepest beliefs, is order – expressed in Greek by two words, *taxis* (cognate with "tactic" and "syntax") and *kosmos* (cognate, ironically, with "cosmetic"). To teach his wife the powers of order, the husband uses examples from the male world: a chorus in drama (as in the Shakespearean theater, all actors in Athens were male), a deployed army, and a Phoenician ship.[9] Within the *oikos* such order is crucial to the household's chief purpose: maximum economic profit. For it is *kosmos* that maximizes both spatial efficiency, human productivity, and that coincidence of aesthetic and moral value in which the Greeks located beauty. With the greatest number of objects most easily accessible in the smallest amount of space, not only can the wife give her husband whatever he asks for instantly, but "place" itself becomes a working person, since "the place itself," the husband explains, "will miss the thing that is not there."[10] Climaxing this panegyric – the first in Western culture – of the economic dividends and aesthetic power of Classical order, the husband claims that *kosmos* can create beauty out of the most ordinarily ugly things – even cooking pots, another of the female jars. Countering the traditional Greek liaison of the ugly and the impure, he declares, "each group appears as a chorus of implements, even the space in the middle appears beautiful, because each thing lies outside it. Just as a circular chorus is not only a beautiful sight itself, but the space in the middle of it also appears beautiful and pure."[11] It is as a microcosm of such *kosmos* that the husband has designed the domestic world, dividing the men's quarters from women's by a bolted door and separating the rest of the household goods "according to tribes."[12] This is the architectural order that the wife maintains by playing the male roles of "law guardian, garrison commander, and legislative council" with her servants inside the house (fig. 2).[13]

But maintaining this order in the *oikos* alone is not enough. In the grand finale to her architectural schooling, the husband explains how and why the wife must mold her mind and body.[14] This part of his

FIG. 2

Marlene Dietrich in a tuxedo on
the set of *Morocco*, 1930

teaching begins with Socrates exclaiming that the wife indeed has achieved a "male mind," and when the husband offers to recount another instance of her immediate obedience, Socrates eagerly accepts, preferring, he says, the virtue of a living woman to the beautiful likeness painted by Zeuxis. This preference for philosophical truth over material artifice turns into the wall that the *oikos* tries to build between the pure and natural beauty of male *kosmos* and women who imitate it, on one hand, and female cosmetic deception, on the other. For once, when the husband caught his wife with white lead and rouge on her face and wearing high heels, he was able to correct her instantly by explaining that just as she would not like him to present counterfeit money, fake gold, or fading purple instead of the real thing, or a body smeared with vermilion and flesh color under the eyes instead of ruddy from natural exercise, so she must present him with a pure body, free of cosmetic deceit. And when she asks how she might make her body as beautiful as possible, the husband recommends exercise through assiduous pursuit of household duties, especially those specialities of *mêtis*, weaving and breadbaking, adding that her visual appearance is stimulating whenever she defeats the maid (her ever-present sexual rival) by being more pure and properly dressed. This doctrine of the auto-architecture necessary to win the man's sexual approval returns us to the play and to Praxagora's invocation of the lamp as tool of pubic depilation.

Depilation as *Female Auto-Architecture*

In requiring women to depilate their genital hair, the architecture of father-rule reaches into the female body's "unspeakable recesses," as Praxagora puts it, using a Greek word (*muchos*) that refers to the innermost part of a landscape or house (fig. 3). Inside these "unspeakable recesses" is the female's pubic hair. Here is the sight and the site that provokes the fetish, the pseudo-phallic prosthesis that worships by mutilating the female genital, simultaneously denying and affirming her castration, her "sameness" with men.[15] And here the woman's architectural power is born. For it is on the model of the matted pubic hair that covers her lack of a penis that the female invented weaving, according to

FIG. 3

Illustration on a cylix by Panaetius of a woman singeing off her pubic hair with a lamp

FIG. 4

Modern styles of depilation. From Wendy Cooper, *Hair: Sex, Society, Symbolism* (New York: Stein and Day, 1971)

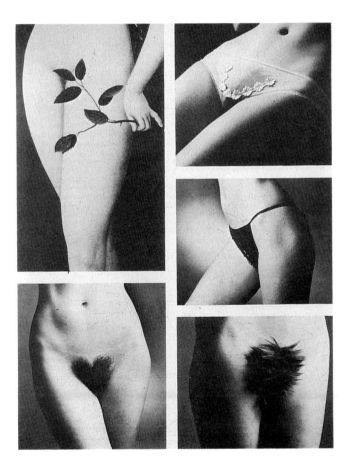

Freud; it is weaving, according to Semper, that is the origin of architecture as vertical space enclosure; and it is cutting, together with weaving, we may add, that constitutes the primary architectural act, the "detail."[16]

In the detail of pubic depilation, the twin strategies of the fetish and the father-ruled house coincide. Each has the same mission: to form the female by cutting her sexuality short.[17] Without such "cosmetic surgery," the female sexuality knows no natural bounds. For in the oppositional categories of Greek thought, the male is dry and limited and the female is unlimited and wet, the two categories being closely connected architecturally. As Aristotle puts it, "the wet is that which is not bounded [*a+oriston*, compare 'horizon'] by any boundary of its own [*oikeios*, 'own'] while being easily bounded [*eu+oriston*] and the dry is easily bound by its own boundary [*eu+oriston*], but with difficulty bounded [*dus+oriston*]."[18] Because the female's wetness – the sign, like the male's erection, of her sexual capacity – knows no intrinsic limit, it must be bound by a formative force outside itself, the institution of father-ruled marriage and its material embodiment in the *oikos*. The trimming of her pubic hair signals the woman's willingness to draw this horizon, to conform herself to Classical *kosmos*. As she weaves the walls that mold the *oikos* and the clothes that veil her body, so the woman trims her genital hair into a particular schema that is epitome of order, the inverted delta, one of the two types of triangles described by Plato in the *Timaeus* as the elementary geometrical forms of the cosmos itself (fig. 4).[19]

At every level of her architectural formation, the female is indoctrinated with a single architectural ideal: to devote her *mètis* exclusively to making herself – her mind, her body, and her house – a parodic imitation of male design and desire. Her architectural imperative is thus to fetishize herself. Ironically, this indoctrination programs the methods and forms of the architectural rebellion staged in the rest of Aristophanes' play. In both her plot to take over the government and in her new urban form, Praxagora combines two basic operations, sectional inversion and extension in plan, that for all their revolutionary ingenuity are, nevertheless, applications of her training to emulate the male. Sectionally, she maintains traditional hierarchy but inverts gender, putting the woman on top, where, true to the self-fetishizing imperative, she can "play the man." In plan, Praxagora extends the household horizontally, turning the *polis* into one big *oikos*, where women will continue to perform their parodic male role. Let us look at the details of her plot and plan.

Praxagora's plot has two phases, first visual and then verbal, and in both the women work as masked men. In order to infiltrate the *ecclesia*, the male-only legislative assembly, and vote in a new regime, the women disguise themselves as men in a glossary of typical fetishes: they put on their husbands' platformed shoes, cloaks, and walking sticks, they suntan their skin, and, in an inversion and displacement upward of pubic depilation, they stop shaving their underarm hair and sew beards on their faces (fig. 5). Dressed up like a man, Praxagora now wins the votes of the male assembly by imitating male speech about women (how often do we all do this?), for she cites women's traditional role – that is, what men traditionally say about women – as the grounds for her proposed gynocracy.

Once the *ecclesia*, packed by the disguised women, votes in Praxagora's new regime, Athens becomes, in effect, a naked female body (in Greek thought, as in many cultures, the earth is understood as female) stripped of all fetishes, all the pseudo-phallic supports of the father-ruled *polis*: private property, marriage, political and judicial institutions, along with the oppositions and hierarchies upon which they stand. Political power is inverted: men stay home while women go out to rule and work, producing and distributing food and clothing as they used to inside the *oikos*. Economic power is extended: all land is held in common and all material goods are donated to a common store, obliterating the difference between own and other's. Women, children, and men, too, become common property, erasing the distinction between legitimate and bastard. The parental function is spread out over the space of each generation with all men of a given age becoming "fathers" and all women, "mothers." Equal access to sexual pleasure is guaranteed by upending aesthetic value: in order to enjoy someone young and beautiful, if you are young and beautiful, you must satisfy someone old and ugly first.

This defetishized social structure – this expansion of the *oikos* to coincide with the *polis* so that the city is one big household for all – is accomplished by Praxagora through architectural procedures that the woman learns at home. Just as women have been taught to devote their

FIG. 5

René Magritte. *The Rape*. 1934.
Oil on canvas, 28 1/2 x 21 in.
The Menil Collection, Houston

FIG. 6

Female putting the Devil to flight
by exposing her genitals.
Illustration by Charles Eisen, ca.
1750, in La Fontaine, *Fables*

mêtis to weaving the walls of the *oikos*, so also, like Penelope, have they learned how to unweave them, when the situation demands. Praxagora's urban plan of (re)constructing the city through demolition is just such a constructive undoing. In her own words, "I declare I will make the city one household by uniting-through-breaking [*syn* 'together' + *rhêggumi*, 'break'] all things into one, so that as a result everyone walks toward one another."[20] And if women are taught to maintain the program of indoor, domestic space, Praxagora knows how to (re)program an outdoors – now wholly domestic – to serve the previously indoor, private function of the male-only symposium: she turns the law courts and stoas into dining rooms, the orator's platform into a pedestal for wine-mixing bowls and water jugs, and from the urns of lots that used to designate judicial assignments, that definitive attribute of direct democracy, each man now draws the letter of his table at the common outdoor dinner.

So to the question, "What will a woman build, if left to her own devices?" the play answers, "She will build as we have taught her." She will turn the city into one big house with herself in power and her sexuality uncontained. She will expose the land as a female genital stripped of every pseudo-phallic stand-in (fig. 6). Female urban form means the end of the "phallus" as architect of all those oppositions – inside versus outside, own versus other's, legitimate versus bastard – and all those hierarchies – male over female, youth over age, beauty over ugliness – all those oppositions and hierarchies upon which Classical value and meaning depend. Female urban form means the death of architecture as phallic differentiation.

What is one to see in this vision of the unadorned, unconfined, uncovered, unfetishized female genital? I conclude with what may be thought of as two "genders" of response. The first is Aristophanes' own, coming in the scene that follows Praxagora's description of her new regime. The scene purports to show how the new law giving sexual preference to the old and ugly affects a beautiful young man. The female is still assimilated to the man-made containers of ceramic jar and house, but with her openings now free of phallic regulation. In dramatizing what the young man suffers from this unfettered genital, the scene becomes, in effect, a defense of the fetish and a demand for its return.

Attempting to avail herself of the new sexual order, an ugly old hag competes with a beautiful young girl for the young man's sexual service, each woman stationing herself in an orifice of the house, one at the window and the other at the door, to hurl abuse at the other. The young man, too, insults the hag. Loaded down, as she is, with white lead and rouge on her face, he likens her to a certain type of ceramic jar, the *lekuthos*, a one-handled jug with narrow neck and deep mouth used for athlete's oil, unguents, makeup, and as an offering for the dead. He charges that her lover is that master pot-painter Death himself, who makes such a *lekuthos* of and for us all. These insults alone do not dissuade the hag. Only as she drags the young man across her threshold, thus inverting the roles of regular marriage, is she finally put to flight, when the young girl warns of incest: "If you establish this law," she cries, "you will fill the entire world with Oedipuses!" But no sooner is the first hag expelled than another arrives, uglier than the first, and then a third arrives, the ugliest of all. Caught in a physical tug-of-war, as each *lekuthos*-like hag tries to drag him into the door of her house, the young man bewails his fate, a synaesthesia of intercourse, castration, and death, and caps it with a vision of compensatory revenge:

"O three-times damned, if I must screw a
putrid woman the whole night and day, and then,
whenever I escape from this one, again have to screw
a Toad[21] who has a *lekuthos* on her jaws.
Am I not damned? Indeed, I am deeply damned,
by Zeus the savior, a man indeed ill-fated,
who will be shut up inside with such wild beasts.
But still, if – as is very likely – I suffer something,[22]
as I sail hither into the harbor under these whores[23] as pilots,
bury me upon the mouth itself of the entrance,
and this woman above, on top of the grave,[24]
tar her down alive, then pour lead
on her feet in a circle around her ankles,
and put her on top above me as a substitute[25] for a *lekuthos*."

In this phantasmagorical vision, entities bear multiple, simultaneous meanings. Intercourse with the female-as-ceramic-embodiment-of-death means imprisonment in her body-as-a-house and being devoured by her castrating *vagina dentata*. This diabolical confinement of the man inverts Zeus' swallowing of Metis and the *oikos'* confinement of the wife. And just as the wife before tried to emulate a "shipshape" *kosmos*, so the female is now the pilot of the male, himself a ship, sailing into the harbor of her voracious genital mouth, upon which he will be buried – but not without his revenge. For in his final words, he envisions a return of the female as fetish – that "monument" (*Denkmal*), in Freud's terms, "to the horror of castration" feared as punishment for incest – and with the fetish, a return of the "phallus" as architectural support. Tarred alive and welded to his tomb at her feet, those perennial objects of the fetishist's sadistic adoration, female *mētis* stands now wholly immobilized, a reduction of the constricting drive of the *oikos* to its logical absurdity. The female as ceramic Pandora is now the parodic *lekuthos*, a pseudo-phallic memorial upon the grave of male glory.

Although certainly representative of the dominant view in subsequent Western tradition, prefiguring as it does the Freudian theory of the fetish, Aristophanes' is not the sole response in Classical thought to the unadorned female genital. The mythology of Demeter offers another reaction in the story of Baubo, who herself prefigures the image of Marilyn birthing the world (figs. 7, 8). When her daughter Persephone is raped by Death, Demeter, goddess of marriage, childbirth, and chthonic fertility, suspends her powers and wanders the now sterile earth disguised as an old woman. Arriving at Eleusis, she is received by the queen Baubo, who offers her food and drink. When the mourning goddess refuses this traditional hospitality, Baubo responds by lifting her skirts and exposing her naked genitals. At this sight, the goddess laughs. She eats and drinks, and with her resumption of human social exchange, the fertility of women and the earth returns. In the tropic power of Baubo's display, in its power to turn mourning and sterility to laughter and fertile intercourse, lies the direction toward another female architecture than the one prefabricated by the Classical *oikos*.[26]

FIG. 7

Figurine of Baubo with torch, found at Priene. Terra-cotta, 4th century B.C.

FIG. 8

Marilyn Monroe birthing the world

1. Aristophanes, *Ecclesiazusae*, ed. with introduction and commentary by Robert Glenn Ussher (Oxford: Clarendon Press, 1973), lines 1–17. All translations from the Greek are my own.

2. In light of this analogy, the Vitruvian ideal of the building as male body appears to be less an original principle than a secondary compensation for the primary correlation between the female and the house.

3. Robert E. Somol, "My Mother, the House," *Princeton Architectural Journal* (1992), 50–71.

4. Hesiod, *Works and Days*, ed. with prolegomena and commentary by Martin Litchfield West (Oxford: Clarendon Press, 1978), lines 96–97.

5. Compare this complex circulation of likeness and hierarchy with the depiction of Pandora on an amphora (British Museum F 147) as a mermaid-like combination of female on the top and *pithos* on the bottom, the *pithos* being a human-sized ceramic pot in which sometimes food and sometimes the bones of the dead were stored. See Otto Lendle, *Die "Pandorasage" bei Hesiod* (Würzburg: Konrad Triltsch, 1957), 80–81, pl. 9. For a similar *mise en abime* of receptacles in the depiction of the female *chôra* in Plato's *Timaeus*, see Ann Bergren, "Architecture Gender Philosophy," in Richard Burdett, Jeffrey Kipnis, and John Whiteman, eds., *Strategies in Architectural Thinking* (Cambridge, Mass.: MIT Press, 1992), 8–46.

6. For *mêtis* as the female's architectural power, see Ann Bergren, "The (Re)Marriage of Penelope and Odysseus: Architecture Gender Philosophy," *Assemblage* 21 (1993), 6–23.

7. Xenophon, *The Oeconomicus*, ed. Arthur Henry Nanson (Cambridge: Cambridge University Press, 1925), ch. 7, paras. 18–36. For an accurate translation of this text in its entirety, see Leo Strauss, *Xenophon's Socratic Discourse: An Interpretation of the* Oeconomicus *with a New, Literal Translation of the* Oeconomicus *by Carnes Lord* (Ithaca and London: Cornell University Press, 1970).

8. For architecture as *maintenant*, the "now" that "maintains," see Jacques Derrida, "Point de folie – maintenant l'architecture," *AA Files-Folio VIII, La Case Vide*, with English trans. by Kate Linker, 1986, 4–19. The French text is reprinted in *Psyché: Inventions de l'autre* (Paris: Galilée, 1987), 477–94.

9. Xenophon, *Oeconomicus*, ch. 8, paras. 3–17.

10. Ibid., ch. 8, para. 10.

11. Ibid., ch. 8, para. 20.

12. Ibid., ch. 9, paras. 2–10.

13. Ibid., ch. 9, paras. 14–15.

14. Ibid., ch. 10.

15. Sigmund Freud, "Fetishism," *The Standard Edition of the Complete Psychological Works of Sigmund Freud,* trans. and gen. ed. James Strachey (London: The Hogarth Press, 1961), vol. 21, 152–57. Compare Charles Bernheimer, "'Castration' as Fetish," *Paragraph* 14 (1991), 1–9: "The purpose of the fetish is to preserve the fantasy that all humans have a penis – the childhood theory of anatomical sameness – and simultaneously to represent a recognition that women lack this organ."

16. Sigmund Freud, "Femininity," *The Standard Edition of the Complete Psychological Works of Sigmund Freud,* trans. and gen. ed. James Strachey (London: The Hogarth Press, 1961), vol. 22, 132: "The effect of penis-envy has a share, further, in the physical vanity of women, since they are bound to value their charms more highly as a late compensation for their original sexual inferiority. Shame, which is considered to be a feminine characteristic *par excellence* but is far more a matter of convention than might be supposed, has as its purpose, we believe, concealment [*verdecken: Decke,* 'cover, ceiling, roof, skin, envelope, coat, pretence, screen'] of genital deficiency. We are not forgetting that at a later time, shame takes on other functions. It seems that women have made few contributions to the discoveries [*Entdeckungen*] and inventions in the history of civilization; there is, however, one technique which they may have invented – that of plaiting and weaving. If that is so, we should be tempted to guess the unconscious motive for the achievement. Nature herself would seem to have given the model which this achievement imitates by causing the growth at maturity of the pubic hair that conceals the genitals. *The step that remained to be taken lay in making the threads adhere to one another* [my emphasis], while on the body they stick into the skin and are only matted together. If you reject this idea as fantastic and regard my belief in the influence of a lack of a penis on the configuration of femininity as an *idée fixe*, I am of course defenceless."

Gottfried Semper, "The Textile Art," *The Four Elements of Architecture and Other Writings,* trans. Harry Francis Mallgrave and Wolfgang Herrmann (Cambridge: Cambridge University Press, 1989), 254–55: "*The beginning of building coincides with the beginning of textiles.* The wall is that architectural element that formally represents and makes visible *the enclosed space as such*, absolutely, as it were, without reference to secondary concepts. We might recognize the *pen*, bound together from sticks and branches, and the interwoven *fence* as the earliest vertical spatial enclosure that man *invented*. . . . Whether these inventions gradually developed in this order or another matters little to us here, for it remains certain that the use of the crude weaving that started with the pen – as à means to make the 'home,' the *inner life* separated from the *outer life*, and as the formal creation of the idea of space – undoubtedly preceded the wall, even the most primitive one constructed out of stone or any other material. The structure that served to support, to secure, to carry this spatial enclosure was a requirement that had nothing directly to do with *space* and the *division of space*. . . . In this connection, it is of the greatest importance to note that wherever these secondary motives are not present, woven fabrics almost everywhere and especially in the southern and warm countries carry out their ancient, original function as conspicuous spatial dividers; even where solid walls become necessary they remain only the inner and unseen structure for the true and legitimate representatives of the spatial idea: namely, the more or less artificially woven and seamed-together, textile walls. . . . In all Germanic languages the word *Wand* (of the same root and same basic meaning as *Gewand*) directly recalls the old origin and type of the *visible* spatial enclosure. Likewise, *Decke, Bekleidung, Schranke, Zaun* (similar to *Saum*), and many other technical expressions are not somewhat late linguistic symbols applied to the building trade, but reliable indications of the textile origin of these building parts." See also "The Four Elements of Architecture," ibid., 102–3, and compare "Structural Elements of Assyrian-Chaldean Architecture," in Wolfgang Herrmann, *Gottfried Semper: In Search of Architecture* (Cambridge, Mass., and London: MIT Press, 1984), 205–6: "It is well known that any wild tribe is familiar with the fence or a primitive hurdle as a means of enclosing space. Weaving the fence led to weaving movable walls of bast, reed or willow twigs and later to weaving carpets of thinner animal or vegetable fiber. . . . Using wickerwork for setting apart one's property and for floor mats and protection against heat and cold far preceded making even the roughest masonry. Wickerwork was the original motif of the wall. It retained this primary significance, actually or ideally, when the light hurdles and mattings were later transformed into brick or stone walls. The essence of the wall was wickerwork. Hanging carpets remained the true walls; they were the visible boundaries of a room. The often solid walls behind them were necessary for reasons that had nothing to do with the creation of space; they were needed for protection, for supporting a load, for their permanence, etc. Wherever the need for these secondary functions did not arise, carpets remained the only means for separating space. Even where solid walls became necessary, they were only the invisible structure hidden behind the true representatives of the wall, the colorful carpets that the walls served to hold and support. It was therefore the covering of the wall that was primarily and essentially of spatial and architectural significance; the wall itself was secondary."

On the relation between the detail and cutting, note the derivation of the term from French *détailler*, "to cut in pieces."

17. Charles Platter, "Depilation in Old Comedy," typescript, 3–4: "The matrix of depilation described by our sources is fundamentally associated with . . . the attempt to control the women of the household whose extravagant sexuality, symbolized by tangled hair, represents a threat to the solid edifice of the family and the social status of the man."

18. Aristotle, *On Coming-to-Be and Passing Away*, trans. Edward Seymour Forster (Cambridge, Mass.: Harvard University Press, 1955), section 329b31–33. See Ann Carson, "Putting Her in Her Place: Women, Dirt, and Desire," in David M. Halperin, John J. Winkler, and Froma I. Zeitlin, eds., *Before Sexuality: The Construction of Erotic Experience in the Ancient World* (Princeton: Princeton University Press, 1990), 135–69, and Platter, 9: "Thus, the male gender, by virtue of its dryness, lends itself to definition and self-ordering. The female, by contrast, has no mechanism for self-limitation, and like water, spreads out until exhausted – like the sleeping *Bacchae* of Euripides and the sexually voracious women who appear in Old Comedy, or until stopped by some limit imposed from the outside."

19. Plato, *Timaeus, Platonis Opera*, ed. John Burnet (Oxford: Oxford University Press, 1965), sections 53c–55c. See F. M. Cornford, *Plato's Cosmology: The* Timaeus *of Plato Translated with Running Commentary* (New York: Harcourt, Brace and Co., 1937), 210–19.

20. Aristophanes, *Ecclesiazusae*, lines 673–74.

21. Greek, *phrunê*, "toad," nickname of many Athenian courtesans because of their complexion.

22. Euphemism for "die."

23. Literally, "hides, toughened skins."

24. Greek, *sêma*, "grave mound, sign."

25. Greek, *prophasis*, "what is said instead," hence "alleged motive, pretext, excuse."

26. For some implications of the figure of Baubo for architectural theory, see Ann Bergren, "Helen and Baubo: Gender in the 'Irreparable Wound,'" in Andrea Kahn, ed., *Drawing, Building, Text* (New York: Princeton Architectural Press, 1991), 107–26.

Crimes in and of the City: The Femme Fatale as Urban Allegory

M. CHRISTINE BOYER

CROSS: You may *think* you know what you're dealing with, but, believe me, you *don't*.

GITTES: That's what the district attorney used to tell me in Chinatown.

– *Chinatown* (1974)

At least one feminist critic of urban form, Rosalyn Deutsche, has criticized a few white male theorists of the postmodern urban condition for adopting the personae of film noir detectives. Pitting the force of rational detection against the irrational power of money (that is, real estate investors, elite residents, and their allies in municipal governments or special municipal authorities), these theorist/detectives attempt to uncover the violent traces of criminal acts of wealth as they have unfolded in the production of urban space.[1] "Men in space," another label Deutsche attaches to these theorists,[2] are far from innocent investigators of treacherous urban terrains risking dangerous encounters with those in power, for they simultaneously perpetrate their own set of crimes against women in the city and cover their own masculine traces with veiled comments and disguised positions. Specifically, these theorists fail to address the role that women traditionally hold in film noir – that of the *femme fatale* (fig. 1). Generally associated with male fears about female sexuality, the *femme fatale* is an ambivalent figure who harbors a threat of enticement, of artifice, of excess, which must be avoided. By hiding the presence of women – making them disappear from, or appear invisible in, sites of the city – theorist detectives desexualize the terrain of the postmodern city. Sue Best, in "Deconstructing Space," agrees with Deutsche, finding

FIG. 1

The *femme fatale* harbors an
uncanny threat to the men she
entices. This secret, never entirely
visible, must be controlled even
by aggressive, often violent means

that such criminal acts against women subsequently enable these same theorist/detectives to achieve the disembodied state of the rational purposive masculine subject who gives renewed form and shape to – or controls and surveils – urban space that long has been considered by geographers to be indeterminate, characterless, neutral, or feminine.[3] These theorists, by not mentioning women in space, implicitly link the dangers of sexual liaison with the dangers of the city.

According to Best, these theorist/detectives "encrypt" the feminine in space by the way they conceptualize it as pure potential matter; yet, subsequently, they appropriate, dominate, and subjugate that space by denying women an appearance in it.[4] The feminine appears only as a concealed secret; it is a code that must be deciphered. By encrypting the feminine in space, gender becomes an object of misrecognition – or non-recognition – and escapes analysis. Thus the feminization of space is implicit in the way metaphors and concepts carry the imprinting of sexual terms; but, at the same time, it escapes awareness, thereby enabling space to "naturally" receive the so-called femininized characteristics of passivity, inertness, staticness, even speechlessness. As Best writes, "[t]his is all done, as it were, under cover [like a true detective]. These theorists continue to do what man has always done: hog the subject position and thereby masquerade as *the* human. It is as if contemporary male writers are played by the binary system and the violent sexual hierarchies it installs, but even after two decades of feminist scholarship the writers in question *still* proceed as if sexuality has nothing to do with textuality."[5]

There is, however, a long history to this sexualization of space, conceptualized by and through the body of woman, and it stretches back at least to the time of Plato, when the metaphoric transference of feminine attributes to spatial concepts appears to have been clearly established. Plato wrote that space as a receptacle

"can always be called the same because it never alters its characteristics. For it continues to receive all things, and never itself takes a permanent impress from any of the things that enter it, it is a kind of neutral plastic material on which changing impressions are stamped by things that enter it, making it appear different at different times. And the things which pass in and out of it are copies of the eternal realities, whose form they take . . . we must make a *threefold* distinction and thinking of that which becomes [birth], that in which it becomes [womb], and the model which it resembles [father]. We may indeed use the metaphor of birth and compare the receptacle to the mother, the model to the father, and what they produce between them to their offspring.[6]"

The metaphoric transference of the female womb onto the spatial receptacle waiting for male impregnation, and of the masculine abstract model onto the disembodied ideal form giver, was clearly delineated by Plato. Best briefly outlines the history of this metaphoric transference in male discourse down to our contemporary "men in space."[7] She finds that Edward Soja, for example, exemplifies the detour men take through the matter of woman while simultaneously disavowing the feminization of space. In his *Postmodern Geography*, Soja declares that space has been denied, denigrated, and reduced to static, passive, and inert matter by the theorization of historians who have elevated the active and dynamic position of time – progress, motion – over the production of space. His desire is to activate feminized space by injecting masculine vigor into it. Thus geography would be reconceptualized and revitalized by the modern and/or postmodern urban, public man. As both Deutsche and Best proclaim, remapped postmodern space now becomes the subjected object of a reformulated cartographer's gaze, which exercises renewed jurisdiction over the urban terrain and establishes fresh alliances with the spectacles of urban violence perpetrated in and against the city and women.

In particular, Deutsche utilizes theorist Mike Davis and his critique of the spatial production of contemporary Los Angeles as exemplary of the gritty tough-guy realism and detached perspective that neo-noir detectives assume. Paradoxically, Deutsche allows that Davis's ground-level "tactics of lived space" puncture the detective's voyeuristic gaze. Thus the concerns and conflicts of Los Angeles's immigrant cultures make an appearance on the urban scene to battle against the evasive and abstract forces of global capital restructuring the space and redefining the uses of the downtown area. Yet Davis remains for Deutsche an exemplary neo-noir detective, ignoring issues of gender, the sexualization of

space, and the embodiment of any and every urban theorist. "By disavowing the question of subjectivity in representations of the city [that
is, woman's place] he disengages urban theory and, strangely, noir as well,
from any dream machinery whatever."[8] Instead, the masculine position
taken up by the theorist/detective is that of the gazer, and the position
of the feminine is that of the gazed upon (image). More precisely, in
noir detective stories, the *femme fatale* is characterized as a destabilizing
force, for she "resists confinement in – or *as* – space";[9] she crosses boundaries and thus threatens male subjectivity. The subsequent work of film
noir, Deutsche relates, is to suppress her image, thus restoring spatial
order and male subjectivity to the center of the picture while ignoring
"how the image of the city, like the image of the woman, is mediated by
the detective's unconscious fantasies and so – whether lucid or bewilder-
ing – is tied up with the mysteries of sexuality."[10]

I read this conflated phrase, "resists confinement in – or *as* – space,"
to mean that the *femme fatale* escapes categorization; she cannot be
pinned down in discrete space nor made accountable to public norms.
She escapes the space of disciplinary order and the meticulous gaze of
the detective. In short, she embodies the irrational – she spreads disorder and disruption and must not be allowed to appear in the same space
as the rational detective lest he be seduced by her powers and deterred
from solving the crime. She must be suppressed and made invisible in
the space in which the detective appears – whether in cinematic space
or in theoretical representations of urban space.[11] Thus Davis transfers
these images of feminine deviance onto the spatial uncertainties and
dangerous encounters of contemporary Los Angeles. Yet it remains the
theorist/detective's role to decipher these anomalies and restore order
to his threatened masculine domain. Davis does so by revealing the
underlying economic causes and effects of Los Angeles's postmodern
spatial violence. But this neo-noir theorist/detective – to make a distinction from Deutsche's argument – is only an analyzer of contemporary
conditions and not an activator. He may solve the crime by revealing its
causes, but he fails to save the innocent from inevitable economic
exploitation and his gaze remains impotent in the restoration of order.
A narration of impotency, of failure of agency and the unleashing of vio-

lence in and against both women and the city – these are the messages that neo-noir detective stories unfurl.

This discussion of the urban analyzer/theorist as the neo-noir detective takes place against Davis's metaphorical serial replay of the 1974 movie *Chinatown* by Roman Polanski.[12] In his replay, the theorist/detective discovers that the contemporary 1980s crisis of downtown Los Angeles as an overbuilt high-rise real estate zone began in the same decade in which *Chinatown* was set – the 1930s – when unscrupulous real estate developers were buying up Los Angeles's orange groves at bargain prices. In each case, Los Angeles is a threatened city: either the flow of water or tax revenues is being criminally tampered with to the financial advantage of real estate operators. In the fictional movie, it is a city under siege by a drought and falling prey to villains like Noah Cross, who manipulates the municipal waterworks and thus adds considerably – for the sake of greed and unquenchable desire – to his real estate holdings. He does so by scandalously rerouting water away from a valley of orange groves and subsequently accumulating all the ruined, worthless land at rock-bottom prices.[13] In the case of contemporary downtown Los Angeles, the city is threatened by the automobile and the spreading highway system that since the 1920s, without cessation, have drawn well-to-do citizens away from the center of the city and into the suburbs. Real estate values in downtown Los Angeles spiraled downward until, as Raymond Chandler wrote, it became a "lost town, shabby town, crook town" where "women with faces of stale beer . . . [and] men with pulled-down hats" resided.[14] After several decades, depressed real estate holdings in the downtown area eventually became ripe for redevelopment, and operators, with the help of municipal authorities, began to subsidize and protect their investments by directing substantial tax revenues away from de-industrialized twilight zones, such as black South Central Los Angeles, and reallocating these monies to low-interest loans for downtown redevelopment, infrastructure, and tax abatement incentives. The same process of de-industrialization and redevelopment took place in many other so-called "soft spots" surrounding the core of central Los Angeles.

I want to argue that the movie *Chinatown* is an allegory and its meaning nowhere explicit, for Chinatown as a place represents the invisible city and is neither knowable nor decipherable. Davis's reference to "*Chinatown*, Part Two?" can be analyzed not as a simple example of how women are rendered invisible by postmodern theorists of space, but as a layered reading of one text through another, facilitating a metaphorical transference of the *femme fatale* onto figurations of place. I assume that Mike Davis might have been aware – but probably unconsciously so – of this allegorical reading of the postmodern city as the *femme fatale*. Nevertheless, his choice of a neo-noir film entitled *Chinatown* as his metaphorical and serial title invites – allows – a more complex rereading of "men in space," but with a twist of difference. So while not disagreeing with Deutsche, I want to consider how these neo-noir detectives express a desire both to know and not to know, to see yet not to see, the conditions of the postmodern city and, thus, to split what is representable from that which remains invisible.

The narrations of film noir are generally located in California, and most often in Los Angeles. But it is a California where, by the 1930s and 1940s, the American Dream of the good life, of wealth and abundance was already beginning to fester. California lacked something – a collective sphere or set of public morals – that would keep private drives for money and power in check. It was a catastrophic utopia grounded in false appearances and betrayed hopes – a condition metaphorically represented through the inversion of beautiful landscapes and pleasant suburban bungalows into film noir sets of darkened city streets and isolated environments that close in on the hero and deterministically control his life (fig. 2).[15] Consequently, this allegorical rereading of film noir, and specifically neo-noir *Chinatown*, enables fatal warnings of impending disaster in both the public and private spheres to reappear under new conditions of postmodernity. Whether or not we heed these warnings as we navigate the passage from modernity to postmodernity depends on how we figure the space of cities as the space of liberation. Therefore it is not, as Deustche assumes, what the film's detective, Jake Gittes, forgets about Los Angeles that seems of central importance as much as it is his failure to see what lies on the surface and, thus, his denial of the subversive message implicit in the articulation of this neo-noir detective story. The rational male gaze of the noir detective or neo-noir cartographer not only connotes the power to render the feminine invisible in space, but also signifies the impotency of the passive observer who witnesses criminal deeds but cannot act to alter their outcome.

Now why did Davis use *Chinatown* as his central metaphor, and what does it mean that the postmodern city is allegorized as the *femme fatale*? The city is generally represented as a site of great ambiguity – both a source of anxiety and a source of pleasure, a utopic and dystopic place. In *Chinatown,* the irrational cannot be represented nor its ambiguities and anomalies resolved. Thus the detective Jake reveals the loss of his powers of detection and the failures of representation. Chinatown is never represented as a place and appears only at the very end of the film; it remains throughout a referenced but invisible site where the "other" is truly monstrous, where everything and anything can happen. The anxieties of the modern city may have been revealed by the manner in which its space was subjected to the surveilling gaze of the white male voyeur; but the postmodern city is represented by a fragmented look not only evading totalizations but also witnessing the impotent powers and innumerable failures of white male purposive rational cartographers. *Chinatown* represents the city of too much knowledge, of enigmatic and suspended judgments, of distasteful positions and information. Displaced from the modern city of patriarchal dominance, we hear the fatal warnings of film noir in the postmodern city: the loosening of paternal authority, the increasing appearance of crimes against the daughter, the disappearance of spaces of enclosure, and the decline of the public sphere.

The feminine has often been allegorized as modernity through the figure of the prostitute, the commodity; as a motif it has been subjected to oblique and fragmented reference (or devaluation and disfigurement) that, nevertheless, embodies within the allowed interstices all the flux, uncertainty, exoticism, sensuousness, wealth of meaning, and "otherness" that both the modern metropolis and the Orient in the nineteenth century unleashed. Christine Buci-Glucksman has written that "the feminine constitutes one of the nineteenth century's 'original historic forms.' . . . The feminine becomes the inevitable sign of a new historic regime of seeing and 'not-seeing,' of representable and unrepresentable."[16] As allegory, the feminine depends on "images, sight, scenes that link the visible and the invisible, life and dream. History presents itself to be seen with all its ambivalence fixed in *tableaux.*"[17] And so the feminine symbolizes all the phantasmagoria and artifice of modernity – images, styles, spectacles, and fictions as well as the destructive tendency of false promises and unfulfilled desires and the melancholic loss of equilibrium and the emptying of experience. The feminine captures the double nature of things: it is both the source of anxieties and the promise of pleasures.

Returning to the history of the detective story, we can begin to examine how film noir attempted in a similar manner to represent the promises of progress and the misgivings over change that modernity inevitably wrought. Edward Dimendberg has pointed out that the noir cycle (1939 to 1959) precisely corresponds to a time of profound spatial transformations in the postwar American city.[18] Massive spatial upheavals were created by the automobile, highway construction, suburban development, and urban redevelopment and these, in turn, produced strong fears that the old centers of cities, long associated with the essence of modernity, were being erased. Having been racked by the machinations of real estate operators, dynamited by urban renewal and evacuated by a middle-class citizenry seeking the safety of the suburbs, the center of the post–World War II city was a site of ruins, threatened with death and decay. The potency of human agency was no longer to be relied upon in a metropolis where vast urban spaces seemed to take on a dominating and crushing power of their own – where alienation and boredom were increasingly apparent and stereotypical preconceptions, such as feminine passivity, might be refuted or sidestepped when a not-so-innocent woman held out a fatal attraction or became the major instigator of crime.[19] One response to this confusion and disorientation was the production of B-rated films, whose very marginality allowed them freedom to express the anxieties and trepidations of postwar American culture. To hint at revolt, to offer a more exhilarating life than bourgeois morality allowed, to wallow in pessimism and misogyny, to depict the urban malaise, to tell the story from the criminal's point of view – these were some of the themes that B-rated films explored. And many of these films now constitute what is called the film noir cycle.[20]

One of the major visual tropes of film noir is the image of the city with a still-vital, if problematic, center: densely massed skyscrapers, dark and shadowy canyon streets, the vertical outlines of skylines, the views from on high, crowded and congested thoroughfares. This was the space of modernity through which film noir characters inevitably strolled: a knowable, mappable terrain with identifiable monuments, favorite haunts, and protected retreats. But these were also the very places that urban renewal programs were threatening with extinction. Kevin Lynch, in his well-known study, *The Image of the City* (written in the late 1950s), nostalgically outlined a place of well-defined nodes, pathways, edges, landmarks, and districts, for he, too, sought to restore the smashed and disintegrating face of the postwar city to a youthful portrait of itself.[21]

In film noir these fears of disfiguration and death resurface, becoming the foreboding images of the nocturnal city: a place of darkened shadows that cover a detective's clues and diminish his powers of sight. Marc Vernet claimed that "the space of night is the space in which the detective, who has everything to gain from seeing without being seen, can be seen without seeing, as the darkness conceals the gleaming surface of an eye or a weapon."[22] Rather than the urban crowd of the nineteenth-century city, into which a criminal could suddenly disappear without leaving a trace, the nocturnal city became the site where traces of a crime – as well as of class distinctions, noise, dirt, and ugliness – were transfigured and erased, only to reassert themselves in an uncanny play of absence-as-presence, of unknown and nightmarish threats.

Dimendberg posits that "darkness" in the postwar city was a lightly coded word for the traumatic memories of World War II. Disguised as entertainment, the film noir cycle could invert these trepidations (the loss of the center of the city and of one's position within it, as well as the unspeakable traumas of the war) and return them to the spectator in an aestheticized, nostalgic, and pleasurable form.[23] Thus film noir represents a twisted variety of the detective story: a nocturnal city that lacks any visualizable form, where the detective often loses his way and the murderous can get away with their crimes. While its cinematographic techniques exploit the montage process to produce cuts and sections of space, fragments and scraps of evidence, they add to the impact of its

FIG. 2
California of the 1930s and 1940s lacked something – it was a catastrophic utopia, and hence film noir inverted its arcadian landscape of suburban bungalows and white picket fences into sets of darkened interiors and threatened spaces

FIG. 3
Barry Fitzgerald looking at the panorama of midtown Manhattan at night, in *The Naked City*. "A city has many faces. . . . And this is the face of New York City – when it's asleep"

narrative form as a flow of possibilities of indeterminate meanings and chance encounters, of themes and variations.[24]

Dimendberg utilizes Ernst Bloch's theory of "non-contemporaneity" or "non-synchronous not of this time" to explore the temporal slippage between the rapidly disappearing city of postwar America and its imaginary reconstruction in film noir. This mix of old and new is yet another name for montage – where anger and pleasure are allowed to work through the material, expressing both a sense of loss and the portentousness of the new, which has yet to be either assimilated or repressed.[25] Film noir experiments with "non-contemporaneity" in order to explain the appearance of a multilayered interpenetration and superimposition of spaces. It builds on the ruins and remains of the historical space of the center of the city: left behind in the disappearing city, the film noir hero resides in seedy hotels with torn window shades and exposed light bulbs hanging from the ceiling, while the *femme fatale* hangs out in two-bit motels or rooms rented by the week. Rather than shock the viewer into rearranging the emptied spaces of the bourgeois city into a utopian order of things-to-come, film noir offers a retreat into a privatized space, allowing its hero to achieve a detached position in which he is not responsible for the crimes he produces in and of the city. Thus film noir misreads, distorts, or refuses to understand its own warnings that the moral formulations of postwar democracy and postwar paternalism were becoming a sham.[26]

Film noir reached its peak in 1950, when fifty-seven films of this type were produced. From this high, the cycle fell to a low of seven in 1958 and 1959. Dimendberg believes this decline had less to do with either a growing taste for realism (or audience boredom with the genre's conventions, as has commonly been assumed) than with the ascendancy of suburban residential areas, the spreading interstate highway system, and the expanding communication networks of radio and television – for this is also the time when non-urban backgrounds and travel accounts begin to manifest themselves in American fiction.[27] Since the American detective story depends on a criminal and a private eye/detective observing the movements of a city's inhabitants, it demands a spatially concentrated city center in order to carry out its discourse on criminality and to impose its legal authority over the urban terrain. A decentralized, fragmenting, and emptying city requires different modes of observation and detection, and relies on different effects of alienation and estrangement.

By repetitiously presenting the detective/private eye hero as a socially detached and uninvolved individual – one who is incapable of establishing relationships with other human beings – film noir denigrated the role of agency. No one was responsible for the crimes that happened in and against the city, nor could the *femme fatale* be stopped. Maybe the detective was guilty for listening to her (probably she was more responsible), but in the standard genre film the lure of money, sex, and death brought inevitable destruction. There are several ways that agency can be denied: by shifting the guilt onto some "other" who resides outside a moral or human order; by failing to awaken from sleep and, thus, maintaining a somnambulent pose in a closed circuit of pleasure; or by becoming addicted to unstoppable drives and unmanageable forces. Myths of the big city are often based on the presence of monsters – alien or man-made – but we are neither connected to nor responsible for them because these monstrous "others" follow laws of their own. In film noir, it is the *femme fatale* who threatens the social order and represents the horror of all that escapes the authority of control.

The city, in film noir, is a locus of alienation and depravity, a dangerous and transitory place of unexpected happenings and surprise endings, a land of used-car lots and fleabag hotels where the hero is entrapped by, and even complicit with, evil.²⁸ Many noir films open with an aerial shot of dark canyon streets of the city below, depicting a sinister force that will defeat the hero. Jules Dassin's *The Naked City* (1948) opens with a panoramic view of Manhattan, a distant and detached viewpoint that attempts to narrate the crime as a series of objective facts – just one of the thousands of stories that the city could tell in an ordinary day (fig. 3). So the seasoned detective tells the novice: "There's your city, Halloran. Take a good look. Jean Dexter is dead. The answer must be somewhere down there."²⁹ As one of its screenwriters, Malvin Wald, commented, "In the *Naked City* it is Manhattan Island and its streets and landmarks that are starred. The social body is, through architectural symbol, laid bare ('naked') as a neutral fact neither, so to speak, good nor bad, but something which, like the human organism itself, can catch a disease (the criminal), and this disease may elude its detectors."[30] In such settings there seems to be an evil or neutral determinism at work: the pleasant suburban bungalows and sunshine streets of Hollywood prewar films have turned into claustrophobic interiors, dark alleys, and the empty spaces of city streets.

Dana Polan argues that woman in the 1940s cinema is often presented as "the enframed world of spectacle,"[31] freed from the bounds of narration and, indeed, able to conflict with narrative form. She disrupts masculine control and inhibits the endeavors of men.[32] In Howard Hawks's *The Big Sleep* (1946), for example, woman is defined as trouble: she lies, she is deceitful, she is a drug addict or alcoholic, she abjures traditional female roles, she talks tough, and she kills. But she is also able to integrate the detective into society, for she tames this isolated figure who once walked the mean streets alone, modulating his sadism and violence, and turns him into an ambivalent character, both tender and tough.[33] But here the feminine and the commodity cross paths. The spectacle is the commodity on display, and the act of showing and revealing often becomes more important than the cause and effect of the story line, the narrative message, or the moral engendered. The *femme fatale* may have acquired new roles, but her progress was often arrested as she was frozen into an image, contained within the camera that men still held.[34]

Interestingly, in *The Big Sleep* not only are the crimes of the daughters those listed above, but they include unpaid gambling debts and being the subjects of pornographic photographs, for which they are blackmailed. Here the camera, usually denoting the power of truth and objective evidence, is transformed into a tool of extortion and sexual fantasy. But the crime, this time, is the relentless commodification of everything and everyone, and the betrayal is the corruption of an economic system that allows women to be reduced to merchandise that can be bought, sold, and traded. Here, too, there is often an inversion. In *The Big Sleep*, originally written in 1939, the captain of industry is a sick and dying man, like the waning power of American industry during the Depression; a man, furthermore, manipulated by his daughters as they also manipulate and are manipulated by his corrupted heirs.

So now let us deal with the demise of agency: the evacuation of the imaginary public sphere in the postwar American city (an invisible city of common values and shared positions), or what Gilles Deleuze referred to as the disappearance of Michel Foucault's "spaces of enclosure" such as the family, the factory, the schools, and, by extension, the centered city, the rule of law and order;[35] and the disruptions of narrative closure by the deceptions and artifice of the *femme fatale*. As we have seen, the detective traditionally functions in society as a restorer of social order. It is his job to uncover the evidence, to construct criminal categories of the self (he assumes there can be no private secret not reducible to some number or some characteristic). Yet Joan Copjec has shown[36] that in order for film noir fiction to be possible, the set of clues can never be closed: there always remains one more piece of evidence to be extracted from the scene of the crime in order to generate suspense and to enable the retelling of the crime as an adventure story. Thus the space that contains the mystery can never be completely described (it remains partially invisible), never closed, and always breachable by the detective. This imaginary closure, then, is what statistics and detective stories share: the probabilities of a crime, of a social event, of disease. But this relationship between statistics and the detective story assumes a public sphere and the notion of a social collectivity.

If we assume an ideal public realm, where the rule of sovereign power reigns and the Oedipal patriarch commands obedience and ensures civic order, then the postwar American city can be contrasted with this ideal as a time and place where private interests, needs, and drives arose to erase any sense of collectivity. Here film noir displayed its warning that this ascendancy held dire consequences for society unless some notion of community, of a sutured totality, could be reintroduced. And this is where Copjec places the role of the voice-over in film noir: it re-introduces community, language, speech, thus framing the endless drive that threatens to destroy the pubic realm. And like Dimendberg analyzing the relationship between film noir and the imaginary centered city, Copjec uses as examples the ascendancy of drive over desire in such anti-urban social policies as suburban expansion, public housing, the federally financed highway systems that destroy the landscape, and regulations mandating segregation. From the perspective of the drive (not desire) one can neither fathom the "other" – be it the *femme fatale* or the city – nor imagine a collective order. The noir detective, who fails to establish relationships and is portrayed as an isolated character existing in places emptied of all desire, increasingly identifies with the criminal until, ultimately, he drives himself to commit criminal acts. Thus the voice-over, for Copjec, exhibits what never can be told within the unfolding of the narrative: the pleasures of private enjoyment that separate the detective from the community and his recurring acts of private satisfaction that inevitably destroy and erode the public terrain.

Let us return, finally, to the neo-noir film *Chinatown* and neo-noir theorist/detectives of social reality such as Mike Davis. *Chinatown* is an allegory of crimes against the daughter (or the city) and of the impotent powers of detection, for the detective can neither save the daughter nor punish the criminal. *Chinatown* has many film noir attributes, but with a twist: the innocent are killed and the patriarchal crimes of incest, murder, and illegal real estate transactions remain unavenged. Like the crimes against the daughter, contemporary real estate practices in central Los Angeles remain unpunished and the spaces of third-world immigrants, black Americans, and the homeless are continuously exploited. In both the film and in Los Angeles, the detectives acknowledge that the motives behind the crimes remain irrational, beyond explanation and knowledge.

As John Belton explains in his discussion of *Chinatown*, the desire for knowledge that normally motivates the average detective is, in this film, transformed into greedy sexual curiosity:[37] "looking" focuses on lurid photographs and presents a critique of the voyeuristic gaze that the cinematic apparatus constructs. Here the sleuth, Jake, whose usual work is to uncover the crimes of sexual liaison, of lovers, of husbands or wives suspected of being unfaithful, cannot read the clues that are right under his own nose. Underscoring the unsavory and pornographic aspects of his nosy work as well as his faulty powers of investigation, Jake's own nose is severely cut and remains bandaged in most every scene (fig. 4). Across the entire length of the film, both Jake and the spectator lose their ability to investigate images and representations. Along with Gittes, the

FIG. 4

Jack Nicholson and Faye Dunaway
in *Chinatown.* The detective Jake's
nose is severely cut and remains
bandaged throughout the film,
underscoring his nosy business of
investigating crimes of passion

spectator misrecognizes what the photographs expose: one photograph is actually *not* evidence of a sexual encounter; another is evidence of a quarrel that remains overlooked as an important clue. The spectator is placed in the position of not being able to decode or trust visual images as they appear on the surface.

Language always plays an important role in detective stories and normally a detective's powers are revealed in the manner in which he demonstrates control over language, especially in his witty repartee. In the opening scenes of *Double Indemnity,* for example, the bantering dialogue and double entendres not only allow the spectator to understand that the amorous relationship between the *femme fatale* and the detective is one of crime and punishment, but also establish the sexual antagonisms to be carried out throughout the film.[38] Thus the detective is consistently given the power of language to be used on the side of rationality, while the *femme fatale* resorts to lies and employs language deceitfully. Both the logic of the detective's reasoning and the prowess of his verbal skills enable him to hold in check, or to contain, the disturbing threat of the irrational.[39] But in *Chinatown* language fails both the detective and the *femme fatale.* Jake never displays the verbal stylistics that usually demonstrate the hard-boiled detective's power over his suspects; indeed, Jake remains relatively silent throughout the film. Verbal style has been transferred to clothing style, allowing the visual cinematic image to take priority over the dialogue. In addition, under patriarchal control, the woman is rendered speechless, unable to articulate or give verbal form to the atrocities of her existence. Evelyn stutters every time she tries to mention her father, and even her explanation of the crime must be physically, not verbally, wrung from her. Her statement "She's my sister . . . my daughter" is incomprehensible to the audience as well as to the detective. When Jake finally recognizes the father's crimes of incest, murder, and real estate manipulation, he finds that the normal powers of language evade him: he is first struck speechless, then when he tries to help, he guarantees that Evelyn will be harmed.[40]

"In *Chinatown,* language . . . and knowledge no longer meet at the crossroads, functioning together to produce knowledge of the Real, but rather fall apart in the contemplation of it."[41] The binary opposition of rational powers of detection against irrational forces of criminality dissolves. Hence the rational thinker comes to the realization that knowledge has limits, that he cannot comprehend the unknowable or control the unnatural. So, too, the powers of language that guide Mike Davis – the neo-noir theorist/detective of contemporary Los Angeles – disintegrate in the contemplation of crimes against the city: he, too, is struck speechless or disarmed as he recognizes that powers of agency lie elsewhere. Everything that once made the center of Los Angeles a gritty city – a place of harsh realities and stark existence, a testing ground for the hardiest of noir detectives – has been eradicated, gentrified, or redeveloped into a sterile and barren corporate core. In the end, we arrive at the pessimistic conclusion that crimes against the city/woman are beyond comprehension, for no one is held accountable and no action appears effective to stop the insatiable drives that have destroyed the public terrain. Thus the spectator can barely hear Jake's final words when he mumbles "to do as little as possible," repeating the advice he once received when he was assigned as a detective to Chinatown. After all, Chinatown is, allegorically, a place where reason has no force and where violence and the irrational reign – where we choose to squander our energy and wealth by doing as little as possible.

1. Rosalyn Deutsche, "*Chinatown,* Part Four? What Jake Forgets about Downtown," *Assemblage* 20 (April 1993), 32–33. Deutsche is referring directly to the work of Mike Davis, "*Chinatown,* Part Two? The 'Internationalization' of Downtown Los Angeles," *New Left Review* (July/August 1987), 65–86, and Derek Gregory, "*Chinatown,* Part Three: Soja and the Missing Spaces of Social Theory," *Strategies* 3 (1990), 40–104. She is also commenting indirectly on the following works of "men in space": Mike Davis, *City of Quartz* (London and New York: Verso Press, 1990), Edward W. Soja, *Postmodern Geography* (London and New York: Verso Press, 1989), and David Harvey, *The Condition of Postmodernity* (London: Basil Blackwell, 1989).

2. Rosalyn Deutsche, "Men in Space," *Strategies* 3 (1990), 130–37, and "Boys Town," *Society and Space* 9 (1991), 5–30.

3. For a more extensive argument that agrees with Deutsche's criticism of these noir detectives, see Sue Best, "Deconstructing Space: Anne Graham's *Installation for Walla Mulla Park* and Jeff Gibson's *Screwballs,*" *Transition Issue* 42 (1993), 27–41, 66–67.

4. Ibid. Best uses the term "encryptment" to emphasize that theories of social space carry the sexualization of space as a kind of ghost or phantom in the concepts which they use, yet they never directly confront these ghosts.

5. Ibid. Best includes, in addition to Harvey and Soja, Fredric Jameson, Michel de Certeau, Dick Hebridge, and Henri Lefebvre.

6. Ibid., 29, and Plato, *Timaeus and Critias,* trans. Desmond Lee (Harmondsworth: Penguin, 1965), 69.

7. Best, 35.

8. Deutsche, "*Chinatown,* Part Four?" 33.

9. Ibid.

10. Ibid.

11. As Joan Copjec argues, the detective extracts one more clue – always on the surface of the scene of the crime but undetectable or remaining invisible before his arrival – and this clue allows him to solve the mystery. There must be a gap, "the distance between the evidence and that which the evidence establishes," something that remains not visible in the evidence, the absence of a final clue that would close or solve the mystery. And this absence makes sexual relations impossible, for the missing clue is the woman. "The Phenomenal Nonphenomenal: Private Space in Film Noir," in Joan Copjec, ed., *Shades of NOIR* (New York: Verso Press, 1993), 177–79.

12. See note 1.

13. Jennifer Bloomer has pointed out to me that the conflation of woman/city is directly related to the many images of water that appear in the film. Not only is water the most important agent in the fertility of the semi-arid lands of Los Angeles and its flow directly related to menstruation, but it also involves fantasies of purification, is endowed with healing powers, and, where it is present, it has turned California into a garden paradise.

14. Quoted by Davis, "*Chinatown,* Part Two?" 68.

15. William Marling, "On the Relation Between American Roman Noir and Film Noir," *Film Literature Quarterly* 21:3 (1993), 178–93.

16. Christine Buci-Glucksman, "Catastrophic Utopia: The Feminine as Allegory of the Modern," in Catherine Gallagher and Thomas Laqueur, eds., *The Making of the*

Modern Body (Berkeley: University of California Press, 1987), 220–29.

17. Ibid., 227.

18. Paul Kerr, "Out of What Past? Notes on the B Film Noir," *Screen Education* 32–33 (Autumn–Winter 1979–80). Quoted by Edward Dimendberg, "Film Noir and Urban Space" (Ph.D. diss., University of California, Santa Cruz, 1992), p. 12.

19. Jon Thompson, *Fiction, Crime and Empire* (Urbana and Carthage: University of Illinois Press, 1993), 36–37, 137–41.

20. Dimendberg, 12.

21. Kevin Lynch, *The Image of the City* (Cambridge, Mass.: MIT Press, 1960).

22. Quoted by Dimendberg, 57.

23. Dimendberg, 64.

24. Ibid., 113.

25. Bloch defined non-contemporaneous elements as "a continuing influence of older circumstances and forms of production, however much they may have been crossed through, as well as of older superstructures. The *objectively* non-contemporaneous element is that which is distant from and alien to the present; it thus embraces *declining remnants* and above all an *unrefurbished* past which is not yet 'resolved' in capitalist terms. . . . Home, soil, and nation are such *objectively* raised contradictions of the traditional to the capitalist Now, in which they have been increasingly destroyed and not replaced." See Dimendberg, 112.

26. Dean MacCannell, "Democracy's Turn: On Homeless *Noir*," in Copjec, *Shades of NOIR*, 279–97.

27. Dimendberg, 253.

28. Dana Polan, *Power & Paranoia* (New York: Columbia University Press, 1986), 259.

29. Quoted by Dimendberg, 78.

30. Quoted by Dimendberg, 80.

31. Polan, 261.

32. Ibid., 288.

33. Paul Coates, *The Gorgon's Gaze* (Cambridge: Cambridge University Press, 1991), 173–76.

34. For comments on *The Big Sleep,* see Ronald R. Thomas, "The Dream of the Empty Camera: Image, Evidence, and Authentic American Style in *American Photographs* and *Farewell, My Lovely,*" *Criticism* 31 (Summer 1994), 428, 433.

35. Gilles Deleuze, "Postscript on the Societies of Control," *October* 59 (1992), 3–7.

36. Copjec, "The Phenomenal Nonphenomenal," 167–97.

37. John Belton, "Language, Oedipus, and *Chinatown*," MLN 106 (1991), 933–50.

38. Ibid.

39. Ibid., 937.

40. Ibid., 944–45.

41. Ibid., 949.

BOYER

Investigating the City – Detective Fiction as Urban Interpretation: Reply to M. Christine Boyer

MARGARET CRAWFORD

Recent rereadings of *Chinatown,* using the film as a metaphor for the act of urban interpretation, raise important questions about the subject positions that inform contemporary urban criticism.[1] Mike Davis, proposing *Chinatown*'s detective, Jake Gittes, as a model for investigating the hidden deals and invisible powers that continue to shape Los Angeles, initiated this discussion. In response, Rosalyn Deutsche has drawn attention to another aspect of the neo-noir genre: the unacknowledged but deeply gendered nature of its representations of urban space. Christine Boyer expands and deepens this critique. Without disagreeing with either Deutsche or Boyer, I would like to offer a slightly different reading of *Chinatown,* examining another distinct genre that also clearly informs *Chinatown:* the hard-boiled detective novel. By focusing exclusively on the noir and neo-noir modes of representation, Davis, Deutsche, and Boyer have ignored both the history and the contemporary discourse of the detective genre. In fact, detective fiction as a popular literary genre has produced a parallel discourse of urban interpretation, developed independently of academic urban studies. Historically linked with both urban reality and the urban imagination, the continuing evolution of the genre offers rich possibilities for rethinking the connections between subjectivity, interpretation, and urban space. Recent detective novels with gay, African-American, and female authors and characters suggest a multiplicity of new positions from which to investigate the city.

It is Walter Benjamin who has drawn attention to the emergence of the detective novel as a uniquely urban literary form,[2] noting that the process of detection is closely linked to the emergence of a city large enough to obliterate the individual criminal's traces in its crowded streets. (The detective story first appeared in the early 1840s, with Edgar Allan Poe's *The Murders in the Rue Morgue* and *The Mystery of Marie Roget*.) Benjamin sees the role of the detective as a successor to the amateur *flâneur* as a privileged observer and interpreter of the city. But unlike the *flâneur*, who derives his pleasures by skimming along the visible surfaces of the city, the detective's goal is to penetrate below the surface to discover the meanings hidden in the city's streets. The detective's unique access to these urban secrets allows him, like a psychoanalyst, to go beyond the purely visible to read the city's collective unconscious. Benjamin follows the detective story in the direction of high art. Tracing the influence Poe had on Baudelaire, he notes that Baudelaire eliminates the detective and his function (solving the crime), maintaining only the heightened and emotion-laden atmo-

sphere that Poe evokes in describing the crime.

An equally important aspect of the detective novel, however, is its realistic representation of actual urban crimes. Poe retells these crimes in ways that highlight the cultural and social themes they embody. *The Mystery of Marie Roget*, for example, is based on the 1840 murder of Mary Rogers, a young New York woman. This crime electrified and obsessed the city much as the violent death of Nicole Simpson recently obsessed Los Angeles.[3] The story of Mary Rogers became a significant cultural event, a text that brought together discussions of female sexuality, social danger, and public safety in a rapidly changing city beset by social transformation and unparalleled cultural diversity. Like the Simpson case, with its narratives of domestic violence, racism, and celebrity in contemporary Los Angeles, the case of Mary Rogers turned private matters – previously considered outside of the purview of public discourse – into both newsworthy information and everyday conversation.

Thus, from its beginnings, the detective novel had a dual relationship to the city. On one hand, it produced literary interpretations that incorporated the mysteries of the urban condition; on the other, it opened up a popular social discourse by representing current concerns about urban life in an accessible fashion, allowing them to be widely and publicly discussed. Significantly, the figure of the female appears prominently in both discourses, inscribed as real and imaginary.

Published between 1930 and 1950, Raymond Chandler's Los Angeles detective novels embodied both of these discourses, overturning the previous genre tradition of the genteel murder mystery.[4] By moving the setting from the drawing room to the streets, he created an alternative set of conventions. Instead of individual psychological motives, social and political corruption motivated the plot and characters. A new model of detection appeared in the character of Philip Marlowe, Chandler's classic hard-boiled private investigator. In Chandler's formula, crime is always doubly rooted: in the public sphere of economic and political corruption, and in the private world of family and sexual disturbances. As in Poe's stories, settings and crimes drawn from social reality were described with a hallucinatory intensity. Chandler's novels combined exaggeratedly tough prose ("lost town, shabby town, crook town . . . [with] women with faces of stale beer . . . [and] men with pulled-down hats") with a social landscape laid out with sharply critical realism. This produced a vision of Los Angeles so potent that, fifty years later, it has acquired the status of an official representation of the city. Several recent books devoted to discovering the "real" settings of Chandler's novels testify to the continued blurring between fiction and history.

As Fredric Jameson has pointed out, Chandler's view of Los Angeles is circular.[5] In Chandler's Los Angeles, already a centerless city where different classes were geographically separate, it was impossible to grasp the social structure as a whole. In this fragmented setting the detective became a privileged figure, moving between rich and poor, and, in the course of investigating a crime, linking the city's separate and isolated parts together. The detective alone could reveal the hidden patterns of the city, the invisible relationships that connect wealth to poverty. Only the detective could comprehend the city as a totality. Chandler's belief that wealth always originated in crime linked crime and corruption as the indissoluble bond between the mansion and the slum. *Farewell, My Lovely* established this familiar pattern, beginning in Florian's, a dive on Central Avenue, the main street of Los Angeles's black district, then moving to an apparently unrelated scene in the Grayle mansion in the exclusive suburb of Pacific Palisades. The plot of the novel operates to connect the two. However, if knowing both sides of town is necessary to fully understand the city, their relationship was never equal. The urban slum was always cast as "other," providing necessary resolution but never existing as a place on its own, only as a counterpoint to the sites of wealth, power, and corruption that truly interested Chandler.

The ability to move comfortably between such disparate locales is the key to the detective's secret knowledge of the city. But, as Jameson shows, the detective's ability to mediate between rich and poor depends on his distance from both. Hard-boiled detectives such as Marlowe are never part of society, but float above it, disengaged from time and space. Unlike the families who hire him, Marlowe had no family. Although the mysteries he solved were rooted in the past, he, himself, had no past; and although the meaning of places was central to his detection, he lived a transient life and belonged to no place. His power was based solely in knowledge, founded in observation and description rather than lived experience. His gaze was always one-way; he described, but was never, himself, described. Claiming to know society as a whole, he did not stand for any genuine close-up experience of it.

Marlowe's unique mobility also gave him access to women from all social classes. Unlike the detective, however, these women were denied mobility – their positions were firmly fixed by their social and urban settings. In contrast to Marlowe – the active, self-created subject – they derived their identities from their fathers and husbands. Women who crossed social boundaries voluntarily, such as the Velma Valento/Mrs. Grayle character in *Farewell, My Lovely*, were punished for their violations. Velma's dramatic self-transformation from red-haired taxi dancer to blond socialite, clearly transgressive, could only have been achieved through crime. Yet, equally criminal behavior on the part of women who stayed in their place were, in Chandler's novels, rewarded with the detective's loyalty. Although, in the course of an investigation, Marlowe invariably uncovered evidence of pervasive public corruption, he never attempted to rectify such social evils. Instead, his resolutions always occurred in the private realm where his loyalties remained, shaped by the mingled impulses of male bonding, chivalry, and sexual desire. This clear separation between public crimes and individual solutions leaves the social order untouched.

Jake Gittes, the protagonist of *Chinatown*, is clearly modeled on Philip Marlowe. He occupies a similar seedy office and his tough and cynical persona masks an equally romantic self-image as a knight errant. *Chinatown*, however, strips the detective of any heroic qualities, revealing the delusions and inadequacies of the hard-boiled role. Jake is able to uncover the film's public crime, the water conspiracy, but incapable of comprehending the private crime of incest. This professional failure is clearly bound up with the gendered subjectivity of the detective's role. Unable to think outside of the accepted categories of petty crimes and sexual peccadilloes that are his stock in trade, Gittes continually misinterprets the nature of the crimes committed in the film. Simultaneously protector/rescuer and seducer/sexual predator, his own ambivalence toward the female protagonists further confuse his perceptions. His incomprehension leads to a double tragedy in which the innocent are killed and the perpetrator of both crimes triumphs. As the movie ends, Jake is handcuffed to a police car, while the police detective reminds him, "After all, it's Chinatown. . . ."

As Boyer notes, Chinatown itself plays an allegorical role in the film, representing the invisible city, neither knowable nor decipherable. Alluded to throughout the film, it becomes actual only as the setting for the final tragedy. In the hard-boiled tradition, the unknowable urban "other" is invariably represented as an ethnic slum. Anything can happen in Chinatown. The role of Chinatown conforms to Chandler's circular image of the city, where corruption connects the white ruling-class with the Asians, African-Americans, or Latinos who also inhabit the city. Deutsche and Boyer demonstrate that women constitute another, equally significant category of "otherness." Thus, Chinatown remains a mystery, a treacherous urban space that hard-boiled perception is incapable of comprehending. If, in *Farewell, My Lovely*, Philip Marlowe can still convincingly link South Central to Pacific Palisades, Jake Gittes is no longer able to do so. Although Los Angeles remains fragmented, the detective's knowledge can no longer bind it together into a single, comprehensible whole. At the same time, public and private acts, rather than existing in separate spheres, as the hard-boiled tradition would have it, are shown to be inextricably linked in urban space. This renders the hard-boiled understanding of the city doubly impossible.

If *Chinatown* struck a strong blow at the pretensions of the male investigator of the city, the genre of detective fiction has continued the process. Over the past ten years, detective writing has developed far beyond the nostalgic sensibility of the neo-noir detective, which continually reinvokes its own fixed categories of interpretation. Interrogating itself, it has dismantled its own assumptions, producing new models of detection that offer a multiplicity of suggestions for new ways of investigating the city. Several contemporary writers have problematized the hard-boiled male role and its relationship to urban knowledge. Joseph Hansen introduced Dave Brandstetter, the first gay detective. Brandstetter's self-consciousness about his gay identity foregrounds the sexual subjectivity suppressed, or taken for granted, in conventional hard-boiled narratives. His always-present awareness of sexual identity and desire, instead of distorting his ability to solve crimes, as it does for Jake in *Chinatown,* actually sharpens his perceptions. This gives him the ability to go beyond a hard-boiled understanding to penetrate another layer of the city, one usually veiled by deceptive appearances.

If Marlowe, Gittes, and their successors are *on* the streets, many current detectives are *of* the streets. Walter Mosely's detective novels, set in Watts and South Central Los Angeles, completely invert Chandler's view of the city, placing its black residents at the center while leaving whites on the periphery. Refuting the detective's claim of understanding the totality of the city, Mosely delineates the boundaries of urban knowledge, recognizing the impossibility of the detective bridging the gap between the two separate realms of the city. For him, South Central or Chinatown can be understood only from the inside. Unlike Philip Marlowe, Mosely's protagonist, Easy Rawlins, is not a professional detective and is reluctantly forced into investigating. He acquires his knowledge not through questioning or intimidating strangers but through friendship and shared histories within a circumscribed community.

Other fictional sleuths challenge even the rationality of detection itself – the source of the male detective's power and knowledge. Romulus Ledbetter, the homeless protagonist of George Dawes Green's *The Caveman's Valentine,* successfully takes on the role of detective, although he lives in a cave in Inwood Park and is beset by paranoid delusions. In a further overturning of genre convention, Ledbetter, who as a transient might be expected to resemble the hard-boiled detective in his lack of social attachment, in fact possesses a devoted middle-class family, who figure prominently in his life.

The most profound transformation of the genre, however, has come from the proliferation of female detectives. In current detective fiction, female writers and characters now outnumber males and dominate the field. This extensive sub-genre has generated a multiplicity of new types of detectives. Professional activities are no longer privileged: any woman can assume the role of detective; any social position, from welfare mother to First Lady, can constitute a vantage point from which to solve crimes and interpret the city and the world. Even the professional female detectives most closely tied to conventional formulas differ considerably from their hard-boiled colleagues. Their lives demonstrate the fluid boundaries between private and public and a far more complex and nuanced subjectivity than that of, say, Philip Marlowe. Female investigators such as Kinsey Milhone or V. I. Warshawski are not separate from society or distanced from everyday life. No longer confined to their offices, they appear in both private and professional settings, allowing the reader to become familiar with their pasts, their neighborhoods, their apartments, their eating habits, and even their mother's china. They also embody multiple roles. Inevitably, any attempt on their part to seek totalizing solutions will invariably be complicated by the presence of family, friends, elderly neighbors, pets, ex-husbands, and past and potential lovers. Subjectivity, rather than being an impediment to the detective's understanding of crime and the city, becomes a mode of understanding them.

A recent Los Angeles detective novel, *North of Montana*, by April Smith, blurs the boundaries between the detective's subjectivity and the city even further. As the title suggests, the plot follows the familiar circular social space of the city, connecting the wealthy Santa Monica neighborhood north of Montana Avenue with the Central American barrio – a recent site of urban "otherness." In the course of an investigation, a female FBI agent, Ana Grey, uncovers her own previously unknown past, discovering that she is part Salvadorian. With part of herself as "other," she occupies a multiple subject position, both inside and outside, detective and object of detection. Like Jake Gittes, she both fails to solve the crime and inadvertently causes the death of an innocent victim. Unlike him, however, she finds hope and redemption – literally on the street in the barrio – that is, in "Chinatown." This reverses the terms of the relationship between the detective and the city, turning Chandler's circular motion back on itself. Instead of the detective attempting to heal the city, or more typically, failing to heal the city, the city has healed the detective.

Thanks to Edward Dimendberg and Marco Cenzatti for their invaluable assistance. I am also grateful to Ernest Pascucci for his insight that popular culture often does the work of theory. See "The City Belongs to That Girl," *ANY* 12 (October 1995).

1. Mike Davis, "*Chinatown*, Part Two? The 'Internationalization' of Downtown Los Angeles," *New Left Review* (July/August 1987), 65–86, and *City of Quartz* (London and New York: Verso Press, 1990), 17–97; Rosalyn Deutsche, "Chinatown, Part Four? What Jake Forgets about Downtown," *Assemblage* 20 (April 1993), 32–33. Also see Rosalyn Deutsche, "Boys Town," *Society and Space* 9 (1991), 5–30.

2. Walter Benjamin, *Charles Baudelaire: Lyric Poet in the Era of High Capitalism* (London: New Left Books, 1974), 43.

3. Amy Gilman Srebnick, "The Death of Mary Rogers, the 'Public Prints' and the Violence of Representation" (paper presented at American Studies conference, UCLA, May 21, 1993).

4. Ernest Mandel points out that after World War I, the detective novel moved from the streets to the drawing room. This can be seen in the British country house subgenre, typified by the work of Agatha Christie as well as in American authors such as Rex Stout and Ellery Queen. Although this genre continued to be popular, after Prohibition American writers turned to urban subjects such as gangsters, organized crime, and corruption. Ernest Mandel, *Delightful Murder: A Social History of the Crime Story* (London: Pluto Press, 1984), 22–39.

5. Fredric Jameson, "On Raymond Chandler," in *The Poetics of Murder: Detective Fiction and Literary Theory* (New York: Harcourt Brace Jovanovich, 1978), 127.

Gendered Spaces in Colonial Algiers

ZEYNEP ÇELIK

The French colonial discourse, developed by a broad base of intellectuals
and military and administrative officers, identified the Algerian woman
as the key symbol of the country's cultural identity.[1] In a typical formulation, J. Lorrain, writing at the turn of the century, called the entire
country "a wise and dangerous mistress," but one who "exudes a climate
of caress and torpor," suggesting that control over her mind and body
was essential.[2] This association extended to the city of Algiers as well.
Popular literature from the colonial period abounds with gendered descriptions that attribute an excessive sensuality to the city. In the turn-of-
the-century travel accounts of Marius Bernard, for example, Algiers is a
lascivious woman whose appeal was evident even in her name: "Algiers!
Such a musical word, like the murmur of waves against the white sand
of the beach; a name as sweet as the rippling of the breeze in the palm
trees of the oases! Algiers! So seductive and easy-going, a town to be
loved for the deep purity of her sky, the radiant splendor of her tur-
quoise sea, her mysterious smells, the warm breath in which she wraps
her visitors like a long caress."[3] Similarly, Lucienne Favre, a woman novelist writing in the 1930s, described the Casbah (the precolonial town
of al-Jaza'ir) as "the vamp of North Africa," endowed with a "capricious
feminine charm" and great "sex appeal."[4] Heralded by Eugène Delacroix's
Les Femmes d'Alger – a painting from the first years of the French occupation that, symbolically, entered the privacy of an Algerian home –
the artistic discourse reiterated this association. Beginning in the 1930s,
Le Corbusier's gendering of Algiers extended this tradition to architecture. Provoking associations between the curved lines of his projects to

modernize the city and the "plasticity" of the bodies of Algerian women, Le Corbusier articulated his enchantment with these women and consistently represented the casbah as a veiled head in his reductive drawings (fig. 1). His choice of words further punctuated the association: the Casbah was "beautiful," "charming," and "adorable."[5] He also likened the city to a female body: "Algiers drops out of sight," he noted as he viewed the city from a boat leaving for France, "like a magnificent body, supple-hipped and full-breasted."[6] The cover sketch of his *Poésie sur Alger* depicts a unicorn-headed, winged female body – supple-hipped and full-breasted (the city/poem?) – caressed gently by a hand (the architect's hand) against the skyline of new Algiers, to be designed by Le Corbusier himself.

While metaphors between cities and female figures are quite common, the exaggerated episode of Algiers stands out, calling for closer analysis. In its historic context, the Casbah presents an evocative case study of gendered spaces. It displays distinctly separate realms, sometimes claimed by the women of Algiers as an alternative to men's public spaces. The gendered spaces of Algiers became truly contested terrains during the colonial era, and their appropriation by the French turned into a major obsession. Focusing on the meanings associated with them and tracing the shifts in the forms of their appropriation, I hope to bring a new perspective to the reading of the colonial city, with references to a specific setting.

The urban fabric of the Casbah, dominated by its short, crooked streets, is a hallmark of the "Islamic city" – a problematic construction by European historians which has recently been subjected to serious revision. Janet Abu-Lughod, the most convincing critic of this concept, has argued, nevertheless, that Islam shaped social, political, and legal institutions, and through them, the cities. She points out that gender segregation was the most important issue here and that, by encouraging it, Islam structured the urban space and divided places and functions.[7] To put it schematically, in the "traditional Islamic city," public spaces belonged to men and domestic spaces belonged to women.

Gender-based and separate turfs prevented physical contact between men and women, and enabled visual privacy. The exteriors of the houses of Algiers reflected the semiotic of sexual segregation: the *mushrabiyyas*

Les Hauts
La Casbah
le bastion 15

FIG. 1

Le Corbusier. Sketch summarizing the essential elements of his design for Algiers. From Le Corbusier, *Poésie sur Alger*, 1950

were literal screens and the asymmetrical arrangement of entrance doors protected the interior of the home from the gaze of passersby. Regardless of the family's income or the size of the building, the houses of the Casbah closed themselves to the street and turned onto a courtyard surrounded by elaborate arcades. The geographic and topographic conditions of Algiers added another element to the houses of the Casbah: rooftop terraces. In contrast to the interiorized courtyards and relatively contrived rooms of the houses, the terraces opened up to neighbors, to the city, to the sea – to the world. The concern for privacy, so dominant in defining the street facades, disintegrated at roof level. It was this alternative realm that the women of Algiers claimed for themselves – as a place of work, socialization, and recreation; indeed, a much more pleasant place than the restricted streets below (fig. 2). The Casbah thus became divided into two realms: on the top, occupying the expanse of the entire city, were the women; at the bottom were the narrow streets belonging to the men.

The French occupation of Algiers (1830–1962) obscured this unusual dual structure by transforming the entire Casbah into an *espace-contre* (counter space) because it contrasted with the European sections of the city in form and in lifestyles, and because its residents continually challenged and opposed the colonizer (fig. 3).[8] Yet, in the typical ambivalence of the colonial condition, thrill and fear of the unknown intertwined with fantasy, and the Casbah opened new vistas for the imagination.[9] The massing and interiority of the Algerian house constituted favorite themes for Orientalist artists who were as much interested in the architectural qualities of the Casbah as in its lifestyles. The rooftop activities of the women, reenacted by painters who turned the top of the Casbah into the sensuous realm of the belly dancer and the ever-reclining odalisque, were depicted with colorful clothes contrasted against the white residential fabric. Interior views of the Algerian house formed another genre, with the stage-set quality of women's *appartements* reinforcing the introverted nature of the domestic realm.[10]

The postcard industry that bloomed around the turn of the century duplicated this dual representation of the houses of the Casbah. Exterior views focused on the narrow, winding streets, while interiors were

FIG. 2

Charles Brouty. Sketch of the rooftops of Algiers. From Le Corbusier, *La Ville Radieuse*, 1938

FIG. 3

Aerial view of Algiers, showing the juncture of the Casbah, on the left, and the French city, on the right

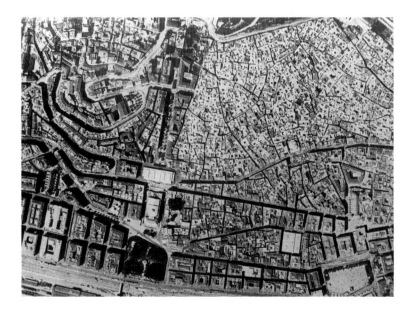

"assembled" as women's environments (often against the ornate arcades of the courtyard) according to familiar Orientalist formulas.[11] Colonial cinematography further reinforced this image in feature films varying from Jacques Feyder's *Atlantide* (1921) and Raymond Bernard's *Tartarin de Tarascon* (1934) to Julien Duvivier's *Pépé le Moko* (1937).

Le Corbusier, too, focused on the courtyards and roof terraces. He argued that the narrow streets of the Casbah were mere passageways, yet, a "miracle" occurred when the door of an Arab house opened, revealing a lovely courtyard where coolness, tranquility, and well-being reigned.[12] Furthermore, Arabs had "conquered the view of the sea for every house" by means of roof terraces that "add[ed] on to each other like a magic and gigantic staircase descending to the sea."[13]

The colonial obsession with the Algerian home grew in proportion to the actual impenetrability of this realm. To Algerians living under French occupation, home carried a special meaning as the place where they found refuge from colonial interventions perpetually confronted in public life. In the words of social historian Djamila Amrane, home was the "inviolable space" where Algerians recovered their identity.[14] It acted as a buffer against colonialism. Furthermore, it constituted an element in the "language of refusal" created by Algerians, a language that involved their whole way of life, from their behavior patterns to their clothing. As Pierre Bourdieu argued, under the constant gaze of Europeans, Algerian society chose to remain tightly closed upon itself by developing innumerable barriers.[15] The home was a most significant shell for this form of resistance.

In this context, spaces occupied by women (and especially women's historically self-defined public realms) become loaded with additional meanings. The colonizer's persistent efforts to appropriate women by incorporating them into modern buildings reveals much about the scope of the role they played in colonial confrontations. Clearly, behind the struggle to appropriate was the desire to control – an issue that emerged predominantly in the designs of the *grands ensembles,* the large housing complexes built for Algerians by the French administration.

From the 1930s on, the French administration regarded housing the Algerians as a major task directly responding to the increase in the "indigenous" population of Algiers and, consequently, to the overcrowding of the Casbah and the emergence of squatter settlements (the *bidonvilles*). Adhering to colonial policies at large, the goal was two-fold: to improve the living standards of local people and to control their environments – both as social engineering tools to secure the French presence. Attempting to refine French colonial policies in order to ensure the legitimacy and durability of the French empire, Albert Sarrault, the former governor of Indochina and minister of colonies, asserted in 1931 that the "historic reality" of colonialism (characterized until then as "a unilateral and ego-tistical enterprise of personal interest, accomplished by the strongest over the weakest" and as "an act of force," not of "civilization") should be corrected. France had to develop a "precise colonial doctrine [relying on] the mirror of its conscience." It was, indeed, France's honor to acknowl-edge the "value of latent races" (*races attardées*) and to see the colonies not simply as markets, but as "creations of humanity." Behind this human-istic facade, however, Sarrault presented the most important issue as the "control of local populations," which would depend on ensuring their loyalty and attachment to the colonizer.[16]

It was in the spirit championed by Sarrault that René Lespès, the foremost scholar of Algiers, explained the political implications of hous-ing in a colonial society. Raising the "material living conditions of our subjects will bring them closer to us," he argued. This was "humanitar-ian work, useful work, necessary work."[17] The president of the Algiers Chamber of Commerce applauded the decision to provide new housing for Algerians because giving them "a taste of hygiene, well-being . . . and a higher degree of civilization" would create a "sentiment of trust in France."[18] In the years to come, the importance of housing as a pacifying device would continue to be emphasized and a massive construction program would be put in action, escalating in scale from the 1950s to the end of French rule.

Control over the domestic spaces of the colonized society was par-ticularly important in the Algerian context because resistance to the French had persisted ever since the 1830s. Increasingly the French admin-istration believed that Algeria could be captured only from the smallest social unit, the family. Therefore, penetrating the spaces that had remained inaccessible to the colonizer became a priority. The architects commissioned to design the *grands ensembles* experimented with a wide range of designs, varying from high-density, low-rise settlements to clusters of apartment blocks; from *"Arabisance"* to pure International Style.[19] Nevertheless, the projects were united by an overriding theme: the attempt to integrate the essential features of the Algerian house; that is, the courtyard and the roof terrace. However, the interpretations varied and often resulted in questionable spaces, which were transformed over time by the residents in response to their needs. Out of approximately forty such projects built in Algiers, two case studies (both from the 1950s) represent intriguing experimentations in French architects' claims to women's spaces.

The spectacularly monumental 200 Colonnes was designed by Fernand Pouillon, who had established himself in Aix-en-Provence and Marseille and who, by 1953, had become chief architect of the city of Algiers. 200 Colonnes sits in the center of a large housing development (called Climat de France, also designed by Pouillon) on a sloped site to the west of the Casbah (fig. 4). The complex provided four thousand dwelling units in blocks planned linearly around communal courts or as single towers. Sizes varied greatly in the search for compositional balance, and site planning required radical interventions to topography.

No other construction in the vicinity matched the dimensions of 200 Colonnes, a massive, rectangular block 233 meters long and 38 meters wide, with a vast courtyard and surrounded by a three-story-high colonnade consisting of two hundred square-shaped columns. The practice of turning the private courtyards of "traditional" houses into one communal space to be shared by all residents was quite common in new housing projects in Algiers, and it sparked heated debate among architects. Essentially, Pouillon's scheme aggrandized the courtyard to the scale of a public square, thereby taking it away from the residents of the building and making it the "agora" of the entire Climat de France development.

With 200 Colonnes, Pouillon deliberately turned away from the "charming" effects of his former projects to create a "more profound, more austere plastique."[20] His references were not only to the residential courtyards of Algiers but also to a long and eclectic legacy that included the towns of Mzab and the ruins of el-Golea and Timimoum in Algeria; Hellenistic agoras and Roman fora; the Place des Vosges and the Palais Royal in Paris; the Court of the Myrtles and the Court of the Lions in the Alhambra Palace in Granada; and Isfahan's great seventeenth-century square, Maydan-i Shah.[21]

The roof terrace was another major feature of 200 Colonnes. Pouillon claimed that in his "new Casbah" he would give Algerian women their semi-private space to work and socialize. Placing small domed pavilions at regular intervals on the immense terrace (as washhouses that would double as centers of gathering), he envisioned a replication of the liveliness of the Casbah rooftops, with women socializing and children playing; clothes drying on the lines would add a picturesque touch to his architecture. Pouillon also made the stairs climbing up to the roof particularly narrow in order to emphasize the domestic and semi-private nature of the passageway and as a reminder of the stepped streets of the old town. However, only the women living on the upper floors used the roof terrace. The majority, loaded down with baskets full of laundry, refused to climb the narrow stairs and, despite the inadequacy of the provisions, chose to wash their clothes in their apartments. To dry them they projected rods from their windows, thus contributing involuntarily to the atmosphere of "authenticity" so cherished by Pouillon.

Pouillon's oversweeping approach to architecture and urban design and his radical interventionism vis-à-vis site conditions present a contrast to the architecture of Roland Simounet. With his responsive and imaginative buildings, Simounet gained respectability among the leading architects of the 1950s despite his relative youth and blatant disapproval of the aesthetic sensibilities of Pouillon, the city's *architecte en chef*.[22] Simounet was greatly influenced by the work of Le Corbusier, but he was also a careful student of Algerian culture, especially the Algerian vernacular. His architecture was shaped by the lessons he learned from European modernism, by his respect for the site, and by his inquiry into vernacular house forms (including squatter settlements) and the patterns of daily life and ritual.

Djenan el-Hasan is the widely published and discussed housing project that established Simounet's reputation. Located near Climat de

FIG. 4

Aerial view of Climat de France
with 200 Colonnes, designed by
Fernand Pouillon

FIG. 5

View of Djenan el-Hasan,
designed by Roland Simounet

France, the 210-dwelling units of Djenan el-Hasan were built to rehouse one thousand former residents of demolished *bidonvilles* in the area. The scheme, described by the architect as "between vertical and horizontal," compactly settled the units on a series of terraces parallel to each other and against the steep slope of the terrain, giving each apartment an uninterrupted view (fig. 5). The lessons that Simounet had learned from the Casbah were interpreted, rationalized, and aestheticized in the stacked, uniform vaulted units. At the same time, the overall image borrowed from the architecture of Le Corbusier, in particular the Roq et Rob project in Roquebrune–Cap Martin (1949), a particularly relevant scheme in the "Mediterranean tradition." Rationalizing the street network of the Casbah, Simounet developed here a complex circulation system of level paths and stepped paths that responded to the site and opened up to small public squares intended for use by men and children.

Simounet's apartments, developed on a strictly modular system derived from Le Corbusier's "Modulor," were either single story or duplex, the latter doubling the former vertically. The first type consisted of a single room and a loggia, which combined the notions of the rooftop terrace and the courtyard. The loggia was intended to function as a living, working, and recreational space – an extension of the house. Unlike the terraces of the houses in the Casbah, this space did not become part of the larger entity but remained linked to the interior space onto which it opened. The placement of a water outlet here was to enable the inclusion of washing facilities, but the further insertion of a toilet (derived from the outhouses in the courtyards of rural domestic architecture) complicated matters by hindering the intended function of this mutant courtyard/roof terrace.

The vaulted roofs could not be reached from the apartment units and, hence, were not designated as useable spaces. Despite their inconvenient form and difficult accessibility, the women of Djenan el-Hasan claimed these rooftops, turning them into work and recreation areas. Thus, the space limitations of the apartments pushed the functions meant to be sheltered in the loggias (such as food preparation) to the rooftops, overruling the inconvenience of jumping from the balcony, down to the roof of the unit in the front row, climbing back up, and working and moving on a curved surface.

As observed in these case studies, French architects were struggling to rationalize, tame, and control indigenous forms. Especially important was the appropriation of women's spaces, into which a great deal of consideration was invested. Nevertheless, this consideration did not achieve access into Algerian women's lives, which remained closed to colonizers – a situation eventually revealed by the active role that women were to play in a war totally unexpected by the French. The pacifying powers of architecture were proven false, as well. With the intensification of the decolonization war, housing project after housing project turned into a resistance center. To cite one example, the residents of Climat de France – deemed by an official report to be politically "less fidgety" than those of the Casbah due to their much better living conditions – took part in public demonstrations. On one memorable day, December 1, 1960, sixty people from 200 Colonnes alone were killed by French forces.[23]

The war of decolonization brought the Casbah to the forefront as a major locus of resistance. In this context, Algerians did not consider the privacy of the family and of women as a sacrosanct issue: resistance fighters were allowed into the houses and onto the rooftops (accessible only through the hearts of houses), facilitating their movements, while other outsiders, including the French forces, were not allowed access. Subsequently, the French forces would blockade the Casbah and occupy not only the streets but also the homes and roof terraces. The surrender of the Casbah is extensively documented by photographs showing armed officers on rooftops – a telling comparison with earlier depictions of the Casbah terraces being "invaded" by women.

Underlying the history of Algiers is a continuing theme that centers on the gendering of urban and architectural spaces. The gendered spaces of Algiers have carried great significance in asserting power, as clearly illustrated by the persistent struggles of appropriation and reappropriation that surfaced so blatantly during the colonial period. Yet, both the pre- and postcolonial eras display a separation of the city into men's and women's realms, albeit in very different contexts.

The current political climate in Algeria calls for extended discussion of women's public and private spaces in contemporary Algiers.

While I cannot engage in that discussion here, I would like to acknowledge the seriousness of the situation by dedicating this essay to the memory of Nabila Djanine, an Algerian woman architect and the leader of a feminist group called The Cry of Women. Nabila Djanine was shot and killed in February 1995.

The material for this article is taken from my forthcoming book, *Urban Forms and Colonial Confrontations: Algiers Under French Rule* (Berkeley: University of California Press, 1997).

1. Winifred Woodhull, *Transfigurations of the Maghreb* (Minneapolis and London: University of Minnesota Press, 1993), 19.
2. J. Lorrain, *Heures d'Afrique* (1899), quoted in Yvonne Knibieler and Régine Goutalier, *La Femme aux temps des colonies* (Paris: Stock, 1985), 40.
3. Marius Bernard, *D'Alger à Tanger* (n.d.), quoted in Judy Mabro, *Veiled Half-Truths: Western Travelers' Perceptions of Middle Eastern Women* (London and New York: I. B. Tauris & Co., 1991), 35.
4. Lucienne Favre, *Tout l'inconnu de la Casbah* (Algiers, 1933), 10. "Sex appeal" is in English in the original.
5. Le Corbusier, *La Ville Radieuse* (Paris: Editions Vincent, Fréal & Cie., 1938), 229.
6. Ibid., 260.
7. Janet L. Abu-Lughod, "The Islamic City – Historic Myth, Islamic Essence, and Contemporary Relevance," *International Journal of Middle East Studies* 19 (May 1987), 162–64.
8. Djaffar Lesbet, *La Casbah d'Alger. Gestion urbaine et vide social* (Algiers: Office des Publications Universitaires, 1985?), 39–48.
9. Colonial relationship is not a symmetrically antagonistic one due to the ambivalence in the positioning of the colonized and the colonizer. Ambivalence is connected to the notion of "hybridity," which depends on the rewriting of the other's original, but transforming it because of misreadings and incongruities and thus making it something different. Expanding the work of Frantz Fanon, cultural critics have focused largely on the ambivalence of the colonized. I would like to extend this notion to the colonizer as well. Among the key texts on the topic are Homi K. Bhabha, "The Other Question," in Russell Ferguson, Martha Gever, Trihn T.

Mihn-ha, Cornel West, eds., *Out There: Marginalization and Contemporary Culture* (Cambridge, Mass.: MIT Press, 1990), 71–87; Homi Bhabha, "Of Mimicry and Man," *October* 28 (October 1984), 125–33; and Benita Parry, "Problems in Current Theories of Colonial Discourse," *Oxford Literary Review* 9 (1987), 27–58.

10. The list of paintings is long. For the depiction of terraces, see, for example, Jules Meunier's *Femmes d'Alger sur les terrasses* (1888) and Marius de Buzon's *Trois Algériennes* (ca. 1927). Among the best-known interior depictions are Delacroix's two versions of *Les Femmes d'Alger* (1832 and 1848) and Auguste Renoir's painting of the same title.

11. For colonial postcards, see Malek Alloula, *The Colonial Harem*, trans. Myrna Godzich and Wlad Godzich (Minneapolis: University of Minnesota Press, 1985).

12. Le Corbusier, *La Ville Radieuse*, 230–31.

13. Le Corbusier, "Le Folklore est l'expression fleurie des traditions," *Voici la France de ce mois* (June 16, 1941), 31.

14. Djamila Amrane, *Les Femmes algériennes dans la guerre* (Paris: Plon, 1991), 45.

15. Pierre Bourdieu, *The Algerians*, trans. Alan C. M. Ross (Boston: Beacon Press, 1961), 157.

16. Albert Sarrault, *Servitudes et grandeur coloniales* (Paris: Sagittaire, 1931), 102–3, 108, 116, 119.

17. René Lespès, "Projet d'enquête sur l'habitat des indigènes musulmans dans les centres urbains en Algérie," *Revue africaine* 76 (1935), 431–36.

18. Louis Morard, "L'Algérie – ce qu'elle est – ce qu'elle doit devenir," *Le Monde colonial illustré* 87 (November 1930).

19. I borrow the term *"Arabisance"* from François Béguin, who defines it as "arabization of architectural forms imported from Europe." See François Béguin, *Arabisances* (Paris: Dunod, 1983), 1.

20. Pouillon's specific reference here is to Diar el-Mahçoul, a housing complex he designed on the hills of Algiers prior to Climat de France.

21. Fernand Pouillon, *Mémoires d'un architecte* (Paris: Seuil, 1968), 206–8; *Travaux nord-africains*, March 7, 1957.

22. Simounet elaborated on the major difference between Pouillon and himself: "Je respecte le site; Pouillon agresse le site" (I respect the site; Pouillon attacks the site). Furthermore, he criticized Pouillon for designing "sans penser aux hommes" (without thinking of men). For Simounet, Pouillon's insensitivity to the site, context, and culture stemmed from his coming directly from France – unlike Simounet, who was "from Algeria." Roland Simounet, interview with the author, Paris, April 16, 1993.

23. Albert-Paul Lentin, *L'Algérie entre deux mondes. Le Dernier Quart d'Heure* (Paris: René Julliard, 1963), 147, 151.

La Donna è Mobile: Agoraphobia, Women, and Urban Space

ESTHER DA COSTA MEYER

For Diana Balmori

This essay will focus on the appearance of agoraphobia, and the imbrication of women, urban space, and pathology.[1] Since this neurosis straddles the fault line between public and private, and affects women in particular, it seems to be a relevant subject of study for us today. Even though agoraphobia cannot be generalized as reflecting the current situation of women, like other urban pathologies, it tells us something about the way space is constitutive of personality. I wish to explore different theories of agoraphobia – sociological, psychological, psychoanalytic, feminist, new historicist – to discover what each of these has to say about this most spatially confining of anxiety disorders, and its relation to women.

Agoraphobia is most commonly defined as the fear of open spaces; or, more literally, the fear of the marketplace. First coined by Dr. Carl Westphal in 1871, the term did not gain common currency until relatively recently.[2] Different authors used *Platzscheu* or *Platzfurcht* (fear of public squares), *Platzschwindel* (dizziness in public squares), *Strassenangst* (fear of streets), *Raumangst* (fear of space), and *Topophobie*. With time, fear of urban spaces came to be identified more correctly with situations located in the public realm: not only streets and squares but, more specifically, crowds, shopping, trains, bridges, tunnels, elevators, and so forth.

In recent years, the incidence of agoraphobia has increased exponentially, currently constituting more than 50 percent of all phobic or psychoneurotic disorders.[3] Its connection to women is beyond dispute: around 85 percent of agoraphobes in this country today are women,[4] and although the vast majority of them are white and affluent, we simply do not know

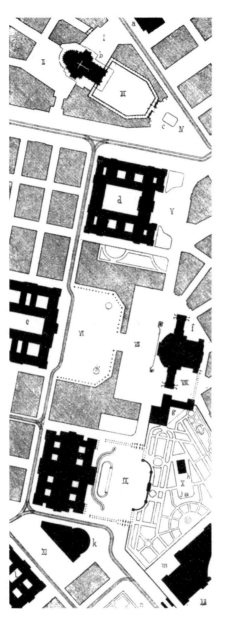

FIG. I

Camillo Sitte's plan for the
Ringstrasse. The Roman
numerals designate the close-
knit squares created by his
infill blocks

enough about the extent of the disease and the forms it takes in other ethnic groups that have no access to psychiatry and lack the resources to stay at home.

One of the first scholars to deal with agoraphobia was the Viennese architect and urbanist Camillo Sitte. Sitte fell back on a literal interpretation of agoraphobia: the fear of open space. Or perhaps it is more fair to say that he was primarily concerned with agoraphobia as a sociological, rather than a pathological, phenomenon. Always attuned to psychological questions, Sitte noticed that many of his contemporaries either scuttled uneasily across large city squares or engaged in long detours, skirting the walls of surrounding buildings. As he wrote in 1889, "Recently a unique nervous disorder has been diagnosed – 'agoraphobia.' Numerous people are said to suffer from it, always experiencing a certain anxiety or discomfort whenever they have to walk across a vast empty place."[5] According to Sitte, only small-scale, enclosed squares took account of what he liked to call "our natural craving for protection from the flank."[6]

Sitte had particular reason to be concerned with agoraphobia. Vienna's old ramparts, which for centuries had served as a boundary – psychological as well as architectural – protecting the historic center, had been torn down to make way for the Ringstrasse, a vast boulevard 190 feet wide and dramatically out of scale with the historic fabric. Perhaps unconscious class fears had something to do with the tensions attaching to the Ringstrasse: from time immemorial the old city had been the seat of the court, the aristocracy, the wealthy bourgeoisie and their servants, while over time, the proletariat was housed in the featureless urban sprawl beyond the walls. The destruction of the ramparts erased the main spatial divide that separated the affluent from the poor and the minorities.

Sitte's proposed redesign for parts of the Ringstrasse added infill architecture to produce small, protective city squares of the sort he had seen in Tuscany and Umbria (fig. 1). His projects, while not carried out, remain a nostalgic, petit bourgeois protest against the inevitable transformation of Vienna into a metropolis. Although they would have helped dispel the malaise of the small-town dweller inured to the shelter and comfort of the capillary street network, his proposals would have worked

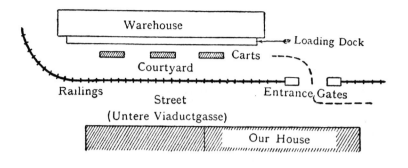

DA COSTA MEYER

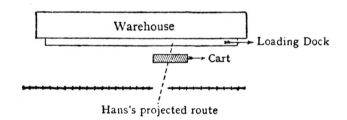

FIG. 2
Freud's diagram showing the
location of Little Hans's house

FIG. 3
Freud's diagram of Little Hans's
projected route

only at the expense of future traffic. His insights were based on an incomplete formulation of the complex social issues involved, but his sensitive reading of the intricacies of urban space remains a valuable tool for town planning even today. And his emphasis on the emotional importance of walls is most perceptive, though it misses the psychosexual connotations that other scholars were later to identify and analyze.

For Sitte's contemporary and fellow citizen Sigmund Freud, who focused on the clinical picture, the fear of urban space was a symptom, not a cause, of aberrant behavior. In Freud's view anxiety neuroses such as agoraphobia were due to repressed, unconscious fears or wishes masquerading as spatial ones, and these fears or wishes were connected not with empty space, but with *urban* (that is, social) space – above all, streets. According to Freud, streets were threatening to those, like affluent or middle-class women, who led a sheltered or repressed life because they held out promises of temptation, sexual fulfillment, and escape from home. This freedom of choice, Freud believed, was a source of great anxiety for the agoraphobe who experienced unconscious guilt for what were, in fact, unconscious desires and, thus, felt the need for a restraining influence like the walls of the house or a companion to walk with.[7]

Linking the etiology of agoraphobia to repressed sexual desire, Freud theorized it as a female malady, at least in his early writings on the subject. As he put it rather crudely in a draft entitled "The Architecture of Hysteria" (1897), "Agoraphobia seems to depend on a romance of prostitution."[8] Yet the first three known patients for whom Westphal earlier had named the disease were, in fact, men, as was the overwhelming majority of cases reported in the medical literature of the day.[9] Freud himself had treated one case of male agoraphobia in 1893 and two in 1895; and though he did not know it at the time, his most important experience with agoraphobic patients was to revolve around a five-year-old boy – the celebrated case of Little Hans.[10] Significantly, this is the only one of Freud's case histories where he makes use of urban plans, however schematic (figs. 2, 3).

When Little Hans developed a fear of going out into the streets and squares of Vienna, Freud correctly saw that space *per se* was incidental to the disease, and incapable of causing trauma. In the case of agoraphobia, buildings and squares have no intrinsic architectural meaning, but are convenient "symbolic substitutes" for repressed feelings.[11] Desire, thwarted by prohibition, transfers itself by metonymy to a nearby object. Urban and architectural space become eroticized through displacement: the final resting place of the repressed and overdetermined signified, at the end of a long metonymic chain. Freud later explained the mechanism and the secondary gains it affords:

"In the case of phobias one can see clearly how this internal danger is transformed into an external one. . . . The agoraphobiac is always afraid of his impulses in connection with temptations aroused in him by meeting people in the street. In his phobia he makes a displacement and is now afraid of an external situation. What he gains thereby is obvious; it is that he feels he can protect himself better in that way. One can rescue oneself from an external danger by flight, whereas an attempt to fly from an internal danger is a difficult undertaking."[12]

As we can see, for Freud there was no easy fit between the urban or architectural signifier and the referent, which is always overdetermined and, thus, partly unavailable. In this sense, we might say that he was a poststructuralist *avant la lettre*. Like all phobias, the story of Little Hans can be broken down into different issues that never exhaust the whole picture: his fear of the streets had to do with, among other things, zoophobia (in his case, a fear of horses). One of Hans's playmates had fallen down while both children were playing horses, and he had also seen a horse fall down in the street. He wished his father, too, would fall down and hurt himself: the Oedipal triangle would then happily resolve itself around Little Hans and his mother. Had Hans limited himself to feelings of love for his mother and ambivalence toward his father, he would not be phobic. "What made it a neurosis," wrote Freud, "was one thing alone: the replacement of his father by a horse. It is this displacement, then, which has a claim to be called a symptom."[13] Displacement – a form of censorship – permitted Little Hans to overcome the ambiguity of his emotions with respect to his father by transferring the aggressive impulses to a substitute object, the horse.

Freud later changed his mind with regard to the origin of agoraphobia in one very important aspect. Reflecting on the case of Little Hans from a distance of several years, he began to revise his earlier view according to which anxiety was the *result* of repressed material. Anxiety, he now believed, was the *cause* of repression: "The majority of phobias go back to an anxiety of this kind felt by the ego in regard to the demands of the libido. It is always the ego's attitude of anxiety which is the primary thing and which sets repression going. Anxiety never arises from repressed libido."[14] What agoraphobes fear is the outbreak of their anxiety attacks.

Be that as it may, Freud successfully isolated the main components of the symptomatology of agoraphobia: the underlying sexual symbolism, the mechanisms of condensation and displacement, and the bipolar world of the patient torn between a fear of obscure forces transferred to urban space, and a home that could be far from nurturing, even in the case of affluent women. Though Freud knew better than to mythologize the home as a benign, sheltering cocoon, he underestimated the extent to which even placid, happy homes could be confining to women. By concentrating on individual cases, which were seen as unique occurrences, he also avoided any correlation between pathology and society. Today, psychoanalysis has moved far beyond its own initial sexist and essentialist explanations, which focused primarily on *women* agoraphobes and disregarded the cultural construction of gender in the pathogenesis of mental illness.

The synchronicity of the appearance of agoraphobia with the rise of the metropolis also anchors it firmly within capitalism. The Industrial Revolution required, among other things, the sexual division of labor and the separation of dwelling from workplace. As a result, the social identities of men and women came to be constituted differently. Yet the doctrine of separate spheres – a male public sphere and a female private sphere – cannot be accepted today except *as* ideology. Numerous historians have underscored the continued presence of women in the public realm throughout the centuries;[15] it was only to men that they had been invisible. Similarly, African-American scholars have shown that in this country, non-Caucasian women often spend more time in the public realm than do men; the relentless focus on the private realm betrays an exclusively white middle-class conception of domesticity.[16]

But the Industrial Revolution also radically altered the class structure and its inscription in the urban fabric. The zoning of land use, which began to be codified in the early decades of the twentieth century, split the proletariat into ethnic subgroups, often driving them out of the historical city with tragic consequences, particularly for working-class women. "It is no accident," according to Gerda Lerner, "that the slogan 'woman's place is in the home' took on a certain aggressiveness and shrillness precisely at the time when increasing numbers of poorer women *left* their homes to become factory workers."[17] Only affluent white housewives could afford to lead cloistered lives secluded in suburbia.

Class plays a powerful role in the geopolitical distribution of agoraphobia over urban space. Just as the equation of obesity with lower-income groups plays a role, however subliminal, in the rise of anorexia,[18] so, too, we must ask to what extent the isolation, if not the suburbanization, of the agoraphobe in this country – her spatial segregation from other ethnic and social groups – may be linked to class fears. Are we dealing with a "pathologic pastorale," if we may be permitted the oxymoron? Is the agoraphobe's attempt to reterritorialize urban space unwillingly complicit with some form of societal discrimination? It seems clear that the semiotics of this anxiety disorder include powerful markers of class and ethnicity, as well as gender. The correlation of urban space and social class is not incidental to the emergence of phobias. Personality evolves in response to specific economic, social, and cultural opportunities made possible in and through the urban environment. According to David Harvey, "Assignment of place within a social-spatial structure indicates distinctive roles, capacities for action, and access to power within the social order."[19] Positionality, we might say, is destiny.

Agoraphobia must, I think, be theorized in relation to capitalism. But we must remember, too, that what we call the public sphere has to do not only with gender, but also with social class and race – issues that vary from culture to culture, and are articulated differently in terms of space. As Susan Bordo notes, "Agoraphobia and anorexia are, after all, chiefly disorders of middle and upper middle-class women – women for whom the anxieties of *possibility* have arisen, women who have the social and material resources to carry the language of femininity to symbolic excess."[20]

If gender is the product of social practices and institutions (disciplines), we must historicize and contextualize agoraphobia, not just pathologize it. Several scholars have done just that, relating cultural factors – not just psychological ones – to the genesis of psychological disorders.[21] Going back to the etymology of agoraphobia, Gillian Brown has reinterpreted it as the fear of the marketplace (or agora), that is, the fear of consumption. In her view, agoraphobia epitomizes the plight of the individual in a market economy and thus can also be seen as a painful and pathologic attempt to circumvent the consumerist role assigned to middle-class women in affluent societies.

With the advent of industrialization, concomitant economic pressures caused severe strains in the traditional value system of American society. The transformation of the home from a place of production to one of consumption had great impact on women's personalities, and led to a drastic change from the Protestant values of thrift and self-denial to an ethic of self-indulgence and self-fashioning. Extending this analysis to the spatial aspect of agoraphobia, we might say that this disorder can be considered, to a certain degree, as a rejection of the commodification of public space made available exclusively for purposes of consumption.

However, withdrawal from the marketplace is no longer feasible: the two realms have become consubstantial. This desperate attempt on the part of agoraphobic women to reprivatize the home and wrest it from commercialism was doomed to failure from the start. With the spread of consumer ideology, the boundary between house and marketplace has eroded.[22] Hence the need for an ideology of domesticity: middle-class women were encouraged to consume but also to stay out of the labor market. Agoraphobia can thus be said to allegorize the sexual division of labor and the inscription of social as well as sexual difference in urban space. It speaks, after all, the same symbolic language as patriarchal society: the gendered antinomy between interior and exterior space reasserts the economic (active) function of the male, and the "non-productive" (passive) one of the middle-class female. Agoraphobia represents a virtual parody of twentieth-century constructions of femininity.[23]

The parodic femininity of agoraphobia is based on a literal interpretation of domesticity as immobility, helplessness, and infantilization – the main stereotype fabricated in the West as a role model for affluent women.[24] Significantly, the vast majority of cases of agoraphobia develops *after* marriage.[25] Transition from a state of total dependency on parents to one of expected independence precipitates a crisis, which may result in agoraphobia. Obviously, an anxiety neurosis as complex as this is always overdetermined. But in light of the escalating number of cases, we cannot be satisfied with purely psychological explanations. The very fact that most cases appear after marriage should alert us to the socio-economic connotations of a disease that keeps women out of the labor force and reiterates their role as housekeepers for their husbands. Agoraphobia is known, to no one's surprise, as "housewives' disease."[26]

In recent years feminist scholars on both sides of the Atlantic have produced a steady stream of challenging literature that treats gender-specific types of neurosis as outlets of resistance to patriarchy: Luce Irigaray, Hélène Cixous, Catherine Clément, and Michèle Montrelay in France and, in the United States, Carroll Smith-Rosenberg, and Elaine Showalter, among others. For these scholars, psychopathology is a form of protest: the hysteric's repressed impulses are articulated symbolically through the body – a fact that implies, from a Lacanian point of view, a refusal of the phallocentric power anchored in language.

Studies on agoraphobia have followed the same trend. Like other forms of psychopathology, it is a language with a syntax of its own. Robert Seidenberg and Karen DeCrow, for example, see it as a strategy of opposition to what we might call the ethic of renunciation usually demanded of married women.[27] It is precisely the somatization of the symptoms that permits the victim to express feelings s/he finds unacceptable. Conversely, agoraphobes avoid situations that give (unconscious) symbolic expression to their hidden fears or wishes: trains (the wish to flee), elevators and tunnels (fear of being trapped in unhappy marriages), and so on.[28] Space perception depends on mastering institutionalized signs, but agoraphobes tend to read them figuratively. Both the places they avoid and those they designate as shelters have to do with distinct typologies which are metaphors for situations they fear or desire. Their spatial codes are personal and hermetic rather than socialized.

The notion that agoraphobia is "body talk" is crucial also for Julia Kristeva, who comes to a similar conclusion from a different perspective. Drawing on the work of Lacan, she sees phobia as a failure of the subject's "signifying system."[29] The [agora]phobic personality, she writes in her analysis of Little Hans's case study, is "incapable of producing metaphors by means of signs alone, . . . the only rhetoric of which he is capable is that of affect, and it is projected, as often as not, by means of *images*."[30] But – and here she departs radically from the others – symbolicity is cathected by a drive that has nothing to do with object choice, and thus bypasses sexual difference.[31]

There can be no doubt that agoraphobia is a coherent signifying system. Its victims stand to gain something from their extreme stance and are prepared to pay exorbitant prices for it. As Freud points out, illness of this kind ends in compromise; Little Hans's fear of going out into the streets served as a ruse for keeping him at home with his beloved mother.[32] Bordo, however, has underscored the self-defeating nature of the agoraphobic protest and its ultimate unwilling and unconscious collusion with the system.[33] Non-discursive, symbolic protest through the body ends up by subserving the hated establishment and reproduces sexual division of labor by keeping women at home; which is to say, it reproduces capitalism.[34]

One of the most perplexing characteristics of this gender-specific disease is the persistence of architectural imagery, a fact that raises several issues. Are the buildings and urban spaces just empty husks to which repressed pathologic behavior attaches itself? Are they, in other words, simply neutral signifiers? Or is there some underlying reason that leads victims of agoraphobia to cast their scenarios of fear and foreboding in architectural terms? If architecture is eroticized through metonymy, which depends on propinquity, why is the garden, for example, not an equally powerful source of affect?

Helène Deutsch, the first woman psychoanalyst to study agoraphobia, was also the first psychoanalyst to analyze the architectural imagery of the house. According to her studies, the act of leaving the protective walls of the home and finding oneself "outside" is associated by many agoraphobics with the act of giving birth.[35] For some psychoanalysts this would explain the high rate of agoraphobia among women. Lest this be taken for an essentialist claim, it should be noted that agoraphobia is one of the rare phobias in which the association of crossing the threshold with parturition occurs in male as well as female patients, thus linking it not to biological sex, but to gender. The equation of home and womb would seem to be so profoundly ingrained that it has the power to feminize male patients. In their regression to intrauterine memories, the agoraphobes' *Lebensraum* shrinks to this tautological condensation of home and maternal body. Their inspired misreading of domestic space is revelatory: after all, "everyone's first environment is a woman."[36]

But architecture has reasons of its own that inflect the slippery referentiality of the word "home." Size, scale, and the anthropomorphic resonances encoded in the articulation of architectural form – all conspire to give it a strong presence in the urban environment. As Denis Hollier writes, "Architecture is society's authorized superego; there is no architecture that is not the Commendatore's."[37] And he quotes Lacan to this effect: "This edifice [Lacan was speaking metaphorically of the psychoanalytic building] is appealing to us. For, metaphoric though this may be, it is perfectly constructed to remind us of what distinguished architecture from building: that is, a logical power organizing architecture beyond anything the building supports in terms of possible use. Moreover no building, unless reduced to a shack, can do without this order allying it with discourse."[38]

As we have seen, agoraphobia was engendered by Western culture even before it was diagnosed for the first time; and femininity, construed as planned helplessness, has still not disappeared from our society. Until relatively recently, children's books often depicted girls immobilized in the house – behind the protection of windows, fences, porches – while boys were shown actively exploring the environment.[39] Although today women may no longer be inexorably trapped in a circularity that culturally constitutes them through images, even the most emancipated women are confronted with another major obstacle that keeps them behind walls. When one woman out of every four in the United States is raped (or one every ten minutes), agoraphobia – the fear of *public* spaces –

takes on a different coloration altogether. In the case of rape victims, public space as such does not exist except as part of a topology of fear. And time, not just space, is also a constituent element of agoraphobia: at night, in most large cities, *all* women are agoraphobic.

Neither the appearance of agoraphobia nor the escalating number of victims is accidental. As Bordo has forcefully demonstrated, psycho-pathologies that emerge within a given society, far from being exceptions to the rule are, in fact, products of that culture.[40] Agoraphobia cannot be reduced to a cultural stereotype – its victims suffer intensely – nor to a purely psychological or individual phenomenon, given the growing incidence of cases. Because of the circumscribed nature of its social distribution, the disease cannot be universalized: it does not represent the female condition. After all, the Duke of Mantua in Verdi's *Rigoletto* was literally correct: even though his famous definition of women was intended sarcastically, today at least – and against all odds – *la donna è mobile*.

DA COSTA MEYER

I wish to thank John Goodman and George Hersey for their suggestions and helpful readings of the manuscript.

1. A longer version of this paper appears in *Assemblage* 28 (1996), 6–15.

2. Carl F. O. Westphal, "Die Agoraphobie: eine neuropathische Erscheinung," *Archiv für Psychiatrie und Nervenkrankheiten* 3 (1872), 138–61. All quotations are from the American edition, *Westphal's "Die Agoraphobie" with Commentary: The Beginnings of Agoraphobia*, commentary by Terry J. Knapp, trans. Michael T. Schumacher (Lanham, Md.: University Press of America Books, 1988).

3. Isaac M. Marks, "Agoraphobic Syndrome," *Archives of General Psychiatry* 23 (December 1970), 539.

4. Iris Goldstein Fodor, "The Phobic Syndrome in Women: Implications for Treatment," in Violet Franks and Vasanti Burtle, eds., *Women in Therapy: New Psychotherapies for a Changing Society* (New York: Brunner/Mazel, 1974), 151.

5. George R. Collins and Christiane C. Collins, *Camillo Sitte: The Birth of Modern City Planning* (New York: Rizzoli, 1986), 183.

6. Ibid., 233.

7. Muriel Frampton, *Agoraphobia* (Bodmin, Cornwall: Thorsons Publishing Group, 1990), 36.

8. Jeffrey Moussaieff Masson, *The Complete Letters of Sigmund Freud to Wilhelm Fliess, 1887–1904* (Cambridge, Mass.: Belknap Press of Harvard University Press, 1985), 248. On this passage and on urban pathology in general, see the illuminating article by Anthony Vidler, "Bodies in Space/Subjects in the City: Psychopathologies of Modern Urbanism," *differences* 5 (Fall 1993), 31–51.

9. Knapp, "Introduction," *Westphal's "Die Agoraphobie,"* 34. See also pp. 28 ff.

10. Sigmund Freud, "Analysis of a Phobia in a Five-Year-Old Boy" (1909), *The Standard Edition of the Complete Psychological Works of Sigmund Freud,* trans. James Strachey, 24 vols. (London: The Hogarth Press, 1973), vol. 10, 3–149. This was an unusual case, as Freud rarely analyzed children. He saw Little Hans only once, and analyzed him by proxy: the child's father, a physician, was an early follower of Freud. Not surprisingly, the mother plays a shadowy role in this tale of two fathers.

11. Ibid., 48.

12. Sigmund Freud, *New Introductory Lectures on Psycho-Analysis,* trans. W. J. H. Sprott (London: Hogarth Press, 1949), 111–12.

13. Sigmund Freud, *Inhibitions, Symptoms, and Anxiety* (1926), trans. Alix Strachey (New York: W. W. Norton, 1989), 25.

14. Ibid., 32. See also Jacques Derrida, "To Speculate – on Freud," in Peggy Kamuf, ed., *A Derrida Reader* (New York: Columbia University Press, 1991), 523.

15. For example, Linda K. Kerber, "Separate Spheres, Female Worlds, Woman's Place: The Rhetoric of Women's History," *Journal of American History* 75 (June 1988), 9–39.

16. Patricia Hill Collins, *Black Feminist Thought: Knowledge, Consciousness, and the Politics of Empowerment* (Boston: Unwin Hyman, 1990), 46–47.

17. Gerda Lerner, quoted in Kerber, 12 (her emphasis).

18. Noelle Caskey, "Interpreting Anorexia Nervosa," in Susan Suleiman, ed., *The Female Body in Western Culture* (Cambridge, Mass.: Harvard University Press, 1986), 178.

19. Quoted in Gillian Rose, *Feminism and Geography* (Minneapolis: University of Minnesota Press, 1993), 18. Space, according to many modern geographers, is not an environment in which social life takes place but "a medium *through which* social life is produced and reproduced." Rose, 19 (her emphasis).

20. Susan Bordo, "The Body and the Reproduction of Femininity: A Feminist

Appropriation of Foucault," in Alison M. Jaggar and Susan R. Bordo, eds., *Gender/Body/Knowledge* (New Brunswick, N.J.: Rutgers University Press, 1989), 22 (her emphasis).

21. Particularly the New Historicists: see Gillian Brown, "The Empire of Agoraphobia," *Representations* 20 (Fall 1987), 134–57, and Walter Benn Michaels, *The Gold Standard and the Logic of Naturalism* (Berkeley: University of California Press, 1987), 3–28. But see also Bordo, "Anorexia nervosa: Psychopathology as the Crystallization of Culture," in Irene Diamond and Lee Quinby, eds., *Feminism and Foucault: Reflections on Resistance* (Boston: Northeastern University Press, 1988), 87–117.

22. Jürgen Habermas, *The Structural Transformation of the Public Sphere*, trans. Thomas Burger (Cambridge, Mass.: MIT Press, 1993), 156. Brown, 142.

23. Bordo, "The Body and the Reproduction of Femininity," 17.

24. See Alexandra Symonds, "Phobias After Marriage, Women's Declaration of Dependence," in Jean Baker Miller, ed., *Psychoanalysis and Women* (New York: Brunner/Mazel, 1973), 297.

25. Kathleen Brehony, "Women and Agoraphobia: A Case for the Etiological Significance of the Feminine Sex-Role Stereotype," in Violet Franks and Esther Rothblum, eds., *The Stereotyping of Women* (New York: Springer-Verlag, 1983), 115.

26. Dianne L. Chambless and Alan J. Goldstein, "Anxieties: Agoraphobia and Hysteria," in Annette M. Brodsky and Rachel T. Hare-Mustin, eds., *Women and Psychotherapy* (New York: Guilford Press, 1980), 123.

27. Robert Seidenberg and Karen DeCrow, *Women Who Marry Houses: Panic and Protest in Agoraphobia* (New York: McGraw Hill, 1983), 31.

28. Chambless and Goldstein, 116, 126.

29. Julia Kristeva, *Powers of Horror* (New York: Columbia University Press, 1982), 35.

30. Ibid., 37 (her emphasis).

31. Ibid., 45.

32. Freud, "Analysis of a Phobia," 139.

33. "On the symbolic level, too, the protest dimension collapses into its opposite and proclaims the utter defeat and capitulation of the subject to the contracted female world." Bordo, "The Body and the Reproduction of Femininity," 21.

34. But see Brown, 154, n. 25.

35. Helène Deutsch, "The Genesis of Agoraphobia," *International Journal of Psychoanalysis* 10 (1929), 69; Milton Miller, "On Street Fear," *International Journal of Psychoanalysis* 34 (1953), 238.

36. Ruth Perry, "Engendering Environmental Thinking: A Feminist Analysis of the Present Crisis," *Yale Journal of Criticism* 6 (Fall 1993), 13.

37. Denis Hollier, *Against Architecture: The Writings of Georges Bataille*, trans. Betsy Wing (Cambridge, Mass.: MIT Press, 1989), ix.

38. Ibid., 32–33.

39. Fodor, 143.

40. Bordo, "Anorexia nervosa," 89. See also her *Unbearable Weight: Feminism, Western Culture, and the Body* (Berkeley: University of California Press, 1993).

"Women Internet" vs. the "Space of Tyranny": Reply to Esther da Costa Meyer

LAURETTA VINCIARELLI

When, in *Rigoletto*, the Duke of Mantua sings the aria, *"La donna è mobile,"* metaphorically stating that woman is volatile and voluble, he is tracing a self-portrait. Indeed, the moral of the drama is that *man* is *mobile,* woman is *not.* Gilda is, in fact, faithful, brave, and heroic to the point of sacrificing her own life for that of the duke.

Was Gilda *mobile?* If mobility is defined as safe movement in urban space, public and private, the answer is no. The fictional Mantua of *Rigoletto* represents, in urban terms, the absolute power of the duke. Public and private spaces coalesce in what I call the "space of tyranny." As for women, they were not only seduced in the streets, but abducted from their homes when convenient for ducal schemes. Gilda's tragic destiny was inevitable. In a Mantua of tyranny, she could not have resorted even to agoraphobia to save herself. However, in the real Mantua of the sixteenth century, Gilda would have been protected by what I call the "Women Internet": communication among not only women in the same household, but all the women in town. From infancy, "Women Internet" would have informed Gilda in minute detail about the physical and moral character of the duke, so that she could not have been deceived, at least not easily.

The segregation of women, conceived in the West at least as early as the Greeks, was never entirely successful. More often it was totally unsuccessful, as shown in both literature and painting. (A few examples from the Roman period would include Petronius' *Satyricon,* Apuleius' *Golden Ass,* and Juvenal's *Xth Satyre.*) The very raison d'être of treatises such as Alberti's *Della famiglia* proves that in the fifteenth century the

157

practice of life was not the one prescribed but, most probably, was closer to that related by Boccaccio in the *Decameron*. From medieval and Renaissance Italian paintings depicting urban scenes, we have a description of urban space where people of all ranks move freely, especially women; for example, Ambrogio Lorenzetti's fresco *Gli effetti del buon governo* at the Palazzo Pubblico in Siena.

With the rise of the middle class and the capitalist economy, segregation of women became more successful. The notions of public and private spaces as we know them today, did, in fact, spring from capitalism. Limiting my observation to central Italy, I can safely say that, as long as agrarian values have resisted the pressures of emerging middle-class values, the majority of public space has been understood and used as an extension of private space, and has been almost entirely controlled by women. Even today, I have seen this phenomenon in Gradoli, a little town north of Rome, in Latium, where 90 percent of the public space is still controlled by women. They inhabit it, they work in it, and they enjoy leisure time in it, keeping alive the "Women Internet."

However, while this situation may still be common in small towns all over central Italy, it is disappearing rapidly. Perhaps this is because women are joining the specialized work force in jobs commonly done away from home, but new work conditions alone do not explain the increasingly muted relationship of women to public space. Instead, this seems to be more the consequence of a change in mentality and social attitudes.

One of the prices people have to pay to be acknowledged as middle class is relinquishing control of public space into the hands of local and regional governments. For example, middle-class Viennese at the turn of this century refused the blurred definition of public and private space implicit in the projects of architect and urbanist Camillo Sitte, who proposed a series of small-scale, enclosed city squares that would have generated a form of public space unsuitable for an efficient performance of the municipal police.

The two urban conditions that I have called the "space of tyranny" and the "space of 'Women Internet'" resurface today in the modern metropolis: the former as a description of critical states of affairs in the metropolitan fringes; the latter as a plausible form of renewal of those fringes – slums that represent, all over the Western world, the other side of the metropolis. The South Bronx in New York during the 1970s and 1980s is a pure example of the "space of tyranny." Neighborhood residents were terrorized and victimized by violent gangs, which, in constant war with each other, were allowed by an indifferent city to control the streets. Consequently, the physical deterioration within the community was tremendous: violent crime, murders, poverty, and disinvestment soared. In *Marisol,* a play by José Rivera, the audience experiences a particularly vivid description of the kind of "continuum of terror" that existed during those years when no private door could interrupt it.

Today, in the mid-1990s, the South Bronx shows signs of improvement. The wars over drugs are somehow under control; some capital is being reinvested there; new housing is being built; and, as a result, both public and private spaces are beginning to reappear. However, even though what is happening is not exactly gentrification, there exists a pervading sense of antagonism between the "old" and the "new" that is palpable. As a result, a philosophy of renewal that "fits the new and old together," based on the involvement of the inhabitants of the area, has begun to emerge. Melrose Commons is an outstanding example. Primarily because of the efforts of one woman, Yolanda Garcia, leader of the neighborhood group Nos Quedamos, the renewal of Melrose is being strongly controlled by its inhabitants, who continue to win innumerable fights with city authorities.

The primary difference between Melrose Commons and many other participatory housing projects is that in Melrose public space is conceived of as an extension of private space; it is safeguarded by the residents who deliberately choose to be responsible for it. It is obvious that this is no middle-class community. Rather, this is a community that relies on itself for protection, knowing that self-defense starts with control. The urban space, public and private, requested by Yolanda Garcia and Nos Quedamos, is that of "Women Internet." In other places in the West, too, in Naples and in Rome, for instance, the urban renewal that really works is that which allows for self-protection and keeps "Women Internet" alive to the advantage of the entire community.

As for myself, I have never felt more secure than in those streets where women sit outside, talking and working, firmly in control of their own surroundings. I think that it is time to reflect on issues of real power versus middle-class status. Yolanda Garcia did not have any hesitation as to which one to select. She chose power – the power of control over her own neighborhood, for the benefit of everybody – and I applaud her.

The Matter of Matter: A Longing for Gravity

JENNIFER BLOOMER

"In one sense, and that deep, there is no such thing as magnitude. . . . Greatness is the aggregation of minuteness; nor can its sublimity be felt truthfully by any mind unaccustomed to the affectionate watching of what is least."

— John Ruskin, *Precious Thoughts*

I shall begin with a tiny thing, the little spot on the body called a birthmark. The birthmark was in times past called a longing mark, the explanation being that it is the image impressed on a baby's skin of an object craved by the mother during her pregnancy. The small caramel marks that ornament the skins of my daughters are shaped, respectively, like a jar of French's mustard and a cucumber. Such images, figures of desired objects, have their analogue in the representations of certain other objects that resemble jars and cucumbers.

Architecture, "the Mother of the Arts," is, after all (as Catherine Ingraham points out in her essay in this volume) not an object art but an object-longing art. And architectural drawings, compositions of lines suggesting form, can be construed as the longing marks of architecture; or perhaps more precisely in this analogy, of the architect who is, with his conception, development, and delivery of product, a kind of mother. The mother, the one who carries weight: gravidity and gravity. This is nothing new or particularly astonishing, but I raise it in order to reconsider the notion of longing and, more particularly, the place of nostalgia, homesickness, the longing for home, in contemporary Western architecture.

I am interested in teasing out the fibers of nostalgia in relation to the practice and discourse of architecture. In opening up this subject – invoking this word tinged with obloquy and often preceded by the qualifier "mere" – I cringe with awareness of the minefield on which I tread. But I am profoundly curious about the polarized response to nostalgia in contemporary architectural discourse. On the one hand, it is placed on a pedestal and made a universal genius of new town planning and architectural style. On the other hand, nostalgia is covered in refusal. But nostalgia *exists*, in all its syrupy sweet, kitschy wonder, in its heartfelt longings, in its achy-breaky desire for something that cannot be had. I am interested in the urge to make it mere, to cover it up, to pretend it isn't there, like a bad zit or a body odor. In the manner of these analogues, nostalgia happens; and it comes with certain pleasures.

The repression of nostalgia is at the core of the project of modernity. Nostalgia is a nineteenth-century disease ever threatening to erupt on the glossy smooth skin of the twentieth. It is, perhaps, like so many repressions, a marker of the animal in us. But, as sentient creatures know deep down inside, any attempt to ignore or repress animal yearnings must always be dominated by an uneasy awareness of their pressures.

In its subjugation of matter by form, the modern concept of design necessarily is dominated by a nostalgia for matter, a fetishization of an imagined absence. Design is the necessity of the new and, in architecture, the big. The possibility of electronic space is the new infinite, eternal design with no bounds, no walls, no enclosure, no stopping. It is the space of going, and certainly not Ruskin's space of repose. The hyperspatial entity, in which space and time form a seamless continuum, is the legitimate heir to the modern project. For a nexus of lines, whether drawn, virtual, simulated, or troped, is the mark of a longed-for object. Form sitting on the lid of its other, matter.

Design is the making of the "always-in-progress New," which is always the "becoming-old." The lust for the New, that telic carrot on a string, like nostalgia, is a longing for something one cannot have, for as soon as the New is materialized, it ceases to be new. And this lust, driven by a neglect of the heavy business of matter, is, in its persistent repressions, intensely nostalgic.

But let us go between the lines, to the heart of the matter, in the belly of the wall:

Lying in the broad, enveloping poché of an ancient castle on Loch Ness, my face catching the gentle breeze off the water through the machicolation, I am cradled in a sac of pure pleasure. The summer breeze, the setting sun, the warmth of the stone, the weight of it, the possibility of the monster – oh, I think I see it, there! No, now it's gone. I am swallowed by this wall, warm, safe, comfortable, but also pricked by longing. It has something to do with the immediacy of the material and its attributes – warmth, weight, odor, color, texture – and the distance of history of which it is a pregnant trace. Other bodies, sharp projectiles, boiling liquids, abject substances, scrambling limbs, the sound of metal on metal, metal on stone, metal on flesh. The howling of dogs. The longing of human animals. Here, in this utterly foreign place, I feel at home. This wall of home and shelter, gravid object swollen with these facts, can be represented with two simple straight, parallel lines.

The track of progress that can be drawn between this pile of stones and contemporary configurations of space is a straight line threatened by ballooning eruptions along its continuum. The line, bulging thing, has swallowed a great deal of *mater* in the hope of hiding her, that little matter of matter. Now you see it, now you don't!

The momentary end of the line, the Now New, is, perhaps, the notion of electronic space. Curiously, to enter this space is to leave home without leaving home. In this space, however, there is no matrix of domesticity; the cozy, sensual matter of home has no place here. Where is the sweet smell of babies, the lovely, slightly sour smell of toddlers? Where is the fat furry twitch of the September squirrel, the slightly unnerving, but endearing, social sounds of hundreds of mother bats nursing hundreds of wee batbabies in the wall just behind the dictionary shelf? As if the Greek, German, French, Latin, Italian, Russian, and English dictionaries speaking together make this little chit chit chit squee sound. The overwhelming wave of delight in finding the first crocus, narcissus, or delicate tips of the peony emerging from the earth in spring? The strange warmth of stone long after the sun has disappeared? There is no place for cyber-domesticity, for electro-sentimentality. Why?

Because this apparent nostalgia-free zone is, in fact, nothing if not nostalgic, a repression of "home-sickness" so extreme that something is not quite being covered up.

The urge to virtual realities of any kind relies on a constant domestic space, whether proximal or distant. The space of domesticity, configured as "real" space, is still, always already, the spatial envelope of the cyberventuring subject who explores the public space of the net or the virtual space of simulation. With his body, that hunk of pulsing meat, in his comfortable, safe, warm, uninterrupted, timeless space, he can project himself anywhere, into anything.

Here, the lines of nerves and the lines of communication form a continuum. It is all transmission of information. Here is an apparent triumph of Aristotelian form over matter, of the rational over the corporeal. With the ostensible obviation – secretion – of the body comes the repression of shame, sentiment, nostalgia, longing. This space of no gravity replicates in certain ways the space of the infant, or even that of the fetus: interactive intake, no responsibility to any body. A nostalgic and sentimental, if not shameful, project in the extreme: the return to the natal home. That dirty place, the matter of *mater*. The relentless drive toward the New is a strangely directed attempt to escape from *Materia*, the old, generative soil, the origin. The New is never dirty; it is always bright, spanking clean, light, full of promise, devoid of weight.

I have a dirty architectural secret: I choose to live in a house designed and built sixty-five years ago by an engineer with an engineer's appreciation of the local climate and an engineer's disregard for style or fashion. I love its beefy masonry walls that, with the shade trees outside, obviate air conditioning in our nasty summers and in which I love to nest and nestle during our nasty winters. I delight in its funky "built-ins," such as the fold-down ironing board in its own little poché space behind the laundry-folding table, which in its 1995 function holds an amazing pile of correspondence, books, slides, and dirty teacups. I am entranced by the 8-inch-wide, 6-foot-deep closet in the part of the downstairs bath plumbing wall unoccupied by plumbing, with its tiny Alice-in-Wonderland door opening out into the hall. It is perfect for storing anything long and skinny. Right now it holds tubes of drawings, rolls of gift-wrapping paper, my loom-warping templates, and a supply of dried corn left over from our fatten-the-squirrels project last fall. And I will not soon forget the thrill of my discovery in the basement of the Herculean 2 x 12 joists beneath the only space in the house where a grand piano can go.

Why does this house-object evoke such blatant nostalgia, such a professionally shameful response? Because I am pleasured by this warm, sheltering thing. I am sentimental about its quirks, mad about its materiality, its weight. Gravid thing, hulking among the wizened yews and cedars, sunk ten feet into the Iowa topsoil, it is going nowhere. It is my home, my burrow, my vessel of children. A catalyst of nostalgia and deeply generated sentiment, this assemblage of rock and tree, metal and molten sand, can be accurately represented less as a construction of lines than as an assemblage of details. For it is in the details, traditionally for philosophers and writers an object burdened with the trope of femininity (and for Mies the momentary dwelling of God), that form and matter, use and pleasure, coincide.

At the coincidence of the exterior and interior of my house are lodged a phalanx of 1930 Pella Rollscreens. Built-in toys, they are technological wonders made in nearby Pella, Iowa, a town built on nostalgia. Pella maintains its old, Dutch immigrant identity: a tiny, tourist attraction of lace, pastries, and an annual Tulip Festival complete with Tulip Princess and tens of thousands of early May cups of color rising from the soil of the town square and its outlying borders and lawns. And, of course, the making of windows of astonishing quality. It is said that the Pella Corporation requires its employees to live in Pella, at home in the body of the family, and not in larger, neighboring, and more diverse Des Moines.

My Pella Rollscreens are markers of the seasons: when the last maple leaf has gone from red to brittle, and the double-glazed casements are levered shut in readiness for the arctic assault to come, it is time to play. Pop, pop, two perfect, thumb-receiving aluminum pads on springs are pushed to the wood of the sill. Then, zoooooop! Look quickly, or you'll miss it! The delicate metal grid, defying gravity in the most astonishing act, disappears upward into the frame of the window, leaving bewildered cobwebs waving bye-bye in its wake. Sometimes, because I adore peeka-boo, I reach up and grab its little rolled aluminum bottom and pull it all the way down, thwack!, to the sill again. Then, pop! pop! It's gone. But, come the first promise of crocus . . . Wheeeere's the screen? There it is! – mediating the boundary of home, the domestic membrane through which spring breezes and summer's gravid air pass, but not the relatively gargantuan bodies of houseflies and errant finches. Pella Rollscreens can be specified on an architectural drawing, but not drawn. Drawn, they are illegible; they simply disappear into the representation of the window's frame. They are a trace in the extreme, an uncanny example of the way that architectural drawings are the longing marks of the architect.

Lodged in the poché of our walls, and in the marrow of our bones, is matter that has been around since the Big Bang. The meat of history and culture: heavy matter. Two parallel lines constitute the longing mark for any wall/vertical planarity of any material, any gravidity. How little such longing marks express – all form, no matter. They form a ghostly, nearly immaterial apparition, like the birthmark, a little nothing, representing little, but signifying much.

BLOOMER

This essay is a small piece from a book manuscript in progress called "The Matter of Matter: Architecture in the Age of Dematerialization."

Battle Lines: E.1027

BEATRIZ COLOMINA

"Anger is perhaps the greatest inspiration in those days when the individual is separated in so many personalities. Suddenly one is all in one piece."

– Eileen Gray, 1942

E.1027. A modern white house is perched on the rocks, a hundred feet above the Mediterranean Sea, in a remote place, Roquebrune at Cap Martin in France (fig. 1). The site is "inaccessible and not overlooked from anywhere."¹ No road leads to this house. It was designed and built between 1926 and 1929 by Eileen Gray for Jean Badovici and herself. Gray named the house E.1027: E for Eileen, 10 for J (the tenth letter of the alphabet), 2 for B and 7 for G. Gray and Badovici lived there most summer months, until Gray built her own house in Castellar in 1934. After Badovici's death in 1956, the house was sold to the Swiss architect Marie Louise Schelbert. She found the walls riddled with bullet holes. The house had clearly been the scene of some considerable violence. In a 1969 letter, she commented on the state of the house: "Corbu did not want anything repaired and urged me to leave it as it is as a reminder of war."² But what kind of war? Most obviously, it was World War II. The bullet holes are wounds from the German occupation. But what violence was there to the house before the bullets, and even before the inevitable relationship of modern architecture to the military? And anyway, to start with, what is Le Corbusier doing here? What brings him to this isolated spot, this remote house that will eventually be the site of his own death?

Eileen Gray. E.1027, Roquebrune–
Cap Martin, France. 1926–29.
View from the sea

"As a young man he had traveled in the Balkans and the near East and had made sketches of strange, inaccessible places and scenes. It was perhaps through a natural, anti-romantic reaction of maturity that later, as a Purist, he proposed to paint what was duplicable and near-at-hand."[3] We will have to go back to Le Corbusier's earlier travels, to the "strange, inaccessible places and scenes" that he had conquered through drawing – at the very least, to Le Corbusier's trip to Algiers in the spring of 1931, the first encounter in what would become a long relationship to this city, or in Le Corbusier's words, "twelve years of uninterrupted study of Algiers."[4] By all accounts, this study began with his drawing of Algerian women. He said later that he had been "profoundly seduced by a type of woman particularly well built," of which he made many nude studies.[5] He also acquired a big collection of colored postcards depicting naked women surrounded by accoutrements from the Oriental bazaar. Jean de Maisonseul (later director of the Musée National des Beaux-Arts d'Alger), who as an eighteen-year-old boy had guided Le Corbusier through the Casbah, recalls their tour:

"Our wanderings through the side streets led us at the end of the day to the rue Kataroudji where he [Le Corbusier] was fascinated by the beauty of two young girls, one Spanish and the other Algerian. They brought us up a narrow stairway to their room; there he sketched some nudes on – to my amazement – some schoolbook graph paper with colored pencils; the sketches of the Spanish girl lying both alone on the bed and beautifully grouped together with the Algerian turned out accurate and realistic; but he said that they were very bad and refused to show them."[6]

Le Corbusier filled three notebooks of sketches in Algiers that he later claimed were stolen from his Paris atelier. But Ozenfant denies it, saying that Le Corbusier himself either destroyed or hid them, considering them a *"secret d'atelier."*[7] The Algerian sketches and postcards appear to be a rather ordinary instance of the ingrained fetishistic appropriation of women, of the East, of "the other." Yet Le Corbusier, as Samir Rafi and Stanislaus von Moos have noted, turned this material into "preparatory studies for and the basis of a projected monumental figure composition,

FIG. 2

Le Corbusier. *Crouching Woman, Front View* (after Delacroix's *Les Femmes d'Alger*). n.d. Watercolor on transparent paper, 19 5/8 x 12 7/8 in. Private collection, Milan

FIG. 3

Eugène Delacroix. *Les Femmes d'Alger dans leur appartement.* 1833. Oil on canvas. Musée du Louvre, Paris

FIG. 4

Le Corbusier. *Graffite à Cap Martin* (*Three Women*). 1938. Mural in Eileen Gray's house E.1027, Roquebrune–Cap Martin

the plans for which seem to have preoccupied Le Corbusier during many years, if not his entire life."[8]

From the months immediately following his return from Algiers until his death, Le Corbusier seems to have made hundreds and hundreds of sketches on yellow tracing paper by laying it over the original sketches and redrawing the contours of the figures. (Ozenfant believed that Le Corbusier had redrawn his own sketches with the help of photographs or postcards.[9]) He also exhaustively studied Delacroix's famous painting *Les Femmes d'Alger dans leur appartement,* producing a series of sketches of the outlines of the figures in this painting, divested of their "exotic clothing" and the "Oriental decor" (figs. 2, 3).[10] Soon the two projects merged: he modified the gestures of Delacroix's figures, gradually making them correspond to the figures in his own sketches. Le Corbusier said that he would have called the final composition *Les Femmes de la Casbah.*[11] In fact, he never finished it. He kept redrawing it. That the drawing and redrawing of these images became a lifetime obsession already indicates that something was at stake. This became even more obvious when in 1963–64, shortly before his death, Le Corbusier, unhappy with the visible aging of the yellow tracing paper, copied a selection of twenty-six drawings onto transparent paper and, symptomatically for someone who kept everything, burned the rest.[12]

But the process of drawing and redrawing the *Les Femmes de la Casbah* reached its most intense, if not hysterical, moment when Le Corbusier's studies found their way into a mural that he completed in 1938 in E.1027. Le Corbusier referred to the mural as *Sous les pilotis* or *Graffite à Cap Martin;* sometimes he also labeled it *Three Women* (fig. 4).[13] According to Schelbert, Le Corbusier "explained to his friends that 'Badou' [Badovici] was depicted on the right, his friend Eileen Gray on the left; the outline of the head and the hairpiece of the sitting figure in the middle, he claimed, was 'the desired child, which was never born.'"[14] This extraordinary scene, a defacement of Gray's architecture, was perhaps even an effacement of her sexuality. For Gray was openly gay, her relationship to Badovici notwithstanding. And in so far as Badovici is here represented as one of the three women, the mural may reveal as much as it conceals. It is clearly a "theme for a psychiatrist," as Le

FIG. 5

FIG. 5

Le Corbusier. *Cabanon*,
Roquebrune–Cap Martin. 1952

FIG. 6

Le Corbusier. Early sketch for
the *cabanon*. December 30, 1951

Corbusier's *Vers une architecture* says of the nightmares with which people invest their houses,[15] particularly if we take into account Le Corbusier's obsessive relationship to this house as manifest (and this is only one example of a complex pathology) in his quasi-occupation of the site after World War II, when he built a small wooden shack (the *cabanon*, figs. 5, 6) for himself at the very limits of the adjacent property, right behind Gray's house. He occupied and controlled the site by overlooking it, the cabin being little more than an observation platform, a sort of watchdog house. The imposition of this appropriating gaze is even more brutal if we remember that Gray had chosen the site because it was, in Peter Adam's words, "inaccessible and not overlooked from anywhere." But the violence of this occupation had already been established when Le Corbusier painted the murals in the house (there were eight altogether) without Gray's permission (she had already moved out). She considered it an act of vandalism; indeed, as Adam put it, "It was a rape. A fellow architect, a man she admired, had without her consent defaced her design."[16]

The defacement of the house went hand in hand with the effacement of Gray as an architect. When Le Corbusier published the murals in his *Oeuvre complète* (1946) and in *L'Architecture d'aujourd'hui* (1948), Gray's house was referred to as "a house in Cap-Martin"; her name was not even mentioned.[17] Later on, Le Corbusier actually got credit for the design of the house and even for some of its furniture.[18] Today the confusion continues, with many writers attributing the house to Badovici alone or, at best, to Badovici and Gray, and some still suggesting that Le Corbusier had collaborated on the project. Gray's name does not figure, even as footnote, in most histories of modern architecture, including the most recent and ostensibly critical ones.

"What a narrow prison you have built for me over a number of years, and particularly this year through your vanity," Badovici wrote to Le Corbusier in 1949 about the whole episode (in a letter that Adam thinks may have been dictated by Gray herself).[19] Le Corbusier's reply is clearly addressed to Gray:

"You want a statement from me based on my worldwide authority to show – if I correctly understand your innermost thoughts – to demonstrate 'the quality of pure and functional architecture' which is manifested by you in the house at Cap Martin, and has been destroyed by my pictorial interventions. OK, you send me some photographic documents of this manipulation of pure functionalism. . . . Also send some documents on Castellar, this U-boat of functionalism; then I will spread this debate in front of the whole world." [20]

Now Le Corbusier was threatening to carry the battle from the house into the newspapers and architectural periodicals. But his public position completely contradicted what he had expressed privately. In 1938, the same year he would go on to paint the mural *Graffite à Cap Martin*, Le Corbusier had written a letter to Gray, after having spent some days in E.1027 with Badovici, in which he acknowledges not only her sole authorship but also how much he likes the house: "I am so happy to tell you how much those few days spent in your house have made me appreciate the rare spirit which dictates all the organization, inside and outside, and gives to the modern furniture – the equipment – such dignified form, so charming, so full of spirit" (fig. 7). [21]

Why, then, did Le Corbusier vandalize the very house he loved? Did he think that the murals would enhance it? Certainly not. Le Corbusier had repeatedly stated that the role of the mural in architecture is to "destroy" the wall, to dematerialize it. In a letter to Vladimir Nekrassov in 1932, he writes: "I admit the mural not to enhance a wall, but on the contrary, as a means to violently destroy the wall, to remove from it all sense of stability, of weight, etc." [22] The mural for Le Corbusier is a weapon against architecture, a bomb. "Why then to paint on the walls . . . at the risk of killing architecture?" he asks in the same letter, and then answers, "It is when one is pursuing another task, that of telling stories." [23] So what, then, is the story that he so urgently needs to tell with *Graffite à Cap Martin*?

We will have to go back once more to Algiers. In fact, Le Corbusier's complimentary letter to Gray, sent from Roquebrune–Cap Martin on April 28, 1938, bears the letterhead, "Hôtel Aletti Alger." Le Corbusier's violation of Gray's house and identity is consistent with his fetishization of Algerian women. One might even argue that the child in this mural reconstitutes the missing (maternal) phallus, whose absence, Freud argues, organizes fetishism. In these terms, the endless drawing and redrawing is a violent substitution that required the house, domestic space, as prop. Violence is organized around or through the house. In both Algiers and Cap Martin, the scene starts with an intrusion, the carefully orchestrated occupation of a house. But the house is, in the end, effaced – erased from the Algiers drawings, defaced at Cap Martin.

Significantly, Le Corbusier describes drawing itself as the occupation of a "stranger's house." In his last book, *Creation Is a Patient Search*, he writes: "By working with our hands, by drawing, we enter the house of a stranger, we are enriched by the experience, we learn."[24] Drawing, as has often been noted, plays a crucial part in Le Corbusier's appropriation of the exterior world. He repeatedly opposes his technique of drawing to photography: "When one travels and works with visual things – architecture, painting or sculpture – one uses one's eyes and draws, so as to fix deep down in one's experience what is seen. Once the impression has been recorded by the pencil, it stays for good – entered, registered, inscribed. The camera is a tool for idlers, who use a machine to do their seeing for them."[25] Statements such as this have gained Le Corbusier the reputation of having a phobia for the camera – despite the crucial role of photography in his work. But what is the specific relationship between photography and drawing in Le Corbusier?

The sketches of the Algerian women were not only redrawings of live models but also redrawings of postcards (fig. 8). One could even argue that the construction of the Algerian women in French postcards, widely circulated at the time,[26] would have informed Le Corbusier's live drawings in the same way that, as Zeynep Çelik notes, Le Corbusier precisely reenacts the images of foreign cities (Istanbul or Algiers, for example) constructed by postcards and tourist guides when he actually enters these cities. In these terms, he not only "knew what he wanted to see,"[27] as Çelik says, but saw what he had already seen (in pictures). He "entered" those pictures. He inhabits the photographs. The redrawings of the *Les Femmes d'Alger* are also more likely to have been realized, as von Moos points out, from postcards and reproductions than from the original painting in the Louvre.[28] So what, then, is the specific role

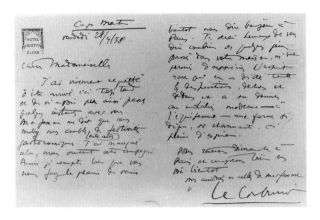

FIG. 7

Letter from Le Corbusier to Eileen Gray, in which he praises E.1027. Roquebrune–Cap Martin, April 28, 1938. Note the letterhead: Hôtel Aletti Alger

FIG. 8

"Femmes kabyles," postcard bought by Le Corbusier in Algiers in 1931

of the photographic image in the fetishistic scene of the *Femmes de la Casbah* project?

The fetish is *"pure presence,"* writes Victor Burgin, "and how many times have I been told that photographs 'lack presence,' that paintings are to be valued *because of their presence!*"[29] This separation between painting and photography organizes the dominant understanding of Le Corbusier's relationship to photography. What these accounts seem to ignore is that here the drawing, the handcrafted artistic meditation, is done "after" the photograph: the art reproduction, the postcard, the photograph.

In fact, the whole mentality of the *Femmes de la Casbah* drawings is photographic. Not only are they made from photographs but they are developed according to a repetitive process in which the images are systematically reproduced on transparent paper, the grid of the original graph paper allowing the image to be enlarged to any scale. This photographic sensibility becomes most obvious with the murals at Roquebrune–Cap Martin. Traditionally, they have been understood as a paradigm of Le Corbusier the painter, the craftsman detached from mechanical reproduction, an interpretation to which Le Corbusier himself has contributed with the circulation of that famous photograph of him, naked, working at one of the murals (fig. 9). This is the only nude image of him that we know, and that it had to be here, in this scene, is telling. What is normally overlooked is that *Graffite à Cap Martin* was not conceived on the wall itself. Le Corbusier used an electric projector to enlarge the image of a small drawing onto the 2.5 x 4 meter white wall where he etched the mural in black.

It is said that in using black Le Corbusier was thinking about Picasso's *Guernica* of the year before, and that Picasso, in turn, was so impressed with the mural at Cap Martin that it prompted him to do his own versions of the *Femmes d'Alger*. Apparently Picasso drew Delacroix's painting from memory and was later *"frappé"* to find out that the figure that he had painted in the middle, lying down, with her legs crossed, was not in the Delacroix.[30] It was, of course, *Graffite à Cap Martin* that he remembered, the reclining crossed-legged woman (inviting but inaccessible), Le Corbusier's symptomatic representation of Gray. But if Le Corbusier's mural had so impressed him, why did Picasso choose not to see the swastika inscribed on the chest of the woman on the right? The swastika may be yet one more sign of Le Corbusier's political opportunism (we must remember that the mural was done in 1938). But the German soldiers, who occupied the house during World War II, may not have seen the swastika either, for this very wall was found riddled with bullet holes, as if it had been the site of some execution.

The mural was a black and white photograph. Le Corbusier's fetish is photographic. Photography, too, has been read in terms of the fetish. Victor Burgin writes: "Fetishism thus accomplishes that separation of knowledge from belief characteristic of representation; its motive is the unity of the subject. The photograph stands to the subject-viewer as does the fetished object. . . . We know we see a two-dimensional surface, we believe we look through it into three-dimensional space, we cannot do both at the same time – there is a coming and going between knowledge and belief."[31]

So if Le Corbusier "enters the house of a stranger" by drawing, could "the house" stand in here for the photograph? By drawing he enters the photograph that is itself a stranger's house, occupying and reterritorializing the space, the city, the sexualities of the other by reworking the image. Drawing on and in photography is the instrument of colonization. The entry to the house of a stranger is always a breaking and entering – there being no entry without force no matter how many invitations. Le Corbusier's architecture depends in some way on specific techniques of occupying yet gradually effacing the domestic space of the other.

Like all colonists, Le Corbusier did not think of it as an invasion but as a gift. When recapitulating his life work five years before his death, he symptomatically wrote about Algiers and Cap Martin in the same terms: "From 1930 L-C devoted twelve years to an uninterrupted study of Algiers and its future. . . . Seven great schemes (seven enormous studies) were prepared *free of charge* during those years"; and later, "1938–39. Eight mural paintings (*free of charge*) in the Badovici and Helen Grey house at Cap Martin."[32] No charge for the discharge. Gray was outraged; now even her name was defaced. And renaming is, after all, the first act of colonization. Such gifts cannot be returned.

FIG. 9

Le Corbusier painting one of
the murals in E.1027

P.S. In 1944, the retreating German Army blew up Gray's apartment in Menton (Saint-Tropez), having vandalized E.1027 and Tempe à Pailla (her house in Castellar). She lost everything. Her drawings and plans were used to light fires.

P.P.S. On August 26, 1965, the endless redrawing of the *Femmes de la Casbah* still unfinished, Le Corbusier went from E.1027 down to the sea and swam to his death.

P.P.P.S. In 1977, a local mason in charge of some work in the house "mistakenly" demolished the mural *Graffite*.[33] I like to think that he did so on purpose. Gray had spent almost three years living on the site in complete isolation, building the house with the masons, having lunch with them every day. She did the same thing when building her house at Castellar. The masons knew her well; in fact, they loved her and they hated the arrogant Badovici. They understood perfectly what the mural was about. They destroyed it. In so doing, they showed more enlightenment than most critics and historians of architecture.

COLOMINA

P.P.P.P.S. Since then, the mural has been reconstructed in the house using photographs. It reemerged from its original medium. The occupation continues.

1. Peter Adam, *Eileen Gray: Architect/Designer* (New York: Harry N. Abrams, 1987), 174.
2. Letter from Marie Louise Schelbert to Stanislaus von Moos, February 14, 1969, as quoted by von Moos in "Le Corbusier as Painter," *Oppositions* 19–20 (1980), 93.
3. James Thrall Soby, "Le Corbusier, Muralist," *Interiors* (1948), 100.
4. Le Corbusier, *My Work*, trans. James Palmes (London: The Architectural Press, 1960), 50.
5. Samir Rafi, "Le Corbusier et 'Les Femmes d'Alger,'" *Revue d'histoire et de civilisation du Maghreb* (Algiers) (January 1968), 51.
6. Letter from Jean de Maisonseul to Samir Rafi, January 5, 1968, as quoted by Stanislaus von Moos in "Le Corbusier as Painter," 89.
7. From several conversations of both Le Corbusier and Ozenfant with Samir Rafi in 1964, as quoted by Samir Rafi in "Le Corbusier et 'Les Femmes d'Alger,'" 51.

8. Von Moos, 91.

9. Conversation of Ozenfant with Samir Rafi, June 8, 1964, as quoted by Samir Rafi in "Le Corbusier et 'Les Femmes d'Alger,'" 52.

10. Von Moos, 93.

11. Rafi, 54–55.

12. Ibid., 60.

13. In *My Work,* Le Corbusier refers to the mural as *Graffiti at Cap Martin.* In "Le Corbusier as Painter," Stanislaus von Moos labels the mural *Three Women (Graffite à Cap Martin),* and in "Le Corbusier et 'Les Femmes d'Alger,'" Samir Rafi labels the final composition from which the mural was derived *"Assemblage des trois femmes: Composition définitive.* Encre de Chine sur papier calque. 49.7 x 64.4 cm. Coll. particulière. Milan."

14. Letter from Marie Louise Schelbert to Stanislaus von Moos, February 14, 1969, as quoted by von Moos, p. 93.

15. Le Corbusier, *Vers une architecture* (Paris: Crès, 1923), 196. The passage here referred to is omitted in the English version of the book.

16. Adam, 311.

17. See Adam, 334–35. No caption of the photographs of the murals published in *L'Architecture d'aujourd'hui* mentions Eileen Gray. In subsequent publications, the house is either simply described as "Maison Badovici" or credited directly to Badovici. The first recognition since the thirties of Gray as architect came from Joseph Rykwert, "Un Ommagio a Eileen Gray – Pioniera del Design," *Domus* 468 (December 1966), 23-25.

18. For example, in an article entitled "Le Corbusier, Muralist," published in *Interiors* (June 1948), the caption of the murals at Roquebrune–Cap Martin reads: "Murals, interior and exterior, executed in sgraffito technique on white plaster, in *a house designed by Le Corbusier and P. Jeanneret,* Cap Martin, 1938 (my emphasis)." In 1981, in *Casa Vogue* 119 (Milan), the house is described as "Firmata Eileen Gray – Le Corbusier" (signed Eileen Gray and Le Corbusier), and an Eileen Gray sofa as "pezzo unico di Le Corbusier" (unique piece by Le Corbusier), as quoted by Jean Paul Rayon and Brigitte Loye in "Eileen Gray architetto 1879–1976," *Casabella* 480 (May 1982), 38–42.

19. "Quelle réclusion étroite que m'a faite votre vanité depuis quelques années et qu'elle m'a faite plus particulièrement cette année." Letter from Badovici to Le Corbusier, December 30, 1949, Fondation Le Corbusier, as quoted by Brigitte Loye in *Eileen Gray 1879–1976: Architecture Design* (Paris: Analeph/J. P. Viguier, 1983), 86; English translation in Adam, 335.

20. "Vous réclamez une mise au point de moi, couverte de mon autorité mondiale, et démontrant – si je comprends le sens profond de votre pensée – 'la qualité d'architecture fonctionnelle pure' manifesté par vous dans la maison de Cap Martin et anéantie par mon intervention picturale. D'ac [sic], si vous me fournissez les documents photographiques de cette manipulation fonctionnelle pure: 'entrez lentement'; 'pyjamas'; 'petites choses'; 'chaussons'; 'robes'; 'pardessus et parapluies'; et quelques documents de Castellar, ce sous-marin de la fonctionnalité: Alors je m'efforcerai d'étaler le débat au monde entier." Letter from Le Corbusier to Badovici, Fondation Le Corbusier, as quoted in Loye, 83–84; English translation in Adam, 335–36.

21. Letter from Le Corbusier to Eileen Gray, Roquebrune–Cap Martin, April 28, 1938, as quoted in Adam, 309–10.

22. "J'admets la fresque non pas pour mettre en valeur un mur, mais au contraire comme un moyen pour détruire tumultueusement le mur, lui enlever toute notion de stabilité, de poids, etc." Le Corbusier. Le passé à réaction poétique, exh. cat. (Paris: Caisse Nationale des Monuments Historiques et des Sites/Ministère de la Culture et de la Communication, 1988), 75.

23. "Mais pourquoi a-t-on peint les murs des chapelles au risque de tuer l'architecture? C'est qu'on poursuivait une autre tâche, qui était celle de raconter des histoires." Ibid.

24. Le Corbusier, Creation Is a Patient Search (New York: Frederick Praeger, 1960), 203.

25. Ibid., 37.

26. About French postcards of Algerian women circulating between 1900 and 1930, see Malek Alloula, The Colonial Harem (Minneapolis: University of Minnesota Press, 1986).

27. Zeynep Çelik, "Le Corbusier, Orientalism, Colonialism," Assemblage 17 (1992), 61.

28. Von Moos, 93.

29. Victor Burgin, "The Absence of Presence," in Burgin, The End of Art Theory: Criticism and Postmodernity (Atlantic Highlands, N.J.: Humanities Press International, 1986), 44 (his emphasis).

30. Rafi, 61.

31. Victor Burgin, "Modernism in the Work of Art," 20th Century Studies 15–16 (December 1976). Reprinted in Burgin, 19. See also Stephen Heath, "Lessons from Brecht," Screen 15 (1974), 106 ff.

32. Le Corbusier, My Work, 50–51 (my emphasis).

33. Von Moos, 104.

Colomina's Web: Reply to Beatriz Colomina

SYLVIA LAVIN

It has often been supposed that the first architecture was domestic and that the first element used to establish this domestic space was a fabric. Even before Gottfried Semper's now-famous enumeration in *The Four Elements of Architecture*, primitive huts were often represented as made of woven sticks or understood to be constructed out of fabric, like a tent (fig. 1). Equally, it has often been supposed that the weaving of textiles is archetypally women's work.[1] Although these traditions are ancient, study of this type of contribution by women to the foundations of architecture has until recently been neglected in favor of emphasizing women's containment by architecture. I would like to suggest that Beatriz Colomina uses the "battle lines" of her paper to spin a web, to weave a fabric that describes a new house, a kind of contemporary hut. Catching within this ensnaring net a complex combination of hitherto unmentionable issues, Colomina offers an understanding of domestic space radically different from that permitted by the long line of primitive huts with which we are familiar.

One of the extraordinary qualities of Colomina's cloth is the huge, almost promiscuous number of threads that she has joined together in its making. I say promiscuous because she has entwined a series of ideas, events, and accidents that would normally be thought of as not properly belonging together. For example, according to more conventional models of historical study, the fact that E.1027 happened to have been occupied during World War II, or that Le Corbusier – long after the house had been designed and built – happened to die there, would have been considered incidental to the proper story of the house itself. But as Colomina so

183

clearly demonstrates, Gray's house never had a proper history. To the contrary, these older models of historical inquiry – based on what have come to be understood as patriarchal notions of autonomy, authorship, and intentionality – betrayed the work of Eileen Gray. Rather than merely erect a new canon in which Gray might have a place, as though she had been simply and benignly overlooked, Colomina reveals how these accidents and happenstances created a history from which Gray was actively excluded. By spinning these new tales, Colomina uncovers the structural conditions that make domestic violence possible and that use the presumed sanctity of the house as shelter for this abuse.

Colomina's essay focuses on containment and occupation as two of the most important of these conditions. The analysis of Gray's house being surveilled by Le Corbusier, its walls being occupied by his murals, evolves, in Colomina's essay, into a strategy complicit with the use of drawing and photography as instruments of colonization, and the use of the media as new tools for the containment of public space. One possibility opened up by this focus is the opportunity to disentangle Gray from Le Corbusier, for the most active agent in the history of E.1027 has been Le Corbusier himself, and his authority, while increasingly undermined and enmeshed in a complex sociohistorical matrix, remains in some way dominant. This concern for male agency and its desire to contain the feminine not only tends to overshadow any independent attention to Gray's work but, by conflating desire with success, also risks reconfining her within the limited status of victim.[2] In contrast, I would like to tug at a few of these threads to see if within these various models of containment and occupation there is ever any possibility of escape.

E.1027 can itself be thought of as a place of escape, for it is one of several houses and environments that Gray built in an effort to begin again – to escape a previous life.[3] Le Corbusier's *cabanon* is even more obviously an escape, as it aligns itself with that whole tradition of rustic retreats from the pressures of urban life (fig. 2).[4] The landscape in which these two houses did battle, so to speak, is also the main feature they share: both use nature as architecture's "other" and as a space of renewal and regeneration. Indeed, E.1027 and the *cabanon* can be seen as versions of primitive huts, not in the sense that they offer themselves as models

FIG. I

Primitive huts in Claude
Perrault's 1684 edition of *Les Dix
Livres d'architecture de Vitruve*

FIG. 2

Le Corbusier's *cabanon* at
Roquebrune–Cap Martin

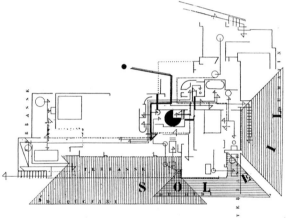

FIG. 3

Eileen Gray. E.1027 living room
with mural by Gray

FIG. 4

Diagrammatic plan of E.1027
showing the passage of the sun

and paradigms of new buildings by posing as originals, but because they seem to offer access to a life outside the rules of civilized behavior and conventional architecture. This aspect of modern primitivism has received a great deal of attention with regard to painting and sculpture, but less so in relation to architecture.

It is in terms of seeking "escape hatches" and "leaks" in the boundaries of normative architecture that some interesting differences between Gray and Le Corbusier emerge. E.1027 is, in fact, riddled with what might be called secret passages, hidden escape routes that have little to do with conventional windows and doors. While Le Corbusier reconsidered the notion of the window, he nevertheless conferred on it the importance of a traditionally privileged architectural element; Gray's work instead suggests other means of relating interiority and exteriority, sociality and subjectivity. The name of the house, E.1027, is written as a cryptogram, both asking and refusing to be decoded. Maps and stencils throughout the house remind the visitor of types of movement uncontainable by architectural interiors and literally invite the spectator *au voyage* (fig. 3).[5] Plans of the house trace the movement of the sun in relation to the movement of occupants, as though attempting to capture these ceaseless peregrinations (fig. 4). Gray herself said that the house had been designed in the "camping style," a style of territorial impermanence, of being on the run, being mobile.[6]

Le Corbusier, in stark contrast, seems to have planted himself on the Roquebrune–Cap Martin site permanently.[7] Although primitivizing, the hut he built for himself is totally stable and entrenched, boxlike and closed off to the external world. The very fact that the *cabanon* was placed so as to serve as an observation platform transformed the site into property, a place that demanded constant surveillance. The way he walked the coastline, marking the territory, was a means of claiming it, almost as though he were leaving his scent and scratches for others to recognize.[8] The clearest articulation of Le Corbusier's attitude toward territorialization and spatial striation seems to lie in his murals. At the time they were painted there was a keen and widespread interest in cave painting, in the marks left on walls by what were presumed to be primitive men. The title Le Corbusier gave them, *graffiti,* is associated with spontaneous and unlettered scratches. His claim that the particular walls of Gray's house that he chose as his easels needed the addition of "spiritual value" (as though he alone could provide the house with a link to some earlier, less compromised age), and the fact that he selected this of all possible places to have himself photographed nude – raw and uncooked – seems to suggest precisely a kind of primitive marking in which Le Corbusier sets himself up as a modern cave painter with the corollary that E.1027 becomes a cave.[9]

Do these two shelters, by Gray and by Le Corbusier, not reveal themselves, then, as differing models of primitive huts? Gray, living on the site like a hunter-gatherer, with her house understood as a tent, and Le Corbusier, dug into the ground, protected by his cave? Above all, did Gray's tent offer her a means to evade the prison in which she said Le Corbusier had placed her? Can the feminine, in fact, be so readily contained? Or, when we repeat the conclusion of Peter Adam, Gray's biographer, that Le Corbusier, by painting his murals on her walls, had raped her, are we not crediting, still, Le Corbusier with a measure of success that we do not confer on Gray?[10] Both these architects held highly developed positions and attitudes toward making and marking, toward stasis and mobility, toward spatiality and containment, that seem to merit equal consideration. By no means do I want to establish a series of simple and gendered oppositions – tent vs. cave, nomadic vs. sedentary – but rather to continue the search for ways to "think difference." When her essay is understood as a fabric woven of differently colored threads, a fabric that changes color depending on the conditions of perception, there emerges a way of "thinking difference" that does not, in Colomina's words, continue the occupation.

1. Within a strictly architectural context, associating the first structures with domesticity begins with Vitruvius in the 1st century B.C. From the Renaissance on, the domestic nature of originary architecture was maintained for a variety of reasons. Palladio, for example, argued that the temple had its origins in domestic space in order to explain and justify his use of the temple front on residential architecture, a conflation otherwise contrary to the rules of decorum. When architectural interest

began to shift beyond iconography and to include issues such as structure, greater attention was paid to the specific forms of these original buildings. Although the Abbé Laugier's hut, first illustrated in the second edition of his *Essai sur l'architecture* (Paris, 1755), which emphasizes the centrality of post and lintel construction, has come to be seen as paradigmatic, other and quite different versions of the hut exist. For example, Claude Perrault's edition of Vitruvius, first published in Paris in 1673, represents the primitive hut as woven out of sticks, as does E.-E. Viollet-le-Duc, in his *Histoire de l'habitation humaine* (Paris, 1875). A.-C. Quatremère de Quincy, in *De l'architecture égyptienne* (Paris, 1803), as well as in others of his numerous publications, argued that one type of hut was in fact a tent, made literally out of fabric. Semper's interest in what one might call alternative modalities of the hut can be seen in this context. See Semper's *The Four Elements of Architecture and Other Writings*, trans. Harry Francis Mallgrave and Wolfgang Herrmann (Cambridge: Cambridge University Press, 1989). For discussions of these traditions, see Joseph Rykwert, *On Adam's House in Paradise* (Cambridge, Mass.: MIT Press, 1981); Sylvia Lavin, *Quatremère de Quincy and the Invention of a Modern Language of Architecture* (Cambridge, Mass.: MIT Press, 1992); Mark Wigley, "Untitled: The Housing of Gender," in Beatriz Colomina, ed., *Sexuality and Space* (New York: Princeton Architectural Press, 1992), 327–89. On weaving and architecture, see Ann Bergren's essay in this volume.

2. In her essay "E.1027: The Nonheroic Modernism of Eileen Gray," *Journal of the Society of Architectural Historians* 53 (September 1994), 265–79, Caroline Constant sought to give the house and its designer their architectural due. However, the complexity of this endeavor is suggested by the organization of her essay, which is structured by a comparison of, and an opposition between, Le Corbusier and Gray. The essay's title accords Gray a negatively marked version of the epithet "heroic" (normally reserved for Le Corbusier), and the inescapable pressure of this structure reveals its effect.

3. Gray more or less abandoned her life in Paris to go to the south of France during the late 1920s. She later left E.1027 to go to Castellar. See Peter Adam, *Eileen Gray, Architect/Designer* (New York: Harry N. Abrams, 1987).

4. It might most profitably be compared to the philosophers' huts and hermitages that were built in eighteenth-century picturesque gardens.

5. In the living room of E.1027 a nautical map of the Caribbean bore the inscriptions "invitation au voyage," from Charles Baudelaire's *Paris Spleen* (1869), and "vas-y-

totor," Gray's nickname for her car. See Constant, 271.

6. For the context in which Gray used the term "camping style," see Adam, 207.

7. Permanence is of course an odd notion in this context, since the hut seems to have reproduced itself on the site. For example, the "Unité de Camping" was built adjacent to the *cabanon* in 1957. Furthermore, necessary extensive rebuildings and renovations of the hut cast doubt on its original permanence.

8. The small shoreline path that runs the full distance between Monte Carlo and Roquebrune is now called the Promenade Le Corbusier. The narrow walkway is marked with street signs and is signaled as a tourist site in the Michelin guide for the French Riviera.

9. In a statement published in "Unité," *L'Architecture d'aujourd'hui* 19, 1948, Le Corbusier described the effect of his murals as "an immense transformation. A spiritual value introduced throughout." Of course, to turn E.1027 into a cave is an attempt to naturalize it, a common approach to the feminine.

10. In discussing Le Corbusier's murals, Adam states: "It was rape. A fellow architect, a man she admired, had without her consent defaced her design" (Adam, 311). This seems a highly rhetorical formulation demanding careful consideration. Adam implies that he is finally articulating something that Gray meant and wanted to say but was unable to. Putting words in Gray's mouth seems a particularly problematic way of addressing her work and the ponderous silence it has had to endure. Adam's completely unsubstantiated yet highly sensational claim takes on the weight of truth as it proliferates and is reiterated in the growing literature on Gray. See, for example, Constant, 278, and Beatriz Colomina's essay in this volume.

Mirror Images: Technology, Consumption, and the Representation of Gender in American Architecture since World War II

JOAN OCKMAN

Two well-known images might be said to define American architecture in the first decades after World War II. One is Lever House, an early icon of International Style modernism, public face of American corporate capitalism (fig. 1). The other is Levittown, embodiment of suburban single-family domesticity, a vision of private life socially traditional and aesthetically conservative (fig. 2). How is this apparent schism in the built representation of postwar America to be explained? Why was a modernist aesthetic acceptable in the public realm but not in the private one? What is the relationship between this – literally and figuratively – high and low architecture? In what follows I shall attempt to answer these questions by postulating the existence of a kind of unstated "bargain" or social arrangement facilitated by basic assumptions about gender roles. From this analysis I shall then consider some significant shifts that have taken place more recently in the context of postmodernism.

It is necessary to begin by redescribing these two emblematic images in terms of the dominant ideologies they represented (fig. 3). The International Style as developed in the corporate and administrative framework of postwar America explicitly embodied the values of *technocracy* – the ethos of rationalism, bureaucracy, and technoscientific progress on which both big business and government were predicated. The exposed high-rise structural frame infilled with the repetitive modulations of an abstract curtain wall reflected the expansionist ambitions and laconic demeanor of American capitalism in an age of cold-war geopolitics.

FIG. 1
Skidmore, Owings & Merrill.
Lever House, New York City.
1952. Photograph by Ezra Stoller,
© ESTO

FIG. 2
Levittown, New York. 1948.
Photograph by Bernard Hoffman,
LIFE Magazine, © 1950, Time, Inc.

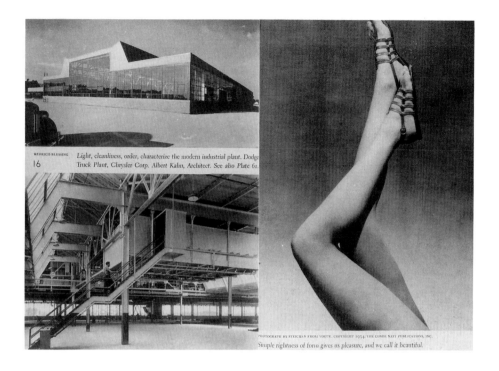

Light, cleanliness, order, characterize the modern industrial plant. Dodge Truck Plant, Chrysler Corp. Albert Kahn, Architect. See also Plate 61.

16

PHOTOGRAPH BY STEICHEN FROM VOGUE. COPYRIGHT 1934 THE CONDE NAST PUBLICATIONS, INC.

Simple rightness of form gives us pleasure, and we call it beautiful.

FIG. 3

Spread from Walter Dorwin
Teague, *Design This Day*, 2nd ed.
(The Studio Publications, 1946).
On the left, Albert Kahn's Dodge
Half-Ton Truck Plant, Chrysler
Corporation, Detroit, photographed
by Ken Hedrich, Hedrich-Blessing,
1938. On the right, photograph
by Edward Steichen for *Vogue*

FIG. 4

Henry Dreyfuss. Evening dress
designed for "*Vogue*'s Woman of
Tomorrow." Photograph by
Anton Bruehl for February 1,
1939, issue of *Vogue*

Ironically, this "strong silent type" came to represent the "new monumentality" that Sigfried Giedion had called for during the war years, although not, to be sure, in the civic sense he had envisioned. Its cold, hard, unornamental, technical image supplied the American government with what it wanted out of its professional elites during the cold-war period. This was, as historian Godfrey Hodgson has put it, "a maximum of technical ingenuity with a minimum of dissent."[1]

Having its major origin in the interwar modern movement in Europe, the postwar International Style was an outcome of the doctrine codified by Henry-Russell Hitchcock and Philip Johnson in their 1932 show at the Museum of Modern Art and of the teachings disseminated by the European emigrés who began at this time to head America's most prestigious schools of architecture. But American postwar modernism also had an indigenous source in the formidable imagery of native American technology: in engineering achievements like the Ford plant at River Rouge, the TVA dam, and, most recently, the arsenal of military production that had brought the United States and its allies to triumph in the war. As a recent exhibition at the National Building Museum in Washington illustrated,[2] the ascendancy of the postwar International Style coincided with the emergence of the American military-industrial complex. American architectural firms, led by offices like Skidmore, Owings & Merrill, designers of Lever House, reproduced these values in their own technically sophisticated and increasingly bureaucratic professional structures. SOM, still a moderate-sized firm at the beginning of the 1940s, got its major breakthrough during the war when it received a $60 million commission from the U.S. government to design a new town for fifty thousand people at Site x of the Manhattan Project, a location near Knoxville, Tennessee, where the atomic bomb was secretly being developed.

It is apparent that the imagery of technological power, highly rationalized and disciplined production, and wealth projected by this postwar architecture was a product of the male-dominated hierarchy whose expression it was and whose values were at stake in it (fig. 4). Geared to optimizing the labor of a new class of capitalist worker whom sociologists would dub "organization man," it reflected a major shift in social orientation. In the earlier phase of modern architecture, the urbanized factory worker had been the protagonist of culture, at least symbolically, and factories and social housing were the inspirational programs. In postwar America, corporate headquarters, embassy buildings, and detached single-family houses became architecture's defining instances, and the man in the gray flannel suit commuting to a wife and children in the suburbs its prototypical occupant (fig. 5). Nor is this characterization belied by the fact that behind the office tower's glass facade, the corporation's CEO furnished his penthouse suite in the style of Louis XIV or the executive dining room like an Edwardian gentleman's club; below, the middle managers, secretaries, and staff worked and lunched in "office landscapes" programmed for maximum functional efficiency. Indeed, the implementation of modernism as the prestige style of corporate capitalism was not a matter of a significant change in taste, as Russell Lynes pointed out in 1949 in his book *The Tastemakers*.[3] Rather, it was a symbolic display of power. The American philosopher George Santayana had observed four decades earlier: "The American Will inhabits the skyscraper; the American Intellect inhabits the colonial mansion. The one is the sphere of the American man; the other, at least predominantly, of the American woman. The one is all aggressive enterprise; the other is all genteel tradition."[4]

In the postwar period this split between the work world and domestic life characterized not only the upper class. For the burgeoning middle class, too, the domestic abode became, if not the place for the ritual enactment of gentility, at least the antithesis to the workaday routine and the repository of bourgeois comfort. The "male" culture of production found its complement in the "female" culture of consumption.

The postwar house thus reflected the other dominant ideology of the postwar period, that of *consumerism*. By the second quarter of this century, mass consumption had become central to the development of American capitalism. Even during the years of World War II, when consumer goods were greatly restricted because of war production needs, the public's appetite for postwar plenitude was whetted by the media and by government-sanctioned advertising (figs. 6, 7). Above all, it was feared that the economy, having reached peak productivity during the years of

FIG. 5

Skidmore, Owings & Merrill.
Manufacturers' Trust Company
Fifth Avenue Branch Bank,
New York City. 1954. View of
vault door through Fifth Avenue
facade. Photograph by Ezra
Stoller, © ESTO

WE'VE GOT THE RANGE

Not the kind that goes in the kitchen — we didn't make those
even in peace times. No, the range we're talking about is the distance
to the nearest Axis outpost from the muzzle of a U. S. howitzer.
Today Briggs men make cartridge cases of steel for these
guns — do it as well as they once made model kitchen and
bathroom fixtures. When folks can buy such things again, the
best will proudly display the name of Briggs.

BRIGGS *Beautyware* PLUMBING FIXTURES

BRIGGS MANUFACTURING COMPANY · DETROIT

FIG. 6

Advertisement for Briggs
Beautyware Plumbing Fixtures,
Architectural Forum, October
1943

FIG. 7

Advertisement for United
States Steel, *Architectural Forum*,
July 1943

FROM A FOXHOLE IN NEW GUINEA
PVT. HOUSTON DREAMS OF *Home*

"OH, BOY, when I get out of this
jungle, I'm going to
build me a sweet little cottage in California and stay there the rest of my
natural life. It won't be big but it'll have
every convenience I can cram into it . . .
a shower with *hot and cold* running
water for each bedroom . . . a handy
little kitchen . . . and a certain girl
named Sally who knows how to make a
juicy steak sit up and say papa."

What kind of homes will the boys
want when they get back from the wars
in 194X? They've been fighting for a
memory of home—a home better than
anything else they've found in foreign
countries. They'll be tired of strange

places—and they'll want something not
too different from the home they left
behind.

One thing you can be sure of, this
mechanized war has given our fighters
a healthy respect for the value and ver-
satility of steel.

For post-war houses, steel will be increasingly important. Because it lends
itself to mass production methods, steel
windows, steel kitchen cabinets, pressed
steel bathtubs, sinks and lavatories can
be made cheaper and will cost less to
install.

Prefabricated steel stairs, clothes
closets, shower cabinets will reduce
costs. Steel roofing, gutters, and down-
spouts will give the most economical
service obtainable over a period of years.

Porcelain enamel, in a variety of colors, will give the architect something
new to work with. It can be made into
attractive paneling for bathrooms and
into colorful maintenance-free shingles
for roofing and a host of other products.

The war has speeded development of
new steels, many of which will be available when the fighting is over. Our new
booklet, "85 Ways to Make a Better
Home" will show you what's new in
steel products. Write for a copy.

U·S·S
BUILDING STEELS

CARNEGIE-ILLINOIS STEEL CORPORATION, *Pittsburgh and Chicago*
COLUMBIA STEEL COMPANY, *San Francisco*
TENNESSEE COAL, IRON & RAILROAD COMPANY, *Birmingham*
United States Steel Supply Company, Chicago, *Warehouse Distributors* · United States Steel Export Company, New York

UNITED STATES STEEL

emerging mobilization, would slide back into a depression if conversion from a military to a domestic economy did not occur rapidly. Postwar planners now spoke of "mobilizing for abundance." Crucial to the viability of the economy's domestic sector was the low- and middle-cost housing market. During the war years, job-hungry architects and an eager building industry indulged in wildly optimistic predictions about the postwar housing market. Nor did their optimism prove unfounded. In the unprecedented boom that followed the war, the suburban dream house became a form of compensation for the privations and sacrifices endured during the years of war and economic stagnation, a realization of the material prosperity to which Americans considered themselves at long last entitled. As the postwar office building became a machine for streamlined white-collar production, so the private house became a machine especially for white middle-class consumption.

It was a machine, however, that dissembled its mechanistic nature. If the American public momentarily became intrigued during the war years with Bucky Fuller's Dymaxion Dwelling Machine (fig. 8) – whose advantages Fuller had been proselytizing for more than a decade with the question, "Madam, do you know how much your house weighs?" – the sheen of a lightweight metal domicile quickly wore off in comparison with the more rooted-looking Cape Coddage offered by a canny developer like William J. Levitt.

"Home, in the American dream, is a quaint little white cottage, shyly nestled in a grove of old elms or maples, bathed in the perfume of lilacs, and equipped with at least one vine-covered wall. Its steep gabled roof, covered with rough, charmingly weathered shingles, shows a slight sag in the ridge. The eaves come down so low that one can almost touch them. Tiny dormers on one side poke themselves through the old roof and let in light through tiny-paned windows to the upstairs bedrooms. In front of the house there is invariably a picket fence, with day lilies poking their heads between the white palings. Let into the fence, at the end of a flagstone walk bordered with alyssum and verbena, is a swinging gate, where husband and wife embrace tenderly as he dashes for the 8:11 and the workaday world." [5]

FIG. 8

R. Buckminster Fuller. Dymaxion
house prototype, manufactured and
erected by Beech Aircraft, Wichita,
Kansas, 1945

This was the nostalgic idyll that George Nelson and Henry Wright set out to dispel in their book of 1945, *Tomorrow's House*, but nothing that they or other modernist proselytizers had to offer seemed able to replace it. Levittown was a margarine substitute, but an appealing one for the thousands of returning GIs and their wives. The fact that like the Dymaxion its Taylorized construction process contradicted its traditionalist image was not a fatal defect for buyers who were, in no small measure, purchasing a life-style, a dream. Moreover, the Levitt was hardly lacking in up-to-dateness; it came equipped with one or more of the latest conveniences, from Bendix washing machines to "built-in" television sets. The idea of the built-in derived from modernist spatial concepts, but Levitt was quick to realize its economic benefit: it qualified equipment to be paid on the mortgage. The buyer was also given, in the later Levitt developments, some limited choice as to plan type, elevation details, and finishes. The marketing strategy of "standardized diversity" catered at least minimally to the deep American desire for individualism.[6] William Levitt appears to have understood the compromise that a large segment of the American public wanted as Fuller and other architects promoting a more radical image of the low-cost house did not. This is not to suggest that Levitt was a populist. He was a businessman. Acknowledging himself that the renderings in his sales brochures could appear deceptive – they portrayed Levittown houses set on spacious, private lawns surrounded by lush foliage – he quipped, "The masses are asses."[7]

But the postwar campaign to redomesticate women after their brief taste of equal employment opportunity in the wartime work force was abetted not only by the tangible amenities of the new suburban dream house but also by its essentialism. Women, voluntarily making room in the job market for the returning veterans, were induced or seduced to return to home and child-rearing through intensive propaganda by government, businessmen, psychologists, religious leaders, and others on behalf of "family values." As one feminist historian has commented, "'Rosie the Riveter' was . . . transformed with dizzying speed from a wartime heroine to a neurotic, castrating victim of penis envy."[8] The mythological imagery of the house as a nest and haven presided over by a nurturing mother figure was fundamental in reestablishing the traditional division

A house with a future

FIG. 9

Cover of a pamphlet by Harwell Hamilton Harris for a promotional series entitled *Revere's Part in Better Living*, published by Revere Copper and Brass Inc., 1943

FIG. 10

Cover of a pamphlet by George Nelson for the series *Revere's Part in Better Living*, 1943

Your children could romp here while you shop...

of labor in the American family. The new tract divisions served in a literal way to enforce the gulf of space and time between private life and
work world. Women's separation increased along the lengthening network of highways; homemaking became increasingly distanced from the
making of history.[9]

Nor, to most women at the time, did it seem a bad bargain. After
the traumatic dislocations of the war, stability and nest building came as
a welcome relief for many. So did economic prosperity, which meant
that the domestic abode, for all its cozy image, did not need to have
humble aspirations (fig. 9). It could be added to, or if rendered obsolete
by the family's changing needs and status, shed for a new and larger
home. Planned obsolescence became an important economic strategy
after the war; an approach similar to that used for selling automobiles
had its application to mass-market housing. Meanwhile, the cornucopia
of new domestic goods churned out by a retooled economy was aggres-
sively marketed to the new generation of housewives, the appointed
"managers of consumption," as Margaret Mead described them in 1948.[10]
While their husbands strove to move upward in the corporate hierarchy,
the "wives of management"[11] attended to the parallel task of keeping up
with the neighboring Joneses. Wartime savings fueled a postwar spending spree, heavily abetted by advertising. Having from its inception
targeted "Mrs. Consumer" as the prime object of its sales pitch, American
advertising increased sixfold between 1920 and 1950 and then doubled
again between 1951 and 1960.[12] Women who had remained on the home
front during the war, encouraged in a time of rationing to be "generals
in their own kitchens," now were assured that the newest gadgetry would
free them from domestic "drudgery" – an oft-repeated Dickensian word.
The myth of the happy housewife – the flawed logic that a streamlined
kitchen was sufficient to liberate a woman from a patriarchal society's
oppression – was parodied by British Pop artist Eduardo Paolozzi in a
1948 collage entitled *It's a Psychological Fact Pleasure Helps Your Disposition.*

Moreover, now that technology had presumably released women
from the burdens of old-fashioned housework, questions remained of
how they should spend their new leisure time. In an ironic turn, the
fundamental capitalist axiom "time is money" was reformulated for a

consumer society. Certainly as far as the advertising industry was concerned, leisure time was time available for consumption, for shopping (fig. 10). In his widely read book *The House and the Art of Its Design,* the architect Robert Woods Kennedy acknowledged, "Our general desire is for women to consume beautifully."[13] During the 1950s the beautiful consumers would play their part. At the beginning of the decade *Fortune* magazine forecast that they would incite $10 billion in spending on home construction and $12 billion on home furnishings.[14] It was Betty Friedan who explosively deconstructed this system ten years later, in 1963, in *The Feminine Mystique.* Stopping short of alleging a conscious conspiracy aimed at women, she wrote, "The perpetuity of housewifery, the growth of the feminine mystique, makes sense (and dollars) when one realizes that women are the chief customers of American business. Somehow, somewhere, someone must have figured out that women will buy more things if they are kept in the underused, nameless-yearning, energy-to-get-rid-of state of being housewives."[15]

It would seem, in short, that the prevailing dichotomy between Lever House and Levittown amounted to a highly efficient, eminently practical, and symbiotic social arrangement. In a society that sought simultaneously to promote maximum productivity and maximum consumption, the public and private spheres had separate but complementary roles to play. Architecture served to reproduce and reinforce this gendered social division, providing an efficacious image for each.

In actuality, of course, the two forms of representation were mirror images of a single system, two sides of the capitalist coin. Both Lever House and Levittown were predicated on highly rationalized and optimized production processes; both were geared to a postwar mass society. Where they differed was in the image they projected, in the one case of elite modernist aesthetics, in the other of midcult taste. Despite his antipathy for the latter, Theodor Adorno acknowledged the fundamental identity of these two antagonistic forms of the contemporary world: "Both [modernism and mass culture] bear the stigmata of capitalism, both contain elements of change. . . . They are torn halves of an integral freedom to which, however, they do not add up."[16]

Meanwhile, the image of architectural modernism, too, was becoming precisely that – an image. In the context of postwar America, of the cold war and McCarthyism, the social idealism that had animated the vanguard architecture of the 1920s began to appear naive or hollow. The postwar glass-grid skyscraper seemed duplicitous in its reference, its elegant, abstract transparency alluding to the utopian vision of a radiant, egalitarian, dynamically open society, while embodying the reality of panoptic, hierarchical bureaucracy. In an influential article published in 1951 entitled "Origins and Trends in Modern Architecture," the architect Matthew Nowicki characterized American architecture at this date as preoccupied more with structure and form than with function. Instead of following function, suggested Nowicki, form now followed form; moreover, he noted, the new architectural formalism was tending toward the "decoration of structure" (this almost twenty years before Denise Scott Brown and Robert Venturi would coin the concept of the decorated shed). Certainly the buildings produced in these years by young architects like Philip Johnson, Edward Durrell Stone, Minoru Yamasaki, and Paul Rudolph, and even older masters like Gropius and Le Corbusier, not to mention Frank Lloyd Wright, were undermining modernist orthodoxy with eclectic and personal inputs. Nowicki probably had in mind Ludwig Mies van der Rohe's famous details at Illinois Institute of Technology and the Lake Shore Drive apartments, where Mies used steel mullions more for expressive purposes than strictly structural ones, in writing, "The symbolic meaning of a support has also been rediscovered, and a steel column is used frankly as a symbol of structure even when it is not part of the structure itself."[17]

And precisely in this revelation of architecture as a system of arbitrary signs, in the dissociation between image and reality, in the use of design for purposes of "corporate identity" and "marketing strategy," in the recognition that modern architecture was simply another historical style – in all this, the transition from modernity to postmodernity took place. With this, I'd like to extend my argument about the relation between technology, consumption, and gender conceptions to the present period, although my comments here can only be very preliminary.

We have said that the postwar International Style was a symbolic representation of the virility of American technology. Starting in World

War II, however, a subtle change began to occur, even if culture was to take a number of years to register it. With the emergence of a so-called postindustrial economy, technological power began to be associated with something besides industrial hardware and large-scale, discrete mechanical objects – besides the rockets, bridges, munitions factories, not to mention grain elevators, airplanes, ocean liners, and plumbing fixtures that had defined modernity earlier. Advanced technology now also came to mean cybernetic processes, software systems, miniaturized electronics, artificial intelligence, telecommunications, and other sophisticated instrumentalities eluding physical form. *The imagination of power* inevitably began to take inspiration from the new logic of global networks, integrated circuits, microchips, smart weapons, virtual fields.[18] The penetration of these often invisible technologies into the unconscious – especially through the impact of advertising and the media on everyday life – served to unleash potent new images and desires. Alison and Peter Smithson wrote in 1956:

"Gropius wrote a book on grain silos,
Le Corbusier one on aeroplanes,
And Charlotte Perriand brought a new object to the office
every morning;
But today we collect ads."[19]

Architecture would remain no less bound than before to rehearse the technocratic background from which it sprang, but the repository from which it would draw its symbolic content would necessarily change with the new modes of production and reception.

At the same time, consumerism would also undergo a change. If gender stereotypes had previously served to reproduce the binary relations of production and consumption – consumption being marked as female and therefore socially less valuable – then increasingly, after World War II, these relations ceased to be so clear-cut. As Robert Bocock has written,

"The modern period was marked by [a] gender division between mothering and consumption, on the one hand, and production and making war on the other. The post-modern has been, by comparison, a period of peace in Western Europe, North America and Japan. This has allowed a change in gender roles for men. No longer required in large numbers as fighters, men, especially younger men, have become consumers too since the 1950s."[20]

Men, too, now construct their identities in terms of what they consume, from sports and cars to movies, food, and clothing. The sociopolitical emergence of gays within capitalist culture, with their frank patterns of consumption, has further challenged the traditional dichotomy that marks consumption as feminine and production as masculine, just as the new politics of childbearing, child rearing, and healthcare have expanded the concept of production to include women's biological reproduction and the whole hitherto excluded economy of the home. At the same time, the increasing participation of women in every echelon of the conventional work force, the shift of the workplace not only from city to suburbs but into the home itself, and the accelerating computerization of both work and everyday life have effectively blurred the lines between production and consumption, public and private realms, undoing the simple bargain between technocracy and consumerism that obtained in the postwar decades. The old dichotomy between home and history has been superseded by public/private relationships deeply inflected by the new commercially and technologically mediated conditions of contemporary life. As German film theorists Oskar Negt and Alexander Kluge have suggested in their book *The Public Sphere and Experience,* our concept of the public realm has to be rethought today across a broadly inclusive and interconnected horizon of social relations.[21] Going beyond traditional liberal civic models, such a reconceptualization of public space would extend to privately owned spaces of commerce and consumption (including, for example, shopping malls), as well as to those less physical and more ephemeral sites where public opinion and consciousness are formed – television and the movies, the print media, the computer internet.

But if the intrusion of commerce and sophisticated technology into every crevice of daily life can hardly be considered cause for comfort, it is also the case that the built representations of postmodern society are no longer charged so heavily with dichotomous gender stereotypes. Both the "softening" of technology and the universalizing of the consumer have obliged architecture to seek new forms of representation. In this context, the initial phase of postmodernist architecture, characterized by the decorative facade treatments of corporate buildings like Johnson's AT&T and civic ones like Michael Graves's Portland, may be described as "cross-dressing" – scandalous with respect to the "strong silent" typology, but symptomatic of the mixing up of technocratic and consumerist values and gender stereotypes in today's society. A current obsession on the part of many architects with using glass on the facade – no longer as a repetitive infill within a clearly articulated and primary structural frame, but as a screening element veiling the structure, or, as Diana Agrest has suggested in an article entitled "Architecture of Mirror/Mirror of Architecture," a reflective element dissolving materiality into paradox and disarticulating the conventional relationships between architectural language and image, surface and depth[22] – offers a further ambiguation of the postwar imagistic clarities.

The ideologies of technocracy and consumerism that we have inherited from the period after World War II are no less entrenched in contemporary architecture than they were at the moment when Lever House and Levittown were conceived. The design and practice of architecture continue to be bound up with the representation of power and the marketing of pleasure. I believe, however, that these twin imperatives are now less reinforced by, and reinforcing of, undesirable gender stereotypes. From a feminist perspective, this is something positive.

1. Godfrey Hodgson, "The Ideology of the Liberal Consensus," in William H. Chafe and Harvard Sitkoff, eds., *A History of Our Time: Readings on Postwar America* (New York: Oxford University Press, 1991), 133.

2. *World War II and the American Dream: How Wartime Building Changed a Nation*, with catalogue edited by Donald Albrecht (Cambridge, Mass.: MIT Press, 1995). See also Elizabeth Mock, ed., *Built in U.S.A. – 1932–1944* (New York: Museum of Modern Art, 1944).

3. Russell Lynes, *The Tastemakers* (New York: Harper & Brothers, 1949), 305–9.

4. George Santayana, *Winds of Doctrine: Studies in Contemporary Opinion* (London:

J. M. Dent, 1913), 188.

5. George Nelson and Henry Wright, *Tomorrow's House: How to Plan Your Post-War Home Now* (New York: Simon and Schuster, 1945), 4.

6. Stewart Ewen, *All Consuming Images: The Politics of Style in Contemporary Culture* (New York: Basic Books, 1988), 229. The unilevel ranch, almost equally popular at this date, especially in the West, represented a less nostalgic image of modern living; it appealed more for its easy life-style, however, than its aesthetic pretensions.

7. John Liell, "Levittown: A Study in Community Development" (Ph.D. diss., Yale University, 1952), 111; cited in Ewen, 227.

8. Karen Anderson, *Wartime Women: Sex Roles, Family Relations, and the Status of Women During World War II* (Westport, Conn.: Greenwood Press, 1981), 176. See also Maureen Honey, *Creating Rosie the Riveter: Class, Gender, and Propaganda During World War II* (Amherst: University of Massachusetts Press, 1984).

9. See Dorothy Dinnerstein, *The Mermaid and the Minotaur: Sexual Arrangements and Human Malaise* (New York: Harper & Row, 1976).

10. Margaret Mead, "The American Family as an Anthropologist Sees It," *American Journal of Sociology* 53 (1948), 454; cited in Robert H. Bremner and Gary W. Reichard, eds., *Reshaping America: Society and Institutions 1945–1960* (Columbus: Ohio State University Press, 1982), 4. It may, of course, be questioned to what extent women actually controlled the purse strings, especially where large purchases were concerned.

11. "The Wives of Management" is the title of a well-known article by William H. Whyte Jr., first published in *Fortune* 44 (October 1951), 68–88, 204–6. Whyte satirically sets out the rules according to which corporate wives should behave.

12. Mary P. Ryan, *Womanhood in America from Colonial Times to the Present* (New York: New Viewpoints, 1975), 260; Douglas T. Miller and Marion Nowak, *The Fifties: The Way We Really Were* (Garden City: Doubleday, 1975), 117.

13. Robert Woods Kennedy, *The House and the Art of Its Design* (New York: Reinhold, 1953), 40.

14. Cited in Ryan, 301.

15. Betty Friedan, *The Feminine Mystique* (1963) (Harmondsworth: Penguin, 1983), 181.

16. Letter from Adorno to Walter Benjamin (1936), cited in Thomas Crow, "Modernism and Mass Culture in the Visual Arts," in Francis Frascina, ed., *Pollock and After: The Critical Debate* (New York: Harper & Row, 1985), 263.

17. Matthew Nowicki, "Origins and Trends in Modern Architecture," *Magazine of Art*, November 1951; republished in Joan Ockman, ed., *Architecture Culture 1943–1968:*

A Documentary Anthology (New York: Rizzoli, 1993), 156.

18. On technology as symbolic form in architecture, a classic essay is Alan Colquhoun's "Symbolic and Literal Aspects of Technology" (1962), republished in Colquhoun, *Essays in Architectural Criticism: Modern Architecture and Historical Change* (Cambridge, Mass.: MIT Press, 1981), 26–30.

19. Alison and Peter Smithson, "But Today We Collect Ads," *Ark* 18 (November 1956), republished in David Robbins, ed., *The Independent Group: Postwar Britain and the Aesthetics of Plenty* (Cambridge, Mass.: MIT Press, 1990), 185.

20. Robert Bocock, *Consumption* (London: Routledge, 1993), 96.

21. See Oskar Negt and Alexander Kluge, *The Public Sphere and Experience* (1972), trans. Peter Labanyi, Jamie Daniel, and Assenka Oksiloff (Minneapolis: University of Minnesota Press, 1993).

22. Diana Agrest, "Architecture of Mirror/Mirror of Architecture," in Agrest, *Architecture from Without: Theoretical Framings for a Critical Practice* (New York: Princeton Architectural Press, 1991), 138–55.

Through the Looking Glass: Reply to Joan Ockman

DENISE SCOTT BROWN

"Things grow curiouser and curiouser," said Alice, as she fell down a hole and grew large then small. And we, as we grow and fall and pass, like Alice, through our own looking glasses, can see a curious new life unfolding before us, challenging us to question old ideas. Today the lenses of gender and ethnicity are upending conventional notions, infusing them with vitality just as, earlier this century, the perspectives of European immigrants and their children enlivened American arts and intellectuality.

Sectional views can engender social reappraisal and effect action. For example, women in the 1970s and 1980s brought changes to work life in America through the provisions they required to help them combine home and work. Among those who flocked to corporations then were women who later left when they hit the glass ceiling. Some started their own businesses, and these incubating enterprises may be signposts to the American economy of the next century. Productivity may rise as a result of women-induced work changes, and work for men and women will never be the same again. The home, too, has changed. As work has become more homely, home has become more work-like. Some of the beneficiaries have been men.

Joan Ockman presents a fascinating thesis on the historical period immediately preceding these changes. *Her* reflections through the looking glass of gender show mid-twentieth century technology and consumption mirroring each other. The technologically based architecture of the American corporation represents, for her, the macho male of the early post–World War II decades and is a metaphor for the military-industrial complex of that time. Inversely, 1950s and 1960s suburbia, typified by Levittown, represents the capitalist environment of maximum consumption, engendered to support postwar increases in goods production. Levittown was primarily a women's world.

These reinterpretations and recombinations of ideas on Modern[1] architecture and suburbia are examples of how new perspectives can mash the conventional wisdom. The word "perspectives" has an architectural ring. In another context, I have referred to a "worm's eye view," using a type of architectural perspective drawing to symbolize history – as I saw it – from the distaff side.[2] Perhaps the oppressed have a worm's eye view. Then who has the bird's-eye perspective on architecture: the king-maker critics? the new theorists? How should we as women and professional architects react to Ockman's gender-based perspectives? We may, in our turn, interpret today's housing and work environments.

In the late 1960s, Robert Venturi and I began our own interpretation of two emerging American environments: the commercial strip via its archetype, Las Vegas; and suburban residential sprawl, typified for us, too, by Levittown. We tried to dissect them using analytic tools derived from architecture, sociology, art history, and other fields. To see our material through other than architectural perspectives, we studied suburban housing environments and the images of houses purveyed by
real estate developers, television, film, and other media.

An important reason for using these commercial images was to question Modern orthodoxy from a perspective of social concern, but that is missed by most architects and critics even today. (It is particularly frustrating to see our work and thought associated with the blatant superficiality of Postmodernism when, in fact, it was derived so obviously from the social planners' critique of the 1960s.[3]) We saluted *early* Modernism not least for its social concern. As Modern images have moved, over the last ninety years, between east and west, Europe and
America, their symbolic meanings have shifted in interesting ways. The flat roof meant left-wing ideals in Germany long before it projected corporate enlightenment in America. Later, Modern architecture was reappropriated by the left as Communist architects borrowed from Oscar Niemeyer and Miami Beach for the Stalin Allee.

Were I to perform our Las Vegas and Levittown studies today, I would take account of America's changing demographic patterns, family forms, and multiculturalism. To the media selected for content analysis I would add retail sales catalogues, particularly for their depiction of house and garden items and clothing. Following Ockman's views of male consumption post-1980, I would examine the ways catalogues sell to men as well as to women.

Another noticeable change is the shifting pattern of workplaces. Levittown started as an outpost but was soon within driving distance of regional shopping malls. Work followed – enough of it to employ many suburbanites near their homes. Now we have "edge city" and even activities once thought to be tied to downtown – for example, financial services – are moving to the suburbs. There is also the prospect of the economy becoming a series of electronically linked cottage industries. This much-heralded shift may have less impact on living and working patterns than is predicted, but already one can learn, earn, and shop at home – all through the same computer screen.

Perhaps, in the end, some cultural activities will remain in the city and urban economies will depend increasingly on these for their support. This pattern has been emerging since the 1980s – for example, on Main Street in the Manayunk section of Philadelphia – if one includes the types of retail commercial uses that prefer old buildings as part of culture and recreation.

SCOTT BROWN

This is not necessarily a death knell for cities, architecture, or architects, but their roles do need rethinking. When and if work and production, goods and services, no longer determine transportation movements and housing choice is not tied to workplace (or the house *is* the workplace), then the whole urban pattern will have changed. Understanding the new work patterns and workplace options could be a challenge to architectural imagination. For example, when costs of travel to work are less constraining on peoples' housing choices, amenity will be an important determinant of location, and architects are strong on finding or defining amenity. Helping people to live and work and build well, in settings that are beautiful, could be an important task for architects.

Rethinking the urban housing environment to suit new family, living and working relationships could be a part of this task. A housing strategy for an urban region should be complex – the opposite of the mass-production, "tin lizzy" solutions architects have propounded for housing problems worldwide. All manner of choices for all manner of groups, cultures, ages, and classes, should exist, in and out of the city. Then the best cities would be those that offer the richest opportunities, many at the neighborhood level rather than at the individual house level. For example, medieval towns had communal food ovens; we, today, share the educating of children and sometimes the care of the elderly. What new apportionment of daily activities between home and neighborhood will best suit the evolving work and family lives of women, men, and children? Should the elementary school and the day care center be near the parents' home or near their workplaces? Architects should be helping to provide, in rich ways, for what is needed now and will be in the near future, given today's social and economic forces of change.

Joan Ockman uses one other lens in her reflection on twentieth-century technology and consumption: the lens of politics. In order for one to agree or disagree with her argument, one would have to know her political stance at the outset. From our studies I would ask: Is Levittown really conservative? Did the capitalists really lead buyers there by their noses? Did the Levittowners believe the ads? Did Levitt really think SCOTT BROWN "the masses [were] asses?" We know how carefully he watched people's reactions to the model houses, and that he built for several markets at once, a few houses at a time, leaving himself options for shifting with buyer preference.

Ockman also mentions "American culture." I'm not sure there is a single American culture. I prefer to talk of "cultures" and then to ask whether different cultures can be aggregated to support general statements about Levittown – or to make input to meaningful designs for city hall. While Ockman has admitted that the capitalists weren't all wrong, that their forecasts weren't all inaccurate, and that some of the changes they generated may even have been good, her statements on architecture in a capitalist society are, for me, too pat and insufficiently supported. Theorists in both architecture and the women's movement are, to my way of thinking, frequently fuzzy: Their speculations lack the discipline of scholarly backing. Now, arguably, the social sciences as "soft" sciences should not be held to the same order of accountability as is physics (the "physics envy" of the social sciences notwithstanding), but the danger lies in architecture and feminist theorists evolving conclusions from anecdotes and stereotypes – the same distortions that women, themselves, have suffered from – rather than from supportable findings. By contrast, the writings of Herbert Gans prove it is possible to make compelling and even polemical observations on cultures and groups without sacrificing scholarly rigor.[4]

I think it's OK for Adorno to make the grand categorical statements quoted by Ockman,[5] given his role in society and the aims of his polemic; but we, as architects and practitioners, makers of concrete things, recommenders of present action, might leave our statements a little more open or produce the research and studies to prove them. And because I can't do that, because I'm a practitioner not an academic (I use academic information for practical, professional purposes; I don't generate it), because I haven't done the research to prove categorical statements, I've learned to say "perhaps." I think this allows one to be more flexible, both as a creative person and as a professional trying to serve clients. Furthermore, ideologies come and go and functional needs change with time, yet our buildings may remain. So as a practitioner I must think of user requirements twenty years from now, not only, as a politician does, of how users may vote two years from now. I must try to persuade my client to think in these terms, too.

In all these ways we architects, *as architects*, should take a different stance from that of the politically identified writer, or from the one we ourselves may take as polemicists, publicists, and politicians – roles as open to us as to anyone else, but we should announce them. Meanwhile, the women's movement, in helping us to see our inherited ideologies in a new light, has opened the doors to all architects to build for new patterns of life and, whether affirming or negating our profession's ideologies, to act as idealists rather than ideologues.

SCOTT BROWN

215

1. "Modern" and "Postmodern" are capitalized to denote a style and an ideology rather than a way of designing buildings today.

2. Denise Scott Brown, "A Worm's Eye View of Recent Architectural History," *Architectural Record* (February 1984), 69–81.

3. Moreover, for the record, when in 1968 we "coin(ed) the concept of the decorated shed" (Ockman), we knew well Matthew Nowicki's concepts as excerpted in Lewis Mumford's *Roots of Contemporary American Architecture* (1952). Criticism of Mies's architecture as the "decoration of structure" was, as I recall, fairly widely made in the 1950s.

4. See, for example, Herbert Gans, *Middle American Individualism: The Future of Liberal Democracy* (New York: The Free Press, 1988).

5. See Ockman, 204.

SCOTT BROWN

Not a Muse: The Client's Role at the Rietveld Schröder House

ALICE T. FRIEDMAN

Notably missing from the history of modern architecture is any substantive discussion of the role of women clients as collaborators in design or as catalysts for architectural innovation. This failure of attention, together with the overvaluing of the individual architect as innovator, has contributed to the "star system" and distorts our understanding of the design process. Moreover, by neglecting the role of convention and gender ideology in shaping both architecture and social relations, historians not only overemphasize individual creativity, but they also perpetuate the false notion that buildings are to be valued primarily as isolated art objects.

Reinserting gender factors into historical inquiry results in a narrative strikingly different from the familiar surveys of architecture. For example, focusing on domestic architecture in Europe and the United States, one finds that a surprisingly large number of the most important houses by prominent architects in this century were designed for women clients or for non-traditional, woman-headed households.[1] The list includes Frank Lloyd Wright's Aline Barnsdall house (1919–23) in Hollywood, California, which was intended to serve as a semi-public residence at the center of a large "art-theater garden"; the Truus Schröder house (1924) in Utrecht, Holland, by Gerrit Rietveld; the Villa Stein–de Monzie (1927) at Garches by Le Corbusier, designed as an exhibition space and residence for four adults (a married couple, Michael and Sarah Stein, and their friend Mme Gabrielle de Monzie and her adopted daughter); Eileen Gray's own house E.1027 (1929), in Roquebrune–Cap Martin (see also Beatriz Colomina's and Sylvia Lavin's essays in this volume); Ludwig Mies van der Rohe's weekend house for Dr. Edith Farnsworth (1945–51) in Plano, Illinois;

Richard Neutra's Constance Perkins house (1955) in Pasadena, California; and Robert Venturi's house for his mother (1963) in Chestnut Hill, Philadelphia – as well as a handful of other, less famous examples.

These houses have a number of characteristics in common. First, they were all designed for relatively well-to-do, highly educated women. Although there is among these women a considerable range in wealth, privilege, and social status (from the heiress Aline Barnsdall to the college professor Constance Perkins), this range is small in comparison with the chasm that divides these women as a group from the majority of the population. Second, the houses were all designed for women who were able to turn to professional architects to work out individual solutions tailored to their needs. Third, the projects were all informed by a simple but radical notion: that the woman-headed household is something that can be actively chosen by women and need not be given second-class status; that such a household is not only a viable social entity but also an architectural entity, worthy of a carefully considered design response. Such representation required a fundamental departure from precedents of type in domestic architecture structured by conventional imagery and social relationships.[2]

While the conditions mentioned above may separate these houses and their clients from the mainstream in some obvious ways, there are fundamental aspects of program, gender, and type in domestic architecture that clearly transcend artistic, economic, and class differences. Since the mid-nineteenth century, conventional thinking about the middle- and upper-class home in Europe and the United States has focused on the idea that it should be protected as a private, family-oriented environment, separate from the public sphere of work.[3] Paired with this is the notion that the home is not only the locus of heterosexual reproduction and socialization but also a stage for ordering social and economic relations. "Home" and "family" have thus been traditionally defined by the patriarchal gender relations that structure them and connect them to the larger society. Nevertheless, while traditional wisdom may have suggested that a woman's place was in the home, it was also true that her status there was awarded to her by her husband and the male-dominated institutions of society as a whole. Within this system, the female-headed household represents a significant disjunction in architectural, economic, and social terms, even for elite women.[4]

Despite the rhetoric of social and technological change, the outlines of the conventional domestic program have remained constant throughout much of this century. Devoted primarily to non-work activities and the care of the body, the twentieth-century house is the locus of family activity as well as a place to entertain and impress guests, including those whose primary contact with family members may be in the workplace. In this context, the typical plan of the American and European single-family home has taken shape: the public and formal spaces, such as living rooms, family rooms, dining rooms, kitchens, and guest bathrooms, are located on the ground floor; the master bedroom, children's rooms, bathrooms, and other private spaces are located in relatively remote, protected areas.

The houses listed above challenge this model, particularly in plan (because it reflects changes in program, the plan, more than any other aspect of design, is the barometer of changes in gender relations that render conventional type-forms irrelevant). When the program shifts away from the patriarchal model, not only do the boundaries between the social environments inside and outside the home begin to blur, but also the spatial allocations within the house itself. For example, in all of these projects, the work/leisure distinction was one of the first elements to go. Work and "public" activities traditionally carried on outside the middle-class home – from light assembly to design work, retail sales, small classes, study groups, or business meetings – were accommodated within the domestic sphere, expanding the program of the home. Multiple functions replaced single-function room designations. In households where children were present, such as the Barnsdall and Schröder houses, conventional spatial divisions between mothers and children were broken down, leading to a more permeable boundary between the areas occupied by different generations and to a greater emphasis on the activities and education of children.

Moreover, ideas about community and individual privacy were redefined and problematized. In some examples, notably the Schröder house, there was a clear effort to provide a separate, private bedroom (however tiny) for the mother and, in that way, to allow her to lay claim to a personal, adult-only area separate from the family's space. In the Villa Stein–de Monzie, where the bedrooms were all on upper floors, the biggest problem was the separation of the suite of private spaces occupied by the Steins from those of Mme de Monzie and her daughter, since the four were close friends but not family members.

Finally, in those houses built for single women, the issue of the bedroom arose because of the ambiguities (either in the mind of the architect or for the client herself) about the sexual and private lives of unmarried women. In some examples, the bedroom disappeared altogether. The most obvious case is the Farnsworth house (intended as a weekend retreat), where the issue of privacy – already challenged by the open plan – was further problematized by the glass exterior walls. In Neutra's Perkins house there is no bedroom, either: the client chose to sleep on a narrow bed next to her drafting board in a small studio off of the main living space. The only real bedroom in the Perkins house is a guest room added at the insistence of the bank that provided the mortgage loan.[5] Clearly, the issue of sexuality (which, in the case of single women, was frequently overshadowed by the spectre of lesbianism) was foreclosed in these projects.

For a variety of reasons, then, houses built for women – whether for themselves alone or for their children as well – reorder the conventions of the domestic program and challenge the values that structure it, producing new, hybrid types and mixed-used spaces. At the same time, this realignment of the categories of patronage, plan, and program opens up a whole new range of questions. To what extent do these and other women clients function as patrons for architects, recapitulating the familiar role of woman as the "guardians of culture"?[6] How many of these women saw themselves as agents of social change, helping generate new prototypes that could be useful in producing innovative housing for other women? How many sought only individual luxuries or monuments to their own wealth and taste? To what extent does the fundamental departure from conventional gender relations and social relations – and, with it, the resulting departure from type – serve as a catalyst for design innovation? Finally, while all of these single-family houses were

designe' women in the United States and
Euro' might they offer for a broader
ran᷍ ..... in housing today?

The Rietveld Schröder House

A closer look at one particularly well known icon of modern architecture, Rietveld's Schröder house, reveals how much basic information has been left out of conventional architectural history (fig. 1).[7] All but one of the widely used introductory texts make no mention of the client or her part in the design process, despite the fact that Truus Schröder's involvement in the project was documented early on and published in a 1958 monograph.[8] All of the texts make much of the house's relationship to the De Stijl movement and to artists such as Theo van Doesburg, concentrating on color, volume, and composition. Only William Curtis discusses the project in detail and credits Schröder, noting that "it seems probable that she inspired some of the more revolutionary aspects of the building like the openness of the upstairs 'free plan' and some of the ingenious built-in furniture."[9] Nevertheless, because this information is not connected to broader questions of gender, nor to social or typological convention, it loses much of its significance.

Although a great deal of information about the Schröder house has been published, very little of it has found its way into the survey books. For example, in a series of interviews conducted in 1982 (she lived in the house until her death in 1985), Schröder described her life history and the circumstances that shaped the design of her house.[10] Truus Schräder was born in 1889 to an upper middle-class Catholic family. She trained as a pharmacist but seems never to have practiced. In 1911, she married F. A. C. Schröder, a lawyer, and the couple settled in Utrecht.[11] Although her first meeting with Rietveld may have occurred during the period of her engagement to Schröder, it is clear that Rietveld's status as a furniture-maker placed him in a world apart from the haut-bourgeois circles in which the Schröders moved (figs. 2, 3). Nevertheless, both Rietveld and Schröder took an interest in contemporary art and design, which ultimately would bring them together.

FRIEDMAN

221

FIG. I

Gerrit Rietveld. Schröder
House, Utrecht, Holland. 1924.
Photographed in 1924

FIG. 2
Truus Schräder, ca. 1910

FIG. 3
Gerrit Rietveld, seated on an early
version of the Red-Blue Chair, in
front of his furniture-making
shop in Utrecht, ca. 1918

Through her sister, An Harrenstein, who lived in Amsterdam, Schröder became aware of a circle of artists and writers who held far greater interest for her than the Utrecht society in which she circulated. This group included Jacob Bendien, Charly Torop, and Kurt Schwitters. Schröder's restlessness was compounded by disagreements with her husband about the upbringing of their three young children. In 1921, at the suggestion of her husband (who was introduced to Rietveld's work by a business associate), Truus Schröder commissioned Rietveld to remodel a room in their house as a private space for her use alone, complete with a day bed, table, and comfortable chairs. The project is significant not only because it brought architect and client together for the first time, but also because it marks Schröder's first venture as a patron. Schröder saw the new room as a place in which she could escape and live as she liked: "I hardly met any people who had a feeling for what was modern. Not through my husband. My husband was eleven years my senior; he had a very busy practice and a great many acquaintances, some of his family lived in Utrecht and they weren't at all interested in that sort of thing. It was only through my sister that ideas came in from outside. We would discuss such things in my room, and then it was mine, only mine."[12]

In his design Rietveld reduced furniture and lighting fixtures to bare essentials, rejecting the luxurious ornament and heavy forms of conventional upper middle-class interiors.[13] Significantly, he seems to have remained open to his client's ideas, giving shape to her suggestions. His own extraordinary ideas about form and color, already apparent in the Red-Blue Chair of 1918, were channeled and challenged by Schröder's critique. This working relationship would structure their collaborations over a period of more than forty years.

When her husband died two years after the remodeling project, Schröder again looked to Rietveld. Her first idea was to find an apartment that Rietveld could renovate for her (her plan was to remain in Utrecht only for the next six years, until the children were out of school, and then to move to Amsterdam).[14] Nevertheless, having discovered a suitable lot at the end of a row of brick houses on the edge of town, Rietveld and Schröder set about designing a new house for her family. Although she had a comfortable income under the terms of her husband's will, her budget was limited: the final cost of the house was approximately the same as for a small, semi-detached dwelling at that time.[15]

When Schröder described her program to Rietveld, she emphasized her need for a home in which parent and children would be brought together in an open space, and in which work activities, such as design, also could be carried out: "I thought it was very good for the children to live in an atmosphere like that, also to have Rietveld often around. To have that experience. To hear those conversations, including those with people who disagreed. In fact, to take part in that exchange of ideas. I was very pleased that the children could share in that."[16] The result was a small house (7 x 10 meters) with a studio, library, workroom, and eat-in kitchen on the ground floor. On the upper floor were the children's bedrooms and a large living and dining area; these "rooms" were actually one large space, which could be partitioned by thin, sliding panels (figs. 4, 5). Although Schröder's own bedroom, also located on this upper floor, was separated from the principal living area by fixed walls, it was not as prominent or large as a traditional parents' bedroom. In the main living space there was a specially designed cabinet made up of storage modules for sewing supplies and stationery, a phonograph, and a movie projector (fig. 6). Each "room" on the upper floor had a washbasin and electrical outlet, which Schröder felt were important to allow individuals to cook "if they wanted."[17] The house not only made a social and artistic statement but also embraced new forms of technology. From the start, it was considered a major contribution to design, and it established both Rietveld and Schröder in the art world.

Throughout the 1920s, Schröder's activities as a patron and artist expanded, and she is listed as co-designer with Rietveld on a number of projects dating from this and the following decade. They completed an important interior renovation of her sister's Amsterdam home in 1926.[18] Between 1930 and 1935, she collaborated with Rietveld on two experimental housing blocks close to her home in Utrecht. Moreover, in the late 1920s her sister, An Harrenstein, with a group of other feminists, founded a magazine, *De Werkende Vrouw*, to which both Schröder and Rietveld contributed articles on architecture and design.[19] Schröder's interest in progressive interior design, and specifically her emphasis on women's work at home, were clearly of a professional nature. An avid reader, she was constantly bringing new ideas to Rietveld's attention and, as she put it, she "urged him to write things down."[20]

It is possible to situate Truus Schröder's feminism and her goals for her house within the broad movement of Dutch and European feminism of the early twentieth century. Although *De Werkende Vrouw* was published for only a short period, its contributors included a number of distinguished feminist philosophers and theorists, and its readers were middle-class intellectuals more interested in art, family, and educational theory than in women's rights in the workplace. Schröder herself never worked outside the home, and her position as a widow with three children compelled her to take a greater interest in household labor and child care than she might otherwise have done.

Like many of her contemporaries, Schröder was broadly influenced by the writings of the Swedish feminist Ellen Key, whose ideas on women's maternal gifts and special role in the home (set forth in a series of books published between the late 1890s and World War 1) were particularly well known in Holland and Germany.[21] Key urged feminists to shift their attention away from the workplace and women's equality *outside* the home to focus on women's unique abilities to nurture and guide their families *within* it. Moreover, Key believed that marriage was unduly restrictive of women's emotional, spiritual, and sexual gifts, and she thus campaigned not only for "free love" and birth-control but also for state support of single mothers.

Although Schröder was never politically active, she nonetheless took a lively interest in housing policy. As a designer she sought to respond to the needs of non-traditional households and believed strongly in women's rights. Her own house is testimony to her ambitious goals and to her concern for broad social and artistic change; her personal circumstances and struggles reinforced that commitment. The Schröder house broke down boundaries between generations and redefined social relations through unconventional design; it contested the structure of the traditional family as well. Rietveld and Schröder were both professional partners and lovers for more than forty years. He was in the house every day and appeared at art events and social gatherings with Schröder,

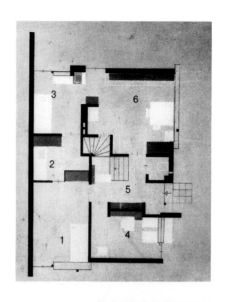

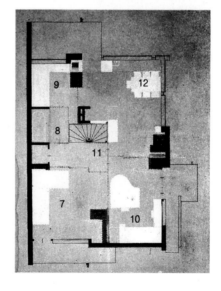

FIG. 4

Schröder House. Plan of the
ground floor. 1. Atelier;
2. Workroom; 3. Service room;
4. Studio; 5. Entry; 6. Kitchen

FIG. 5

Schröder House. Plan of the
upper floor 7. Girls' room;
8. Bathroom; 9. Truus Schröder's
room; 10. Boy's room;
11. Staircase; 12. Living-dining
room

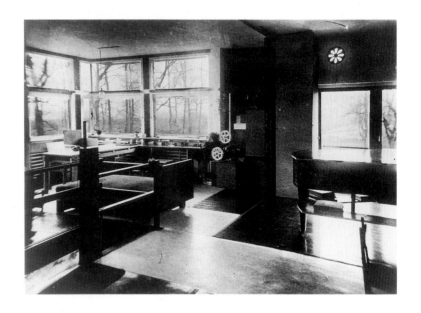

FIG. 6

Schröder House. Interior, with
the living-dining room and
the corner of the boy's room.
Photographed ca. 1924

despite the fact that his own wife and six children also lived in Utrecht (Rietveld moved into Schröder's house only after his wife's death, and he lived there with Schröder from 1958 until his own death in 1964). As a mixed-use family home and design studio, it went beyond the more familiar type of the artist's studio to suggest a new model for a small family house and workshop.

The lessons of the Schröder house are many. First, it is clearly the result of a collaboration between a man and a woman, each of whom brought distinctive skills and interests to the project. Second, the client's role was critical to the outcome: not only did Schröder act as patron and partner, but it was she who created both the program and the opportunity to work it through. This collaboration – which took ideas off the drawing board into the real world where they were challenged by material, economic, social, and artistic conditions – was indispensable; without it there would have been no architecture, only drawings and models. Finally, the house included a number of successful design innovations: a flexible, open plan on the upper floor, in which rooms were screened by moveable partitions, allowing for both privacy and community for mother and children (although noise seems to have been a constant problem while the children remained in the house);[22] large, open windows, which extended the interior space out to the street and garden and flooded the house with light; brilliant colors and intimate scale; a small, private room apart from the open area in which the parent could be both close to her children and separate from them; a ground floor of small, fixed-wall rooms in which privacy and quiet could be found. Clearly the Schröder house is both a richly meaningful work of architecture and an essay on the meaning of privacy and community.

Ultimately, the Schröder house and other houses built for women clients reveal the narrowness of conventional approaches to the history and design of domestic architecture. Failure to recognize and understand the radical decisions that produce significant buildings blunts our awareness of the social choices that can be and have been made. Too often buildings are discussed solely in formal terms, while the political and ideological context of the design process remains obscure. The future of historiography and the future of design go hand in hand: if historians

FRIEDMAN

and teachers do not have the information or the analytic approaches to make the process known, then architects and students cannot be blamed for falling back on conservative type forms as the starting point for design; certainly they cannot be faulted for failing to recognize the importance of planning for social change. The charge to feminist historians and critics is clear: to reveal, through research that begins with individual lives and choices, the cultural conditions in which buildings are produced, and to confront the relationships of power that structure the physical environment and produce the sociopsychological conditions in which the lives of men and women are lived.

1. The work presented here is drawn from my book on women clients and twentieth-century architecture, to be published by Harry N. Abrams in 1997. The section on the Schröder house is taken from a chapter of that book written in collaboration with Maristella Casciato and draws on her unpublished paper "Models of Domesticity in the Twentieth-Century Dwelling: The Case of the Schröder House (1924)."

2. For an extended discussion of this issue, see my article "Just Not My Type: Gender, Convention, and the Uses of Uncertainty," in Karen A. Franck and Linda H. Schneekloth, eds., *Ordering Space: Types in Architecture and Design* (New York: Van Nostrand Reinhold, 1994), 331–34. The problem of designing for non-traditional households is considered in detail in Franck and Sherry Ahrentzen, eds., *New Households, New Housing* (New York: Van Nostrand Reinhold, 1991).

3. The literature on this subject has grown over the last decade. For an overview, see Leslie Kanes Weisman, *Discrimination by Design: A Feminist Critique of the Man-made Environment* (Urbana and Chicago: University of Illinois Press, 1992), and Gwendolyn Wright, *Building the Dream: A Social History of Housing in America* (Cambridge, Mass.: MIT Press, 1981). Clifford E. Clark Jr., *The American Family Home 1800–1960* (Chapel Hill and London: University of North Carolina Press, 1986), provides a useful survey of social and architectural developments.

4. This research is incorporated into two important articles on housing for single parents and female-headed households: Sherry Ahrentzen, "Overview of Housing for Single-Parent Households," and Jacqueline Leavitt, "Two Prototypical Designs for Single Parents: The Congregate House and the New American House," both in Franck and Ahrentzen. See also Eugenie Ladner Birch, ed., *The Unsheltered*

Woman: Women and Housing in the '80s (New Brunswick, N.J.: Center for Urban Policy Research, 1985).

5. On Farnsworth, see my "Domestic Differences: Edith Farnsworth, Mies van der Rohe, and the Gendered Body," in Christopher Reed, ed., *Not at Home: The Suppression of Domesticity in Modern Art and Architecture* (London: Thames and Hudson, forthcoming). The information about the Perkins house is drawn from a series of interviews I conducted with the client at her home in January 1989.

6. On women as patrons of the arts, see Kathleen D. McCarthy, *Women's Culture: American Philanthropy and Art, 1830–1930* (Chicago: The University of Chicago Press, 1991), and Karen J. Blair, *The Torchbearers: Women and Their Amateur Arts Associations in America 1890–1930* (Bloomington: Indiana University Press, 1994).

7. On the Schröder house, see Paul Overy et al., *The Rietveld-Schröder House* (Cambridge, Mass.: MIT Press, 1988). This volume includes an interview with the client conducted by Lenneke Büller and Frank den Oudsten in 1982 (first published in *Lotus International* 60 [1988], 33–57).

8. On Rietveld, see Theodore M. Brown, *The Work of G. Th. Rietveld, Architect* (Utrecht: A. W. Braun, 1958), and Marijke Kuper and Ida van Zijl, eds., *Gerrit Th. Rietveld: The Complete Works* (Utrecht: Centraal Museum Utrecht, 1992). The surveys include Kenneth Frampton, *Modern Architecture: A Critical History,* 3rd ed. (London: Thames and Hudson, 1992), 144–46; Manfredo Tafuri and Francesco dal Co, *Modern Architecture* (New York: Rizzoli, 1986), vol. 1, 112; and Spiro Kostof, *A History of Architecture: Settings and Rituals,* 2nd ed. (New York: Oxford University Press, 1995), 702.

9. William J. Curtis, *Modern Architecture since 1900,* 2nd ed. (Englewood Cliffs, N.J.: Prentice-Hall, 1987).

10. Ibid. Schröder's contribution was also the subject of an important pamphlet written by Corrie Nagtegaal, who lived in the house as a tenant/companion in the last years of Schröder's life (*Tr. Schröder-Schräder, Bewoonster van het Rietveld Schröderhuis* [Utrecht: 1987]). I am grateful to Ms. Nagtegaal for her generosity in sharing her research and experiences with me.

11. Overy et al., 21.

12. Büller and den Oudsten, "Interview with Truus Schröder" in Overy et al., 47.

13. Kuper and van Zijl, cat. nos. 51, 84.

14. Büller and den Oudsten, 52.

15. The house cost somewhere between 6,000 guilders (Schröder's recollection in ibid.,

FRIEDMAN

78) and 11,000 guilders (Overy et al., 22, after Brown, 155, n.38). A figure of 9,000 guilders is cited, without source, in Kuper and van Zijl, 101.

16. Büller and den Oudsten, 93.

17. Ibid., 60. How this would work in practice in such a small space is unclear.

18. Kuper and van Zijl, cat. no. 107. A surgery and guest room by Schröder and Rietveld were completed in 1930 (cat. no. 156).

19. Truus Schröder-Schräder, "Wat men door normalisatie in den woningbouw te Frankfurt a/d Main heeft bereikt" (What Has Been Achieved by the Standardization of Housing in Frankfurt a/d Main) 1 (no. 1–2, 1930), 12–14, and "Een inliedend woord tot binnenarchitectuur" (An Introductory Note on Domestic Architecture) 1 (no. 3, 1930), 93–94. Gerrit Rietveld, "De stoel" (Chairs) 1 (no. 9, 1930), 244, and "Architectuur" (Architecture) 1 (no. 11–12, 1930), 316–18.

20. Büller and den Oudsten, 92.

21. On Key's influence, see Richard J. Evans, *The Feminist Movement in Germany 1894–1933* (London: Sage Publications, 1976), and Katharine S. Anthony, *Feminism in Germany and Scandinavia* (New York: H. Holt and Co., 1915). See also Kay Goodman, "Motherhood and Work: The Concept of the Misuse of Women's Energy, 1895–1905," in Ruth-Ellen Joeres and Mary Jo Maynes, eds., *German Women in the Eighteenth and Nineteenth Centuries* (Bloomington: Indiana University Press, 1986), 110–27. Key's works influenced Frank Lloyd Wright, and it was Wright's lover Mamah Borthwick Cheney who was designated as Key's official English translator in 1909. See Anthony Alofsin, *Frank Lloyd Wright: The Lost Years, 1910–1922: A Study of Influence* (Cambridge, Mass.: MIT Press, 1994), and his "Taliesin: To Fashion Worlds in Little," *Wright Studies* 1 (1991), 44–65.

22. Büller and den Oudsten, 57.

Housing for a Postmodern World: Reply to Alice T. Friedman

GHISLAINE HERMANUZ

The thesis that to design for women is – at least potentially – to design for a different social order is intriguing. It assumes that political and ideological conditions can engender specific architectural responses that lead to socially relevant forms. Thus understanding both "the cultural conditions in which buildings are produced and . . . the relationships of power that structure the physical environment and produce the socio-psychological conditions in which the lives of men and women are lived" (see Alice T. Friedman's essay in this volume, p. 230) is key to the design of housing that is relevant to women. If, indeed, as Friedman suggests, women are the challengers to conventions that have traditionally constrained the design of the residential environment, it is imperative to recognize the different societal, cultural, and economic forces that affect women's lives, for these life circumstances expand the concept of home for women beyond the confines of its interpretation by a singular class or cultural group.

The house Friedman discusses, namely Rietveld's Schröder house, clearly articulates the different sets of premises that women clients, when given the opportunity to suit their own homes to their specific needs, have used to redefine the domestic environment. From conventional definitions of privacy and publicness, and the traditional concept of the sacrosanct bedroom, to the notion of separation of workspace and domestic space, Truus Schröder questioned accepted notions and substituted original answers tailored to her own individual life-style. Schröder's house seems to suggest that a model for the spatial reordering of the domestic program exists, and that it consists of blurring the boundaries between the private and public spheres as well as questioning the social relationships of traditional family life.

Whether these findings are universal and hold true within the realm of collective housing (as opposed to that of the individual single-family home) and whether they apply across class and cultural boundaries are the pivotal questions to raise relative to the design of gender-specific dwelling spaces. For the Schröder house to be meaningful as an archetype of a new domestic environment, the lessons learned from it must illustrate more than a successful process of individuation. In fact, it must establish a conceptual and programmatic breakthrough relevant to housing for all women. If the Schröder house is more than the expression of class privileges – indeed, if it is the expression of a socially responsible domestic environment – the choices and priorities implied in it will ultimately produce better homes for all. To find a definition of domesticity with relevance for women globally and, thus, to understand the meaning of "home" in our postmodern world, a look at some ideas that have evolved from debates among grassroots women internationally brings new insight to the issue.

In September 1995, the Fourth World Conference on the Status of Women, a summit meeting of women called by the United Nations, was held in Beijing. The issue of housing was, surprisingly, absent from the conference's initial agenda. Because of the pressure put on the United Nations by groups of grassroots women involved – by choice and necessity – in providing homes for their communities, issues of shelter, housing, and the role of women in their development were eventually discussed. These women (from Africa, Asia, Latin America, and across the United States and Europe) proposed a platform that defined housing, and therefore homes, as that essential institution that roots people in a place and a culture. In a joint statement prepared for Beijing, they also stressed the creation of communities as the ultimate goal of housing development. They asked for recognition of the informal household economy and domestic work, both controlled by women, as the most valuable economic activities of developing societies.[1]

Home, thus defined in political terms as the nexus of social and economic activities, is the place that offers women equitable access to resources and a stake in their community. It is a means to overcome poverty and re-create a community. Home is also the place that provides safety in the midst of the insecurities created by fluctuating economies. It is not only the space where women's traditional reproductive role unfolds but also a place that can fulfill much deeper yearnings for empowerment and control over one's life. Indeed, for these women home is the very source of their empowerment. Control, security, community building, and economic sustenance are key concepts in defining what housing for women should be.

The Beijing declaration asked that housing be viewed as a social and economic investment. As a social investment it gives women access to the basic services they are entitled to from society, allowing them to redefine their reproductive and nurturing roles; as an economic investment it gives them a place in the production system and, thus, in the defini-tion of development policies – from land use to transportation patterns.[2] If the Schröder house gives us a glimpse of a possible model for a mod-ern house-type (albeit one that is bound up in its own class conventions), grassroots women have defined for us the paradigm of housing for our postmodern society.

But what is domesticity in a postmodern society? Is it within the realm of collective housing or within the realm of the private house that this concept will find a new definition? The dilemma of finding the proper, formal architectural response to this fundamental challenge of domesticity as social program still needs to be explored. Differentiating between ruptures with conventions and the replacement of one conven-tion with another is another dilemma. For instance, blurring the separa-tion between private sphere and public realm within the home can be seen as representing women's efforts to transcend domesticity; but it could just as well be the expression of a middle-class trend toward the frag-mentation of social units into single autonomous entities, rather than a collective redefinition of the social space. Understanding the impact of today's economic reality on the home's potential for change is yet another key aspect of design for postmodernity. What if housing provided support for more than the reproduction of labor power? Three projects, repre-senting work done for women and with women as clients, will illustrate the import of these questions.

Domesticity Redefined: Three Case Studies

The first project is a proposal for housing women released from prison in a facility located on New York City's Lower East Side. The brief from the sponsor, the Women's Prison Association, called for an environment supportive of these women's effort to reestablish themselves in the larger community and renew close ties with their children. In discussions of the program, the clients defined their bedroom as the most private space within the dwelling unit – not as the sacrosanct marital room centered on a large bed, or even as the showcase of a consumption-oriented society – but as a place for total privacy (figs. 1, 2). The transformation of the domestic program that the women deemed essential was based on the collectivization of certain domestic tasks: sharing of child care and some housekeeping activities, provided that sharing created an economic advantage. Sharing a kitchen was acceptable only to the degree that it made for a more rational use of space; control over food provisions and cooking remained individual. Here collectivization, not individuation, was the dynamic of change. Yet, it is the very process of collectivization which led to an increased need for a totally private sphere, no matter how small.

The second project, proposed for Harlem, was sponsored by the Inner City Labor Alliance (ICLA), which represents several minority labor unions in the New York region. The ICLA had asked its membership to describe their ideal home.[3] The result of that consultation was an innovative apartment program focused on redefining the parents' bedroom. While its privacy was maintained, the bedroom was transformed into a polyvalent space. The bed, still a major element in the room, shared space with an entertainment center, a workspace, a hobby space, and a storage space. The importance of the parents' room required its location in the most prominent place in the building's footprint – the corners – where it would enjoy light from and views in two directions. The living room, ceded to children and guests, was more anonymous and smaller in size. In this project, the boundary between public and private realms was redefined in response to a restructuring of family relationships, which are often no longer hierarchical. Parity and separateness between parents' world and children's world was the core of the unit's design. Linkages to the larger community were expressed symbolically with the parents' bed-sitting room offering visual connections to the surrounding neighborhood.

The third project is in the Williamsburg-Greenpoint section of Brooklyn, where a multicultural group of women has been struggling to revitalize and transform the neighborhood for more than ten years.[4] Here the architect was asked to respond to a brief for the development of housing that encouraged self-sufficiency rooted in interdependence with the community.[5] This concept led to specific design principles. Dwelling units had to foster companionship, support, and sharing of domestic chores. The addition of a door between individual dwelling units made it possible for two families to merge their family spaces while still maintaining privacy. Separately accessible rooms could accommodate a helper, a guest, or an older relative. Numerous community spaces, centrally located and directly accessible from the outside, were included to allow for a variety of functions that could provide economic benefits for residents (fig. 3). Additional spaces devoted to economic enterprises increased the relative size of the building's communal spaces, and individual spaces could be devoted to collective use, which offered neighbors choices rather than imposing on them a single pattern of social relationships.

Although they do not constitute a definite answer to the questions raised at the beginning of this essay, these three examples show that identifying, and then responding to, a changing social program can lead to significant formal changes. They also suggest that revolutionary changes are hard to confront and respond to. For instance, when domesticity is redefined in collective terms – when domestic work is recognized for its value to the economy and elevated to productive status – it may be that those activities should leave the dwelling altogether. If this were to happen, would it mean the demise of the concept of home, which, without its individualized domestic work function, would then lose its raison d'être? Most socially driven changes to the house program seem to force the admission that the home is not a world unto itself but a link to the services and the development opportunities of the larger society. According to this view, the house could become the foundation of a socially

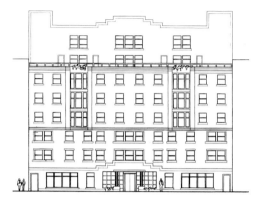

FIGS. 1, 2

City College Architectural Cente.
(CCAC) in collaboration with
Conrad Levenson Architects.
Proposal for Women's House, 308
East 8th Street, New York. 1987.
The mother's bedroom is the
smallest of the two rooms. Because
it occupies the farthest, most
remote corner of the unit, this tiny
room offers total privacy

FIG. 3

Katrin Adam with Barbara
Marks. Neighborhood Women's
Inter-Generational Housing,
Williamsburg-Greenpoint,
Brooklyn. 1984. At ground level,
rooms directly accessible from
the outside can become shared
spaces that "outsiders" can enter
without interfering with the
privacy of the residential areas

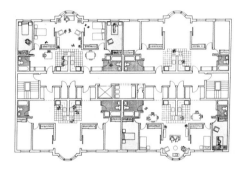

HERMANUZ

238

responsible urbanism, instead of an introverted world of isolation and privilege. Rather than blur the boundary between private and public realms, this urbanistic function of the dwelling begs for its intensification. These examples also suggest how important it is to define women's role beyond domesticity.

Housing for Postmodernity

In the nineteenth and early twentieth centuries, movements to reform conditions in the workplace also led to the transformation of the nineteenth-century industrial city into the modern metropolis of today, and the introduction of public health measures, zoning, new transportation systems, and suburban residential development. Similarly, the struggles of women in the residential realm today – in support of women's right to survive in an often hostile and unsupportive environment – must look beyond the individuation of the home as the only way to reflect changed socioeconomic conditions; only then will they lead to a different urbanism and a different home environment for postmodern times. Such efforts must recognize new forms of households: extended, nuclear, multilocational, polygynous, those headed by men or women, single or not, and even by children. They must challenge present building norms and design standards that conflict with the economic behavior of diverse households and communities. And they must lead to new dwelling types that do not preclude opportunities for economic development but, instead, allow for a symbiotic relationship with the social services of the larger community and the fostering of equal access to resources.

HERMANUZ

These new housing designs will acknowledge the economic value of women's contributions within the household and within the community, giving them parity with traditionally recognized economic endeavors. Women's struggles to control, transform, upgrade, and maintain their houses will lead to the creation of sustainable environments. For houses to become homes, in women's terms, they must be changed from mere shells, tailored to specific life-styles, to the building blocks of communities and equitable economic structures upon which social structures can develop.

1. HIC (Habitat International Coalition), Women & Shelter Network, International Council of Women, GROOTS International, and UNCHS, "Women in Human Settlements Development" (Habitat, 1995).

2. Jo Beall and Caren Levy, "Moving Toward the Gendered City" (paper prepared for the Preparatory Committee for Habitat II, Geneva 1994, University College, London, 1994).

3. Joint design studio project between City College Architectural Center (CCAC) and Columbia Community Design Workshop (CCDW), A. Philip Randolph Village, housing development proposal for the Inner City Labor Alliance, spring 1991.

4. Sandra Shilen, "Grassroots Women Reclaiming and Rebuilding Communities: Neighborhood Women's Renaissance" (paper presented at OECD conference Women in the City: Housing Services and the Urban Environment, Paris, 1994).

5. For a complete analysis of this project, which was designed by architect Katrin Adam, see Leslie Kanes Weisman, *Discrimination by Design: A Feminist Critique of the Man-Made Environment* (Urbana and Chicago: University of Illinois Press, 1992), 150–52.

HERMANUZ

Claiming the Public Space: The Mothers of Plaza de Mayo

SUSANA TORRE

To my "disappeared" Argentinian classmates, and to their mothers

The role of women in the transformation of cities remains theoretically problematic. While women's leadership in organizations rebuilding communities and neighborhoods and their creation of new paradigms for monumentality are sometimes noted in the press, these interventions have yet to inform cultural discourse in the design disciplines or in the history and theory of art and architecture.

The largest body of current feminist scholarship on women in urban settings is concerned with the construction of bourgeois femininity in nineteenth-century European capitals.[1] Within this framework, women are seen as extensions of the male gaze and as instruments of the emerging consumer society and its transformative powers at the dawn of modernity. In other words, they are described as passive agents rather than engaged subjects.[2] When women have assumed transformative roles, feminist critics and biographers have seen them as exceptional individuals or female bohemians, publicly flaunting class and gender distinctions; in contrast, women in general, and working-class women in particular, are presented as unintentional agents of a collective social project, acting out assigned scripts. As a class, women share the problematic status of politically or culturally colonized populations. Both are seen as passively transformed by forced modernization rather than as appropriating modernity on their own and, through this appropriation, being able to change the world that is transforming them.

From this perspective it is difficult to see the current individual and collective struggle of women to transform urban environments as anything of cultural significance, or to reevaluate the enduring influence of traditional female enclaves originated in the premodern city. Many of these enclaves continue to serve their traditional functional and social roles, like the public washing basins in major Indian cities or the markets in African villages, while others have persisted as symbolic urban markings, like the forest of decorated steel poles that once held clotheslines in Glasgow's most central park. Some of these enclaves have even become a city's most important open space, like River Walk in San Antonio, Texas, where women once congregated to wash laundry and socialize.

A literature is now emerging, focused on the participation by marginalized populations in the transformation of postmodern cities and establishing the critical connection between power and spatiality, particularly within the disciplines of art and architectural history and architectural and urban design.[3] To these contributions, which have revealed previously unmarked urban sites as well as the social consequences of repressive urban planning ideologies, should be added feminist analyses of women's traditional urban enclaves and of women's appropriations of public sites that symbolized their exclusion or restricted status. These appropriations, whether in the form of one of the largest mass demonstrations ever held on the Washington Mall (in favor of abortion rights) or in the display of intimacy in very public settings (such as the private offerings and mementos that complete Maya Lin's Vietnam Memorial and compose the monumental Names Quilt commemorating AIDS victims), continue to establish women's rights not merely to inhabit but also to transform the public realm of the city. It is in such situations that women have been most effective in constructing themselves as transformative subjects, altering society's perception of public space and inscribing their own stories into the urban palimpsest.[4]

As in all instances where the topic of discussion is as complex as the transformative presence of women in the city – and particularly when this topic does not yet operate within an established theoretical framework – the main difficulty is to establish a point of entry. In the present essay I propose entering this territory through the examination of one dramatic case of a successful, enduring appropriation: the Mothers of the Plaza de Mayo in Argentina.⁵ This small but persistent band of women protesters first captured international attention in the mid-1970s with their sustained presence in the nation's principal "space of public appearance," as Hanna Arendt has called the symbolic realm of social representation, which is controlled by the dominant political or economic structures of society. This case illustrates the process that leads from the embodiment of traditional roles and assigned scripts as wives and mothers to the emergence of the active, transformative subject, in spite of – or perhaps because of – the threat or actuality of physical violence that acts of protest attract in autocratic societies. As we will see, this case is also emblematic of architecture's complicity with power in creating a symbolic system of representation, usually of power hierarchies. The hegemony of this system has been threatened ever since the invention of the printing press and is now claimed by electronic media and its virtual space of communication. Finally, the Mothers of Plaza de Mayo's appropriation of the public square as a stage for the enactment of their plea is a manifestation of *public space* as social production. Their redefinition of that space suggests that the public realm neither resides nor can be represented by buildings and spaces but rather is summoned into existence by social actions.

The Mothers of the Plaza de Mayo

In March 1976, after a chaotic period following Juan Perón's death, a military junta wrested power from Perón's widow, Isabel, in order (as the junta claimed) to restore order and peace to the country. The first measures toward achieving this goal were similar to those of General Pinochet in Chile three years earlier, and included the suspension of all civil rights, the dissolution of all political parties, and the placement of labor unions and universities under government control. It would take seven long, dark years for a democratically elected government to be restored to Argentina, which at last permitted an evaluation of the extent of open kidnappings, torture, and executions of civilians tolerated by the military. Because of the clandestine, unrecorded activities of the paramilitary groups charged with these deeds, and because many burial sites still remain undisclosed, agreement as to the exact number of "disappeared" may never be achieved, but estimates range from nine thousand to thirty thousand. Inquiries to the police about the fate of detainees went unanswered. Luis Puenzo's 1985 film, *The Official Story*, offers glimpses into the torture and degradation endured by thousands of men, women, and even babies, born in detention, some of whom were adopted by the torturers' families.

"Disappearances" were very effective in creating complicitous fear: many kidnappings were conducted in broad daylight, and the victims had not necessarily demonstrated open defiance of the military. In fact, later statistics show that almost half of the kidnappings involved witnesses, including children, relatives, and friends of those suspected of subversion. Given the effectiveness of arbitrary terror in imposing silence, it is astonishing that the public demands of less than a score of bereaved women who wanted to know what had happened to their children contributed so much to the military's fall from power. Their silent protest, opposed to the silence of the authorities, eventually had international resonance, prompting a harsh denunciation of the Argentinean military, which led, finally, to the demise of state terrorism and the election of a democratic government.

The actions of the "Mothers," as they came to be known, exemplified a kind of spatial and urban appropriation that originates in private acts that acquire public significance, thus questioning the boundaries of these two commonly opposed concepts. Gender issues, too, were not unimportant. The Mothers' appropriation of the plaza was nothing like a heroic final assault on a citadel. Instead, it succeeded because of its endurance over a protracted period, which could only happen because the Mothers were conspicuously ignored by the police, the public, and the national press. As older women they were no longer sexually desirable, and as working-class women they were of an inferior ilk. Nevertheless, their motherhood status demanded conventional respect. Communicating neither attraction nor threat, they were characterized by the government as "madwomen." The result of their public tenacity, which started with the body exposed to violence, eventually evolved into a powerful architecture of political resistance.

Plaza de Mayo is Argentina's symbolic equivalent of the Washington Mall. It is, however, a much smaller and very different kind of space: an urban square that evolved from the Spanish Plaza de Armas, a space that has stood for national unity since Creoles gathered there to demand independence from Spain in May of 1810. The national and international visibility of Plaza de Mayo as *the* space of public appearance for Argentineans is unchallenged. Originally, as mandated by the planning ordinances of the Law of the Indies, its sides were occupied by the colonial Cabildo, or city council, and the Catholic Cathedral. Today the most distinctive structure is the pink, neoclassical Casa Rosada, the seat of government.

Military exercises, executions, and public market commingled in the plaza until 1884, when Torcuato de Alvear, the aristocratic mayor, embarked on a Haussmanian remodeling of the center of Buenos Aires shortly after important civic structures – such as Congress and the Ministries of Finance and Social Welfare – had been completed. A major element of Alvear's plan was Avenida de Mayo, an east-west axis that put Congress and the Casa Rosada in full view of each other. Such a potent urban representation of the checks and balances of the modern, democratic state was achieved through selective demolition, including the removal of the plaza's market stalls and the shortening of the historic Cabildo's wings by half their original length. Currently, the plaza's immediate area includes several government offices, the financial district, and the city's most famous commercial street, Florida. This densely populated pedestrian thoroughfare links Avenida de Mayo to Plaza San Martin, another major urban square. A plastered masonry obelisk, the May Pyramid, erected on the square in 1811 to mark the first anniversary of the popular uprising for independence, was rebuilt as a taller, more ornate structure and placed on the axis between Congress and the Casa Rosada. In this new position, it became a metaphorical fulcrum in the balance of powers.

The now well-known image of a ring of women with heads clad in white kerchiefs circling the May Pyramid evolved from earlier spontaneous attempts at communication with government officials (fig. 1). At first, thirteen wives and mothers of the "disappeared" met one another at the Ministry of the Interior, having exhausted all sources of information about their missing children and husbands. There a small office had been opened to "process" cases brought by those who had filed writs of *habeas corpus*. One woman well in her sixties, Azucena Villaflor de Vicente, rallied the others: "It is not here that we ought to be," she said. "It's the Plaza de Mayo. And when there are enough of us, we'll go to the Casa Rosada and see the president about our children who are missing."[6] At the time, popular demonstrations at the plaza, frequently convened by the unions as a show of support during Juan Perón's tenure, were strictly forbidden, and gatherings of more than two people were promptly dispersed by the ever-present security forces. The original group of thirteen women came to the plaza wearing white kerchiefs initially to identify themselves to one another. They agreed to return every Thursday at the end of the business day in order to call their presence to the attention of similarly aggrieved women. The Mothers moved about in pairs, switching companions so that they could exchange information while still observing the rule against demonstrations. Eventually they attracted the interest of the international press and human rights organizations, one of which provided an office where the women could congregate privately. Despite this incentive to abandon the plaza for a safer location, the Mothers sustained a symbolic presence in the form of a silent march encircling the May Pyramid. That form, so loaded with cultural and sexual associations, became the symbolic focus of what started as a literal response to the police's demand that the women "circulate."

The white kerchiefs were the first elements of a common architecture evolved from the body. They were adopted from the cloth diapers a few of the Mothers had worn on their heads in a pilgrimage to the Virgin of Luján's sanctuary. The diapers were those of their own missing children, whose names were embroidered on them, and formed a headgear that differentiated the Mothers from the multitude of other women in kerchiefs on that religious march (fig. 2). In later demonstrations the Mothers constructed full-size cardboard silhouettes representing their missing children and husbands, and shielded their bodies with the ghostly blanks of the "disappeared."

By 1982, the military had proven itself unable to govern the country or control runaway inflation of more than 1000 percent per year. The provision of basic services was frequently disrupted by the still powerful

FIG. 1

The circular march around the
May Pyramid

FIG. 2

Mothers clad in kerchiefs embroidered with the names of their
relatives and the dates of their
disappearance, 1985

FIG. 3

Celebration in Plaza de Mayo
with scarves signed by the supporters of the Mothers. The Casa
Rosada is in the background

TORRE

247

Peronista labor unions, and many local industries had gone bankrupt due to the comparative cheapness of imported goods under an economic policy that eliminated most import taxes. Then, in the same year, the military government embarked on an ultimately ruinous war with Great Britain over the sovereignty of the Falkland/Malvinas Islands. With the help of the United States satellite intelligence and far superior naval might, Great Britain won with few casualties, while Argentina lost thousands of ill-equipped and ill-trained soldiers. The military government, which had broadcast a fake victory on television using old movie reels rather than current film footage, was forced to step down in shame by the popular outcry that followed. Following the collapse of the military government, the Mothers were a prominent presence at the festivities in Plaza de Mayo, their kerchiefs joyously joined as bunting to create a city-sized tent over the celebrants (fig. 3). They have continued their circular march to this day, as a kind of living memorial and to promote their demands for full accountability and punishment for those responsible for the disappearance of their husbands and children.

After the election of a democratic government, the military leadership was prosecuted in civil rather than military court, resulting in jail sentences for a few generals and amnesty for other military personnel. Although the amnesty was forcefully contested by the Mothers and other organizations, the protest was seen by many as divisive. Nevertheless, the Mothers and a related organization of grandmothers pressed on with attempts to find records about disappearances and fought in the courts to recover their children and grandchildren. Then, early in 1995, more than a decade after the restoration of democratic government, a retired lieutenant publicly confessed to having dumped scores of drugged but still living people from a helicopter into the open ocean, and he invited other military men on similar assignments to come forth. The Mothers were present to demonstrate this time as well, but now the bunting had become a gigantic sheet that was waved overhead as an angry, agitated sea.

The Mothers were able to sustain control of an important urban space much as actors, dancers, or magicians control the stage by their ability to establish a presence that both opposes and activates the void represented by the audience. To paraphrase Henri Lefebvre, bodies produce space by introducing direction, rotation, orientation, occupation, and by organizing a *topos* through gestures, traces, and marks.[7] The formal structure of these actions, their ability to refunctionalize existing urban spaces, and the visual power of the supporting props contribute to the creation of public space.

What is missing from the current debate about the demise of public space is an awareness of the loss of architecture's power to represent the *public*, as a living, acting, and self-determining community. Instead, the debate focuses almost exclusively on the *physical space* of public appearance, without regard for the social action that can make that environment come alive or change its meaning. The debate appears to be mired in regrets over the replacement of squares (for which Americans never had much use) with shopping malls, theme parks, and virtual space. But this focus on physical space – and its ideological potential to encompass the public appearance of all people, regardless of color, class, age, or sex – loses credibility when specific classes of people are denouncing their exclusion and asserting their presence and influence in public life. The claims of these excluded people underscore the roles of *access* and *appearance* in the production and representation of public space, regardless of how it is physically or virtually constituted. They also suggest that public space is produced through public discourse, and its representation is not the exclusive territory of architecture, but is the product of the inextricable relationship between social action and physical space.

TORRE

1. An excellent example is Elizabeth Wilson's *The Sphinx and the City* (London: Virago, 1991).

2. See Alain Touraine, *Critique of Modernity* (Oxford: Blackwell, 1995), especially the chapter entitled "The Subject."

3. See Sophia Watson and Katherine Gibson, eds., *Postmodern Cities and Spaces* (Oxford: Blackwell, 1995).

4. A different approach has been taken by Jennifer Bloomer in her Urban Still Life

project, which proposes to replace heroic (male) statues with domestic (female) tableaux, apparently without challenging the symbolic order of the nineteenth-century city.

5. The Mothers of Plaza de Mayo's activities have been extensively documented from a human rights point of view. See Josephine Fisher, *Mothers of the Disappeared* (Boston: South End Press, 1989), for interviews with the leaders and bibliographical references.

6. Quoted in John Simpson and Jana Bennett, *The Disappeared and the Mothers of the Plaza: The Story of the 11,000 Argentinians Who Vanished* (New York: St. Martin's Press, 1985).

7. Henri Lefebvre, *The Production of Space* (Oxford and Cambridge, Mass.: Blackwell, 1991).

The Politics of Underestimation

MARION WEISS

"It was never about proving that women can do anything a man can do, but about being judged as individuals by the same standard as men in any job for which they can qualify. . . . It was about the privilege of serving one's country without artificial barriers based solely on gender. In short, women's struggle for a place in the armed forces has been about seeking the full rights and responsibilities of citizenship."

– Major General Jeanne Holm, USAF (Ret.)[1]

This is the story of my involvement for more than five years in the Women's Memorial and Education Center at Arlington National Cemetery, a project that is still a work in progress, caught in the messy laboratory of practice. To work as the architect and as a woman on a "women's project" – a project in the monumental corridor of Washington, D.C. – for a woman general and her board composed largely of other women generals has been a unique experience.

But this is also the story of a particular moment in time, when the politics of underestimation will have enabled a permanent change to the physical core of the most symbolically laden city in the United States. True power in architecture begins not with the architect but with a site and the aspirations of an enlightened client. In this case the site had been perceived as a remnant in spite of its central location on the monumental axis, and the client represented a group of individuals perceived as peripheral to the history of this country in spite of their critical role in its military service. The client, Brigadier General Wilma Vaught, USAF Retired, is the power behind the realization of this visionary project, and her will has been fueled by a desire to transform this country's perception of the women who have served in its defense, to create a monument that will give physical recognition to the collective contribution of a group of individuals previously denied recognition on the basis of gender. Finally, it is a story about the efficacy of the review process for public work in the capital city of the United States.

"Without clear-cut authority, the [women's] . . . ability to influence decisions and coordinate actions depended on perceptions of their relationship to the power structure. In this respect they shared a number of severe handicaps. Because they were totally without military experience, their credibility was always in doubt. Because they held low rank in a hierarchy of top brass, they lacked military clout. Because they were women, it was difficult to be taken seriously. . . . The best things the line directors had going for them were their backgrounds; basic intelligence, an ability to get along with people; the fact that the men were basically unsure of themselves where women were concerned. [They] had no precedents to fall back on so [they] had to chart [their] own course."

– Major General Jeanne Holm, USAF (Ret.)[2]

The history of women in the United States military has been one of persistence, courage, and foresight in the face of repeated frustrations and the built-in institutional resistance of a tradition-bound military subculture. It is a history set against the background of peace and war, social evolution, and advancement in the technology of warfare. It is ultimately a disturbing history of consistently inequitable treatment in both opportunity and recognition. The perceived need for a memorial to women in the military implicitly recognizes that ours is not an egalitarian society without discrepancies in treatment and opportunity, and that there is still the need to confer separate status and recognition for women's contributions.

The initiative to hold a national design competition for a women's memorial was not unprecedented; competitions had been held for the Vietnam and Korean war memorials. However, securing for the competition one of the last sites remaining on the monumental axis was a highly unprecedented achievement. In 1985, Congresswoman Mary

Rose Oakar, chairperson of the House Subcommittee on Libraries and Memorials, had introduced legislation for a memorial to honor women who have served in the Armed Forces of the United States, and to authorize the incorporation of the Women in Military Service for America (WIMSA) Foundation to establish the memorial on federal lands in the District of Columbia or its environs.

In the spring of 1988, the National Park Service assisted the WIMSA Foundation in identifying potential sites within the National Capital Beltway but well outside the monumental corridor: one near Washington National Airport, another near the National Park Service headquarters at Haines Point, and a third in a yet more isolated location. At the conclusion of a guided tour of the sites, the director of the National Park Service, returning to the office at Arlington National Cemetery, drove the site selection team past the cemetery gateway with its 240-foot neoclassical hemicycle/retaining wall on axis with the Lincoln Memorial (fig. 1). General Vaught, aware that she had never known the purpose of that structure or what the site was for, said to the director, "I've never understood that thing. What is it? What does it mean? Is it available?" The director, unable to answer any of her questions, offered to find out.

To understand the significance of the cemetery gateway site, it is necessary to understand its historical context. Washington is a city that has been built, modified, extended, built again; equally, the politics of the city are layered and entrenched. The utopian idea of a monumental city set in a virgin landscape belonged to the nineteenth century of L'Enfant and Jefferson, but the plan of monumental Washington as we know it today was determined in the first quarter of the twentieth century, the same era that also saw the establishment of the Commission of Fine Arts and the National Capital Planning Commission.

The hemicycle wall, at best a dry piece of classicism, was designed in the 1920s by William Kendell of McKim, Mead & White long after the original partners in the firm had died. Devoid of meaning today, the hemicycle wall and forecourt, marked by 60-foot-high pylons, are streaked by thick white and yellow stalactites formed primarily by calcium compounds that leak steadily through the concrete reinforced stone retaining wall. Trees and weeds grow within the most deteriorated joints of the wall.

Aerial view of existing hemicycle/
retaining wall and Arlington
National Cemetery

General Vaught, having given military briefings for twenty-eight years, was exceptionally well qualified to seek site approval from Congress as well as the many commissions and advisory groups that participated in the review process. She recognized that the embarrassing condition of the site, clearly caused by lack of funds to restore and maintain it, was a strategic advantage, and she was confident that site approval would be granted because the WIMSA Foundation was prepared to incorporate into the competition brief the restoration of the hemicycle wall and entrance to Arlington National Cemetery. Additionally, the WIMSA Foundation was prepared to establish a $1 million endowment, which would assist the Park Service in the maintenance of the site after the memorial was built.

On July 28, 1988, the final steps in site selection were accomplished with approval of the hemicycle site by the National Capital Planning Commission and the Commission of Fine Arts. Six weeks later, the extraordinarily thorough preparation by WIMSA and General Vaught resulted in approval by Congress of both the site and the competition design program – a shorter approval period than previously had been achieved for any Washington memorial site.

A national design competition was soon announced and entries were reviewed in June and November 1989. Jurors included artist Mary Miss, architect Romaldo Giurgola, *Boston Globe* critic Robert Campbell, and three women veterans. The competition brief articulated concern for the relationship of the new women's memorial to existing historic structures on the site, and emphasized that restoration and preservation of the historic hemicycle and cemetery gateway were to be integral parts of any design concept. In addition to the memorial itself, the brief called for a 30,000-square-foot education center to be included in the design.

In our preliminary studies for the competition, my partner, Michael Manfredi, and I were powerfully struck by the quality of light defining the family of Washington monuments at night and, by contrast, the darkness that enshrouded the gateway to Arlington National Cemetery. We were also taken by the remarkable view of the city from the site and the carpet of tombstones that stretched behind the wall in the other direction. Our winning scheme proposed four stairs thrusting through the blank niches of the hemicycle wall, and a crown of ten 40-foot-high

FIG. 2

Conceptual model of memorial
with glass spires

glass spires symbolizing the collective nature of the memorial (fig. 2). Our intent was to celebrate the many individuals whose strength reflected collective rather than singular acts of heroism and bravery. The memorial gallery of the education center, located in our scheme behind the hemicycle wall, was to be lit during the day by natural light brought in through the glass spires; at night the spires would join the other illuminated memorials of monumental Washington. The four stairs, breaking through the old wall and ascending to the cemetery above, symbolized women's breaking through of barriers and gradual ascension through the ranks of military service. The stairs also connected the lower level of the memorial with the cemetery level above, making accessible expansive views of the cemetery and the city. The education center, incorporating the hemicycle wall as its only visible facade, was buried, its roof forming a public terrace that met the gravesites and looked back to the city of Washington.

During the first half of 1991, informal reactions to our design by various public agencies and advisory groups required us to prepare additional material for submission to the National Capital Planning Commission. Meetings with preservation review boards revealed their collective concern about penetrations into the existing hemicycle wall that might "damage the historic fabric." In response, reports were prepared by architectural historians demonstrating the precedent for modifying significant historic structures within the monumental axis. We incorporated minor modifications into the design and employed computer imaging to describe the project's appearance by night and by day.

In June 1991, a revised design was presented to the National Capital Memorial Commission, whose members expressed overall satisfaction with the design except for two elements – the spires and the stairs, which were deemed too visible and intrusive for this historically significant site. The commission's recommendations included eliminating the stairs and the spires; or changing the glass spires into marble obelisks like others already present in the cemetery; or lowering them below the 4-foot-high balustrade of the upper terrace so that they would not be visible from the Lincoln Memorial. (The glass spires were viewed as incompatible with the traditional structures in place on the site, and Jacqueline Kennedy expressed concern about night lighting, which she felt might diminish the importance of the Kennedy Flame located on axis with and up the hill from the Women's Memorial.) The director of the National Park Service, also chairman of the National Capital Planning Commission, informed General Vaught that he would not advance our project for the necessary review by other commissions unless we incorporated the recommendations of his commission, which we were unwilling to do. It was a discouraging end to two years of hard work.

Rather than abandoning the project, we met with General Vaught and asked if she would be willing to allow us to present to her and her design advisory board an alternative design scheme based on our original concept. In her typically positive manner, General Vaught agreed. We were immobilized for nearly a month. Light and passage remained the critical ideas, but the parameters and possibilities had been redefined. Finally, with the meeting date only a few days away, we realized that there was another way to employ light to express collective contribution. Our new concept emerged from personal contacts over the previous year and a half with some of the women whom this memorial would be commemorating. They were sharp, direct, modest about their singular contributions, and passionate about the contributions of their respective units of service. We spent a lot of time getting to know one group of women in particular – former military aviators now in their seventies and who continue to fly recreationally. They told us many stories of women pilots whose lives were lost in World War II while transporting injured fighter planes back to neutral territory for repairs (male fighter pilots were considered too valuable to be put at risk for such maintenance missions). Individual recollections like these led us to conclude that the richness of these women's stories could best be conveyed in their own words; no single quote could express the diversity of their experiences and sacrifices. The project needed to make vivid the many voices versus the singular.

In our final scheme, the four stairs still invade the wall selectively, but the gallery behind the wall is lit internally by an arc of 150 glass tablets (figs. 3, 4). Like unbound pages of a journal, the tablets are inscribed with individual quotes that carry the voices of those who served; and

WEISS

FIG. 5

Model of interior of memorial gallery with arc of glass tablets above

their collective memories cast legible shadows into the gap between the wall and the cemetery. At night a horizon of light is transmitted through the glass arc, which is nearly invisible by day (fig. 5).

Our preparation for the next round of approvals became increasingly tactical. General Vaught took the lead, explaining that success in Washington is achieved by patiently "filling in all the squares." She listened carefully to each of the commissions' concerns, read the transcripts of their comments, and prepared lists of items to which we had to respond. She began each meeting with, "We've listened to you carefully, we hope you feel we've responded to your concerns, and we need your help." Staff members of the various commissions became our allies as General Vaught demonstrated her flexibility and desire to "do the best thing for the Memorial and the Gateway to the Cemetery." Eventually, approvals and memoranda of understanding were secured from the National Capital Memorial Commission, the National Capital Planning Commission, the Advisory Council for Historic Preservation, the District of Columbia Historic Preservation Office, the Virginia State Historic Preservation Office, Arlington National Cemetery, the National Park Service, and the National Commission of Fine Arts. Groundbreaking occurred in June 1995 in a televised ceremony at Arlington National Cemetery with the president, Mrs. Clinton, and the secretary of defense present. Construction is scheduled for completion in 1997.

Working on the Women's Memorial has not involved, as one might have expected, long discussions of gender, of "otherness," of separate status, of feminine symbolism, nor of the physical distinctions of form celebrating women versus men. The desire voiced by many newscasters and reporters – to see the memorial as a statue of a woman – was adeptly handled by General Vaught, who replied: "There has been too much time and too broad a set of jobs that military women have held for any statue to do justice to these women's contributions. . . . What uniform would be timeless, what job would be the appropriate one to give form to?" Rather, the project has reinvented a historically significant site in order to provide a powerful symbolic tribute to women patriots.

Design of the Women's Memorial and Education Center has been an experience that should forever destroy the myth of Howard Roark, of the architect as autonomous artist, indifferent to the dynamic circumstances and uncertainties inherent in the design and review processes. The "success" of our project is not the central issue. What remains salient is the passion and commitment of our client and her prescient understanding that what was most critical to the Women's Memorial was that it be located within the center of monumental Washington, not at its periphery.

1. Major General Jeanne Holm, U S A F (Ret.), *Women in the Military: An Unfinished Revolution*, rev. ed. (Novato, Calif.: Presidio Press, 1982), 508.
2. Ibid., 35.

Confessions in Public Space

LYNNE BRESLIN

Architects in practice most often recognize private and public domains
as they are defined by conditions of physical boundedness. In common
law, property ownership means the exclusive private right to determine
occupancy, use, and form. The public interest, however, is asserted by
establishing zoning and building codes and, in some municipalities, regulations concerning materials, heights, and other design features that
strictly determine the conditions for development of that private property.

In architectural theory a division is often made between the private
(domestic) space and the public realm. However, with the development
of new institutions beginning in the late Enlightenment, this simple
private/public division breaks down, generating a progressive crisis of
signification, identification, and function. The hospital, school, and
prison are reconfigured to assume characteristics and functions of both
the private and public realms. In the hospital, for example, our most private acts – giving birth and dying – are performed in public. The very
notion of a public realm comes increasingly under attack as society's
consensus on values weakens and the opportunity to celebrate shared
values, urbanistically, is undermined. Consensus may be legally expressed
and politically arbitrated, but the public internalizes the resulting laws
less and less and relies, instead, on paid surveillance. Thus public codes
of behavior and private impulses often conflict in the daily occupation
of public spaces. In 1904, the New York City subway opened to a week
of public celebration of this newest of civic amenities, but today, ninety
years later, crime so threatens public order that the subway must now
be secured by a separate transit police force. Living/sleeping – common

acts on subway trains and in stations – are outlawed on the grounds that private behavior is not appropriate in public spaces.[1]

The role of visibility and of the "gaze" is also of great importance in defining the public realm.[2] In the United States, the violation of privacy (spying, wiretapping) is legally justified if the public interest is perceived to be threatened. Jeremy Bentham and Michel Foucault recognized (almost two hundred years apart) that any society that maintains a "watch" over its citizens prepares them for subtle (or not-so-subtle) assaults on individual rights facilitated by ever-more invasive technologies that can make a private realm public, despite the opaqueness of space. However, without such technologies opaqueness renders a public space private, leaving it vulnerable to anti-social conduct. Thus parks are often renovated to increase the visibility of pedestrians and police so that such private acts as vagrancy, drug use and dealing, and other crimes are discouraged.

The dialectic of private and public allows us to define ourselves both as individuals (private persons) and as public citizens (members of a polis). The nature of our private identification – the acknowledgment of our individuality (depending on gender, race, nationality, values, politics) – has spatial and architectural implications. Similarly, our ability to identify public spaces, our readiness or reluctance to project ourselves into those public spaces, and our actions in those spaces depend on our well-being in, and psychological evaluation of, such spaces.

The Museum as Articulation of Public and Private

Nationality and identity as the particularized versions of private and public are often mobilized by the museum experience. The accounting of individual/private acts in relation to the public or national interest becomes a qualitative standard for the polis. Yet the continuing implosion of public and private makes the discerning of potential for individual and social expression even more critical. While some modern critics have reviled the museum as a desiccated, encyclopedic, diachronic venture that buries culture and history, Andreas Huyssen argues otherwise. In his essay "Escape from Amnesia: The Museum as Mass Medium," he points out that in museums there is the possibility of "people experiencing the never-ceasing negotiations between self and other."[3] In its building design, its collections, and its curatorial approaches, the museum foregrounds issues of memory, representation, and narrative.

The museum as an institution began as one of the great Enlightenment projects – the material objectification of knowledge and the ordering of matter and culture (science, people, art, and history). In the late 1960s, the emergence of several new types of museums, accompanied by new attitudes toward design and curating, not only demonstrated an expansion of interest in the museum as a public/social forum – a clearly "spectacular" operation – but also shifted its focus from an objectified majority (defined according to the dominant values of a white European male elite) to a particular, subjective marginality that embraces gender as well as race, class, national origin, religion, age, and numerous other sociopolitical subsets.[4]

The Smithsonian's National Museum of American History in Washington, D.C., is a good example of this shift. Originally a repository of artifacts of high culture and officially sanctioned historical interest, the American History museum later began to collect everyday objects – the private stuff of popular culture. At about the same time, new museums and museum exhibitions of interest only to small segments of the population began to attract growing and increasingly mainstream audiences. From the Musée des Arts Populaires (with its collection of toys, cooking equipment, clothing, instruments) to the Museum of Humor, the National Museum of Women in the Arts, the Museum of Television and Radio, African-American museums, Native American museums, Jewish museums, and children's museums, we have witnessed an almost endless desire for the absorption of the popular, the marginal, the ephemeral, and the peripheral – for restructuring it into transcendent significance.

Huyssen points out in his essay that the public craves the sharing and experience of the materiality of everyday objects. This need for actualizing a public realm in the shared reexperience of common histories, everyday occurrences, and aesthetic moments has been mobilized in two recent Smithsonian exhibitions: *From Field to Factory*, which traced African-American migration from the southern to the northern states; and *A More Perfect Union and the U.S. Constitution*, the story of the legally sanctioned treatment of Japanese Americans during World War II, including the interning of most of the West Coast Japanese-American population. Both exhibitions made more explicit an official but personalized accounting of a problematic history and a marginalized identity within a nation. Both said a great deal about American legal wrongdoing and officially sanctioned violation of minority rights, and both were designed so as to compel the museum visitor to experience and perceive these violations personally and privately. For example, at two adjacent entryways to *From Field to Factory* marked "White" and "Colored," the museum visitor was forced to take a stand, to choose an identity, to act as "White" or "Colored" in embarking on this historical passage through a series of one-to-one oral histories. In *A More Perfect Union*, the visitor had to accept the confidences of a father recalling his humiliation at internship and discrimination – at his separation from the majority. Whether or not visitors were able to accept as authentic these victims' testimonies (relating what it was like to live behind fences and the lingering tug of guilt and inferiority) remains to be fully evaluated, but the drama of dispossession and dislocation because of the accident of birth is no longer left to nuance and inference. The point made in these exhibitions is the vulnerability and powerlessness of the private individual in a public realm where the will of the majority is left morally unchallenged.

This implosion of public history and (marginalized) private identity is further explored in the United States Holocaust Memorial Museum in Washington, D.C. At the entrance, each visitor is given a passport and an assumed identity (close in age and gender-matched to the visitor's identity) so that the events of the exhibition can be experienced in a more direct way. At significant junctures, passports are electronically updated to note the changing circumstances of the visitor's assumed identity (now you are living in the ghetto, now you are interned in a camp, now you escape and work with the underground – though in the majority of the forty thousand real cases depicted in this exhibition, death was the victim's fate). The visitor follows a promenade that leads through one of the cattle cars used to transport victims to the Nazi concentration camps and past a real barracks and crematorium from Auschwitz. The visitor's experience is manipulated so that objective distancing of fact and past history via the safety net of simulation is not possible. Here the museum creates not simply a context – a mise en scène – but rather a setting for emotionally laden artifacts that viscerally recall past existence. This shift to the material – to real, intense fragments of horror – demands emotional as well as intellectual engagement.

Another example of this design strategy is *Assignment Rescue: The Story of Varian Fry*, an exhibition for the United States Parks Service installed in temporary exhibition space in the Holocaust Memorial Museum (figs. 1–3).[5] The client's directive was to communicate that legal and moral action are not always the same, and that when law and morality come into conflict, the greater good is to act morally, even if this means violating the law. This message was conveyed through the story of Varian Fry and his work during a thirteen-month period beginning in the fall of 1940 as a representative of the Emergency Rescue Committee in Marseille, France. Fry's mission was to save as many as possible of the artists, intellectuals, writers, and politicians trapped in Nazi-occupied and Vichy France. Identity, identification, and party membership become morally compromising conditions. Public/private, objective/subjective are the issues in this particular examination of a repressed event.

Private artifacts – diaries, personal effects, private letters, postcards to loved ones, confidential memoranda, souvenir photographs, government forms, and oral histories that reveal much information of a very personal nature – engage the visitor, who, through several exhibition strategies, is forced into complicity. In order to understand what is going on, the visitor quite naturally looks through slightly ajar doors, into open drawers, closets, and suitcases, louvers, and one-way mirrors; the visitor cannot help but overhear, oversee. Without quite realizing it, the visitor penetrates the sanctioned space of the museum, crossing over the line, the invisible but tangible wall that is supposed to separate visitor from the museum staging. The story is a "secret," documented only incidentally with photographs of the peripherally permitted and the officially allowed that never explicitly depict events or reveal the rescue maneuvers. A

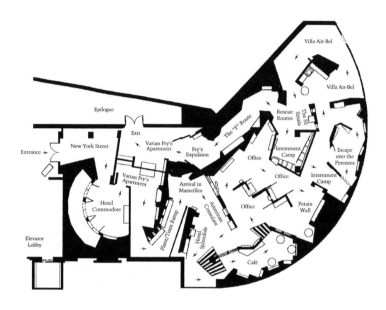

FIG. 1

Assignment Rescue, exhibition
floor plan

FIG. 2

The "F" Route

Fry and his staff constantly
refined their clandestine strategies
as border patrols became stricter,
the Vichy government changed its
exit visa policies, old escape routes
were discovered, and new ones
had to be established and tested.
Fry enlisted a refugee couple,
Johannes and Lisa Fittko, to help
him organize what would become
one of the committee's most successful escape routes to Spain –
the "F" Route

FIG. 3

The Villa Air-Bel

The intensity of Fry's work began to take a personal toll. He and his staff endured interrogations, searches, and constant surveillance by the distrustful French and American authorities. When several of his colleagues decided to rent a villa on the outskirts of Marseille, Fry seized the opportunity to move in and escape the relentless pace of his work for a few hours each day. Several Surrealist artists and their families who were waiting to receive their visas completed the company.

From the Villa Air-Bel, Fry wrote to his wife, "I now live in a château about half a mile out, and none of my clients knows where. It is a delightful big house, with an incredible Mediterranean view from the terrace. Besides four members of my staff, André Breton and Victor Serge and their wives live with us. They too are clients, but of the delightful rather than the pestiferous kind. Breton is particular fun: I like Surrealists. The first night, for instance, he had a bottle full of praying mantises, which he released on the tablecloth at dinner and had walking round like so many pets"

series of walls that separate, hide, and reveal double dealings creates a space in which the visitor experiences the conditions that in 1940–41 ensnared the hunted, the refugee, and Fry himself.

Assignment Rescue is an exhibition that progressively demands not spectator approbation, but an intrusive behavior, which challenges the normally conditioned, passive experience of museum-going. The distinction between authentic and facsimile, while recognized, is muted and consigned a less important role in the orchestration of a psychologically invested surrealistic enactment of Fry's mission. The angled, lateral, obsessive spaces introduce the visitor to a world – Marseille in the 1940s – where it was impossible for the private person (refugee or rescuer) ever to occupy the center, to freely observe the monumental (public) city. The visitor/refugee is always relegated to the periphery, deprived of the "gaze." Public collapses into private through the confession of private acts in public space.

1. See Henri Lefebvre, *The Production of Space,* trans. Donald Nicholson-Smith (Oxford and Cambridge, Mass.: Blackwell, 1991). Philosophers from Hegel to Lefebvre have claimed that each age engenders paradigmatic forms and types that express a consensus of the polis, its philosophy and culture in public architecture (the Renaissance *palazzo* might be seen as a confusion between domestic and public architecture, but since the nobility ruled, their homes and places of business inevitably assumed a public presence).

2. Since the 1950s, the discourse of the "spectacular" society and the postmodern have elaborated on the shrinking of *both* the private and public realms. Baudrillard discusses the implosion of the public and private realm into the television box and computer screen. Guy Debord routinely points out that in our universal condition – that of a spectator society – private experience has been so mediated that the individual can no longer experience authentic emotions. S/he looks to a conditioned response (inculcated through the mediated medium that circumscribes any and all experience) for instructions on how to react. As our private capacity is diminished, our ability to meet in unmediated public space erodes.

3. Andreas Huyssen, "Escape from Amnesia: The Museum as Mass Medium," in *Twilight Memories: Marking Time in a Culture of Amnesia* (New York: Routledge,

1994). Huyssen presents Baudrillard's attitude toward the museum – a "simulation machine like television . . . extending sometimes towards the preservation of districts – whole areas of cities" as a modernist attitude. "For Baudrillard, musealization is the pathological attempt to preserve, control and dominate the real in order to hide the fact that the real is in agony due to the spread of simulation. . . . Musealization is precisely the opposite of preservation, it is killing, freezing, sterilising, dehistoricising, and decontextualizing." Huyssen skillfully argues that Baudrillard's depiction of the exploded museum as imploded world never acknowledges "any of the vital attempts to work through repressed or marginalized pasts or acknowledges the current to create alternative forms of museum activities" (30).

4. I view gender as a subset of the marginal because, grouped with race, class, national origin, religion, and age (to mention only some), it is related to the larger social political issues of marginality. The countercultural protests in the America of the 1960s gave voice to groups publicizing their differences from the majority. Postmodernism took the political movements of feminism, civil rights, anti-war, and Marxism and elaborated on the conditions of marginality (the emphasis of the particular) granting license to individuals to focus on and celebrate difference. Thirty years ago, individuals often repressed their difference to maintain entitlement, while today mainstream culture and commerce (if not politics) embrace and market marginality. Museums have often addressed the lack of information and documentation to better depict difference. As institutions, museums are not simply capitalizing on the desire for more information but are instrumental in enabling their audience to construct identities. Material culture and history are necessary for self-education as well as majority education.

5. Conceptualized and designed by Lynne Breslin: Architecture and Design. The design team, led by Breslin and including Meira Kowalsky and Dennis Balk, worked closely with the Exhibitions Department of the Holocaust Memorial Museum, headed by Susan Morgenstein, Lauriston Marshall, Elizabeth Berman, and Marvin Liberman. Breslin was also responsible for the interior design of the temporary exhibition gallery on the concourse level.

Diversity by Design: Feminist Reflections on the Future of Architectural Education and Practice

LESLIE KANES WEISMAN

Teaching and practice in service of social justice and environmental responsibility have historically been considered marginal to the central concerns of architecture. Those who are committed to these goals often find themselves "outsiders within an inner circle of privilege."[1] However, I am optimistic that the current identity crisis in architectural education and practice – about which there is a plethora of recently published books and articles[2] – will cause the margins and the center to change place. I fear that if they do not, the practice of architecture may well become anachronistic and irrelevant.

The fundamental question facing architectural education and practice today is not how better to train future architects to compete against one another in a diminishing job market and professional role; but, rather, how to improve the quality of architectural education and practice as inherently interrelated, life-affirming models for understanding the world at large, and each person's special "belongingness" to it. Lynda H. Schneekloth puts the question this way:

"How do we situate ourselves within the academy that simultaneously privileges us and excludes others and is therefore a form of oppression that subjugates other knowledges and peoples? We who are located in the university and are trained by the university as professionals, are implicated in the production and reproduction of the existing truths that marginalize and empower. We have the intellectual tools and time to engage in a sustained critique of the culture, to resist the elitist claims of the university, and to transform the deformation resulting from participation in oppression. This work is one of our most emancipatory projects."[3]

In the industrialized Western world of the nineteenth and twentieth centuries, almost all design and technology has been based on the disassembling of organic wholes into fragmented parts. Both physical space and social place have been shaped by dichotomies: cities and suburbs, workplaces and dwellings, architecture and nature, women and men, rich and poor, black and white, young and old, gay and straight, able-bodied and disabled. Today, we stand at the foothills of the twenty-first century, facing a future in which the old, dichotomous paradigms simply will not work. The disastrous consequences of global homelessness, poverty, and environmental degradation, and the escalation of social chaos, violence, and disharmony worldwide require healing and the restoration of wholeness within the art of living. The bleak and hostile environments of most American cities must be transformed into places of health, regeneration, and conviviality.

Architecture, too often regarded as a matter of style, is now a matter of survival. After eleven thousand years of building to protect ourselves from the environment, we are now discovering that our designs often diminish our health and the viability of the planet. The global need for housing, healthcare, and environmental restoration have far-reaching consequences for all of humanity's future. Architects have a particularly important and creative role to play in addressing these problems.[4]

I write as an architectural educator who believes that it is professionally myopic and morally irresponsible to teach students to evaluate architectural work in terms of aesthetics, building performance, and cost without also teaching them to consider whether what they are designing is ecologically intelligent and socially just. I also write as a feminist who believes that equal rights for women are not worth having in a society that would force people to choose between the pain of a woman who is the victim of domestic violence and an African-American man who is beaten by police officers who are just "doing their job." In such a society, no one has a monopoly on suffering. Moreover, if we fail to see and understand the systemic connection between the behavior of those who rape the earth and those who rape women – if we say we will stop doing violence to the environment and its precious biodiversity but remain neutral and unmoved by the overwhelming global violence against women, children, and people of color – those who hold power in society will simply be free to continue to displace the tragedies of oppression and exploitation from one locus or group to another. To achieve a feminist future in which all people and all life matters, we will have to move beyond the politics of exclusion, intolerance, and competing special interests; we will have to recognize the interdependence among all of humanity, the natural world, and the products of human design; and we will have to learn to think and act out of that recognition.

Recognizing the Challenges

The Global Need for Housing Today, one quarter of the world's population – more than one billion people – do not have adequate housing. Since the 1960s, major wars in Eastern Europe, Asia, Latin America, Africa, and elsewhere have created a vast refugee population of some thirty million people, 75 percent of them women and children. An estimated 100 million people worldwide are homeless.[5]

In the United States in 1989, twenty-nine million people needed low-income housing, including eleven million children and four million elderly; yet only one in four of those in need had access to it. Two and one-half million Americans are displaced from their homes each year. Homelessness, which afflicts three million Americans, continues to grow by leaps and bounds among all ages, races, and household types, but especially among minority women and children.[6] From the miserable refugee camps in Bosnia and Rwanda and the squalid shanty towns of South Africa, to the deplorable public housing projects of North America, the need to provide decent, affordable housing is crucial worldwide; and that need will escalate as the global population continues to expand throughout the twenty-first century.

Today, although many individual faculty members offer studio courses that address housing design relative to urban renewal and the needs of the homeless, the poor, low-income households, and immigrant groups, few architecture schools require courses that analyze the social and political contexts in which housing is designed and built. Yet an understanding of housing economics, manufacturing processes, real-estate development, land-use zoning, government housing programs, political systems, and community organization is essential if architects are to be effective advocates of housing as a basic right available to all people as well as designers of houses for the affluent.

Architecture and Healthcare Equally crucial will be the need to provide innovative healthcare environments that contribute to healing and human welfare. Advances in medicine and nutrition have made important contributions to extending the average lifespan. In the next forty years the population eighty-five and older will quadruple in the United States. The Census Bureau estimates that by the year 2020, for every hundred middle-age persons, there will be 253 senior citizens;[7] and as the population continues to age, there will be a dramatic increase in the numbers of people with some form of mobility, vision, or hearing impairment, as well as those suffering from Alzheimer's disease and other dementias. The traditional skilled nursing home will not be an appropriate residential setting, either financially or psychologically, for a significant number who will only require a minimal or moderate level of assisted care.

In addition to the burgeoning aging population, the AIDS pandemic will cause the demand for health-related services and facilities to soar. In 1994, there were one million Americans with AIDS or HIV trying to gain access to an appallingly inadequate healthcare system with beleaguered healthcare facilities. The World Health Organization estimates that worldwide there are currently ten million people infected with HIV and that by the year 2000, that number will grow to forty million. Harvard University, however, predicts that by that date 100 million people will be living with HIV, ten million of them children under the age of five years.[8]

Despite the need for design expertise in healthcare that these statistics project, there is currently a paucity of courses and programs on the subject available in architecture schools.[9] Who in this last decade of the twentieth century is being taught to design barrier-free, assisted-living arrangements with built-in healthcare and support services for the frail elderly and people with Altzheimer's or AIDS? Who will provide small-scale, family-oriented neighborhood wellness centers where preventive medicine is practiced? New regional hospitals providing state-of-the-art technology for those in need of specialized care? Hospice settings to ease the pain of terminal illness? In the future, redesigning existing healthcare settings and creating new environments for care and cure will offer design professionals a major challenge for which few architecture students are being prepared.

"Lifespan" Design As four-generation families become the norm in the next few decades, new transgenerational or "lifespan" design standards will have to be developed and used to construct new buildings and adapt existing spaces so that people of all ages and with different levels of physical ability can live and work independently. ("Lifespan" design conceptually expands the more familiar term "universal design," which implies, quite impossibly, that "one size fits all.") Buildings and spaces designed according to "lifespan" principles would be dynamic, not static; changeable over time in response to social and environmental factors and the changing needs, activities, and life circumstances of the people who use them. "Lifespan" design embodies a philosophy of process and architectural transformation that will require architects and designers to change their priorities from designing buildings of permanence and monumentality to designing buildings and spaces that survive, like living species, by adaptive evolution.[10]

Although there are notable exceptions,[11] few architecture students are presently being introduced to these issues. Practitioners – obliged to design to code in order to avoid lawsuits – are learning to comply with the complex regulations for accessibility set forth in the Americans with Disabilities Act (ADA), but it is the spirit not the letter of the ADA that both architecture students and practitioners should be responding to by exploring the potential for innovation inherent in "lifespan" design.

Restoring the Environment In the future, environmental restoration, a new cross-disciplinary field dedicated to the science and art of healing the earth, will employ huge numbers of people around the world in cleaning up and repairing the damage done to our water, land, and air, and in restoring regional habitats and ecosystems to protect endangered species. This emerging "green consciousness" should have a profound impact on architectural education and practice as designers begin to understand the consequences of the choices they make. For example, design practitioners, through lack of awareness and, until fairly recently,

lack of choice, have specified building materials that come from threatened or non-renewable resources; materials that are mined, harvested,
or manufactured in a manner that creates pollution or in other ways is
harmful to the environment, and is destructive of certain cultures. Architects and designers also have unknowingly specified toxic building products and HVAC systems that create indoor air pollution ("sick building
syndrome"), a phenomenon that costs the United States $60 billion a year
in absenteeism, medical bills, and lost worker productivity. (The EPA
ranks poor indoor air quality as the fourth highest health risk out of
thirty-one classes of pollution.)[12]

More than half of the energy that is consumed in the United States
every year goes into constructing and maintaining the built environment;
and wasted construction materials represent 20 percent of the contents
of all landfills in the U.S. or thirty-one and a half million tons of waste.[13]
"Green architecture" is not a trend; it is an ethical responsibility for all
architecture students and practitioners.

At present, architectural offices generally score higher than architec-
tural schools on the environmental literacy test. Organizations like the
American Institute of Architects (AIA), Architects, Designers and Planners
for Social Responsibility (ADPSR) and groups like the Rocky Mountain
Institute (RMI) have developed impressive resource guides, bibliographies,
and databases on green building technologies, materials, and products.
Some educational programs, like the Center for Regenerative Studies at
California State Polytechnic University, Ball State University, and Yester-
morrow Design/Build School in Warren, Vermont, are pioneering in
training future architects to be environmentally responsible designers. Still,
there are relatively few practitioners and even fewer graduating students
who know how to integrate sustainable design principles into their work;
most are unprepared even to challenge energy-wasteful building conventions.

Cultural Pluralism in Neighborhood Regeneration Thirty years of continuous immigration from Latin America, the Caribbean, and Asia has dramatically shifted demographics in the United States and will ultimately
change America's view of race. Currently, 13 percent of the nation's population is African-American; nearly 10 percent, or twenty-five million, is

Hispanic. Another three and a half million are Chinese, Japanese, Koreans, Filipinos, Vietnamese, and Laotian Hmong, and hundreds of thousands are dark-skinned East Indians, Pakistanis, and Bangladeshis. The 1990 census identified nearly three hundred "races," six hundred Indian tribes, seventy Hispanic groups, and seventy-five combinations of multiracial ancestry.[14] These demographic changes will have no less an impact on architectural education and practice than on society as a whole.

All across the United States, ethnically and racially diverse middle- and working-class people are struggling to regenerate deteriorated inner-city neighborhoods through collective activism dedicated to creating affordable homes and safe streets (see also the essays in this volume by Ghislaine Hermanuz and Lauretta Vinciarelli). As agents of social change and urban renewal, these neighborhood groups should be able to form powerful partnerships with socially concerned architects. How can an architectural education that continues to define professional expertise in relation to the history of white, heterosexual, Euro-American male consciousness prepare students to function as effective professionals in pluralistic communities? How will students be sensitized to "difference" when they are encouraged to suppress their own gender, race, and class identities in the process of becoming "professional"?

Equal Access to Electronic Information Like ecological awareness and multi-culturalism, information technology will also transform societies. In the coming decades, access to the information highway will be the basis for generating wealth and power and determining the fundamental ability to function in a democratic society. In 1994, American consumers spent $8 billion on personal computers, just a little less than the $8.3 billion they spent on television sets.[15] Not surprisingly, access to the new technology breaks down along gender, race, and class lines. Wealthy and upper middle-class families, white males, and affluent school districts form the bulk of computer owners and users. The impact of this disparity is reflected in a study that determined that those who can use computers earn 15 percent more than those in similar jobs who cannot.[16] This statistic reveals one of the most troubling questions of the information age: in an era in which success is increasingly identified with the ability to gain access to cyberspace, will the new technology only widen the gap between women and men, rich and poor, white and non-white, educated and undereducated?[17]

Computers have already had a significant impact on architectural practice. Computer-aided design has eliminated entry-level drafting jobs, increased the productivity and profitability of firms using the technology, and "eliminated the barriers of time and distance that once protected firms from [long distance] competition. . . . By the year 2000, any two person design firm [will be able to] do work anywhere."[18] The implications for architectural education are clear: students who graduate without computer skills will be seriously handicapped in the job market; and schools that fail to provide their graduates with these tools will risk their status as accredited degree programs.

Learning From Feminism

Increasingly, architecture schools are being criticized for graduating students who discover that their "status is low, their chances at designing something satisfying are slim . . . and their earnings stand scant prospect of being commensurate with the length of their training."[19] Some argue that "the implicit guarantee that the school prepares the student for the world of work verges on dishonesty."[20] Feminist pedagogy – with its attention to collective processes, redefining power relationships, deconstructing false dichotomies (for example, between theory and practice, client and professional), and eliminating inequities in gender, race, class, disability status, and sexual orientation – can be especially useful in constructing a new model of architectural education and practice attuned to today's real problems and possibilities. Four feminist educational principles deserve discussion.[21]

Employ Collaborative Learning Educators should develop and use teaching methods in which interdependent, team problem solving and "co-creativity" are practiced and rewarded over competitive, solitary problem solving and individual creativity. In the discipline of architecture, which has historically applauded the solo virtuoso designer, reconceptualizing and valuing the different roles and contributions of individuals within a collective design process represents a radical change. Nevertheless, collaborative learning in small groups is important preparation for a world in which most problems, whether scientific, corporate, or architectural, will be solved in teams.

Share Authority and Knowledge Teachers must share their authority and question their monopoly over knowledge so that students are empowered to direct their own learning, and so that people in other disciplines and with different life experiences can join in the problem-solving discourse. In the future, the boundaries of the problem to be solved – not the boundaries of a single academic discipline – will determine what knowledge is needed and where it can best be found. These changes will be facilitated by the growing and ultimately universal use of computers in the classroom. As tools for learning, computers will dramatically change both the locus of information and the traditional role of the teacher as oracle versus the student as passive recipient of hand-me-down knowledge. In the techno-university, education will shift from experts giving answers to students seeking answers.[22]

Eliminate False Dichotomies Teachers must create learning situations that connect academic theory and knowledge with applied practice, establishing collaborative relationships among architects, clients, and user groups. The best way to teach students about cultural difference is to involve them with people who are different from themselves – not easily accomplished within the narrow confines of the traditionally elitist university dominated by privileged white males. Further, although architecture has always been a service profession, it has traditionally served only those who can afford to pay for it.

Faculty can address these concerns by arranging for students to work as volunteers on real projects for non-profit organizations that engage contemporary social and environmental problems. The non-profit organizations and the constituencies they serve become, in effect, pro bono clients.[23] Be it through design/build studios, community design centers, design/research studios, or elective and required courses, service learning raises students' confidence in their own abilities to meet the challenges of the real world, in which they will practice. As important, they learn that being an architect – with all the formal and technological demands the role involves – and working for social justice and a sustainable future do not have to be at odds.

Emphasize Ethical Values and Interconnectedness Teachers should inspire and challenge students to use their creative abilities to improve our world by changing what they find today into what is needed tomorrow; into what is fair and just for all people and all life on our planet. When we design, we affect the lives of others by our decisions. When students discover that they are accountable to others, they begin to design in an empathic mode, entering into peoples' plights and identifying with their concerns. And when this happens, students, educators, and practitioners cannot remain neutral or detached from the processes and products of their own design; they are summoned to compassionate action in which they seek to empower others through their work, rather than merely imposing their own images on the world.

Reexamining Professional Boundaries

To prepare architects for professional practice in a world characterized by global telecommunications, environmentally responsible lifestyles, and increasingly aging and pluralistic societies worldwide, architecture must become a more research-oriented, knowledge-based profession; and the conventional professional boundaries of the discipline must be reexamined. Architects must learn how better to solve problems in interdisciplinary teams with experts in natural resource conservation, economics, politics, art, medicine, behavioral and social sciences, law, and engineering. They must learn to work in innovative partnerships with low-income, non-profit, and culturally diverse groups. They must be taught how to use design as a tool to create, rather than respond to, public policy, legal regulations, and building codes. They must be taught not only to design buildings but also to diagnose them for their healthfulness, energy efficiency, and accessibility. The public's growing interest in healthy buildings and barrier-free design must be translated into an architecture where both function and form celebrate the environmental message and human diversity. "Green architecture" and "accessible design" must evolve beyond the inclusion of environmental control systems and wheelchair ramps which, while functionally and morally important, have hardly produced visually inspiring architecture.

Several initiatives that address the need to redefine the architecture profession are worth mentioning. For example, the *Code of Conduct for Diversity in Architectural Education,* published in 1992 by the Association of Collegiate Schools of Architecture, states:

"Given current demographic trends, architectural education – and ultimately the architectural profession – will be denying itself the best pool of young talent, if major segments of the population are not encouraged and welcomed to the study of architecture. If students of architecture are not encouraged to be sensitive to the pluralism of our culture, they will not be able to serve the diverse range of clients with whom they will eventually be working. Students who learn to develop a sensitivity to the diverse cultural traditions of the world will be better prepared to take on the challenges of working in the global marketplace. This is important not just for the career development of individual students, but also for the competitive advantage of both the profession and national interests."[24]

In support of this statement, the National Architectural Accrediting Board has asked all school visitation teams to put more emphasis on evaluating how a school's curriculum and administrative policies and practices "contribute to and enrich gender, racial and ethnic diversity in architectural education."[25] Similarly, the American Institute of Architects has established a Diversity Program to provide women and "minority" members – defined in the broadest sense to include diversity by gender, race, creed, ethnic origin, age, disability, or sexual orientation – with equal access and influence at all levels of the Institute and profession. California Women in Environmental Design (CWED), based in San Francisco, has created a booklet entitled *Design = Leadership, A New Perspective for Designing a Better Future,* that provides design students and professionals, political and business leaders, and community groups with guidelines for determining the impact of a proposed design upon the public good at all scales, from a single building to a regional plan. *Project EASE: Educating Architects for a Sustainable*

Environment, has held two planning conferences in which invited participants with expertise in sustainable development, architectural education and practice, landscape architecture, planning, environmental science, and architectural and ecological research have evaluated existing program content throughout North America in light of "the demands of sustainability, changing demographics, social and cultural change . . . and the need to restore architects to leadership positions in the world community."[26]

The politics of human and environmental exploitation that defined the twentieth century must be replaced in the twenty-first century with an ethic of interdependence that values human difference, fosters relationships of human equity, and acknowledges humanity's debt to the earth. As the form givers in our society, architects have a professional opportunity and civic responsibility to contribute their expertise toward that end. But to effectively do so, traditional architectural education and practice must undergo creative change today.

1. Sharon E. Sutton paraphrases bell hooks's phrase in "Contradictory Missions of a Tempered Radical's Teaching," Jeffrey Howard, ed., *Praxis I: Faculty Casebook on Community Service Learning* (Ann Arbor: ocsl Press at the University of Michigan Press, 1993), 152.

2. For examples on architectural practice, see Thomas Fisher, "Can This Profession Be Saved?" *Progressive Architecture* (February 1994), 5–49, 84; and Dana Cuff, *Architecture: The Story of Practice* (Cambridge, Mass.: MIT Press, 1991). For examples on architectural education, refer to Greig Crysler, "Critical Pedagogy and Architectural Education," *Journal of Architectural Education (JAE)* 48 (May 1995), 208–17; Thomas Dutton, ed., *Voices in Architectural Education, Cultural Politics and Pedagogy* (New York: Bergen and Garvey, 1991); and Sharon E. Sutton, "Seeing the Whole of the Moon," in Schoem Frankel and Zuniga Lewis, eds., *Multicultural Teaching in the University* (Westport: Praeger Publishers, 1993), 161–71.

3. Lynda H. Schneekloth, "Partial Utopian Visions," in *Women and the Environment,* Human Behavior and Environment series 3, Irwin Altman and Arza Churchman, eds. (New York: Plenum Press, 1994), 288–89.

4. In the future, successful problem solving will require an increasingly sophisticated collaboration among many different specialists. When I refer to architectural education and practice in this essay, I do so for the sake of brevity and mean also to include those practicing, teaching, and studying in the related professions of inte-

rior design, industrial design, product design, landscape architecture, and planning.

5. Mim Kelber, ed., *Official Report of the World Women's Congress for a Healthy Planet* (New York: Women's Environment and Development Organization, 1992), 3.

6. *Safety Network, The Newsletter of the National Coalition for the Homeless* 6 (June 1989), 1; and Jane Midgley, *The Women's Budget,* 3rd ed. (Philadelphia: Women's International League for Peace and Freedom, 1989), 16.

7. Melinda Beck, "The Geezer Boom," *Newsweek,* special issue, "The 21st Century Family" (Winter/Spring 1990), 66.

8. Erik Eckholm, "Aids, Fatally Steady in the U.S., Accelerates Worldwide," *New York Times,* June 28, 1992, E8.

9. The University of Wisconsin–Milwaukee offers courses in gerontology and architecture; Texas A&M and Clemson University teach health-facilities design; Harvard lists a number of professional development courses in universal design, hospital design, and the design of assisted-living facilities; and New York University School of Continuing Education established a certificate program in healthcare design in 1994. The American Institute of Architects (AIA), in cooperation with the Association of Collegiate Schools of Architecture (ACSA), has developed a Design For Aging Curriculum Resource Package, which was tested by architecture faculty at ten ACSA schools in Spring 1995. The National Symposium on Healthcare Design, based in Martinez, Calif., holds annual conferences that bring together design educators, practitioners, healthcare providers, and manufacturers specializing in health-related environments.

10. For further discussion about the impact of changing demographics and other social trends on the future of housing design, see "Redesigning the Domestic Landscape" in Leslie Kanes Weisman, *Discrimination by Design: A Feminist Critique of the Man-Made Environment* (Urbana: University of Illinois Press, 1992).

11. Adaptive Environments in Boston, Mass., has developed an excellent model curriculum on universal design which was tested in twenty-two schools in 1993–94.

12. "Healthy Buildings and Materials," AIA Building Connections Series Videoconferences; "Building Green, Audubon House," videotape (New York: National Audubon Society, 1993); and National Audubon Society and Croxton Collaborative, Architects, *Audubon House, Building the Environmentally Responsible, Energy-Efficient Office* (New York: John Wiley & Sons, 1994), 38.

13. "Resource Flows and Efficiencies," AIA Building Connections Series Videoconferences (Washington, D.C.: American Institute of Architects, 1993).

14. Tom Morganthau, "What Color is Black?" *Newsweek,* February 13, 1995, 64–65.

15. Suneel Ratan, "A New Divide Between Haves and Have Nots?" *Time,* special issue,

"Welcome to Cyberspace" (Spring 1995), 25.

16. Ibid.

17. The Women, Information Technology, and Scholarship (WITS) Group at the Center for Advanced Study, University of Illinois at Urbana-Champaign, has developed a series of recommendations and action steps that individuals and organizations can take to ensure gender equity in global communications networks.

18. Fisher, 46.

19. Ibid., 47.

20. Thomas Saint, as quoted in ibid.

21. Feminist pedagogy is currently used by many design educators, in both traditional universities and in alternative educational settings like the Women's School of Planning and Architecture (WSPA) and Sheltering Ourselves: A Women's Learning Exchange (SOWLE). WSPA was cofounded in 1974 and operated until 1981 as a national summer program open to all women interested in the environmental design professions and trades. For a history of the organization, its goals and curricula see Leslie Kanes Weisman, "A Feminist Experiment, Learning From WSPA, Then and Now" in Ellen Perry Berkeley with Matilda McQuaid, eds., *Architecture, A Place For Women* (Washington, D.C.: Smithsonian Institution Press, 1989), 125–33. SOWLE, based at the Women's Research and Development Center, Cincinnati, Ohio, has been operating since 1987 as an international association of women who are personally and professionally involved in issues of housing and economic development for women and their families. SOWLE's learning exchanges are designed in a variety of formats accessible to women of diverse racial and educational backgrounds.

22. Claudia Wallis, "The Learning Revolution," *Time* (Spring 1995), 50.

23. For more information on service learning see Susan DeLuca-Dicker, "Building a Revolution, Using Architecture and Education to Instigate Social Change," *Interiors & Sources* 6 (January/February 1993), 38–43; and Leslie Kanes Weisman, "An AIDS Education," *The Construction Specifier* 46 (August 1993), 78–80.

24. The Association of Collegiate Schools of Architecture, *Code of Conduct for Diversity in Architectural Education* (Washington, D.C.: ACSA, 1992), 2.

25. Letter from John M. Maudlin-Jeronimo, AIA, Executive Director of the National Architectural Accrediting Board, Inc. (NAAB), to NAAB Visiting Team Members, January 5, 1994.

26. Published materials on Project EASE are forthcoming. The project is headed by Marvin E. Rosenman, Professor and Chair, Department of Architecture, College of Architecture and Planning, Ball State University.

Resisting the Patriarchal Norms of Professional Education: Reply to Leslie Kanes Weisman

SHARON E. SUTTON

Power. Many people conceive of it as a somewhat negative characteristic of the human psyche, encompassing the capacity to exert force, manipulate, coerce, and even destroy. Having power in the sense of control or domination means having superior physical strength, economic resources, or public distinction; it accrues to the wealthy, to politicians, corporate executives, and famous athletes.[1] Being without power – being powerless – is being unable to exercise choice, deferring to others who are supposedly more qualified, reacting to someone else's agenda rather than setting one's own. Being powerless suggests a state of dependence, alienation, or disenfranchisement; it is the domain of the poor, women, persons of color, and even those professional students who are trained to conform to white middle-class norms in university settings.

In an earlier era, when relationships were more circumscribed and resources more plentiful, hierarchical conceptions of authority were less damaging than they are in today's multicultural society because control – whether of nature or society – necessarily results in exploitative uses of the earth's assets. Leslie Kanes Weisman draws a connection between degradation of the physical environment and a dichotomized social world-view that assigns greatly varied status and worth to different individuals, which, in turn, affects their access to natural resources.[2] As development ethicist Rajni Kothari wrote in 1990: "Modern humanity, and in particular Western technological humanity, has accumulated wealth by denying the rights of others to share in nature's bounty. These 'others' include marginal communities (tribes and small villages), future generations, and other species. Inequality, nonsustainability, and ecological instability all arise from the selfish and arrogant notion that nature's gifts are for private exploitation, not for sharing."[3]

287

A sustainable society rests not only on the willingness of the powerful to share resources but also on the participation of many persons, including those who traditionally have been cast as powerless, in democratic decision making. Such power sharing is essential in the fields of planning and design, where broad-based cooperation is a prerequisite to lasting environmental solutions. As the amount of undeveloped, uncontaminated land disappears; as escalating violence within and between nations increasingly determines how space is designed and used; as car-oriented, privatized United States life-styles are promulgated worldwide via global communications systems, planners and designers[4] will require more empowering, inclusive approaches to authority.[5]

But how will students learn such approaches in university settings that are governed by patriarchal norms of control and domination?[6] How can faculty engage aspiring professionals in critically reflecting on whether their work is, in Weisman's words, "ecologically intelligent and socially just"? How can feminists achieve a pedagogy that allows persons who traditionally have been marginalized in their fields to simultaneously succeed in and resist the patriarchal norms of professionalization? These are the questions I address in this essay.

Power versus Empowerment

Ecofeminist Starhawk differentiates three forms of authority: power-over, power-with, and power-from-within.[7] Power-over shapes most institutions – from the halls of Congress to corporations, schools, churches, hospitals, and even our families. It is the power of prison guards, the military, or drug dealers who use weapons or physical force to exert control. It is the power of corporate executives, university presidents, or faculty who have named roles that entitle them to enforce obedience. It is the power of white men as well as educated, wealthy, heterosexual, and able-bodied persons whose favored socioeconomic status grants them certain inherent rights. Starhawk compares the consciousness of power-over to seeing the world with a high-beam flashlight that illuminates the details of discrete elements but does not reveal the fabric of space in which these elements are interrelated. This conception of power can be found in most of the earlier leadership literature, which placed great emphasis on the personal style and skills of a charismatic individual.[8]

Unlike power-over, Starhawk's other two forms of authority are not tied to material privilege. Power-with is the ambiguously structured influence that is wielded among equals. It is the authority of good parents or teachers who guide young persons in realizing their own capacities. It is the authority of the elders, clan mothers, or chiefs in indigenous societies who are listened to because of their wisdom and judgment. It is the authority of poets, public speakers, or songwriters who provide intellectual leadership through their clarity of thinking. The strength of power-with does not come from an ability to outdo others but rather from a desire to connect with and nurture them; it is not driven by the status-seeking that prevails in power-over but rather by a commitment to assume responsibility and make a difference on behalf of others. While power-over concentrates authority in the hands of properly credentialed persons, power-with grows as relationships multiply within a culture of shared responsibility and mutual respect. In recent leadership literature, power-with is referred to as transactional leadership, in which followers are acknowledged as vital to any leader's ability to bring about change, no matter how charismatic that person might be.

Starhawk's third type of influence is known as power-from-within, a spiritual endeavor that is anything but objective or externally controlled. Power-from-within stems from idealism, magic, love, hope, and persistence; it is accessed through a sense of connectedness to the universe of human beings and nature; it comes from an ongoing struggle to develop greater awareness of self and other. Expressed through such vehicles as poetry, ritual, surprise, or humor, power-from-within is perhaps more available to young persons than it is to those who are ensconced in the status quo. Francis Moore Lappé and Paul Martin DuBois applauded this form of influence as a way of addressing controversial environmental issues, noting a citizens group in Kentucky that used drama to call attention to the dumping of waste in their community. The group staged a funeral on the steps of the state capitol, complete with music, a hearse, and many bereaved citizens, who demanded that the governor either sign a death certificate for the state of Kentucky or implement a moratorium on dumping. Their performance focused attention on an important problem and everyone had a good (empowering) laugh in the process.[9] Other examples of power-from-within include such rituals as the singing of "We Shall Overcome" during the civil rights movement, the embroidering of Circle of Life squares by displaced Peruvian women, and the painting of graffiti by disenfranchised ghetto youth.

Professional Education as Enculturation into Power-Over

Schools of planning and design ought to be extraordinary sources of power-with and power-from-within. Since no one person can bring about change in something as complex as the physical environment, schooling in these disciplines ought to engage students in transdisciplinary collaboration, community organizing, and political activism. Since planning and designing are about envisioning alternative futures, schooling ought to increase students' awareness of the societal inequities that are made visible through built form, and encourage them to resist restating those inequities in their own work. Since a more sustainable society will only come into being if more privileged groups (planners and designers among them) limit their own consumption, schooling ought to encourage students to critique those professional values and assumptions that encourage exploitation of nature's bounty.

Unfortunately, such an empowering education would contradict the norms of professionalization whose very purpose is to prepare students for exercising power over given bodies of knowledge. Professionalization is the last step in a lifelong process of ranking and rating; it restricts membership in various fields to those with specified levels of education and training, thus creating occupational monopolies that are controlled by persons who already are within the inner circle.[10] Unlike those whose authority derives from ownership of capital or property, the power-over of middle-class professionals lies in ownership of specialized knowledge and thus in the capacity to define the reality of other persons.

In licensed fields such as architecture and landscape architecture, power-over is especially apparent – in the accreditation of schools, internship requirements, registration exams, and enforcement of codes and zoning ordinances – advancement being contingent on conformity to explicit as well as implicit professional standards. For example, to excel within the culture of architecture one must be able to stay up for nights on end to finish school projects, fill out countless forms and get numerous recommendations to take the state board exams, sacrifice private life to ninety-hour work weeks, and design in the prevailing architectural style. And, as in other areas, family class background plays a potent role in determining the opportunities that are available to individuals at given points in their careers, as do gender and race.

Over time, such enculturation processes reinforce patriarchal norms and coopt the idealism of planners and designers, rendering them powerless to address contemporary environmental challenges. As leadership scholar John W. Gardner noted:

"All too often, on the long road up, young leaders become 'servants of what is rather than shapers of what might be.' In the long process of learning how the system works, they are rewarded for playing within the intricate structure of existing rules. By the time they reach the top, they are very likely to be trained prisoners of the structure. This is not all bad; every vital system re-affirms itself. But no system can stay vital for long unless some of its leaders remain sufficiently independent to help it to change and grow."[11]

A professional worldview that is promulgated from a position of privilege to protect its own cache of credentialed expertise cannot be responsive to today's explosive global changes, especially relative to the physical environment. As Weisman notes, students need more organic, inclusive paradigms to address the problems of sheltering and caring for transgenerational, culturally diverse families. At the same time, they must learn how to use new technologies to enhance rather than destroy the beauty of nature and the specialness of individuals. Such challenges require a new generation of planners and designers who are sufficiently independent of the self-serving aspects of their fields. What kind of education would empower students to exercise authority in concert with socioeconomically disadvantaged groups? How can students be enculturated into their exclusionary professional roles while becoming more inclusive in their thinking? How can educators, especially women and persons of color, who already occupy marginal positions in academia, break with patriarchal norms in their pedagogy without risking their own and their students' ability to reap the rewards of mainstream society?

The Paradoxes of Professional Education in a Sustainable Society

"I imagine an alternative praxis of architecture that simultaneously embraces two seemingly contradictory missions. In this alternative approach, we use our right hand to pry open the box so that more of us can get into it while using our left hand to get rid of the very box we are trying to get into. With part of ourselves, we work to achieve power and authority within the traditions of the dominant culture. . . . With another part of ourselves, . . . we reject the dominant voice's power-over mentality because it is inappropriate to the power-with mentality that is required to bring about social change."[12]

Education in a sustainable society involves contradictions for students and faculty alike, and this is especially true for women, persons of color, and those non-materially privileged persons who manage to access the ivory towers. Weisman proposes a feminist pedagogy that emphasizes collective, non-hierarchical problem-solving processes that strive for a more ecological worldview through an ongoing critique of social injustice. Such a pedagogy necessarily means that faculty must assume paradoxical roles and, at the same time, decide just how far out of the mainstream to venture. Feminist pedagogy requires that we simultaneously strive for professional excellence as defined by the dominant culture while seeking to serve the interests of those who have been marginalized by that culture's power structure. It requires that we indulge ourselves intellectually and, at the same time, critique our privilege to do so. It requires that we struggle against oppression while acknowledging our own complicity – however unintentional – in perpetuating injustice through our participation in the credentialing process.

Given these paradoxes, feminist faculty might elect one of many avenues along a continuum of resistance to the power-over of the patriarchy. Some might choose more conventional routes, seeking ways to create alternative learning spaces within traditional contexts – a choice that is the least costly because it does not challenge institutional hierarchies. Others might choose the path I have taken, working within the mainstream while seeking to transform it. bell hooks and others have written about the duality of being inside an institution while struggling against its traditions, referring to this position as one of creative marginality, "a site one stays in, clings to even, because it nourishes one's capacity to resist."[13] Some activist faculty might opt out of professional education and find other venues for affecting the physical environment. This choice exacts the highest price because it means sacrificing the security of conferred status and mainstream credentials. I might have pursued this path, but I felt obliged to pry open academia's doors for other women and persons of color.

Each of these different horizons is equally valuable and necessary to igniting a widespread movement within the fields of planning and design. Students in these fields already learn critical skills for contributing to today's environmental challenges, including the capacity to synthesize disparate information and project alternative futures. Faculty can encourage them to use these abilities to engage so-called powerless persons in collective problem-solving while assiduously resisting the prevailing acceptance of domination and exploitation. Most movements are embodied not in institutional contexts but in books, speeches, popular songs, or memories of people and events. Power-with and power-from-within – empowerment – comes to those, often without titles or named roles, who have the courage to challenge normative thinking and inspire risk-taking visions of social and environmental justice.

1. Francis Moore Lappé and Paul Martin DuBois, *The Quickening of America: Rebuilding Our Nation, Remaking Our Lives* (San Francisco: Jossey-Bass, 1994).

2. Of the industrialized countries, the United States has the widest income gap between rich and poor. The well-to-do, who earn about 95 percent of their income from exploitative land development, reap eleven times the income of the poor, thus providing a striking example of the connection between the domination of nature and the domination of people.

3. Rajni Kothari, "Environment, Technology, and Ethics," in J. Ronald Engel and Joan Gibb Engel, eds., *Ethics of Environment and Development: Global Challenge, International Response* (Tucson: The University of Arizona Press, 1990), 27–35.

4. I use the term "planners and designers" because I believe that the environmental problems Weisman outlines in her essay cannot be addressed by single disciplines but, rather, require broad transdisciplinary collaboration. Although a number of

individual planners and designers are making valuable contributions, they are limited by prescribing solutions according to their own disciplinary focus. Thus the neo-traditional urban designers look at town-making without taking into account the rural environment; conservationists focus on farmland and open space without considering the need for reducing dependence on the automobile; and the "fur, feather, and fin" ecologists ignore human ecology, especially with respect to race, gender, and class. Contemporary environmental problem-solving requires collaboration among the many persons who plan and design natural and built space, and this linked term, "planners and designers," is meant to suggest such an inclusive approach.

5. The term "empowerment" generally refers to the processes through which disadvantaged persons seek to increase their fair share of resources. I use the word to include, as well, the processes through which privileged persons gain the courage to share their advantages.

6. "Patriarchy" literally refers to that condition (still existing in some cultures) in which a man owned his wife, children, and perhaps slaves. I use the term "patriarchal norms" more broadly to indicate a condition of dominance and dependence in which some persons have institutionally conferred authority over others. For example, the behavior of faculty and students is typically governed by patriarchal norms, regardless of the gender of either group.

7. Starhawk, *Truth or Dare: Encounters with Power, Authority, and Mystery* (San Francisco: Harper & Row, 1987). Starhawk's definition of power is but one of many in the literature, but it provides particularly useful insights into the inner, spiritual resources of individuals and groups.

8. The notion of leadership as a way of ordering social life was first articulated in 1869 by the English scientist Sir Francis Galton, who put forth the "Great Man" theory, according to which leaders possessed universal savior-like characteristics that were fixed, largely inborn, and applicable in all situations.

9. Lappé and DuBois.

10. Barbara Ehrenreich, *Fear of Falling: The Inner Life of the Middle Class* (New York: Pantheon), 1989.

11. Thomas E. Cronin, "Reflections on Leadership," in William E. Rosenback and Robert L. Taylor, eds., *Contemporary Issues in Leadership*, 3rd ed. (Boulder: Westview Press, 1993), 7–25.

12. Sharon E. Sutton, "Finding Our Voice in the Dominant Key," in Jack Travis, ed., *African-American Architects in Current Practice* (New York: Princeton Architectural Press, 1991), 13–15.

13. bell hooks, *Yearning: Race, Gender and Cultural Politics* (Boston: South End Press, 1990), 150.

The Pen Is Mightier Than the Building: Writing on Architecture 1850–1940

DIANE FAVRO

As the current raging discourses reveal, architecture is as much about words as about actual buildings. From Vitruvius to Peter Eisenman, architects have relied on texts to promote their work, explain their theories, document their careers, and glorify their lives in an attempt to ensure their places in history. The written word, after all, reaches a far larger audience and endures far longer than place-bound buildings, and it is not subject to the ravages of the elements, economics, and changing social needs.

From the mid-nineteenth century through the period between World Wars I and II, publications by architects proliferated.[1] The first American publishing boom in architecture occurred just after the Civil War, when the number of new books per year rose from eleven in 1868 to twenty in 1882. One architect, the Gothic Revivalist Ralph Adams Cram, founded or edited four well-known journals, wrote art criticism for the *Boston Transcript*, and authored more than one hundred articles and twenty-four books. Not surprisingly, the written voice of the American practitioner of architecture during this period was decidedly male. Largely excluded from the profession, women took up their pens to address, instead, larger issues of the built environment.[2] Public reception of their writings had widespread implications for fields related to architecture – implications either ignored or minimized by the profession and the histories it condoned.

The social mores of early American society tended generally to muffle the voices of women, who were not expected to speak out – even when dealing with sanctioned "female subjects." For example, a manual of manners from 1837 advised American women to work hard at household chores but warned, "Honorable as is the performance of these daily duties, it is bad taste to say much about them."[3] The Victorian female had been programmed to assume the self-effacing and largely anonymous position of "the woman behind her man" (or the woman behind her country). Writing was an acceptable activity for the genteel woman of the nineteenth century only as long it was undertaken to improve her skills as wife and homemaker. Ideally, writing was to be done at home (family duties permitting), isolated from the corrupting influences of the male business world. Considered a hobby, not an occupation, women's writing was not meant to compete with men's efforts. Those women who did make writing a career operated in completely different spheres from male authors, remaining in the background (that is, the home) and denigrating or subordinating their own personalities for the good of others.

As the emotional, nurturing sex, women wrote about feelings more than about ideas. They addressed audiences composed of other middle- and upper middle-class women or young people, and their topics were those socially identified as "female": child rearing (including education of the young) and domesticity. Assuming the role of cultural custodians, women also wrote about the arts in America, delving into criticism and history. Their written works were generally small in scale and modest in intent: articles, short stories, diaries, letters, and pamphlets; often they published anonymously or in collections, with no one contributor dominant.

The same generalities applied when nineteenth-century American women writers turned to topics relating to the built environment. They championed the architectural achievements of individual (male) practitioners and of America as a whole. Generally, women writers were relegated to the position of *adjuncts to* or *servicers of* the profession, viewed by their contemporaries (especially architects) as mere mediators between the profession and the public. Similarly, women who wrote on domesticity and social reform were seen as mere conduits for teaching other women how to cope with the concerns of family and society. Thus, their production was further devalued because it addressed primarily female (by definition lower status) audiences. Assuming roles of self-denial and speaking on behalf of others, women writers fell outside the accepted parameters of high culture and, instead, operated in the antipodal realm of mass culture.

Architects as Authors

The earliest American texts relating to architecture were pragmatic"how to" books aimed at (male) amateurs expanding the built environment of a new nation.[4] However, by the later part of the nineteenth century, architects began to define themselves as educated professionals, not builders. As a result, writing about architecture changed character. Male architects wrote to exalt architecture as an art or science, and the architect as an independent artistic genius toiling to bring forth the truth. This notion quickly became ingrained in the American imagination. In the 1934 edition of *The Book of the School,* architect and University of Pennsylvania professor Paul Cret stated that architecture "has for its main object the development of the artist's personality." By the turn of the century, design, history, and representation had been added to the predominantly technical curricula of the recently established architecture schools. Elevating their discourse, architects more and more were writing for a select audience of their peers and an educated elite from which they hoped to attract worthy clients.

The male voice was singular and headily self-promotional. Like artists, genius-architects wanted to be thought of as working alone to create masterpieces. Beyond articles in professional journals, the most desirable venues were autobiographies and monographs on individual architects or firms.[5] Naturally, individual authorship was important; few men published with co-authors or in anthologies. And while the architect might pass the pen to a professional writer, he was always careful to maintain some degree of control. The results were predictably sympathetic as, for example, the 1915 commissioned monograph on McKim, Mead & White, a production which has its contemporary counterpart in the far more numerous and lavish Rizzoli and *A.D.* publications.

In contrast to their male peers, women architects rarely wrote. Julia Morgan, one of the most prolific practitioners (male or female) on the West Coast, with more than five hundred projects to her credit, scrupulously avoided being what she disparagingly labeled "a talking architect." Not only did Morgan decline to write about her own work or ideas, she refused interviews and did not seek publication of her projects.[6] Various rationales for such behavior are conceivable: self-promotion and advocacy of independent ideas were contrary to contemporary bourgeois ideals of femininity; women architects had to work harder and longer than their male peers, leaving little time for authorship; and, in general, women designed houses, not monuments, emphasizing the social aspects of design and client satisfaction (topics of marginal interest to a profession concerned with the apotheosis of the genius-architect). Moreover, strong restrictions on the architectural education available to women gave them scant opportunity to develop the fluency necessary to participate in more avant-garde discourse.

Likewise, until the middle of the twentieth century, few female practitioners published in the professional press. Architecture journals only grudgingly accepted contributions by female writers, naturally giving preference to the few women who had acquired architectural training. Not surprisingly, activist articles promoting women's entry into the profession were infrequent. A female writer of the nineteenth century, whether trained as an architect or not, was most likely to have her article published if she promoted male achievement, the male vision of the profession, or women's traditional roles.[7] Consequently, the majority of articles by women dealt with sanctioned female subjects such as domestic design, the decorative and pictorial arts, and history.[8] No female architect of the period wrote an autobiography. Yet, while their male peers more or less ignored them, women writers on architecture were readily accepted by the broad popular audience in America, which was greatly affected by their output.

Promoting Home Economics

The house dominated architecture in nineteenth-century America and, as the acknowledged realm of women, was naturally the topic of greatest coverage by female writers. Most had no training as architects; instead, they drew on their first-hand knowledge as homemakers as well as on their educations in the arts, teaching, philosophy, and, by the first decades of the twentieth century, the newly defined fields of home economics (including interior design) and landscape design.[9] Responding to the clearly gendered divisions between work and living spaces fostered by the Industrial Revolution, women writers guided other middle- and upper middle-class American women in their efforts to create comfortable, attractive, healthy homes. A spate of housekeeping books emerged, focused on everyday strategies for running a home.[10] In line with the professionalization of other fields, several writers identified housekeeping as a domestic science, in effect arguing for its consideration as a female profession. They advised not only on cooking, cleaning, and child rearing, but also on architectural design and the technical aspects of heating, ventilation, plumbing, lighting, and construction.

For example, the much studied book by Catherine Beecher and Harriet Beecher Stowe, *The American Woman's Home* (1869), explored the centralization of the kitchen and other mechanical services. The feminist Charlotte Perkins Gilman wrote on the physical organization of the home and apartment building, and the socialization of housework in *Women and Economics* (1898) and *The Home: Its Work and Influence* (1903). Greta Gray's *House and Home* (1923) was published in the popular Lippincott's Home Manuals series and served as both a manual for women at home and as a textbook for students at the burgeoning teachers' colleges and other female-oriented institutions emphasizing domestic science and home economics. Concurrently, a number of home magazines aimed at a female readership appeared, many of them edited and staffed primarily by women, for example, *Woman's Home Companion*, founded in 1873, and *The Ladies' Home Journal*, founded in 1883 (fig. 1).[11] These popular periodicals explored all aspects of domestic life, frequently juxtaposing fashions with house plans and technical information on house construction and maintenance.

Teaching Etiquette and Cultivating Taste

In 1831, the English writer Mrs. Frances Trollope caused an uproar with her book *Domestic Manners of the Americans*, in which she lambasted the coarse, immoral, and uncultured life-styles of this relatively new country's citizenry – as well as the disgraceful architecture of its major cities. Women across the country took up the gauntlet, publishing numerous books and articles on etiquette, all interwoven with moralism. Etiquette books not only taught middle-class women how to behave socially but underscored the significance of environment in determining behavior. These culminated with the authoritative and comprehensive writings of Emily Post, who in her newspaper columns and especially in her popular book *The Personality of a House* (1930) dealt with interior design and behavior, advising that male environments should be based on the man's occupation while female environments should respond to how a woman looks.[12]

Mariana Van Rensselaer, identified as America's first professional female art critic, was one of several women who honed America's taste by evaluating art and the built environment for the general public. She wrote for both popular magazines (*Century, Atlantic Monthly*) and professional journals (*American Architect, American Architect and Building News*). In a piece for the *North American Review* entitled "Client and Architect," Van Rensselaer argued that clients should defer to the elevated taste and knowledge of the American architect.[13] Sarah Hale, editor of *Godey's Lady's Book* magazine (published alternately as *Godey's Magazine;* fig. 2) from 1837 to 1877, led successful campaigns to make Bunker Hill and Mount Vernon national monuments, acknowledging women's role as, "the preserver, the teacher or inspirer, and the exemplar."[14] In a nationalistic gesture she announced in 1854 that *Godey's* would publish only projects by American designers for the popular series Lady's Book Houses. Louisa C. Tuthill, who wrote the first book on American architectural history in 1841 (*History of Architecture, from the Earliest Times; Its Present Condition in Europe and the United States,* published 1848), explained in a letter to her publisher that her objective was "to improve the public taste by bringing the topic before readers of all classes, and furnishing correct models for imitation." But, like her male counterparts, Tuthill did not incorporate the efforts of early women designers into her history.

Advocating Reform

Early on in America's history, women had assumed responsibility for the general care of the soul; in architecture this translated into the promotion of community projects and morally uplifting designs.[15] By the twentieth century, women writers were actively attempting to shape devel-

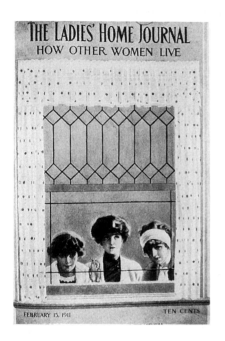

FIG. 1

1911 theme issue of *The Ladies' Home Journal*, which focused on "How Other Women Live"

FIG. 2

Cover of *Godey's Magazine*, 1896, edited by Sarah Hale

11.15. H. S. Phillips, "The Woman That Saved the Union," poster for *Godey's Magazine* (1896).

opments in social reform. For example, Alice Constance Austin wrote a number of articles in socialist publications outlining the design of an efficient, supportive, centralized community with communal cooking and laundry services, and a printing shop run by women.[16] Gilman created an entire feminist utopia in her novel *Herland* of 1915, first serialized in a monthly magazine. Composed entirely of women, this society fashioned a rational, peaceful, prosperous, and ecologically sound environment focused on the collective raising of children (reproduction was by parthenogenesis).

The social worker and peace advocate Jane Addams reached a national audience with such works as *Democracy and Social Ethics* (1902), which prompted her campaign for cleaner urban environments, healthy living and work environments, and humane urban design. Her autobiographical account of an urban settlement house, *Twenty Years at Hull House* (1910), became a classic of reform literature, and in 1931 she won the Nobel Peace Prize. Later in the century, planner Catherine Bauer capitalized on the opportunities for improving low-income housing offered by the New Deal; she analyzed the socialized housing experiments of Europe and promoted a human-scale American solution (*Modern Housing*, 1934). And while no female architects of the period wrote about their lives, several reformers penned boastful autobiographies, such as *The Living of Charlotte Perkins Gilman*, published posthumously in 1935.

High versus Popular Culture

While the architecture profession in the early twentieth century considered women's writings on the built environment as, at best, a promotional service and, at worst, frivolous, the cultural impact of these publications was significant. Reaching a broad audience (as early as 1851, *Godey's Lady's Book* magazine boasted seventy thousand subscribers), these writings helped forge unified, distinctly American ideas about the house, the city, and architecture in general. Although wide distribution did not immediately shake the ivory tower of the profession, in the end, American (male) architects could not ignore the value of popular acclaim. Recognizing the need to attract a broader audience, in 1891 the profession established the *Architectural Record*, a journal edited by male journalists, not architects, and targeted at the educated layman, an audience reached by neither technical professional journals nor the popularizing "ladies' magazines." Nevertheless, the profession's low opinion of "lady writers" and its adamant distancing of itself from "feminine" or popular concerns had long lasting and deleterious results. Proclaiming the autonomy of architecture as art and demonstrating an open hostility to mass culture, male architects in the early twentieth century fostered a radical separation of themselves from domestic economy, functionality, health, morals, and social reform – all the topics of women's writings. The most famous architects of the day presented themselves as being above concern with budgets and lower-status users, much to the detriment of their clients and the profession as a whole. The problematization of high and low culture, male and female, also segregated and devalued the related fields of interior and landscape design that women had pioneered.

In the area of history, male architects focused on the high cultures represented by European architecture, deriding or ignoring the multiculturalism evident in the popular histories written by women. For example, Tuthill's pivotal history of architecture was devalued because she took a subjective, inclusive approach to the past, discussing, alongside European examples, the architecture of a wide range of cultures, including Persian and "aboriginal" American. Architects favored, instead, the encyclopedic *A History of Architecture on the Comparative Method* (1896), a heavy tome in which the British architect Banister Fletcher and his son, Banister Flight Fletcher, adopted a more scientific approach, presenting a veritable taxonomy of past architecture. Although the Fletchers avoided any hint of popularization by focusing their first edition on the major monuments of Europe, in the revised fourth edition of 1901, Banister Flight Fletcher did expand the contents to include other cultures – but he placed them under the pejorative heading of "non-historical."

The New Woman

As Victorian social worker Helen Bosanquet noted, "In reference to the outside world, man has power and woman 'influence.' Within the home woman has the active power and man 'influence.' "[17] For women authors in the late nineteenth and early twentieth centuries the equation was reversed. "Lady writers" had great influence in the outside world, while male architectural authors had power in the much smaller professional realm. Women addressed a broad, nationwide, public audience, and ultimately shaped architectural developments as forcefully as their male counterparts. Operating outside the gender restrictions of the profession, women authors had the opportunity to succeed. Many did just that, claiming the right to autonomy as authors at a time when women could not do so as designers. Equally important, women explored and advanced issues displaced from the profession by both pure misogyny and by the gendering of high and mass culture.

Gradually, economic and theoretical transformations compelled American male architects to venture out from their ivory tower and into female domains. Faced with declining opportunities after the depression of the 1890s, architects began to concern themselves increasingly with the middle-class house and urban reform movements.[18] While women's writings on gendered subjects continued to flourish in the early decades of the twentieth century and to be appreciated by the masses, their dominant voice softened. Simultaneously, various social theories, including the neo-Marxian Frankfurt School, abandoned the notion of mass culture as feminine and equated it instead with streamlining, technological reproduction, and masculine objectivity.[19] The genderized dichotomy between high and mass culture blurred and shifted after World War I, encouraging more crossover between topics and authors.

Complementing this shift in ideological ground were transformations in the educational and vocational possibilities for women. With increased access to education, the suffrage movement, health and dress reforms, women redefined themselves. Since the 1890s, mainstream media had described the ideal of the New Woman as an independent, intelligent, educated individual able to interact and compete with men as an equal. By the 1920s, living examples of the New Woman walked the streets of America. Greater numbers of women entered the expanding service and public sector occupations, while others became influential clients of architecture, either individually or collectively. In particular, women took leadership positions as critics and editors for respected art and literary publications, including Dora Marsden of *The Egoist, An Individualist Review,* Harriet Monroe of *Poetry,* and Emma Goldman of *Mother Earth.* Their highly visible and public participation in the discourse on high art further defeated the old gendering of mass culture and facilitated women's direct participation in the profession of architecture.

After World War I, more women became architects and took an active part in professional discourse. Currently, women writers on architecture come from such diverse backgrounds as professional practice, teaching, history, theory, criticism, and journalism. Having cast aside the role of *servicers to* the profession, they occupy positions of power both in architecture and in popular culture. Most significantly, they shape the discourse of the profession as major contributors to ongoing debates and as editors of not only the home journals of enduring popularity but of important professional journals as well. Today, when women write about architecture, both the public and the profession listen.

1. American architectural writers naturally drew upon English models; see Henry-Russell Hitchcock, *American Architectural Books, New Expanded Edition* (New York: Da Capo Press, 1976), vi; Nikolaus Pevsner, *Some Architectural Writers of the Nineteenth Century* (Oxford: Clarendon, 1972); and Andrew Saint, *The Image of the Architect* (New Haven: Yale University Press, 1983), 96–114. Some of the earliest discussions of architecture in America are to be found in the writings of philosophers, including Thoreau and Emerson; see Don Gifford, ed., *The Literature of Architecture: The Evolution of Architectural Theory and Practice in Nineteenth-Century America* (New York: E. P. Dutton & Co., 1966), 92–126, 172–197.

2. The process of women's entry into the profession is explored in a number of works, including the essays in Susan Torre, *Women in American Architecture* (New York: Whitney Library of Design, 1977), and Ellen Perry Berkeley and Matilda McQuaid, eds., *Architecture, A Place for Women* (Washington, D.C.: Smithsonian Institution Press, 1989). See also Gwendolyn Wright, "On the Fringe of the Profession: Women in American Architecture," in Spiro Kostof, ed., *The Architect* (New York: Oxford University Press, 1977), 297–98.

3. The quote comes from a book written by "A Lady": *The Young Lady's Friend* (Boston: American Stationers' Company, John B. Russell, 1837), 41. On the

endurance of societal pressures to keep women invisible in the professional realm, see Denise Scott Brown, "Room at the Top? Sexism and the Star System in Architecture," in Berkeley and McQuaid, 237–46.

4. In the first half of the nineteenth century, few architects had professional training and thus relied on pattern books and manuals, among them Dr. William Thorton's *Town and Country Builders' Assistant* (1797), Minard Lafever's *The Young Builder's General Instructor* (1829) and *The Modern Builder's Guide* (1833), and Asher Benjamin's *The Country Builder's Assistant* (1797) and *The American Builder's Companion* (1806). These were based upon English examples such as *British Architect* by Abraham Swan, reissued in 1775 for an American audience; see Helen Park, *List of Architectural Books Available in America before the Revolution* (Los Angeles: Henessey and Ingalls, 1973).

5. Ralph Adams Cram wrote *My Life in Architecture* in 1936; some twelve years earlier, the prolific Louis Sullivan had devised a new genre merging philosophy and life experience in *Autobiography of an Idea.* Authorship was an important means of promotion for American architects who, as professionals, were not allowed to advertise until the 1970s. Architects often used biographies and other writings to validate their careers, present a revisionist life-style, or attack their rivals; see Lisa Koenigsberg, "Life-Writing: First American Biographers of Architects and Their Works," in Elisabeth Blair MacDougall, ed., *The Architectural Historian in America* (Hanover: University Press of New England, 1990), 41–58.

6. Only at the urging of her engineering associate Walter Steilberg was Morgan's work published, in *Architect and Engineer in California* 55 (1918), 39–107; see Sarah Boutelle, *Julia Morgan, Architect* (New York: Abbeville, 1988), 16, 46. Natalie Kampen and Elizabeth G. Grossman, "Feminism and Methodology: Dynamics of Change in the History of Art and Architecture" (Wellesley, Mass.: Wellesley College Center for Research on Women, Working Paper no. 122, 1983).

7. Reflecting the national cultural insecurity, professional journals were more likely to publish articles by foreign women; see Lisa Koenigsberg, "Mariana Van Rensselaer: An Architecture Critic in Context," in Berkeley and McQuaid, 47–48.

8. Two American women architects published architectural histories in the early twentieth century: Lois Lilley Howe and Eleanor Raymond; Keith Morgan and Richard Cheek, "History in the Service of Design: American Architect-Historians, 1870–1940," in MacDougall, 75.

9. In 1867, Louisa Tuthill wrote *True Manliness: Or, The Landscape Gardener. A Book for Boys and Girls.* Landscape design became an accepted field for women and was

avidly promoted by Van Rensselaer and other writers; see Koenigsberg, "Mariana Van Rensselaer," 49–50. On the history of landscaping architecture in general, see Anne Peterson, "Women Take Lead in Landscape Art," *New York Times* (March 13, 1938), 1; Deborah Nevins, "The Triumph of Flora: Women and American Landscape, 1890–1935," *Antiques* 127 (April 1985), 913; and Catherine R. Brown and Celia N. Maddox, "Women and the Land: A Suitable Profession," *Landscape Architecture* 72 (May 1982), 64–69. On women in interior design, see Emma M. Tyng, "Women's Chances as Bread Winners, Part VIII: Women as Interior Decorators," *The Ladies' Home Journal* (October 1891), 4; and C. Ray Smith and Allen Tate, *Interior Design in 20th Century America: A History* (New York: Harper & Row, 1987).

10. Dolores Hayden, *The Grand Domestic Revolution* (Cambridge, Mass.: MIT Press, 1981); Gwendolyn Wright, "The Model Domestic Environment: Icon or Option?" in Torre, 22–24.

11. Middle-class women from both urban and rural contexts formed a large constituency whose commonalities overrode the particularities of locale. Their patronage made the nineteenth century into "the century of the woman's magazine"; Frank L. Mott, *A History of American Magazines, 1741–1850* (Cambridge, Mass.: Harvard University Press, 1930).

12. Post claimed familial knowledge of architecture; she dedicated *The Personality of a House* to the "memory of the architects of my family." On the evolution of the etiquette book tradition, see Arthur Meyer Schlesinger, *Learning How to Behave: A Historical Study of American Etiquette Books* (New York: Macmillan, 1946). Post in effect anthropomorphizes various portions of the house; see Leslie Kanes Weisman, *Discrimination by Design: A Feminist Critique of the Man-Made Environment* (Urbana: University of Illinois Press, 1992), 92–97.

13. Mariana Van Rensselaer, "Client and Architect," *North American Review* 151 (September 1890), 390. This article so closely captured the profession's vision of itself that the American Institute of Architects recommended it be distributed at the convention of 1890 and made Van Rensselaer an honorary member. The article was subsequently reprinted in *AABN* 40 (April 1893), 11–12; Koenigsberg, "Mariana Van Rensselaer," 45.

14. Sarah Josepha Hale, *Manners, or Happy Homes* (Boston: J. E. Tilton, 1868), 21. Hale also successfully lobbied to make Thanksgiving Day a national holiday.

15. Doris Cole, *From Tipi to Skyscraper: A History of Women in Architecture* (Boston: i press, 1973), 34–49.

16. On Austin's community designs, see Hayden, 242–48.

17. Helen Bosanquet, *The Family* (1906); quoted in Elizabeth Roberts, *A Woman's Place: An Oral History of Working-Class Women, 1890–1940* (Oxford: Blackwell, 1984), 117.

18. Wright, *Moralism and the Model Home*, 222.

19. This shift was further accelerated by the rise of modernist ideology after World War I. In many ways modernism was reactionary, responding to the female threat of mass culture. Several basic modernist tenets were antithetical to those championed in women's writing, including nationalism and traditionalism. Huyssen characterizes an ideal modernist work as displaying male characteristics of experimental (that is, scientific) approaches, autonomy, irony, ambiguity, individualism, effacement of content, and erasure of subjectivity; see Andreas Huyssen, *After the Great Divide: Modernism, Mass Culture, Postmodernism* (Bloomington: Indiana University Press, 1986), 48, 53–55; my thanks to Anne Bermingham for the reference. On modernism as a professional ideology, see Magali Sarfatti Larson, "Emblem and Exception: The Historical Definition of the Architect's Professional Role," in Judith R. Blau, Mark E. La Gory, and John S. Pipkin, eds., *Professionals and Urban Form* (Albany: State University of New York Press, 1983), 70–76.

DIANA AGREST is principal, Agrest and Gandelsonas Architects, New York, and adjunct professor of architecture at Columbia University and The Cooper Union. She has taught at Princeton, was formerly Bishop Professor at Yale, and was a fellow at the Institute for Architecture and Urban Studies. Among her publications, which include numerous critical essays, are *Agrest and Gandelsonas: Works* (Princeton University Press, 1994), *Architecture from Without: Theoretical Framings for a Critical Practice* (MIT Press, 1991), and *A Romance with the City: The Work of Irwin S. Chanin* (The Cooper Union Press, 1982).

DIANA BALMORI is principal for design, Balmori Associates, Inc., in New Haven, Connecticut, and a critic in the School of Architecture and the School of Forestry and Environmental Studies at Yale University. She is co-author of *Redesigning the American Lawn* (Yale University Press, 1993), *Transitory Gardens, Uprooted Lives* (Yale University Press, 1993), and *Beatrix Ferrand's American Landscapes: Her Gardens and Campuses* (Sagapress, 1985). Among her current projects are the master plan for the University of Texas (Austin), the Gwynns Falls Greenway in Baltimore, and the NTT Shinjuku Headquarters in Tokyo.

ANN BERGREN is professor of Classics at the University of California, Los Angeles, and teaches architectural theory at the Southern California Institute of Architecture. She has taught Classics at Princeton and architectural theory at Harvard, worked in the office of Eric Owen Moss, and is currently a student in the Master of Architecture program at the Harvard Graduate School of Design. Her writing on architecture has been published in *ANY (Architecture New York)*, *Assemblage*, *Princeton Architectural Journal*, *Harvard Architectural Review*, and *Strategies in Architectural Thinking*.

JENNIFER BLOOMER is associate professor of architecture at Iowa State University and a past fellow of the Chicago Institute for Architecture and Urbanism. She serves on the editorial boards of *ANY (Architecture New York)* and *Assemblage*, and in 1992 delivered the Annual Discourse of the Royal Institute of British Architects. Author of the widely acclaimed *Architecture and the Text: The (S)crypts of Joyce and Piranesi* (Yale University Press, 1993), she is currently writing a book of essays tentatively titled "The Matter of Matter: Architecture in the Age of Dematerialization".

M. CHRISTINE BOYER is William R. Kenar, Jr., Professor of Architecture at Princeton University, past chair of the City and Regional Planning Program at Pratt Institute, and formerly associate professor of architecture, planning, and preservation at Columbia

309

University. She is the author of *CyberCities: Visual Perception in the Age of Electronic Communication* (Princeton Architectural Press, 1996), *The City of Collective Memory: Historical Imagery and Architectural Entertainment* (MIT Press, 1994), *Manhattan Manners: Architecture and Style 1850–1900* (Rizzoli, 1985), and *Dreaming the Rational City: The Myth of American City Planning* (MIT Press, 1983).

LYNNE BRESLIN is adjunct assoicate professor of architecture at Columbia University and principal, L. Breslin: Architecture & Design, New York. She has also taught at Princeton, Pratt Institute, The Cooper Union, and Parsons School of Design. *Assignment Rescue,* installed in the temporary concourse gallery at the United States Holocaust Memorial Museum in Washington, D.C., is one of her most recent exhibition designs. She has written widely on Japanese design, including an essay in Botand Bogner, ed., *The New Japanese Architecture* (Rizzoli, 1990).

ZEYNEP ÇELIK is professor of architecture at the New Jersey Institute of Technology. She is the author of *Displaying the Orient: Architecture of Islam at Nineteenth Century World's Fairs* (University of California Press, 1992), *The Remaking of Istanbul: Portrait of an Ottoman City in the Nineteenth Century* (University of Washington Press, 1986, and University of California Press, 1994), and co-editor and co-author of *Streets: Critical Perspectives on Public Space* (University of California Press, 1994).

BEATRIZ COLOMINA is an architect and historian who teaches at Princeton University. Her books include *Privacy and Publicity: Modern Architecture as Mass Media* (MIT Press, 1994), which was awarded the 1995 AIA International Architecture Book Award, and, as editor, *Sexuality and Space* (Princeton Architectural Press, 1992), awarded the 1993 AIA International Architecture Book Award. She serves on the editorial board of *Assemblage* and is currently a Samuel H. Kress senior fellow at the Center for Advanced Studies in the Visual Arts, Washington, D.C., where she is working on a book on the relationships bewteen war and modern architecture.

PATRICIA CONWAY is professor of architecture at the University of Pennsylvania and past dean of Penn's Graduate School of Fine Arts. A founding partner of Kohn Pedersen Fox and former president of Kohn Pedersen Fox Conway, she was named Designer of the Year by *Interiors* magazine in 1987. She is the author of *Art for Everyday: The New Craft Movement* (Clarkson Potter, 1990) and *Ornamentalism: The New Decorativeness in Architecture and Design* (Clarkson Potter, 1982), which was nominated for the American Book Award, and she chaired the "Inherited Ideologies" conference at Penn in 1995.

MARGARET CRAWFORD is chair of the history and theory program at the Southern California Institute of Architecture. She has also taught at the University of California (San Diego) and the University of Southern California.

Her publications include, as co-editor, *The Car and the City* (University of Michigan Press, 1991), *Building the Workingman's Paradise: The Architecture of the American Company Town* (Verso Press, 1995), and numerous articles on the American built environment.

ESTHER DA COSTA MEYER is assistant professor in the Department of the History of Art and the School of Architecture at Yale University. She has lectured at the University of Iowa, Harvard, and Columbia and is the author of *The Architecture of Antonio Sant'Elia* (Yale University Press, 1995).

DIANE FAVRO is associate professor of architecture and urban design at the University of California (Los Angeles). She has also taught at Bilkent University, Ankara, Florida A&M, and San Francisco State College. Her publications include, as co-editor and co-author, *Streets: Critical Perspectives on Public Space* (University of California Press, 1994), "Ad-Architects: Women Professionals in Magazine Ads," in Ellen Perry Berkeley and Matilda McQuaid, eds., *Architecture: A Place for Women* (Smithsonian Institution Press, 1989), and *The Urban Image of Augustan Rome* (Cambridge University Press, 1996).

ALICE T. FRIEDMAN is professor of art and co-director of the architecture program at Wellesley College. She has also taught at Harvard and has several publications in progress, including a study of the role of women clients in the making of the modern house (Harry N. Abrams, 1997). Other publications include "Just Not My Type: Gender, Convention and the Uses of Uncertainty," in Karen Franck and Lynda Schneekloth, eds., *Type and Ordering of Space* (Van Nostrand Reinhold, 1994), and "Architecture, Authority and the Female Gaze" (*Assemblage,* Fall 1992).

GHISLAINE HERMANUZ is professor of architecture at the City College of New York, director of the City College Architectural Center, and principal, Hermanuz, Ltd. Formerly associate professor of architecture and assistant dean at Columbia, she has published *At Home in Harlem: An Architectural Walking Tour* (CCAC, 1992), *Sustainable Development in Industrialized Countries: The Challenge of Decent and Affordable Housing for All* (United Nations Committee on Shelter and Community, 1990), and "Infill: A Remedy to Harlem's Deterioration," in Deborah Norden, ed., *Reweaving the Urban Fabric* (Princeton Architectural Press, 1989).

CATHERINE INGRAHAM is associate professor of architecture at Iowa State University and editor of *Assemblage.* She has taught at the University of Illinois (Chicago), Harvard, and Columbia, and is a past fellow of the Chicago Institute for Architecture and Urbanism. Her many publications include "What's Proper to Architecture," in Kevin Alter and Elizabeth Danze, eds., *Regarding The Proper* (University of Texas Press, 1995) and "Initial Proprieties: Architecture and the Space of the Line," in Beatriz Colomina, ed., *Sexuality and Space* (Princeton Architectural Press, 1992).

SYLVIA LAVIN is assistant professor of architectural history and theory at the University of California (Los Angeles). She has taught at Harvard, Columbia, Southern California Institute of Architecture, and the University of Southern California. She is the author of numerous publications on eighteenth-century French architectural theory, including *Quatremère de Quincy and the Invention of a Modern Language of Architecture* (MIT Press, 1992). She is currently working on a book concerned with modern architecture and the culture of psychoanalysis.

DIANE LEWIS is a practicing architect at Diane Lewis, Architect, New York, and associate professor of architecture at The Cooper Union. She has also taught at Harvard, Yale, and other schools in the United States, Europe, and Australia, and was recently a visiting scholar at the Architectural Association, London. In 1976 she was awarded a Rome Prize. She is co-editor of *The Education of an Architect* (Rizzoli, 1987). Other writings and projects have been widely published in the art and literary press, and her work has been exhibited internationally.

MARY MCLEOD is associate professor of architecture at Columbia University and a director of the Society of Architectural Historians and of the Architectural League, New York. Her publications include, as co-editor, *Architecture, Criticism, and Ideology* (Princeton Architectural Press, 1985), "Undressing Architecture: Fashion, Gender and Modernity" in Deborah Fausch et al., eds., *Architecture in Fashion* (Princeton Architectural Press,

1994), and "Architecture and Politics in the Reagan Era" (*Assemblage* 8, 1989).

JOAN OCKMAN is director of the Temple Hoyne Buell Center for the Study of American Architecture at Columbia University and adjunct professor of architecture there. She has held editorial positions on *The New Yorker, Skyline,* and *Oppositions,* was senior architecture editor at Rizzoli, and director of publications for Columbia's Graduate School of Architecture, Planning and Preservation. Her first book, *Architecture Culture 1943–1968: A Documentary Anthology* (Rizzoli, 1993), was named Book of the Year by the 1994 AIA International Architectural Book Awards program and *The New York Times.*

DENISE SCOTT BROWN is a principal in Venturi, Scott Brown and Associates, Inc., Philadelphia, and a theorist, educator, and writer. Her work over the last thirty-five years on urban design, architecture, and urban planning ranges from the Sainsbury Wing of the National Gallery in London to a plan for downtown Memphis, and has earned her awards that include the ACSA-AIA Topaz Medallion (1996), the Philadelphia Award (1993), the National Medal of the Arts (1992), and the Order of Merit of the Republic of Italy (1987). Among her published writings are *Urban Concepts* (Academy Press, 1990) and, with Robert Venturi and Steven Izenour, *Learning from Las Vegas* (MIT Press, 1972).

SHARON E. SUTTON is professor of architecture and urban planning at the

312

University of Michigan. She brings to her work a varied background in music, psychology, and the graphic fine arts as well as experience in conflict management. Sutton's research, which spans several countries, focuses on youth, culture, and the environment. A recipient of the American Planning Association's Education Award and a former Kellogg national fellow, Sutton is the author of several books on the role of place in learning, including *Weaving a Tapestry of Resistance* (Bergin and Garvey, 1996).

SUSANA TORRE is past director of the Cranbrook Academy of Art in Bloomfield Hills, Michigan, and former chair of the Department of Architecture at Parsons School of Design, New York. She has also taught at the University of Sydney, Australia, Columbia, Yale, Carnegie-Mellon, University of Cincinnati, Syracuse University, and the New Jersey Institute of Technology. She was a member of the editorial collective of "Making Room: Women in Architecture" (*Heresies* 3, 1981) and editor of *Women in American Architecture: A Historic and Contemporary Perspective* (Whitney Library of Design, 1977).

LAURETTA VINCIARELLI is adjunct associate professor of architecture at Columbia University. She has taught as well at the City College of New York, the University of Chicago, and Pratt Institute. Her drawings, paintings, and completed architectural projects are represented in the permanent collections of The Museum of Modern Art, New York, the archive of the Venice Biennale, and the Italian

Archive of Drawings. She lectures widely, most recently at Harvard, Yale, Princeton, Rice, Tulane, Cranbrook, and the Architectural Association, London.

LESLIE KANES WEISMAN is associate professor and past associate dean of architecture at New Jersey Institute of Technology and, recently, George A. Miller Visiting Professor at the University of Illinois, Champaign-Urbana. She has also taught at M.I.T., Brooklyn College, and the University of Detroit, and was co-founder of the Women's School of Planning and Architecture, New York. Among her publications is the award-winning *Discrimination by Design: A Feminist Critique of the Man-Made Environment* (University of Illinois Press, 1992). She is the 1994 recipient of the ACSA National Creative Achievement Award for contributions to the advancement of architectural education.

MARION WEISS is partner, Weiss/Manfredi Architects, New York, assistant professor of architecture at the University of Pennsylvania, and visiting critic at Yale University. In 1991 she won the AAUW Outstanding Emerging Scholar Award; she was also featured in the June 1990 issue of Japan's *Space Design Journal*, devoted to "American Women in Architecture." She and her partner, Michael Manfredi, are winners of the New American Green competition, the Bridging the Gap competition, and the two-stage competition for the Women in Military Service for America Memorial and Education Center at Arlington National Cemetery project, now in construction.

Index

Page numbers in *italic* denote illustrations.

Photograph Credits